MW00757459

3 CREATING

Chapter 5
OUTLINING YOUR SPEECH
→ Page 137

Chapter 6
ORGANIZING THE SPEECH BODY
→ Page 173

Chapter 7
INTRODUCING AND CONCLUDING YOUR SPEECH
→ Page 195

4 PRESENTING

Chapter 8
USING LANGUAGE SUCCESSFULLY
→ Page 215

Chapter 9
DELIVERING YOUR SPEECH
→ Page 237

CHAPTER 10
USING PRESENTATION AIDS
→ Page 261

5 LISTENING & EVALUATING

Chapter 11
LISTENING
→ Page 299

Chapter 12
EVALUATING SPEECHES
→ Page 317

8 SPEAKING ON SPECIAL OCCASIONS

Chapter 16
SPEECHES FOR SPECIAL EVENTS
→ Page 443

9 SPEAKING IN PROFESSIONAL & GROUP SETTINGS

Chapter 17
ON-THE-JOB SPEAKING
→ Page 471

Chapter 18
SPEAKING IN SMALL GROUPS
→ Page 493

NCA STUDENT OUTCOMES FOR SPEAKING AND LISTENING
→ Page 507

GLOSSARY
→ Page 523

BIBLIOGRAPHY
→ Page 533

NOTES
→ Page 535

CREDITS
→ Page 536

INDEX
→ Page 541

DETAILED CONTENTS
→ Page 554

DK Guide to Public Speaking

LISA A. FORD-BROWN

Columbia College

Allyn & Bacon

Boston Columbus Indianapolis New York San Francisco Upper Saddle River
Amsterdam Cape Town Dubai London Madrid Milan Munich Paris Montréal Toronto
Delhi Mexico City São Paulo Sydney Hong Kong Seoul Singapore Taipei Tokyo

Text design, page layout, and cover design:
Stuart Jackman

Editorial Director: Daryl Fox
Editor-in-Chief, Communication: Karon Bowers
Director, Market Research and Development: Laura Coaty
Director of Development: Meg Botteon
Development Editor: Brenda Hadenfeldt
Editorial Assistant: Megan Sweeney
Associate Development Editor: Angela Mallowes
Media Producer: Megan Higginbotham
Marketing Manager: Blair Tuckman
Managing Editor: Linda Behrens
Associate Managing Editor: Bayani Mendoza de Leon
Production Manager: Raegan Keida Heerema
Project Coordination: Integra Software Services, Inc.
Cover Photos (*clockwise from top left*): © Ladi Kim/Alamy, GK Hart/Vikki Hart, © The National Trust Photolibrary/Alamy, © vario images GmbH & Co.KG/Alamy
Visual Research Manager: Rona Tuccillo
Senior Manufacturing Buyer: Mary Ann Gloriande
Printer and Binder: RR Donnelley & Sons Company/Crawfordsville
Cover Printer: Lehigh-Phoenix

For permission to use copyrighted material, grateful acknowledgment is made to the copyright holders on pp. 536–540, which are hereby made part of this copyright page.

Library of Congress Cataloging-in-Publication Data

Ford-Brown, Lisa A.
DK guide to public speaking / Lisa A. Ford-Brown.
    p. cm.
  ISBN-13: 978-0-205-75011-5
  ISBN-10: 0-205-75011-7
1.   Public speaking—Handbooks, manuals, etc. I. Ford-Brown, Lisa A. II. Title.
PN4129.15.F67 2012
  808.5'1—dc22   2010044658

4 5 6 7 8 9 10—DOC—13 12 11

Allyn & Bacon
is an imprint of

www.pearsonhighered.com

ISBN-13: 978-0-205-75011-5
ISBN-10:   0-205-75011-7

Preface

The inspiration for this book was a 2008 study by a leading research institution concluding that students use a textbook for less than 15 percent of their study time for their public speaking course. The picture that emerged from 25 hours of interviews and more than 300 diary entries was this: Although students found textbooks to be useful when studying for quizzes, they did not find them at all useful for guidance while developing their speeches. As a result, *DK Guide to Public Speaking* was created to give students the practical information and examples they seek right up front, supported with the concepts and theories instructors know students need.

To test students' experiences, usability studies were commissioned for this text. Students from two- and four-year colleges used *DK Guide to Public Speaking* for tasks such as creating oral citations, evaluating central ideas (thesis statements), and locating and selecting sources. These studies resulted in many hours of video feedback that helped hone the text in areas students find most challenging in creating a speech.

The insights of more than 300 public speaking instructors, including a Faculty Advisory Board of nearly 50, ensure the text meets the needs of students and faculty in a conceptually, theoretically, and pedagogically sound way.

Combining its comprehensive coverage with the powerfully visual DK design, the student- and instructor-tested *DK Guide to Public Speaking* offers an easy-to-navigate resource with dynamic visuals, current examples, and concise instruction that will equip students with the tools and confidence to be effective speakers.

→ See pages vi–xi for highlights and features of the book.

Origins of *DK Guide to Public Speaking*

Extensive student feedback

Student diary studies and usability testing highlighted the challenging areas that students need their public speaking text to address and demonstrated how the design of the material could help. Students emphasized that they look for practical information and easy-to-find examples to provide them with the guidance they want, when they need it most—during their speech preparation.

Thorough instructor reviews

Focus groups, editorial reviews, and ongoing feedback from the Faculty Advisory Board helped to ensure the text facilitates the conceptual and theoretical outcomes for public speaking.

Expert collaboration

To create this vision, *DK Guide to Public Speaking* paired an award-winning public speaking teacher with one of the world's leading guidebook designers. Working in tandem with the publisher, this team took significant course content and developed it into an engaging visual presentation.

Features

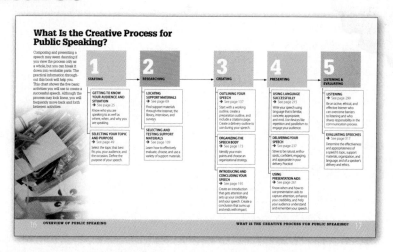

1

Designed for easy use and navigation: Tabs and process charts help students quickly find answers to questions on any part of the speech process or type of speaking. Blue cross-references guide students to related sections.

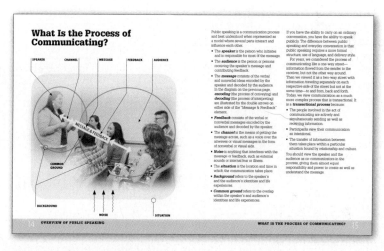

2

Presents concepts visually, supported by text: The pairing of visuals and detailed explanations allows students to get an overview at a glance and read on for specifics.

3

Driven by examples: Diverse examples of varying lengths are used extensively throughout, from student, community, business, historical, political, special occasion, and other speaking situations. Many are annotated to teach students in context. End-of-chapter case studies apply concepts to extended examples.

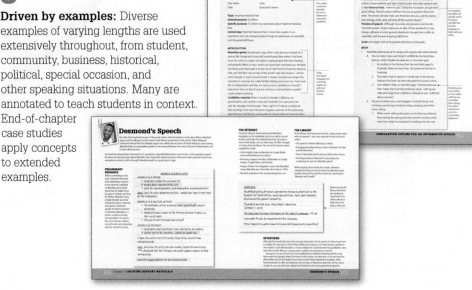

4

Emphasizes confidence-building: Starting with a section in the Overview chapter on overcoming apprehension, the text then features blue "Confidence Booster" sections throughout to give students insights and positive reinforcement on ways to deal with fears and to ensure they are well prepared.

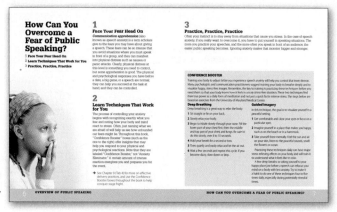

5

Applies public speaking skills in business settings: A practical chapter on "On-the-Job Speaking" (Chapter 17) offers strategies for how to create successful business presentations and speak more effectively in meetings, interviews, and other key workplace settings.

6

Emphasizes ethics at every stage:

Building from the introductory material on ethics and avoiding plagiarism in the Overview chapter, "Practicing Ethics" sections are integrated throughout the text to give students insights into ethical issues to keep in mind when dealing with each part of the speech process.

PRACTICING ETHICS

Sometimes impromptu speaking will make you feel like you are being "put on the spot" or asked to speak without preparation. Remember: Most of the time you will be asked for impromptu comments because you are an expert on the subject or have something critical to add. Therefore, ethically, it is your responsibility to never make up information to sound good or to get through the moment. Be honest.

7

Includes Checklists and Tip boxes for practical application: Extensive use of checklists gives students practical tools to help create and evaluate their speeches at each stage of the process. Tip boxes provide useful information and advice along the way.

CHECKLIST for Evaluating a Special Occasion Speech

❑ Does my introduction include an attention-getter, credibility material, statement of relevance, and preview?

❑ Does the body of my speech have an appropriate organizational strategy and supported main points?

❑ Is my language clear, vivid, and appropriate?

❑ Does my conclusion include a summary, an audience reaction statement, and a WOW ending?

❑ Is the length of my speech appropriate?

❑ Is my delivery dynamic and enthusiastic? If appropriate, am I delivering the speech extemporaneously? Do I maintain almost constant eye contact?

TIP: Responding from the Audience

As an audience member to a toast, if you pick up your glass at the beginning of the toast, don't put it down until the end. You should always raise your glass and sip some liquid, or you will appear impolite or seem to suggest that you don't agree with the toast.

8

Highlights how to evaluate speeches: A unique chapter on "Evaluating Speeches" (Chapter 12) teaches students how to better evaluate and critique their own work and that of others. In addition, chapters on subjects such as informative and persuasive speaking offer further tips on evaluating specific types of speeches and messages.

Introduction

Jessamyn had trouble keeping her thoughts together when giving a speech. When she enrolled in her first public speaking class, she told a classmate, "I get so nervous, I can't remember my next thought." Jessamyn thought she was not able to give a good speech. Then her professor required each student to turn in an outline for each speech given in the class. At first, Jessamyn found outlining tedious. However, when she practiced the speech, she noticed it made more sense to her, and she could more easily tell how long it would be. She could tell it was a bit short, so she added more statistics to make one of her points.

The best part came the day of the speech. She remembered each point without looking down at her note cards as much as before. She got through the speech as she had planned. Jessamyn was less nervous and even had a bit of fun giving the speech. For the first time, she walked away from the lectern proud of her accomplishment. After a few more speeches, Jessamyn realized that the time she took to outline was helping her create better speeches and be more confident.

Now you are ready to learn how to develop this essential tool for giving a successful speech. Because creating an effective outline is so important and complex, Tab 3 is divided into three chapters designed to break apart the process into manageable portions. The three chapters work in concert with each other. This chapter explains the qualities and components of outlines and the different types of outlines.

CHAPTER 5 CONTENTS

Why Do You Need an Outline? 138

What Are the Parts of an Outline? 140
1 Introduction 141
2 Body of the Speech 141
3 Conclusion 141
4 Source Page 141

How Can You Create an Effective Outline? 142
1 Record the Topic, Specific Purpose, and Central Idea 143
2 Use Full Sentences 143
3 Cover Only One Issue at a Time 144
4 Develop the Introduction and Conclusion 145
5 Use Correct Outline Format 146
6 Use Balanced Main Points 148
7 Employ Subordination 148
8 Plan Out Formal Links 150
9 Use Proper Citations 151

What Are the Different Types of Outlines? 152
1 The Working Outline 152
2 The Preparation Outline 154
3 The Delivery Outline 158

What Can You Use to Link Your Speech Parts Together? 160
1 Transitions 161
2 Signposts 162
3 Internal Previews 162
4 Internal Reviews 163

How Do You Cite Sources in Your Outline? 164

How Do You Create a Source Page? 166
1 Follow the Overall Format Requirements 167
2 Create Proper Entries for Each Source 167

Sophia's Speech 170

CHAPTER 6: Organizing the Speech Body 173

CHAPTER 7: Introducing and Concluding Your Speech 195

Tab 3 Review 214

CHAPTER 5 CONTENTS

Why Do You Need an Outline? 138

What Are the Parts of an Outline? 140
1 Introduction 141
2 Body of the Speech 141
3 Conclusion 141
4 Source Page 141

How Can You Create an Effective Outline? 142
1 Record the Topic, Specific Purpose, and Central Idea 143
2 Use Full Sentences 143
3 Cover Only One Issue at a Time 144
4 Develop the Introduction and Conclusion 145
5 Use Correct Outline Format 146
6 Use Balanced Main Points 148
7 Employ Subordination 148
8 Plan Out Formal Links 150
9 Use Proper Citations 151

9

Highlights a learning objective in each chapter heading: Chapter headings are in question-and-answer format—to ask common questions that beginning speakers have and to provide clear answers. Each chapter-opening contents section also serves as a list of learning objectives for that chapter.

Speaking Competencies: Basic Skills

In order to be a **competent speaker**, a person must be able to compose a message and provide ideas and information suitable to the topic, purpose, and audience. Specifically, the competent speaker should exhibit the following competencies by demonstrating the abilities included under each statement on pages 508–513.

Determine the purpose of oral discourse.

ABILITIES	REFER TO...
• Identify the various purposes of discourse.	**Tab 1 STARTING**
• Identify the similarities and differences among various purposes.	**Overview** Overview of public speaking, 1–23
• Understand that different contexts require differing purposes.	**Chapter 2** Identify the general purpose of your speech, 50–51
• Generate a specific purpose relevant to the context when given a general purpose.	Identify the specific purpose of your speech, 58–59
	Tab 6 SPEAKING TO INFORM
	Chapter 13 The informative speech, 333–367
	Tab 7 SPEAKING TO PERSUADE
	Chapter 15 The persuasive speech, 402–441
	Tab 8 SPEAKING ON SPECIAL OCCASIONS
	Chapter 16 Speeches for special events, 443–469
	Tab 9 SPEAKING IN PROFESSIONAL & GROUP SETTINGS
	Chapter 17 On-the-job speaking, 471–491
	Chapter 18 Speaking in small groups, 492–505

10

Correlates with NCA learning outcomes: Learning objectives are based on the outcomes described in Part One of "Speaking and Listening Competencies for College Students" by the National Communication Association. A detailed section in the back of the book provides a guide to where each outcome is addressed in *DK Guide to Public Speaking.*

11

Based on how students do research: The research chapters in Tab 2 (Chapter 3, "Locating Support Materials," and Chapter 4, "Selecting and Testing Support Materials") are designed from the ground up around the astounding array of digital and print resources available to students. Coverage emphasizes how to evaluate sources and cite them orally and in written form.

12

Covers presentation aids in a truly visual way: Chapter 10, "Using Presentation Aids," takes full advantage of the cutting-edge and visual nature of the text to explain and showcase the variety of aids available to students today—and the best ways to maximize their use.

Supplements

Unparalleled Support Will Help Bring Your Course to Life!

FOR INSTRUCTORS

INSTRUCTOR'S MANUAL
(ISBN: 0-205-02866-7)
Prepared by Maggie Sullivan, Loras College, this comprehensive, peer-reviewed resource offers a chapter-by-chapter guide to teaching with this innovative book! Each chapter features learning outcomes, a detailed lecture outline (based on the accompanying PowerPoint™ presentation package), discussion questions, activities, and content quizzes. There also are many suggestions for incorporating visual elements from the book and multimedia resources from MySpeechLab in your lectures and assignments.
Available at www.pearsonhighered.com/irc.com
(access code required)
Print and Digital

TEST BANK
(ISBN: 0-205-02867-5)
The fully reviewed Test Bank, prepared by Janice Ralya Stuckey, Jefferson State Community College, contains multiple choice, true/false, completion, short answer, and traditional essay questions. Unlike any other public speaking test bank available, we also offer visual essay questions that require students to evaluate and discuss key visual elements from the book. Each question has a correct answer and is referenced by page, skill, and topic.
Available at www.pearsonhighered.com
(access code required)
Print and Digital

MYTEST COMPUTERIZED TEST BANK
(ISBN: 0-205-02864-0)
This flexible, online test-generating program includes all questions found in the Test Bank, allowing instructors to create their own personalized exams. Instructors also can edit any of the existing test questions and even add new questions. Other special features include random generation of test questions, creation of alternate versions of the same test, scrambling of question sequence, and test preview before printing.
Available at www.pearsonmytest.com
(access code required)
Digital only

POWERPOINT™ PRESENTATION PACKAGE
(ISBN: 0-205-02865-9)
Prepared by Christa Tess, Minneapolis Community & Technical College, this text-specific package provides a basis for your lecture with visually enhanced PowerPoint™ slides for each chapter of the book. In addition to providing key concepts and select art from the book, these presentations bring the book's exciting, visual presentation to life with pedagogically valuable animations as well as detailed instructor notes.
Available at www.pearsonhighered.com/irc
(access code required)
Digital only

CLASSPREP
(Instructional Support Library)
New from Pearson, ClassPrep makes lecture preparation simpler and less time-consuming. It offers the very best class presentation resources (art and figures) from all of our texts, videos, lecture activities, audio clips, classroom activities, and more—in one convenient online destination. You may search through its extensive database of tools by content topic or by content type (video, audio, activities, etc.).
ClassPrep is in the Instructor's section of MySpeechLab.
Digital only

A GUIDE FOR NEW PUBLIC SPEAKING TEACHERS, 5/e
(ISBN: 0-205-82810-8)
This handy guide helps new teachers prepare for and teach the introductory public speaking course more effectively. It covers such topics as preparing for the term, planning and structuring your course, evaluating speeches, utilizing the textbook, integrating technology into the classroom, and much more!
Available at www.pearsonhighered.com/irc
(access code required)
Print and Digital

PEARSON CONTEMPORARY CLASSIC SPEECHES DVD
(ISBN: 0-205-40552-5)
This exciting DVD includes more than 120 minutes of video footage. Each speech is accompanied by a biographical and historical summary that helps students understand the context and motivation behind each speech. Speakers featured include Martin Luther King, Jr., John F. Kennedy, Barbara Jordan, the Dalai Lama, and Christopher Reeve.
DVD only

FOR STUDENTS

FREE APP FOR APPLE iPHONES, iPADS, AND iPODS: "DKPS iCHECK"

This handy new app gives students quick and easy access to all 50 of the "Checklists" from *DK Guide to Public Speaking* FREE of charge. Students can download iCheck directly on to their iPhone, iPad, or iPod Touch from the Apple iTunes App Store with no restrictions, fees, or pass codes. Research shows students value Checklists more than any other learning aid in a public speaking text. Now they can reference them on the spot—whether preparing to conduct an interview, doing research in the library, or even getting ready to give a speech, the DKPS iCheck App is there to help.
Digital Only

PUBLIC SPEAKING IN THE MULTICULTURAL ENVIRONMENT

(ISBN: 0-205-26511-1)
Prepared by Devorah A. Lieberman, Portland State University, this booklet helps students learn to analyze cultural diversity within their audiences and adapt their presentations accordingly.
Available for purchase.
Print only

THE SPEECH OUTLINE

(ISBN: 0-321-08702-X)
Prepared by Reeze L. Hanson and Sharon Condon of Haskell Indian Nations University, this workbook includes activities, exercises, and answers to help students develop and master the critical skill of outlining.
Available for purchase.
Print only

SPEECH PREPARATION WORKBOOK

(ISBN: 0-135-59569-X)
Prepared by Jennifer Dreyer and Gregory H. Patton of San Diego State University, this workbook takes students through the stages of speech creation—from audience analysis to writing the speech—and includes guidelines, tips, and easy-to-fill-in pages.
Available for purchase.
Print only

STUDY CARD FOR PUBLIC SPEAKING

(ISBN: 0-205-44126-2)
Colorful, affordable, and packed with useful information, the Pearson/Allyn & Bacon Study Cards make studying easier, more efficient, and more enjoyable. Course information is distilled down to the basics, helping students quickly master the fundamentals, review a subject for understanding, or prepare for an exam. Because they are laminated for durability, they can be kept for years to come and pulled out whenever students need a quick review.
Available for purchase.
Print only

PEARSON PUBLIC SPEAKING STUDY SITE

This open-access student Web resource features practice tests, learning objectives, and Web links organized around the major topics typically covered in the Introduction to Public Speaking course. The content of this site has even been correlated to the table of contents for your book.
Available at www.abpublicspeaking.com.
Digital only

VIDEOLAB CD-ROM

(ISBN: 0-205-56161-6)
This interactive study tool for students can be used independently or in class. It provides digital video of student speeches that can be viewed in conjunction with corresponding outlines, manuscripts, note cards, and instructor critiques. Following each speech, there are a series of drills to help students analyze content and delivery.
Available for purchase.
CD-ROM only

FOR INSTRUCTORS AND STUDENTS

MYSPEECHLAB

MySpeechLab is a state-of-the-art, interactive, and instructive solution for public speaking courses. Designed to be used as a supplement to a traditional lecture course or to completely administer an online course, MySpeechLab combines a Pearson eText, MySearchLab™, MediaShare, multimedia, video clips, activities, research support, and tests and quizzes to completely engage and support students. Go to www.myspeechlab.com to learn more and see a tour. Access code required for the full site.
(See next page for complete description.)

Groundbreaking and Multifaceted Media Support with

The new MySpeechLab for *DK Guide to Public Speaking* provides state-of-the-art media for both instructors and students. It combines pedagogy and assessment with an extensive collection of videos, speech preparation tools, assessments, research support, and multiple newsfeeds—to make learning more effective for all types of students.

It also provides a convenient video upload tool (MediaShare) that allows students to post videos of their speeches for feedback and review.

VIDEO-RELATED ONLINE FEATURES

Videos and Video Quizzes: An extensive variety of interactive videos provides students with the opportunity to watch and evaluate sample speeches, both student and professional. Select videos are annotated with instructor feedback or include short, assignable quizzes that report to the instructor's gradebook. Professional speeches include classic and contemporary speeches, as well as video segments from communication experts.

AmericanRhetoric.com: Through an exclusive partnership with AmericanRhetoric.com, MySpeechLab incorporates many great speeches of our time (without linking out to another site and without advertisements or commercials!). Many speeches also are accompanied by assessment questions that ask students to evaluate specific elements of those speeches.

ABC News Feed: MySpeechLab provides online feeds from ABC News, updated hourly, to help students choose and research their speech topics.

MediaShare: With this engaging video upload tool, students are able to upload their speeches for their instructor and classmates to watch (whether face-to-face or online) and provide online feedback and comments at time-stamped intervals. Instructors also have the option to include a speech evaluation rubric (to fill out themselves or for peer evaluations) and a final grade for each student's speech. Grades can be exported from MediaShare to a SCORM-compliant .csv spreadsheet that can be imported into most learning management systems.

MYSPEECHLAB FEATURE HIGHLIGHTS

eText: Identical to the content and design of the printed text, *DK Guide to Public Speaking* eText provides students access to their text whenever and wherever they need it. In addition to contextually placed multimedia features in every chapter, the eText allows students to take notes and highlight, just like a traditional book.

Competency Check: Review the National Communication Association's "Outcomes for Speaking and Listening" and use media and other content from MySpeechLab to help achieve mastery of these outcomes.

HELPFUL ONLINE TOOLS

MyOutline: This helpful outline tool offers step-by-step guidance for writing an effective outline, along with tips and explanations to help students better understand the elements of an outline and how all the pieces fit together. Outlines that students create can be downloaded to their computer, emailed as an attachment, or saved for future editing. Instructors can select from several templates or create their own outline structure and template for students to use.

Topic Selector: This interactive tool helps students get started generating ideas and narrowing down topics. It is question based, rather than drill-down, to help students really learn the process of selecting their topic. Once they have selected a topic, students are directed to credible online sources to further the research process.

Building Speaking Confidence Center: Students will find self-assessments, strategies, video, audio, and activities that provide additional guidance and tips for overcoming speech apprehension—all in one convenient location of MySpeechLab.

Flashcards: Review important terms and concepts from each chapter online or on your mobile device, such as the iPhone, iPad, BlackBerry, Droid, and more. In addition to standard text-based flashcards, all terms and definitions also are available video-based, with students stating each term and its definition.

Audio Chapter Summaries: Every chapter includes an audio chapter summary for online streaming use, perfect for students reviewing material before a test or instructors reviewing material before class.

ONLINE ASSESSMENT TOOLS

Speech Evaluation Tools: Instructors have access to a host of evaluation tools to use in the classroom as well as an assortment of evaluation forms, rubrics, and guides for students and instructors. Don't forget, Pearson's MediaShare described on the previous page takes speech evaluation to a whole new level!

Student Self-Assessments: Online self-assessments, including the PRCA-24 and the PRPSA, allow students to assess and confirm their comfort level with speaking publicly. Instructors can use these tools to show learning over the duration of the course via MyPersonalityProfile, Pearson's online self-assessment library and analysis tool. MyPersonalityProfile enables instructors to assign self-assessments at the beginning and end of the course so that students can compare their results and see where they have improved.

Student Study Plan: Pre- and post-tests for each chapter test students on their knowledge of the material in the course. The tests generate a customized study plan for further assessment and focus students on areas in which they need to improve using links to the textbook, as well as the top media items that can assist in improving their results.

Online Course Administration: No matter what course management system you use—or if you do not use one at all but still wish to easily capture your students' grades and track their performance—there is a MySpeechLab option to suit your needs.

A **MySpeechLab** access code is no additional cost when packaged with new copies of *DK Guide to Public Speaking*. To get started, contact your local Pearson Publisher's Representative at www.pearsonhighered.com/replocator.

Acknowledgments

This book was a labor of love for many people and I was blessed to work with a great team and to have folks from my professional as well as personal lives offering support. Some journeys can be lonely adventures, but this one showed me the true value and brilliance of an ensemble working creatively and passionately together.

Karon Bowers (Editor-in-Chief, Communication) set the ball rolling by noticing that this funny little redhead had a unique approach. During the process, Karon was always willing to offer guidance, wisdom, and a bit of humor. Brenda Hadenfeldt (Development Editor) was amazing. She calmed me when I needed it, offered thoughtful and intelligent advice when I veered from the path, and energized me when I slowed. One day, we will share a Tang pie with Lulu. Stuart Jackman (Design Director for DK Education) is a master of design, and working with him was like having blinders removed from my eyes and creative spirit. His awe-inspiring artistic talent and incredible knowledge of how to teach visually lifted this book beyond my dreams. Our collaboration was truly life changing, as it made me a better teacher, and I can't wait to see how it lifts my students. Laura Coaty (Director, Market Research and Development) was another creative genius behind the idea for this book and provided valuable insights at every stage. She also pulled us back when we made a wrong turn (what great colors!) and became the best cheerleader the project could have. Laurie Panu (Senior Publisher's Representative) noticed something in me that I didn't realize could be such an asset; she said that I "play in the sandbox well with others." Thank you, my friend.

Others at Pearson and Dorling Kindersley to whom I am eternally grateful for their insight and efforts include Daryl Fox (Editorial Director), Blair Tuckman (Marketing Manager), Sophie Mitchell (Publisher for DK Education), and Megan Sweeney (Editorial Assistant), and everyone in development, editorial, marketing, permissions, media, and production who worked so hard to make this project happen.

Many thanks to Tharon Howard, Director of the Clemson University Usability Testing Facility, and his team, including Wendy Howard, for conducting the pivotal diary study that inspired this project. Their insightful findings and recommendations gave our book team a student-centered roadmap we followed from start to finish. Their additional student usability testing of early prototypes also informed the layout, navigation, and use of examples throughout the text.

In addition, thanks are due the many undergraduate students at both Clemson University and Tri-County Technical College who participated in these important studies. By quantifying their actions and articulating their needs, these students helped us better understand their study habits and what they needed that they were not getting from traditional public speaking textbooks.

Many Faculty Advisory Board members, focus group participants, and reviewers (listed on pages xviii–xx) also provided valuable feedback along the way. Working with such wonderful and talented educators was an awe-inspiring and humbling experience.

Possibly one of the most important support groups an academic writer can have is a team of great student and research assistants. Steven Dotson, Crystaldawn Howell, Charity J. Hunter, and Karissa Scott blessed this project with endless hours of research, advice, speech outlines, topic ideas, and proofreading and kept "Doc" from pulling her hair out. I thank you and my hairdresser thanks you.

For years, my students have influenced what and how I teach. These Columbia College students went a step further by offering speech ideas, outlines, and modeling for photos included in this book: Michelle E. Arnold, Jeff Barringer, Caitlin Jenkins Campbell, Andria Caruthers, Desiree Chong, Rachel Coleman, Tori Gehlert, Ashley Hardy, Candace Johnson, Katherine Mancuso, Milos Milosavljevic, Logan Park, Kylie E. Stephenson, Jessica Ucci, Christopher Vietti, and Rachel K. Wester.

I would also like to thank Dorinda K. Stayton, Kimberly Albrecht-Taylor, Brendan Chan (University of Texas at Austin), and the Rev. John Yonker (Columbia, Mo.) for offering their amazing talents in the form of complete speech manuscripts.

Throughout this project, I have been fortunate to enjoy the support and assistance from many colleagues on the Columbia College campus. I wish to thank: President Gerald Brouder, Terry Smith, Mark Price, Lori Ewing, Terry Obermoeller, the Humanities Department, and the Professional Development Committee for supporting and recognizing the value of this book. With a layout artist in London and editorial support all across the United States, technology played a significant role in this process. I would like to thank the entire Columbia College Technology Services group and specifically mention the following: Kevin Palmer, Stefanie McCollum, and B.J. Donaldson. Megan Pettegrew-Donely and Kaci Smart provided some much-needed photographs. Other CC folks who offered input—or just held my hand—are Lucia D'Agostino, Janet Caruthers, Lynda Dunham and her staff, Danny Campbell, Johanna Denzin, Ann Schlemper, Lizbeth Metscher, Julie Estabrooks, Tim Ireland, and David Roebuck. I am grateful and proud to call you my colleagues.

I would like to thank several exceptional educators who have influenced me both professionally and personally: C. Sue Davis, Harriet McNeal, Dan P. Millar, Elyse Pineau, Ron Pelias, David Worley, Mary Carol Harris, and John T. Warren. I am sincerely indebted to Sheron J. Dailey for helping me proofread and for challenging my ideas. Only a true mentor and friend would read every page as if it were her own. I am a better teacher because of these colleagues, and there is a bit of each of them in the pages of this book.

I am extremely grateful to the Ford and Brown families for all the support and understanding. I would especially like to thank Lea Ann Camp, Ross G. Brown, and Gwenneth Brown for their excitement, support, and encouragement.

Finally, I must recognize my life partner, Bruce Brown. Thank you for encouraging me to do this project, putting up with my strange sleeping habits (lack of), my almost constant talking about ideas, and my endless mood swings. You offered insight when I needed it, fed the pups and chicks when I didn't have time, and knew when it was time to just leave me to my computer.

What an adventure this was, and I dedicate this book to ALL of you.

FACULTY ADVISORY BOARD

From the very beginning, the members of the Faculty Advisory Board offered valuable criticism, insight, ideas, and enthusiasm. Thank you all for your time, energy, and wisdom.

Shae Adkins, Lone Star College–North Harris; **Allison Ainsworth,** Gainesville State College; **Mary Alexander,** Wharton County Junior College; **Julie Allee,** Indiana University South Bend; **Barbara Baron,** Brookdale Community College; **Kate Behr,** Concordia College; **Constance Berman,** Berkshire Community College; **Kimberly Berry,** Ozarks Technical College; **Kirk Brewer,** Tulsa Community College, West Campus; **Ferald Bryan,** Northern Illinois University; **Rebecca Carlton,** Indiana University Southeast; **Gary Carson,** Coastal Carolina University; **Wendy R. Coleman,** Alabama State University; **Diana Cooley,** Lone Star College–North Harris; **Karin Dahmann,** Blinn College; **Natalie Dorfeld,** Thiel College; **Kelly Driskell,** Trinity Valley Community College; **Robert D. Dunkerly,** College of Southern Nevada; **Steve Earnest,** Coastal Carolina University; **Katrina Eicher,** Elizabethtown Community and Technical College; **Kristina Galyen,** University of Cincinnati; **Jo Anna Grant,** California State University, San Bernardino; **Tressa Kelly,** University of West Florida; **Sherry Lewis,** University of Texas at El Paso; **Daniel Leyes,** Brookdale Community College; **Terri Main,** Reedley College; **Anne McIntosh,** Central Piedmont Community College; **James McNamara,** Alverno College; **Donna Munde,** Mercer County Community College; **John Nash,** Moraine Valley College; **William Neff,** College of Southern Nevada; **Karen Otto,** Florida State College at Jacksonville; **Maria Parnell,** Brevard Community College, Melbourne ; **Katherine Rigsby,** University of South Alabama; **Kristi Schaller,** University of Georgia; **Michael Shannon,** Moraine Valley Community College; **Pam Speights,** Wharton County Junior College; **Janice Stuckey,** Jefferson State Community College; **Christa Tess,** Minneapolis Community and Technical College; **Jane Varmecky,** Tulsa Community College, Southeast Campus; **Jenny Warren,** Collin County Community College, Spring Creek; **Rebecca Weldon,** Savannah College of Art and Design; **Susan Wieczorek,** University of Pittsburgh at Johnstown; **Susan Winters,** University of Cincinnati; **Brandon Wood,** Central Texas College; and **Quentin Wright,** Mountain View College.

FOCUS GROUP PARTICIPANTS

Carolyn Babcock, Savannah College of Art and Design; **Cameron Basquiat,** College of Southern Nevada; **Shirene Bell,** Salt Lake Community College; **Linda Brown,** El Paso Community College, Transmountain Campus; **Dawn Carusi,** Marietta College; **Helen Chester,** Milwaukee Area Technical College; **Russ Church,** Middle Tennessee State University; **Kathleen D. Clark,** University of Akron; **Janis Crawford,** Butler University; **Dale Davis,** University of Texas at San Antonio; **Ella Davis,** Wayne County Community College; **Shannon Doyle,** San Jose State University; **Jeanne Dunphy,** Los Angeles City College; **Jennifer Fairchild,** Eastern Kentucky University; **Jeff Farrar,** University of Connecticut; **Katie Frame,** Schoolcraft College; **Kathy Golden,** Edinboro University of Pennsylvania; **Don Govang,** Lincoln University; **Joy Hart,** University of Louisville; **James Heflin,** Cameron University; **Terry Helmick,** Johnson County Community College; **Wade Hescht,** Lone Star College–North Harris; **Heather Hundley,** California State University, San Bernardino; **Lynae Jacob,** Amarillo College; **Jim Kuypers,** Virginia Tech; **Libby McGlone,** Columbus State Community College; **Terri Moore,** Brevard Community College, Melbourne; **Tim Pierce,** Northern Illinois University; **Sherry Rhodes,** Collin County Community College, Courtyard Center; **Rebecca Robideaux,** Boise State University; **David Schneider,** Saginaw Valley University; **April DuPree Taylor,** University of South Alabama; **Paaige Turner,** Saint Louis University; **Julie Weishar,** Parkland College; and **Charla Windley,** University of Idaho.

REVIEWERS

Donald Abel, Amarillo College; Helen Acosta, Bakersfield College; Brent Adrian, Central Community College, Grand Island; Bob Alexander, Bossier Parish Community College; Krista Appelquist, Moraine Valley Community College; Brenda Armentrout, Central Piedmont Community College; Ann Atkinson, Keene State College; Jackie Augustine, Victor Valley College; Kevin Backstrom, University of Wisconsin Oshkosh; Cynthia L. Bahti, Saddleback College and Orange Coast Colleges; Elise Banfield, Genesee Community College; Kristin Barton, Dalton State College; Jennifer Huss Basquiat, College of Southern Nevada; Polly Begley, Fresno City College; Tim Behme, University of Minnesota, Twin Cities; Belinda Bernum, Mansfield University; Denise Besson-Silvia, Gavilan College; Melanie Lea Birck, Bossier Parish Community College; Mardia Bishop, University of Illinois; Carol Bliss, California State Polytechnic University; Tonya Blivens, Tarrant County College, Southeast Campus; Robert Boller, University of Hawaii at Manoa; Beverly McClay Borawski, Pasco-Hernando Community College; Jeffrey Brand, Millikin University; LeAnn Brazeal, Kansas State University; Heather Brecht, Ithaca College; Michele Bresso, Bakersfield College; Stefne Lenzmeier Broz, Wittenberg University; Barbara Ruth Burke, University of Minnesota; Donna Burnside, University of Texas at Brownsville; Nicholas Butler, Arizona State University; Dennis Cali, University of Texas at Tyler; Marybeth Callison, University of Georgia; Mary Carver, University of Central Oklahoma; Connie Caskey, Jefferson State Community College; Jennifer Chakroff, Kent State University; Angela Cherry, Laney College; Robert Christie, DeVry College; Carolyn Clark, Salt Lake Community College; Benjamin J. Cline, Western New Mexico University; Cindy Cochran, Kirkwood Community College; Jodi Cohen, Ithaca College; Teresa Collard, University of Tennessee at Martin; Leslie Collins, Modesto Junior College; Ron Compton, McHenry County College; Linda Carvalho Cooley, Reedley College; Jim Cunningham, Embry Riddle Aeronautical University; Andrea Davis, University of South Carolina Upstate; Quinton D. Davis, University of Texas at San Antonio; Tasha Davis, Austin Community College, Round Rock; Isabel del Pino-Allen, Miami Dade College; Susan Dobie, Humboldt State University; Natalie Dudchock, Jefferson State Community College; Ann Duncan, McLennan Community College; Janine W. Dunlap, Freed-Hardeman University; Kristen Eichhorn, SUNY Oswego; Marty Ennes, West Hills College Lemoore; Heather Erickson, Emerson College; Diane Ferrero-Paluzzi, Iona College; James M. Floss, Humboldt State University; Jeffrey Fox, Northern Kentucky University; Rebecca Franko, California State Polytechnic University; Barbara Franzen, Central Community College; Stacy Freed, University of Tennessee at Martin; Todd S. Frobish, Fayetteville State University; Mark S. Gallup, Lansing Community College; Joseph M. Ganakos, Lee College; Laura Garcia, Washington State Community College; Kevin M. Gillen, Indiana University South Bend; Donna Goodwin, Tulsa Community College; Donna Gotch, California State University, San Bernardino; Robert Greenstreet, East Central University; Howard Grower, University of Tennessee; Angela Grupas, St. Louis Community College, Meramec; Karen Hamburg, Camden County College; Carla Harrell, Old Dominion University; Richard Harrison, Kilgore College; Vickie Harvey, California State University, Stanislaus; Linda Heil, Harford Community College; Anne Helms, Alamance Community College; Linda Hensley, Southwestern College; Lisa Katrina Hill, Harrisburg Area Community College, Gettysburg; Tim Horne, University of North Carolina at Charlotte; Allison Horrell, Spartanburg Community College; Marcia W. Hotchkiss, Tennessee State University; Christopher Howerton, Woodland Community College; Teresa Humphrey, University of South Carolina Aiken; Mary Hurley, St. Louis Community College at Forest Park; Nancy Jennings, Cuyamaca College; Robert Kagan, Manchester Community College; Pamela Kaylor, Ohio University Lancaster; Rebecca M. Kennerly, Georgia Southern University; Peter Kerr, Asbury University; Susan Kilgard, Anne Arundel Community College; Ray Killebrew, Missouri Baptist University; Sandra King, Anne Arundel Community College; Loretta Kissell, Mesa Community College; Brian Kline, Gainesville State College; Krista Kozel, Dona Ana Community College; Staci Kuntzman, University of North Carolina at Charlotte; Kristina Langseth, Minneapolis Community and Technical College; Cindy Larson-Casselton, Concordia College; Jeffrey Lawrence, Ivy Tech Community College, Columbus/Franklin; Michael Lee, College of Charleston; Robert Leonard, Sinclair Community College;

Lindstrom, Minneapolis Community and Technical College; Darren Linvill, Clemson University; Karen Lollar, Metropolitan State College of Denver; Steve Madden, Coastal Carolina University; Kristen Majocha, University of Pittsburgh at Johnstown; Reed Markham, Daytona State College, DeLand; Ginger K. Martin, Guilford Technical Community College; Sujanet Mason, Luzerne County Community College; Leola McClure, MiraCosta College; James R. McCoy, College of Southern Nevada; Dee Ann McFarlin, North Central Texas College; Deborah Socha McGee, College of Charleston; Miriam McMullen-Pastrick, Penn State Erie, The Behrend College; James McNamara, Alverno College; Delois Medhin, Milwaukee Area Technical College; Shellie Michael, Volunteer State Community College; Josh Miller, Los Angeles Valley College; Barbara Montgomery, Colorado State University, Pueblo; Eric Moreau, College of Southern Nevada; Lynnette Mullins, University of Minnesota, Crookston; Heidi Murphy, Central New Mexico Community College; Thomas Murray, Fitchburg State University; W. Benjamin Myers, University of South Carolina Upstate; Alexa Naramore, University of Cincinnati; Kay E. Neal, University of Wisconsin Oshkosh; Mary T. Newman, Wharton County Junior College; Rebecca Nordyke, Wichita State University; Christine North, Ohio Northern University; Erin Obermueller, Concordia College–New York; Elizabeth Reeves O'Connor, Rochester Institute of Technology; Tami Olds, Northern Virginia Community College; Mary Oulvey, Southwestern Illinois College; Mariusz Ozminkowski, California Polytechnic State University, Pomona; Deborah Panzer, Nassau Community College; Daniel Paulnock, Saint Paul College; Jean Perry, Glendale Community College; Charlotte Petty, University of Missouri at St. Louis; Shirlee Pledger, Fullerton College; Mihaela Popescu, California State University, San Bernardino; Mike Posey, Franklin University; Shelly Presnell, Shasta College; Ann Preston, St. Ambrose University; C. Thomas Preston, Gainesville State College; Marlene M. Preston, Virginia Tech; Shannon Proctor, Highline Community College; Brandi Quesenberry, Virginia Tech; Rita Rahoi-Gilchrest, Winona State University; Michele Ramsey, Penn State Berks; Rasha Ramzy, Georgia State University; Paul R. Raptis, Gainesville State College; Jessica Reeher, SUNY Oswego; Catherine Reilly, Dominican College; Elizabeth Richard, Saint Louis University; Maryanna Richardson, Forsyth Technical Community College; William Richter, Lenoir-Rhyne University; Heather Ricker-Gilbert, Manchester Community College; B. Hannah Rockwell, Loyola University Chicago; Terry Rogers, Casper College; Estrella Romero, Riverside City College/Riverside Campus; Douglas Rosentrater, Bucks County Community College; Kimberly Ross-Brown, Bluegrass Community and Technical College; Chip Rouse, Stevenson University; Tracy Routsong, Washburn University; Noreen M. Schaefer-Faix, Defiance College; Lisa Schroeder, Southwestern Oklahoma State University; Sydney Scott, Pace University; Jeff Shires, Purdue University North Central; James R. Shoopman, Embry Riddle Aeronautical University; Kate Simcox, Messiah College; June Smith, Angelo State University; Shelley Larson Soleimani, Oakland Community College; Kalisa Spalding, Elizabethtown Community and Technical College; Denise Sperruzza, St. Louis Community College, Meramec; Ruth Stokes, Trident Technical College; Wendell Stone, University of West Georgia; Jacob Stutzman, Oklahoma City University; Robert L. Strain, Florida Memorial University; Erik Stroner, Iowa Central Community College; Tammy Swenson-Lepper, Winona State University; Judy Szabo, Northeastern Junior College; Ann Taylor, Northern Kentucky University; Michael Tew, Eastern Michigan University; Miki Thiessen, Rock Valley College; Ryan Thompson, McLennan Community College; Greg Toney, Tri County Technical College; Jill Trites, University of Minnesota; Judi Truitt, Volunteer State Community College; Suzanne Uhl, Mt. San Jacinto College; Shannon VanHorn, Valley City State University; Lauren Velasco, Foothill College; Pamela S. Wegner, Black Hills State University; Deborah Wertanen, Minneapolis Community and Technical College; Patty Wharton-Michael, University of Pittsburgh at Johnstown; Charlene Widener, Hutchinson Community College; Robert L. Williams, Moberly Area Community College; Tyrell Williams, St. Phillip's College; Mark J. P. Wolf, Concordia University Wisconsin; Justin Young, Trine University; and Tony Zupancic, Notre Dame College.

DK Guide to Public Speaking

How Will Public Speaking Help You?

When Jenna and Sergei enrolled in public speaking classes, both saw it as a waste of time and dreaded it more than anything. Jenna worried that she wouldn't find anything interesting to say. Sergei was nervous and thought he would never want or need to use public speaking skills beyond class.

Before their classes ended, Sergei and Jenna felt differently. Jenna realized that a speech about Ramen noodles could be interesting if she used dynamic language and delivery as well as unique support materials. She discovered this popular college snack helped fight hunger in Japan after World War II. Jenna developed confidence in speaking and went on to own a consulting firm inspiring small business owners.

Sergei learned that his nervousness could be an asset and he could give a good speech. He still got nervous but knew how to positively channel his anxiety. Sergei joined the Mock Trial Club—something he would have passed up before his class. Even more astounding, he found he enjoyed it and changed his major to pre-law.

You may not yet see the benefit of learning to speak effectively, either. The extraordinary events that might happen in our lives, requiring us to step to the lectern, are hard to predict. But no matter what career you pursue, the influence that effective speaking will have on your life is significant. You will find yourself needing to defend a decision, promote your business, protect your family, or take a stance. These events require that you move beyond everyday skills and develop competent public speaking skills. This book will help you step up to those challenges.

OVERVIEW OF PUBLIC SPEAKING CONTENTS

How Can You Be a Successful Public Speaker? — 2
1 Be Audience Centered — 3
2 Select Appropriate Topics — 3
3 Be Knowledgeable — 3
4 Use Appropriate Verbal and Nonverbal Behavior — 3
5 Use Appropriate Appeals — 4
6 Be Creative but Organized — 5
7 Select Appropriate Delivery Styles — 5
8 Practice Again and Again — 5
9 Boost Your Confidence — 5

How Can You Overcome a Fear of Public Speaking? — 6
1 Face Your Fear Head On — 6
2 Learn Techniques That Work for You — 6
3 Practice, Practice, Practice — 7

How Can You Be an Ethical Public Speaker? — 8
1 Be Everything Required of a Successful Speaker — 9
2 Be Open to Differences — 9
3 Select and Use Reliable Evidence, Logic, and Reasoning — 9
4 Be Sensitive to the Power of Language — 9
5 Be Dedicated and Thorough in Citing Sources — 10
6 Accept Responsibility for Your Communication — 11
7 Support and Endorse Freedom of Expression — 11

When Will You Use the Skills Offered in This Book? — 12
1 In Your Public Life — 12
2 In Your Professional Life — 13
3 In Your Personal Life — 13

What Is the Process of Communicating? — 14

What Is the Creative Process for Public Speaking? — 16

Using the Steps in This Book — 23

CHAPTER 1: Getting to Know Your Audience and Situation — 25

CHAPTER 2: Selecting Your Topic and Purpose — 49

Tab 1 Review — 68

How Can You Be a Successful Public Speaker?

1 **Be Audience Centered**
2 **Select Appropriate Topics**
3 **Be Knowledgeable**
4 **Use Appropriate Verbal and Nonverbal Behavior**
5 **Use Appropriate Appeals**
6 **Be Creative but Organized**
7 **Select Appropriate Delivery Styles**
8 **Practice Again and Again**
9 **Boost Your Confidence**

We often know when we hear or see successful public speakers, even if we can't always put our fingers on why we like them. Good public speaking habits seem to slide right on by, unnoticed, while the speakers can move us and change our lives.

So what makes a good speaker? Scholars have wrestled with this question for centuries, but deep down, you already know the answer. Think about President John F. Kennedy or Martin Luther King, Jr. Search the Internet for recent famous commencement speeches by entrepreneur Steven Jobs or celebrities like Ellen DeGeneres, Jon Stewart, or Rachel Maddow, and think about what you like. Even if you disagree with their viewpoints, it is hard to deny that they all had or have good communication skills. Like you, they initially had certain skills that needed more work as well. For example, former Prime Minister of England Margaret Thatcher reportedly took voice-training courses to change her high voice to a lower one—a pitch that was culturally perceived to be authoritative.

Beginning speakers often see perfection as the key to success, only to be disappointed. No one is perfect, but successful public speaking grows out of the following qualities.

1

Be Audience Centered

Have you ever heard someone say, "You can't understand me until you have walked in my shoes?" This phrase symbolizes theorist and philosopher Kenneth Burke's notion of identification, as discussed in his book *A Rhetoric of Motives*. **Identification** (also called *empathy*) is the human need and willingness to understand as much as possible the feelings, thoughts, motives, interests, attitudes, and lives of others. As human beings, we are born separate but spend much of our lives looking for what we share with others. Good public speakers know that being audience centered allows them to help the audience connect with the speakers and their topics.

→ See Chapter 1 (Tab 1) for how to analyze your audience.

→ See Chapter 11 (Tab 5) for how to be a better listener.

2

Select Appropriate Topics

You cannot be audience centered if the topic is not appropriate to your audience and the occasion. However, you must be true to yourself as well. Locating a topic that fits you as well as your audience and the situation is the foundation of a good speech.

→ See Chapter 2 (Tab 1) for how to select and narrow your topic.

3

Be Knowledgeable

When the great artist Michelangelo was 88 years old, he allegedly wrote, "I am still learning." To be a successful speaker, you must be diligent and know as much as possible about your topic, audience, occasion, language, and methods of delivery right up to the moment the speech ends.

→ See Chapter 1 (Tab 1) for how to get to know your audience.

→ See Chapter 2 (Tab 1) and Chapters 3 and 4 (Tab 2) for how to learn about your topic.

→ See Tab 4 to learn about language and delivery options.

4

Use Appropriate Verbal and Nonverbal Behavior

Think about how you talk to your best friend compared with how you speak to someone like your mother or grandfather. Most likely, you do not use the same verbal and nonverbal language with your friend that you do with an older relative. The same goes for speaking effectively in public. Speakers must think about the topic, audience, situation, and intent of their speeches when they select their verbal and nonverbal behavior.

→ See Chapters 8 and 9 (Tab 4) for tips on appropriate behavior.

5
Use Appropriate Appeals

The great philosopher Aristotle wrote in the *Rhetoric* about the influence certain appeals (also called *proofs*) have on the credibility of a speaker and his or her speech. Aristotle argued that your credibility and that of your speech stems from *logos, ethos*, and *pathos*. Aristotle as well as other scholars reference yet another appeal that is topic specific and, therefore, not used as frequently. That appeal is *mythos*.

Logos appeals to your audience's ability to reason or work through your ideas logically. You use this sort of appeal when you organize a speech and support your speech with material that your audience will accept through reasoning.

→ See Tabs 2, 3, and 7 for help with developing stronger logic skills.

Ethos is the appeal of reliability. Your audience must view you and your support materials as reliable. You use this appeal when you demonstrate to the audience that you have their best interest in mind and are confident in the quality of your support materials as well as of the sources you quote. Your audience must view you as trustworthy, competent, objective, and enthusiastic for you to have high ethos.

→ See the section "How Can You Be an Ethical Public Speaker?" on pages 8–11 for more information about building your reliability.

→ See Tab 2 for information on maintaining source credibility.

Pathos references appealing to the audience's emotions to maintain their interest or to convince them of your intent. You create pathos through effective use of support materials and language. Speakers engaging an audience's emotions must be careful to balance this appeal with ethos and logos.

→ See Chapter 4 (Tab 2) for how to effectively use support materials.

→ See Chapter 8 (Tab 4) for more on effective language usage.

Mythos appeals to your audience's need for group membership and connection to the group's traditions, identity, and values. Appealing to a U.S. audience's sense of patriotism since 9/11 has become a popular political campaign technique and is a classic use of mythos. As with pathos, you create mythos through effective use of support materials and language, as well as your perceived credibility.

→ See Chapter 4 (Tab 2) for how to effectively use support materials.

→ See Chapter 8 (Tab 4) for more on effective language usage.

You must use a combination of these appeals to get your audience to listen, to understand your message, and, ultimately, to react the way you intend. Skillful and ethical speakers learn when and how to use appeals appropriately.

→ See Chapter 14 (Tab 7) for more discussion of using appeals.

6
Be Creative but Organized

Individuality, uniqueness, imagination, resourcefulness, and vision are all qualities of creativity. Imagine if Martin Luther King, Jr., had said "I have a hope" rather than "I have a dream." Imagine if Michael Jackson hadn't envisioned the video for "Thriller." We might not have one of the greatest speeches of all time, or music videos as we now know them might never have happened. Both men contributed something unique by being creative and resourceful yet organized in a manner acceptable to their audiences. Good speakers think outside the box and take chances that will set them apart from others.

→ Tabs 1–5 will show you how to be creative and organized when composing and presenting your speech.

7
Select Appropriate Delivery Styles

As with your verbal and nonverbal behavior, you must select the appropriate style of delivery. For example, reading from a manuscript about your trip to the state fair will seem strange and too formal. Most of the speeches you will give in a class or your everyday life will be extemporaneous. Speaking *extemporaneously* requires you to practice sufficiently, logically organize the speech, and use minimal notes while giving the speech.

→ See Chapter 9 (Tab 4) for a detailed description of delivery styles.

8
Practice Again and Again

In the first century BCE, Roman author Publilius Syrus wrote, "Practice is the best of all instructors." Most often, beginning students do not practice enough or exactly as they plan to give their speeches. Bad habits (such as putting off writing a speech until the last minute, just reading over the speech instead of practicing it, or practicing it only once) can cause many problems. Practicing helps you hone all your skills, locate issues that are not working within the speech, and develop confidence. Let your mind and body become familiar with your speech.

→ See Chapter 9 (Tab 4) for rehearsal guidelines.

9
Boost Your Confidence

Boosting your confidence will go a long way toward making you a better speaker. You will begin to actually enjoy giving a speech (Yes, you will!) if you work on how you feel about your abilities. Like creating a speech, boosting your confidence is a process that takes work and time. Most people have some level of anxiety about public speaking, and the next few pages will help you start to control that anxiety.

> **TIP: Speech Anxiety**
>
> Remember that nervousness is normal—even important—and can help energize you!

How Can You Overcome a Fear of Public Speaking?

1 **Face Your Fear Head On**
2 **Learn Techniques That Work for You**
3 **Practice, Practice, Practice**

1
Face Your Fear Head On

Communication apprehension (also known as *speech anxiety*) is a term scholars give to the fears you may have about giving a speech. These fears can be so intense that you avoid situations where you must speak in front of a group, and they can manifest into physical distress such as nausea or panic attacks. Clearly, physical distress at this level is something you need to control, but some apprehension is good. The physical and psychological responses you have before a date, a big game, or a speech are normal; they can help you succeed at the task at hand, and they can be controlled.

2
Learn Techniques That Work for You

The process of controlling your anxiety begins with recognizing exactly what you fear and noting how your body and mind react to stress. Often, just naming what we are afraid of will help us see how unfounded our fears might be. Throughout this book, "Confidence Booster" boxes (such as the one to the right) offer insights that may help you respond to your physical and psychological reactions. Note that they are labeled "Confidence Booster," not "Anxiety Eliminator." A certain amount of intense reaction energizes you and prepares you for the event.

➜ See Chapter 9 (Tab 4) for more on effective delivery practices, and use the Confidence Booster boxes throughout the book to help conquer stage fright.

3
Practice, Practice, Practice

Often your instinct is to stay away from situations that cause you stress. In the case of speech anxiety, if you really want to overcome it, you have to put yourself in speaking situations. The more you practice your speeches, and the more often you speak in front of an audience, the easier public speaking becomes. Ignoring anxiety makes that monster bigger and stronger.

CONFIDENCE BOOSTER

Training your body to adjust *before* you experience speech anxiety will help you control that inner demon. Many psychologists and communication practitioners suggest training your body to breathe deeply and to visualize happy, stress-free images. Remember, the key to training is practicing these techniques before you need them so that your body learns how it feels in a truly stress-free situation. These two techniques find their true power as a daily form of meditation and not just a quick fix for intense stress. The steps below are based on exercises from the University of Maryland Medical Center.

Deep Breathing

Deep breathing is a great way to relax the body.

1 Sit straight or lie on your back.

2 Slowly relax your body.

3 Begin to inhale slowly through your nose. Fill the lower part of your chest first, then the middle and top part of your chest and lungs. Be sure to do this slowly, over 8 to 10 seconds.

4 Hold your breath for a second or two.

5 Then quietly and easily relax and let the air out.

6 Wait a few seconds and repeat this cycle. If you become dizzy, slow down or stop.

Guided Imagery

In this technique, the goal is to visualize yourself in a peaceful setting.

1 Get comfortable and close your eyes or focus on a particular spot.

2 Imagine yourself in a place that makes you happy, such as on the beach or in a hammock.

3 Take yourself there mentally. Feel the sun and air on your skin, listen to the peaceful sounds, smell the flowers or ocean.

Practicing these techniques daily can have major stress-relieving effects on your body and will train it to understand what it feels like to relax.

A few deep breaths or taking yourself to your happy place just before a speech can refocus your mind on a body with less anxiety. Try to make it a habit to do one of these techniques four to five times daily, especially during potentially stressful times.

How Can You Be an Ethical Public Speaker?

1 **Be Everything Required of a Successful Speaker**

2 **Be Open to Differences**

3 **Select and Use Reliable Evidence, Logic, and Reasoning**

4 **Be Sensitive to the Power of Language**

5 **Be Dedicated and Thorough in Citing Sources**

6 **Accept Responsibility for Your Communication**

7 **Support and Endorse Freedom of Expression**

Being ethical means much more than just following the rules. Rules are part of the equation, but ethics grows out of our need to develop social relationships with others and our responsibilities within those relationships. If you were the only person on an island, your ethics would be of no concern because your actions would affect only you. However, you are not the only human being on an island, and you must construct and maintain relationships with others. To do so, others must view you as trustworthy, competent, objective, and passionate about what you do and support.

Adhering to the following qualities will help you be an ethical public speaker and build a strong relationship with your audience. To help you build that strong relationship, numerous "Practicing Ethics" boxes appear throughout this book. Ethics should become a part of every decision you make as you create your speech; it is not simply something to consider only when you read this section. So use these boxes to help and remind you every step of the way.

1
Be Everything Required of a Successful Speaker

Earlier in this Overview, you learned the nine qualities of a successful speaker. These qualities are the foundation of an ethical speaker as well. You have a responsibility to the audience to give a speech that is well researched and well crafted from your audience's perspective. Likewise, creating a well-crafted speech is self-respecting, because a solid speech will boost your confidence and credibility in the eyes of the audience.

→ See Tabs 1–5 for more on developing the qualities of a successful speaker.

2
Be Open to Differences

More than 6,000 different languages are spoken in the world. This fact alone makes it necessary to be open to differences in our current global culture. Language is only a small segment of what makes us unique. As an ethical speaker, you must work at recognizing every member of your audience and respect his or her needs and motives. Avoid **ethnocentrism**, or the assumption that your own group or culture is better than all others. Create a sense of inclusion, not exclusion. Be respectful and helpful.

→ See Chapter 1 (Tab 1) to help you get to know your audience.

3
Select and Use Reliable Evidence, Logic, and Reasoning

To be ethical, you must dedicate yourself to using reliable evidence, tight organization, and careful reasoning (avoiding fallacies). When speaking publicly, you have the opportunity to alter people's lives. Be careful with that responsibility. As Aristotle wrote in "De Caleo" ("On the Heavens"), "The least initial deviation from the truth is multiplied later a thousandfold."

→ See Chapter 4 (Tab 2) for how to select evidence.
→ See Tab 3 for help with organizing a speech.
→ See Chapter 14 (Tab 7) for how to create sensible reasoning and avoid fallacies.

4
Be Sensitive to the Power of Language

Words have the power to heal and to destroy. As an ethical speaker, you must be aware of your language choices and their power. Overly emotional language can cloud your audience's ability to reason. Offensive language directed at someone's race, ethnicity, religion, gender, or culture is inappropriate at the very least and can be the fuel for hate groups at its worst. Use language for the good of others.

→ See Chapter 8 (Tab 4) for how to use language effectively and ethically.

5

Be Dedicated and Thorough in Citing Sources

Avoiding plagiarism is all about protecting the words, ideas, and illustrations created by someone else, no matter if the creation is published or unpublished. When you intentionally or accidentally use all or a portion of the words, ideas, or illustrations created by someone else without giving proper credit, you commit the unethical and potentially harmful act of *plagiarism*. Plagiarism is not acceptable and may prevent you from passing a class, get you placed on academic probation, or force you to resign from a position. Recognizing the different types of plagiarism and adhering to preventive techniques will help you avoid plagiarizing in your speech.

- *Blatant plagiarism* can occur either when speakers take an entire speech or document and present it as their own or when a speaker takes parts of information from other sources and links the parts together, creating an entire speech out of someone else's words. Both of these forms are clearly intentional and highly unethical acts. In both forms, the speaker claims the words of others as his or her own and makes no attempt to recognize the original author.

- *No-citation plagiarism* occurs when speakers fail to give source credit to a specific part of their speech that has been taken from another source. This form of plagiarism can occur once or several times throughout a speech, even when the speech is created mainly by the speaker or when other sources are cited correctly. This form of plagiarism may be accidental but is still unethical. Be sure that you have carefully cited all your sources.

→ See Tab 2 for more details on how to cite sources correctly.

PRACTICING ETHICS: HOW TO AVOID PLAGIARISM

- Read and make sure you understand your institution's and instructor's plagiarism policies.
- Do your research early so that you have enough time to properly prepare.
- Keep detailed notes on any sources you use and the specific material you find there.
- Use your own words, sentence structure, and organizational structure.
- Utilize a variety of sources.
- Make sure that you cite sources of quotations, paraphrased material, facts, definitions, and statistics.
- Cite the sources of illustrations, pictures, drawings, graphs, photos, videos, tables, maps, and other such items if you did not create them yourself.
- Follow the class assignment rules for citing sources on your outline, source page, and during your speech.

REMEMBER

Whether blatant or no-citation, intentional or accidental, plagiarism is highly unethical and can be damaging. Be diligent in citing your sources during your speech and on your outline. Citing sources will build your credibility.

6
Accept Responsibility for Your Communication

In this age of very open disclosure and easy access to recording devices, we cannot always predict the long-term effects related to what we say or do. Make sure you are willing to stand by your words and actions, not only in the immediate short-term speaking situation, but in the long term as well.

7
Support and Endorse Freedom of Expression

The *First Amendment* of the U.S. Constitution (adopted in 1791) states, "Congress shall make no law… abridging the freedom of speech, or the press…." As a public speaker, you are morally and legally obligated to comply with laws that protect others. Practicing the previous six guidelines will help you protect the rights of others. Keep the following practices in mind as well:

- Be careful to debate ideas rather than to attack people.
- Keep your feelings, especially if you feel angry, in check.
- Above all, remember that the First Amendment is a form of protection and empowerment, not censorship and disenfranchisement.

It just seems to be a human trait to want to protect the speech of people with whom we agree. For the First Amendment, that is not good enough. So it is really important that we protect First Amendment rights of people no matter what side of the line they are on.[1]

FLOYD ABRAMS,
attorney and Constitutional law expert

When Will You Use the Skills Offered in This Book?

1 In Your Public Life
2 In Your Professional Life
3 In Your Personal Life

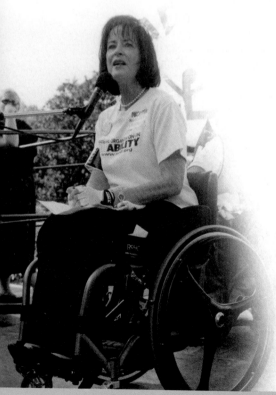

1
In Your Public Life

Taking the time now to understand the public speaking process will help you:

- Improve your ability to speak out about issues in your community and larger society.
- Become more culturally sensitive.
- Become a better consumer of public communication from others through the development of your critical thinking skills.

Engaging in public speaking is empowerment at its purest. We live in a country that honors its people with the freedom of speech, and as citizens, we can use that freedom to improve our lives and those of future generations. Someday, you may find yourself the president of a local community project to keep children drug-free. You may find yourself appointed the neighborhood spokesperson when a large corporation wants to purchase land in your neighborhood for a new construction project. When family members struggle to pay their medical bills, you may find yourself speaking out for medical reform. You will encounter numerous times throughout your life when you will need to have the courage to speak out publicly on issues that concern you and those you care about.

2
In Your Professional Life

Individuals who develop effective communication skills get better grades, more promotions, higher pay, and more overall success in their educational and professional careers. No matter what major you select or what profession you end up working in, you will need to be an effective speaker.

Learning how to outline or cite sources is as important in a science research class as it is in a speech class, and learning how to listen will help you in all your classes, as well as in your professional relationships. Today, most two-year and four-year college courses in any field have an oral presentation requirement. When looking for a job, you will find that most employers place a high emphasis on good written and oral communication skills when hiring and evaluating their employees. The basic job interview is quite possibly the most difficult persuasive communication most of you will undertake.

3
In Your Personal Life

Personal benefits relate to your self-esteem and self-development. When you engage in public speaking, you learn more about yourself and others, as well as how to be a better listener and overall person. The self-esteem benefit may be the most important at this point in your public speaking mission. Most beginning speakers have some fear or stage fright related to giving a speech. Ironically, the single best way to beat the stage-fright monster is to give many speeches. Once you realize you can give a speech and that most audiences are more forgiving than you think, you will find confidence in yourself that you didn't know existed. So get up to that lectern, give that speech as you practiced it, pat yourself on the back, and conquer that monster!

→ See Chapter 9 (Tab 4) for more on effective speech delivery and the Confidence Booster boxes throughout the book for help with conquering stage fright.

If I had to go back to college again — knowing what I know today — I'd concentrate on two areas: learning to write and to speak before an audience. Nothing in life is more important than the ability to communicate effectively. [2]

PRESIDENT GERALD R. FORD

What Is the Process of Communicating?

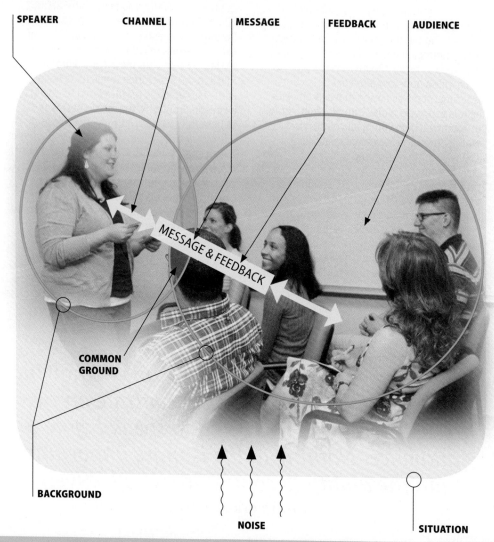

SPEAKER   CHANNEL   MESSAGE   FEEDBACK   AUDIENCE

MESSAGE & FEEDBACK

COMMON GROUND

BACKGROUND

NOISE

SITUATION

Public speaking is a communication process and best understood when represented as a model where several parts interact and influence each other.

- The **speaker** is the person who initiates and is responsible for most of the message.
- The **audience** is the person or persons receiving the speaker's message and contributing feedback.
- The **message** consists of the verbal and nonverbal ideas encoded by the speaker and decoded by the audience. In the diagram on the previous page, **encoding** (the process of conveying) and **decoding** (the process of interpreting) are illustrated by the double arrows on either side of the "Message & Feedback" element.
- **Feedback** consists of the verbal or nonverbal messages encoded by the audience and decoded by the speaker.
- The **channel** is the means of getting the message across, such as a voice over the airwaves or visual messages in the form of nonverbal or visual aids.
- **Noise** is anything that interferes with the message or feedback, such as external sounds or internal fear or illness.
- The **situation** is the location and time in which the communication takes place.
- **Background** refers to the speaker's and the audience's identities and life experiences.
- **Common ground** refers to the overlap within the speaker's and audience's identities and life experiences.

If you have the ability to carry on an ordinary conversation, you have the ability to speak publicly. The difference between public speaking and everyday conversation is that public speaking requires a more formal structure, use of language, and delivery style.

For years, we considered the process of communicating like a one-way street—information flowed from the sender to the receiver, but not the other way around. Then we viewed it as a two-way street with information traveling separately on each respective side of the street but not at the same time—to and from, back and forth. Today, we view communication as a much more complex process that is transactional. It is a **transactional process** because:

- The people involved in the act of communicating are actively and simultaneously sending as well as receiving information.
- Participants view their communication as intentional.
- The transfer of information between them takes place within a particular situation bound by relationship and culture.

You should view the speaker and the audience as co-communicators in the process, giving them almost equal responsibility and power to create as well as understand the message.

What Is the Creative Process for Public Speaking?

Composing and presenting a speech may seem daunting if you view the process only as a whole, but you can break it down into workable parts. The practical information throughout this book will help you. This chart shows the five basic activities you will use to create a successful speech. Although the process may look linear, you will frequently move back and forth between activities.

1 STARTING

GETTING TO KNOW YOUR AUDIENCE AND SITUATION
→ See page 25

Know who you are speaking to as well as where, when, and why you are speaking.

SELECTING YOUR TOPIC AND PURPOSE
→ See page 49

Select the topic that best fits you, your audience, and the occasion. Define the purpose of your speech.

2 RESEARCHING

LOCATING SUPPORT MATERIALS
→ See page 69

Find support materials through the Internet, the library, interviews, and surveys.

SELECTING AND TESTING SUPPORT MATERIALS
→ See page 109

Learn how to effectively evaluate, choose, and use a variety of support materials.

3
CREATING

OUTLINING YOUR SPEECH
→ See page 137

Start with a working outline, create a preparation outline, and include a citations page. Create a delivery outline to use during your speech.

ORGANIZING THE SPEECH BODY
→ See page 173

Identify your main points and choose an organizational strategy.

INTRODUCING AND CONCLUDING YOUR SPEECH
→ See page 195

Create an introduction that gets attention and sets up your credibility and your speech. Create a conclusion that sums up and ends with impact.

4
PRESENTING

USING LANGUAGE SUCCESSFULLY
→ See page 215

Write your speech using language that is familiar, concrete, appropriate, and vivid. Use devices like repetition and parallelism to engage your audience.

DELIVERING YOUR SPEECH
→ See page 237

Strive to be natural, enthusiastic, confident, engaging, and appropriate in your delivery. Practice!

USING PRESENTATION AIDS
→ See page 261

Know when and how to use presentation aids to capture attention, enhance your credibility, and help your audience understand and remember your speech.

5
LISTENING & EVALUATING

LISTENING
→ See page 299

Be an active, ethical, and effective listener who can overcome barriers to listening and who shares responsibility in the communication process.

EVALUATING SPEECHES
→ See page 317

Determine the effectiveness and appropriateness of a speech's topic, support materials, organization, and language, and of a speaker's delivery and ethics.

1 STARTING

GETTING TO KNOW YOUR AUDIENCE AND SITUATION

Knowing who you will be speaking to, as well as where, when, and why you are speaking, is fundamental to creating a speech.

All of your decisions during the speech-making process need to consider these factors.

- Who will be in the audience? What are the audience's beliefs, values, attitudes, or personal, social, or other traits?

- Where will the speech take place? What are the specific characteristics of the location that could affect my speech?

- What time of day will my speech take place? Will there be other speeches? What will happen before and after?

- Why is the audience gathered? Is it a special occasion?

➔ Chapter 1 shows you how to get to know your audience and situation.

SELECTING YOUR TOPIC AND PURPOSE

Your speech topic and purpose must interest you and should be appropriate to your audience and the occasion.

Here are some suggestions to help you in the selection process.

- Evaluate your speech assignment or speech invitation for hints about a topic or the type of speech you need to give.

- Create a list of possible topics by:

  - Brainstorming, or free-associating, about possible ideas

  - Exploring topic ideas related to the type of speech you are giving (to inform, to persuade, or to accentuate an event)

  - Searching the Internet, newspapers, or other media for ideas

- Review your list and select the topic that best fits you, your audience, and the occasion.

- Narrow your topic by writing a single, complete sentence about your topic and what you want to cover in the speech.

  - Do some preliminary research to see if you can locate enough appropriate and current information on the topic.

  - Think of three to five main points you might make about your topic, and create a working outline to guide your research.

➔ Chapter 2 shows you how to select an appropriate topic.

OVERVIEW OF PUBLIC SPEAKING

2 RESEARCHING

LOCATING SUPPORT MATERIALS

With the advent of the Internet, locating and collecting support materials has never been so easy or exciting. However, you can locate great materials in many places.

- **Start with your own personal knowledge and possessions**
  Personal materials should primarily be used at the beginning of your research and not the only type of sources you consult.

- **Search the Internet**
  Use search engines to locate Web sites, online references, virtual libraries and archives, and blogs.

- **Check out the library, either online or in person**
  The library offers books, special collections, periodicals, government documents, reference material, online databases, and interlibrary loans.

- **Conduct interviews or surveys related to your topic**

→ Chapter 3 shows you how to locate support materials.

SELECTING AND TESTING SUPPORT MATERIALS

Support materials are the substance that fills the content of your speech. You should always:

- **Use a variety of materials** (examples, facts, definitions, statistics, or testimony)

- **Evaluate the materials**
  - Are the materials accurate?
  - Are the materials recent?
  - Are the materials complete?
  - Are the materials reliable?
  - Are the materials appropriate?

- **Use the materials in an effective manner**
  - Do the materials have a purpose?
  - Are you presenting the materials in a variety of ways?
  - Do your delivery techniques make the materials stand out?
  - Do you correctly and effectively cite the sources of the materials?

→ Chapter 4 discusses support materials in detail.

3 CREATING

OUTLINING YOUR SPEECH

You need to lead your audience through your speech, and outlining helps you create a logical structure.

All preparation outlines should adhere to formal outline rules, and citations should follow a style manual, such as MLA or APA. Your preparation outline should include:

- An introduction and a conclusion
- A body containing main points and support materials
- Links between each part to guide the audience
- Citations within the outline and a source page

Create a delivery outline, out of key words and phrases, to use during your actual presentation.

→ Chapter 5 shows you how to create outlines.

ORGANIZING THE SPEECH BODY

Using an appropriate organizational strategy for the body of your speech is essential.

You choose a strategy by:

- Identifying your main points
- Considering your speech goal (to inform, to persuade, to accentuate)
- Considering what your audience knows or needs to know about your topic

Organizational strategies include chronological, topical, spatial, causal, order of intensity, comparative, problem–solution, refutation, and Monroe's motivated sequence.

→ Chapter 6 explains the organizational strategies and shows you how to use them.

INTRODUCING AND CONCLUDING YOUR SPEECH

Your introduction and conclusion are the first and last opportunities you have to dazzle your audience, so dedicate time to crafting effective ones.

Your introduction should launch your speech by using this format:

- Attention-getter: Begin with material that grabs your audience's attention.
- Credibility material: Build your credibility by stating why you should give this speech.
- Relevance to audience: Build the audience's interest in you and your topic.
- Preview of speech: Introduce the topic and preview your main points.

Your conclusion should wrap up your speech with impact. Use this format:

- Summary statement: Briefly recap the speech's main ideas.
- Audience response statement: Tell your audience how you want them to respond to the speech.
- WOW statement: Provide closure with a memorable "wow" ending.

→ Chapter 7 shows you how to create effective introductions and conclusions.

PRESENTING

USING LANGUAGE SUCCESSFULLY

Language is powerful, and you need to use it effectively.

Your speech should:

- Use language that is familiar, concrete, precise, and accurate.
- Use vivid language for emotional appeal.
- Use repetition and parallelism to help your audience remember points.
- Use language that is appropriate for you, your audience, and the occasion.

➜ Chapter 8 shows you how to make effective language choices.

DELIVERING YOUR SPEECH

Successful delivery takes practice.

You should aim to:

- Be natural
- Be enthusiastic
- Be confident
- Be engaging verbally and nonverbally
- Be appropriate

Remember to use your voice and body effectively. Vary your voice in rate, pitch, volume, and other characteristics. Be sure your appearance is appropriate, make eye contact, and use facial expressions and gestures to emphasize points in your speech.

Above all, practice, practice, and practice your speech some more!

➜ Chapter 9 offers guidance on effective delivery techniques.

USING PRESENTATION AIDS

Not all speeches require presentation aids, but when you do use them, they can be beneficial.

Effective presentation aids can:

- Capture your audience's attention.
- Enhance your credibility if they are well made.
- Increase your audience's understanding of complex ideas or statistics.
- Improve your audience's ability to remember parts of your speech.

You can use audio or video clips, items, models, maps, graphs, charts, and/or pictures to enhance your speech.

To be effective, presentation aids should be:

- Easy to see
- Kept simple
- Appropriate for you, your audience, and the occasion
- Well made

➜ Chapter 10 helps you determine if you need presentation aids and shows you how to craft them.

5 LISTENING & EVALUATING

LISTENING

As a college student, you spend most of your day listening. As a speaker, you need to help your audience listen successfully. Listening effectively is an ethical responsibility—as well as a necessity for gaining information and critically evaluating the communication of others. Our ability to listen influences our personal, professional, and public lives.

Effective listening faces several barriers that we must continually overcome:

- Environmental barriers, such as a siren
- Physiological barriers, such as a head-ache or hearing impairment
- Psychological barriers that occur in our heads, such as racism or sexism
- Linguistic barriers or verbal and nonver-bal issues, such as not understanding slang or an unfamiliar nonverbal symbol

To overcome these barriers:

You must understand what listening is and accept your share of the responsibility in the communication process. As a speaker, help your audience listen more effectively by knowing who they are, grabbing their atten-tion, creating a message that is interesting and easy to follow, controlling the environ-ment, and paying attention to audience feedback. As an audience member, actively listen (concentrate by focusing on the verbal and nonverbal) and listen critically (assess the message, reserve your personal reactions, and be open minded).

EVALUATING SPEECHES

Learning to give evaluations of your own and others' speeches, and to accept other people's evaluations of your speeches, begins with viewing the process as a *good* thing. An evaluation is a form of assessment, an act of appreciation, or a means of self-improvement.

When you are evaluated or you evaluate someone else, you should consider:

- Is the topic appropriate?
- Did the speech use effective support materials?
- Was the speech organized effectively?
- Was the speaker's delivery effective?
- Were the language choices appropriate and effective?
- Was the speaker ethical?

Effective evaluation begins with being truthful, specific, sensitive, helpful, and positive.

→ Chapter 11 explains the listening process and shows you how to be a better listener.

→ Chapter 12 will show you how to use feedback to improve and how to be a constructive evaluator.

Using the Steps in This Book

Creating a speech is a lot like running a race, solving a puzzle, or playing a video game. You evaluate the other players and the situation; you research your options; you organize your strategy; and you plan an effective attack or move. You select a path to take, and you follow it, one step at a time, to the finish line. In the first five tabs of this book, you will encounter the tools and activities to help you along the path of creating the best communicative events you can. In the last four tabs, you will see those tools and activities put into practice when creating an informative, persuasive, or special occasion speech, as well as when communicating in a professional setting or a small group.

As American civil rights activist Jesse Jackson once said,

"If my mind can conceive it, and my heart can believe it, I know I can achieve it." [3]

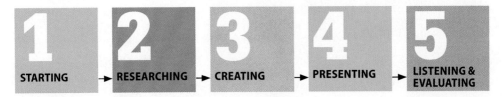

Use the steps in this book to conceive a great speech and to believe in your heart of hearts that you can deliver it. Take a deep breath, stand tall, walk to the lectern, and believe in yourself. You can achieve success and confidence in speaking!

1

GETTING TO KNOW YOUR AUDIENCE AND SITUATION

Introduction

Think about how you feel when someone cannot remember your name. Or does not look at you when speaking to you. Or gives you advice without learning who you are, what your needs are, or what motivates you. These behaviors can make you feel like you do not exist or are not important or that what you believe does not matter.

Speaking to an audience that you have not taken the time to learn about creates similar feelings. It is a necessity and your ethical responsibility as a speaker to appreciate your audience if you want to succeed. Like a good friendship, a connection with your audience is not easy or something that just happens. You have to work at it. So let's get started and learn about your audience.

OVERVIEW OF PUBLIC SPEAKING   1

CHAPTER 1 CONTENTS

Why Do You Need to Know Your Audience?   26
1 You Want to Get Your Audience's Attention and Good Will   27
2 You Will Build Your Speaking Competence   27

What Do You Need to Know About Your Audience?   28
1 Attitudes   28
2 Beliefs   29
3 Values   29

What Specific Traits Do You Need to Investigate?   30
1 Personal Traits   30
2 Psychological Traits   32
3 Social Traits   33

Why Do You Need to Know the Speaking Situation?   36

What Do You Need to Know About the Speaking Situation?   38
1 Place and Audience Size   38
2 Time   39
3 Occasion   39

How Do You Locate Audience and Situation Information?   40
1 Stop, Think, and Brainstorm   40
2 Interview   41
3 Survey   42
4 Research   43

How Can You Adapt to Your Audience During the Speech?   44
1 Adapt to External Noise   45
2 Adapt to Internal Noise   45

Chang's Speech   46

CHAPTER 2: Selecting Your Topic and Purpose   49

Tab 1 Review   68

Why Do You Need to Know Your Audience?

1 You Want to Get Your Audience's Attention and Good Will

2 You Will Build Your Speaking Competence

Famous stage, radio, and film star Fanny Brice once said,

"Your audience gives you everything you need.... There is no director who can direct you like an audience." [1]

Although Brice was speaking of acting, her comments apply to public speaking as well.

Being in tune with your audience comes from knowing about the audience members and will benefit your speech in important ways.

1
You Want to Get Your Audience's Attention and Good Will

Audiences want you to do the work to grab and keep their attention. One way to do this is to recognize their **egocentrism**, or the tendency for your audience to be interested in things that relate and matter to them. Audiences want you to recognize that they are a unique group of individuals, not one mass without personality, which means crafting your speech to be **audience centered**. This approach begins the moment you start selecting your topic and continues to the moment you finish delivering your speech.

Speaking from an audience-centered standpoint begins with **audience analysis**—a systematic investigation of characteristics that make your audience unique. Audience analysis helps you answer such questions as:

- What ideas should be covered for this audience?
- How much information will they need?
- What language and support materials will work best for them?
- What could be potential audience expectations and reactions?
- What obstacles could affect the speech?

2
You Will Build Your Speaking Competence

Speaking competence relates to how well you communicate with others. No matter if you find yourself communicating with an audience that is similar or one that is significantly different with multiple diverse social, personal, or cultural identities, your communication will be considerably better if you demonstrate an effective speaking competence, or what Stephen Littlejohn and Karen Foss in *Theories of Human Communication* call intercultural competence. According to Littlejohn and Foss, this competence has three components:

Identity knowledge means knowing what is distinctive about an audience.

Mindfulness means being conscientiously aware of those distinctions. Paying attention to your audience's distinctiveness is an ongoing process. It becomes part of every decision you make from the moment you accept a speaking engagement to the moment you finish the event.

Negotiation skill is the ability to respond to audience differences through sensitivity, politeness, willing adjustment, and collaboration. Littlejohn and Foss suggest that you have achieved effective negotiation when your audience understands you and feels respected.

CONFIDENCE BOOSTER

Analyzing your audience to know their point of view—and to see them as individuals instead of a mass of people—has the added benefit of helping you feel more comfortable in front of them. Think about the fact that it is easier to talk to a friend than a stranger. That feeling has a lot to do with knowing how your friend might react to you and your topic. In turn, this knowledge allows you to think through the best means for getting the best reaction from your friend. Speaking to a public audience is no different, so do not cheat yourself out of this potential confidence booster. Spend the time necessary to get to know your audience.

What Do You Need to Know About Your Audience?

1 Attitudes

2 Beliefs

3 Values

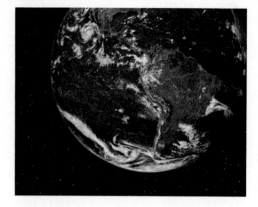

1
Attitudes

Attitudes are persistent psychological responses, predispositions, or inclinations to act one way or feel a particular way—usually positive or negative—toward something. For instance, you might like New York City better than Chicago, you may not trust anything found on the Internet, or you may like to date men that are tall and have dark hair. The longer someone holds an attitude, the more information he or she usually has to support it—and the harder it is to change.

2
Beliefs

Beliefs are those things a person accepts as plausible based on interpretation and judgment, such as believing in a religion or philosophy. For example, you may believe it is the responsibility of humans to take care of the planet, Internet bullying is harmful, the earth's seasons are caused by its tilting on its axis, or the United States has a responsibility to help other countries in times of disaster. Some beliefs may be easily accepted with only a little knowledge, whereas others take time to accept or may be very controversial.

3
Values

Values relate to worth or what a person sees as right or wrong, important or unimportant, desirable or undesirable. Values are our principles, such as cherishing family over professional success. Other examples of values held by many in the United States are independence, progress, freedom of speech, life, good health, honesty, wealth, and education. When you are from or belong to a country, culture, or religion, you may be expected to hold and share common values with the other members.

Beliefs, values, and attitudes make up the audience's **identity.** Of course, you will never fully know your audience's specific beliefs, values, and attitudes about every issue in your speech, but knowing as much as possible about them will help you make your speech more meaningful and you more confident.

What Specific Traits Do You Need to Investigate?

1 **Personal Traits**
2 **Psychological Traits**
3 **Social Traits**

1

Personal Traits

Personal traits (sometimes referred to as *demographics*) include age, gender, sexual orientation, household type, education, occupation, income, and disabilities. Each characteristic can potentially provide insight into what's important to your audience, how they will feel about given issues, and what they accept as true. For example, older adults who lived through the Great Depression and World War II tend to worry about consuming too much of certain products because they lived through times of great need or heavy rationing. The chart on the facing page, adapted from *When Generations Collide* by Lynne Lancaster and David Stillman, describes some generational trends you can consider to help you understand your audience better.

CHECKLIST for Personal Traits

❑ What's the age range of my audience? What's the average age?

❑ What's the gender ratio?

❑ Who are the audience members specifically? What do I know about their occupations? Education? Households? Disabilities?

❑ What's the average income or socioeconomic level?

❑ What might the audience already know about my potential topics?

NOTE: Not all of these questions will apply to every speaking event, but you should do your best to know as much as possible about the audience.

GENERATIONAL TRENDS

Be aware that focusing too much on trends can lead to ***stereotyping***, which is false or over-simplified generalizing applied to individuals based on group characteristics. Allow the trends to guide but not dictate your interactions.

Born before 1945 (*Traditionalists*)	Defining word: **loyal** Marry once, "save for a rainy day," little formal education, conservative, respect authority and America, not easily persuaded.
Born 1946–1964 (*Baby Boomers*)	Defining word: **optimistic** More educated, committed to belonging, political, very competitive, spend rather than save, divorce and remarry, cynical of and challenge authority.
Born 1965–1980 (*Generation X*)	Defining word: **skepticism** Product of divorce, single parents, or blended homes; resourceful and independent; count on peers and friends more than family; influenced by media; struggle with money.
Born 1981–1999 (*Millennials or Generation Y*)	Defining word: **realistic** Smart, confident, practical, techno-savvy, concerned about personal safety, influenced by friends and media, appreciate diversity, can be very biased.

PRACTICING ETHICS

- Be respectful of gender and sexual orientation. No matter whether your audience is predominately male or female, or gay or straight, being insensitive will hurt your reputation and perpetuates negative stereotypes.
- Recognize that you may have few "traditional" household members in your audience. According to the Population Reference Bureau, only 7 percent of all U.S. households in 2002 were "traditional."
- Remember that high levels of education do not always equate with intelligence. College graduates are not smart about everything, and some very intelligent people are self-taught. However, the more education your audience has, the more they are exposed to different topics and language.
- Be cautious about connecting income levels and occupations—not all lawyers are highly paid, for instance.
- Consider that you may have audience members with disabilities. They often have unique insights and may have certain communicative challenges.
- Understand that personal traits can change, due to significant events, trends, and opportunities during a particular time in history. For example, after the tragedy of September 11, 2001, many U.S. citizens—regardless of age—were more concerned about country and family.
- Avoid negative stereotyping. *Understand* commonalities and differences, but don't compartmentalize.
- Above all, respect diversity, all the time!

2

Psychological Traits

The **psychological traits** of your audience pertain to their needs and motivations. In *Motivation and Personality*, psychologist Abraham Maslow outlined a classic theory demonstrating how people's needs motivate them to respond in certain ways. For example, if buying or doing something will help people satisfy a need, they will more likely make that purchase or do that activity. Maslow fine-tuned his theory by identifying five levels of needs, which are *hierarchical*. In other words, you must fulfill some of the basic needs before the other needs become crucial. **Maslow's hierarchy of needs** is best represented as a pyramid, with basic needs at the bottom, giving support to the higher levels.

SELF-ACTUALIZATION NEEDS

SELF-ESTEEM NEEDS

SOCIAL NEEDS

SAFETY NEEDS

PHYSIOLOGICAL NEEDS

Physiological needs are related to continued existence, such as food, water, general comfort, and sex. These are the most pure and most necessary for a person to continue to live. A speech on "How to Eat Healthy on a Budget" highlights this level of need.

Safety needs relate to what we need to feel secure, such as a roof over our heads and safety in our own homes. A speech demonstrating how to be ready in times of disaster evokes this type of need.

Social needs are those feelings we have about belonging. Most of us want to give and receive love, be close to others, and be supported. We have a strong need to feel a part of groups, such as family, friends, or religion. Pep rallies and speeches given during new student orientations on college campuses strive to fulfill this need.

Self-esteem needs relate to our strong need for respect from others we view as important, much as you may have felt when you were a teenager and wanted your parents to trust you and be proud of you. Pride, prestige, self-respect, accomplishment,

recognition, and the need for success are aspects of this need. Speeches given at graduations usually focus heavily on this need.

Self-actualization needs relate to the need to feel achievement connected to personal identity, independence, happiness, and potential. An example of a self-actualization speech would be seven-time winner of the Tour de France and cancer survivor Lance Armstrong giving a motivational speech to a group of young cancer survivors. His LiveSTRONG motto characterizes this need.

CHECKLIST for Psychological Traits

❑ What needs might my audience have?

❑ Is there a level of needs where my audience has significant concerns?

❑ Because of their needs, will my audience be positive, apathetic, or negative toward my potential speech topics?

❑ How might I use their needs to show relevance to my topic or to persuade them?

3
Social Traits

Your audience's *social traits* relate to how they are affected by or identify with other groups of people. Two types of groups can influence your audience—those by choice and those by birth.

SOCIAL TRAITS BY CHOICE

The "by choice" group are people your audience members choose to connect with, like political parties, hobby communities, athletic teams, and religious, professional, social, or civic organizations. Studying these group connections can give you obvious but significant insights into how your audience will relate to you and your topic. For example, avid hunters may react negatively to a speech arguing for new hunting regulations unless they see a benefit to hunters or the animal population.

SOCIAL TRAITS BY BIRTH

The second group includes those relationships your audience members have with others by birth and by growing up within certain societies—specifically race, ethnicity, and culture.

Race is the biological differences of humankind, based on physical markers, such as color and texture of hair, color of skin and eyes, shape of facial features, bodily build, and proportions.

Ethnicity stems from our national and religious affiliations.

Culture is the system that teaches a set of objectives and rules that help us survive and gain societal acceptance within our community. Individuals learn, share, and convey culture from generation to generation.

Race, ethnicity, and culture mold a person's identity and, therefore, will directly influence how he or she responds to issues.

Given how diverse our towns, offices, schools, and digital lives have become, understanding the social traits of the audience is a speaker's ethical imperative and key to potential success. However, simply knowing you have a diverse audience is not that helpful. The following pages look at some ways audience members' race, ethnicity, and culture can impact your speech.

CHECKLIST for Social Traits

❏ What organizations will sponsor the speaking event?

❏ What organizations might be represented at the event?

❏ What other social affiliations might influence my speech (such as hobbies or athletic teams)?

❏ What professions might be represented?

❏ What religions might be represented?

❏ What cultures, ethnicities, and races might be represented?

U.S. POPULATION DIVERSITY

According to the U.S. Census Bureau in 2010, the nation is getting more racially and ethnically diverse, as well as much older.

We are a country built and empowered by our diversity. As a speaker, you must be aware of and sensitive to diverse points of view when you select a topic and source materials, create an argument, use specific language, or choose your delivery style.

Given their different cultural heritages, their personal struggles, and the struggles represented in previous generations of their families, "minorities" have unique perspectives, needs, and motivations that you must keep in mind. For example, they tend to consider issues such as equal opportunity, immigration laws, English as the official U.S. language, and minority representation in high-level government and private offices more carefully than people in the "majority."

Consider diversity an opportunity rather than an obstacle, with greater opportunity and greater appreciation in almost every stage of your speech process. The next page highlights some cultural characteristics that might help you shape your speech for a particular culture or a multicultural audience.

CHANGES IN U.S. POPULATION DIVERSITY (each figure = 1%)

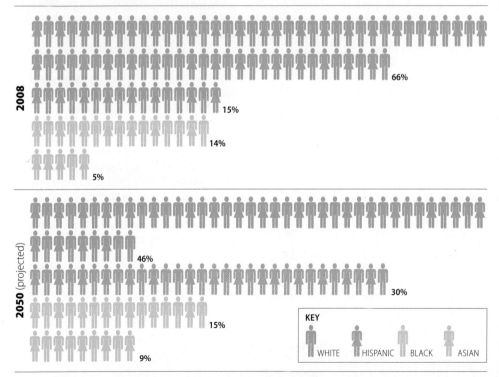

CULTURAL TENDENCIES

In *Culture's Consequences*, Geert Hofstede's Value Dimension model offers a helpful way to look at cultural tendencies and might help you adapt appropriately to a culture (or cultures). Keep in mind that these are tendencies, not individual responses. You will rarely, if ever, find someone who fits them exactly. Let them guide, not define, your interactions. Adapted from Samovar, Porter, and McDaniel's *Communication Between Cultures*, this table explains the tendencies.

HOFSTEDE'S FIVE DIMENSIONS OF CULTURE

DIMENSION	EXPLANATION	EXAMPLE COUNTRIES	AUDIENCE RESPONSE
High Power vs. Low Power	High-power cultures have clear, defined lines of authority and responsibility	High-power countries Guatemala, Mexico, Venezuela, Arab countries	High-power audiences will respond well to material from credible sources
	Low-power cultures blur these lines	Low-power countries Germany, Costa Rica, Great Britain, Denmark, U.S.	Low-power audiences like equality and options
Individual vs. Collectivist	Individual cultures stand for self	Individual countries U.S., Australia, Great Britain, Canada, Netherlands, Italy, France, Denmark, Germany	Individual audiences will respond better to an emphasis on personal reward
	Collectivist cultures stand for the group	Collectivist countries Venezuela, Pakistan, Costa Rica, Peru, Taiwan, Chile, South Korea	Collectivist audience will respond best to an emphasis on community and a sense of duty
Competitive vs. Nurturing	Competitive cultures stress competitiveness, assertiveness, ambition, wealth, and material possessions	Competitive countries Japan, Austria, Venezuela, Italy, Ireland, Greece, Switzerland, Mexico, Great Britain, U.S., Germany	Competitive audiences will respond to emphazing strength, winning, gaining an edge, and material success
	Nurturing cultures stress relationships, quality of life, sexual equality, and care of the environment	Nurturing countries Sweden, Norway, Chile, Costa Rica, Netherlands, South Korea, Denmark, Finland, Portugal, Thailand	Nurturing audiences will respond well to nurturing language, caring behavior, and equality
High-uncertainty Avoidance vs. Low-uncertainty Avoidance	High-uncertainty cultures strive to avoid uncertainty and ambiguity through stability	High-uncertainty countries Greece, Portugal, Japan, Peru, Spain, France, Costa Rica, Mexico, Israel, Belgium	High-uncertainty audiences need clear logic, detailed information, and small steps to initiate change
	Low-uncertainty cultures are tolerant of the unusual, new ideas, and other people	Low-uncertainty countries Singapore, Jamaica, Denmark, Ireland, U.S., India	Low-uncertainty audiences don't need as much detail, are willing to be more adventurous, and embrace change
Long-term Orientation vs. Short-term Orientation	Long-term cultures value persistence, thriftiness, future, a strong work ethic, structure, and status	Long-term countries China, Taiwan, Japan, South Korea, Brazil	Long-term audiences respond to detail, persistence, and seeing what benefit there is for the future
	Short-term cultures emphasize time and are concerned with short-term results, try to "cheat" old age, seek quick gratification, and deemphasize status	Short-term countries Great Britain, Canada, the Philippines, U.S.	Short-term audiences want quick results with almost instant gratification. How will this get the job done?

WHAT SPECIFIC TRAITS DO YOU NEED TO INVESTIGATE?

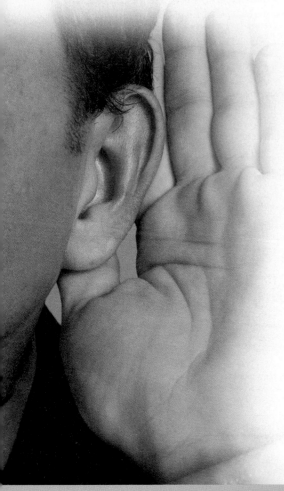

Why Do You Need to Know the Speaking Situation?

Let's look back at the transactional process of communication. Notice that the entire process takes place within the situation (in this case, the classroom).

If you remember from the Overview, the situation is the location and time in which the communication takes place, and it encircles the entire communication process.

Much of the noise that can negatively affect communication resides in the communicative situation and could influence the outcome of your speech at any time. In many ways, understanding and predicting potential negative or positive issues related to the situation is as important as selecting the right topic. If you and your audience are not comfortable with the situation, this will make it difficult—at best— for you to get the most productive responses to your speech. At worst, you could face a complete communication breakdown between your speech and the audience.

→ See the Overview (Tab 1) for a detailed discussion of the communication process.

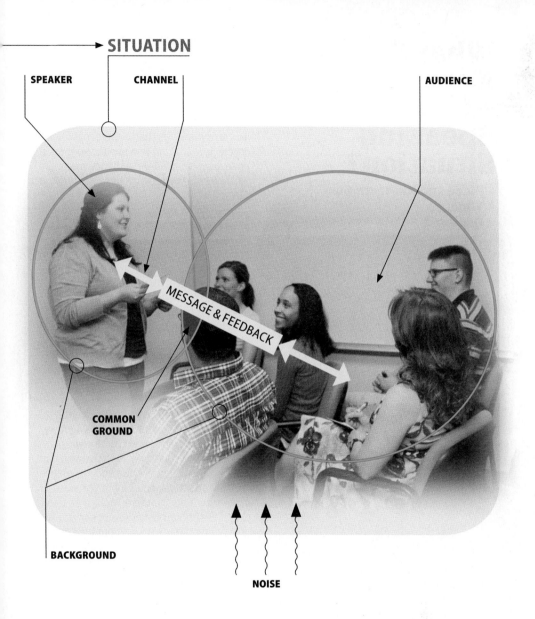

SITUATION

SPEAKER CHANNEL AUDIENCE

MESSAGE & FEEDBACK

COMMON GROUND

BACKGROUND

NOISE

What Do You Need to Know About the Speaking Situation?

1 **Place and Audience Size**
2 **Time**
3 **Occasion**

1

Place and Audience Size

Imagine this scene: You are a shorter-than-average person about to give a commencement address from behind a solid wooden lectern, on a stage that is three feet above the floor where the first few rows of your audience are sitting. These audience members will see only the top of your head, if they can see you at all.

Or: Imagine giving a speech outdoors on a windy day—from loose manuscript pages.

Both of these examples highlight how important it is to consider the environment where you will be speaking and to plan ahead. A simple, short platform for the first speaker prevents embarrassment. A manuscript printed on heavy paper and attached in a binder prevents the second speaker's need to run after flying pages.

You may be in a public speaking class and know that your classroom is where you will give the speech. But such familiarity is a luxury you rarely have, and even in the classroom, you need to prepare. What if someone has taken the lectern to another room? You should always try to visit the space prior to your speech so that you can make changes if necessary and possible.

Think about any equipment you need and make sure it will be there. Make a backup plan if the equipment does not show up or is not working. Also, find out how large the audience will be. Audience size could influence how formal (for larger audiences) or informal (for smaller ones) your style can be. For a large audience, you may need more equipment, such as a microphone. Use the checklist at left to help you prepare.

2
Time

Time has two factors. The first are general elements related to the time of day, day of the week, rotation of speakers, events before the speaking event, and length of speaking time. Each element has the potential to influence your speech positively or negatively. For instance, holding audience attention during an after-dinner speech can be challenging because the audience has just eaten and may be tired.

The second factor is time's influence on your relationship with the audience. For example, if this is the first time the group hears you speak, you will likely be careful to build your credibility (ethos). If they have heard you speak many times and have responded favorably, you might be a bit less formal. Think about how your professor or your boss related to you when you first met. How does she or he relate to you now? Is there a difference? Has your relationship evolved over time?

Use the checklist below to see how time will affect your speech.

CHECKLIST for Time

❑ How much time will I have to speak?

❑ How early should I arrive?

❑ What day of the week and time of day will I speak? How might these influence my speech? Is either of these culturally significant for my audience?

❑ Where do I fall in the rotation of speakers? How might someone else's speech influence mine?

❑ Is there late-breaking news I should consider?

❑ Is this the first time this audience will hear me speak?

❑ What is my relationship with this audience? How can I improve my speech based on that relationship?

3
Occasion

Think about *why* your audience is gathered to hear your speech. How might the occasion influence their feelings about you and your topic? Are they a captive audience, required to be there, who do not feel like they can leave? Or are they a voluntary audience, who made the choice to hear your speech.

Audiences required to attend an event, such as students at graduation or employees at a job-required meeting, can be apathetic, negative, or impatient. You might even experience some of these reactions in your classroom, as your audience has to be there regularly and must listen to many speeches. Captive audiences are not impossible to reach, but you must be more dynamic and interesting to gain their attention.

Mood is another consideration. Is the situation celebratory? Somber? Businesslike? Your speech should reflect and respect the appropriate mood.

Use the checklist below to assess your occasion.

CHECKLIST for Occasion

❑ What does the audience expect out of this event?

❑ What will be the mood of the day?

❑ Why are they here?

❑ How will they respond to the topic?

❑ Is this a special occasion? What is the relationship of any other speakers to the occasion?

❑ Does this audience have any social norms or expectations I should know about?

❑ Who's in charge of the event, and what is their relationship with the audience?

How Do You Locate Audience and Situation Information?

1 **Stop, Think, and Brainstorm**
2 **Interview**
3 **Survey**
4 **Research**

Adapting to your audience and situation begins immediately after you receive a public speaking assignment or engagement. The more you can predict about your audience early in the speech-making process, the better you can prepare. If you don't know your audience, you could choose an inappropriate topic or select the wrong source materials. There are several methods for collecting audience and situation information prior to the speaking event.

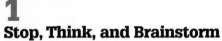

1
Stop, Think, and Brainstorm

As a speaker, you should start your audience analysis by thinking about what you already know, followed by brainstorming with others about the audience and situation. Simply taking the time to be mindful of what you (or someone close to you) might know could save valuable time. Turn to friends, relatives, teachers, or peers and ask them what feelings or knowledge they might have about the audience and your potential speech ideas. Sometimes fresh eyes can see connections and issues that we cannot when we are so involved in the process.

For example, you may decide to give a speech to help classmates through the tough times of finals week. This topic can be common, requiring you to focus on unique subtopics or to locate exceptional support materials. Speaking with a campus counselor or student life office may help you focus on a unique topic or subtopics related to your classmates' needs or your school's culture. In this situation, you are not conducting an interview about your speech so much as you are using a knowledgeable person as a sounding board or helpful idea generator to develop your speech topic.

2
Interview

Interviewing someone connected with the speaking event, a person familiar with the audience membership, and members of the audience are excellent ways to learn about your audience and situation. The interview can be in person, over the phone, by e-mail, or by regular mail. Although not usually as formal as an interview conducted to gather support materials, many of the same techniques apply here.

→ See Chapter 3 (Tab 2) for more on how to conduct an interview.

BASIC INTERVIEW GUIDELINES

- Think about what you need to know about the audience and situation. What will help you select or develop your topic? What will help you relate to the audience?
- Plan your questions to get the best responses.

    Open-ended questions allow the interviewee to give a detailed response and often will give you valuable information that you had not anticipated.

    Closed-ended questions are used when you want general, quantifiable information.

OPEN-ENDED QUESTION
What's it like living in the new student apartment complex?

 This question allows interviewees to talk about anything related to the complex and does not lead them into giving only positive or only negative comments.

CLOSED-ENDED QUESTION
Do you prefer living in a traditional style residence hall rather than an apartment layout?

 This question could be answered with a simple yes or no and assumes the interviewees can compare the two types of living situations.

- Be willing to add questions that come to mind as you conduct the interview, but make sure you are conscious of how long the interview is running. Remember that the person you are interviewing has a busy life, too.
- Always end the interview by asking if you have missed anything important that would help you understand your audience better. Your interviewee may have insights that you didn't expect.

3
Survey

Written surveys or questionnaires are helpful for gathering information from a large pool of people—and often from your audience. Surveys may contain open- and closed-ended questions but should tend toward the closed-ended.

→ See Chapter 3 (Tab 2) for a detailed discussion on question construction for surveys.

Suppose you are giving a speech on the reaction to dedicated bike lanes in your city.

You could ask a closed-ended question:

Are you satisfied with the new dedicated bike lanes on the city streets? ❑ Yes ❑ No

Or an open-ended question:

How do you feel about the new dedicated bike lanes on the city streets?

For a speech topic on city smoking bans, your survey might look like this:

Use familiar language.	**Smoking Ban Questionnaire**
Use a clean, consistent structure for the overall questionnaire.	1. What is your age?_____
Ask necessary demographic questions.	2. What is your sex? Male _____ Female _____

Ask only one thing in each question.	3. What is your educational level?
	    High school _____ Some college _____
	    College _____ Other (please specify) _____

Make no assumptions about your respondents.	4. What is your approximate annual income?
	    Less than $10,000 _____ $10,000–$25,000 _____
	    $25,000–$50,000 _____ $50,000–$75,000 _____
	    $75,000–$100,000 _____ More than $100,000 _____

	5. What are your smoking habits?
	    Never smoked _____ Past smoker _____
	    Smoke on occasion _____ Smoker _____

Use neutral responses—don't be biased or leading.	6. What are your feelings about the proposed smoking ban in public buildings?
	    Against it _____ For it _____
	    Not concerned _____ Other (please specify) _____

4

Research

Simple detective work can be a great way to analyze your audience, especially if they are part of a larger group or organization. Often groups and organizations publish information about their membership, goals, mission, facilities, activities, and accomplishments. The information might be on the Internet (does the group have a Web site?) or in brochures, press releases, newspaper and magazine articles (can you locate a city magazine promoting local groups?), or annual reports.

Opinion polls, census data, almanacs, local and city government archives, and historical societies are good sources as well. You may find some of them online or through your local library. These sources are useful for general data about a population. For example, how many African Americans hold college degrees?

www.gallup.com

www.pewresearch.org

www.firstgov.gov

www.census.gov

www.infoplease.com

How Can You Adapt to Your Audience During the Speech?

1 Adapt to External Noise
2 Adapt to Internal Noise

No matter how much you prepare for your audience, you cannot think of everything ahead of time. The communication process has too many variables that can change the outcome.

Earlier in this chapter, we reviewed the transactional process of communication. If you look back at it, you will notice that "noise" pushes into the process. This noise may interrupt the audience's ability to listen and your ability to communicate.

Chapter 11 will talk more about the importance of listening—for both the speaker and the audience—as well as how noise becomes a barrier to active listening. For now, you should realize that effective listening can only happen when the speaker and audience members are willing to work at it, by identifying and eliminating the noise.

→ See Chapter 11 (Tab 5) for more on how speakers and audience members can effectively listen to one another.

1
Adapt to External Noise

External noise occurs or originates outside of the mind or body and can be classified into two categories.

Environmental barriers:
sounds, movement, light, darkness, heat, cold, hard seats

Linguistic barriers:
misread verbal and nonverbal messages, such as slang, jargon, technical words, body language that differs across cultures

Anything from a loud lawn mower outside the window, to a computer that will not connect to the Internet, to a campus emergency the morning before your speech can change the best-laid plan, making it difficult for you to listen to your audience and for them to listen to you. Just remember:

- Stay calm.
- Pay attention to the noises affecting you and your audience.
- Be willing to adjust (such as pausing for the noisy lawn mower to pass or eliminating the noise if possible).

2
Adapt to Internal Noise

Internal noise occurs or originates inside of the mind or body and can be classified into two categories.

Physiological barriers:
hunger, sickness, disabilities, pain

Psychological barriers:
negative thoughts about the topic, distraction outside of the situation (such as a fight with a partner), fear, egocentrism, racism

Adapting to internal noise may require more work than adjusting to external noise. Points to keep in mind:

- If your audience's attention is wandering, call on members, move around the room, or vary your delivery to prompt them to listen.

➔ See Chapter 9 (Tab 4) for more on delivery.

- Be a creative, dynamic speaker and your audience will want to listen.
- Pay attention to the nonverbal behavior of your audience. The way people are sitting or their facial expressions are great feedback on how to adapt to the moment. For instance, if listeners seem confused, slow down and offer more examples to help them understand.
- Anticipate a potentially negative response and lessen the effect.

➔ See Tab 7 for more on how to influence your audience's responses.

- Ultimately, realize your audience is ethically responsible for listening to you.

In most cases, the audience will view you as a better speaker for being in enough control to handle problems—and to pull them back into the speech.

Chang's Speech

Chang is the president of the student body at a small liberal arts college. The college plans to build a new residence hall but needs to raise student fees to help fund the project. In his role as student president, Chang must conduct several informational sessions about the project and the fee increase. Several of his friends are excited about the new hall but concerned about the fee increase. Chang knows he needs to get a better idea of how the fee increase will influence his audience.

Chang brainstormed about who might give him the best information related to this project.

> PEOPLE TO TALK TO
> Admissions Director
> Financial Aid Director
> Dean of Student Life
> Building Committee

FOCUSING IN ON THE SITUATION

Chang made an appointment to meet with the Dean of Student Life at the college. The Student Life Office will make all of the arrangements for Chang's speeches and is familiar with the makeup of the student body.

To open on a friendly note, Chang briefly chatted with the dean before jumping into the interview but was careful not to go over the time allotted for the meeting.

Before the meeting, Chang constructed interview questions designed to gather the information he needed.

This interview helped Chang see how the residence hall will be a great new addition. He also learned that the college is working on ways it can help the students deal with the increased fees. However, he still wants to know how the majority of students feel about the project so that he can tailor his speech to increase their knowledge and not just reinforce their current beliefs or attitudes.

Meeting with Dean Ortiz
July 10th @ 1:00
Reece Hall 203

1. When and where will I give these presentations?

2. How many will attend?

3. How will the room be configured?

4. What prompted the College to decide to build the new hall?

5. Were students a part of that decision? Were students a part of the process?

6. What will the hall look like and how will it be different from the ones we have now?

7. How much will the fees increase?

8. How will that affect our current students? Will there be students who can't continue in their education because of the increase? Are there plans for the College to help those students in some way?

9. Can you think of anything else I need to know to help me inform my peers about this decision?

SURVEYING THE POTENTIAL AUDIENCE

Because a good cross-section of the student body can be found at the Student Union, Chang created a survey and asked students at the union to complete it.

Chang greeted each student and explained his survey. He made a conscious effort to survey equally across class rank and between males and females.

Proposed Residence Hall and Fee Increase Questionnaire

1. What is your class rank? _____

2. What is your sex? _____ Male _____ Female

3. Do you live on campus or off? _____On campus _____Off campus

4. What are your feelings about the building of a new hall?

_____ Support it even with the fee increase   _____ Oppose it because of the fee increase

_____ Would support it without the fee increase   _____ Oppose it no matter what

Other (please specify): _____
_____

5. If you support the building of the new hall, what is your number one reason for doing so?

_____ Need more rooms on campus   _____ Other halls are old

_____ Closer to my classes   _____ Like the new building design options

Other (please specify): _____
_____

6. If you oppose the building of the new hall, what is your number one reason for doing so?

_____ I don't care because I will graduate before it is finished

_____ I like the other halls

_____ I don't see why we need it

_____ I don't like the new building design options

_____ I don't support the fee increase

Other (please specify): _____
_____

AUDIENCE'S ATTITUDES, BELIEFS, AND VALUES

After collecting a good number of surveys, Chang studied the information so that he could use it to understand the students' concerns and needs. Everyone was excited about the hall, especially those who might get to live there. Most students saw a need for a new hall but were concerned about the fee increase. Of the students who opposed the hall, 95 percent did so because of the increase. Chang decided that he would focus his speeches on how the college planned to help students deal with the fee increase rather than why they needed a new hall.

2

SELECTING YOUR TOPIC AND PURPOSE

Introduction

The key to any good speech is a first-rate topic. If you are using this book in a beginning speech class, selecting a good speech topic may seem like a challenge. Unless your instructor limits you, your topic could be almost anything. Any topic that is suitable for you, your audience, and the classroom situation is appropriate—which may seem overwhelming.

However, outside of your speech class, most of your public speaking opportunities will be professional or social. Your expertise may limit your topic choices, or someone else may tell you what your topic should be. Even so, you will still need to define carefully your purpose and central idea to help keep you on track when building your speech. In either case, starting your topic selection process early is crucial to your success. Speech topics can reach a dead end when they are not appropriate, or when you cannot locate enough information in a timely fashion. Also, allowing your brain to "chew" on your topic early will help you generate ideas, making the speech easier to prepare.

Imagine that you are planning a vacation. For weeks before the trip, you think constantly about what you will do, where you will eat, and what you will take. You make reservations and arrangements. By the time the vacation comes around, you are so prepared and excited that packing will seem easy and you will be ready to go. Giving your speech that same amount of time and excitement will result in a better, more enjoyable speech and will give you enormous confidence.

OVERVIEW OF PUBLIC SPEAKING 1

CHAPTER 1: Getting to Know Your Audience and Situation 25

CHAPTER 2 CONTENTS

How Do You Select a Topic? 50
  1 Identify the General Purpose of Your Speech 50
  2 Create an Idea Bank 51
  3 Select Your Topic 54

How Do You Narrow Your Topic? 56

How Do You Create a Central Idea? 58
  1 Identify the Specific Purpose of Your Speech 58
  2 Identify the Central Idea of Your Speech 60
  3 Evaluate Your Central Idea 62

How Do You Construct a Working Outline? 64

Maria's Speech 66

Tab 1 Review 68

How Do You Select a Topic?

1 **Identify the General Purpose of Your Speech**

2 **Create an Idea Bank**

3 **Select Your Topic**

1

Identify the General Purpose of Your Speech

Identifying the general purpose of your speech will help you narrow your topic options. The **general purpose** is the unrestricted aim of your speech, which can fall into three different categories.

To inform. The giving of information is the aim of this general purpose. Speeches focusing on topics such as "How to Make a Kite," "The History of Hershey's Chocolate," and "The Life and Career of Gilda Radner" are examples of speeches to inform.

To persuade. When your goal is *to reinforce*, *to change*, or *to influence* the attitudes, values, beliefs, or actions of your audience, you aim to persuade. Speeches arguing for health care reform or rallying members of the Republican party to support a candidate are examples of speeches to persuade.

To accentuate a special occasion. *To entertain*, *to celebrate*, or *to commemorate* is the aim of a special occasion speech. A wedding toast, a graduation speech, or a speech given by a breast cancer survivor to women recently diagnosed with breast cancer each has the aim to accentuate a special occasion.

If you are giving a speech for class, the assignment likely tells you the general purpose. When you are invited to speak, the audience or the occasion may dictate your general purpose. In some cases, you may have the flexibility to choose. For a commencement speech, for example, unless the invitation indicates your purpose, you can choose to inform, persuade, inspire, or entertain.

TIP: General Purpose
You can have only one general purpose—to inform, to persuade, or to accentuate (entertain, celebrate, etc.). Using an entertaining delivery style does not necessarily make your purpose to entertain. Your general purpose is your overriding goal for the whole speech.

2
Create an Idea Bank

An **idea bank** is a list of general words and phrases that could be potential speech topics for you. Here's how to create an idea bank.

- Evaluate your speech assignment, the audience, and the speaking situation. Often this will help you limit your potential topics.

→ See Chapter 1 for how to evaluate your audience and situation.

- Write down your idea bank by hand. Using paper rather than a computer allows your mind to see connections and to jump more quickly from idea to idea.

- Make a list of potential topics. The next few pages will show you how to use brainstorming, exploring your general purpose, and searching to make your topic list. Include as many ideas as you can that you find interesting.

CONFIDENCE BOOSTER

One reason beginning speakers are nervous about giving speeches is self-doubt, often manifesting itself in a belief that they are not good at speaking or do not have anything to offer the audience. This self-doubt often leads to speakers selecting topics they think the *audience* will like but are not topics the *speakers* know well or are passionate about. If giving a speech seems daunting to you, try to select a topic that is familiar and will be interesting to research. You can then keep your research focused, spend more time practicing, and use your nervous energy to feed your excitement.

BRAINSTORMING

Brainstorming is when you "free associate," or jump from one word or concept to another. The best way to start brainstorming is to take a personal inventory of your hobbies, interests, experiences, abilities, talents, values, attitudes, or beliefs. If you have trouble getting started, working with another person who knows you well may help. Record these concepts in your idea bank. Below is one example of an idea bank created by brainstorming.

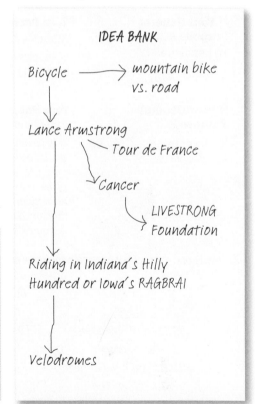

IDEA BANK

Bicycle ⟶ mountain bike vs. road

Lance Armstrong

Tour de France

Cancer

LIVESTRONG Foundation

Riding in Indiana's Hilly Hundred or Iowa's RAGBRAI

Velodromes

EXPLORING YOUR GENERAL PURPOSE

Using another method to make an idea bank, *exploring your general purpose,* you can create columns for the different types of speeches and topic categories that fit your purpose. The following table offers some categories you can use to generate ideas.

→ See Tabs 6, 7, and 8 for step-by-step discussions of how to create the types of speeches related to each general purpose.

If Your General Purpose Is...	Your Potential Topic Categories Are...
To inform: To describe	Object, person, animal, place, or event
To explain	Concept or issue
To demonstrate	Process

If Your General Purpose Is...	Your Potential Topic Categories Are...
To persuade:	Attitudes, beliefs, values, behaviors/actions, or policies
	(For topics under any of these categories, think about reinforcing, changing, or creating new attitudes, beliefs, etc.)

If Your General Purpose Is...	Your Potential Topic Categories Are...
To accentuate a special occasion:	Entertainment, celebration, commemoration
	(These categories are not as straightforward and will depend on the goal of the speech. You must adapt to the occasion as well as the audience. Most special occasion speeches take place at events like weddings, graduations, christenings, retirement parties, funerals, award ceremonies, inaugurals, dinners, holiday celebrations, fund-raisers, campaign banquets, conferences or conventions, and so on.)

Below is one example of an idea bank created by exploring a general purpose.

IDEA BANK		
Places	*To inform*	*Animals/Insects*
Island of Anguilla	*To describe*	Canaries
Gettysburg		Golden Retrievers
Mississippi Headwaters		Butterflies
San Diego Zoo		Bobcats in Missouri

SEARCHING FOR TOPIC IDEAS

A third way to create an idea bank is *searching*, when you simply browse print publications, reference works, Web sites, or other media and materials for subject ideas.

For example, you can look through acceptable journals or magazines you already have access to at home or in a library, such as:

- The Sunday paper in your area
- *Time*
- *Newsweek*
- *The Week*
- *Smithsonian*
- *National Geographic*
- *The American Heritage Dictionary*
- Encyclopedias

You can also watch a news broadcast, search an academic database at the library, or navigate the vast world of the Internet. A few places you might look include:

- About.com
- Ask.com
- Librarians' Internet Index
- Lycos Topics
- MSN Directory
- Yahoo! Directory

The idea bank shown on this page is one example created by searching—in this case, a search of the Librarians' Internet Index.

> **IDEA BANK**
> *Ideas from Librarians' Internet Index*
>
> Bubbles – How to make tools & solution
> Fortune-telling
> Kites
> Pioneer life
> Digital vs. film cameras
> Women photographers
> Juggling
> Political memorabilia (19th & 20th centuries)

3
Select Your Topic

Now that you know your general purpose and have an idea bank full of potential topics, you can select your topic. Ask yourself a series of focus questions to help identify topics that will work well and eliminate topics that will not.

- Which topics in my idea bank will work for my general purpose?
- Which topics fit the speech assignment or request?
- Which topics are most familiar to me?
- Which topics am I most comfortable speaking about?
- Which topics have positive aspects for the audience, occasion, speaking event, or timing of the event? Which topics might cause a negative reaction from the audience or are not appropriate?
- Which topics are new or unique to this audience?
- Which topics are worth the audience's time and attention?

For example, suppose you are volunteering at the local Historical Society and you create the idea bank below because the Society wants you to give an informative talk. You ask yourself the focus questions and cross out topics, such as "kites," that do not relate to the Society's exhibits, because those topics may not interest visitors. You reason that visitors might like to hear a talk related to the recreated pioneer village on the property. Connecting this thought to your hobby of woodworking, you think that investigating how the pioneers built their homes will be a good topic. It passes the test created by the focus questions.

Idea Bank for Historical Society

- ~~Bubbles — How to make tools & solution~~
- ~~Fortune-telling~~
- ~~Kites~~
- (Pioneer life / Building homes)   Pony Express
- ~~Digital vs. film cameras~~
- ~~Women photographers~~
- ~~Juggling~~   ghost towns
- ~~Political memorabilia (19th & 20th century)~~

TIP: Judging Topics

Be careful not to judge a topic too quickly. Some topics may appear to be a waste of time but can be used creatively. For example, making bubble tools and solutions may seem unworthy for a college class. However, if your audience consists of several parents or elementary education majors, or if it is close to finals week, you might be giving your audience information they can use to involve their children or students in the creative process or a great activity to alleviate the stress of studying.

Finally, before you commit to a topic, do some preliminary research to see if you can locate current, quality materials on the topic. As you research, ask these questions:

- Are there enough materials to create a speech that fits into my allotted speech time?
- Is there a variety of quality materials for the topic?
- Will I be able to locate and review the materials in time to prepare effectively for my speech?

If you are having trouble finding support materials, you may want to return to your idea bank for a new topic.

➜ Tab 2 explains how to do research and evaluate support materials.

PRACTICING ETHICS

Remember these ethical guidelines when selecting a topic.

- Your topic should fit the audience and the occasion.
- Your topic should be worth the audience's time.
- Your topic should be appropriate to you.
- You should not feel like you need to hide something about the topic from your audience.
- Your topic should not be harmful to you or your audience.
- Your topic should not break any laws or rules set by the organization sponsoring or housing your speaking event.
- Your topic selection should allow you enough time to effectively prepare your speech.
- Persuasive topics should focus on issues, not on individuals.
- Ultimately, you should be able to live with the consequences of your choices.

TIP: Starting Early

Remember that you need time to write and rehearse the speech. The day before your speech is too late to find or receive a large amount of research materials.

How Do You Narrow Your Topic?

Narrowing your topic may not seem all that difficult or important, but the scope of your topic can make or break your speech.

A well-defined, specific topic will help you:

- Achieve the general purpose of your speech. A topic that is too broad will not be thorough enough to be informative, persuasive, or celebratory.

- Reduce the time you spend researching and writing the speech.

- Increase your confidence for giving the speech. If you feel you are trying to cover too much material in a few minutes or you cannot remember all of the speech, your nervousness will increase. A narrow topic allows you to focus on an appropriate amount of material and to feel confident that your speech is not overloaded.

- Effectively deliver your speech at a comfortable rate. A speech that tries to cover too much will run long or seem rushed because you will talk too fast. A narrow topic helps keep the length down and allows you to speak at an understandable rate.

- Keep your audience focused on your topic. A well-defined topic will help audience members follow your speech and can prevent their minds from wandering.

Although you can narrow your topic in different ways, the main result of any method you use should be a focused, effectively written *central idea* (thesis statement). Your instructor may prefer a certain method, or the following steps can help you create a focused speech topic.

IDENTIFY THE SPECIFIC PURPOSE OF YOUR SPEECH	The *specific purpose* of your speech is a single statement that combines your general purpose, your audience, and your objective. The *objective* is the outcome or behavior you want your audience to experience or adopt after hearing your speech. ➔ See pages 58–59.
IDENTIFY THE CENTRAL IDEA OF THE SPEECH	The *central idea* (also called a thesis statement, theme, or subject sentence) is a concise, single sentence summarizing and/or previewing what you will say in your speech. ➔ See pages 60–61.
EVALUATE YOUR CENTRAL IDEA	Once you have created an initial central idea, you need to evaluate it. An effective central idea is vital to a successful speech because everything you say in your speech should relate back to this one complete statement. ➔ See pages 62–63.
CONSTRUCT A WORKING OUTLINE	A *working outline* is a brief sketch of the body of your speech. The working outline will contain what you have composed so far—your topic, general purpose, specific purpose, and central idea—plus working main points to guide your research. ➔ See pages 64–65.

How Do You Create a Central Idea?

1 **Identify the Specific Purpose of Your Speech**

2 **Identify the Central Idea of the Speech**

3 **Evaluate Your Central Idea**

1

Identify the Specific Purpose of Your Speech

Identifying your specific purpose is the first step in creating a focused central idea. The **specific purpose** of your speech is a single statement that combines your general purpose, your audience, and your objective. The **objective** of the specific purpose describes the outcome or behavior you want your audience to experience or adopt. Notice how the specific purpose examples at the top of the next page identify what the speakers want their audiences to take away from the speeches.

CHECKLIST for Evaluating a Specific Purpose

❏ Does my specific purpose contain my general purpose, my audience reference, and my objective for the speech?

❏ Is my specific purpose an infinitive statement (to inform, to convince, to motivate, to inspire)?

❏ Am I using clear, concise language?.

❏ Does my specific purpose identify exactly what I want to discuss?

❏ Does my specific purpose focus on only one speech topic?

❏ Does my specific purpose relate to the audience? Does it work with the occasion and time? Is it appropriate for me?

❏ Am I trying to do too much? Will it fit the time?

EXAMPLES OF SPECIFIC PURPOSES

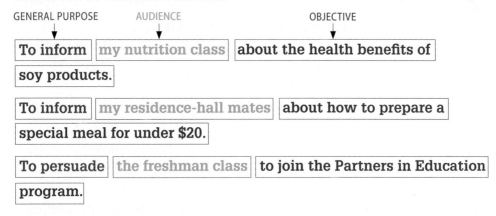

GENERAL PURPOSE   AUDIENCE   OBJECTIVE

To inform | my nutrition class | about the health benefits of soy products.

To inform | my residence-hall mates | about how to prepare a special meal for under $20.

To persuade | the freshman class | to join the Partners in Education program.

The above examples follow these guidelines for composing a specific purpose:

- Begin with an infinitive form ("To…") that reflects the general purpose, such as "To inform," "To persuade," or "To commemorate."
- Specify the audience. In the first example, the audience is "my nutrition class."
- State the objective. In the first example, the objective is to give the audience information "about the health benefits of soy products."
- Use clear, concise language. Avoid filler words or technical or long descriptions. For instance, the first example does not say, "the *awesome* health benefits of products *made with the fermented juice of a native Asian bean.*"
- Focus on only one speech topic. "The health benefits *and manufacturing* of soy products" would be two distinctly different speech topics.

Returning to your pioneer homes speech, you could construct a specific purpose this way:

GENERAL PURPOSE   AUDIENCE   OBJECTIVE

To inform | Historical Society visitors | about how pioneers built homes.

Your specific purpose should contain the key information and be concise, as the pioneer example shows. Once you have constructed a specific purpose, always evaluate it using the checklist to the left.

If you have a sound specific purpose, you are ready to identify and compose your central idea.

2

Identify the Central Idea of Your Speech

The **central idea** (also called a *thesis statement, theme,* or *subject sentence*) is a concise, single sentence summarizing and/or previewing what you will say in your speech. Any decision you make about your main points or support materials should connect back to the theme of this central idea.

How the central idea differs from the specific purpose can seem confusing, but the difference lies in how each functions. First, the specific purpose identifies the objective of your speech. Then, the central idea summarizes and/or previews the ideas your speech will cover in order to achieve its objective. Here are a few examples demonstrating how the specific purpose relates to the central idea. The objective of each specific purpose is shown in blue.

If Your Specific Purpose Is...	Your Central Idea Could Be...
To inform my nutrition class about the health benefits of soy products.	Today's market offers several soy products that are beneficial to our health.
To inform my residence-hall mates how to prepare a special meal for under $20.	You can prepare a special home-cooked meal with a few basic utensils, an eye for a bargain at the supermarket, and your residence-hall kitchenette.
To persuade the freshman class to join the Partners in Education program.	As college students, we need to give back to the community by joining the Partners in Education Program, which pairs our college with a local elementary school.

Notice how the second central idea example—preparing a special meal—previews the speech's possible main points (utensils, supermarket bargains, and kitchenette). Some instructors may require you to preview your main points in this way as a standard part of your central idea.

WHAT DOES AN EFFECTIVE CENTRAL IDEA INCLUDE?

Let's compose a central idea for the speech on pioneer home building. Start by looking at your specific purpose and identifying your objective.

SPECIFIC PURPOSE

To inform Historical Society visitors **about how pioneers built homes.**

OBJECTIVE

Your central idea will then summarize and/or preview what you will cover in your speech to achieve your objective. Here is one possible central idea:

CENTRAL IDEA

Pioneers moving westward built homes using available materials, basic hand tools, and general construction skills.

Notice how this example:

- Considers what your audience—the Historical Society visitors identified in your specific purpose—will need or want to know.
- Previews what your speech will include: in this case, the "available materials, basic hand tools, and general construction skills" pioneers used to build homes. This information comes from your preliminary knowledge and research.
- Focuses on only one speech topic: how pioneers built their homes.
- Uses simple, clear language that is not figurative or ambiguous. In the pioneer example, you could list the types of materials and tools, but if these types are no longer common, including them here could be confusing.
- Is a complete sentence, with a noun phrase and a verb phrase.
- Is a declarative statement, not a question.

These are all qualities your central idea should have in order to be effective.

→ The next two pages show you how to evaluate a central idea for these qualities.

3

Evaluate Your Central Idea

To evaluate your central idea for effectiveness, study it from two perspectives. First, check the mechanics; that is, make sure your central idea is written correctly with the proper parts, construction, and focus. Secondly, assess your central idea as it relates to your speech event and audience. Use the following guidelines and the checklist on the next page to help you evaluate.

MECHANICALLY SOUND

To be mechanically sound, your central idea should meet all four of the following criteria.

▪ **Your central idea should be a complete sentence.** A complete sentence contains a noun phrase and a verb phrase and can stand alone.

INCORRECT:
Positive aspects of the low-impact Kickbike, a bicycle-scooter hybrid.

CORRECT: | The noun phrase
The Kickbike, a European bicycle-scooter hybrid, is a low-tech, low-impact, and high-intensity piece of exercise equipment.
| The verb phrase

Although the incorrect example ends with a period, it is only a noun phrase; without a verb phrase, it is not a complete sentence. The correct version contains both noun and verb phrases and can stand alone.

▪ **Your central idea should be written as a statement, not a question.**

INCORRECT:
How safe is the radiation emitted by your cell phone?

CORRECT:
Cell phones emit tiny amounts of radiation, which scientists believe may be linked to certain types of brain cancer.

Asking a question—as in the incorrect example—can help you think about your speech, but your central idea needs to be a declarative sentence, as in the correct example.

> **TIP: Refining Your Central Idea**
> Keep in mind that your central idea might change slightly as you do research and organize the speech. Be open to refining it as you move through the creative process.

- **Your central idea should use clear, specific, and direct language.** To be clear, use language familiar to the audience and words that are concrete. Avoid vague or filler language and qualifying phrases that can lessen the impact of your central idea.

INCORRECT:

Some believe basically that the radiation silently emitted from cell phones can cause cancer.

CORRECT:

Cell phones emit tiny amounts of radiation, which scientists believe may be linked to certain types of brain cancer.

In the incorrect example, "some believe" is vague—who are the "some"? "Basically" is a filler word that serves no purpose, and "silently" is unnecessary because all radiation is silent. The correct example drops the filler words and specifies "scientists believe," as well as what types of cancer may be caused by the radiation.

- **Your central idea should focus on only one speech topic.**

INCORRECT:

Kickbikes and elliptical trainers are low-impact, high-intensity pieces of exercise equipment.

Two nouns connected with a conjunction ("and") may indicate you have more than one speech topic.

CORRECT:

The Kickbike, a European bicycle-scooter hybrid, is a low-tech, low-impact, and high-intensity piece of exercise equipment.

CORRECT:

An elliptical trainer is a low-impact and high-intensity piece of exercise equipment.

In the incorrect example, "Kickbikes" and "elliptical trainers" are two equal topics that could each get a speech-length treatment. Notice how each of the correct examples previews possible points ("low-tech," low-impact," etc.) while focusing on a single speech topic.

APPROPRIATE FOR THE EVENT AND AUDIENCE

Because your central idea is a culmination of your broad topic, general purpose, and specific purpose, your central idea should, at this stage, be appropriate and focused enough for the event. However, you need to continue to assess if the topic is still narrow enough for the time allotted, interesting enough to grab your audience's attention, unique enough to not waste their time with something they already know, and accessible enough to not be too technical or confusing for them.

CHECKLIST for Evaluating a Central Idea

❑ Is the central idea written as one complete sentence?

❑ Is the central idea written as a statement (not a question)?

❑ Does the statement use clear, simple, and direct language?

❑ Does the central idea focus on only one speech topic?

❑ Can I cover this central idea in the time allotted for my speech?

❑ Is the central idea worth my audience's time and attention?

How Do You Construct a Working Outline?

The construction of a speech is a creative process, with many ways you can approach it. Some beginning students and their instructors find that creating a working outline at this point helps them focus and transition into the research phase of creating a speech.

A **working outline** is a brief (usually handwritten) sketch of the body of your speech. This outline will help you stay on track while researching your speech and give you direction on what to look for. The working outline will contain what you have composed so far—your topic, general purpose, specific purpose, and central idea—plus working main points to guide your research. The working main points may or may not be the main points you use in your final outline, but they serve the same purpose. Main points, which you will learn more about in Chapter 5, are the skeletal structure, or backbone, that makes up the body of your speech; they are the two to five most important ideas to know about your topic. **Working main points** are early drafts of your main points. They may be awkward in format and can change significantly as you research your topic.

→ Chapter 6 (Tab 3) explains how to finalize your main points as you compose your speech.

CHECKLIST for Evaluating Working Main Points

❑ Does each main point cover *only one* key idea?

❑ Are my main points similarly constructed (are they parallel)?

❑ Am I roughly balancing the time spent on each point?

❑ Do my main points relate back to the central idea?

To construct your working main points:

1.

Turn to your central idea for categories. Write down your central idea and highlight its important issues. Evaluate the highlighted issues to see if you can discover two to five main categories with one distinct key idea per category.

CENTRAL IDEA:

Pioneers moving westward built homes using available materials, basic hand tools, and general construction skills.

CATEGORY	**CATEGORY**	**CATEGORY**
Basic hand tools	General construction skills	Available materials
KEY IDEA	**KEY IDEA**	**KEY IDEA**
What hand tools did pioneers use to build homes?	What were the general construction skills?	What materials were available for pioneers to use?

2.

Sum up each of your categories with a statement or question as shown in each key idea above. These are your working main points. Your final main points must be statements, but for now, questions may seem easier to formulate and may help focus your research. Write in complete sentences, make your points parallel in structure, and balance them so that you will spend roughly equal time on each.

TOPIC: Pioneer life

GENERAL PURPOSE: To inform

SPECIFIC PURPOSE: To inform Historical Society visitors about how pioneers built homes.

CENTRAL IDEA: Pioneers moving westward built homes using available materials, basic hand tools, and general construction skills.

MAIN POINT #1: What materials were available for pioneers to use?

MAIN POINT #2: What hand tools did pioneers use to build homes?

MAIN POINT #3: What were the general construction skills?

The preliminary research you did when selecting your topic can help you compose working main points, which will continue to evolve as you prepare your speech. Use the checklist on the left to evaluate your working main points.

Maria's Speech

Maria is a student taking an Introduction to Speech class as part of her associate degree program. Her assignment is to give a seven-minute persuasive speech on something she passionately supports. When Maria first read the assignment, her heart sank. Like many of her friends, Maria didn't think she was passionate about anything. She decided to give the techniques of brainstorming, exploring her general purpose, and searching a try.

SELECTING A TOPIC

Because Maria knew her general purpose (to persuade), she sat down with pen and paper to create her idea bank. To fill the bank, she read through news sites on the Internet for ideas, talked to her mom about ideas, browsed through the magazine *The Week*, and simply looked around her parents' home for ideas. Maria came up with several topic ideas but crossed off the ones that she decided were not appropriate for her audience or for her. Then she crossed off the overused and highly charged topics.

Issues at school	Issues in my town	National or global issues
~~parking~~	zero waste efforts	~~nuclear weapons~~
~~student fees~~	~~rough roads~~	abuse → child → women → elderly
campus food	~~condoms in schools~~	dieting
~~dating~~	no smoking law	~~global warming~~
binge drinking	homelessness	endangered species

Dad's honeybees

Finally, with only a few topics left, Maria's mind jumped from endangered species to her dad's honeybees. Maria lives in a part of the country with a lot of vineyards and orchards. Her dad raises honeybees to help the local farmers pollinate their crops. Several years ago, the bees began dying off from colony collapse disorder. Because most of her classmates were from the local area, Maria knew that the future loss of all honeybees would influence their lives, and she had also found a topic she was passionate about for personal reasons.

IDENTIFYING HER SPECIFIC PURPOSE AND CENTRAL IDEA

With her broad topic in hand, Maria moved on to writing her specific purpose and central idea.

TOPIC:
Endangered species

GENERAL PURPOSE:
To persuade

SPECIFIC PURPOSE:
To persuade my class that the U.S. honeybee population is dying off.

CENTRAL IDEA:
Without human intervention, an unknown cause will wipe out the common honeybee by 2035.

TOPIC:
Endangered Species

GENERAL PURPOSE:
To persuade

SPECIFIC PURPOSE:
To persuade my class that the U.S. honeybee population is dying off.

CENTRAL IDEA:
Without human intervention, an unknown cause will wipe out the common honeybee by 2035.

   I.   FIRST (WORKING) MAIN POINT: Why are honeybees an essential link in our food chain?

   II.   SECOND (WORKING) MAIN POINT: What is killing the honeybee?

   III. THIRD (WORKING) MAIN POINT: How can we prevent the extinction of the honeybee?

CONSTRUCTING A WORKING OUTLINE

With her central idea formulated, Maria set out to do some preliminary research. Her father had several books and articles on the subject, and she also found several current, reputable Web sites. For example, Penn State University and the University of California–Davis both had conducted a lot of research on the honeybee problem. Maria felt confident she could get a lot of quality information for her speech and even discovered ideas for working main points. Before she called it a night, she had her working outline completed.

Tab 1: Review

OVERVIEW REVIEW QUESTIONS

1. What makes a successful speaker? An ethical speaker?
2. How can you work at decreasing speech anxiety?
3. What is the transactional process of communication? Identify and explain each part.

CHAPTER 1 REVIEW QUESTIONS

1. Why is analyzing your audience and situation important?
2. What do you need to know and investigate about your audience?
3. What should you know about the speaking situation?
4. How do you locate audience and situation information?

CHAPTER 2 REVIEW QUESTIONS

1. What is the process for narrowing your topic?
2. What is a specific purpose? What questions should you ask when evaluating your specific purpose?
3. What is a central idea? What questions should you ask when evaluating your central idea?

TERMS TO REMEMBER

Overview
identification (3)
logos (4)
ethos (4)
pathos (4)
mythos (4)
communication apprehension (6)
ethnocentrism (9)
plagiarism (10)
blatant plagiarism (10)
no-citation plagiarism (10)
First Amendment (11)

speaker (15)
audience (15)
message (15)
encoding (15)
decoding (15)
feedback (15)
channel (15)
noise (15)
situation (15)
background (15)
common ground (15)
transactional process (15)

Chapter 1
egocentrism (27)
audience centered (27)
audience analysis (27)
speaking competence (27)
identity knowledge (27)
mindfulness (27)
negotiation skill (27)
attitudes (28)
beliefs (29)
values (29)
identity (29)
personal traits (30)
stereotyping (31)

psychological traits (32)
Maslow's hierarchy of needs (32)
social traits (33)
race (33)
ethnicity (33)
culture (33)
external noise (45)
environmental barriers (45)
linguistic barriers (45)
internal noise (45)
physiological barriers (45)
psychological barriers (45)

Chapter 2
general purpose (50)
idea bank (51)
brainstorming (51)
specific purpose (58)

objective (58)
central idea (60)
working outline (64)
working main points (64)

Introduction

Research is the act of investigating, evaluating, and summarizing information. The research activities in Chapters 3 and 4 will help you find effective **support materials** (or *evidence*)—information that explains, elaborates, or validates your speech topic. Support materials come from different types of **sources** (books, magazines, journals, blogs, Web sites, interviews, etc.).

For example, Logan is preparing a speech on basketball and wants to use some startling statistics about one of the best professional basketball players of all time. However, he also wants to choose a player not everyone in his class knows. Logan asked a librarian for help. She recommended first searching the Internet for a list of great players and then looking for a specific player from that list. Within minutes, Logan had the opening to his speech.

> Which NBA player became the only player to average more than 50 points per game for an entire season? Who still has the best rebounding record of all time, with 23,924? Who was nicknamed the "Big Dipper"? According to NBA.com, if you answered Wilt Chamberlain, you are correct.

Because of the Internet and the quality of U.S. libraries, you (and Logan) have a vast amount of information at your fingertips, making research easier than ever. If you live in a small town and do not have a library down the street, you can still do some solid research online. If you do live near public or academic libraries, these research facilities contain materials you will not find online and employ staff trained in research and eager to assist you.

CHAPTER 3 CONTENTS

What Does the Internet Have to Offer You? 70
 1 Search Engines 72
 2 Commercial Web Sites 74
 3 Nonprofit Organization Web Sites 75
 4 Blogs 76
 5 Personal Web Sites 77

How Can You Use the Internet to Access Libraries? 78

What Does the Library Have to Offer You? 80
 1 The Catalog 81
 2 Databases 82
 3 Books 84
 4 Newspapers 85
 5 Magazines 86
 6 Newsletters 87
 7 Journals 88
 8 Special Collections or Rare Books 89

What Can You Find Both on the Internet and in Libraries? 90
 1 Government Resources 91
 2 Reference Works 92

How Can You Gather Support Materials in an Interview? 94
 1 Prepare for the Interview 95
 2 Conduct the Interview 96
 3 Use Media-assisted Interviews if Necessary 97

How Can You Gather Support Materials with a Survey? 98
 1 Create the Survey 99
 2 Conduct the Survey 101

How Do You Take Good Research Notes? 102
 1 Prepare to Research 102
 2 Use a Note-taking System 103
 3 Know the Appropriate Style Manual 104

Desmond's Speech 106

CHAPTER 4: Selecting and Testing Support Materials 109

Tab 2 Review 136

What Does the Internet Have to Offer You?

1 **Search Engines**

2 **Commercial Web Sites**

3 **Nonprofit Organization Web Sites**

4 **Blogs**

5 **Personal Web Sites**

The Internet, with its vast amounts of information, is most effective when used correctly and ethically, which begins with understanding how it works. First, you should recognize the difference between the Internet and the World Wide Web (the Web):

The **Internet** is the massive worldwide network of hardware, connecting millions of computers together so that they can receive and retrieve information.

The **Web** is an information-sharing model built on top of the Internet that allows us to access all that information. When you log in to a Web **browser**, such as Internet Explorer or Mozilla Firefox, you are surfing the Web.

Material available on the Web can be categorized based on ease of access:

The **visible Web** includes anything you can access through a general search engine, such as Google.

The **invisible Web** (or *deep Web*) references information that is not accessible through a general search engine, either because the information has not been indexed by that search engine or because you need a special gateway (like a database) to access it. Often, the best way to access information on the invisible Web is through your institution's library, which will have numerous databases. Most libraries allow patrons to access the databases via the Internet at all times.

> **TIP: Personal Sources**
> Don't forget to consider your own available personal sources. If your topic is something you are interested in, you may own books, objects, memorabilia, records of an event, video, pictures, or other related items. This is often a great place to start your research.

The following pages will show you how to locate and use search engines, types of Web sites, and blogs in your research.

Web sites usually consist of multiple, unified pages beginning with a home page. A Web site may be created and maintained by an individual, group, business, or organization. The contents of a Web site might include images, video, articles, facts, statistics, digital documents, and links to related Web sites.

→ See Chapter 4 (Tab 2) for a detailed discussion on evaluating all sources.

Use common sense—don't believe everything you read on the Internet.

WHAT SHOULD YOU EVALUATE?	HOW CAN YOU EVALUATE THIS INFORMATION?	TIPS
Accuracy: Does the information seem plausible?	• Check for citations. • Investigate the authors. • Verify content with other sources.	• Citations are usually located at the bottom of the page. • Look for an "About Us" link to find information or Google the authors. • Locate the same information in other sources.
Responsibility: Who is responsible for this Web site? What are their qualifications related to your topic?	• Look at the page header. • Study the site address (URL) for clues. • Scroll to the bottom of the home page for copyright information.	• Look for author information and research their qualifications. • A .org, .gov, or .edu extension may signify a more reliable source than .com or .net sites.
Impartiality: Could this site be biased? How are the site creators affiliated?	• Check for advertisements that may indicate a bias. • Check for a mission statement. • Consider who the site is targeting as an audience.	• Some Web sites pay to be the top results in a search engine. They may be called sponsored links. • Look for a link such as "Our Mission," "FAQ," or "About Us" to find more information.
Currency: When was this site created? Is it important to your topic to have the most current information possible?	• Check for a copyright date or date of last update at bottom of home page. • Verify content with other sources.	• If a site has no copyright date, look for a date when material (such as an article or blog entry) was posted. • Look at citation dates for recent dates.

1
Search Engines

From a Web browser, **search engines** are the specific tools you use to search for information on the Web. A search engine sends out what is called a *spider* to fetch everything it can that is related to a key term or terms you have typed into the engine. The engine will then send back **hits**, or a list of Web pages, files, images, and other items related to the terms. This section lists some of the most common and effective engines, but many more are available.

Note that scholarly materials are commonly housed in databases, which often have limited access on the invisible Web. You will need to access most databases through a library.

→ See "What Does the Library Have to Offer You?" on page 80.

GENERAL SEARCH ENGINES

Google	www.google.com
Yahoo!	www.yahoo.com
Bing	www.bing.com
AltaVista	www.altavista.com
Lycos	www.lycos.com

METASEARCH ENGINES

Metasearch engines are search engines that search other, often smaller or unknown, engines and specialized sites—great for doing a large sweep to see what is on the Web.

A9	www.a9.com
Dogpile	www.dogpile.com
Excite	www.excite.com
Mamma	www.mamma.com
Metacrawler	www.metacrawler.com

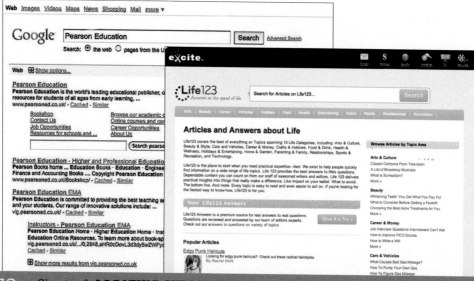

SEARCHING THE INVISIBLE WEB

Because the invisible Web is not accessible via general search engines, use these sites.

Infomine	infomine.ucr.edu
Google Scholar	scholar.google.com
Alexa	www.alexa.com
Complete Planet	www.completeplanet.com
High Wire	highwire.stanford.edu
Directory of Open Access Journals	www.doaj.org

WEB DIRECTORIES

To locate only Web sites, use Web directories. They are not inclusive, so use them wisely.

The Open Directory Project	www.dmoz.org
Google Directory	www.google.com/dirhp

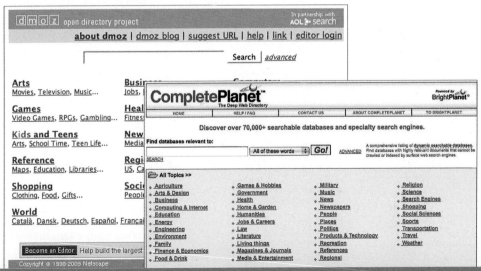

2
Commercial Web Sites

Commercial Web sites are sites created and maintained by for-profit businesses or organizations. These Web sites are typically promotional sites but can include newspapers, television networks, and video and image services (e.g., YouTube or Google Maps).

For a speech on relief efforts for Haiti, Tobi found an article listing several U.S. corporations that donated to the efforts. However, she wanted more detail about what some of the companies were actually doing. So, Tobi searched the companies' commercial Web sites for details. On the Monsanto site (shown below), she found this quotation to use in her speech.

> We believe agriculture is key in the long-term recovery of Haiti. That's why we've donated more than $4 million worth of conventional corn and vegetable seeds to be made over the next 12 months in support of reconstruction efforts. The donated seeds include corn, cabbage, carrot, eggplant, melon, onion, tomato, spinach, and watermelon.

Leading into this quotation, Tobi used the oral citation shown at the end of this page.

ADVANTAGES
- Can offer information unavailable in print
- May be current (be sure to check dates)
- May be seen by your audience as reliable information about the business or company

DISADVANTAGES
- Are often biased toward the interests of the site owner or paid advertisers, if any
- May require verifying information with other sources or may not be verifiable
- May not credit all sources of information

WHEN TO USE
- To locate information about a company
- To gather support materials from sites of respected news organizations
- To find current or popular culture materials
- To find presentation aids (cite the sources)

TIPS ON LOCATING
- Use a search engine to find a specific site if you have one in mind, or search on your topic to locate related sites.

SAMPLE ORAL CITATION
"According to the feature story 'Monsanto Donates Corn and Vegetable Seeds to Haiti' located on Monsanto.com on May 14, 2010, Monsanto has made efforts to help."

3

Nonprofit Organization Web Sites

Nonprofit organization Web sites are sites for local, national, and international not-for-profit organizations dedicated to issues or causes, such as UNICEF, MADD, the Special Olympics, or the Magic Johnson Foundation. Their URLs often end with ".org."

Suppose you are researching a speech on a UNICEF program for a service learning assignment. You and your classmates are required to participate in civic responsibility activities as part of your degrees, and you want to inform your audience about an opportunity. On the UNICEF Web site, you discover information about UNICEF's "Achieving Zero" program, under this banner headline:

> **24,000 children die every day from preventable causes. We believe that number should be zero.**

The headline grabs your attention so effectively that you write it down as a potential attention-getter for your speech. The site (shown below) contains numerous stories from specific countries, a bar graph demonstrating progress in lowering the child mortality rate, and how your audience can help. You can use the site to collect some support materials and follow related links, like "People & Partners," to help find additional sources. See the end of this page for a sample oral citation.

ADVANTAGES

- Can provide background and current information about a service or issue
- Are usually considered reliable sources and may link to other reliable sources
- Tend to use accessible language

DISADVANTAGES

- Have set goals or agendas, which may bias how information is presented
- May not include author credentials
- May accept paid advertisements, which could signal that the site's information is biased (verify the information with other sources)

WHEN TO USE

- To locate detailed information about a particular issue or organization
- To locate emotional appeal examples

TIPS ON LOCATING

- Search online using the name of the organization or the issue it supports.

SAMPLE ORAL CITATION

"This graph, from the article 'Achieving Zero,' found June 1, 2010, on unicefusa.org, demonstrates the progress so far in reducing child deaths worldwide."

4
Blogs

A ***blog*** is a Web site or page that contains regular postings by its author(s)—often in the form of a journal—and may allow visitors to comment. Blogs exist for almost any topic. When created by authorities, they can offer unique, credible information; but keep in mind that most blogs will represent specific opinions or points of view. Types of blogs include:

- Personal blogs (including Twitter)
- Corporate blogs (used internally for communication or externally for marketing)
- Subject blogs (politics, travel, fashion, education, law, music, etc.)
- Media blogs (comprised of videos, links, sketches, photos, etc.)

Bruce enjoys studying presidential history and airplanes, so he decided to combine his two interests into a speech about Air Force One. On the White House blog (shown below), Bruce found information he could draw from to create his speech, such as:

> ...the President and his travel companions enjoy 4,000 square feet of floor space on three levels, including an extensive suite for the President that features a large office, lavatory, and conference room. Air Force One includes a medical suite that can function as an operating room, and a doctor is permanently on board....

See one of Bruce's oral citations at the end of this page.

ADVANTAGES
- Can provide current information
- Can be helpful in gauging public opinion
- Can offer unique material

DISADVANTAGES
- Are often biased toward the opinions of the blogger(s)
- May require verifying information with other sources
- May not credit all sources of information

WHEN TO USE
- To find examples of public opinion
- To find new developments about your topic (to verify with other sources)
- To gauge if a topic is controversial or of current general interest

TIPS ON LOCATING
- Use blog search engines (Google Blog Search, Blogarama, Bloglines, Technorati).

SAMPLE ORAL CITATION
"According to the White House blog on July 14, 2010, Air Force One totals 4,000 square feet of floor space on three levels."

HOUSE *PRESIDENT BARACK OBAMA* ★ ★ ★ ★ THE WHITE HOUSE ★ ★ ★ ★ Get Email Updates | Contact Us

PHOTOS & VIDEO   BRIEFING ROOM   ISSUES   *the* ADMINISTRATION   *the* WHITE HOUSE   *our* GOVERNMENT

White House · Air Force One

Air Force One

The Executive Branch
The Legislative Branch
The Judicial Branch
The Constitution

Federal Agencies & Commissions
Elections & Voting
State & Local Government
Resources

Flickr   iTunes
MySpace   LinkedIn

LATEST NEWS & UPDATES

THE WHITE HOUSE BLOG

Read the Blog

THE VICE PRESIDENT *of the* UNITED STATES

No matter where in the world the President travels, if he flies in an Air Force jet, the plane is called Air Force One. Technically, Air Force One is the call sign of any Air Force aircraft carrying the President. In practice, however, Air Force One is used to refer to one of two highly customized Boeing 747-200B series aircraft, which carry the tail codes 28000 and 29000. The Air Force designation for the aircraft is VC-25A.

Air Force One is one of the most recognizable symbols of the presidency, spawning

5
Personal Web Sites

Personal Web sites are created by groups or individuals and focused on topics of personal interest. These sites, if created by a credible source, can offer personal or expert testimony. Much like blogs, personal Web sites can be created by anyone with the skills and equipment, and they may represent specific opinions.

Karissa is an art major who likes to work in nontraditional forms. Recently she has been working with fiber, and she came across a print of a quilt by fiber artist Annette Kennedy. Inspired by her work, Karissa decided to select Kennedy as one of the nontraditional artists she would speak about to a class. Karissa accessed the artist's personal Web site (shown below), where she found digital images of Kennedy's works and information about the artist. During the speech, Karissa used this direct quotation from the artist's biography:

I love and am inspired by the beauty in nature. I have always been an avid amateur photographer. These things coupled with my love of fabric and color lead me to my journey of creating landscape and pictorial art quilts from personally taken photographs.

Karissa also found several images to display during the speech

ADVANTAGES

- Can be reliable support if author is a recognized expert on your topic
- Can offer unique material

DISADVANTAGES

- Can be written by anyone, regardless of his or her credentials (research the author's credibility)
- May require verifying information with other sources
- Are often promotional or biased toward the opinions of the author
- May not credit all sources of information

WHEN TO USE

- To find material that humanizes your topic
- To find personal information about the site author(s)

TIPS ON LOCATING

- Use the search engines discussed on pages 72–73 to locate Web sites.

SAMPLE ORAL CITATION

"According to the official Web site of Annette Kennedy, *Mountain Chapel* is an award-winning work from 2008."

Fiber Earthspaces
Annette Kennedy
fiber artist

Mountain Chapel

I love and am inspired by the beauty in nature. I have always been an avid amateur

How Can You Use the Internet to Access Libraries?

The facing page shows you an example of a library's online portal. Most libraries allow you to access at least some of their services online, and searching these portals is an effective way to do preliminary research on the library's holdings and resources, as well as to access online databases or reference material. Online access is also extremely helpful when you realize you need more information or you forget a citation and cannot get back to the physical library quickly. Most library portals allow you to:

- Search their catalogs and databases just as you would if you were sitting in the library (see the librarian for any special log-on requirements for databases).

- Utilize other services such as those noted on the library portal example on the next page. So explore your library portal and learn what it has to offer.

However, do not cut corners! Don't be afraid to go to the library! The reference librarian can save you time, as his or her job is to help you find information and resources. If researching is a relatively new process for you, begin with a face-to-face discussion with your librarian. He or she can help you learn how to use the resources designed to make your search faster and more effective. Whenever you ask a librarian for help, take the following items with you:

- Your speech assignment and any notes you have about it

- Your working outline

- Any research you have already completed

→ The next sections of this chapter will tell you more about the resources inside a library.

Locate online writing help

You may find a list of Internet links related to your research needs or writing skills. For example, your library might have links to sites on evaluating Web material, writing essays, and avoiding plagiarism.

Contact a librarian

If you can't go to the library in person, you may be able to e-mail or chat with a librarian about a specific research question.

eBook search

Some library catalogs allow searches for eBooks.

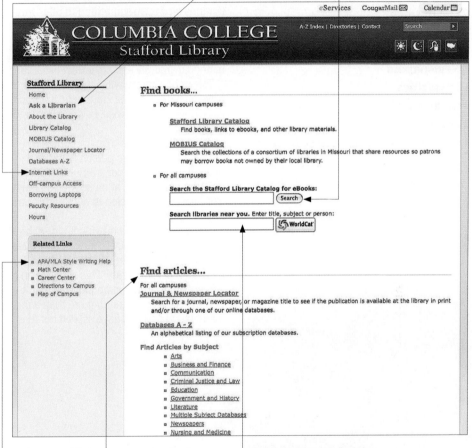

COLUMBIA COLLEGE
Stafford Library

eServices   CougarMail ✉   Calendar 🗓

A-Z Index | Directories | Contact   Search ▶

Stafford Library

Home
Ask a Librarian
About the Library
Library Catalog
MOBIUS Catalog
Journal/Newspaper Locator
Databases A-Z
▶Internet Links
Off-campus Access
Borrowing Laptops
Faculty Resources
Hours

Related Links

- APA/MLA Style Writing Help
- Math Center
- Career Center
- Directions to Campus
- Map of Campus

Find books...

- For Missouri campuses

Stafford Library Catalog
Find books, links to ebooks, and other library materials.

MOBIUS Catalog
Search the collections of a consortium of libraries in Missouri that share resources so patrons may borrow books not owned by their local library.

- For all campuses

Search the Stafford Library Catalog for eBooks:
[   ] (Search) ◀

Search libraries near you. Enter title, subject or person:
[   ] 🔍 WorldCat'

Find articles...

For all campuses
Journal & Newspaper Locator
Search for a journal, newspaper, or magazine title to see if the publication is available at the library in print and/or through one of our online databases.

Databases A - Z
An alphabetical listing of our subscription databases.

Find Articles by Subject
- Arts
- Business and Finance
- Communication
- Criminal Justice and Law
- Education
- Government and History
- Literature
- Multiple Subject Databases
- Newspapers
- Nursing and Medicine

Style manual help

You can get help with creating citations and formatting your outline.

Article search

This section allows you to search for articles, journals, newspapers, and databases in its collection.

Search multiple libraries

Some campus libraries have reciprocity arrangements with other libraries, allowing you to borrow or consult a wider range of materials and saving you valuable time.

What Does the Library Have to Offer You?

1 **The Catalog**

2 **Databases**

3 **Books**

4 **Newspapers**

5 **Magazines**

6 **Newsletters**

7 **Journals**

8 **Special Collections or Rare Books**

You should always include the library in your research adventures. In most college towns, you have a library on or affiliated with your campus, as well as a public library. In some larger cities, you may find additional libraries dedicated to specialized topics. All of these libraries may have something to offer your speech topic.

The college library will have more academically oriented information, such as historical analysis and scientific research.

The public library will offer you access to more local history and statewide statistics, as well as popular books, newspapers, and magazines.

Special libraries are usually connected or related to a famous person (such as a presidential library), company, organization, government agency, or museum. You may need special permission to access the stacks in these libraries.

Many libraries also provide an interlibrary loan (ILL) service. ILL allows you to request items located at other libraries that will be delivered to your library. This service can give you access to much more material, but it can be time consuming (often more than a month for delivery) and can have associated fees.

TIP: Know Your Requirements
Most college speech assignments require that you use a certain amount of material from the library, rather than relying only on the Internet. Check your assignment and ask your instructor.

1
The Catalog

All libraries have a catalog system, typically an electronic search engine, designed to help you locate materials physically owned by the library. Items in the library's database are cataloged according to subjects and related subjects as assigned by the Library of Congress. Usually you can search for publications by title, author, or subject. The librarian can help you determine what search terms to use to target your research. You should always pay attention to the related subjects listed for other possible routes to take in your search. The tips given earlier for search engines are helpful here as well.

Contact a librarian: You can ask a librarian a question.

Chinook University**Libraries**
University of Colorado at Boulder

Hours | Off-Campus Access (VPN) | Chinook Home | Libraries Home | CU-Boulder Home

How do I...?   Ask Us: email | chat | phone   Log in to My Chinook

Chinook > Find by Advanced Keyword

Find by Advanced Keyword

SEARCH TIPS

Search by: Any Field / **for:** _____ And /
                   Any Field / **for:** _____ And /
                   Any Field / **for:** _____

Submit   Clear Form

Optional Limits:

Collection: All Collections /
Year: After ____ and Before ____
Material Type: ANY /
                     Videorecordings: Choose one /
                     Sound Recordings: Choose one /
Electronic Version: ☐
Location: ANY /
Language: ANY /
Publisher: _____
Items that are available: ☐
Sort by: Date /
                     Submit

Find Journals/Serials | Find Articles & More | Reserves | More search options »

Prospector | WorldCat.org | Research and Subject Guides | CU Digital Library (CU-DL) | E-Journal Finder
New Titles 🔊 | Suggest a Title for Purchase | Interlibrary Loan | Reserve a Group Study Room

Colorado   Contact University Libraries: email | chat | phone
University of Colorado at Boulder   University Libraries, 184 UCB, 1720 Pleasant Street, University of Colorado Boulder, CO 80309-0184
                                     Libraries Information 303-492-8705 | Research & Instruction 303-492-7521
                                     © Regents of the University of Colorado

TIP: Visiting Other Libraries
If you want to use a library you are not affiliated with, check the library's Web site or call for its visiting patron policies. In many cases, a letter of introduction from the director of a library where you are already a patron will help you gain access.

Multifaceted search
This library lets you search all its collections and locations. You can also search items by format (print, audio, etc.) and other criteria.

Finding materials
You can locate books, articles, and other materials by searching catalogs and databases.

2
Databases

Although search engines like Google can help you find general information, they do not access everything, and you will usually need to do deeper research to find the highest quality support materials.

Most libraries subscribe to **databases**, or extensive collections of published works—such as magazine, newspaper, and journal articles—in electronic form, making them easy to search and locate. Databases contain descriptions and citation information about articles (title of article and publication, author, publication date, etc.), and they often include the full text of the articles. A database itself is not a source you will cite in your speech; it is a portal for finding a large amount of support materials from many different sources, all in one place.

Different databases may focus on different subject areas. For instance, ERIC (Education Resources Information Center) covers education research. Others specialize in arts, sciences, law, or business. Your reference librarian can tell you what databases are available at your library and what disciplines they cover, to help you choose the ones most relevant to your topic. Your library's Web site will likely include a link to these databases.

You search in databases much like you search in the library's catalog or with a search engine. A search screen from one common database (JSTOR) is shown on the next page. Just as with a search engine, you have options for basic and advanced searching. You may be able to limit your search by discipline or subject, to full-text articles only (rather than a description or abstract), to recent articles only, or by the language an article is written in.

Multiple-subject databases contain sources across a vast spectrum of disciplines and periodicals. Use these to research broadly and then to narrow your topic. Some common ones include:

- Academic Search Elite/EBSCOhost
- LexisNexis
- JSTOR
- Project MUSE

Specialized databases contain sources related to specific disciplines or topics. Use these to focus your research once you have your topic narrowed. Some common ones include:

- Bloom's Literary Reference Online (literary criticism and resources)
- CQ Weekly (coverage of acts of Congress)
- ERIC (education)
- OVID (science and health care)
- Standard & Poor's NetAdvantage (business)

TIPS: Using Databases

- Search in the database as you would search with an Internet search engine.
- Use databases to help you narrow your topic.
- Start with a full-text search. You might find everything you need, not only information in abstract form.
- Put limits on your search by defining attributes.
- Search more than one database.
- Ask your librarian for help if you have questions or find using a database intimidating.

Basic search
Enter key terms related to your topic.

Advanced search
Investigate how you can limit your search or do a detailed search.

Search tips
Pay attention to tips the site might offer. Different tips may appear on each page.

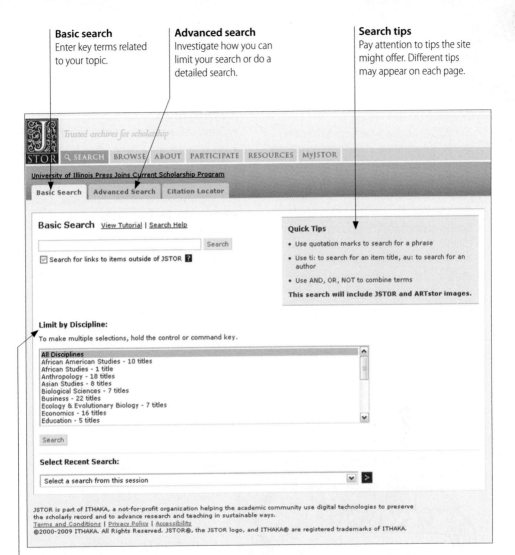

Trusted archives for scholarship

🔍 SEARCH BROWSE ABOUT PARTICIPATE RESOURCES MyJSTOR

University of Illinois Press Joins Current Scholarship Program

Basic Search **Advanced Search** **Citation Locator**

Basic Search View Tutorial | Search Help

[   ] Search

☑ Search for links to items outside of JSTOR ?

Quick Tips

• Use quotation marks to search for a phrase
• Use ti: to search for an item title, au: to search for an author
• Use AND, OR, NOT to combine terms

This search will include JSTOR and ARTstor images.

Limit by Discipline:
To make multiple selections, hold the control or command key.

All Disciplines
African American Studies - 10 titles
African Studies - 1 title
Anthropology - 18 titles
Asian Studies - 8 titles
Biological Sciences - 7 titles
Business - 22 titles
Ecology & Evolutionary Biology - 7 titles
Economics - 16 titles
Education - 5 titles

Search

Select Recent Search:

[Select a search from this session   ▼] ▶

JSTOR is part of ITHAKA, a not-for-profit organization helping the academic community use digital technologies to preserve the scholarly record and to advance research and teaching in sustainable ways.
Terms and Conditions | Privacy Policy | Accessibility
©2000-2009 ITHAKA. All Rights Reserved. JSTOR®, the JSTOR logo, and ITHAKA® are registered trademarks of ITHAKA.

Discipline search
Some sites allow broad searches, such as by academic discipline.

3
Books

You might use any of several types of books for support materials. A book may be written by a single author, multiple authors, corporate authors, or government authors.

Types of books include:

- Nonfiction books (when credible, offer factual information about people, places, events, things, animals, etc., and are written by reliable authors)
- Fiction books (authors invent creative stories)
- Edited collections (compilations of essays or articles, written by multiple authors but related topically)
- Anthologies (compilations of short stories, poetry, or plays)

Janie has been asked to give a presentation on preserving pickles at a local farm show. In the book *The Beginner's Guide to Preserving Food at Home,* she found lists of equipment needs and numerous recipes. Before giving the audience a couple of the recipe examples, Janie included an oral citation (see sample in next column). Also, Janie included the source on printed copies of a recipe she distributed to the audience at the end of her speech.

ADVANTAGES

- Often considered extremely reliable
- Usually contain a large amount of detailed information
- Often have bibliographies or source notes leading you to additional material
- Often contain quotable passages for emotional appeals

DISADVANTAGES

- May not have current information (check the copyright date and verify information with current sources)
- Require more time to read and glean information, due to length

WHEN TO USE

- To find important detail and contextual information about your topic
  - To locate facts, statistics, and examples

TIPS ON LOCATING

- Search for your topic on sites like Amazon or Library of Congress (www.loc.gov) to identify books to seek at the library.
- Search the library catalog.

SAMPLE ORAL CITATION

"In her 2009 book *The Beginner's Guide to Preserving Food at Home,* Janet Chadwick offers several easy pickle recipes."

4
Newspapers

Newspapers are published daily, weekly, or biweekly and can be local, national, or international. They contain news, information, opinions, and advertisements. Articles tend to focus on politics, crime, business, health, art/entertainment, society, and sports.

In the wake of the 2010 Gulf of Mexico oil spill, Ross argues to stop off-shore oil drilling until new regulations are in place. Because the Gulf spill is a relatively new event at the time of his speech, Ross turns to newspapers for much of his information. Ross found this information in the July 23, 2010, online edition of the *Wall Street Journal*:

> According to testimony…, the Deepwater Horizon experienced a series of power losses, computer crashes and other issues in the months before the explosion, and hundreds of items were overdue for maintenance. But in a March 29 email, a BP manager praised workers on the rig for completing 63 of 70 maintenance items. It wasn't immediately clear whether the email referred to the same maintenance issues.

See one of Ross's oral citations at the end of this page.

ADVANTAGES
- Often viewed as current and reliable
- Feature condensed information
- Use accessible language

DISADVANTAGES
- Rarely cite references
- May not give background information
- May require finding other in-depth sources
- May be outdated quickly

WHEN TO USE
- To find current facts and statistics
- To locate extended examples
- To support current events or topics

TIPS ON LOCATING
- Search the library databases.
- Public libraries often carry local and some national newspapers.
- Academic libraries often carry local, national, and international newspapers.
- Ask a librarian how to find archived issues.
- Some newspapers are also online (note that online editions can be different).

SAMPLE ORAL CITATION
"A July 23 *Wall Street Journal* online article, 'BP Managers Named in Disaster Probe' by Ben Casselman and Russell Gold, said testimony in a federal investigation indicated several reasons to anticipate a major incident."

5
Magazines

Magazines are published on a regular schedule (weekly, monthly, or quarterly) and contain a range of articles, often related to a theme or focus. Magazines are generally financed by advertisements as well as a purchase or subscription price.

Magazines can be local, regional, national, or international. Some focus on popular culture (e.g., *Vogue* or *GQ*), whereas others tend toward educational topics (e.g., *Scientific American* or *National Geographic*). Magazines, especially for general readers, often use accessible and vivid language.

For example, Nico wants colorful examples for his speech about king penguins. He finds an article describing the responsibilities of adult penguins with chicks, and he draws from it to conjure up an effective image:

> According to Tom O'Neill, in his September 2009 *National Geographic* article "Every Bird a King": "During this three-month period, the adults peck at all trespassers.... Researchers figure that a king penguin parent devotes four hours and 2,000 pecks a day to fighting off interlopers."

See the end of this page for another sample from Nico's speech.

ADVANTAGES
- Often viewed as current and reliable
- Feature condensed information
- Use accessible language

DISADVANTAGES
- May not give background information
- May require finding other in-depth sources
- May be outdated quickly

WHEN TO USE
- To find facts, statistics, and examples
- To support current events or topics

TIPS ON LOCATING
- Search the library databases.
- Libraries often have many magazines and may archive old issues.
- Some magazines have Web sites, but they may differ from print versions or contain only old issues.

SAMPLE ORAL CITATION
> "The king penguin is the second largest type of penguin. It can be as tall as three feet and weigh an average of 30 pounds, according to the September 2009 *National Geographic* article 'Every Bird a King' by Tom O'Neill."

6
Newsletters

Newsletters are regularly distributed mini-publications produced by clubs, churches, societies, associations, businesses, and government agencies. Their purpose is to provide concise information about a group or one main topic of interest. Newsletters can be delivered in printed or electronic form.

Because strokes are the third leading cause of death and the most common cause of adult disability, Sean wants to inform his classmates about causes, types, and signs of strokes. In a National Institutes of Health newsletter, Sean found this list of signs and used it in his speech as well as on his presentation aids:

SIGNS OF STROKE

If you see or have one or more of these symptoms, call 911 right away:

• **Sudden numbness or weakness of the face, arm, or leg, especially on one side of the body**

• **Sudden confusion, trouble speaking or understanding**

• **Sudden trouble seeing in one or both eyes**

• **Sudden trouble walking, dizziness, or loss of balance or coordination**

• **Sudden severe headache with no known cause**

See Sean's oral citation at the end of this page.

ADVANTAGES

- Contain information specific to an organization or topic
- Offer material not found elsewhere
- Give information in condensed form

DISADVANTAGES

- May give incomplete information
- May use specialized language
- May not cite sources or authors
- May be biased or promotional

WHEN TO USE

- To locate information on specific groups or topics
- To find a group's stance on an issue
- To discover or follow current events

TIPS ON LOCATING

- Search for a Web site maintained by the group or author of the newsletter.
  - May be in a library's periodical or reference section; ask your librarian.
  - Contact the organization.

SAMPLE ORAL CITATION

"According to the May 2010 issue of 'News in Health,' published by the National Institutes of Health, these are potential signs of a stroke."

7
Journals

Journals are academic and professional publications issued at regular intervals, such as quarterly. Journals typically use *peer review*, in which experts in the appropriate field evaluate the articles before they are accepted for publication.

Journals are topic specific and tailored for a certain audience. For example, the *Journal of the American Medical Association* is written for medical professionals. Journals exist in most major fields.

Mitali is majoring in film. In her film history class, she must give a presentation on the films of Martin Scorsese. The assignment states that the presentation must include critical reviews as well as Scorsese's film history. So, Mitali turns to some of the journals of her field. In the *Journal of Film and Video*, she finds this article.

> **"Geographies of Desire: Postsocial Urban Space and Historical Revision in the Films of Martin Scorsese"**

Mitali found some descriptive quotations in the article, and the endnotes offered other articles she could research for support materials. See the end of this page for how she began one of her oral citations.

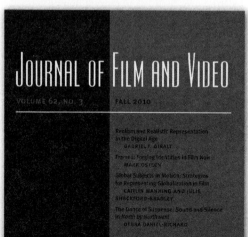

ADVANTAGES
- Have extremely high credibility
- Are written and reviewed by experts or specialists in the field
- Include extensive bibliographies where you may find further sources

DISADVANTAGES
- Are written in a formal style that may need to be adapted for your audience
- Use language specific to the field that may be difficult to understand

WHEN TO USE
- To find detailed facts and statistics
- To locate expert testimony
- When highly credible sources are needed
- With a highly educated audience

TIPS ON LOCATING
- Many databases include full-text versions of journals.
- Academic libraries often carry selected scholarly/professional journals in print.

SAMPLE ORAL CITATION
"In her article, 'Geographies of Desire: Postsocial Urban Space and Historical Revision in the Films of Martin Scorsese'—published in the Spring/Summer 2010 issue of the *Journal of Film and Video*—Professor Sabine Haenni argues that..."

8
Special Collections or Rare Books

Many libraries house special collections or rare books that are unique to that library. Items in special collections may include rare books, historical records (archives), manuscripts, personal correspondence, photographs, or physical items and artifacts.

Because these items are rare, fragile, and often valuable, they are usually stored in a controlled environment known as *closed stacks*. You cannot check out these items and may need to present identification or a letter of reference to gain access, if access is available. Specialized libraries offer vast collections that can benefit you if your speech is on a related topic.

For example, if your speech is about Mark Twain's life, you might visit the special collections of the Hannibal Free Public Library in Missouri if you live in that area. Hannibal was Twain's boyhood home, and the library holds information and artifacts related to his life and writings. You might find a photo or a rare edition of a Twain book for a presentation aid. If you cannot visit, you could contact the library or access its digital exhibits online. You may find other special archives online as well.

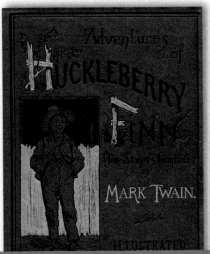

ADVANTAGES
- Contain unique, often engaging material
- Can offer many primary sources
- Can be extensive at some libraries

DISADVANTAGES
- May be far away or difficult to locate
- May not allow access to everyone
- May require you to view materials under special conditions
- May not allow you to touch or photocopy the items

WHEN TO USE
- To find unique facts, statistics, and examples (especially extended) from rare materials

TIPS ON LOCATING
- Search online for special libraries.
- Many collections may not be electronically searchable, so think about locations related to your topic and check their local libraries for special collections.
- Ask your local reference librarian for help.

SAMPLE ORAL CITATION
"This image, from the Internet Archive, is the cover for the 1885 first edition of the book *Adventures of Huckleberry Finn*."

What Can You Find Both on the Internet and in Libraries?

1 Government Resources

2 Reference Works

Although you can often locate many of the previously discussed sources online and in libraries, the most common sources that consistently reside in both places are government resources and reference works.

Government resources are valuable for locating up-to-date statistics and information on current events being discussed by government officials.

For example, when Ivan wrote a speech to argue for installing red-light cameras in his hometown, he located this key statistic on the city's Web site.

> **Nationwide, it's estimated that red-light running causes more than 9,000 crashes each year.**

See the end of page 91 for an oral citation from Ivan's speech.

Meanwhile, for her speech on the basic elements of building architecture, Sara used the dictionary to help her define the word *quoin* in language useful to her novice audience. She found at merriam-webster.com that a quoin is:

> **...a solid exterior angle (as of a building).**

See page 93 for Sara's sample oral citation.

The next few pages will give you tips on using government references and reference works, as well as hints on how to orally cite these types of sources.

CONFIDENCE BOOSTER

Allowing yourself to take the necessary time to effectively research your topic will not only help you compose a great speech but also increase your confidence. When you spend time building your knowledge about a topic, you become more comfortable talking about it.

1
Government Resources

Government resources are information sources created by local, state, and federal governmental agencies. They can include books, reports, bills, pamphlets, maps, Web sites, or other documents.

ADVANTAGES
- Are often viewed as highly credible
- Are often very current
- Often contain information not available elsewhere
- Often have extensive bibliographies where you might find further material

DISADVANTAGES
- The quantity of publications can be overwhelming
- May not include citation information
- May be difficult to locate the specific publication you are looking for

WHEN TO USE
- To locate statistics and facts
- To locate policy information
- To locate practical information. Agencies often publish "how-to" programs, such as how to start a business or create school lesson plans.

TIPS ON LOCATING
- Local and state publications:

  Search the Internet using the city or state name, or ask your librarian how to locate government holdings.

  Public libraries are often good sources of local and state publications.

  Check the state library, which may be housed in the state capital.

- Federal resources:

  Go to www.usa.gov/Agencies/Federal/All_Agencies/index.shtml for a list of Web sites.

  The Government Printing Office Web site (www.gpoaccess.gov) offers information about federal government publications and libraries.

  Consult the printed guidebook *E-government and Web Directory: U.S. Federal Government Online.*

SAMPLE ORAL CITATION
"Columbia, Missouri, recently installed two red-light cameras to catch drivers running red lights. The city's official Web site notes that more than 9,000 accidents occur yearly nationwide due to drivers running lights."

2
Reference Works

A reference work is a compilation of information such as facts, data, and definitions arranged for easy access. Many printed reference works have a corresponding Web site.

Some examples are:

- Dictionaries (general and subject specific)
- Encyclopedias (general and subject specific)
- Thesauruses
- Yearbooks or annuals (e.g., *Statistical Abstracts, The World Almanac, Book of Facts, Facts on File Yearbook, Yearbook of Higher Education, Yearbook of Agriculture*)
- Atlases (contain maps, charts, and tables about places from around the world)
- Grammar handbooks and style manuals
- Books of quotations
- Medical reference books
- Biographical reference books (e.g., *International Who's Who, Who's Who of Women, Current Biography, Biography Index*)
- City directories

ADVANTAGES

- Are great places to begin your research
- Are useful places to get brief statistics, facts, and quotations
- Are helpful in constructing your outline

DISADVANTAGES

- May offer information that is too brief
- Can focus on obscure facts or definitions that are not popularly acceptable or used
- May be user-created sites, such as Wikipedia, which may not always be accurate and so are not viewed as credible. The source lists within these types of references may help you locate reliable primary sources, but always check with your instructor to see if using such user-created references is acceptable for your assignment.

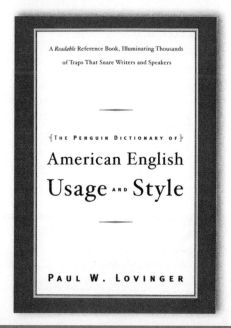

A *Readable* Reference Book, Illuminating Thousands of Traps That Snare Writers and Speakers

{THE PENGUIN DICTIONARY OF}

American English
Usage AND Style

PAUL W. LOVINGER

Dictionaries may be general or specialized.

WHEN TO USE

- To locate brief definitions or segments of information
- To locate statistics and facts
- To assist you in using language effectively
- To start your research and get a broad base of information to build upon

SAMPLE ORAL CITATION

"As defined at merriam-webster.com, the quoin of a building is a solid exterior angle."

TIPS ON LOCATING

- Check the reference section of your library or ask a reference librarian.
- Typing in a key word or phrase or asking a search engine a question will pull up many of these online references. The following are some commonly used Internet references:

>   Merriam-webster.com
>   Onelook.com
>   Infoplease.com
>   Biography.com
>   Refdesk.com
>   The World Factbook
>   Bartlett's Familiar Quotations

Online references can often be located by searching for a key word or phrase.

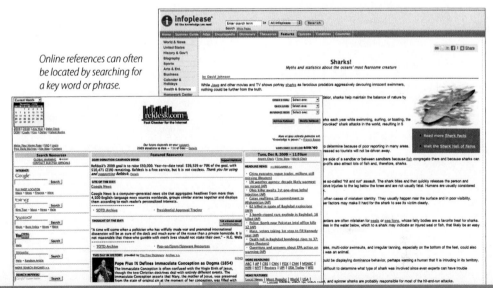

How Can You Gather Support Materials in an Interview?

1 **Prepare for the Interview**
2 **Conduct the Interview**
3 **Use Media-assisted Interviews if Necessary**

Interviews are information-gathering sessions where you (the *interviewer*) ask either one person or a group (the *interviewee/ interviewees*) a series of prepared questions. As a student at an institution of higher education, you have access to many experts across numerous fields, as well as a large number of people who could offer lay testimony. Conducting personal interviews could offer you:

- Excellent expert information not available by other means
- Firsthand experience or feelings about the topic
- Leads on where and how to locate other support materials
- The ability to increase the credibility of your speech as well as to make your speech more personable
- Insight into your audience's perspective, if you interview them directly

TIP: Finding People to Interview

When conducting your research, look for organizations related to your topic. Think about groups, societies, businesses, clubs, institutions, associations, or museums that might have helpful information or publications. Interview someone if you can. For example:

- If you are doing a speech on inexpensive spring break travel packages or how to prepare for a flight with all the new regulations, interview a travel agent.
- If you need local or state history, interview someone at a historical society or museum.
- If you need information on composting, interview someone at the local extension agency, agricultural school, or farmer's market association.

1
Prepare for the Interview

SET UP A TIME AND A LOCATION

- Set the time around your interviewee's schedule. Set start and end times and stick to them. Most interviews should last no longer than 30 to 60 minutes.

- Select a location that is comfortable for the interviewee and that is quiet, with few interruptions (away from phones if possible).

- Reconfirm the time and place with your interviewee.

WRITE YOUR QUESTIONS

- Research the interviewee's background, and be sure your questions are appropriate to his or her expertise.

- Ask questions that help you gather the types of support materials (examples, facts, etc.) you need.

- Use more open-ended questions than closed-ended questions. ***Open-ended questions*** encourage discussion or longer responses. This type of question may start with *who, what, where, when, why,* or *how.*

  For example:

  How do you feel about the proposed emergency notification system?

  Closed-ended questions prompt only "yes" or "no" answers. For example:

  Do you support the proposed emergency notification system?

- Collect information that will establish your interviewee's credibility with your audience:

  What's your exact title?
  How long have you worked for your company?

DECIDE HOW TO RECORD THE INTERVIEW

- Note taking alone may work if you plan to summarize and the interview is brief.

- Use audio or video recording for direct quotations, detailed facts or statistics, or complex material. Take notes as a backup. As an ethical interviewer, you must have permission to audio or video record an interview. Some schools might require written permission, or you might just document the permission at the beginning of the recorded interview. After you have turned on the recording device, you might say to the interviewee:

  Are you aware I am recording this interview? Do I have your permission to do so? Thank you, and if at any time you would like me to stop the recording, just say so.

PRACTICING ETHICS

When you conduct interviews for a speech, remember:

- Always be respectful of your interviewee's time.

- Always get permission from your interviewee if you want to make an audio or video recording of the interview.

2
Conduct the Interview

To conduct a successful interview, you should:

- Pay attention to your appearance. Be well-groomed and dress appropriately.
- If you are using any equipment, make sure it works.
- Arrive on time and begin the interview on time.
- Thank the interviewee for his or her time.
- Explain your topic and speech goal.
- Give the interviewee time to respond to each question.
- Allow yourself to think of *follow-up questions*, or new questions that occur to you based on the interviewee's answers so far. However, be careful not to do this too often or you may run out of time.
- Ask the interviewee to clarify anything if you do not understand.
- Be an active listener.

→ See Chapter 11 (Tab 5) for listening tips.

- Near the end of the interview, check your notes to see if you have the information you need.
- End your interview with a question like:

  Is there anything else I should know?

  Is there anyone else you recommend I speak with?

- End the interview on time.
- Thank the interviewee again, and ask if you can follow up if questions arise later.
- Take a few minutes immediately after the interview to make additional notes while the conversation is still fresh in your mind.
- Send the interviewee a thank-you note. If appropriate, you might offer to share your outline or invite him or her to your speech.

Use the checklist on this page to help prepare for and conduct your interview.

SAMPLE ORAL CITATION FOR INTERVIEW MATERIAL

"In a personal interview I conducted last month, local dentist Dr. Marvin Jones said that his office will donate supplies and a day of free checkups to support the city's health literacy campaign in schools."

CHECKLIST for Interviewing

- ❑ Did I set up an appropriate time and place for the interview?
- ❑ Do my questions collect background information as well as necessary support materials?
- ❑ Are most of my questions open-ended?
- ❑ Do I have a means for recording the interview?
- ❑ On the day of the interview, am I well-groomed and dressed appropriately?
- ❑ Do I have everything I need to conduct the interview (questions, notebook, recorder, address, etc.)?
- ❑ After the interview, did I send a thank-you note?

3
Use Media-assisted Interviews if Necessary

Sometimes meeting face-to-face for an interview is impossible. When necessary, you can use the telephone, e-mail, or instant messaging to conduct the interview. However, realize that these forms of information collection are not as effective as sitting face-to-face with the interviewee. You cannot use as many questions with e-mail, and instant messaging will force an interviewee to take longer to respond. Also, people tend to craft their written words differently and more carefully. You might lose the dramatic effect of an oral narrative and will certainly lose the nonverbal responses from your interviewee. Still, when you need testimony from a particular person or group, media-assisted interviews are better than no interview at all.

Most of the guidelines on preparing for and conducting in-person interviews will still apply for media-assisted interviews. In general, always follow good etiquette and be respectful of your interviewee and his or her time. A few reminders and tips:

- Set up a specific time for a phone interview.
- For an interview via e-mail or a similar method, contact the interviewee in advance to formally request the interview.
- If you are sending written questions, limit how many you ask. Proofread them for any errors in spelling or grammar.

PRACTICING ETHICS

When using information collected from an interview, you have an ethical responsibility to:

- Report the information as accurately as possible. Quote and paraphrase correctly and in context. You might even ask the interviewee to listen to your speech or read over the outline prior to the speech event.
- Protect the interviewee from painful effects that might occur when you reveal something intimate or distressing about them to a larger audience. If an interviewee has requested anonymity or if you think you should protect his or her identity for any reason, use a pseudonym in your speech instead of an interviewee's real name. During the speech, inform the audience that you have changed the name to protect the privacy of the individual. If you feel that the person's identity is crucial to your speech, consult with your instructor.

How Can You Gather Support Materials with a Survey?

1 Create the Survey

2 Conduct the Survey

Surveys are similar to interviews in that their purpose is to collect information. However, they help you collect quantifiable information from a large group of individuals known as the **population**. The responses given to survey questions are not as wide open as in an interview, and the survey is usually self-administered—requiring careful construction of the questions.

Depending on your survey's focus, you can collect opinions and/or factual information from the individuals in your population. The polls we hear about prior to major elections are examples; they are statistics collected by administering surveys. When collecting support materials for a speech, you use surveys in the same way.

For example, if you are giving a persuasive speech on your school's intentions to install an emergency notification system that will notify students, staff, and faculty of an emergency, knowing how the student body and staff feel about this system would help you focus your speech as well as give you statistics related to community opinion.

Surveys can be beneficial because they:

- Are a valuable way to collect information from a large number of people
- Allow you to collect a wide variety of information
- Are relatively easy and economical to administer
- Can be simple to interpret, if your survey is simple and brief

You can find many survey tools available online for free. Search using phrases such as "free survey tools" or "free survey maker."

1
Create the Survey

Most surveys are short and self-administered, so crafting your questions is very important. Unlike interviews, surveys benefit from using more closed-ended questions. Before you begin writing questions, take a few moments to focus on what specific information you want to collect, including demographic information important to your data and topic.

→ See Chapter 1 (Tab 1) for more information about demographics.

As you create your questions, use clear and appropriate language, ask about only one issue in each question, and try to accommodate all possible answers.

INEFFECTIVE:

1. Tell me why you shop at the farmer's market and what you buy?

....

This is really two open-ended questions in one that may take too long to answer. The respondents may give incomplete responses or answer only one of the questions.

EFFECTIVE:

1. Out of the following reasons, why do you shop the farmer's market? Please check all that apply.

.... Value

.... Quality of products

.... Variety of organic products

.... Location of the market

.... Supporting local farmers

.... Other

Please explain

....

This question asks about only one issue and offers specific responses plus an option to add one not there. You could quickly gather information with this question.

CHECKLIST for Surveys
❏ Am I asking only one thing in each question?
❏ Am I using language that is clear and appropriate to my respondents?
❏ Did I use mostly closed-ended questions?
❏ Did I keep the questionnaire short and simple?

Continuing with the farmer's market topic, a more developed survey would look like this.

→ See page 42 for another sample survey.

Make questions easy to read in an consistent format

FARMER'S MARKET SURVEY

1. Are you from Jackson City?
   .... Yes
   .... No

2. If you are not from Jackson City, do you live in Lawrence County?
   .... Yes
   .... No

3. What is your sex?
   .... Female
   .... Male

4. What is your age?
   .... Younger than 20
   20–39
   40–59
   .... 60 or older

5. How often do you visit the farmer's market?
   .... First time
   .... Weekly
   .... Every two weeks
   .... Monthly
   .... Periodically during the season

6. Why do you shop the farmer's market? (Check all that apply.)
   .... Value
   .... Quality of products
   .... Variety of organic products
   .... Location of the market
   .... Supporting local farmers
   .... Other
   Please explain ....
   ....

7. Which products do you **regularly** purchase? (Check all that apply.)
   .... Organic vegetables
   .... Vegetables
   .... Plants
   .... Cut flowers
   .... Cheese
   .... Meat
   .... Eggs
   .... Honey
   .... Homemade baked goods
   .... Handmade products
   .... Other
   Please explain ....
   ....

Use very specific language

2
Conduct the Survey

Once you have your survey written and reproduced (if necessary), you are ready to administer it. Most likely, you will only survey a **sample**, or portion, of the population you are researching.

Determining your sample size can be complicated if you need a low margin of error (high reliability) that what you say about the population is correct. The primary guidelines for selecting and determining the size of your survey sample are the following:

Select individuals who represent subgroups across the entire population. Your sample should represent different genders, ages, races, religions, social statuses, and so on, if these are important to your survey. Achieving a representative sample can be difficult. To help achieve the appropriate variety:

- Be sure you ask demographic questions in the survey so that you can see if you are getting a representative sample.
- Select individuals randomly (e.g., every tenth student) from a general and complete list, such as your campus phone directory or e-mail directory.

Survey a large enough sample. "Large enough" means that you are reasonably confident that your sample represents the population and that your audience will find your results credible.

Factor in the location. Be aware of how the location where you are going to conduct the survey can influence the results. Surveying students in the science building may mean that most of your respondents will be science majors—which may or may not be appropriate, depending on your survey's goals.

SAMPLE ORAL CITATION FOR SURVEY MATERIAL

"In my February survey of 85 out of the 120 new employees here at the plant, more than two-thirds indicated a high level of satisfaction with their jobs."

TIP: Review Your Questions

Surveys are a great way to get information about your topic, but an effective survey takes time and thought to create. Once you have drafted a survey, you might be wise to let someone who knows how to create an effective survey (like an instructor) take a look at it.

How Do You Take Good Research Notes?

1 **Prepare to Research**
2 **Use a Note-taking System**
3 **Know the Appropriate Style Manual**

1
Prepare to Research

Before you begin your research:

- Use Chapter 4 to guide you on the types of support materials you may find and how you might use each type.

- Create a list of types of support materials you may want to locate.

- Use the checklist below as you research, to keep in mind five important characteristics of effective support materials.

→ Chapter 4 (Tab 2) helps you prepare to research and shows you how to choose effective support materials.

CHECKLIST for Evaluating Support Materials

❑ Is the information accurate?

❑ Is the information current and timely?

❑ Is the information complete? Am I missing anything?

❑ Will my audience view the information and the source as trustworthy?

❑ Is the information suitable for my audience?

2
Use a Note-taking System

Detailed note taking is the key to good research. Most students use one of three basic methods:

- Take handwritten notes on note cards or sheets of paper.
- Photocopy or print pages containing support materials.
- Use a combination of written note taking and copying/printing.

Any of these methods can be effective, but handwritten notes (either alone or in combination with copying/printing) can work especially well when creating a speech. If you have your support materials on individual cards or sheets of paper, you can easily categorize the pieces into a strategy; you can physically lay them out in the order you plan to insert them into the speech. This method can be more effective for the beginning researcher and may save time later.

Although photocopying is faster than writing, you may not be as selective about the type, quality, or quantity of support materials—which can make creating your outline more confusing.

Some sample handwritten notes are shown here.

TOPIC: SAVE THE ENVIRONMENT

Quotation from Silent Spring:

"Then a strange blight crept over the area and everything began to change. Some evil spell had settled on the community: mysterious maladies swept the flocks of chickens; the cattle and sheep sickened and died. Everywhere was a shadow of death."

Information for citation:

Carson, Rachel. Silent Spring. Boston: Houghton Mifflin, 1962. 2. Print.

REMEMBER, no matter what method you use, you will need to include specific citation information.

TIP: Keeping Track

If you use a combination of note taking and photocopying, make sure you have a method to match your notes with the right photocopy so that you can create accurate source citations.

TOPIC: BIRTH DEFECTS

Statistics:

- About 120,000 babies (1 in 33) in the United States are born each year with birth defects.
- A birth defect is an abnormality of structure, function, or metabolism (body chemistry) present at birth that results in physical or mental disabilities or death.
- Birth defects are the leading cause of death in the first year of life.

From: http://www.marchofdimes.com/pnhec/4439_1206.asp

(I have a photcopy of this page in speech folder)

3
Know the Appropriate Style Manual

Most beginning speech classes require students to use the style manual of either the *Modern Language Association (MLA)* or the *American Psychological Association (APA)* to cite sources properly in the written outline. Creating your speech outline and oral citations will be much easier if you adhere to your assigned style as you take your notes. Most major style formats will require some or all of the following information.

- Author and/or editor names
- Title of the main source (book, magazine, newspaper, Web site, etc.)
- Title of a specific article, essay, or other item being used from within a larger main source
- Publisher or, for a Web site, the sponsoring organization
- Date of publication
- Date of retrieval for electronic sources
- Web address (URL) for a Web site
- The issue, volume, and/or number of a periodical (especially a journal), if given
- The name of the database you used to access a source, if applicable
- The digital object identifier (DOI), if one is given and you are using APA style
- Page numbers

Collect as much of this information as you can while you are researching, even if you are not sure how much of it you will need, to avoid having to search for it again later. Photocopies of title pages and copyright pages, or printouts of Web pages that show URL information in the headers and footers, can help serve as backups to your notes.

Citing your sources correctly on your outline and during your oral presentation is the only way to prevent plagiarism.

REMEMBER

There are two types of plagiarism:

- **Blatant plagiarism**—occurs either when speakers take an entire speech or document and present it as their own or when speakers take parts of information from other sources and link them together, creating an entire speech of someone else's words.

- **No-citation plagiarism**—occurs when speakers fail to give source credit to a specific part of their speech that is borrowed from another source.

Beginning speakers often use books, Internet sources, and periodicals as their major sources. Here are a few examples for how to cite these sources using MLA and APA styles.

PRINTED BOOK
MLA STYLE:
Lear, Linda. *Rachel Carson: Witness for Nature*. New York: Holt, 1997. Print.

APA STYLE:
Lear, L. (1997). *Rachel Carson: Witness for nature*. New York, NY: Henry Holt.

FROM THE INTERNET
MLA STYLE:
Centers for Disease Control and Prevention. "2009 H1N1 Flu: Situation Update." *CDC.gov*. CDC, 2 Oct. 2009. Web. 3 Oct. 2009.

APA STYLE:
Centers for Disease Control and Prevention. (2009, October 2). 2009 H1N1 flu: Situation update. Retrieved from http://www.cdc.gov/h1n1flu/update.htm

PRINTED PERIODICAL (e.g., newspaper)
MLA STYLE:
Cailler, Daniel. "Mayor Favors Use Tax for Online Shoppers." *Columbia Daily Tribune*, 6 Oct. 2009: A12. Print.

APA STYLE:
Cailler, D. (2009, October 6). Mayor favors use tax for online shoppers. *Columbia Daily Tribune*, p. A12.

➔ See Chapter 5 (Tab 3) for a more detailed discussion of style formats.

TIPS: Collecting Citation Information

- When recording information for a Web site citation in APA style, be sure to note the address (URL). This is the most commonly forgotten piece of information, and you must include it all on your APA reference pages.

- When conducting research, carry or keep your style manual handy so that you can refer to it for citation specifics. The majority of libraries have the most recent version of the commonly used manuals in their reference collections.

Desmond's Speech

Recently, Desmond read an issue of *Newsweek* online, which included an article about Nelson Mandela's legacy and his influence on the current South African government. In the article, "Father Disfigure," Desmond noticed that Eve Fairbanks argues thus: within the very heart of South African consciousness, Mandela holds an unassailable position as "the national liberator, the savior," and even "its Washington and Lincoln rolled into one."

Desmond has always been interested in U.S. presidents, especially Washington and Lincoln, so this quotation piqued his interest in learning more about Mandela. Also, Desmond's speech instructor discussed other powerful rhetoricians and political activists, and he thought Mandela would be a good speech topic.

PRELIMINARY RESEARCH

Before committing to this topic, Desmond did some quick preliminary research to see what he could find on Mandela and to think about how he might focus his speech. Simply searching for "Nelson Mandela" using Google brought up a host of potential source materials and options. Desmond quickly decided he wanted to talk about Mandela as a person, a political activist, and a president. He spent a few more minutes making research notes and evaluating what he needed to locate.

MANDELA RESEARCH NOTES

MANDELA AS A PERSON:
- Need facts about his personal life
- Need a basic timeline of his life!
- Look for autobiographies and biographies mentioned online

Note: Look for more magazine articles... could save time to not read all the biographies.

MANDELA AS A POLITICAL ACTIVIST:
- The Fairbanks article mentions "anti-apartheid"—need a definition
- Mandela became leader of the African National Congress in 1961—verify date
- Why was he arrested and imprisoned?

MANDELA AS PRESIDENT:
- Need dates and significant issues during his presidency
- Locate text of his speeches... maybe an audio clip

(I have the entire text of his Nobel Peace Prize speech from nobelprize.org)

Note: Interview the professor who teaches South African history
***I should do this first because she might suggest places to find information.

Look for images/photos for presentation aids

THE INTERNET

Using the Internet, Desmond located Mandela's biography on the nobelprize.org site as well as several articles and books that looked interesting. He made a note to find books, such as *Great Souls: Six Who Changed a Century*, from the library. The rest of his Internet search supplied him with:

- A list of eight books by Mandela on Google Books (some with limited access online)
- Numerous images and video of Mandela on Google Images, Google Video, and YouTube
- Images of three *Time* Magazine covers with Mandela's image (Mandela was *Time*'s Man of the Year in 1993)
- Mandela quotations from www.brainyquotes.com

THE LIBRARY

At the library, Desmond searched the catalog and located what he wanted—plus new material he had not found online:

- *The Speeches of Nelson Mandela* (a video)
- A biography by Mary Benson, *Nelson Mandela: The Man and the Movement*
- Three of Mandela's books and two informative articles
- *The Penguin Book of Twentieth-Century Speeches*, containing the text of a Mandela speech

While helping Desmond locate a book, a librarian mentioned seeing an article written by Mandela about Gandhi. Desmond located that article by searching for "Mandela and Gandhi."

APARTHEID

An official policy of racial segregation formerly practiced in the Republic of South Africa, involving political, legal, and economic discrimination against nonwhites.

*Searched onelook.com, then Yahoo! Education (October 5, 2009)

The American Heritage Dictionary of the English Language, 4th ed.

Copyright © 2006 by Houghton Mifflin Company.

http://education.yahoo.com/reference/dictionary/entry/apartheid

Before leaving the library, Desmond also looked up "apartheid" in an online reference linked from the library's Web site.

INTERVIEWS

Although Desmond had more than enough information for his speech, he felt unsure how to explain the importance of the African National Congress, so he interviewed a professor who studies South African politics. He also realized he could interview his grandfather, who came from South Africa as a young man, to gather personal source material.

During his research, Desmond noted organizations related to Mandela and his work. None were local groups where Desmond could conduct an interview, so he searched the official Web sites for the Nobel Peace Prize and the Nelson Mandela Foundation. Both had information to offer, including the text of many of Mandela's speeches. At the end of Chapter 4, you can read more about how Desmond selected material for his speech.

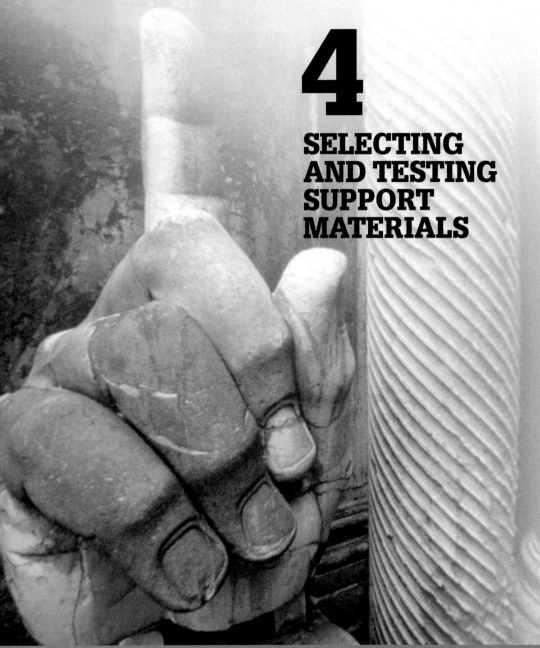

4

SELECTING AND TESTING SUPPORT MATERIALS

Introduction

You do research every day. For example, have you ever looked in your closet to see which clothes are clean, then evaluated your clothing options based on what you will do during the day? That's research. Have you searched the Internet for the best price on a TV? That's research. Have you looked around town for the cheapest food prices? That's research. However, for your research to be effective, you have to know what information is worth paying attention to.

In your speech research, this means you must select the best support materials possible. The goal of this chapter is to help you recognize and evaluate various types of support materials.

The act of research in itself has much to offer. Approach your research as an activity leading to new horizons, new knowledge, improved practices, and increased alternatives. Allow yourself to enjoy research, and you might learn something about yourself. Conducting research can help build your self-confidence by proving that you have a tenacious talent to persevere and to solve problems. It will help you develop critical thinking skills that will serve you well in preparing your speech—and in almost every aspect of life. Above all, conducting research will sometimes confirm your beliefs and can, at other times, offer new alternatives.

That's research!

> *What is research, but a blind date with knowledge.*[1]
>
> WILL HENRY

CHAPTER 3: Locating Support Materials   69

CHAPTER 4 CONTENTS

What Types of Support Materials Can You Use in Your Speech?   110
  1 Facts   110
  2 Definitions   110
  3 Testimony   111
  4 Examples   112
  5 Statistics   114

How Do You Determine What Types of Sources and Support Materials to Use?   116
  1 Consider Primary vs. Secondary Sources   117
  2 Consider Scholarly vs. Popular Sources   118
  3 Consider Your Own Personal Knowledge   119
  4 Consider Your Topic Needs   120

What Do You Evaluate in Your Support Materials?   122
  1 Accuracy   122
  2 Currency   123
  3 Completeness   124
  4 Trustworthiness   124
  5 Suitability   125

How Do You Use Support Materials Effectively?   126
  1 Use Your Materials Purposefully   126
  2 Use Your Materials in Different Ways   127
  3 Use Quotation and Paraphrasing Effectively   128
  4 Use Delivery Techniques to Enhance Your Materials   129

How Do You Cite Sources Orally?   130
  1 Collect the Necessary Content   130
  2 Create and Deliver Oral Citations   132

Desmond's Speech   134

Tab 2 Review   136

What Types of Support Materials Can You Use in Your Speech?

1 **Facts**

2 **Definitions**

3 **Testimony**

4 **Examples**

5 **Statistics**

1
Facts

Facts are verifiable bits of information about people, events, places, dates, and times. Most audiences will accept a fact with minor support or a simple oral citation and will not require an extended logical argument to prove the fact. The fact must be typical and from a recent reliable source. For example:

> **The Golden Gate Bridge opened to traffic on May 28, 1937.**

> **Hawaii and Alaska became U.S. states in 1959.**

2
Definitions

For a classroom speech on digital piracy, Jonah used a definition to gain his audience's attention:

> **When you hear the word piracy, do you think of *Pirates of the Caribbean*? Or do you think about buying cheap bootlegged copies of DVDs or music? If you answered yes to the latter question, you know that "the illegal trade of software, videos, DVDs, and music" is "digital piracy." According to the 2010 *Webster's New World Finance and Investment Dictionary,* this form of piracy "occurs when someone other than the copyright holder copies the product and resells it for a fraction of the cost that the legitimate producer charges."**

In general, **definitions** are brief explanations designed to inform your audience about something unfamiliar. As you can see in Jonah's speech, a definition can also be used as a language or persuasive device. How you define a word or phrase can persuade your audience to focus their attitudes or beliefs about that word or phrase in a particular way.

3

Testimony

You use **testimony** as support material when you use the firsthand knowledge or opinions of yourself or others. Testimony tends to be interpretive or judgmental.

Personal testimony is from your own personal experience or point of view. For example, Monica, a student, included her own story in an informative speech on adoption:

> **Imagine you are six years old and your little sister is three, and the state takes you away from your birth parents. Imagine not knowing where you will live, where you will go to school, or if your little sister will go with you. That was my life when I was six. But my story has a happy ending: My sister and I were adopted by great people we now call Mom and Dad.**

Monica's audience will probably view her expertise on this subject as high because she lived the experience. However, relying entirely on your own personal testimony can backfire. Supporting your knowledge with other forms of evidence is always important, even for many experts. Most speech assignments also require sources outside of your own personal experience.

Lay testimony (or *peer testimony*) occurs when an ordinary person other than the speaker bears witness to his or her own experiences and beliefs. When Senator John McCain included "Joe the Plumber's" comments in the October 15, 2008, presidential debate, he was using the testimony of an ordinary person in an effort to demonstrate problems with then-Senator Barack Obama's plan to solve the economic crisis.

Prestige testimony draws its effectiveness from the status of the person testifying, which often stems from his or her popularity, fame, attractiveness, high-profile activities, or age, if older. For example, advertisements and political statements that feature famous movie stars or sports figures are using prestige testimony. This testimony tends to be less credible logically but may appeal emotionally.

Expert testimony is testimony from a person the audience recognizes as an expert. The expert must be in a field related to your topic—a doctor for a medical topic, a teacher for an education topic, a scientist for a scientific topic, and so on. An expert's specialty can also be a factor; an eye doctor, for instance, is not an expert on heart surgery. Identifying your source's expertise to your audience is crucial:

> **According to Kathleen Sebelius, the U.S. Secretary of Health and Human Services, the H1N1 flu virus does not seem to be as strong as anticipated. However, individuals should stay home if they are sick, and everyone should consider getting the vaccine— especially those at risk.**

Identifying Sebelius's title lends credibility to her testimony—and to your speech.

CHECKLIST for Testimony

- ❏ If I am using personal testimony, do I support it with other sources?
- ❏ If I am using lay testimony, will my audience identify with the people giving the testimony and view them as credible?
- ❏ If I am using prestige testimony, will the audience view the person's reputation positively?
- ❏ If I am using expert testimony, do I tell my audience why the person is an expert?
- ❏ Are all the testimonies I use relevant to my topic?
- ❏ Is the person testifying free of bias?

4

Examples

Examples are specific instances or cases that embody or illustrate points in your speech. The content of the examples may embody or illustrate items, people, events, places, methods, actions, experiences, conditions, or other information. They act as samples, patterns, models, or standards that help your audience understand and accept your points. Effective examples bring life to your speech, making your topic vivid and concrete for your audience.

Examples fall into three categories: brief, extended, and hypothetical.

BRIEF EXAMPLES

Specific instances illustrating a single general notion are **brief examples**. You use this type of example to quickly illustrate something, and you can use several back-to-back to demonstrate frequency.

EXTENDED EXAMPLES

(also known as *stories, narratives, illustrations,* or *anecdotes*)

Extended examples are more detailed examples, allowing the audience to linger a bit longer on the vivid, concrete images the examples create. You can use a narrative or story in your introduction as an attention-getting device; in speeches with a general purpose to inspire; or as support material where you need to help your audience understand or make connections to your point or access their emotional responses. A good story must use language and imagery effectively to create—or transport the audience to—the world being described. The story has to fit together and be plausible in the eyes of the audience.

➔ See Chapter 8 (Tab 4) for more on effective language usage.

CHECKLIST for Examples

❏ Will the audience view my example as typical?

❏ Will the audience see the example as relevant?

❏ Will the audience find the example believable?

❏ Is the example representative of the larger group or category that it stands for?

❏ Do I have enough examples to support my point?

❏ Am I sure that no counterexamples can disprove my point?

HYPOTHETICAL EXAMPLES

Examples based on the potential outcomes of imagined scenarios are **hypothetical examples;** they gain their power from future possibilities. An effective hypothetical example requires the speaker and the audience to have faith that the projected outcome *could* occur. In other words, the example is not real in the present but could happen in the future.

A brief example in a speech about active senior citizens might look like this:

> Today's older adults are redefining what "older" means. George H. W. Bush, for example, celebrated his 85th birthday in June 2009 by skydiving from 10,500 feet over Maine.

Suppose you are preparing a persuasive speech on controlling the spread of HIV in South Africa. You find the article "Women, Inequality, and the Burden of HIV" in the February 17, 2005, issue of the *New England Journal of Medicine*. Editing a small portion of the article, you create an extended example:

> Thandi Dlamini grew up in a crowded four-room house with 13 family members. As the youngest girl, she was charged with cooking, cleaning, and caring for her elders. At age 19, she met her first boyfriend. From the perspective of Thandi and the other women in her community, he was quite a catch—he was older, unmarried, and financially stable. She dreamed that one day he would offer to pay her *lobola* (bride price) and she would have her own home. Several months after meeting, he and Thandi had sexual intercourse, and she says this was her first encounter.
>
> Nine months later, she gave birth to a daughter, Zama. The baby was sick from the beginning and by six months of age was seriously failing to thrive. After being tested for HIV, Thandi was given three tragic pieces of information: she had given her daughter HIV, no treatment was available, and Zama would not live long.
>
> *Ichilo*. Disgrace. *Amahloni*. Shame. This is how Thandi describes her feelings after leaving the hospital. Thandi's boyfriend left after he heard about the baby, and Zama died shortly after that.

For instance, a speech on emergency preparedness could use a hypothetical example about local risks:

> Cities like ours along the Mississippi River would experience great destruction if an earthquake erupted on the New Madrid Fault. One hundred years ago, when the fault last erupted, the force was so intense it changed the path of the Mississippi. That was before we settled the area and built many of our homes and businesses in the big cities near the fault. If a similar quake occurred today, we could have major destruction and fatalities. Recovery would take months. Would you have enough food and water for your entire family for a week? Do you have an emergency plan to react to a quake or to contact family members? Do you have necessary medical supplies? Are you prepared?

5
Statistics

Statistics are numerical facts or data that are summarized, organized, and tabulated to present significant information about a given population (people, items, ideas, etc.). When you use statistics correctly, your audience will view them as factual and objective. Statistics should not scare or confuse you or your audience.

Descriptive statistics aim to describe or summarize characteristics of a population or a large quantity of data. For example:

> Katie Smith, a WNBA Detroit Shock player and the 2008 MVP, has a career average of 15.8 points, 2.8 steals, 3.1 rebounds, and average playing time of 34.7 minutes per game as of August 3, 2009 (wnba.com).

The average (or *mean*, see the chart on the next page) of Smith's statistics over her career gives the audience an idea of her talent in a brief snapshot. As another example, if you survey your entire speech class and calculate the percentage results of the survey, you are generating descriptive statistics.

Inferential statistics aim to draw conclusions about a larger population by making estimates based on a smaller sample of that population. For example:

> President Barack Obama's job approval rating, after hitting a low point of 52% in the middle of last week, has edged back up to 56% for the latest three-day period, July 31 through August 2 (Gallup.com).

This example says that 56% of all Americans approved of Obama's work. Yet the Gallup data, like most poll statistics in the news, are inferential. They come from only a portion of the population; if the poll is trustworthy, the portion is assumed to be representative of the whole.

As another example, if you poll only *one-third* of the students taking speech classes at your school and then make predictions about *all* students taking speech classes there, you are calculating inferential statistics.

USING STATISTICS

- Make sure your statistics are accurate. Check any calculations to confirm that they are correct.

- Verify important statistics from multiple sources for better validity.

- Do research to confirm that the collection, interpretation, and reporting methods for the statistics were ethical and valid and the sample is representative.

- If the statistics are based on a poll, any differences shown by the poll should be less than the poll's margin of error.

- Explain clearly to your audience what the numbers mean. Brief examples and visual aids often help make statistics understandable.

➔ See Chapter 10 (Tab 4) for help with creating presentation aids.

- Use statistics in moderation. Too many can make your audience stop listening.

- Inform your audience of any biases the source of the statistics may have.

- Report the statistics in a manner that does not twist their meaning.

- Comparing statistics can help explain them. Be sure to compare like things.

Different statistical data can make different measurements as well. A mean, a median, and a mode are some of the most common measurements used in speeches.

WHAT IS IT?	HOW DO YOU FIND IT?	EXAMPLES
A **mean** is an average of a set of numbers.	Add up all the numbers in a set and divide the sum by the number of items in the group.	Four speech scores: 88, 86, 81, 92 The sum: $88 + 86 + 81 + 92 = 347$ Divide sum by number of scores: $347 \div 4 = 86.75$ The mean: 86.75
A **median** is the "middle value" in your set of numbers after you have placed them in increasing order. The median separates the lower half of your sample from the upper half (e.g., those in the lower half of an income range and those in the upper).	When you have an *odd* amount of numbers, place your numbers in increasing order and simply locate the middle number.	Five speech scores: 88, 86, 81, 92, 84 Place in increasing order: 81, 84, 86, 88, 92 The median: 86
	When you have an *even* amount of numbers, place your numbers in increasing order and locate the two middle numbers; then add them together and divide by two.	Four speech scores: 89, 86, 81, 92 Place in increasing order: 81, 86, 89, 92 Locate the two middle numbers: 86, 89 Add them and divide by two: $86 + 89 = 175 \div 2 = 87.5$ The median: 87.5
A **mode** is the number that occurs the most in your set.	Place your numbers in increasing order and look for the number that repeats the most.	Set of speech scores: 84, 92, 75, 69, 84, 86, 91, 74, 84, 91 Place in increasing order: 69, 74, 75, 84, 84, 84, 86, 91, 91, 92 The mode: 84

CHECKLIST for Statistics
❑ Are my statistics accurate?
❑ Do I explain them clearly?
❑ Have I been careful not to use too many?

TIP: Modes
You may have more than one mode if multiple numbers occur with the same frequency, and you may not have a mode at all if each number in your set occurs only once.

How Do You Determine What Types of Sources and Support Materials to Use?

1 **Consider Primary vs. Secondary Sources**

2 **Consider Scholarly vs. Popular Sources**

3 **Consider Your Own Personal Knowledge**

4 **Consider Your Topic Needs**

Think about the last time you researched a topic for a paper or another project. If you were diligent in looking for material, you probably ended up with a wide variety and a large quantity of materials that was daunting at first. You had to cull through the stack and select the best types of material for your project.

Researching for a speech is a similar process, and one of the first steps to determining effective support materials is to consider the different types of support materials and if they are appropriate for your topic, your audience, and your speaking occasion.

Often a class speech assignment or a course's expectations specify what types of support materials or sources are appropriate. For example, many college-level courses require that you use only primary and scholarly sources. So if you are giving your speech as a class assignment, start with what the assignment tells you. Speech invitations outside of the classroom will usually be more open and even vague about such expectations. In either case, your decisions about sources and support materials should be based on your knowledge of the topic, the audience's knowledge and expectations, and the significance of the occasion.

Ultimately, selecting the best types of support materials available for your speech is your responsibility. Your own opinions or knowledge is not enough to create an effective speech. The discussion on the next few pages will help you see the benefits of the different types of sources and their relationship to your topic needs.

1
Consider Primary vs. Secondary Sources

One of the first source and support material considerations you need to make is whether to use primary or secondary sources or both. Each of these types of sources plays an important role in formal speech composing.

WHAT IS IT?	EXAMPLES
Primary sources are the original sources of the information. Primary source material is the closest to what is being reported on or studied; it is not being quoted by a second party.	Original research reports, photographs, graphics, videos, or documentaries; historical brochures or pamphlets; autobiographies; novels; poems; some speeches; letters; e-mails; diaries; blogs; some Web sites; eyewitness accounts Interviews, surveys, or field research you conduct about your topic
Secondary sources cite, review, or build upon other sources. Secondary sources quote or paraphrase primary sources.	Most newspaper and magazine articles; some journal articles; reviews; biographies; reprinted photographs or graphics; some Web sites quoting other sources Most speeches you give are themselves secondary sources. Rarely, if ever, should you give a speech where you do not use information from other primary and secondary sources to support your speech.

WHEN DO YOU USE PRIMARY OR SECONDARY SOURCES?

Both primary research and secondary sources will offer strong support materials for certain topics. Sometimes, one is better than the other, but you will usually use both.

For example, if you are giving a speech about parking needs on your campus or the potential need for an on-site day care at your corporate headquarters, you will need to do primary research to get a feel for the local needs. Using secondary research from other institutions or corporations who have positively implemented the program that you are arguing for will strengthen your argument even further.

In another speech, you might focus mostly on cancer statistics collected by physicians at major medical clinics to motivate your audience to stop smoking or to incorporate healthier eating habits. When you quote these statistics, you are using information from a secondary source. However, sprinkling personal narratives from real people you personally interview throughout those statistics humanizes the numbers and allows you to use primary source materials as well.

2

Consider Scholarly vs. Popular Sources

The basic differences between scholarly and popular sources are as follows.

WHAT IS IT?	CHARACTERISTICS	EXAMPLES
Scholarly sources are written for readers who are specialists in their academic or professional fields.	• Are written by authors with academic credentials related to your topic • Discuss and research topics at length • Use very technical language • Aim to educate specialists • Cite all sources supporting the research	Articles in journals, books, research databases, or on professional Web pages
Popular sources are written for general readers.	• Are often written by journalists • Tend to be short discussions • Use common language • Aim to educate and/or entertain the general public • Often cite no sources or give sources that are brief and incomplete	Articles in newspapers, magazines, newswires, popular culture databases, and news-related Web pages

WHEN DO YOU USE SCHOLARLY OR POPULAR SOURCES?

Choosing to use scholarly or popular sources depends heavily on your topic and your audience, but you will always use at least one type and may use both. The main reason you would rely on one more than the other resides in the *credibility of the author* and the *reliability of the information*.

Most audience members will view scholarly research as more trustworthy and accurate than information from popular sources. However, some topics will not need that level of integrity or will relate more to popular culture than to academia. Even within these two categories, you will discover varying degrees of credibility and reliability. A well-regarded popular source that focuses on a particular subject is credible and reliable for a speech on that topic, such as *Fortune* magazine for finance issues, whereas you will be hard-pressed to find an audience that values information from the many tabloids on the market today.

3

Consider Your Own Personal Knowledge

Relying on your own personal knowledge for an *entire* speech is rarely, if ever, a good idea. Even when you know a considerable amount about your topic, you need to demonstrate to your audience that your knowledge is credible. The best way to do that is to cite other material supporting your ideas or position. Your audience has an ethical responsibility to use critical thinking skills when listening to your speech, and you have the ethical responsibility to demonstrate your trustworthiness.

WHEN CAN YOU USE YOUR OWN PERSONAL KNOWLEDGE?

Use your personal experience to build your own ethos and to give a personal face to your topic. Your personal experience can be an excellent source of examples, definitions, facts, and emotional appeal. Remember the earlier example from the speaker who had been adopted by loving parents? Again, use

other sources for the bulk of your speech, to support your ideas and establish your credibility and reliability. Without support, your personal knowledge may be dismissed by your audience. Use your personal experience as an added value to your speech, not a crutch or a substitute for research.

An *ineffective* use of personal experience would be giving a speech about your summer vacation to Africa without including other sources or with only a step-by-step account of your trip and your opinion of it. An *effective* use of personal experience would be to use information gathered from reliable online sources, travel industry sources, historical documents from places you visited, and published travel guides, articles, and books on Africa for the bulk of the speech. Then you could add your personal experience throughout, giving life to the facts. For example, vividly describing a sunset while on safari will bring to life the basic information you want to tell about Africa. Your credibility will soar.

CONFIDENCE BOOSTER

Being proud of your speech goes a long way to building your confidence. If you know you have unique, interesting, accurate, current, and reliable materials, you can be proud of your speech and excited about giving it.

4

Consider Your Topic Needs

Some topics demand special consideration when you are selecting your sources or support materials.

For example, if you are at a professional meeting to discuss the latest techniques for treating autism, you will need to use more scholarly publications or papers presented at other professionally respected conferences. Primary sources are a must in this case.

If you wanted to give a speech in the weeks following Jimmy Johnson's fourth NASCAR title on November 22, 2009, you would need to use current event sources like NASCAR magazines, the sports section of the newspaper, and/or Internet sites.

Use the chart on the next page for suggestions to guide your selection decisions. For instance, if your topic's special demand is that it is controversial—such as arguing for or against the death penalty—some types of support materials you might focus on are those that downplay the emotional aspects and appeal most to an audience's logic: statistics, examples, expert testimony, definitions, and facts. The types of sources that will then help you locate these strong support materials are scholarly sources, highly respected or focused popular sources, and primary sources.

The guidelines in the chart are only suggestions, not steadfast requirements or limitations. Remember, always keep your relationship with the topic as well as your audience in mind as you make your decisions about support materials and sources.

TOPICS WITH SPECIAL DEMANDS	TYPES OF SUPPORT MATERIALS	TYPES OF SOURCES
Controversial or highly emotional topics	Statistics, examples, expert testimony, definitions, facts	Rely more on scholarly or highly respected or focused popular sources. Primary sources are a necessity.
Topics with a purpose to incite emotions or inspire	Examples (particular narratives), lay and expert testimonies	Popular sources tend to contain more emotionally evocative examples and lay testimony. Expert testimony will more often be found in scholarly sources or your own primary research (interviews and surveys).
Technical topics	Definitions, facts, brief examples, statistics	Rely more on scholarly or highly respected or focused popular sources. Primary sources are a necessity. If the audience is unfamiliar with the topic, you will need to include definitions of technical terms.
Abstract topics	Definitions, facts, brief examples (particular narratives)	Use more scholarly or highly respected or focused popular sources.
Topics relating to current events	Statistics, examples, testimony, facts, definitions	Current events will require you to rely more on popular sources because the topics are too new to appear in scholarly sources. Scholarly sources may offer historical comparisons to the current topic.
Unique topics	Examples, definitions, testimony, facts	Depends on the topic and what types of sources are available for it. You may need to do your own primary research, such as interviewing an expert related to the topic.
Topics your audience knows well	Depends on the topic, but unique examples, statistics, facts, and testimony will help you inspire the audience to listen.	Depends on the topic, but the key here is finding unique information to keep your knowledgeable audience interested and learning.

What Do You Evaluate in Your Support Materials?

1 **Accuracy**

2 **Currency**

3 **Completeness**

4 **Trustworthiness**

5 **Suitability**

1

Accuracy

Several years ago, a student majoring in biology wanted to persuade her class to be open to the potential of cloning for medical reasons. She began her speech with an extended example of the successful 2005 cloning of Snuppy, a dog. Snuppy was reported to be the first clone to survive for an extended period of time. A few months before the speech, however, news broke that the South Korean scientist who had reportedly cloned Snuppy had lied about the dog being a clone. The student used only one source, the original news release about Snuppy, and failed to verify it with any other sources—making her speech inaccurate.

Accuracy is an ethical consideration for the original creators of the information and for you. Accurate support materials must meet two standards.

- First, the information should be verifiable from the original source as well as supported by multiple sources. You should use only materials that you can verify as accurate or are from an extremely reliable source.

- Second, you must use your support materials within their original context. Do not twist the information to fit an agenda that does not match the author's intent.

The accuracy of the information's creator or source is out of your control. However, you can attempt to verify information with other sources, evaluate your sources for accuracy, and always use sources that are extremely reliable. Even trusted sources can occasionally report false information. Your ethical responsibility is to present the most accurate, verifiable support materials possible.

2
Currency

If your audience knows more recent information about your topic than your speech reflects, your credibility and the potential for your speech to achieve its general purpose will drop considerably.

- First, you must make sure you have the most current information possible about your topic, which is not as easy as it sounds.

  For instance, if you are researching online, you can easily pull up outdated Web pages that seem to have current information. Always check the copyright date of the page or the last time it was updated. Usually, you can find that information at the bottom of the first page (the home page). If you cannot locate a date, verify the information with another source.

- Second, if your topic is not one that is changing rapidly, a good general research rule to follow is to use information published or collected in the last five years. Some exceptions might be if your topic is historical, the older material is very important, or no recent information is available.

- Third, you need to be as current as possible with your information right up to the moment you give your speech. Changes can happen quickly, especially if your topic is unpredictable or related to current events. You are responsible for knowing about new developments that affect your topic.

  For example, suppose you had been scheduled to give a speech on August 5, 2009, and your topic was why the United States should intervene and bring home two U.S. journalists, Euna Lee and Laura Ling, imprisoned in North Korea. You would have needed to make radical last-minute adjustments, because the women were released and flown home early that day.

Some of the best speech topics are unpredictable (which is what makes them interesting), so do not be afraid of these topics. Just be diligent and stay on top of the latest information.

TIP: Staying Current

Listening to a national news show while you are dressing, driving, cleaning, or cooking is an easy way for you to stay current. You can also subscribe to a respected national paper or news magazine or read one online. *The Week* magazine is an excellent condensed version of a week of information.

3
Completeness

Particularly if you intend to inform or persuade your audience, you need a sufficient amount of comprehensive, detailed information to achieve your goal. Two or three examples are not enough to demonstrate or prove your central idea or even show a trend. Persuasive speeches especially need complete information behind them to be ethical and influential.

For example, in recent years, many U.S. cities have supported the use of tasers by law enforcement personnel. As new data and more examples are available about the potential harm these devices can render, more citizens are changing their views about tasers. Two or three examples might illustrate a minor point about the hazards of tasers but are not complete enough to sway opinion or effectively inform an audience of how harmful tasers are overall. To give complete information, you may need to summarize several types of examples or incorporate wide-ranging national statistics about injuries or deaths caused by tasers.

TIP: Sufficient Support

There is no formula for how much support is enough, but you can get an indication by thinking about what you are asking your audience to understand or agree to. The more you want your audience to accept or change—or the less your audience already knows about the topic—the more support materials you need.

4
Trustworthiness

Your support materials' trustworthiness is similar to your ethos: it is measured by the opinion of your audience, not you. If your *audience* does not have the necessary information or respect to view your support materials as trustworthy, they are not.

- Select materials from trustworthy sources and help your audience view them as such. The audience should see the author or creator of the information as an expert on the topic. Provide the audience with the author's or creator's credentials (education, training, position, and/or other experience that relates to your topic).

- Select materials from unbiased sources. The author or creator of the materials should not have a hidden agenda—or if there is one, you need to inform your audience of that bias or not use the materials.

- Be particularly diligent in holding electronic sources to high standards of credibility. As noted earlier, the Internet provides a lot of information, but anyone can easily create or change a Web site. Always ask:
  - What is the purpose of the site?
  - What type of site is it?
  - Who sponsors the site? Who contributes?
  - Are there advertisements on the site, and, if so, how might they bias the information?
  - When was the site created? Has it been updated recently?

5
Suitability

Your support materials are suitable when your audience is able to view the materials as relevant to them, to the topic, and to the occasion. To demonstrate suitability:

- Use support materials with a purpose that is clear and concrete.

→ See the section "Use Your Materials Purposefully" on page 126.

- Use materials that relate back to your central idea.

- Include information that shows your audience why the materials are relevant to them, to the topic, and to the occasion.

For example, suppose you are from a country where water shortages are a concern, and you want to give a persuasive speech about water conservation to students in an area of the United States where water is abundant. Using data, examples, personal narrative, and other information related only to other countries currently experiencing water shortages, such as several along the equator, will not resonate with your U.S. audience. You must use at least some support materials demonstrating the effects of water shortages within the United States.

You never want to have a moment when your audience questions why you just said something or views your materials as awkward or inappropriate.

PRACTICING ETHICS

Manipulating your support materials to prevent your audience from being rational—or to make them overly emotional—is extremely unethical behavior. Remember these ethical guidelines when using support materials.

- Present hypothetical examples as such—not as factual.

- Present prestige testimony honestly and not as expert testimony.

- Interpret and represent statistics fairly and accurately.

- Use a variety of support materials and sources.

- Include and note primary sources orally during your speech.

- Research thoroughly for alternate points of view.

- Use and quote materials in their correct context. Do not omit information.

- Use reliable, trustworthy sources.

- Give proper oral citations (include some variation of the date of publication, type of publication, title, author, and highlights of author's credentials).

- Disclose any agendas or biases a source might have.

How Do You Use Support Materials Effectively?

1 **Use Your Materials Purposefully**
2 **Use Your Materials in Different Ways**
3 **Use Quotation and Paraphrasing Effectively**
4 **Use Delivery Techniques to Enhance Your Materials**

1
Use Your Materials Purposefully

From the previous discussion, you know that support materials should be suitable. In other words, your audience needs to know the reason, rationale, or function for nearly everything you include in a speech, and that is acutely true of your support materials. You will use most support materials for one of four purposes.

- To clarify unfamiliar or abstract information
- To create and hold your audience's attention
- To help your audience remember important aspects of your speech
- To prove a claim your speech makes

Whenever you use support materials, you should be able to use one of these four purposes to answer this question: "Why am I using this material?" If you can't, the material is likely just filler, and you should replace it.

2

Use Your Materials in Different Ways

You can employ different approaches when using support materials. Here are four common ones to try.

Direct: The easiest and most common way to use support materials is to be simple and straightforward. Here, you identify and use materials for what they are: examples, facts, definitions, testimony, or statistics. In the speech, the materials are presented in a manner that simply identifies them and draws strength from direct use.

For example, for a class speech on Argentine football (soccer) player Diego Maradona, Felipe creates this sentence:

> **In the 1986 World Cup quarter-final round, Diego Maradona scored two goals now known as the "Hand of God" and the "Goal of the Century."**

This statement is a direct use of support materials—in this case, Felipe simply presents facts as facts. Many beginning speeches use a combination of examples, facts, definitions, testimony, and/or statistics, presented directly, to support their topics.

Comparison: When you use support materials to point out similarities between two or more ideas, things, factors, or issues, you are using them as a **comparison**. For example, Felipe wants to assert that Maradona was as great a player as the famous Brazilian, Pelé:

> **Diego Maradona and Pelé each made it to four FIFA World Cup finals.**

Felipe's comparison of their similar career statistics, like World Cup finals, helps make his point.

Contrast: When you use support materials to point out differences between two or more ideas, things, factors, or issues, you are using them in **contrast**. Felipe tries this:

> **Pelé won three FIFA World Cups in his career, whereas Diego Maradona won only one.**

Felipe's contrast of the players' World Cup successes is correct, but highlighting this contrast might suggest that Pelé was a better player than Maradona, not that they were equal.

Analogy: An **analogy** helps explain the unfamiliar by comparing and contrasting it to what is familiar. The key to using analogy is that your audience must be familiar with one of the two things being compared and contrasted. There are two types of analogies:

- **Literal analogy** compares and contrasts two like things.

  > **Although Maradona and Pelé came from different playing backgrounds, their similar career successes make them the greatest footballers of all time.**

  Felipe can discuss Pelé and Maradona as two like things—successful players. You might use literal analogy if you are advocating once choice over another, such as supporting one political candidate over another, by comparing and contrasting their views.

- **Figurative analogy** compares and contrasts two essentially different things.

  > **Diego Maradona is like a god to many Argentines.**

  Felipe can use this analogy to highlight Maradona's popularity. One common figurative analogy is comparing and contrasting business practices and sports strategies.

3

Use Quotation and Paraphrasing Effectively

Most of the time, you will summarize your support materials by gleaning out important information, incorporating it in your own words, and crediting ideas with citations. Quoting your sources at key points can provide compelling additional support.

Directly quoting support materials from a source is generally more effective than paraphrasing. However, in a speech, direct quotation is not always possible, and you must interpret long, unwieldy quotations by paraphrasing.

Quote precisely if the material is short and says something better than you can about your topic or is memorable (amusing, clever, expressive, gripping, or convincing). In a written text, you signal a direct quotation with quotation marks or, for longer passages, a block format. Use a **block quotation** when the quotation is more than four lines of printed text. Block quotations are further indented, do not use quotation marks, and place parenthetical information after the end punctuation. For example:

> In his March 2010 *National Geographic* article "Africa's Last Frontier," Neil Shea writes:
> Dunga Nakuwa cups his face in his hands and remembers his mother's voice. She has been dead nearly two years, but for Dunga's tribe the dead are never very far away. (102)

In a speech, signal a direct quotation orally by using a technique such as:

> Neil Shea writes in his *National Geographic* article, "Dunga Nakuwa cups his face...."

Paraphrase when the section you wish to use is too long (more than two to three sentences, as a general rule), wordy, unclear, vague, or difficult or awkward for you to say. **Paraphrasing** restates the content of the material in a simpler format and in your own words, using language appropriate for your audience. For example, here is a section of text from Aristotle's *Rhetoric:*

> The modes of persuasion are the only true constituents of the art: everything else is merely accessory. These writers, however, say nothing about enthymemes, which are the substance of rhetorical persuasion, but deal mainly with non-essentials.

Here is how a speaker might paraphrase this for an audience unfamiliar with Aristotle:

> According to the *Rhetoric*, Aristotle believed that logic was the only true method of persuasion and that everything else was merely ornamentation. Other (classical) scholars focused on less vital aspects of rhetoric and ignored the enthymeme (the classical logical argument).

The bulk of your speech should be your words and organization. If you quote or paraphrase too much, the speech is not original. Your audience expects to hear your words.

REMEMBER TO CITE!

If you are summarizing, quoting, or paraphrasing the words, ideas, concepts, or thoughts of others, you must orally cite the source and note the citation in your outline. Make sure you follow an acceptable style manual.

➜ See the section "How Do You Cite Sources Orally?" on page 130.

➜ See Chapter 5 (Tab 3) for more information on written citations and style manuals.

4

Use Delivery Techniques to Enhance Your Materials

Delivery techniques can make or break a segment of great support material. This may seem redundant, as delivery can make or break an entire speech. However, beginning speakers can unwittingly fall into poor delivery habits when they use support materials, particularly extended examples, narratives, or statistics.

Suppose a student uses the *National Geographic* quotation discussed earlier as an attention-getting device in a speech about how tourists, missionaries, and merchants are destroying tribal culture. Imagine the student delivering this in a dry monotone voice:

> **"Dunga Nakuwa cups his face in his hands and remembers his mother's voice. She has been dead nearly two years, but for Dunga's tribe the dead are never very far away. In the villages they are buried just below the huts of the living, separated from hearths and sleeping skins by only a few feet of dry, depleted soil. They remain near in the mind, too. This is why Dunga still hears his mother: When will you take revenge on your brother's killers?" This quotation, from Neil Shea's March 2010 *National Geographic* article "Africa's Last Frontier," demonstrates how tradition remains a significant part of this tribe's culture.**

Now, reread the passage and imagine the student pausing briefly after the first sentence, making good eye contact, building his or her voice in intensity. Imagine the student memorizing the one line from the mother and delivering that line with a slightly different inflection, complete eye contact, and a pause before citing the source. Wouldn't this delivery style hold your attention better as a listener?

Good delivery can bring your support materials to life if you practice just a few techniques and observe these suggestions.

- Understand your materials—and deliver them in a way that shows you do.

- Practice saying aloud the entire support material segment, especially if the material is a long narrative or example. Become so familiar with the words that they seem like your own. Practice statistics to the point that you do not need to look at your notes to remember them. Internalizing your support materials will help demonstrate their importance.

- Employ dramatic effect. Speak with enthusiasm that is appropriate for your topic and the occasion. Use dramatic pauses, stress important words, and vary the pace of your words to help access the emotional potential of the materials. If you are bored or unexcited about your material, your audience will be, too.

- Use repetition and/or restatement to help your audience understand and remember your support materials.

- Consider using presentation aids to reinforce what you are saying. Presentation aids are exceptionally helpful when presenting statistical information. Conversely, refrain from putting extended examples on a visual aid and simply reading them to your audience.

➜ See Tab 4 for detailed help with delivery and presentation aids.

How Do You Cite Sources Orally?

1 **Collect the Necessary Content**
2 **Create and Deliver Oral Citations**

1

Collect the Necessary Content

You know that when you write a paper, you need to cite your sources. When you write and give a speech, you also need to use citations. *Citations* are the credits for the original sources of the support materials you are using.

As a speechwriter in a class, you will need to use both oral and written citations—oral during the speech and written ones on the outline. Chapter 5 will help you with written citations, and writing style manuals offer specific guidelines on how to format written in-text citations and source pages for your outlines.

Here we are concerned with the oral citations. During a speech, the oral citations you use must always be incorporated so that the audience clearly hears them, because listeners do not have the outline or source page. Compared to a written paper, however, your oral citation is not as detailed. Your first citation of a source will be the most detailed, and any later reference to the same source needs just enough information to connect it back to the original.

For example, Nina is doing a presentation on actor and director Tom Hanks. Her speech focuses on his historical films. She needs to cite an article from *Time* Magazine.

> **As Douglas Brinkley notes in his March 2010 *Time* article, "The World According to Tom," the only facts Hanks recalled from history lessons about World War II were that Japan bombed Pearl Harbor on December 7, 1941, and America retaliated on August 6, 1945, by dropping an A-bomb on Hiroshima.**

This could be Nina's first oral citation for this source during her speech.

This chart suggests the potential content of your first oral citations for different sources. Use it to help you collect the necessary information for your oral citations.

Your oral citation should include enough information that proper credit is given and that an audience member could locate the item being cited if he or she desires to do so.

CONTENTS OF ORAL CITATIONS

TYPE OF SOURCE	WHAT TO INCLUDE IN YOUR ORAL CITATION
Web site	Identify it as a Web site, title of Web page, site sponsor, and either the date of publication, last update, or when you accessed it; may include article title
Magazine or journal	Identify it as an article, name of magazine or journal, author and qualifications, and date of publication; may include article title
Newspaper	Identify as an article, name of paper, author and qualifications, and date of issue; may include article title
Book	Identify that it is a book, title, author and qualifications, and date of publication
Government document	Title, name of agency or branch of government publishing it, and date of publication
Brochure or pamphlet	Identify it as a brochure or pamphlet, title, who published it, and date of publication
Reference works	Title and date of publication
Videotape, DVD, or CD	Title of tape or disk and date
Television or radio	Title of the show, channel or network, and date of broadcast
Interview conducted by you	Identify yourself as the interviewer, name and identity of the person interviewed, and date of interview

If you need to create a written text of your speech (such as an outline), or a works cited or reference page, you will need more specific information.

→ See Chapter 5 (Tab 3) for more information on written citations and style manuals.

The next section will offer you examples and advice on how to construct and deliver your oral citations.

2
Create and Deliver Oral Citations

The main rule of oral citation is to make sure you cite everything you borrow from another source. This includes words, phrases, sentences, paragraphs, photos, diagrams, video and audio clips, graphs, and so on. If the item is not original to you, you must cite the source.

Your citations should not be too repetitive, misplaced, or boring. You want your audience to listen to them. Follow these suggestions:

Use variety when possible. Once you have given a detailed oral citation, subsequent citations for the same source can be shorter. For example, recall that Nina's first citation was very detailed:

> As Douglas Brinkley notes in his March 2010 *Time* article, "The World According to Tom," the only facts Hanks recalled from history lessons about World War II were that Japan bombed Pearl Harbor on December 7, 1941, and America retaliated on August 6, 1945, by dropping an A-bomb on Hiroshima.

Her second citation of this source might use the author's last name and the article title.

> Again, Brinkley, in his article "The World According to Tom," states that Hanks….

If Nina cites the same article again, she might only include:

> According to Brinkley,…

After you have cited a source three or four times, if the citations are close together, you can use a simple citation like Nina's last one.

Do not put every citation at the beginning or end of a quotation, summary, or para-phrase. Write them in different ways. Variety is the key to avoiding ineffective repetition and keeping your audience's attention.

Place your citations with the information being borrowed. A common error is to group all citations together at the beginning of a point or add them on to the end of the speech.

> INEFFECTIVE:
> The material from this section of my speech came from a special issue of *Time* Magazine, April 19, 2010, Rachel Carson's book *Silent Spring,* and the spring 2010 *Nature Conservancy* Magazine.

The proper way to orally cite your sources is to cite each at the time you use it in the speech. If you have a lot of summarized information from one source, you might use this type of oral citation to begin the section:

> The information summarized in my next point comes from the 1999 book *Classical Rhetoric for the Modern Student* by Edward Corbett and Robert Conners.

If using visuals from another source, it is best to cite the source on your presentation aid and to orally note the citation during the speech.

> CITATION ON A PRESENTATION AID:
> Carl Zigrosser, *Prints and Drawings of Käthe Kollwitz.* New York: Dover, 1969. Print.
>
> ORAL CITATION:
> This 1927 self-portrait of Käthe, from the book *Prints and Drawings of Käthe Kollwitz,* depicts a solemn Käthe.

To draw your audience's attention to the written citation, you might gesture at its location on the aid. Placing the written citation in the same location on every aid will help guide your audience's eyes to it each time.

Be enthusiastic about your sources. Be proud of the research you did to support your speech. Speak clearly and maintain good volume as you cite sources. Use a variety of inflection that demonstrates your enthusiasm.

Practice saying your citations when you rehearse your speech. If you practice, you will remember better to include your citations; they will become more familiar; and you can further craft them to be effective. The chart below shows the five types of support materials and gives sample beginnings for orally citing each type.

SAMPLE ORAL CITATIONS

TYPE OF SUPPORT MATERIALS	BEGINNING OF AN ORAL CITATION
Examples	"As Desdemona says in Shakespeare's *Othello*..." "Let me give you two examples of identity theft. The first comes from the May 10th issue of *Newsweek*..."
Facts	"As published in the July 2009 issue of the *Conservationist*, a lunar moth lives..."
Definitions	"*Time* Magazine—in its April 12, 2008, issue—defines..."
Testimony	"In an interview I conducted last October with Dr. James Wing in our history department, Dr. Wing said..." "As Chantal Smith, an eyewitness to the plane crash, said in January..."
Statistics	"According to the National Transportation Safety Board's Web site, accessed on May 6, 2010, the percentage of railroad accidents due to..." "In a June 2009 issue of *Lancet*, available online at..."

➔ Chapter 5 (Tab 3) on outlining and Chapter 9 (Tab 4) on delivery will offer more examples and advice.

CHECKLIST for Oral Citations

❑ Does my citation include the necessary information?

❑ Am I citing everything borrowed from another source?

❑ Am I presenting my oral citations in a variety of formats?

❑ Are my citations properly placed?

❑ Have I practiced saying my citations within my speech, and do they seem to be a natural part of the speech?

Desmond's Speech

At the end of Chapter 3, you met Desmond, a student researching for a speech on Nelson Mandela. Desmond used an article he had recently read in *Newsweek* and an initial Internet search as starting points for his research, and then he made his decision to do an informative speech on the life of Mandela as a man, an activist, and a president. Once he had mapped out some research notes and a working outline, Desmond located more than enough information. Now, Desmond must evaluate and select the best materials for his speech.

SELECTING THE TYPES OF SUPPORT MATERIALS AND SOURCES NEEDED

As Desmond selected support materials, he wanted to use as many primary sources, such as Mandela's biographies, as possible. He found a lot of Web sites on Mandela, but many did not have credentials listed or only seemed to be using material he could find in a primary source.

Because Mandela is such a popular figure, Desmond decided to use many of the popular sources, like *Time* Magazine. He was confident he could verify that material. Also, because Desmond's audience members are young adults in a speech class, he decided to limit direct quoting of scholarly sources. Instead, he would use them for verification—unless he found a quotation that was perfect for the speech. The respected Web sites that he located, such as the sites for the Nelson Mandela Foundation and the Nobel Peace Prize, would help increase Desmond's ethos, too.

EVALUATING AND USING EFFECTIVE SUPPORT MATERIAL

With many of his sources in front of him, Desmond began to evaluate and place the support materials he needed for each of his main points. In class, Desmond learned that the materials must be accurate, complete, from a trustworthy source, and suitable for his audience.

Desmond looked at some of the information he found on Wikipedia. He knew his instructor would not accept Wikipedia as a final source, so he would have to verify this information elsewhere in order to use it.

> ### NOTES FOR OUTLINE
>
> • Mandela as president:
>
> "South Africa's first multi-racial elections were held on April 27, 1994."
>
> The African National Congress (ANC) won 62% of the vote and Mandela was inaugurated May 10, 1994.
>
> (Find another source to verify this information)

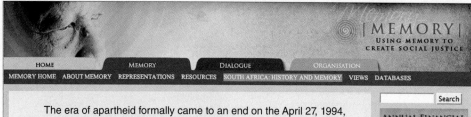

Search

ANNUAL FINANCIAL
STATEMENTS

MANDELA DAY IS A
CALL TO ACTION
TO MAKE THE
WORLD A BETTER
PLACE, ONE SMALL
STEP AT A TIME

The era of apartheid formally came to an end on the April 27, 1994, when Nelson Mandela voted for the first time in his life – along with his people….

Rolihlahla Nelson Dalibunga Mandela was inaugurated as President of a democratic South Africa on May 10, 1994.

Many of Desmond's printed primary sources were written before Mandela became president, so he could not use them to verify information about the presidency. However, Mandela's biography on the Nelson Mandela Foundation Web site is regularly updated. Desmond validated recent facts through this reliable source.

CREATING CITATIONS

As Desmond placed support material in his evolving preparation outline, he began to draft his oral citations for a photo and quotations.

Desmond found another quotation he wanted to use, and from his notes, he knew it came from one of two biographies he researched in his college library. Desmond was unable to check the books out, however, because they are autographed and kept in the library's special collections; and he realized now he didn't specify which book the quotation is from. He will have to return to the library to verify the correct source (Mandela's book *Long Walk to Freedom*).

This image, taken from CNN.com on March 12, 2010, shows Mandela just after his release from prison in 1990.

In his 1993 acceptance and Nobel Lecture, found on Nobelprize.org, Mandela states, "We stand here today as nothing more than a representative of the millions of our people who dared to rise up against a social system whose very essence is war, violence, racism, oppression, repression, and the impoverishment of an entire people."

"Our message was that no sacrifice was too great in the struggle for freedom."

(Needs citation – which book was this from?)

Tab 2: Review

CHAPTER 3 REVIEW QUESTIONS

1. What is the difference between the visible and invisible Web?

2. How do you evaluate Internet sources? Why is evaluating online sources important?

3. What are the different types of Web sites available? Choose one type and explain how and why you might use it as a source.

4. What is a database and how can you use it in your research?

5. What kinds of information can interviews offer?

6. What are three steps for taking good research notes? Explain.

CHAPTER 4 REVIEW QUESTIONS

1. What is testimony? Explain the four types.

2. How do the three types of examples differ from one another?

3. What is the difference between descriptive statistics and inferential statistics?

4. What are the five characteristics you should evaluate in your support materials? Explain each.

5. What are four purposes that support materials can be used for?

6. What is paraphrasing and when should you use it?

7. What are four suggestions for creating and delivering oral citations? Explain each.

TERMS TO REMEMBER

Chapter 3
support materials (69)
sources (69)
Internet (70)
Web (70)
browser (70)
visible Web (70)
invisible Web (70)
Web sites (71)
search engines (72)
hits (72)
blog (76)
databases (82)
interviews (94)
open-ended questions (95)
closed-ended questions (95)
follow-up questions (96)
surveys (98)
population (98)
sample (101)

Chapter 4
facts (110)
definitions (110)
testimony (111)
personal testimony (111)
lay testimony (111)
prestige testimony (111)
expert testimony (111)
examples (112)
brief examples (112)
extended examples (112)
hypothetical examples (112)
statistics (114)
descriptive statistics (114)
inferential statistics (114)
mean (115)
median (115)
mode (115)
primary sources (117)
secondary sources (117)
scholarly sources (118)
popular sources (118)
comparison (127)
contrast (127)
analogy (127)
literal analogy (127)
figurative analogy (127)
block quotation (128)
paraphrasing (128)
citations (130)

Introduction

Jessamyn had trouble keeping her thoughts together when giving a speech. When she enrolled in her first public speaking class, she told a classmate, "I get so nervous, I can't remember my next thought." Jessamyn thought she was not able to give a good speech. Then her professor required each student to turn in an outline for each speech given in the class. At first, Jessamyn found outlining tedious. However, when she practiced the speech, she noticed it made more sense to her, and she could more easily tell how long it would be. She could tell it was a bit short, so she added more statistics to make one of her points.

The best part came the day of the speech. She remembered each point without looking down at her note cards as much as before. She got through the speech as she had planned. Jessamyn was less nervous and even had a bit of fun giving the speech. For the first time, she walked away from the lectern proud of her accomplishment. After a few more speeches, Jessamyn realized that the time she took to outline was helping her create better speeches and be more confident.

Now you are ready to learn how to develop this essential tool for giving a successful speech. Because creating an effective outline is so important and complex, Tab 3 is divided into three chapters designed to break apart the process into manageable portions. The three chapters work in concert with each other. This chapter explains the qualities and components of outlines and the different types of outlines.

CHAPTER 5 CONTENTS

Why Do You Need an Outline?	138
What Are the Parts of an Outline?	140
1 Introduction	141
2 Body of the Speech	141
3 Conclusion	141
4 Source Page	141
How Can You Create an Effective Outline?	142
1 Record the Topic, Specific Purpose, and Central Idea	143
2 Use Full Sentences	143
3 Cover Only One Issue at a Time	144
4 Develop the Introduction and Conclusion	145
5 Use Correct Outline Format	146
6 Use Balanced Main Points	148
7 Employ Subordination	148
8 Plan Out Formal Links	150
9 Use Proper Citations	151
What Are the Different Types of Outlines?	152
1 The Working Outline	152
2 The Preparation Outline	154
3 The Delivery Outline	158
What Can You Use to Link Your Speech Parts Together?	160
1 Transitions	161
2 Signposts	162
3 Internal Previews	162
4 Internal Reviews	163
How Do You Cite Sources in Your Outline?	164
How Do You Create a Source Page?	166
1 Follow the Overall Format Requirements	167
2 Create Proper Entries for Each Source	167
Sophia's Speech	170
CHAPTER 6: Organizing the Speech Body	173
CHAPTER 7: Introducing and Concluding Your Speech	195
Tab 3 Review	214

Why Do You Need an Outline?

"Why do I need an outline?" is possibly the question most frequently asked by beginning speakers. One of the best ways to see the value of an outline is to think of it as a piece of architecture.

Visualize the tallest building in your town or on your campus. Think about how each nail, each beam, each panel, and each floor support relates to the next. What would happen if a beam were missing or in the wrong place? The result would be disastrous, right? What happens if a doorway is missing or too small and you can't get from one room to the other? (Sounds like a moment out of *Alice in Wonderland*, doesn't it?)

Doorways, stairwells, and halls allow us to move smoothly through a building by linking the rooms and floors together. Architects create a sound structure and use elements of design such as space, line, shape, texture, and color to design a safe, functional, and pleasing building. Without a plan, the building could be useless, unsightly, and likely to fall apart.

The same is true for a speech. Successful speeches contain distinctive features and components that are carefully structured for a particular function and pleasing effect. The process of outlining your speech will help you build that strong foundation and will make the process of creating a speech faster as well as easier.

Many students see outlining a speech as just busywork required by the instructor and do not see its value at first. Like most things worth creating, a speech is more than just the sum of its parts.

You must be selective in what materials you use, and you must build them in a way that will hold your speech together and allow your audience to move easily through your information. Your outline is the blueprint you use to make sure everything is properly supported, in the right place, and easy to maneuver.

Think about the last time you wrote a paper. You probably went through several drafts of the paper, crafting exactly what you wanted to write, making sure that readers could follow your essay and feel that they gained something from your paper. For most writers, that perfect paper does not happen on the first try.

Crafting a successful speech is a similar process. When you prepare a speech, you need to go through the stages of inventing; researching; drafting; editing; proofreading; and, when possible, peer reviewing before you give the speech. Creating outlines is the most effective way for you to achieve these important steps.

An outline helps you:

- Ensure that your main points relate to your central idea.
- Select the appropriate organizational pattern and keep it consistent.
- Make sure your subpoints are related and subordinate.
- Evenly distribute your support materials and investigate the quality of the material.
- Formulate links between parts of the speech.
- Design a speech your audience can follow and recall.
- Create a permanent record of your speech.

So, creating an outline is more than just busywork!

CONFIDENCE BOOSTER

Knowing your material is the best way to lower your anxiety, and the best way to learn it is to be exceedingly meticulous, comprehensive, and systematic when creating the outline of your speech.

What Are the Parts of an Outline?

1 Introduction
2 Body of the Speech
3 Conclusion
4 Source Page

Creating a visual image in your mind of a basic outline will help you understand its parts and help you create an outline. Here is the basic blueprint for most outlines.

INTRODUCTION

Link

I.   First main point

    A. First subpoint of I

        1. First subpoint of A

           a. First subpoint of 1

           b. Second subpoint of 1

        2. Second subpoint of A

    B. Second subpoint of I

Link

II.   Second main point

    A. First subpoint of II

    B. Second subpoint of II

        1. First subpoint of B

        2. Second subpoint of B

Link

III.   Third main point

    A. First subpoint of III

    B. Second subpoint of III

Link

CONCLUSION

SPEECH BODY

1
Introduction

The *introduction* opens the speech, grabs the audience's attention, and focuses it on the topic.

→ See Chapter 7 (Tab 3) for how to create an introduction.

2
Body of the Speech

The *body* contains the central portion of the speech, including the main points, the multiple layers of subordinate points, and the links. It is, essentially, what you want to tell your audience about the topic.

Main points are the essential ideas you must cover or the main claims you wish to make, and they directly relate to your central idea. Most speeches will have two or three main points, but some speeches (usually process or persuasive) will have more— around five.

Subpoints (also called *subordinate points* or *supporting points*) offer information to support and relate back to the main point. You can have multiple layers of subpoints (e.g., your subpoints can have their own subpoints).

Links (also called *transitions*) act much like hyperlinks on your computer, which serve to make a logical jump between two places on your computer. Links in your speech will make logical connections between parts of your speech.

→ See "What Can You Use to Link Your Speech Parts Together?" on page 160.

3
Conclusion

The *conclusion* ends your speech and takes one last moment to reinforce your main ideas as well as to "wow" your audience.

→ See Chapter 7 (Tab 3) for how to create a conclusion.

4
Source Page

Many instructors will require a page at the end of your preparation outline that indicates the sources you used in your speech. You will create this page just as you do for a formal research paper, often using the style manual for the *Modern Language Association (MLA)* or the *American Psychological Association (APA)*. Style manuals are guides for writing and documenting research. Your instructor may require you to purchase a style manual, or you may just use the one located in your library's reference section. Make sure you have the correct style manual and that it is the most current. Certain software packages (including Word) can help you adhere to a style, although you should always check the citations and page format for accuracy.

→ See "How Do You Create a Source Page?" on page 166.

How Can You Create an Effective Outline?

1 Record the Topic, Specific Purpose, and Central Idea

2 Use Full Sentences

3 Cover Only One Issue at a Time

4 Develop the Introduction and Conclusion

5 Use Correct Outline Format

6 Use Balanced Main Points

7 Employ Subordination

8 Plan Out Formal Links

9 Use Proper Citations

In this section, you will encounter the nine qualities of an effective outline. It is important to note that not all of the qualities are necessary for different types of outlines. For example, you will not include full sentences in the outline you use for delivering your speech (the delivery outline). However, full sentences are almost always a requirement in the outline you create as you craft your speech (the preparation outline). If you are not sure what your assignment requires, ask your instructor.

A section later in this chapter will discuss the three types of outlines and their uses. However, for now, you should realize that correct preparation outline format is the basis of all types of outlines, and it is important that you begin early to use as many of the qualities as possible.

Let's look at each of the nine qualities as well as how two speakers, Jessamyn and Zamir, work to incorporate each into their outlines. Jessamyn is a big NFL football fan and wants to give her class a brief history of the game. Zamir owns a café in the City of Jackson and is concerned about an overabundance of pigeons. His café has an outdoor seating area, where pigeons have become a problem and a potential health hazard. His speech proposes that the city institute a plan to decrease the pigeon population.

➜ See "What Are the Different Types of Outlines?" on page 152 for examples of complete outlines.

1
Record the Topic, Specific Purpose, and Central Idea

You should include the topic, specific purpose, and central idea at the top of the outline as a title framing the speech. Doing so will help you keep these elements of your speech in the forefront of your mind as you create the rest of the outline.

Topic: ....

Specific Purpose: ....

Central Idea: ....

2
Use Full Sentences

You should write each outline component in full sentences. Writing in full sentences forces you to think in complete thoughts and will help you learn the speech as well as gauge its length. If you use only words or phrases in the preparation outline, you may struggle for the right words when giving the speech. Below, see how Jessamyn rewrote her working points as full sentences.

INCORRECT

I. The beginning of football
   A. Two different sports
      1. English soccer player 1823 and rugby
      2. Between 1880 and 1883, Yale's rugby players changed rules

CORRECT

I. The game of football has come a long way since its beginnings.
   A. Football is actually adapted from two different sports (Ominsky).
      1. While playing soccer in 1823, an English soccer player got frustrated and picked up the ball and started running with it, creating the sport of rugby.
      2. Between 1880 and 1883, as rugby grew in popularity, one of Yale's rugby players conceived a new set of rules for the game, very similar to today's football game.

3
Cover Only One Issue at a Time

Covering only one issue at a time in each outline component will help you keep your speech simple enough for delivery and will keep you from writing the speech as a manuscript. The best way to adhere to this quality is to write only one sentence per component in the body of the speech. For example, Zamir noticed that his first point looked more like a paragraph:

INCORRECT

I. The City of Jackson needs to institute a plan to decrease the numbers of pigeons that infest it each year, breeding everywhere and roosting on buildings, because they spread diseases to humans and other animals and contaminate our waterways. The pigeons...

Avoid using words like **and**, **or**, **because**, or **but** to connect two independent issues in one sentence.

Zamir corrected this problem by breaking the paragraph down into points, each containing only one issue at a time.

CORRECT

I. The City of Jackson needs to institute a plan to decrease the number of pigeons.
    A. Each year, thousands of pigeons flock to the city.
        1. They breed everywhere.
        2. They roost on many buildings.
    B. Pigeons spread disease.
        1. They carry germs that affect humans.
        2. They carry germs that affect animals.
        3. They can contaminate our waterways.

4

Develop the Introduction and Conclusion

Most instructors suggest creating your introduction and conclusion after you create the body of the speech (Chapter 7 will show you how). For now, recognize that they are an integral part of the preparation outline. Beginning speakers tend to cut corners in the development of a speech by deciding to improvise the introduction and conclusion as they speak. This practice sets you up for serious problems at critical moments in the speech. Speech anxiety is often the highest at the beginning, making the practice of "thinking on your feet" frustrating and often impossible. Therefore, you may forget crucial parts of the introduction and conclusion. Polish and practice them as you do the rest of the speech. Below are Jessamyn's NFL speech introduction and conclusion. Notice the major parts in each one.

EXAMPLE OF INTRODUCTION

Attention material: A friend of mine used to say that she thought the game of football looked like a bunch of chickens running around with their heads cut off.

Relevance to audience: If you are anything like my friend, then you probably don't appreciate the fall and winter seasons the same as I do. My hope is that during the next few minutes you will develop an understanding and appreciation for the sport of National Football League (NFL) football.

Credibility material: As sister to a high school player, a daughter of a military football coach, and an unwavering fan of the game, I enjoy watching and playing the sport with my brothers.

Preview of speech: Today, I want to share a brief history of the game of football, the development of the NFL, and how the league is set up today.

EXAMPLE OF CONCLUSION

Summary statement: The NFL is a complex association, but once you have an understanding of football's history, the development of the NFL, and how the league is currently set up, it is much easier to comprehend.

Audience response statement: So now that you have a basic working knowledge of the NFL, the next time you are flipping through the channels on a Sunday afternoon, maybe, just maybe, you will turn on a football game and enjoy it like I do.

WOW statement: Join me for some FOOOOTBALL!

→ See Chapter 7 (Tab 3) for how to create effective introductions and conclusions.

5
Use Correct Outline Format

The format of an outline should be very systematic, helping you to logically structure your speech and aiding you in your delivery. You should always use correct outline formatting in the body of the speech. The following guidelines will help you.

DISTINGUISHING MAIN POINTS

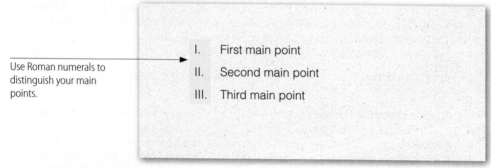

Use Roman numerals to distinguish your main points.

I.   First main point

II.   Second main point

III. Third main point

PATTERN OF SYMBOLS

Use a consistent pattern of symbols (e.g., uppercase letters, numbers, and lowercase letters).

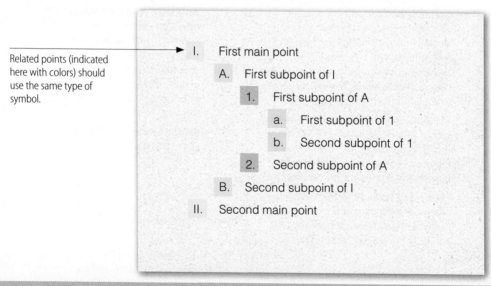

Related points (indicated here with colors) should use the same type of symbol.

I.   First main point
  A. First subpoint of I
    1. First subpoint of A
      a. First subpoint of 1
      b. Second subpoint of 1
    2. Second subpoint of A
  B. Second subpoint of I
II.   Second main point

SUBPOINTS

Each subpoint must have at least two subdivisions if it has any. Think of it like cutting up an apple. If you cut up an apple, you have at least two pieces. You may end up with more pieces, but you cannot divide something without a result of at least two.

For example, subpoint A has two subdivisions, 1 and 2 (indicated here with colors).

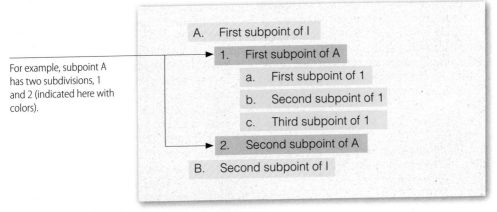

A. First subpoint of I
1. First subpoint of A
  a. First subpoint of 1
  b. Second subpoint of 1
  c. Third subpoint of 1
2. Second subpoint of A
B. Second subpoint of I

ALIGNMENT OF POINTS IN YOUR OUTLINE

Your main points should line up closest to the left margin of the page, and each subsequent subdivision should be indented further to the right.

Each main point should align left, and each level of subpoints should be indented further to the right.

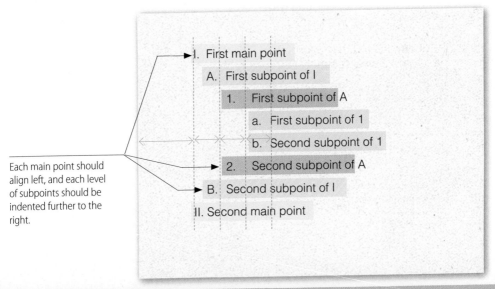

I. First main point
A. First subpoint of I
  1. First subpoint of A
    a. First subpoint of 1
    b. Second subpoint of 1
  2. Second subpoint of A
B. Second subpoint of I
II. Second main point

6
Use Balanced Main Points

Your main points should be equal in importance to each other. They will directly relate to the overall topic but should not overtly relate to each other. Each main point should coordinate with the others. For example, Jessamyn created these three relatively balanced main points. Point 1 is a bit shorter in duration, but points 2 and 3 are almost equal:

Specific purpose: To inform my audience about the National Football League (NFL).

I. A brief history of the game of football explains the evolution of the NFL.

II. The NFL has come a long way since its beginnings.

III. Today, the NFL has a unique organizational setup.

Notice that each point is unique and relates back to the specific purpose.

➔ See Chapter 6 (Tab 3) for details on how to logically organize your main points.

7
Employ Subordination

The components of your outline following each main point should be properly subordinate to the point above them. In other words, any statement that comes under a point must *not* be equal to or of greater importance than the point directly above it. An easy test for this is to read the main point, mentally insert "because" or "for," and then read the subpoint. If doing so makes a logical connection between the main point and the subpoint, the subpoint is subordinate.

Let's return to Zamir's speech on pigeon control to demonstrate how this works. On the next page, see how Zamir works through the first main point to check for subordination. He uses the *"because* or *for"* test to make sure he has followed the principle of subordination.

> I. The City of Jackson needs to institute a plan to decrease the number of pigeons.
>   A. Each year, thousands of pigeons flock to the city.
>   1. They breed everywhere.
>   2. They roost on many buildings.
>   B. Pigeons spread disease.
>   1. They carry germs that affect humans.
>   2. They carry germs that affect animals.
>   3. They can contaminate our waterways.

First, Zamir tested the connections between the main point and its subpoints A and B:

Main point I

The City of Jackson needs to institute a plan to decrease the number of pigeons **because** each year, thousands of pigeons flock to the city.

Subpoint A

Main point I

The City of Jackson needs to institute a plan to decrease the number of pigeons **because** pigeons spread disease.

Subpoint B

Then, he tested the connections between a subpoint, such as B, and its subpoints (1, 2, and 3):

Subpoint B | B's subpoint 1

Pigeons spread disease **because** they carry germs that affect humans.

Subpoint B | B's subpoint 2

Pigeons spread disease **because** they carry germs that affect animals.

Subpoint B | B's subpoint 3

Pigeons spread disease **because** they can contaminate our waterways.

8
Plan Out Formal Links

You should include links between major components of the speech. An effective speaker will lead the audience almost effortlessly from one point to another, and formal links will make this seem smooth, not jolting. Jessamyn used this link between her first main point about the history of the NFL and her second main point about the NFL's current structure:

> Now that we understand the formation of the National Football League, let's look at the structure of the NFL today.

Jessamyn placed the link on her preparation outline here:

II. The NFL has come a long way since its beginnings.
   A. Football is actually adaptations made to two different sports (Ominsky).
      1. While playing soccer in 1823, an English soccer player got frustrated and picked up the ball and started running with it, creating the sport of rugby.
      2. Between 1880 and 1883, as rugby grew in popularity, one of Yale's rugby players conceived a new set of rules for the game, very similar to today's game.

   ► (**Link**: Now that we understand the formation of the National Football League, let's look at the structure of the NFL today.)

III. Today, the NFL has a unique organizational setup.

➔ See "What Can You Use to Link Your Speech Parts Together?" on page 160 for how to write effective links.

9
Use Proper Citations

You should include in-text citations within the outline itself and a page with sources listed according to an acceptable style manual.

In the speech outline, you can do your in-text citations one of two ways, depending on what your instructor requires or what works best for you. Your first option is to follow your style manual. In this example, Jessamyn followed the MLA style of using *parenthetical citations*, or placing the citation information in parentheses at the end of a sentence:

II. The NFL has come a long way since its beginnings.

  A. Football is actually adaptations made to two different sports (Ominsky).

Alternatively, Jessamyn could incorporate the citation into the outline text to help her remember to give it during the speech. This method is especially useful for beginning speakers.

For example:

II. The NFL has come a long way since its beginnings.

  A. According to Dave Ominsky and P. J. Harari, in their 2008 book *Football Made Simple: A Spectator's Guide*, football is actually adaptations made to two different sports.

Before you decide how to cite your sources within the outline text, make sure you first check your instructor's requirements for the speech. Your instructor may stipulate how you create in-text citations.

→ See "How Do You Cite Sources in Your Outline?" and "How Do You Create a Source Page?" on pages 164 and 166.

PRACTICING ETHICS
Using proper citations in your outline will help you remember to cite your sources orally, preventing you from plagiarizing portions of your speech.

What Are the Different Types of Outlines?

1 The Working Outline
2 The Preparation Outline
3 The Delivery Outline

1

The Working Outline

Working outlines are usually handwritten attempts to organize your thoughts as you progress through the early stages of creating a speech—especially as you do research. These outlines will change often and will be a combination of complete thoughts, words, and phrases. Think of them as a way to record your thoughts, narrow in on your main points, and play around with organizational strategies. Your working outline is mostly for your eyes only. You should attempt to use correct outline form, but this is still a very free-flowing stage. For example, Steven is giving a classroom speech about fair trade chocolate. His topic, specific purpose, central idea, and working outline are shown on the next page.

Steven remembered how important it is to formulate and record his topic, specific purpose, and central idea as he created his working outline. Doing so helps him remain focused during his research. He plans to refer back to his specific purpose and central idea often so that he does not stray from his goal.

<u>Topic</u>: Fair Trade Chocolate

<u>Specific Purpose:</u> To inform my audience about fair trade chocolate.

<u>Central Idea:</u> Fair trade chocolate is more than just expensive chocolate; it is responsible chocolate.

Like many beginning students, Steven found it helpful to create his potential main points as questions during this stage of the speech process. This can help Steven stay focused as he conducts research that answers each of the questions. Later, he will change his main points into declarative sentences.

I.   What is fair trade chocolate?

II.   Why is chocolate an issue?
      A.   process of harvesting and where
      B.   chocolate is harvested by slaves

III. Where can you purchase fair trade chocolate locally?
      A.   stores
      B.   online
      C.   what's not fair trade

2
The Preparation Outline

Preparation outlines (also known as *formal* or *full-sentence outlines*) will be much longer and more detailed than working outlines. Designing a preparation outline allows you the opportunity to give the necessary time, effort, and thought to creating a successful speech.

The entire outline will adhere to correct outline form. The introduction, body, and conclusion will be clearly marked and connected with detailed links. The outline will end with a complete and correct source page, listing all the sources cited in the speech. You should follow your instructor's requirements for how to present the outline, but in most cases, it will be:

- Typed
- Double spaced
- Formatted in a specific and consistent way
- Handed in prior to or on the day you give your speech

The basic format of a preparation outline should look similar to the template at right. This template is the standard pattern you can use to create most speech outlines.

Student name	Class
Date	Instructor name

Topic
General purpose
Specific purpose
Central idea

INTRODUCTION
    Attention-getter
    Credibility material
    Relevance to audience
    Preview of speech

(Link from introduction to first main point)

BODY
  I. First main point
    A. Subpoint
    B. Subpoint
      1. Subpoint of B
      2. Subpoint of B
      3. Subpoint of B

(Link between first and second main points)

  II. Second main point
    A. Subpoint
    B. Subpoint
      1. Subpoint of B
      2. Subpoint of B
    C. Subpoint

(Link between second and third main points)

  III. Third main point
    A. Subpoint
      1. Subpoint of A
        a. Subpoint of 1
        b. Subpoint of 1
      2. Subpoint of A
    B. Subpoint
    C. Subpoint

(Link to conclusion)

CONCLUSION
    Summary statement
    Audience response statement
    WOW statement

      Works Cited (or References)

Steven's preparation outline looked like this.

Steven Barker   COMM 110
October 22, 2010   Dr. Smith

Topic: The facts surrounding fair trade chocolate are astounding.
General purpose: To inform
Specific purpose: To inform my audience about fair trade chocolate.
Central idea: Today, I want to share what fair trade chocolate is, why chocolate is an issue, and where you can purchase fair trade chocolate.

INTRODUCTION
Attention-getter: Raise your hand if you have had any chocolate today. Raise your hand if you have had any chocolate in the last week. How about the last month? Or the last year?
Relevance to audience: For those of you who raised your hands and even those of you who didn't, what you are about to hear will surely make you think twice before the next time you eat a chocolate candy bar.
Credibility material: As a member of the Christian Social Justice Committee, I have become concerned about fair trade chocolate.
Preview of speech: Fair trade chocolate is becoming a global concern in our culture today. To understand its impact, we have to answer the following three questions. What is fair trade chocolate? Why is chocolate an issue? Where can one buy fair trade chocolate?

(**Link:** First, what is fair trade chocolate?)

BODY
I. Fair trade, according to FairTradeFederation.org, is an economic partnership based on dialogue, transparency, and respect.

A. Fair trade essentially is a combination of several ideals.
  1. It is set in place to provide safe work environments for industries.
  2. It allows for adequate levels of pay for all employees in industry.
  3. It prevents the practice of slavery in all associated industries.
  4. It ensures the rights of children.
B. Fair trade chocolate is chocolate that is harvested and prepared by individuals who receive fair wages for the work that they do.

(**Link:** Second, why is chocolate such an issue?)

II. Chocolate harvested by slaves is such a big issue because of the limited product alternatives for consumption in the United States.
  A. It is estimated that there are more than 27 million modern-day slaves throughout the world (Batstone).
  B. The manner in which the chocolate-harvesting slaves are procured as well as how they are treated is horrendous.
    1. According to the 2001 documentary *Slavery*, these slaves are sometimes bought from parents for as little as $30.
    2. They are also taken from street corners in neighboring countries after being promised food and wealth.
  C. Ghana Africa grows cocoa for export.
    1. It is the world's largest exporter of cocoa beans.
    2. It is also the largest among the slave industry.
  D. The United States is the world's largest importer of cocoa beans.

(**Link:** Finally, where can one buy free trade chocolate?)

III. There are several places to purchase free trade chocolate.
  A. The Internet is the best place to purchase chocolate.
    1. Sweetearth.com deals specifically with fair trade.
    2. So does Divine Chocolate at divinechocolateusa.com.

B. The Mustard Seed, which is located in downtown Columbia, is a fair trade only store that sells Divine Chocolate.

C. Kaldi's Coffee also sells fair trade chocolate. Their store is located in downtown Columbia right next to the Mustard Seed.

D. Some common chocolates are not fair trade.

   1. Hershey, Nestle, Mars, and Lindt chocolates make up more than 75 percent of the chocolate that most stores carry.

   2. These brands of chocolate are not slave free.

As you can see, free trade chocolate is available locally and via the Internet.)

CONCLUSION

Summary statement: Fair trade chocolate has become a big issue throughout the world today. Now you know what fair trade chocolate is, why chocolate has become an issue, and where you can purchase fair trade chocolate.

Audience response statement: You can now make an informed choice to eat responsible chocolate, or not.

WOW statement: I will leave you today with a gift. This is a sample of Divine Chocolate. This is what chocolate should taste like, because no little kid was forced to make it for you. This chocolate is slave free and guilt free. It is Divine!

Works Cited

"About Fair Trade." *FairTradeFederation.org*. Fair Trade Federation, 2007. Web. 19 Oct. 2009.

Batstone, David. *Not for Sale: The Return of the Global Slave Trade—and How We Can Fight It*. New York: Harper, 2007. Print.

Slavery. Dir. Kate Blewett and Brian Woods. Narr. Kate Blewett and Brian Woods. British Broadcasting Channel, 2001. Film.

3

The Delivery Outline

Delivery outlines will maintain the tight structure of the preparation outline but will eliminate much of the detail because you will know it by memory after writing the speech and doing some preliminary practicing. Create and use this outline as early as possible in the rehearsal stage of your speech. It is important that your "mind's eye" becomes familiar with the layout of this outline. You know you have become familiar enough with it when you can anticipate moving on to the next note card or page without looking down. This outline should assist you but not be a crutch. If you find that you want to read directly from it most of the time, it has too much detail. A delivery outline will also have delivery and presentation hints highlighted at key points during your speech. You should set up your delivery outline format with what you find the most useful and comfortable. The following is only one example, showing the note cards Steven used during his speech.

Intro.   CARD # 1

- Raise your hand if you have had any chocolate today. Raise your hand if you have had any chocolate in the last week. How about the last month? Or the last year?
- As a member of the Christian Social Justice Committee
- What fair trade chocolate is (slide)
- Why chocolate is an issue
- Where you can purchase fair trade chocolates

(**Link:** First, what is fair trade chocolate?)

                                                                       CARD # 2

I. Fair trade, according to FairTradeFederation.org, is an economic partnership based on dialogue, transparency, and respect.
   A. Combination of several ideals (slide)
      1. Safe work environments for industries   SLOW
      2. Allows for adequate levels of pay for all   DOWN
      3. Prevents practice of slavery
      4. Ensures the rights of children
   B. Harvested and prepared by individuals that receive fair wages

(**Link:** Second, why is chocolate such an issue?)

CARD # 3

II. A big issue—limited product alternatives for consumption in the U.S.
   A. David Batstone, in *Not for Sale: The Return of the Global Slave Trade—and How We Can Fight It*, states more than 27 million modern-day slaves throughout the world
   B. Horrendous procurement and treatment (slide)
      1. According to a 2001 documentary entitled *Slavery*, these slaves are sometimes bought from parents for as little as $30.
      2. Taken from street corners promised food and wealth
   C. Ghana, Africa   (slide)
      1. World's largest exporter of cocoa beans
      2. Largest among the slave industry
   D. The U.S.—world's largest importer of cocoa beans

      (Link: Finally, where can one buy free trade chocolate?)

CARD # 4

III. There are several places to purchase free trade chocolate. (slide)
   A. The Internet
      1. SweetEarth.com
      2. DivineChocolateUSA.com
   B. Locally
      1. The Mustard Seed
      2. Kaldi's Coffee
   C. Common chocolates that are not fair trade.
      1. Hershey, Nestle, Mars, and Lindt chocolates make up more than 75 percent of the chocolate that most stores carry.
      2. These brands are not slave free.

CARD # 5

- Fair trade chocolate has become a big issue throughout the world today. Now, you know what fair trade chocolate is, why chocolate has become an issue, and where you can purchase fair trade chocolate.
- You can now make an informed choice to eat responsible chocolate, or not.
- I will leave you today with a gift.

(Begin to pass out candy.)

- This is a sample of Divine Chocolate. This is what chocolate should taste like because no little kid was forced to make it for you. This chocolate is slave free and guilt free. It is Divine!

What Can You Use to Link Your Speech Parts Together?

1 **Transitions**
2 **Signposts**
3 **Internal Previews**
4 **Internal Reviews**

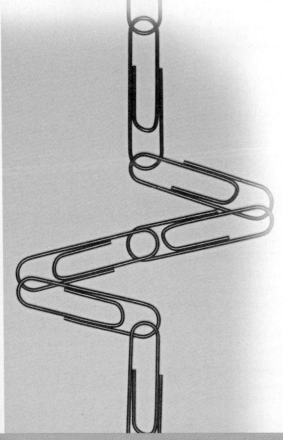

On page 141, you learned that links are one of the important parts of your speech's body. Links (also called transitions and connectives) make logical connections between the parts of your speech.

Think of a computer hyperlink—usually a word, symbol, image, or other element in a document or on a Web site that links, when you click on it, to another section in the same document/site or to a completely new document/site. Just as a hyperlink serves to make a jump between two related places, a speech link creates a bridge between two sections of your speech.

Many instructors require your speech links to be part of your preparation outline. Transitions, signposts, internal previews, and internal reviews are four types of links you can use.

1
Transitions

Transitions are words or phrases signaling movement from one point to another as well as how the points relate to each other. Transitions fall into the following categories.

TYPE OF TRANSITION	EXAMPLES
Time transitions are words and phrases that demonstrate a passing of time.	Let's move on to... Now that we have... We are now ready... In the future... Meanwhile... Later... Next...
Viewpoint transitions demonstrate a change in your view of a situation.	On the other hand... However... Conversely... Although... But...
Connective transitions simply unite related thoughts.	Also... Another... In addition... Moreover... Not only... but also...
Concluding transitions signal the end of a section within the speech or the ending of the entire speech.	Therefore... Thus... As a result... Finally... In conclusion... To summarize...

2
Signposts

Signposts are words or phrases that signal to the audience where they are with regards to related thoughts and/or what is important to remember. Some of the most common signposts are:

- First... Second... Third...
- Argument #1... Argument #2... Argument #3...
- My first reason... My second reason...
- Above all, remember...
- Keep in mind...
- The most important aspects are...

For example:

> The first step in preparing a strawberry patch is to locate a well-drained, sunny location.

After presenting the details of how to select a great place for the strawberry patch, you would use the same type of signpost to signal the remaining steps as you progress through the speech, offering details for each.

> The second step is to prepare the soil in the patch prior to planting....

> The third step is to select the best type of strawberry plants for your location and usage....

> The fourth step is to place the plants in the ground properly....

> The fifth step is to care for the plants to produce the best fruit possible....

3
Internal Previews

As links, **internal previews** are like mini introductions and look like detailed signposts. These statements tell the audience what will be covered next in the speech. Here are a few examples:

> Let's look at how the NFL consists of 32 teams, two conferences, and four divisions.

> To prepare the tomatoes for drying, you need to select the best fruits, wash them, and thinly slice them. Let's look at the preparation process in greater detail.

> There are many reasons why we need universal health care. However, I would like to focus on how a universal system would decrease the numbers of uninsured citizens, improve the access to proper care for those already insured, and help regulate the cost of care.

An internal preview is a great way to link your introduction and the body of your speech. It can act as the preview of your full speech, as in the last example above.

TIP: Signposts

Be careful to avoid conflicting or repeating signposts. For example, if your speech is on baking a cake, you might correctly say, "The first step is to gather ingredients." But you should then avoid signposts that make your subpoints sound similar, such as "The first ingredient is flour. The second is eggs." By the time you get to your second main point of "The second step is to mix," your listeners will be confused.

4
Internal Reviews

Internal reviews (also known as *internal summaries*) are like mini conclusions. They summarize what you have just covered in the previous section of your speech. Here are a few internal review examples:

It is our responsibility to offer health care to every U.S. citizen, to improve access, and to lower care costs that force a need for a universal system.

Knowledge, persistence, and charisma are what make a great salesperson.

To review, you need a well-drained and sunny location, loamy soil, and certain nutrients to create the best strawberry patch.

The steps for preserving tomatoes by drying are selecting tomatoes that dry well, preparing them for the drying process, using the proper drying process for the equipment you have, and storing the tomatoes in a dry, cool place.

Often you will combine internal previews and internal reviews with a transition, as these examples do.

Now that you have selected the right location for the strawberry patch, prepared the soil, and purchased the correct plants for your climate, it is time to plant the strawberries properly.

Now that we have discussed the evolution of football and the establishment of the NFL, we can move on to considering....

TIPS: Effective Links

• Creating your links ahead of time and placing them in the correct spots will help you remember to use them, and you won't struggle for words during the delivery of the speech. You should write out the links completely on the preparation outline. You might also use an abbreviated version of your links in your delivery outline so that you remember to include them.

• You can use nonverbal cues to add emphasis to your links. Pausing, gesturing, changing locations or facial expressions, and increasing or decreasing your pitch or rate are some ways to help signal that a link is occurring.

How Do You Cite Sources in Your Outline?

As discussed in the Overview, citing your sources—in speeches and in writing—is an ethical responsibility and the only way to prevent plagiarism. Whenever you borrow words or concepts, directly quote something, or paraphrase, you need to cite the source. If what you are discussing is not common knowledge for most of your audience, you need a citation. When in doubt, cite a source.

Most speech instructors will ask you to follow your style manual. However, the instructor may offer instructions on how to handle citations unique to the public speaking forum. Be sure to check with your instructor. Some general guidelines are:

- Cite your sources within the outline, followed by a source page at the end of the outline.

- Incorporate citations into the text of the outline, record them parenthetically, or use a combination of both.

- Unless the citation is part of the outline text, place it at the end of a sentence.

- The information within the citation should point to the source listed on the source page at the end of your outline.

Your style manual offers detailed discussions of how to cite effectively; however, the following chart offers a few general rules and examples for citing sources within your outline.

→ See Chapter 4 (Tab 2) for details on how to cite sources orally.

MLA CITATIONS	APA CITATIONS
Use the author–page number method.	*Use the author–publication date method.*
One author, parenthetical citation: "…can help you save time and money" (Smith 345).	**One author, parenthetical citation:** "…can help you save time and money" (Smith, 345).
One author, in-text citation: According to Smith's article in the November issue of… (345).	**One author, in-text citation:** According to Smith (1990), you can…
Two to three authors, parenthetical citation: (Smith, Baker, and Jones 456)	**Two to six authors, parenthetical citation:** (Smith, Baker, & Jones, 1990)
Two to three authors, in-text citation: According to Smith, Baker, and Jones, the people agreed with the candidate (456).	**Two to six authors, in-text citation:** Smith, Baker, and Jones (1990) found that the people agreed with the candidate.
More than three authors: (Wilson et al. 85)	**More than six authors:** (Wilson et al., 1990)
No author identified: *Begin with the first few words of the source on the source page (usually the title).* "Only 10 percent polled agreed" ("Politics Today" 45).	**No author identified:** *Begin with the first few words of the source on the source page (usually the title).* "Only 10 percent polled agreed" ("Politics Today," 1990).
Corporate or group authors: *The name of the group serves as the author.* (Food and Drug Administration 123)	**Corporate or group authors:** *The name of the group serves as the author.* (Food and Drug Administration, 2009)
No page number available: (Food and Drug Administration)	**No date available:** (Food and Drug Administration, n.d.)

REMEMBER

When citing Web pages, you may not know the author, or the material may have been created by corporate or group authors.

How Do You Create a Source Page?

1 **Follow the Overall Format Requirements**
2 **Create Proper Entries for Each Source**

As with citing sources within the text of your outline, your style manual will guide the creation of your source page. Again, you need to pay attention to any instructions given in class, because an oral speech can have unique sources that your instructor may want included.

For example, APA style does not usually include personal communications (private letters, memos, e-mails, personal interviews, telephone conversations, etc.) on the source page. Many speech instructors, however, do want them cited formally on the outline and orally in the speech. In most cases, the speech instructor wants *all* sources included in your speech cited, including downloaded video, music, Internet documents, personal interviews, photos, and so on. In other public speaking situations, you may find that having a handout ready for distribution and including your source page will be helpful so that your audience can retain information better or do further investigation.

> **REMEMBER**
> Honesty about where you get your materials is the best policy and will build your credibility with your audience.

1
Follow the Overall Format Requirements

The following are general guidelines for creating the layout of the source page.

- Make sure you are using the most current and appropriate style manual for your class.
- If you are using MLA style, the source page uses the title "Works Cited," which is centered.
- If you are using APA style, the source page uses the title "References," which is centered.
- With either MLA or APA, your source page should:
  - be double spaced
  - use a hanging indent
  - list sources in alphabetical order
  - use the same font (style, color, and size) as the text of the outline
  - use standard one-inch margins

The chart on the following pages shows you—at a quick glance—some differences between these two styles. Check your style manual for a more detailed description for creating a source page.

2
Create Proper Entries for Each Source

Each style manual gives detailed instructions on how to create the entries on the source page. You will want to refer often to your manual on how to create entries. The table on the following page outlines the most common sources used in a speech, according to MLA or APA. The key to a successful source page is to select a style and stay with it consistently. Remember to double check for proper format if you are using software to create your source page. Software can make mistakes or be out of date.

CHECKLIST for Creating an Outline

❑ Did I include the topic, specific purpose, and central idea?

❑ Did I use full sentences?

❑ Do I have only one sentence for each outline component? Does each sentence cover only one idea?

❑ Did I create a complete introduction and conclusion?

❑ Am I using correct outline format?

- Am I using Roman numerals for the main points, and are they closest to the left margin?
- Am I using uppercase letters, numbers, and lowercase letters for the appropriate levels of subpoints?
- Does each subpoint have at least two divisions?

❑ Are my main points equal in importance to each other?

❑ Do the components of my outline follow correct subordination?

❑ Did I include links?

❑ Did I include the in-text citations and a source page?

MLA AND APA AT A GLANCE

Book - MLA	Hurston, Zora Neale. *Their Eyes Were Watching God.* New York: Harper, 1990. Print.
Book - APA	Hurston, Z. N. (1990). *Their eyes were watching God.* New York, NY: Harper & Row.
Newspaper - MLA (Print and database)	Danielsen, Aarik. "Heritage in the Hand." *Columbia Daily Tribune* 18 Oct. 2009: C1+. Print.
	"Additional Fake Lipitor Recalled: Illinois Wholesaler Takes Action after FDA Issues Warning." *Kansas City Star* 18 June 2003: C1. *NewsBank.* Web. 28 Sept. 2009.
Newspaper - APA (Print and database)	Danielsen, A. (2009, October 18). Heritage in the hand. *Columbia Daily Tribune,* pp. C1, C2.
	Additional fake Lipitor recalled: Illinois wholesaler takes action after FDA issues warning. (2003, June 18). *The Kansas City Star,* p. C1. Retrieved from NewsBank.
Magazine - MLA (Print and database)	"Drug Safety: Partnership for Safe Medicines Arms Public against Counterfeit Drugs." *Biotech Business Week* 15 Dec. 2008: 54-56. Print.
	"Drug Safety: Partnership for Safe Medicines Arms Public against Counterfeit Drugs." *Biotech Business Week* 15 Dec. 2008: 1513. *LexisNexis.* Web. 28 Sept. 2009.
Magazine - APA (Print and database)	Drug safety: Partnership for safe medicines arms public against counterfeit drugs. (2008, December 15). *Biotech Business Week,* 54–55.
	Drug safety: Partnership for safe medicines arms public against counterfeit drugs. (2008, December 15). *Biotech Business Week,* 1513. Retrieved from LexisNexis Academic News Search.

Web page - MLA (With government author)	United States. Dept. of Health and Human Services. Food and Drug Administration. "Counterfeit Medicines—Filled with Empty Promise." *U.S. Food and Drug Administration*. Dept. of Health and Human Services, 1 Sept. 2009. Web. 3 Sept. 2009.
Web page - APA (With government author)	U.S. Department of Health and Human Services, U.S. Food and Drug Administration. (2009, September 1). *Counterfeit medicines—filled with empty promise*. Retrieved from http://www.fda.gov/Drugs/ResourcesForYou/ucm079278.htm
Interview conducted by speaker - MLA	Jones, Timothy. Personal interview. 1 Nov. 2009. Jones, Timothy. Telephone interview. 1 Nov. 2009. Jones, Timothy. E-mail interview. 1 Nov. 2009.
Interview conducted by speaker* - APA	**APA normally does not recognize undocumented sources such as interviews. Because speakers often use interviews as source material, your instructor may ask you to include them as shown below.* Jones, T. (2009, November 1). Personal interview. Jones, T. (2009, November 1). Telephone interview. Jones, T. (2009, November 1). E-mail interview.

TIP: Examples of APA and MLA

Looking at correct source pages can help you visualize how to put one together. The sample on page 361 follows APA format and the sample on page 157 follows MLA.

Sophia's Speech

Sophia's grandparents and parents moved from Naples, Italy, to the United States two years before she was born. She notices that they are sometimes confused by commonly used phrases that have another meaning than the literal meaning of the words. The one that stumped her grandfather the most was "son of a gun." Sophia's English teacher called them idioms, so she decided to do an informative speech on the origin of a few common ones she knew.

HER WORKING OUTLINE

Before heading to do research, Sophia took a few moments to think about what her main points might be and asked a few friends to name some idioms they use. From this, she created her working outline.

Topic: Idioms

General purpose: To inform.

Specific purpose: To inform my listeners about some common idioms.

Central idea: Today, I would like to share some common idioms and their meanings.

Main Point # 1: "It's raining cats and dogs."

Main Point # 2: "Let the cat out of the bag"

Main Point # 3: "Son of a gun"

Main Point # 4: "Real McCoy"

HER PREPARATION OUTLINE

Locating information about her idioms was easier than she thought it would be. Sophia found a lot of information on the Internet and in a few books at her library. Her next step was to create the preparation outline. Sophia made sure to format the page as her instructor required; she created her introduction and conclusion, wrote in full sentences, used proper outline format, cited her sources within the text of the outline, and created her Works Cited source page (Sophia used the MLA manual).

Sophia Ucci
April 28, 2010

SPCM 101
Dr. Craig

Topic: Linguistic Urban Legends—Idioms or Word Myths

Gene

Spec

Cent
mean

INTR

Atten
chick
confu
few o
urban
evide
moral
Today
as "w

Credi
Actua
When
becau
some
them

Relev
idiom

Preview of speech: After polling some friends, I discovered that "it's raining cats and dogs," "let the cat out of the bag," "son of a gun," and "real McCoy" are common word myths used by people our age. So today, I would like to tell you what each of these means and the origin of that meaning.

(**Link:** Let's begin with "it's raining cats and dogs.")

BODY

I. "It's raining cats and dogs" is a commonly used expression when it is raining extremely hard.

  A. In the 1700s, animals would live in the thatched roofs of people's homes (Wilton).

    1. When it rained, the roof would become slippery and the animals would slip and come tumbling off the roof onto the ground.

    2. Although the saying seems logical, it is not completely factual.

    3. The animals that lived in the roofs were animals such as rats, mice, and insects.

    4. Occasionally there was a cat, but for the most part, the animals were varmints.

    5. So, this saying remains a myth.

(**Link:** There is, though, another saying that has to do with a cat.)

HER DELIVERY OUTLINE

With her preparation outline completed, Sophia created the delivery outline she would use during her speech. Because she likes to give her speeches without a lectern, she put her delivery outline on stiff note cards. She is now ready to practice, practice, and practice some more.

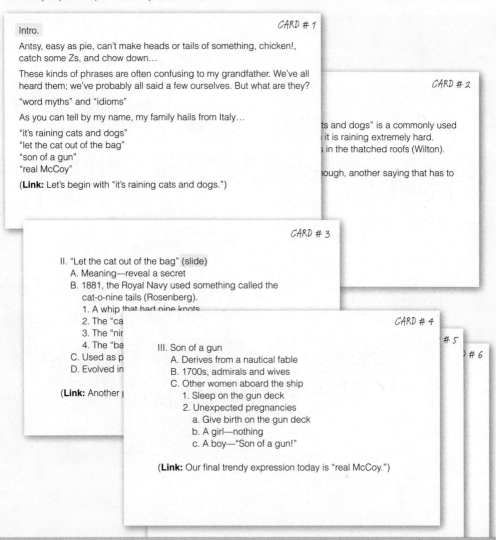

CARD # 1

Intro.

Antsy, easy as pie, can't make heads or tails of something, chicken!, catch some Zs, and chow down…

These kinds of phrases are often confusing to my grandfather. We've all heard them; we've probably all said a few ourselves. But what are they?

"word myths" and "idioms"

As you can tell by my name, my family hails from Italy…

"it's raining cats and dogs"
"let the cat out of the bag"
"son of a gun"
"real McCoy"

(**Link:** Let's begin with "it's raining cats and dogs.")

CARD # 2

ts and dogs" is a commonly used
it is raining extremely hard.
s in the thatched roofs (Wilton).

ough, another saying that has to

CARD # 3

II. "Let the cat out of the bag" (slide)
   A. Meaning—reveal a secret
   B. 1881, the Royal Navy used something called the
      cat-o-nine tails (Rosenberg).
      1. A whip that had nine knots
      2. The "ca
      3. The "nir
      4. The "ba
   C. Used as p
   D. Evolved ir

(**Link:** Another

CARD # 4

III. Son of a gun
   A. Derives from a nautical fable
   B. 1700s, admirals and wives
   C. Other women aboard the ship
      1. Sleep on the gun deck
      2. Unexpected pregnancies
         a. Give birth on the gun deck
         b. A girl—nothing
         c. A boy—"Son of a gun!"

(**Link:** Our final trendy expression today is "real McCoy.")

5

6

6

ORGANIZING THE SPEECH BODY

Introduction

The goal of Chapter 5 was to help you see the benefits of outlining, including how outlines can create the necessary structure for your speech to achieve its specific purpose. This chapter, however, will take you through more micro-level structuring by offering you ways (strategies) to organize your main points or the body of your speech.

A *strategy* is a plan designed to achieve a goal—in this case, your specific purpose. Strategy is concerned with the relationship and arrangement of your main points. In other words, your strategy is not about how you explain your main points (the content) but is about how your main points relate to and follow each other (the organization), to achieve your goal to inform, persuade, or accentuate a topic.

For example, if you are giving a demonstration speech in a chemistry class about a chemical reaction, the order of the steps is important to the outcome of the reaction and your audience's comprehension. If you complete steps out of order, the results could be disastrous.

In any speech, the strategy you use to order your main points can make or break an argument. The strategy you use can assist or hinder your audience's learning about or appreciation of a person, animal, place, event, object, concept, issue, or process. Helping you select the right strategy for you, your general purpose, your topic, and your audience is the goal of this chapter.

CHAPTER 5: Outlining Your Speech   137

CHAPTER 6 CONTENTS

What Organizational Strategies Can You Use in Your Speech?   174
1 Chronological   176
2 Topical   177
3 Spatial   177
4 Causal   178
5 Order of Intensity   178
6 Comparative   179
7 Problem–Solution   180
8 Refutation   181
9 Monroe's Motivated Sequence   182

How Do You Select the Best Strategy?   184
1 Consider Your General Purpose   185
2 Consider Your Topic   185
3 Consider Your Audience   185

How Do You Make a Speech Out of a Strategy?   186
1 Discover Your Main Points   186
2 Create Your Main Points   188
3 Expand with Subpoints   190

Pedro's Speech   192

CHAPTER 7: Introducing and Concluding Your Speech   195

Tab 3 Review   214

What Organizational Strategies Can You Use in Your Speech?

1 **Chronological**

2 **Topical**

3 **Spatial**

4 **Causal**

5 **Order of Intensity**

6 **Comparative**

7 **Problem–Solution**

8 **Refutation**

9 **Monroe's Motivated Sequence**

Most speakers choose from nine basic organizational strategies: chronological, topical, spatial, causal, order of intensity, comparative, problem–solution, refutation, and Monroe's motivated sequence.

Chapter 5 noted that there are three main parts to a speech: the introduction, the body, and the conclusion. The strategy you select will help you organize the body of your speech.

When you select a strategy, you will consider which one works best with your general purpose, the topic, and the audience. Because these three elements are constantly interacting with and reacting to each other, you may find that you can use more than one strategy effectively—and that is fine. Trust your instincts to select one that seems the best for your purpose, topic, and audience and for you as the speaker. The following pages will help you understand in greater detail how each strategy works.

CONFIDENCE BOOSTER

Selecting the right strategy and sticking to it is a powerful confidence booster. The time you spend making sure you follow the strategy will help you become more familiar with the details of your speech. A major contributor to low confidence is not knowing what your next thought might be. Likewise, a well-organized speech will help you look and feel confident and trustworthy.

ORGANIZATIONAL STRATEGIES FOR SPEECHES

STRATEGY	WHAT IS IT?	WHEN MIGHT YOU USE IT?	WHAT TYPES OF SPEECH USE IT?
Chronological	Strategy based on moving through time or sequential steps	Useful for speeches about a process or development over time or plan of action	Informative Persuasive Special occasion
Topical	Strategy highlighting the natural subtopics or divisions within a speech topic	Ideal when your topic has inherent subtopics	Informative Persuasive Special occasion
Spatial	Strategy describing the arrangement of space related to an event, place, or object	Useful when you need to walk your audience through a space or setting	Informative Special occasion
Causal	Strategy based on cause-to-effect or effect-to-cause	Effective for speeches focusing on causes or consequences of something already present or possible	Informative Persuasive Special occasion
Order of intensity	Strategy based on ordering from least to most, easy to difficult, or neutral to intense	Notable for building on the audience's understanding, concerns, or interests related to a topic	Informative Persuasive
Comparative	Strategy that explains or argues by comparing something to something else	Great when topics are abstract, technical, or difficult; beneficial for showing advantages	Informative Persuasive
Problem–solution	Strategy demonstrating a problem and then advocating a solution	Useful when trying to change attitudes or when calling for a particular solution	Informative Persuasive
Refutation	Strategy based on countering someone else's argument	Beneficial when there is a strong opposing side to an issue and you counter it	Persuasive
Monroe's motivated sequence	A five-step strategy that motivates an audience to action based on their needs	Excellent strategy for a call to action speech	Persuasive

1

Chronological

You will use the ***chronological strategy*** when you need to move through steps in a process or develop a timeline. Depending on the topic and your general purpose, you might move forward or backward through the process or timeline for effect. This type of arrangement is especially helpful when stressing the history of an event, person, or thing or when demonstrating a process.

For example, a process speech might look something like this:

Specific purpose: To inform my audience how to use a compost bin.

Central idea: Composting is an easy way to save space in our landfills while growing great vegetables or flowers.

I. There are many types of composting bins, making it important to select the right one for your needs and budget.

II. Where you position your composting bin can make composting either effortless or grueling.

III. A few simple steps will help you maintain a sweet-smelling, productive compost pile.

IV. Using the "black gold" from your pile will supply you with a bounty of produce or flowers.

Here, each main point walks the listener through the major steps of composting. The subpoints should do the same.

A timeline example might look like this:

Specific purpose: To inform my audience about the space shuttle.

Central idea: Created in the 1970s and scheduled to retire in 2010, NASA's space shuttle program has made space history.

I. The 1970s were the foundation years for the shuttle.

II. The 1980s were the first years of shuttle missions.

III. The 1990s demonstrated the true power of the shuttle but were shrouded by disaster.

IV. The period from 2000 to 2010 marked the progress toward retiring the shuttle fleet.

In this example, each main point covers a major section of the space shuttle's historical timeline. This speech logically proceeds from oldest date to most recent. However, some chronological speech topics can also cover a timeline in reverse.

TIP: Demonstration Speeches

When you give a demonstration speech (a "how to do it" speech), you can use the chronological strategy to create a step-by-step organization.

2
Topical

You will use the **topical strategy** (also called the *categorical*) when there is a strong inherent or traditional division of subtopics within the main topic. If you give a speech about chocolate, for example, a natural topic division could be white, milk, and dark. For a topic like taking a vacation to Orlando, you might divide the topic according to how people traditionally think about vacations—places to see, places to eat, and places to stay.

Specific purpose: To inform my audience about techniques to improve their schoolwork.

Central idea: To succeed in school, you need to organize your life, carefully manage your time, and focus mentally.

I. Organization is the process of giving structure and order to your work.

II. Time management is controlling or directing time into useful chunks.

III. Mental focus is realizing what you have to do and concentrating hard on that single item.

Notice how each main point takes on a different subtopic—organization, time management, and mental focus. As individual subjects, these may seem unrelated, but in relation to the central idea and main topic, they are logically connected.

3
Spatial

A **spatial strategy** recognizes space as a way to arrange the speech. This strategy is useful when you want to discuss your topic in relationship to a physical setting, a natural environment, or proximity. Examples might be speaking about your tour through the White House, room by room; telling the new freshman class about your campus, building by building; or speaking about historical sites like Gettysburg or Mount Vernon. A speaker can even arrange an informative speech about the human tooth spatially by beginning at the outermost part, the enamel, and working in to the soft center, or dental pulp.

Specific purpose: To inform my audience about the Grand Canyon.

Central idea: Carved by the Colorado River, more than 277 miles long, and more than a mile deep in places, the Grand Canyon National Park is like three parks in one when you visit the North Rim, the South Rim, and the Inner Canyon.

I. The North Rim has a much higher elevation than the South, making it cooler with better views of the Canyon.

II. The South Rim is more accessible and has several historical sites.

III. The Inner Canyon is the unpredictable lifeline of the park.

The spatial strategy is often a useful way to deal with a setting as large as the Grand Canyon. It helps you divide the space (North Rim, South Rim, and Inner Rim) into more manageable parts.

4
Causal

You will use the **causal strategy** when you want your audience to understand the cause and effect or consequences of something. With this strategy, you can either trace the path that leads up to a certain result or backtrack from the effect to the cause. Which way you go depends on what is most important to your specific purpose.

For example, explaining the causes leading up to the economic crisis beginning in 2009 would be a great candidate for this type of arrangement.

Specific purpose: To inform my audience about the causes of the current economic crisis.

Central idea: The current economic crisis in the United States can be explained by examining the chain reaction created by the declining housing market and global financial ramifications.

I.   An unsustainable real estate boom brought prices the average family could not afford.

II. Bank losses created a major loss of capital.

III. The average person feels the effects of a recession.

Depending on your topic, you may have one cause leading to a single effect, a single cause leading to several effects, or several causes leading to one effect.

5
Order of Intensity

When you use an **order of intensity strategy** (also called *climactic*), you arrange your main points in order from least to most, easy to difficult, or neutral to intense. You will determine this order based on your audience's needs and understanding of the topic.

Specific purpose: I want my audience to agree that the United States needs to take action to fight obesity.

Central idea: Reversing the obesity rate in the United States should be a top priority.

I.   Obesity can directly impact your everyday life.

II. Obesity has direct consequences on the quality of your health.

III. Obesity can kill you.

This example uses the order of least to most. Obesity's impact on daily life is less intense than its potential to cause death.

6
Comparative

The ***comparative strategy*** uses the practice of compare and contrast. In an informative speech, you might use this strategy with new, abstract, technical, or difficult-to-comprehend topics. Here, you compare your topic to something the audience knows—for example, comparing the U.S. banking system to the European system or comparing your school to another similar to it. This pattern only works when the two things you are comparing are comparable or analogous.

Specific purpose: To inform new students about college life.

Central idea: Comparing what college might be like to your high school experience will help you anticipate the next four years.

I. Your classroom experience will be unlike your high school class expectations.

II. Your social life will be different from what it was in high school.

III. Your everyday life responsibilities will be different.

Notice how this first example uses the comparative strategy for informative purposes. This approach helps the audience understand and follow the speech by comparing the unknown (college life) with the familiar (high school experience).

In a persuasive speech, this strategy can be used to convince an audience that one thing is better than another, by comparing the two. This is a common practice used by many salespersons and is often referred to as ***comparative advantage***.

Specific purpose: To convince my audience to purchase an LCD television.

Central idea: Current LCD televisions are better than plasma televisions.

I. The positive qualities of current LCD screens make them better products than plasma screens.

II. Both types of televisions have potential negatives, but the LCD works best for most homes.

III. The price difference makes the LCD a better purchase.

This persuasive example compares and contrasts LCD and plasma televisions by outlining both the positive and negative differences of each. The speech aims to demonstrate that the LCD is a better choice overall.

TIP: Limit Comparisons
Don't get carried away with the number of comparisons you make, which can be confusing to the audience. In a short presentation, such as those you are likely to give in class, five or fewer comparisons will suffice.

7
Problem–Solution

You will use the **problem–solution strategy** when you want to show your audience how to solve a problem, making it an arrangement suited for a persuasive speech. With this strategy, your speech will have two main sections dedicated to the "problem" and the "solution." For example:

Specific purpose: To convince my audience that artificial sweeteners are dangerous.

Central idea: Artificial sweeteners are an easy alternative for the calorie-conscious, but the toxic effects of these chemicals should prompt consumers to seek safer choices.

I. **(problem):** Artificial sweeteners like Splenda, sucralose, aspartame, and saccharin cause major side effects that can be potentially dangerous.

II. **(solution):** Gradually decreasing your intake of artificial sweeteners by drinking more water, unsweetened tea, or naturally flavored drinks is the solution to preventing future problems and improving your overall health.

Some persuasive speeches using the problem–solution format may need more than two main points. Why? First, you may need to expand your strategy when the problem and/or solution is so complex that you need more than one main point for either or both, to help your audience understand your position. Secondly, you may need to expand your points if you think your audience might be unwilling to accept the idea that there is a problem or that your proposed solution is the best.

Specific purpose: To convince my audience that there is a serious problem with the education system in our town.

Central idea: As members of this community, we need to recognize the current problems with educating our children and to swiftly seek effective solutions to those problems.

I.   **(problem):** The 2009 standardized test results show that our students at all levels are behind in math, reading, and writing skills.

II. **(problem):** At the high school level, we see a decline in the sciences as well.

III. **(problem):** Our high school dropout rate is one of the highest in the state.

IV. **(solution):** We need to implement a program to evaluate and update the curriculum in all these areas.

V.   **(solution):** We need to attract more motivated and successful educators to our schools.

VI. **(solution):** We need to improve our class facilities.

TIP: Informative Speeches
The problem–solution strategy can be used with informative speeches when your audience is familiar with the problem and solution but not the reasons behind the decision. Here, you use the strategy to simply inform them.

8
Refutation

The **refutation strategy** works only for persuasive speeches and is most common in a court of law. Outside of the courthouse, you would most often use this pattern when you want to change a current policy, program, or viewpoint. You begin your refutation by outlining and dismantling the opposing side, which paves the way for you to persuade the audience to accept your point of view. This strategy is most effective when you are pushing for an exact end result and you need to discredit the opposing point of view by showing it is wrong, harmful, or misinformed.

A refutation has four main steps.

1. State the opposing point of view.
2. Describe the outcomes and consequences of the opposing point of view.
3. Present the argument and evidence for your point of view.
4. Show how your plan is preferable to the point of view you are refuting.

A speech supporting President Obama's health care plan over one proposed by the Republican party (GOP) would follow this strategy.

Specific purpose: To persuade my audience to support President Obama's proposed health care plan.

Central idea: The Obama administration's proposed health care plan will be more effective than that proposed by the GOP.

I. The GOP believes their proposed health care plan is better for several reasons…

II. These reasons could have several outcomes and consequences.

III. President Obama believes the White House's plan will serve the people of America better.

IV. The President's plan is better than the GOP's for the following reasons…

Notice how the speaker states the opposing point of view (the GOP's) in the first point and the consequences of that view in the second main point. The third main point then presents President Obama's plan, and the last point demonstrates the speaker's preference.

PRACTICING ETHICS

Honesty and reliability are key traits of ethical persuasion. Don't mislead your audience into believing something is harmful or wrong if it isn't.

9
Monroe's Motivated Sequence

Developed by Alan Monroe of Purdue University in the 1930s, **Monroe's motivated sequence** is really a more detailed problem–solution strategy. Basing the speech on what motivates the audience, the speaker convinces the audience that the speaker has the solution to their needs. If you remember the discussion about audience needs and motivations in Chapter 1, you should see the benefit of this strategy, which has five stages:

- Attention—During this stage, you begin to direct your audience's attention toward your topic.

→ See Chapter 7 (Tab 3) for ideas on creating attention-grabbing devices.

- Need—Here, you demonstrate for your audience that they need a change by suggesting that a problem exists and they need to solve it.

- Satisfaction—At this stage, you propose the solution to the problem and support it as the best one with the appropriate evidence. The audience must feel that your plan will work.

- Visualization—With the problem highlighted and the solution suggested, you now help the audience visualize how great the situation will be after they implement the plan. In other words, help them visualize the benefits.

- Action—Now, call them to action or tell them exactly what they must do to achieve the solution you have suggested.

The motivated sequence has an added benefit: Its stages correspond to all parts of a speech.

Speech Outline	Motivated Sequence
Introduction ◄———	Attention Stage
Body	
First main point ◄———	Need Stage
Second main point ◄———	Satisfaction Stage
Third main point ◄———	Visualization Stage
Conclusion ◄———	Action Stage

PRACTICING ETHICS

Monroe's motivated sequence, by its nature, allows you to manipulate people's needs, which can be based on an emotional reaction rather than on logic. Be careful and ethical when you appeal to your audience's emotions to change their minds and to take action. There are always consequences with actions. Help your audience make ethical and safe choices.

This example demonstrates how you would outline a speech using this strategy.

Specific purpose: To convince my audience that we need to save the mountain gorilla.

Central idea: The extinction of the mountain gorilla, who shares almost 98 percent of its genetic makeup with humans, could greatly cost humankind.

Introduction (attention stage): The mountain gorilla is one of the world's most endangered species with fewer than 740 remaining in Africa, and none has ever survived captivity (UC Davis).

I. (need stage): The mountain gorilla shares almost 98 percent of its genetic makeup with humans, so many of the diseases, malnutrition, and habitat concerns afflicting the gorillas could affect the human population as well.

II. (satisfaction stage): If this gorilla is to survive and the delicate balance of the ecosystem be maintained, we must safeguard the gorillas of Rwanda, Uganda, and the Democratic Republic of the Congo.

III. (visualization stage): During the past 10 years, the Mountain Gorilla Veterinary Project's medical program has helped increase the gorilla population by 17 percent, making the mountain gorilla the only great ape whose numbers are rising, not falling (UC Davis).

Conclusion (action stage): You can help save the mountain gorilla by supporting research and conservation efforts through donations to organizations like the African Wildlife Foundation or the Diane Fossey Gorilla Fund International or by spreading awareness of these issues.

According to O. C. Ferrell and Michael Hartline in their book *Marketing Strategy*, marketers use a slightly different version of the motivated sequence—known by the acronym AIDA—when selling products or services, which you could use for a slightly different speech.

A – Awareness: Attract the attention of the customer.

I – Interest: Raise customer interest by focusing on advantages and benefits.

D – Desire: Convince customers that they want and desire the product or service.

A – Action: Lead customers toward taking action and/or purchasing.

TIP: When to Use AIDA

The AIDA strategy works best with audiences that are not negative or hostile about your topic or solution. Asking a negative or hostile audience to change their minds and take action on that change is often too much to ask. Using the problem–solution strategy would be better in this case.

How Do You Select the Best Strategy?

1 Consider Your General Purpose
2 Consider Your Topic
3 Consider Your Audience

It is important to stress that the focus of this chapter is the organizational strategy at the *main point level* of your speech. In other words, you will use one of the previously discussed strategies to develop and arrange your main points. Doing so gives you the main strategy for your speech. The difficult part of selecting a strategy is that most speeches can use more than one strategy. However, you must consider your general purpose, topic, and audience when selecting the best strategy for your speech.

1
Consider Your General Purpose

Some of the strategies work for all types of speeches and some work only for informative or persuasive speeches. Likewise, special occasion speeches are usually chronological or topical. Starting with your general purpose will allow you to begin to narrow the list of strategies a bit.

2
Consider Your Topic

Your topic may lead you to a strategy. For example, if your topic is how to make candles, you are going to teach your audience a process. Demonstration or how-to-do-it speeches, such as one on creating candles, will use the chronological strategy because you are moving sequentially through steps. If your topic is homelessness and you want your audience to support a proposed solution to fight homelessness in your community, you will probably use a strategy like problem–solution, Monroe's motivated sequence, or comparative. Still other topics have natural divisions within them, so they fit nicely into the topical strategy.

3
Consider Your Audience

Finally, think about what your audience knows or how they might be interested in your speech. For example, if you are giving a speech about a very complex topic that the audience will have some trouble understanding, the comparative strategy may be helpful because it will help them understand the topic by comparing and contrasting it to something they are familiar with.

If your audience is strongly opposed to your viewpoint, use a strategy like refutation to ease them into seeing the potential problems or issues with their competing viewpoints.

CHECKLIST for Selecting an Organizational Strategy

❑ Am I using a strategy that will work for my general purpose (to inform, persuade, or accentuate)?

❑ Does my topic suggest a strategy? For example, a speech on the history of Mardi Gras calls for a strategy related to time (chronological).

❑ What does my audience need to know or what perspective do I want them to accept about my topic? What strategies would help them achieve the goals I have for them?

❑ Is the topic a difficult subject for my audience? Which strategies would produce the best results?

How Do You Make a Speech Out of a Strategy?

1 **Discover Your Main Points**
2 **Create Your Main Points**
3 **Expand with Subpoints**

1

Discover Your Main Points

As noted in Chapter 5, your main points are the major themes or thoughts you want to discuss about your topic. Sometimes the strategy you select to use for the speech will suggest the focus of the main points. For example, with the problem–solution strategy, you know you will have at least one main point for the problem and one for a solution.

However, you may not be ready to select a strategy until you have discovered your main points. Remember, creating a speech is not a perfectly linear process.

The best way to discover your main points is to make a list of everything you want to convey in the speech. Although there are numerous ways you could do this, the method shown at right works for many beginning students.

TIP: Seeing Connections
If you have trouble seeing themes or connections, try writing each comment in a complete sentence on the individual cards or pages. This method will also help you create your preparation outline.

Return to your specific purpose and central idea to make a list of answers to the following question: What details or thoughts do I want to express in my speech?

Put each individual answer to this question on a single note card or piece of paper. Make sure you put only one detail or thought on each card or piece of paper.

Now study these notes for themes or connections that might allow you to group them under broader themes.

Select the two to five most important themes as your main points for your speech. On average, most audience members can only remember two to five main points; do not get carried away with too many. Your time restraints may only allow for two or three.

What details do I want to express in my speech on the history of Mardi Gras?

Relationship to Catholicism

Founders: Le Monyne Brothers – March 3, 1699, est. of Point du Mardi Gras

1702 est. of Mobile as the first capital of French Louisiana

1720 – Biloxi

1723–New Orleans

Translate Mardi Gras

— 1600–1700S

1837–first documented parade

1870–Twelfth night revelers and King Cakes

1857–hard times for the festival and how the people saved it

— 1800S

1918-1919–cancelled because of WWI

1920-1930–struggled because of Prohibition and the Depression

1940-1990s–growth

This year

1990S–PRESENT

HISTORY – lends itself to a chronological strategy

THREE THEMES FOR MAIN POINTS COULD BE

2

Create Your Main Points

Effective main points will take some time to create. Doing so now will help you stay on track and save time. Aim for the following qualities to make your main points effective.

COMPLETE SENTENCES

Your main points should be complete thoughts, not only words or phrases. They should contain at least a noun and a verb.

Creating complete sentences will help you think in complete thoughts when you give the speech. Complete sentences will also help you be exact about what you want to say during each section of the speech.

For instance, the following incorrect example could be about anything related to candle making. You could be speaking about the history of candle making, the dangers of candle making, the mass production process, or the process of making candles at home.

INCORRECT:
I. Candle making

CORRECT:
I. The process of candle making is simple enough to do at home.

The correct example clarifies what you will speak about.

ONE IDEA IN EACH POINT

You should introduce only one idea in each main point. Watch for words like "and," "or," or "but" connecting two independent issues in one sentence.

→ See Chapter 5 (Tab 3) for discussion of covering only one issue at a time.

DECLARATIVE SENTENCES

Write your main points in declarative sentences, which should not be difficult because you tend to write most of your papers, letters, and notes this way. A declarative sentence simply states fact or argument and does not ask your audience to respond or take action. It states the main point you are making. Declarative sentences never end in a question mark.

INCORRECT:
I. Are LCD screens better than plasmas?
II. What are the pros and cons of an LCD and a plasma screen?
III. Which screen is cheaper?

CORRECT:
I. The positive qualities of current LCD screens make them better products than plasma screens.
II. Both types of televisions have potential negatives, but the LCD works best for most homes.
III. The price difference makes the LCD a better purchase.

COORDINATION

Your main points should adhere to coordination; that is, as much as possible, the main points are balanced or equal to each other in weight and level of ideas. They should not overtly relate to each other but should directly relate to your specific purpose.

For example, suppose your specific purpose is this:

To inform my audience about a few of the most influential American women painters.

In the following incorrect example, the main points relate back to the specific purpose, but they are unbalanced. You would spend most of the speech time on point one.

INCORRECT:

I. From the founding of this country through the mid-twentieth century, several American women painters influenced the art world.

II. Contemporary American women painters continue to set the new standard.

Instead, you might divide your main points into three significant periods of development. Doing so will allow you to coordinate and balance the amount of information to the artist highlighted. Plus, you will end with the most significant period of development for women painters. For example, few significant women artists in America were working prior to the 1800s, so your first main point could cover 1800–1874, marking the first significant period for female American painters. Your second main point could cover 1875–1974, and the last point could cover the new revolution of female painters from 1975 to the present.

CORRECT:

I. From 1800 to 1874, American women painters created genre art to appeal to the popular masses.

II. From 1875 to 1974, American women painters gained somewhat limited acceptance as professionals.

III. From 1975 to the present, American women painters have gained significant acceptance.

Within each main point, you would strive to select a similar number of influential painters to focus on and balance the information you have on each.

PARALLELISM

You use **parallelism** effectively when you arrange your words, phrases, or sentences in a similar pattern, which can help your main points stand out. For example, simply starting each main point with the same beginning pronoun can signal when you begin a new point and make it easier for your audience to remember the points.

I. Your classroom experience will be unlike your high school class expectations.

II. Your social life will be different from what it was in high school.

III. Your everyday responsibilities will be different.

→ See Chapter 8 (Tab 4) for further discussion on using parallelism throughout your speech.

At this point, you should have the best strategy and main points for your topic and audience. Now you can begin to give body or substance to your speech.

CONFIDENCE BOOSTER
Parallelism, like repetition or mnemonic devices, can help you remember your speech. If you use the devices, you will spend less time looking at your notes and you will have more confidence in remembering the key issues.

3

Expand with Subpoints

The subpoints are the filling or content that give your speech substance. Subpoints elaborate on each of the main points. Their job is to clarify, emphasize, or provide detail for the main point they support. In the subpoints, you will use your support materials (statistics, facts, testimony, examples, etc.). You can have multiple layers of subpoints. Your subpoints can also have subpoints. The number of subpoints and layers will vary depending on how much materials you have to convey or need to use. Remember, adhering to proper outline format will help you see how your subpoints relate to the main points and to each other.

I. First main point

    A. First subpoint of I

        1. First subpoint of A

            a. First subpoint of 1

            b. Second subpoint of 1

        2. Second subpoint of A

    B. Second subpoint of I

II. Second main point

Related subpoints (indicated here by colors) should use consistent symbols and alignment.

➜ See Chapter 5 (Tab 3) for a more detailed discussion on outline format.

Follow these suggestions when creating your subpoints.

- You should use full sentences.
- You should introduce only one idea in each subpoint.
- You should adhere to coordination and subordination. Each subpoint on the same level should coordinate or be equal with each other subpoint. Those subpoints directly below a main point or a subpoint should be subordinate, or secondary, to the point above them.

- Your subpoints do not need to follow the same organizational strategy you used for you main points. They can have a strategy of their own or be arranged as a formal argument.

➜ See Tab 7 for more information on argumentation.

COMMON ORGANIZATIONAL PROBLEMS

If you follow the outlining and organizational suggestions in Chapter 5 and this chapter, you should not have many, if any, organizational problems. However, it is smart to watch out for the more common ones.

COMMON ORGANIZATIONAL PROBLEM	PREVENTION/SOLUTION
Your selected organizational strategy does not fit the topic or audience.	• Before you commit to a strategy, always consider what your audience needs to know (or do) about your topic. • While you consider the audience's needs, keep your general purpose, specific purpose, and central idea in mind. • Then select the strategy that helps you best fulfill the audience's needs as well as your goal for the speech.
You stop adhering to the arrangement of the strategy at some point during the speech.	• Refer to your textbook several times during the process of creating your outline to refresh your memory about the strategy you are using. • Set up an outline shell or template that mirrors the strategy before you start filling in support materials.
You have too many main points.	• Remember that most classroom speeches will only have time for two or three main points unless the strategy calls for more. • Longer speeches might make up to seven main points work, but your audience will have trouble remembering more than that. • If you feel like you need more main points, check your specific purpose. It may be too broad or you may have strayed from it.

You do not have enough time for the body of the speech.	• Check to see if you are spending too much time on the introduction or conclusion. Remember, the approximate formula for breaking down your speech time is:
	    Introduction: 15%
	    Body: 75%
	    Conclusion: 10%

You are spending too much time on one or two main points and cannot cover the rest efficiently.	• Try to keep each of your subpoints equal under a given main point. This is called a **standard of balance.** No one will be timing how long you stay on a point, but you do not want to shortchange a point.

Pedro's Speech

Pedro attends a university that requires students with a sophomore standing or below to live on campus. Students exempted from this policy are either married, single parents, residents with a permanent address within the local county, over the age of 22, or classified as military veterans. Pedro would like to see this policy changed. Overcrowded residential halls, cafeterias, and parking lots are making life on campus miserable for many students. Some have even transferred to other schools.

PEDRO'S SPECIFIC PURPOSE AND CENTRAL IDEA

Pedro will give his speech at a campus assembly. The audience will include both students and administrators. He knows the majority of students agree with him, so his primary concern is to get the administrators to see the key problems with the policy. Pedro crafted the following specific purpose and central idea.

Specific purpose: To persuade my audience that more students should be allowed to live off campus.

Central idea: Our university's increased enrollment has caused overcrowding in the residence halls and parking lots, so the university should relax the campus housing policy.

HIS ORGANIZATIONAL STRATEGY OPTIONS

After reviewing the nine different strategies he could use to arrange his speech, Pedro came up with this list of alternatives for a persuasive speech. Almost immediately, the problem–solution strategy seemed the best fit for his speech topic and mixed audience. He could demonstrate for the students and the administration what the current problems are and then offer a solution.

~~Causal~~

~~Comparative~~

~~Chronological~~

~~Order of Intensity~~

~~Monroe's Motivated Sequence~~ ←

Pedro immediately eliminated the first four because they did not fit his topic or specific purpose.

This option would only work if Pedro is calling his audience to action.

Problem–Solution

~~Refutation~~ ←

Refutation strategy will not work because the reasons for the original policy were good, but other issues are causing the policy to fail now.

CREATING HIS SPEECH

Following the description for a problem–solution strategy as well as the proper way to write his main points, Pedro created two main points.

I. In recent years, Blackhawk University has seen a significant increase in student enrollment, putting a strain on campus resources.

II. If the university adjusts the on-campus living requirement for students, then Blackhawk can continue to increase admissions.

After considering the information related to the problem, Pedro constructed his subpoints.

I. In recent years, Blackhawk University has seen a significant increase in student enrollment, putting a strain on campus resources.
   A. For the past four years, locating enough rooms for students has been difficult.
   B. Parking on campus is difficult at best.

II. If the university adjusts the on-campus living requirement for students, then Blackhawk can continue to increase admissions.
   A. Resource strain could be reduced if students were allowed to move off campus after completing 24 hours of classes instead of 48.
   B. Resource strain could be further reduced if students with a 3.5 GPA or higher in their first semester and a high school GPA of 3.6 or higher could appeal to move off campus after their first semester.

With this main structure of his speech completed, Pedro is ready to fill in the support for his two main points and create his introduction and conclusion.

7

INTRODUCING AND CONCLUDING YOUR SPEECH

Introduction

Think about how the networks on television work to get you to watch a program. They give a tidbit just as the previous show ends, and then they try to draw you into staying with the program before they go to the first break. They never show the first commercial until you are laughing or in suspense so that you will want to "stay tuned." Likewise, if it is a weekly series, they will leave you at the end of the program excited and motivated to return, often with a "WOW" moment. You are hooked and will respond the way they want by returning to the show the following week.

The same is true for the introduction and conclusion of a good speech. The introduction must grab your audience's attention first and foremost. Your conclusion needs to let them down easy but offer a "WOW" moment. Your audience should be eager to respond to the topic as you intended. If you leave your audience breathless, speechless, or wanting to clap, you have given them a "WOW" moment and a powerful speech.

CHAPTER 5: Outlining Your Speech 137

CHAPTER 6: Organizing the Speech Body 173

CHAPTER 7 CONTENTS

What Should Your Introduction Do? 196
1 Capture Your Audience's Attention 196
2 Build Your Credibility Early 197
3 Demonstrate Audience Relevance 197
4 Introduce the Topic and Preview the Speech 197

What Are Effective Attention-Getters? 198
1 Facts and Statistics 199
2 Quotations 199
3 Stories, Narratives, Illustrations, or Anecdotes 200
4 Humor 200
5 Questions 201
6 References to Historical or Recent Events 201
7 References to Self, Occasion, or Audience 202
8 References to Prior Speeches 202
9 Displays of Talent 203

How Do You Organize an Introduction? 204

What Should Your Conclusion Do? 206
1 Signal the Ending 207
2 Summarize 207
3 Elicit a Response 207
4 Create an Impact One Last Time 207

What Can You Use as a "WOW" Statement? 208
1 Quotations 208
2 Stories, Narratives, Illustrations, or Anecdotes 208
3 Humor 209
4 Rhetorical Questions 209
5 Challenges to the Audience 209
6 References Back to the Introduction 209

How Do You Organize a Conclusion? 210

Lacey's Speech 212

Tab 3 Review 214

What Should Your Introduction Do?

1 **Capture Your Audience's Attention**
2 **Build Your Credibility Early**
3 **Demonstrate Audience Relevance**
4 **Introduce the Topic and Preview the Speech**

Many beginning speakers miss the importance of literally *launching* into their speech. The introduction should be one of the most exciting, moving, and interesting moments of the speech. Think of the emotional and physical feelings you have when you hear or say the word *launch*; that is exactly what your introduction should feel like.

1
Capture Your Audience's Attention

Think about the noise and distractions you hear as you enter a room of people, like a classroom. People are talking about the weather, recent events, family issues, or dating or work problems. They are moving chairs, shuffling papers, texting, or checking messages. Their minds and bodies are wandering, and you have to get them to focus on you and your topic. As people who love fishing or the Texas Longhorns would say, you have to "hook 'em," or capture their attention.

This function of the introduction may be the most important—you have to get the audience's attention before you can do anything else with your speech. Good speakers spend a lot of time crafting their attention-getters.

Take a look at the following attention-getter used by Andalee, a student, for her speech on laundry skills.

> Classes have been in session a few weeks now, and I bet the laundry monster is about to bust out of your closet. You may not have a clean pair of socks or, worse yet, a clean outfit for your date tomorrow night. Maybe you did a load and everything white came out pink because you missed sorting out a red sock. Add in special laundry care instructions or a stain, and your stress level over how to do your laundry hits the top of the chart. How much bleach do you really need to use? Does liquid fabric softener go in before the rinse cycle or during? Should you use enzymes? Heck, what are enzymes?

Andalee uses anecdotes, questions, and other attention-grabbing tactics.

➔ See "What Are Effective Attention-Getters?" on page 198 for more details.

2
Build Your Credibility Early

Your introduction should begin to reveal your credibility as a speaker with ethical consideration for your audience and a relationship with the topic. As discussed in the Overview, Aristotle referred to the speaker's credibility as *ethos*. The audience needs to perceive you as kind, competent, caring, honest, and excited about your topic and speech event. You can start establishing ethos in the introduction by:

- Being confident—practice your introduction until you are sure of it and your abilities
- Demonstrating your knowledge of the topic
- Pointing out what you have in common with the audience or topic
- Making it evident that you are sincere and concerned for the audience's well-being

Building your credibility in the introduction does not need to be complicated. In most speeches, employing an effective delivery style and using a simple sentence begins the process. You will continue to build credibility throughout the speech. In her laundry speech, Andalee drew on her experience:

> As a mother of a toddler and as a spouse, I wash laundry all the time! I have spent a lot of time researching the best and cheapest way to keep our clothes looking great.

TIP: Delivering the Introduction
Using an energetic delivery from the introduction of your speech onward can also build interest and get your audience excited about the topic.

3
Demonstrate Audience Relevance

Audiences want to know quickly why your speech is relevant to them. An early statement about what your topic has to offer can demonstrate that they have something to gain from listening to you. For example, Andalee highlighted relevance by adding this statement after establishing her credibility:

> As a college student like you, I have to use time wisely and keep the cost of replacing damaged clothes or purchasing expensive laundry aids to a minimum.

4
Introduce the Topic and Preview the Speech

After capturing your audience's attention, you need to give listeners a preview of what they can expect from your speech. This step moves the focus from you to the essence of your speech and usually consists of a single sentence or two, briefly outlining your speech. For example:

> Today, I want to help you see that doing the laundry doesn't have to be stressful or expensive. Actually, it can be quite easy if you take the time to properly sort your laundry, purchase a few basic cleaning items, and follow proper washer and dryer techniques.

In these two sentences, Andalee has given a quick preview of what her speech will cover.

What Are Effective Attention-Getters?

1 **Facts and Statistics**

2 **Quotations**

3 **Stories, Narratives, Illustrations, or Anecdotes**

4 **Humor**

5 **Questions**

6 **References to Historical or Recent Events**

7 **References to Self, Occasion, or Audience**

8 **References to Prior Speeches**

9 **Displays of Talent**

An ***attention-getter*** is something you say, show, or do to get your audience to focus on you and on the topic and goal of your speech. In most cases, it should be the first words spoken or the first images or actions shown.

Rarely should you say or show anything extra before you begin your speech. Otherwise, you might diminish the power of your attention-getter, as well as your speech itself. For example, in most classroom speeches, you do not need to state your name or make any other statements; rather, you should simply launch into your speech.

Attention-getters have a big job, so spend time crafting them, trying them out on someone else, and practicing them until they sound natural.

Attention-getters need you to be as creative as possible. They need to be unique, startling, awe inspiring, or otherwise compelling in order to hook your audience's attention. Remember the last time you saw a movie trailer that completely mesmerized you? In a short period of time, the music, graphics, words, actions, actors, and/or special effects caught your attention so much that you stopped whatever else you were doing. Perhaps you even held your breath as you watched it. Although few speakers have the resources to create an attention-getter at the level of most movie trailers, you can create the same effect with just a little work.

Generally, you will use one of the nine creative tactics discussed in this section.

1
Facts and Statistics

Facts and statistics can help you point to a remarkable situation or problem. They can be very vivid or shocking even though they are condensed. For example:

> According to the Centers for Disease Control and Prevention at cdc.gov, heart disease is the leading cause of death for women. In 2006, 315,930 women died from heart disease. That was more than one in every four, or 26%, of deaths. In 2006, about 6.9% of all white women, 8.8% of black women, and 6.6% of Mexican American women were living with some type of coronary heart disease. Almost two-thirds of the women who died had no previous symptoms. Around the same number of women and men die each year of heart disease in the United States. Heart disease is no longer a "man's disease."

Facts and statistics work best if they are unfamiliar to the audience; they can then have a shock value and engage the audience. In the example above, the facts and statistics about cardiovascular disease may surprise listeners, as many view it as a disease more likely to strike men.

2
Quotations

Quotations are words or passages written or said by someone else. For an attention-getter, you want a succinct and interesting quotation from someone who will raise your credibility. You may use word-for-word quotations or paraphrases. The words or passage may come from a speech, novel, poem, short story, play, TV or movie dialogue, or another similar source.

> "To stand at the edge of the sea, to sense the ebb and flow of the tides, to feel the breath of a mist moving over a great salt marsh, to watch the flight of shore birds that have swept up and down the surf lines of the continents for untold thousands of year, to see the running of the old eels and the young shad to the sea, is to have knowledge of things that are as nearly eternal as any earthly life can be," writes the famous environmental activist Rachel Carson, in her 1941 book *Under the Sea-Wind*.

TIPS: Using Attention-Getters
- Facts and statistics are most effective if they are previously unknown to the audience and come from a reliable source.
- Make sure you give the name of the person you are quoting and his or her qualifications or relationship to your topic. Include enough of an oral citation to direct your audience to the appropriate source.
- If the quotation is long—requiring you to read it—practice it over and over for dramatic effect. You want to maintain as much eye contact as possible.
- If you are using pictures and video for illustration, practice with them to smoothly incorporate them into the speech. Do not just tack them on to the beginning.

PRACTICING ETHICS
Remember to cite your attention-getter's source. Giving the source at the end of the attention-getter is often most effective.

3
Stories, Narratives, Illustrations, or Anecdotes

Stories, narratives, illustrations, or anecdotes are vivid accounts that can personalize your speech by helping the audience identify with the topic. The accounts should be interesting, evoking, and entertaining. You should not need to explain them. Be creative and selective. The accounts can be true or fictional, from your personal life or from broader arenas. Be careful if you are telling your own story, because you may become too emotional or the audience may have such heightened empathy for you that it is hard for them to listen.

Here's a short example.

> Zohar is a nine-month-old boy. He does not have the comforts of growing up that you and I have. Zohar coughs violently. An IV pumps medicine into his shriveled arm—medicine that may soon run out. His ribs show clearly through his fragile skin. Zohar's parents hold his tiny hands and pray for his recovery, but Zohar has malaria and severe malnutrition. He is near death. Zohar is only one—one of thousands who will die, one of millions affected. Zohar was born in the region of Darfur, in a country called Sudan, on the continent of Africa, where children just like him are being forced out of their homes by violence as we speak. Journalist Emily Wax, in her June 2004 *Washington Post* article "In Sudan, Death and Denial," introduces us to Zohar and his family.

This example has just enough emotional appeal to draw the audience in.

4
Humor

Humor can build a positive relationship with your audience and lighten up a dry or complex topic. However, you must be careful when using humor if you want to be effective and ethical. Any use of humor should:

- Relate to your audience, topic, and/or occasion
- Be funny (try it out on someone else)
- Not be demeaning to a particular group of people
- Be understandable to your audience (be careful of using humor across cultures or subcultures that might not understand the joke)

If you are giving a speech in an introduction-to-college class on how to study for exams, you might tell a joke like this:

> One day, a professor was giving a big test to his students. He handed out all of the tests and went back to his desk to wait. Once the test was over, the students all handed the tests back in. The professor noticed that one of the students had attached a $100 bill to his test with a note saying, "A dollar per point."
>
> The next class, the professor handed the test back out.
>
> This student got back his test and $64 change. (*pause*)
>
> Clearly, there must be better ways to get a good grade on an exam than this joke from teach-nology.com might suggest. Today, I would like to offer you some advice….

You might get a few laughs if your humor is relevant, understandable, and appropriate.

5
Questions

You can use a question or a series of questions to direct your audience's attention to your topic. The questions can be asked in a manner to get a direct response or posed as **rhetorical questions** when you do not want a response but simply want to focus audience attention. Here are some examples:

Response-evoking questions:

> By a show of hands, how many of you are not allowed by the university to bring a car to campus? (*wait*) How many of you had trouble finding a parking place on campus today? (*wait*) How many of you have had to park far away at night and then walk home alone? (*wait*)

Rhetorical questions:

> Are you tired of taking the bus to the mall or bumming a ride because the university won't allow you to bring a car to campus? Are you sick of being late to class because you can't find a parking place? Are you mad that you have to walk home from a far away parking lot at night? If so…

Both types of questions can have some problems that you need to be aware of and try to prevent. The response-evoking questions can take a lot of time, they can sidetrack your audience too much, and the answers to the questions may not be what you expect. Rhetorical questions can cause audience members to linger too long in the thoughts or feelings you evoked, resulting in them becoming sidetracked. Beginning speakers often perceive questions as the easiest method and rely too heavily on them, lessening their effectiveness. Use the best method, not the easiest.

6
References to Historical or Recent Events

Depending on the purpose of your speech, the audience, the timeliness of your speech, and your relationship to those factors, referring to a historical or recent event can be an effective attention-getter. In some situations, it might even be necessary, if that event is momentous. For example, many speeches given in the months after September 11, 2001, began with a reference to that horrific event.

In a more recent example, President Barack Obama made the following references in a health care speech to Congress on September 9, 2009.

> Madame Speaker, Vice President Biden, Members of Congress, and the American people:

> When I spoke here last winter, this nation was facing the worst economic crisis since the Great Depression. We were losing an average of 700,000 jobs per month. Credit was frozen. And our financial system was on the verge of collapse.

> As any American who is still looking for work or a way to pay their bills will tell you, we are by no means out of the woods. A full and vibrant recovery is many months away. And I will not let up until those Americans who seek jobs can find them; until those businesses that seek capital and credit can thrive; until all responsible homeowners can stay in their homes. That is our ultimate goal. But thanks to the bold and decisive action we have taken since January, I can stand here with confidence and say that we have pulled this economy back from the brink.

7

References to Self, Occasion, or Audience

When your background, the speaking occasion, and/or the audience has a special relationship to the speech topic, referring to these elements as your attention-getter can be effective as well as important to setting the tone of the speech.

For example:

> Good morning, Chairperson Allen, members of the restoration committee, the staff, and all of you from the community. It is my pleasure and honor to deliver the keynote address at this rededication of Smithburg's Community Library.
>
> What a great day for a celebration of a building that has stood the test of time and brought so much joy to so many people. Your many hours of work and fund-raising to make this day possible shine brighter today than the sunlight against the blue backdrop of the clear sky.
>
> As a former member of this town, I spent countless hours as a child reading books or attending the library's programs while waiting for my mother to finish work. For many of Smithburg's children during the 1960s, this was our second home. The community library can and should be the heart of a small town.

Although not necessary to do all three, notice how this speaker refers to the audience, the occasion, and her background.

8

References to Prior Speeches

When someone else speaks prior to you and his or her speech was significantly important or moving, referring to that speech can be a great way to begin. Doing so will take your audience back to the emotions felt at that earlier time. However, this form of attention-getter can be difficult to craft if you do not have enough time between the previous speech and yours.

> Yesterday, in his State of the College address, President Jones outlined the growth this grand institution has experienced in the last few years. As he noted, we are experiencing great success. Quoting the Swedish soccer manager, Sven-Göran Eriksson, President Jones reminded us that "The greatest barrier to success is the fear of failure." Today, I am here not to talk about barriers. I am….

This speaker clearly had a day to incorporate a prior speech into his or her speech. If you are speaking immediately after someone else, a reference of this sort can be difficult for the beginning speaker.

9
Displays of Talent

With some topics and if you have a related talent, you can grab your audience's attention through a brief display of that talent. For example, if you are giving a speech about the importance of being multilingual and you can speak several languages fluently, you might start the speech off by saying "hello and welcome" in a few different languages. Or, when speaking to a group interested in learning American Sign Language, you could begin by signing a short statement. You might even use more nonverbal and/or artistic ways to gain an audience's attention, such as doing a short segment of a dance routine or singing a song that relates to the topic.

The key to this attention-getter is to be sure your talent is strong enough to increase your ethos. Equally important, the talent must have a significant relationship to the topic and audience.

LOCATING ATTENTION-GETTERS ON THE INTERNET

STATISTICS:
www.gallup.com
www.census.com
www.prb.org
www.data.gov
www.library.vanderbilt.edu/romans/fdtf
www.usa.gov/Citizen/Find_Services.shtml

QUOTATIONS:
www.bartleby.com
www.bemorecreative.com
www.famous-quotes-online.com
www.coolnsmart.com
www.toomanyquotes.com
www.brainyquotes.com

STORIES:
www.inspirationpeak.com

HUMOR:
www.funny-jokes-online.com

HISTORICAL/RECENT EVENTS:
aad.archives.gov/aad

GREAT SPEECHES:
www.americanrhetoric.com/speechbank.htm

CHECKLIST for Using an Attention-Getter

❏ Will my attention-getter work?

❏ Is my attention-getter appropriate for the occasion?

❏ Does my attention-getter relate to my topic, audience, or the occasion? Will my audience easily see that relationship?

❏ Have I made sure that my material is not inappropriate or offensive to my audience?

How Do You Organize an Introduction?

Most speech instructors suggest creating the body of the speech before you write either the introduction or conclusion. You need to know the tone and content of your speech before you can introduce or conclude it.

Once you are ready to write your introduction, its major parts should correspond to the four functions discussed earlier in this chapter. Your introduction should be no more than 15 percent of the total speech time, so you usually have under a minute to carry out these functions.

Any introduction should start with a good attention-getter, but you can present the other parts in just about any order. Beginning speakers often have the impulse to introduce themselves first. However, if you will be introduced or if the audience already knows you, this step is not necessary. Remember that the first thing you do or say should be designed to grab the audience's attention.

The template below and the example on the next page suggest the two most common arrangements for the parts of an introduction.

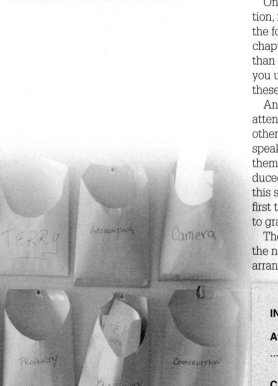

INTRODUCTION

Attention-getter: ....
....

Credibility material: ....
....

Relevance to audience: ....
....

Preview of speech: ....
....

Jameel is creating a speech on compulsive shopping for his class assignment. After many drafts and revisions, his introduction looks like this:

INTRODUCTION

Attention-getter: Shopping—it's the American pastime. It gives us a temporary high and a feeling of enjoyment we can't find quite the same way in other activities. As Robert Coombs suggests in his 2004 book, the *Handbook of Addictive Disorders*, "Almost all of us have purchased goods at some time to cheer ourselves up, and many see money and material possessions as tangible signs of personal success. We use consumption to improve our image, self-esteem, or relationship with others." But the questions are how far is too far, and how much is too much? And should you consider yourself or a loved one a compulsive shopper?

Relevance to audience: According to a 2006 survey by the Stanford University School of Medicine, 5.8 percent of the U.S. population—about 17 million people—are compulsive shoppers. That means two of us in this room might be considered compulsive shoppers.

Credibility material: Personally, I enjoy the many highs of shopping and have at times spent more than I should on one trip to the mall. But does that make me a compulsive shopper?

Preview of speech: In this speech, I will explore compulsive shopping as an addictive disorder, who tends to have the disorder, and how it can be treated.

Jameel has correctly included all four parts of an introduction. What attention-getter tactics can you identify? How has Jameel applied some of those tactics to other parts of his introduction?

CHECKLIST for Your Introduction
❏ Do I have an effective attention-getter?
❏ Do I begin to establish my credibility?
❏ Do I establish relevance between my audience and the topic?
❏ Do I preview the speech?

CONFIDENCE BOOSTER
Most beginning speakers experience their strongest communication apprehension in the first few minutes of a speech. A solid and creative introduction can help you feel more comfortable. Never plan to just "wing" or improvise your introduction. Be prepared; practice the introduction completely and multiple times. Doing so will help you feel more relaxed.

What Should Your Conclusion Do?

1 **Signal the Ending**
2 **Summarize**
3 **Elicit a Response**
4 **Create an Impact One Last Time**

The best way to think about a conclusion is to see it as almost the reverse of your introduction, or that they are very similar and frame your speech. You will use some of the same tactics in the conclusion that you did in the introduction. Although you usually will not need to demonstrate your credibility with the topic or show the relevance to the audience at this point in the speech, you do need to review what you have said, tell the audience what you want them to do, and "WOW" them one last time. Ultimately, your conclusion should provide closure, leaving your audience enlightened and satisfied.

Do not rush creating your conclusion or cut short the process because you think you can craft it as you give the speech. Your conclusion is the last moment you have to increase your audience's understanding and appreciation, persuade them, or entertain them. Take advantage of this significant moment.

The next few pages will help you harness the power of your conclusions.

1
Signal the Ending

Think of this function like the end of a good movie or book. Throughout, the viewer or reader has moved along a path that builds to one defining moment—the ending. In speeches, you need to signal that ending. The most common ways to signal that the end is near are:

- A vocal change, such as slowing down and beginning to lower your intensity
- A physical change, such as moving from behind the lectern (often accompanied by a vocal change)
- A language signal, such as "In conclusion…" or "Today, we have…"

Once you have signaled the conclusion, you should not bring up new information about your topic. Otherwise, you are taking your audience back to information that should be in the body of the speech, which is confusing.

2
Summarize

This is your last chance to tell your audience about your topic in a way that will help them remember it. This statement should effectively and concisely restate your speech's main points.

For example, a speech informing your audience about counterfeit medicines popping up for sale in places like the Internet could have a summary statement such as:

> We've learned a lot about counterfeit medicine today. However, what's important to remember is, first, counterfeit medicine is widespread; second, counterfeit medicine is difficult to contain; and third, there are steps you can take to protect yourself from counterfeits.

3
Elicit a Response

Ideally, you do not want your audience to come away from your speech as passive vessels—taking in your speech but doing nothing with it. Therefore, you need to elicit, or bring forth, the response you wish them to have in relation to your topic. In other words, tell the audience what you want them to do with the information you have just given them. For example:

> Now that you know that counterfeit medicines can be a problem, it is time for you to take action to protect yourself and your loved ones.…

Or, as another example, at the end of a toast:

> Please join me in toasting our new mayor.…

4
Create an Impact One Last Time

Finally, the very end of your speech should take one last moment to really make your speech memorable and leave your audience with an intense feeling. That feeling should almost compel them to clap enthusiastically. That is the "WOW" moment of a speech. Because this moment is important to the effectiveness of your conclusion, the next section of this book will help you craft an effective "WOW" statement.

What Can You Use as a "WOW" Statement?

1 Quotations
2 Stories, Narratives, Illustrations, or Anecdotes
3 Humor
4 Rhetorical Questions
5 Challenges to the Audience
6 References Back to the Introduction

1 Quotations

When using a quotation to end a speech, the quotation may have a direct relationship with the topic or may be somewhat metaphorical in capturing the essence of the topic.

For example, for a speech related to the Apollo 11 landing or a speech motivating the audience to volunteer, you could end with:

> As Neil Armstrong said, "That's one small step for man; one giant leap for mankind."

2 Stories, Narratives, Illustrations, or Anecdotes

These devices help humanize your topic and can appeal one last time to your audience's emotions. In a conclusion, keep them as short as possible and try not to read them directly, which would lower their impact.

For example:

> I would like to end with a story about my grandfather. During World War II, he….

Emotional power (pathos) can be an effective way to help your audience remember your speech.

TIP: Use Attention-Getter Techniques
The best way to think about a "WOW" statement is to treat it like the attention-getter in the introduction. Many of the techniques you can use to grab your audience's attention can dazzle them at the conclusion of the speech as well.

3

Humor

Laughter is a positive experience for most individuals and can ease an audience out of your speech. Remember to make any use of humor relate to your audience, topic, and/or occasion; test the material to see if it is really funny; avoid demeaning humor; and make sure your audience will understand the joke.

For example, you might end a speech on reducing stress with this bumper-sticker saying:

> "Stress is when you wake up screaming and you realize you haven't fallen asleep yet."

4

Rhetorical Questions

A series of rhetorical questions can focus how you want your audience to think about your topic and the goal.

For example, in a speech to persuade college students to help in an afterschool program, these questions could end the speech:

> See these children? (*click to slide 5*) Do you want them to end up like other inner-city children? Do you want them to be another crime statistic?

This speaker pairs the rhetorical questions with an image to increase the effect.

5

Challenges to the Audience

Ending by challenging your audience to act in a certain way can focus their attention on that behavior.

For example, adding a few more questions to the previous example challenges the audience to make a proposed response.

> See these children? (*click to slide 5*) Do you want them to end up like other inner-city children? Do you want them to be another crime statistic? Do you have 20 minutes a week that you could give toward changing the lives of these children? I do, and I hope you will join me in volunteering in the Glenwood afterschool program.

6

References Back to the Introduction

This type of "WOW" statement creates a frame for your speech by referring back to the attention-getter you used in your introduction.

For example, if you use the first few lines of a poem to start a speech, you might end with more of the poem. Or, if you tell a story at the beginning, returning to that moment of emotional appeal and finishing the story can nicely frame your speech.

➜ See page 211 for an illustration of this technique.

PRACTICING ETHICS

Be ethical when using humor. Many jokes and humorous stories can be inappropriate or derogatory. Review the discussion about the ethical use of humor in attention-getters (page 200) if needed.

How Do You Organize a Conclusion?

Your conclusion should be approximately 5 percent of your speech time. This is not much time, and you do not want to leave your audience feeling either like you suddenly stopped speaking or you went on forever after you signaled the ending. So it is important to spend some time constructing your conclusion.

> **CONCLUSION**
>
> **Summary statement:** ....
> ....
>
> **Audience response statement:** ....
> ....
>
> **WOW statement:** ....
> ....

As in your introduction, the organization of your conclusion can vary; but generally, the above template and the example on the next page show the basic order. Remember to always end with a "WOW" statement.

For the end of his classroom speech about unrest in Darfur, Kyril crafted this succinct and moving conclusion.

CONCLUSION

Summary statement: I hope my speech today has offered you some insight into the Darfur issues. We have discussed the history of Darfur, why the violence in the region continues to worsen, and how we can make an effort to bring about peace.

Audience response statement: My purpose in giving this speech is to persuade you that even as citizens of the United States, we can take action to save lives.

WOW statement: Remember nine-month-old Zohar from the beginning of my speech? Zohar did not make it—and he became one of the thousands who died. To his parents, Zohar was their only child. To the world, Zohar is a statistic. Your actions could make Zohar, a child and someone's son, one of the last to be a statistic.

Kyril has correctly included all three parts of a conclusion. Notice how his "WOW" statement refers back to a story in his introduction and finishes that story, to end on a note of emotional appeal.

CHECKLIST for Your Conclusion

❑ Do I signal the ending of the speech?
❑ Do I end the speech soon after signaling the conclusion?
❑ Do I restate my main points?
❑ Do I challenge the audience?
❑ Do I have the best possible "WOW" statement ending my speech?
❑ Do I have the necessary oral citations, if any are needed?

Lacey's Speech

Lacey is from St. Louis, Missouri, and is attending college nearby. She has to give an informative speech in class, and many of her classmates are from other states or countries. Because fall break is just around the corner, Lacey decides to tell them about her hometown of St. Louis in hopes they might travel there over their three-day weekend.

CREATING AN EFFECTIVE INTRODUCTION

After conducting the research and writing the body of her speech, Lacey was ready to create her introduction.

The attention-getter

Lacey knew a lot about the city, but she found some unique facts that she didn't know and decided to turn those into a series of questions as her attention-getter.

> Do you know where the first kindergarten was founded? Where Dr. Pepper and 7-Up were first introduced? Where ice cream and peanut butter were invented? Where the first lung cancer surgery was performed? You may be surprised that one city is the answer to all of these questions, and it is only about an hour and half away. The answer—St. Louis, Missouri, according to the St. Louis Convention and Visitors Commission at explorestlouis.com.

Demonstrating her credibility

Being one of the few students in the class from Missouri, Lacey saw a natural connection to demonstrating her credibility.

> My family has lived in St. Louis for generations, and during the past 18 years, I've come to love the city for many reasons. It's one of my favorite places in the world to be.

Showing audience relevance

Lacey's speech is scheduled a week before the college's three-day fall break. Lacey knows everyone will want to get away but may not have a lot of money for travel. She decides that this is a great way to show her audience what her speech has to offer them.

> Because our fall break is next week and we are all looking for something special to do on a college student's budget, I thought I would introduce you to what St. Louis has to offer—just a short car ride away.

Previewing her speech

Lacey's last step in her introduction is to preview her speech for the audience.

> I'm going to tell you about three of the main attractions that make St. Louis a great place to visit: first, the St. Louis Arch; second, the home of the St. Louis Cardinals baseball team, Busch Stadium; and lastly, Forest Park.

CREATING AN EFFECTIVE CONCLUSION

With her introduction and the body of her speech completed, Lacey had only one more part to finish—her conclusion.

Signaling the ending and summarizing

As Lacey creates her conclusion, she reminds herself to keep it short and to not introduce new material after she signals the ending of the speech and summarizes her points.

> So if you're feeling bored, broke, and still want to have an exciting weekend, you should make the hour and a half drive to St. Louis. The historical Gateway Arch, the new Busch Stadium, and beautiful Forest Park are all affordable and waiting for you and your friends.

Eliciting a response

Just as she did in the introduction, Lacey reminds the audience that what she wants them to do is go to her hometown for an inexpensive but exciting weekend.

> Don't wait until the weekend is over. Fill up your car, grab some snacks, and head east on Interstate 70. You can't miss it. I'm heading home to all St. Louis has to offer and I hope you do, too.

Concluding with a "WOW" statement

Lacey's grandmother's favorite movie is *Meet Me in St. Louis* with Judy Garland. Lacey has seen it several times, and she knew it offered a "WOW" ending for her speech in a song sung by Garland.

> As Judy Garland sang,
>   "Don't tell me the lights are shining
>   Anyplace but there
>   We will dance the 'Hoochie-Koochie'
>   I will be your 'Tootsie-Wootsie'
>   If you will meet me in St. LOO-eee"

Tab 3: Review

CHAPTER 5 REVIEW QUESTIONS

1. List and briefly explain the nine qualities of an effective outline.
2. What are the three different types of outlines, and why should you use each one?
3. Explain the four different types of links and give an example of each.
4. Using the appropriate style manual for your class, create a source page entry for this book.

CHAPTER 6 REVIEW QUESTIONS

1. Name three strategies you could use for an informative speech, and explain why each is an effective choice for informing.
2. Name three different strategies you might use for a persuasive speech, and explain why each is an effective choice for persuading.
3. How should you determine which strategy is the best for your speech?
4. What are the five main qualities you should adhere to when creating your main points? Briefly explain them.

CHAPTER 7 REVIEW QUESTIONS

1. What are the four functions of a speech introduction?
2. What are nine types of attention-getters you can use? Write an example of one.
3. What are the four functions of a speech conclusion?
4. What are six types of "WOW" statements you can use? Write an example of one.

TERMS TO REMEMBER

Chapter 5
introduction (141)
body (141)
main points (141)
subpoints (141)
links (141)
conclusion (141)
working outlines (152)
preparation outlines (154)
delivery outlines (158)
transitions (161)
signposts (162)
internal previews (162)
internal reviews (163)

Chapter 6
strategy (173)
chronological strategy (176)
topical strategy (177)
spatial strategy (177)
causal strategy (178)
order of intensity strategy (178)
comparative strategy (179)
comparative advantage (179)
problem–solution strategy (180)
refutation strategy (181)
Monroe's motivated sequence (182)
parallelism (189)
standard of balance (191)

CHAPTER 7
attention-getter (198)
quotations (199)
rhetorical questions (201)

Introduction

These quotations from famous speeches throughout history demonstrate the power of language. You may recognize most of them and may even be able to quote one or two. King's repetition of the evocative phrase "I have a dream," Truth's use of a straightforward rhetorical question, and Henry's as well as Clinton's use of parallelism help etch these quotations into our minds. Like these speakers, you can learn to harness the power of language. This chapter will offer you advice, examples, and tools for using language to its fullest potential to help your speech be a success. You will learn why language is powerful, how to use it effectively, and how to boost your language's distinctiveness.

CHAPTER 8 CONTENTS

What Makes Language So Important?	216
1 Meaning	216
2 Culture	218
3 Power	219
How Can You Use Language Effectively?	220
1 Be Correct	220
2 Be Clear	222
3 Be Specific	223
4 Be Appropriate	224
5 Use Oral Style	226
6 Be Distinctive	227
How Can You Boost Your Distinctiveness?	228
1 Use Vivid Language	228
2 Use Speech Devices	232
Lewis's Speech	234
Chapter 9: Delivering Your Speech	237
Chapter 10: Using Presentation Aids	261
Tab 4 Review	298

"*Ain't I a woman?*"[2]

SOJOURNER TRUTH

"*I know not what course others may take; but as for me, give me liberty, or give me death!*"[3]

PATRICK HENRY

"*And let us heed the call so that we can create a world in which every woman is treated with respect and dignity, every boy and girl is loved and cared for equally, and every family has the hope of a strong and stable future.*"[4]

HILLARY RODHAM CLINTON

What Makes Language So Important?

1 Meaning
2 Culture
3 Power

1
Meaning

To understand how you use language, it is important to realize that *language* or, more precisely, *words* are symbols that you create, learn, and use to express your thoughts and feelings. Words are:

- **symbolic:** A word represents what it is referring to either by association, resemblance, or convention.

- **arbitrary:** The relationship between the word and what it stands for is random, subjective, or coincidental.

For example, think about the word *book*. Nothing about the letters that make up that word, or their arrangement, directly or logically relates to the thing you are reading from right now. That relationship is understood only when you learn to associate the word (*book*) with pages bound between two covers.

The movie *The Miracle Worker*, about the life of Helen Keller, features a scene in which Annie Sullivan teaches blind and deaf Helen the sign for water—a key breakthrough, as Helen connects the word and the object together. At that moment, the word *water* became the symbol for that cold, wet substance Helen had felt for years; previously, she had no word or language to express it. The word now had meaning for Helen.

In their book, *The Meaning of Meaning*, Charles K. Ogden and Ivor A. Richards demonstrate how words (symbols) relate to the things they represent. Ogden and Richards created the "triangle of meaning" represented in the illustration on the next page.

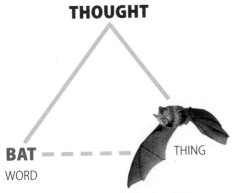

THOUGHT

BAT – – – – – – THING

WORD

bat—a usually wooden implement used for hitting the ball in various games (www.merriam-webster.com)

CONNOTATIVE MEANING

The **connotative meaning** of a word is the emotional and personal reaction you might have to a word. Your reaction could be anywhere on a continuum from an emotional avalanche (a significant positive or negative response to a word) to an emotional famine (no real response at all). Let's return to the bat example.

What if you are highly afraid of bats (the mammal)? Some people exhibit fear at just the thought of the word. Nothing in the word itself or its denotative definition should elicit that response, but those individuals have had an experience with or a knowledge of bats that adds that connotative meaning for them. For instance, maybe they were once attacked by a scared bat or they know that bats can carry rabies.

Conversely, what if you are a zoologist and your specialty is the study of the red bat? Your response to hearing the word would more likely be excitement and interest.

These differences in the emotional and personal reactions to a word add to your understanding and meaning of a word. The denotative and connotative meanings work in tandem to create your overall understanding and response to most words. As a speaker, you should always be aware that your audience may not have the same denotative or connotative meaning in mind for a word you use. For example, some younger speakers often use *girl* with a positive intent when referring to any woman, but that word choice might have a negative connotative meaning for some older women.

Notice that the bottom of the triangle is broken, and no direct relationship connects the word (bat) to the thing (the animal). Instead, the word must go through your thought process to reach the connection to the living animal. In your mind, if the word is familiar, you have two meanings that help you then come up with a definition of the thing represented. They are the *denotative* and *connotative* meanings of a word.

DENOTATIVE MEANING

The **denotative meaning** of a word is the accepted meaning and is the one found in the dictionary. For example,

> bat—nocturnal … flying mammals that have wings formed from four elongated digits of the forelimb covered by a cutaneous membrane and that have adequate visual capabilities but often rely on echolocation (www.merriam-webster.com)

Sometimes a word can have more than one denotative meaning. Then, you must pay attention to the context surrounding the word. For example, the word *bat* could refer not to the animal but to a piece of sporting equipment.

2
Culture

Language is one of the means individuals use constantly to create, share, and transmit their cultural identity.

Culture is learned patterns of beliefs, values, attitudes, norms, practices, customs, and behaviors shared by a large group of people. Samovar, Porter, and McDaniel—in their book *Communication Between Cultures*—argue that:

- Culture is dynamic, or in a constant process of reinvention.
- Culture is shared.
- Culture is transmitted from generation to generation.
- Culture is based on symbols; the most important is language.

The online and social networking cultures you may belong to are examples of how connected language and culture are to each other. Since the Internet explosion of the last century, cyber-culture members have had to learn many new words, phrases, and grammatical conventions. Cyber-cultures tend to change almost daily, so their language is extremely dynamic. If you want to practice the proper norms, customs, and behavior, you have to stay on top of the current language—words and terms like *blogging, texting, tweeting, hashtag, skype,* and *apps.*

As a speaker, you are part of multiple cultures that influence your language choices. However, none is more important to the public speaker than the culture/cultures represented in the audience and connected to the speech topic. If you have the opportunity to give the same speech to different, diverse audiences, your language may be radically different.

The limits of my language mean the limits of my world.[5]

LUDWIG WITTGENSTEIN
philosopher

PRACTICING ETHICS

The words you choose to use can create meaning and cultural identity, influence feelings and attitudes, move people to action, or empower or break down individuals and groups. Carefully selecting your words is one of your most important ethical practices when giving a speech.

- Use emotionally rich language sparingly and when appropriate. Do not cloud your audience's judgment by using language that incites strong emotions that cannot be supported logically.

- Use appropriate language.

→ See the section "Be Appropriate" on page 224 for suggestions.

- Realize that your connotative meaning for a word may not be offensive, but to someone else the word could seem extremely inappropriate. Remember that listeners' interpretations of a word is part of the message being conveyed.

3

Power

Do you know the children's rhyme "Sticks and stones may break my bones, but words will never hurt me"? Parents often recite this to children when someone has called the child a hurtful name. Although the rhyme's intent is to teach a child to view words as powerless, words are anything but powerless. Here are some powers of language.

- As the previous two sections demonstrate, language helps you understand and create meaning, and through language, you create, share, and transmit cultural identity—and that is powerful.

- Language allows you to name experiences or things. For example, before Bill Wasik, senior editor for *Harper's Magazine*, staged the first "flash mob" in 2003, the experience did not exist as named. You may now know that a flash mob is "a group of people summoned (as by e-mail or text message) to a designated location for a specific time to perform an indicated action before dispersing" (www.merriam-webster.com). You have language to describe the act—and that is powerful.

- Language can bring people together for a common cause. For example, once you understood the meaning of the term *flash mob*, you could then participate in one. This ability to gather or mobilize is powerful.

- Language can persuade you to act a certain way. Maybe you persuade a friend to join you in a flash mob. Your language allows you to negotiate with that friend. Persuasion is powerful.

- Unfortunately, language has the power to create and maintain inequality, to control, to hurt, and to disempower. This power can be conscious or unconscious, and history contains numerous examples. For instance, much of Adolf Hitler's power came from his ability to use language and to deliver persuasive speeches.

  Or think about the current use of the word *terrorist*. What images come to mind when you say or hear the word? Would you consider Timothy McVeigh (Oklahoma City bombing) or Theodore Kaczynski (the Unabomber) to be a terrorist? In news reports following the May 2010 failed car bombing in Times Square, several reports suggested that the bombing was an act of "terrorism" or "international terrorism" before a motive or a suspect was identified. Terrorism is commonly defined as politically motivated actual or threatened violence. A terrorist's nationality or religion has nothing to do with being labeled a terrorist, but since 9/11, many people tend to associate the label with certain national or religious ties. Today, some people may not consider Timothy McVeigh or Theodore Kaczynski terrorists because they are U.S. citizens, even though their acts were seemingly politically motivated. In these cases, language is powerful in misleading and damaging ways.

- Fortunately, language creates equality, frees, heals, and empowers as well. People such as Mahatma Gandhi, Mother Teresa, Bono, and Princess Diana have used their language skills for these reasons—and that is powerful.

How Can You Use Language Effectively?

1 **Be Correct**
2 **Be Clear**
3 **Be Specific**
4 **Be Appropriate**
5 **Use Oral Style**
6 **Be Distinctive**

1

Be Correct

When you think that something is correct, you usually think it is free from error or complying with standards. "Correct" applies to language as well. Your language should be free, as much as possible, of interpretation error and should adhere to certain standards. Using language incorrectly often leads to misunderstanding and low speaker ethos (credibility). When speakers use language incorrectly, they tend to use the wrong word, mispronounce words, and/or use incorrect grammar.

Selecting an incorrect word can occur when the speaker is not familiar with the best word for the situation—or selects one that sounds similar to the correct word, which is called **malapropism**. Although malapropisms can be amusing, they can cause confusion. Because of their humor, you see them used in comedy scripts like this example from the November 23, 2000, episode of NBC's *Friends*.

> **Joey: "No, a moo point. Yeah, it's like a cow's opinion. It just doesn't matter. It's moo."**

Joey means *moot point*— a point that is irrelevant or unimportant. Another word commonly misused for *moot* is *mute*. But *mute* means a person is unwilling or unable to speak. These incorrect examples may be humorous, but using either *moo* or *mute* for *moot* is incorrect and confusing.

Incorrect pronunciation of words can also cause confusion. Make sure you know how to pronounce a word correctly. Beginning speakers often have trouble with names of people and foreign places. If you are unsure how to pronounce something, look it up or ask someone.

→ See Chapter 9 for more on pronunciation.

Although you can be a bit less formal with your grammar in an oral presentation, you still want to adhere to correct grammar rules. Do not equate informal with incorrect. Here are four common errors.

ERROR #1: MISPLACED MODIFIER

This error occurs when you place a modifier too far away from what it is modifying. For example:

INCORRECT:
The man caught a bass wearing a purple hat.

CORRECT:
The man, wearing a purple hat, caught a bass.

ERROR #2: PRONOUNS

There are three common pronoun errors. First, make sure your pronouns are in agreement (plural vs. singular) with the nouns they refer to. For example:

INCORRECT:
Everyone wants their own piece of the pie.

CORRECT:
Everyone wants his or her own piece of the pie.

Second, make sure you use the correct form of a pronoun for its function in the sentence. Use pronouns such as *I, she,* and *he* as subjects; use forms such as *me, her,* and *him* as objects.

INCORRECT:
Him and me are best friends.

CORRECT:
He and I are best friends.

He and *I* are subjects in the above examples. Below, *her* and *me* are objects, receiving the action of Mom's yelling.

INCORRECT:
Mom yelled at she and I.

CORRECT:
Mom yelled at her and me.

Third, if you are using the third-person singular pronouns (*he, she, one,* and *it*), use *doesn't, does not,* or *does.* For all other pronouns (*I, you, we,* and *they*), use *don't, do not,* or *do.*

INCORRECT:
She don't want to go.

CORRECT:
She doesn't want to go.

ERROR #3: *WENT* VERSUS *GONE*

When using a helping verb (like *has* or *have*), use the past participle form of a verb. For example:

INCORRECT:
I should have went to the party.

CORRECT:
I should have gone to the party.

ERROR #4: SUBJECT/VERB AGREEMENT

If you use a singular noun in the present tense, use a singular verb. Plural nouns use plural verbs. For example, the following sentence refers to only one of many coats; therefore, the noun is singular and the verb should be, too.

INCORRECT:
One of these coats are mine.

CORRECT:
One of these coats is mine.

This example demonstrates a plural noun and plural verb agreement.

INCORRECT:
The peacocks is beautiful.

CORRECT:
The peacocks are beautiful.

Or, if the noun phrase consists of two nouns linked by *and*:

INCORRECT:
The cat and the dog is in the barn.

CORRECT:
The cat and the dog are in the barn.

2

Be Clear

In your speech, more so than in writing, it is imperative that you use language your audience will recognize and understand. Language clarity means that your audience immediately recognizes and understands your word choices. Because listeners do not have the opportunity to pause your speech and go check a dictionary, your language must be as clear as possible for them.

Also, if you use language that your listeners use on a regular basis, you will build a rapport with them, which, in turn, will build your ethos in their eyes. Keeping your language clear and familiar is highly contingent on knowing your audience.

→ See Chapter 1 (Tab 1) for details on getting to know your audience.

These guidelines will help you keep your language clear and familiar.

- Select a style and level of language appropriate to your audience.
- Be cautious with **jargon**, or specialized or technical language, which might be confusing. If you use it, do so sparingly and define words that could be unfamiliar.

- Be cautious with abbreviations and acronyms, which can be confusing to a listener. An **abbreviation** is the shortening of a word to stand as the whole word. For example:

limo	limousine
Net	Internet
bro	brother
stats	statistics

An **acronym** is a word formed from the initials or other parts of several words.

NATO	North Atlantic Treaty Organization
NCA	National Communication Association or
	National Cheerleaders Association
CEO	Chief Executive Officer
JPEG	Joint Photographic Experts Group

Use abbreviations and acronyms sparingly, if at all, and always explain them the first time you use them in a speech.

> **TIP: Intercultural Audiences**
> Jargon, abbreviations, and acronyms can be unfamiliar and confusing to intercultural audiences. Be especially sensitive to language with diverse audiences.

3
Be Specific

Getting your message across in a straightforward manner is necessary in a speech. Think about the most difficult book you have ever read. Then think about how many times you reread passages to understand them—or completely started over. Your audience cannot do that when you are giving a speech. They hear things once, maybe twice if you repeat something for them. In an instant, they must interpret your message and formulate a response and/or commit it to memory. Here are some steps that will help you stay specific.

- Be concrete. Concrete words create precision, clarity, and vividness. They focus on a person, object, action, and/or behavior and help listeners create a complete and, hopefully, accurate image. For example:

ABSTRACT:
The person saved the child.

CONCRETE:
Mr. Campbell saved the newborn from the burning car.

Being concrete does not always mean using many more words. Selecting words that are more descriptive or precise is more concrete as well. For example:

ABSTRACT:
Puck and Zelda are dogs.

CONCRETE:
Puck and Zelda are golden retrievers.

- Eliminate unnecessary words.
- Speak primarily in the active voice. In the active voice, the subject is doing the action stated in the verb. In the passive voice, the subject is the receiver of the action.

ACTIVE:
The dog caught the mole.
PASSIVE:
The mole was caught by the dog.

Occasionally, passive voice can be effective when you want to emphasize the receiver of the action more than the doer. But use it sparingly. This example from the Declaration of Independence uses passive voice for effect.

We hold these truths to be self-evident, that all men are created equal, that they are endowed by their Creator with certain unalienable Rights, that among these are Life, Liberty, and the pursuit of Happiness.

- Avoid *clichés*. Clichés are overused words or phrases that have lost their effect from overuse. Some examples:

Live and learn	Needless to say
A matter of time	To tell the truth
Before I knew it	Cut to the chase
What goes around comes around	Without a doubt

- Avoid fillers. *Fillers* are sounds, words, or phrases that serve no purpose and do not help your audience understand the message. Often, you can find a more concise way to say something, or you can eliminate the word or phrase. Some examples:

INSTEAD OF	SAY
a number of	several

INSTEAD OF	SAY
due to the fact that	because

AVOID FILLERS SUCH AS
ah, um, like, you know, or **actually**

4

Be Appropriate

The type of language you use should suit you, your audience, and the situation. Always remember that you are cocreating your message with your listeners. Their denotative and connotative definitions of a word may or may not be the same as yours. This disconnect in meaning can have adverse effects on your message and your ethos. Your success depends on selecting appropriate language that is constructive, not destructive. Therefore, it is important to:

AVOID ETHOS-REDUCING LANGUAGE

- Avoid slang and profanity. Using these may seem funny or acceptable with a particular audience, but, they are more likely to reduce your credibility in the eyes of your audience. Some audiences may even laugh, but, generally speaking, this language will lower your ethos. You will gain very little and lose a lot.

- Avoid **doublespeak**, or constructing language that disguises or distorts what you mean. Using euphemisms, jargon, or inflated language—or simply not making sense—produces doublespeak. **Euphemisms** are less-direct words or phrases that are used to replace harsh, distasteful, or offensive language. For example, companies often use the word *downsizing* instead of *layoffs* to cover up the effects on employees.

USE CULTURALLY APPROPRIATE AND UNBIASED LANGUAGE

- Avoid singling out personal traits or characteristics (such as age, disability, race, sex, sexual orientation, educational level, and so on) when they do not relate to the subject at hand. Do not use personal traits or characteristics to simply identify someone. For example:

INCORRECT:
The gay student had coffee.

The student's sexual orientation has nothing to do with the consumption of coffee.

- Use the name for an individual or group that they prefer, such as:

African American or black; Asian or Asian American; American Indian or Native American; white or Caucasian; Hispanic, Latino, or Chicano

Gay, lesbian, bisexual, or transgendered (avoid homosexual)

A person with a disability or a person with cancer (avoid disabled person or cancer victim/patient). This is the "person-first" rule.

- Avoid language that promotes stereotypes. Some examples to avoid:

women's work, catching a man, woman driver, spinster, Mr. Mom

- Avoid examples, photographs, or phrases that promote stereotypes. For example, do not show photos of only minority men when discussing violence or use examples that suggest career women lack homemaking skills.

- Use gender-neutral language. The table to the right offers a few suggestions.

USING GENDER-NEUTRAL LANGUAGE

AVOID	USE INSTEAD
man or mankind	person, human being, or humankind
man and wife	husband and wife couple or partners is even better
chairman or chairwoman; fireman; congressman; councilwoman	chair or chairperson; firefighter; congressperson; councilmember
sportsmanship	fair play or positive attitude
actress	actor
housewife	homemaker, parent, or caregiver
mothering	parenting
pronoun *he* to represent both male and female or situations generally viewed as masculine (such as sports) pronoun *she* in situations generally viewed as female	the plural *they*, or replace with *one*, *you*, or *he or she* You can also reword to avoid using pronouns: INCORRECT: "On average, each nurse was disappointed with her raise." CORRECT: "On average, each nurse was disappointed with the raise." or "On average, nurses were disappointed with their raises."
girl or boy (over the age of 18)	woman or young woman; man or young man
Miss and Mrs.	Ms. to refer to married and unmarried women (as you would use Mr.) Always refer to women as you would men. Use full names, last names only, or title (Ms.) and name.

5

Use Oral Style

If you have ever read a transcript of a verbal conversation, you know that the way people speak is radically different from the way they write. Likewise, if you have ever heard someone read a paper aloud, you know this format is much harder to follow than a conversational delivery and requires greater concentration on the part of the listener.

When you give a speech, you want to use an oral, or verbal, style rather than a written style. In oral style, you use more everyday language, personal pronouns such as *we* or *you* contractions, and shorter sentences that put the subjects and verbs closer together. Here are the major differences between written and oral styles.

CHARACTERISTICS OF ORAL STYLE	CHARACTERISTICS OF WRITTEN STYLE
Informal language	Formal language
Animated language	Technical language
Simple sentence structure	Complex sentence structure
Personally tailored messages	Impersonal messages
Repetition and restatement	Detailed and complex thoughts

For example, Makenna gave a speech to her class about counterfeit drugs, making the mistake of writing it like a paper. One of her main points was as follows:

> The next reason why the market for this form of counterfeiting is growing can be attributed to the Internet. It provides a platform to advertise the phony drugs and also reaches out to a large number of people. CEO of Pharmaceuticals Security Institute and Partnership board member Thomas T. Kubic states that one of their members accessed more than 1000 sites selling medicine online and found that 97 percent of them did not comply with state and federal laws or did not observe patient safety and pharmacy practice standards. Two-thirds of the sites offered drugs that were not FDA approved and illegal for sale ("Drug Safety," 2008).

In their evaluations, Makenna's classmates said the speech was difficult to understand. This same paragraph might have been more effective if Makenna had used oral style:

> The Internet is the next reason why we are seeing a growth in the counterfeit drug market. The Internet provides an easy means for advertising phony drugs while reaching a large number of potential customers. According to Thomas Kubic, CEO of Pharmaceuticals Security Institute and Partnership board member, one of their members accessed more than 1000 sites selling drugs. This member found that 97 percent of the sites did not comply with state and federal laws or did not observe patient safety and pharmacy practice standards. And two-thirds of the sites offered drugs that were not FDA approved and were illegal for sale ("Drug Safety," 2008).

6

Be Distinctive

As this segment from the 2004 Democratic National Convention speech of then-Senator Barack Obama demonstrates, the right language can paint an emotional picture in the minds of those listening. Most U.S. citizens barely (if at all) knew this young Illinois senator, but his speech left a lasting impression that night. Read it aloud for the full effect of the language's distinctive style.

> Tonight is a particular honor for me because, let's face it, my presence on this stage is pretty unlikely. My father was a foreign student, born and raised in a small village in Kenya. He grew up herding goats, went to school in a tin-roof shack. His father—my grandfather—was a cook, a domestic servant to the British.
>
> But my grandfather had larger dreams for his son. Through hard work and perseverance, my father got a scholarship to study in a magical place, America, that shone as a beacon of freedom and opportunity to so many who had come before.
>
> While studying here, my father met my mother. She was born in a town on the other side of the world, in Kansas. Her father worked on oil rigs and farms through most of the Depression. The day after Pearl Harbor, my grandfather signed up for duty, joined Patton's army, marched across Europe. Back home, my grandmother raised a baby and went to work on a bomber assembly line. After the war, they studied on the G.I. Bill, bought a house through F.H.A., and later moved west all the way to Hawaii in search of opportunity.
>
> And they, too, had big dreams for their daughter. A common dream, born of two continents.
>
> My parents shared not only an improbable love, they shared an abiding faith in the possibilities of this nation. They would give me an African name, Barack, or "blessed," believing that in a tolerant America, your name is no barrier to success. They imagined —They imagined me going to the best schools in the land, even though they weren't rich, because in a generous America, you don't have to be rich to achieve your potential.

By using language that stood out from the norm—that was unique, attention grabbing, and memorable—Obama became a national success almost overnight. Many commentators and political analysts marked that speech as the beginning of his move to the White House. Yes, the story he tells is exceptional, but it is how he tells it that makes it distinctive.

The next section of this chapter offers you strategies and examples for how to make your language distinctive.

CHECKLIST for Using Language Effectively

❏ Is my language correct?

❏ Is my language clear? Do I avoid jargon?

❏ Is my language specific? Do I use concrete words and active voice?

❏ Is my language appropriate? Do I avoid biased words?

❏ Do I use oral style?

❏ Is my language distinctive?

How Can You Boost Your Distinctiveness?

1 **Use Vivid Language**
2 **Use Speech Devices**

1

Use Vivid Language

When you think of something being vivid, you think of it as bright, glowing, vibrant, colorful, dramatic, and flamboyant. Vivid language is everything you can think of that is contradictory to dull, uninteresting, dry, lifeless, or lackluster.

You can bring life and vividness to your speech by using language that appeals to your audience's senses or by embellishing your words so that they are remarkable and memorable.

APPEALING TO THE SENSES

Senses are the physiological methods humans use to perceive things around them. Attributed to Aristotle, in his *De Anima*, the traditional classifications for human senses are seeing, hearing, smelling, tasting, and touching. More recently, movement and bodily tension have been added.

When you develop your speech, using language that evokes or appeals to one or more of these senses can be a powerful tool—to bring an object to life, vividly explain a technique, invoke passion, or simply entertain. Although you will not want every sentence to use a sensory appeal and you will not use every appeal in one speech, you will want to use enough appeals to keep the audience interested and listening. So think about how you can take an ordinary statement and make it a sensory image. Use the chart on the next page to help you.

SENSES	WHY MIGHT I APPEAL TO THIS PARTICULAR SENSE?	EXAMPLES
Sight (visual)	To make a visual comparison between things or to restore a visual image from memory	"The water on the floor glimmered in sunlight."
Sound (auditory)	To help the listener understand how something sounds or to evoke a sound memory	"As the wind blew, you could hear the cracking and splitting of the tree limbs."
Smell (olfactory)	To take a person back to a place, time, or feeling, as people often associate smell with a memory	"Many people remember the smell of cookies or turkey baking when they think of great Christmas memories, but I don't. My favorite memory is the cool leathery smell of the brand-new football my Dad gave me when I was eight."
Taste (gustatory)	To associate the taste of something with something known or to restore taste memory	"It tastes like chicken." "The sweet rolls were chewy and buttery with a hint of almond."
Touch (tactile)	To create the feel of something or evoke a relationship/feeling between the person and the object touched	"Think about the last time you really played a video game and how the controller warmed to your intensity and vibrated softly as you fought your battle."
Movement (kinetic)	To create speed or direction or to evoke the sense of how something moves	"You can experience no better feeling than the graceful motion of your body at an insanely fast speed, crisscrossing down a mountain on a snow-board."
Tension (kinesthetic)	To create/evoke bodily tension or lack thereof	"As he reacted to his anger, you could see his jaw and fists clench."

CONFIDENCE BOOSTER

Building your vocabulary will help you feel more comfortable speaking. If you have a broad and varied vocabulary, you can be more powerful, creative, and interesting when developing your speech. Here are a few suggestions to build your vocabulary.

1. Read more.

2. Actively pursue words. Look them up when you do not know them.

3. Make a habit of learning a new word every day.

4. Work new words into your everyday speech.

5. Work word puzzles and games, and play around on word sites.

6. Read a dictionary or a thesaurus.

EMBELLISHED LANGUAGE

Just as you can decorate, enhance, or beautify your home, your appearance, and even your car, you can enhance your words. However, when you think about words that embellish a speech, you are doing more than just making them fancier. You are making them more remarkable and memorable. Read this section toward the beginning of Martin Luther King, Jr.'s Lincoln Memorial Address, given in Washington, D.C., August 28, 1963. King made his speeches remarkable and memorable. Read it aloud for the full effect.

> So we have come here today to dramatize an appalling condition. In a sense we have come to our nation's capital to cash a check. When the architects of our republic wrote the magnificent words of the Constitution and the Declaration of Independence, they were signing a promissory note to which every American was to fall heir.
>
> This note was a promise that all men would be guaranteed the inalienable rights of life, liberty, and the pursuit of happiness. It is obvious today that America has defaulted on this promissory note insofar as her citizens of color are concerned. Instead of honoring this sacred obligation, America has given the Negro people a bad check which has come back marked "insufficient funds." But we refuse to believe that the bank of justice is bankrupt. We refuse to believe that there are insufficient funds in the great vaults of opportunity of this nation.

King uses evocative language, as well as metaphor, to compare the rights granted in the Constitution and Declaration of Independence with a promissory note to all Americans.

In the very next paragraph, King continues to paint his image of a check representing freedom and justice.

> So we have come to cash this check—a check that will give us upon demand the riches of freedom and the security of justice. We have also come to this hallowed spot to remind America of the fierce urgency of now. This is no time to engage in the luxury of cooling off or to take the tranquilizing drug of gradualism. Now is the time to rise from the dark and desolate valley of segregation to the sunlit path of racial justice. Now is the time to open the doors of opportunity to all of God's children. Now is the time to lift our nation from the quicksands of racial injustice to the solid rock of brotherhood.

As you can see from these segments, the language grabs listeners' attention and directs them to the denotative and connotative meanings the speaker wished to convey.

Often, you can combine an appeal to senses with embellished language to boost the effectiveness of your message, as this student did in a speech about traveling to the Bahamas. Look at how Gwenn revised her description of water:

LESS DISTINCTIVE:
The water was an amazing color.

MORE DISTINCTIVE:
The color of the water was like a fusion of the blue in a bright sky and the green of a lush meadow.

Gwenn is appealing to sight by describing a past memory as well as to movement (kinetic) in the fusion (a joining together). She tops off those appeals by explicitly comparing the color of the water (simile) to the sky and a meadow.

You can use techniques called ***tropes*** to transform ordinary words. Adapted from Edward Corbett and Robert Connors, *Classical Rhetoric for the Modern Student*, this chart explains the most common tropes.

TROPE	WHAT IS IT?	EXAMPLES
Simile	An explicit comparison between two things, using *like* or *as*	busy as a bee, clear as a bell, cold as ice, common as dirt, crazy as a loon, cute as a button After applying the motion sickness patch, my mouth was dry as a bone.
Metaphor	An implied comparison	"Every day is an uphill battle." "Your home is your castle." "That outfit is a train wreck."
Personification	Giving human traits to an object, idea, or animal	"My computer hates me." "The camera loves you" "Art is a jealous mistress." "The wind was howling." "Opportunity knocked." "The sun greeted me this morning." "Snow had blanketed the city." "Time waits for no one."
Oxymoron	Connecting two ordinarily contradictory words together	act naturally, Hell's Angels, jumbo shrimp, Led Zeppelin, Iron Butterfly, found missing, deafening silence, unbiased opinion, original copies, same difference, almost exactly, Great Depression
Hyperbole	The use of exaggeration for emphasis	"I told you a million times to clean your room." "After the race, my legs weighed a ton." "My sister will buy anything that is on sale."
Irony	The use of words to convey a meaning that is the opposite of its literal meaning	"I am overjoyed at the thought of going to the dentist." "I am so brilliant that I locked myself out of my car."
Onomatopoeia	Words that imitate the sounds they represent	achoo, ahem, baa, bah, bang, bark, beep, boink, boo, buzz, chatter, chirp, clang, clap, click, cluck, ding-dong, fizz, smack
Rhetorical questions	Asking a question, but not for the purpose of receiving an answer	"If you prick us, do we not bleed? If you tickle us, do we not laugh? If you poison us, do we not die? And if you wrong us, shall we not revenge?" —William Shakespeare, *The Merchant of Venice*, 3:1

2

Use Speech Devices

Like embellishing words, the techniques of manipulating word order—known as *schemes*—can help you create distinctive language. Here, you can repeat sounds, words, phrases, sentences, and grammatical patterns. You can juxtapose contrasting ideas, change word order, or omit words to create a particular rhymes that appeals to the ear and makes your words unforgettable.

Think about the nursery rhymes you learned as a child. They were fun to say and hear as well as easy to remember because they contained speech devices. Many of them used devices of repetition, like this one.

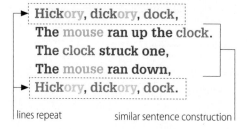

Hickory, dickory, dock,
The mouse ran up the clock.
The clock struck one,
The mouse ran down,
Hickory, dickory, dock.

lines repeat   similar sentence construction

Martin Luther King, Jr., often used rhythm and repetition in his speeches. You can see these devices in his speech example on page 230 and in this powerful conclusion to his Lincoln Address:

> This will be the day when all of God's children will be able to sing with a new meaning, "My country, 'tis of thee, sweet land of liberty, of thee I sing. Land where my fathers died, land of the pilgrim's pride, from every mountainside, let freedom ring." And if America is to be a great nation, this must become true. So let freedom ring from the prodigious hilltops of New Hampshire. Let freedom ring from the mighty mountains of New York. Let freedom ring from the heightening Alleghenies of Pennsylvania! Let freedom ring from the snowcapped Rockies of Colorado! Let freedom ring from the curvaceous peaks of California! But not only that; let freedom ring from Stone Mountain of Georgia! Let freedom ring from Lookout Mountain of Tennessee! Let freedom ring from every hill and every molehill of Mississippi. From every mountainside, let freedom ring.
>
> When we let freedom ring, when we let it ring from every village and every hamlet, from every state and every city, we will be able to speed up that day when all of God's children, black men and white men, Jews and Gentiles, Protestants and Catholics, will be able to join hands and sing in the words of the old Negro spiritual, "Free at last! Free at last! Thank God Almighty, we are free at last!"

Repetition is only one type of device, or scheme, that you can utilize. Again adapted from Corbett and Conners, this chart (page 233) explains common speech devices used by speakers today.

SCHEME	WHAT IS IT?	EXAMPLES
Repetition	Replicating the same words, phrases, or sentences for emphasis	"… And on that path to freedom, Harriett Tubman had one piece of advice. **If you** hear the dogs, **keep going**. **If you** see the torches in the woods, **keep going**. If they're shouting after you, keep going. Don't ever stop. **Keep going**. If you want a taste of freedom, **keep going**. Even in the darkest of moments, ordinary Americans have found the faith to **keep going**." —Hillary Rodham Clinton, 2008 DNC speech
Assonance	Repeating a similar vowel sound	We need to meet and greet. "… the **odious apparatus** of Nazi rule." —Winston Churchill
Alliteration	Repetition of initial consonants in two or more words in close proximity	"Already American vessels have been **searched**, **seized**, and **sunk**. —John F. Kennedy, *Profiles in Courage* She placed the cold clammy cloth on his forehead.
Parallelism	Duplicating the same grammatical patterns more than once	"We have seen the state of our Union in the endurance of rescuers, working past exhaustion. We've seen **the unfurling of flags, the lighting of candles, the giving of blood, the saying of prayers**—in English, Hebrew, and Arabic." —George W. Bush, address to Congress, 2001 **"Tell me and I forget. Teach me and I may remember. Involve me and I will learn."** —Benjamin Franklin
Antithesis	Juxtaposition of contrasting ideas, often in parallel structure	"That's one small step for **man**, one giant leap for **mankind**." —Neil Armstrong, July 21, 1969 "We have found ourselves **rich in goods**, but **ragged in spirit**." —Richard Nixon, first inaugural speech
Anastrophe	Reversing expected word order to gain attention	Cold and damp was the wind. "Ask not what your country can do for you; ask what you can do for your country." —John F. Kennedy, inaugural speech
Asyndeton	Deliberately omitting conjunctions	"We shall **pay any price, bear any burden, meet any hardships, support any friend, oppose any foe** to assure the survival and the success of liberty." —John F. Kennedy, inaugural speech **"I came, I saw, I conquered!"** (Veni, Vidi, Vici!) —reportedly written by Julius Caesar

Lewis's Speech

Lewis traveled to Greece last summer and wants to give an informative speech on a few highlights of Greece and the places he visited. He has created his outline and practiced a few times, but he thinks the speech lacks excitement. He has asked Zoe, a classmate, to listen to his speech as he rehearses and offer suggestions for how he can make it better.

Zoe finds the organizational strategy (topical) and the support materials effective. Her initial comments:

"Lewis, I really like your speech and it's very informative. Lots of detail, but not so much that you can't cover each of your main points. Talking about traveling to Greece could be difficult to narrow, but you do a good job of giving snapshots of a few places to visit. I think the issue is with language. You are very matter-of-fact with the details, and we lose the ambience of Greece. We need to find some places where you can bring Greece to life for the audience. Let's look at your outline."

USING LANGUAGE EFFECTIVELY

Before turning to Lewis's outline, Zoe explained some general written comments she made during the speech.

Zoe's first comment refers to Lewis's tendency to use fillers a lot.

Her second one refers to Lewis's inclination to say "you guys" instead of just "you." Lewis was not even aware that he said it. They decided to have Lewis give the speech a few more times, and each time he started to say "like," "you know," or "you guys," Zoe would raise her hand. Lewis was soon able to eliminate the habit.

- Watch saying "like" and "you know" all the time

- Drop the "you guys"—mainly at the beginning and end of speech

- Your relevance statement may insult someone

For her third comment, they turned to the outline to see how Lewis had constructed his relevance-to-audience statement. This is what he had:

Relevance to audience: Americans don't travel much outside of their own country, which means you are missing out on some amazing ancient wonders of the world. As you get older and more financially secure, you should consider traveling to faraway places like Greece.

Zoe's concern was with the first sentence, given that Lewis is an international student. She felt that because most students in the class were from the United States, they could be offended by the suggestion that "Americans don't travel." Lewis dropped the sentence and stated instead, "As you get older and more financially secure, you should consider traveling to faraway places to seek out some of the amazing wonders of the world—places like Greece."

USING VIVID LANGUAGE

Zoe suggested that places such as the attention-getter could be stronger if Lewis used vivid language to paint enticing images of Greece for his listeners.

This was his current attention-getter:

Attention-getter: Did you know that Greece is the first country that steps into the stadium in the athletes' parade in the modern Olympic games? That honor is because the first Olympic games took place in ancient Olympia, in Greece, in 776 BC. Speaking of games, did you know that the popular yo-yo toy, the second-oldest known toy in the world, originated back in ancient Greece, around 3,000 years ago?

Zoe noted that it was interesting information, especially the yo-yo part, but not a strong attention-getter if the purpose of the speech is to motivate people to be interested in traveling to Greece. She suggested that Lewis create a vivid mental image that pulls the audience into Greece. He could even use photos to support the language.

So, Lewis changed his attention-getter to appeal to many of the audience's senses and incorporated a bit of repetition.

Attention-getter: Imagine sitting at an outdoor café on the edge of the sea, the bright sunlight dancing across the waves, the ocean spray hitting your skin, and the wind whisking through a field of lavender. Imagine the taste of fresh bread pulled apart, dipped in fresh olive oil and herbs. Imagine standing in the center of a field where ancient athletes played the first Olympic games, as the roar of thousands of spectators filled them with inspiration. Imagine Greece.

After creating his new attention-getter, Lewis decided to adjust his speech to this "imagine" theme periodically, to return his audience to that initial feeling.

9
DELIVERING YOUR SPEECH

Introduction

Think about someone you consider a good speaker and the first time you saw him or her speak. Think about how the speaker's use of voice kept you interested in the topic and signaled what was important. Think about what the speaker did with his or her hands, arms, and face to create and reinforce a message. What did the speaker wear? Did the clothing seem appropriate to the speech and occasion? Do you think the speaker gave this speech without rehearsing it several times?

Because you found this speaker effective, he or she probably spent some time thinking about gestures, voice, use of space, clothing, and other delivery issues. Odds are, the speaker practiced that speech several times before giving it.

A public speech is a presentation that merges the written speech with the oral presentation, and both are open to interpretation. Your message and delivery work together to create the whole experience. Therefore, delivery is important. Effective delivery does not draw attention to itself and uses both verbal and nonverbal elements to assist the message on its way to the audience. Effective delivery is natural and engaging, and it demonstrates confidence. This chapter will help you employ a delivery style that can help your audience understand, appreciate, and enjoy your message.

We are what we repeatedly do; excellence, then, is not an act but a habit.[1]

WILL DURANT,
summarizing Aristotle

CHAPTER 8: Using Language Successfully   215

CHAPTER 9 CONTENTS

What Are the Elements of Vocal Delivery?   238
1 Pitch   238
2 Volume   239
3 Rate   239
4 Pause   240
5 Variety   241
6 Pronunciation   242
7 Articulation   243
8 Dialect   243

What Are the Elements of Physical Delivery?   244
1 Appearance   244
2 Eye Contact   245
3 Facial Expression   246
4 Gestures   246
5 Movement   247
6 Posture   247

What Are the Methods of Delivery?   248
1 Extemporaneous Speaking   249
2 Manuscript Speaking   250
3 Memorized Speaking   250
4 Impromptu Speaking   251

How Do You Rehearse an Extemporaneous Speech?   252
1 Read Aloud the Preparation Outline   253
2 Prepare Your Delivery Outline   253
3 Prepare Your Presentation Aids   253
4 Practice Multiple Times   254
5 Do a Final "Dress Rehearsal"   255
6 Prepare for Questions   255

How Should You Prepare for the Day of the Speech?   256

Harriet's Speech   258

CHAPTER 10: Using Presentation Aids   261

Tab 4 Review   298

What Are the Elements of Vocal Delivery?

1 **Pitch**

2 **Volume**

3 **Rate**

4 **Pause**

5 **Variety**

6 **Pronunciation**

7 **Articulation**

8 **Dialect**

1

Pitch

Pitch is how high and low your voice is in frequency and is determined by how fast or slow your vocal cords vibrate. The greater the number of vibrations per second your cords move, the higher the pitch. Two aspects determine how fast your cords will vibrate.

The first is the length and thickness of the vocal cords. For example, in general, women's vocal cords tend to be short and thin, allowing the cords to vibrate fast. Therefore, their voices are usually higher in pitch than men's.

The second aspect is how relaxed or stressed your body is. When you are excited, tense, or frightened, the muscles around your voice box (larynx) unconsciously tighten, raising the pitch of your voice. To demonstrate how this works, say this phrase calmly: "The tree is falling." Now, imagine your friends are standing near the tree and you must save them by yelling, "The tree is falling!" During the second demonstration, your voice is clearly louder—but it is also higher in pitch, signaling your friends to the danger.

You already know from the Overview chapter that former British Prime Minister Margaret Thatcher trained her high feminine voice to be lower. Pitch is something you can work on if your voice is extremely high or low; and, as with many elements in your speech, variety in pitch is important. A constant pitch, known as **monotone**, is distracting and boring. Varying your pitch (*inflection*) will help you demonstrate enthusiasm, excitement, concern, and dedication to the topic.

2
Volume

Like your stereo volume, your vocal *volume* is how loud or soft your voice is. Some speech instructors would say the appropriate volume is just a bit louder than your normal speaking voice. However, you need to consider the size of the room and audience, the level of environmental noise, and whether you must project on your own or will be using a microphone.

Aim for a volume that can vary and still be heard in the back row of the audience when you are at your softest—and not hurt you at your loudest. If you speak in a perpetually soft voice that can just barely be heard, your audience may think you are unsure or timid. Not varying the volume can sound boring or apathetic. A loud voice can make your audience stop listening and can damage your vocal cords.

Pay attention to the cues your audience sends you about your volume. They may lean forward if you are too quiet and turn their heads slightly to hear you better. If you are too loud, they may lean back, lower their chins slightly, and frown.

If you are from a culture where speaking softly is more acceptable, you might have trouble recognizing when you are too quiet. Practice your speech with someone who will tell you to keep raising your voice until you reach a good volume, and then rehearse at that level several times. You may feel like you are yelling; that's normal. Relax and practice the new level until it seems more comfortable.

3
Rate

Your vocal *rate* is the speed at which you speak. The average rate a person can speak is between 120 and 150 words per minute. In parts of the country, people may speak faster (e.g., New York City) or slower (e.g., some southern states). You can manipulate your rate to add excitement, exhilaration, or urgency to your speech. The key to a good overall rate is to pay attention to your audience. If your audience seems bored, speeding up may help. If the topic is difficult and they appear confused, slowing down would be helpful. If you feel out of breath during your speech, that is a good indication that you are talking too fast. Slow down, let your audience catch up, and allow yourself to breathe.

TIPS: Using a Microphone

If a room or audience is too large, the acoustics are poor, or you are physically unable to project your voice, you will need to use a microphone.

- If possible, practice your complete speech with the sound system to uncover problems.
- Perform a second sound check 30 minutes or so before the event starts.
- Periodically, pay attention to the sound person. He or she may signal you when an issue arises (for example, if you forget to turn on the microphone).
- Determine the type of microphone and how far or close you need to be to it.
- Beware of distracting vocal sounds (popping sharp consonants or heavy breathing) or nonverbal sounds (hitting the lectern) that might be amplified by the system.
- Be careful not to make side or private comments that might be heard over an open microphone. Always assume that the microphone is on, until you are a safe distance from it.

4

Pause

A vocal **pause** can be used for more than just slowing down your speaking rate. Pauses can allow your audience to linger on a thought, in order to apply meaning or gauge significance. Also, pauses can be used as a tool for enhancing or emphasizing a point, and they can draw your audience's attention to a point you are about to make.

Maybe you once had an elementary school teacher who used this technique to get your class under control. Your teacher stood at the front of the room with hands on hips or arms crossed and yelled out, "Class!" He or she then waited. Eventually each child realized that the silence had a significant meaning: The class was to get a time-out.

At the end of his inaugural address on January 20, 1961, John F. Kennedy provided an excellent example of how pauses can focus an audience's attention on the message and evoke a major reaction. Each line break represents a pause (capitalization indicates increased volume), and you can listen to the speech on YouTube.

> **And so, my fellow Americans,**
> **ask NOT**
> **what your country can do for you;**
> **ask what you can do for your country.**
>
> **My fellow citizens of the world,**
> **ask NOT**
> **what America will do for you,**
> **but what together we can do**
> **for the freedom of man.**

REMOVING VOCAL FILLERS

Do not be afraid to use pauses to help avoid using vocal fillers. As you learned in Chapter 8, fillers are extraneous sounds and words like *ah, um, like,* or *you know.* Most pauses that are uncomfortable for a speaker are not significant to the audience, but the fillers become distracting.

The process of removing vocal fillers from your speech will take time and a lot of patience. In the end, it will be worth it, and you will appear and feel much more confident.

- Practicing your speech numerous times will help you become familiar with your topic, which will decrease the time it takes you to recall what to say next. Speakers tend to use vocal fillers when struggling for their next word or sentence. But make sure to use enough natural pauses that you do not speed through your speech.

- Realize that removing vocal fillers is a process. The first step is to make a conscious effort to recognize that you are using fillers. Then, you must work to recognize that when and why you use them. The next step is to preempt the usage, which takes time, dedication, and patience.

- Having a friend or family member signal you each time you use a filler during a rehearsal might be beneficial.

- Record your speech and listen to it. Hearing how fillers detract from your delivery can inspire you to use them less.

5
Variety

German writer Jean Paul Richter once noted that the "variety of mere nothings gives more pleasure than the uniformity of something." Although "mere nothing" is never effective in a speech, Richter's point does have some merit. As the previous discussion of volume, pitch, rate, and pause suggests, vocal variety is a necessity if you want to give an effective speech. You use vocal **variety** when you fluctuate, change, or adjust your volume, pitch, rate, and pauses. To do so brings your voice and, therefore, your words to life, filling them with expression and animation. To be an effective speaker, you must employ vocal variety.

To understand what vocal variety can do for your speech, locate a video clip of a famous speech. AmericanRhetoric.com and YouTube have several, such as former President Ronald Reagan's "tear down this wall" speech—remarks delivered in front of Brandenburg Gate in Germany on June 12, 1987.

Here is the basic text of the most famous portion of the speech:

> General Secretary Gorbachev, if you seek peace, if you seek prosperity for the Soviet Union and Eastern Europe, if you seek liberalization: Come here to this gate! Mr. Gorbachev, open this gate! Mr. Gorbachev, Mr. Gorbachev, tear down this wall!

As Reagan speaks these now-famous words, his voice deepens, slows at times, and rises in volume to punch the ending. If written poetically to simulate the vocal variety President Reagan used, this same section would look like the following. End-of-line breaks represent longer pauses or breaks, added spaces between words represent short pauses, and capitalization represents increased volume and intensity in his delivery.

> General Secretary Gorbachev,
> if YOU seek peace,
> if you seek prosperity for the Soviet Union and Eastern Europe,
> if YOU seek liberalization:
> Come here to THIS gate!
> Mr. Gorbachev,
> open THIS gate! (applause)
> Mr. Gorbachev,
> MR. GORBACHEV,
> TEAR DOWN THIS WALL!

His effective delivery inspired listeners around the world. Listen to a recording for yourself and see if you, too, can feel the energy when he speaks.

6
Pronunciation

Correct **pronunciation** is the standard or commonly accepted way to make a word sound. For example, do you know someone who says the word *picture* like the word *pitcher*? The word *picture* should be pronounced "pik-tchure," and *pitcher* should be pronounced "pit-chure."

Poor pronunciation can, at the very least, slow down your audience's listening skills as they try to figure out what you intend or, in the worst case cause complete misunderstanding.

Recognizing when you mispronounce a word can be difficult, as you may not know you are doing it. Ask your friends and family to pay attention and tell you when you mispronounce a word. If you are unsure of how to pronounce a new word, look it up or ask someone who should know. Many online dictionaries allow you to play sound recordings of correct pronunciations.

Not knowing how to correctly pronounce words can also significantly lower your ethos. Be diligent and find out the correct way to pronounce the words you plan to use in your speech.

SOME COMMON MISPRONUNCIATIONS

CORRECT SPELLING	MISPRONUNCIATION	CORRECT PRONUNCIATION
Affidavit	Af-fi-david	Af-fi-davit
Asked	Aks	Askt
Barbed wire	Bob wi-re	Barbed wi-er
Clothes	Close	Clōthes
Especially	Ex-pecially	Es-pecially
February	Feb-u-ary	Feb-ru-ary
Hierarchy	Hi-archy	Hi-er-archy
Jewelry	Jew-le-ry	Jew-el-ry
Library	Li-berry	Li-brer-y
Nuclear	Nu-cu-lar	Nu-cle-ar
Theater (or theatre)	The-ate-er	The-uh-ter

TIP: Pronunciation
If you know you have trouble pronouncing a word and cannot break the habit, use an alternative word if possible.

7
Articulation

Articulation is how completely and clearly you utter a word—for example, saying "morning" instead of "mornin'." Closely linked, and often used synonymously with articulation, is **enunciation**, or the distinctiveness and clarity of linked whole words—for example, saying, "Did you eat yet?" instead of "Jeat yet?"

Speaking fast, mumbling, running words together, and dropping vowels or consonants (as in "drinkin'") are all considered poor articulation or enunciation—commonly referred to as "lazy speech." Audiences may view these habits as inappropriate for a public speech, which can harm your ethos.

Mumbling is a common problem for beginning speakers. If you have this habit, make a conscious effort to eliminate it. Warming up your mouth can help. Before entering the speech location, open your mouth wide several times, stretching your jaw muscles (be careful if you have medical issues with your jaw), then hum as you rapidly vibrate your lips together. Like an athlete stretches, you need to warm up your mouth's muscles.

8
Dialect

All cultures and subcultures have unique elements in their speech known as dialects. A **dialect** is how a particular group of people pronounces and uses language. Dialects can be regional (e.g., the South) or ethnic (e.g., Jewish English).

Dialects are important for establishing and maintaining cultural identity, so you do not automatically need to avoid using dialect. However, if your dialect is significantly different from that of your audience, it can distract them and decrease your effectiveness.

When a dialect interferes with communication, it is usually because grammar and vocabulary cause the misunderstanding. For example, in the Boston area, you might hear a water fountain called a bubbler or a rubber band called an elastic.

When speaking outside of your region or culture, use the more standard vocabulary. Doing so will help you prevent misunderstanding and distraction while maintaining your individual identity.

CHECKLIST for Vocal Delivery

❏ Is my volume appropriate for this space and the audience size? Do I need to use a microphone?

❏ Am I using both low and high pitches? Do I need to regulate my natural pitch?

❏ Is my rate too fast or too slow?

❏ Am I using pauses effectively?

❏ Do I use enough vocal variety?

❏ Am I pronouncing all my words correctly?

❏ Am I mumbling, running my words together too fast, or clipping consonants or vowels?

❏ Will my dialect distract the audience?

What Are the Elements of Physical Delivery?

1 **Appearance**
2 **Eye Contact**
3 **Facial Expression**
4 **Gestures**
5 **Movement**
6 **Posture**

1

Appearance

If you know of her, two things come to mind when you think of Lady Gaga—her music and her appearance. Although her appearance is not what makes her a good singer, it is part of the persona she wishes to create, helping her stand out and be memorable.

Similarly, you should not underestimate the influence your appearance can have on your speech. **Appearance** includes your dress and grooming choices. Once you walk into a room, the people around you begin to form first impressions about you. Unlike Lady Gaga, you should rarely, if ever, draw attention to your appearance, because you want your audience to focus on your message. Your appearance should improve your ethos and support your message. Here are some guidelines:

- Always be well groomed.
- Dress for the occasion. You want to dress a bit better than what is expected for the occasion and the audience.
- Consider environmental issues. Wearing black on a hot, sunny day may make you sweat and appear more nervous.
- Use your appearance to support your topic. (Wearing a suit for a speech on changing motor oil in a car will seem odd.)
- Think about the mood, attitude, or image you want to project.
- Avoid wearing distracting items like flashy colors or jewelry.

2
Eye Contact

If there is one piece of advice effective speakers understand, it is to make eye contact. You must establish and maintain eye contact with your audience if you want them to stay focused on you and your message and view you as trustworthy. In addition, eye contact enables you to obtain feedback during the speech.

Although cultural norms differ, Western culture prefers **direct eye contact**, or briefly looking straight into the eyes of the other person. During a public speaking occasion, you can accommodate this cultural preference by randomly selecting several people in the audience to make direct eye contact with. Choosing those audience members who are actively listening to your speech and smiling will help boost your confidence as well.

Direct eye contact
Choose several audience members to make direct eye contact with. As an audience member, help the speaker by being an active listener and maintaining eye contact with him or her.

The beginning speaker often uses ineffective eye contact. Familiarize yourself with the ineffective practices in the chart below. If you recognize yourself in any of these categories, try to self-regulate the behavior or ask a friend to watch you during your speech.

INEFFECTIVE EYE CONTACT	WHAT IS IT?	EFFECTIVE SOLUTION
The Bobber	A speaker who bobs up and down rhythmically from notes to audience	Practice the speech so you don't rely on your notes so much, or shorten your delivery outline.
The Stargazer	A speaker who looks above and beyond the audience	Don't be afraid to look at your audience. Most audiences are friendly.
The Obsessor	A speaker who looks at only one or two audience members during the whole speech	Use more of the space in front of the audience, forcing you to look at more people, and practice including most of the audience.
The Obliterator	A speaker who tends to look at only one side of the audience and forgets the rest	Prior to the speech, familiarize yourself with the edges of the audience in all directions. Move around and use more of the space in front of the audience during the speech.

3
Facial Expression

Facial expressions are the use of facial muscles to convey your internal thoughts or feelings. Many animals use facial expressions, but humans seem to be the masters of this form of communication. Although you have thousands of different expressions, only six seem to be universal.

UNIVERSAL EXPRESSION	HOW DO YOU MAKE IT?
Happiness	Raise mouth corners into a smile
Fear	Raise brows, open eyes fully, and open mouth slightly
Surprise	Arch brows, open eyes wide to expose more white, and drop jaw open slightly
Disgust	Raise upper lip and wrinkle nose bridge (which raises cheeks)
Anger	Lower brows, press lips together firmly, and bulge eyes
Sadness	Lower mouth corners and raise inner portion of brows

Here are some keys to using effective facial expressions.

- Match your expressions to your verbal message.
- Keep your expressions natural. Avoid overdoing or exaggerating them.
- When speaking across cultures, consider the universality of your expressions.

4
Gestures

You use *gestures* when you use your body or parts of it (hands, arms, eyes, or head) to convey a message and feelings during your speech. The gestures used during a speech are usually either emblems or illustrators.

Emblems are speech-independent and culturally learned gestures that have a direct verbal translation. When you shrug your shoulders to convey "I don't know" or form a circle with your thumb and index finger on the same hand to communicate a feeling of "OK," you are using emblems. Winking, nodding yes, waving hello, and rolling your eyes are emblems, too. An emblem may not mean the same thing in another culture, so be careful.

Illustrators are speech-dependent and closely linked to what is being said. They help you demonstrate words or messages in a speech. For example, if you put up one finger as you say, "my first point," you are using an illustrator.

Effective gestures should:
- Vary, so that they do not become rhythmic and distracting
- Be appropriate to the speech, audience, and occasion
- Be purposefully used and add to your message

5
Movement

Movement refers to your use of motion and space during the speech. How to use space depends, as always, on your needs, the topic, the audience, and the occasion.

If the topic and the event are extremely formal, such as a graduation ceremony, standing to the side of the lectern or moving around on the stage is less acceptable. However, most speech events will allow some flexibility with movement and will be better if you use it. Standing completely still can make you seem rigid or unapproachable and can cause any nervous tension in your body to intensify.

Lecterns (especially with microphones) are useful tools but can be a barrier between you and your audience. If you want to build a friendlier and more approachable relationship, avoid using a lectern. If possible, stand to the side or move around periodically. You should avoid pacing, however. Just remember to make your movement purposeful, not distracting, and consistent with your verbal message. If a microphone is necessary, try to use a lapel or wireless one.

6
Posture

Posture is the position of your body during your speech and, like your facial expressions, can convey inner thoughts and feelings you have about yourself, your audience, the topic, and the situation. If you are nervous, your body might be rigid and straight. If you are very relaxed, depressed, or tired, your shoulders might droop or you might lean against the table or lectern. If you close off your body by hiding behind a lectern or crossing your arms, you appear less approachable.

Conversely, if you are somewhat at ease and excited about your speech, your body will be open (front of the body visible), mostly relaxed but energized, and straight but not stiff. This posture is more natural and inviting to the audience. It conveys that you are enthusiastic and comfortable with your audience, topic, and situation. Your posture can significantly influence your ethos.

Bad posture
Crossing your arms or leaning against the lectern

Good posture
More natural and inviting to the audience

CHECKLIST for Physical Delivery

❏ Is my appearance well groomed and appropriate?

❏ Am I employing good direct eye contact?

❏ Am I varying my facial expressions, gestures, and movements? Are they natural?

❏ Does my posture convey enthusiasm for my topic, the audience, and the occasion?

What Are the Methods of Delivery?

1 Extemporaneous Speaking

2 Manuscript Speaking

3 Memorized Speaking

4 Impromptu Speaking

To speak to an audience of conference attendees, Mia carefully researched her topic, created a preparation outline, and rehearsed her speech with a delivery outline several times before presenting the speech.

President Laurer gave a speech he read from a manuscript to the faculty, staff, and public on the state of the university.

The chief executive officer of the Pennington Corporation gave a speech for the company banquet that he had memorized.

When a business advisory board asked Jeff to comment on his new potential product line, he took a moment to gather his thoughts and gave a quick summary of its potential and cost.

Each of these speakers is using one of four different acceptable methods of speech delivery—extemporaneous, manuscript, memorized, or impromptu—for his or her particular situation. Mia gave an extemporaneous speech. President Laurer used manuscript delivery. The CEO gave a memorized speech. And Jeff delivered his speech impromptu.

The following sections explain each method and will help you decide when each type of delivery is appropriate for your speeches.

Each method has pros and cons, making it better for certain speeches and situations. Whichever method you employ, follow these guidelines.

- Be as natural and comfortable as possible. This means you have rehearsed enough so that the speech flows smoothly but not as if you are a machine speaking. Your speech should sound conversational.

- Connect with your audience. Building a connection to your audience is easier with the extemporaneous and impromptu methods, because you can tailor or tweak your speech to the audience's needs in the moment. However, good manuscript and memorized speeches can build connections when you employ effective techniques such as direct eye contact and a natural delivery style.

- Be enthusiastic and confident! If you are not, your audience will not be excited or believe you. Practice, practice, practice, and you will begin to believe in your speech and your abilities. While you are presenting your speech, you should not worry about whether you can give a good speech; rather, you should think about how you can adapt and adjust to make the speech even better.

The most common acceptable method is extemporaneous speaking. Outside of the classroom, your role in society or your profession, the topic, and the occasion will signal if you need to use an alternative. In the classroom, your assignment or instructor will guide you.

1
Extemporaneous Speaking

WHAT IS IT?

Extemporaneous speaking is considered the most acceptable contemporary method of delivery. Here, you plan out, rehearse, and deliver the speech from a key-word/phrase outline.

WHEN SHOULD YOU USE IT?

This type of delivery is more audience centered than others because it is speaking "with" your audience and not "at" them. When your goal is to give an audience-centered speech, this is the method to use. In fact, you should try to use this method most of the time. Most classroom speeches require extemporaneous delivery.

DELIVERY TECHNIQUES

With the extemporaneous style, you will expand on the brief notes you have in front of you as you speak. You have rehearsed the speech so that you are not scrambling for something to say, which allows you to adapt to the audience and to sound more natural. Preparing the speech effectively and rehearsing it enough to become very comfortable with the topic is essential to this type of delivery.

➜ See also "How Do You Rehearse an Extemporaneous Speech?" on page 252.

2
Manuscript Speaking

WHAT IS IT?

Manuscript speaking occurs when you read directly from a word-for-word copy of the speech.

WHEN SHOULD YOU USE IT?

This form of delivery is used when you must be careful about what you say and you must present the speech exactly as planned, so that you do not omit important details or misstate critical information. Politicians, researchers, government officials, news broadcasters, commentators, corporate leaders, and other speakers often use this method when accuracy is crucial or when the media will report on or analyze the speech.

DELIVERY TECHNIQUES

Manuscript speaking can distance you from the audience. Your eye contact may be poor and you may be tied to a lectern or prompting device, which will serve as a wall between you and your audience. When you give a manuscript speech, work on making as much eye contact as possible, keep your gestures high and not hidden by the lectern or prompter, and keep your voice dynamic. Rehearse the manuscript five, 10, 15 times—whatever it takes for you to be comfortable with your delivery and message. Mark delivery tips on the manuscript. Speakers who use this technique effectively will appear to be delivering the speech almost without the aid of the manuscript.

3
Memorized Speaking

WHAT IS IT?

A memorized speech is another method that allows you to deliver a speech exactly as written. *Memorized speaking* means you rehearse the speech so much that you commit the full text to memory.

WHEN SHOULD YOU USE IT?

This delivery is used for many of the same reasons as the manuscript speech. Some speakers also employ this method when accuracy and the appearance of spontaneity are equally important. Storytellers, religious leaders, and speakers giving special occasion speeches may use this delivery.

You may find memorized delivery helpful during sections of a speech that you primarily deliver using another method. For example, you might memorize a quotation or your introduction and conclusion.

The downsides are that you might forget what comes next and it is more difficult to respond to audience feedback. So use this method for brief speeches, such as toasts.

DELIVERY TECHNIQUES

The key to an effective memorized speech is to rehearse it a lot and make it sound fresh. Keep your excitement high and use effective verbal and nonverbal delivery techniques. You might memorize the entire speech or a few sections that you will weave together.

4

Impromptu Speaking

WHAT IS IT?

Impromptu speaking is the only method of delivery that has very little, if any, preparation or rehearsal. If any outline is used, it is simply notes jotted down quickly.

WHEN SHOULD YOU USE IT?

Even though this is the least-prepared type of speech, often uses a very basic organizational strategy, lacks solid evidence, and uses simplistic language, impromptu speaking is the type of delivery we use the most in our everyday lives. You use this type of delivery when answering a question in a public forum (like the classroom), when you need to offer information or dispute an issue during a meeting, or when you are asked to address an audience at a moment's notice.

DELIVERY TECHNIQUES

The best technique for impromptu speaking is to always be prepared with appropriate knowledge and information. Avoid being unprepared for classes, meetings, or events where you might be called upon to offer comments or answer questions. Look through the agenda for a moment when you might be asked to participate. You will almost always be asked to respond about something you should or do know. These steps will help you put your thoughts together.

- Pay close attention during the event. To be and appear competent, you need to know what was said and what was asked of you.

- Think about your purpose for addressing this particular audience. What are the listeners' needs and interests? How does your expertise relate to them?

- If you have time, write down key words, phrases, or ideas and think about a logical order. If you do not have time to write something down, pause and gather your thoughts. People will wait briefly if they see you are thinking about an answer. Sometimes you can buy yourself time by standing or walking to the front of the room. It is remarkable how little time you really need to gather your thoughts if you are prepared.

- Try to limit your remarks to two or three points at most.

- Think about what evidence you can offer to support your points.

- Try to connect your comments to information presented earlier, if possible.

- Base your response in your personal knowledge and experiences.

PRACTICING ETHICS

Sometimes impromptu speaking will make you feel like you are being "put on the spot" or asked to speak without preparation. Remember: Most of the time you will be asked for impromptu comments because you are an expert on the subject or have something critical to add. Therefore, ethically, it is your responsibility to never make up information to sound good or to get through the moment. Be honest.

How Do You Rehearse an Extemporaneous Speech?

1 **Read Aloud the Preparation Outline**

2 **Prepare Your Delivery Outline**

3 **Prepare Your Presentation Aids**

4 **Practice Multiple Times**

5 **Do a Final "Dress Rehearsal"**

6 **Prepare for Questions**

REHEARSAL NOTE

There is no magical formula for how many times you need to rehearse your speech for each of the following steps. The key is: as much as you need to move successfully to the next step. If you read your preparation outline aloud two times and feel you are ready to make the delivery outline, then do so. However, if you find yourself struggling to remember details when using the delivery outline, you need to back up a step. Check your logic, and read the preparation outline aloud several times. If you have not spent enough time with the details or if the logic is flawed, your speech will be hard to remember.

Rehearsing is an individual process that will be specific to you. Do not assume that if your friend can give a speech with only two rehearsals, so can you. Pay attention to what does or does not work for you, and adapt your rehearsals to your needs. Be willing to improve your rehearsal practices. Even an excellent speech has room for improvement.

1
Read Aloud the Preparation Outline

At this step in the rehearsal process, you want to read aloud the preparation outline several times. Pay attention to the order of your points, how much support material you are using, and the order of the support materials. Include your links as well to see if they smoothly transition between points and parts of the speech. Read aloud the introduction and conclusion to see if they are interesting and flow well. Read the preparation outline one more time at a reasonable pace and time yourself. Make changes where necessary to correct issues or to adhere to the time limit. At this point, you should be under the time limit, because you have not added verbal and nonverbal techniques or presentation aids that will take up time during your speech. Once you feel like you have a solid speech, move on to the next step.

TIP: Preparation Outline
You should have your preparation outline done at least two days before the speech event or in the time frame required by your instructor. You cannot prepare your delivery outline or rehearse the speech effectively if your preparation outline is incomplete. Most speakers need to practice over the course of several days to make a speech sound conversational, so give yourself time to spend with your finished preparation outline.

2
Prepare Your Delivery Outline

Now, you want to reduce your preparation outline to only key words, phrases, and important quotations, statistics, or details. Try not to include too much of the introduction or the conclusion. You will tend to read it if you do, and direct eye contact is crucial.

Add delivery cues after you have what you think is the final delivery outline. Include any delivery cues you need at the moments you think you might need them. Remember to note cues for presentation aids.

➔ See Chapter 5 (Tab 3) for more help creating a delivery outline.

3
Prepare Your Presentation Aids

Next, prepare the presentation aids exactly as you will use them in the speech event. Do not cut corners here. You want to practice with the finished aids to discover any problems and to make them seem a natural part of your speech.

➔ See Chapter 10 (Tab 4) for more on using and creating presentation aids.

TIP: Delivery Outline
If your hands tend to shake when you give a presentation, use stiff paper, note cards, or something like a file folder or clipboard to support your delivery outline. This will allow you to feel comfortable when picking up your notes or not using a lectern.

4
Practice Multiple Times

Now it is time to put your speech on its feet. At this point, you want to practice your speech exactly as you plan to give it. Here are some hints.

- At this stage, always practice from the delivery outline. If you discover that you are struggling with any part, read over the preparation outline and then return to practicing with the delivery outline.

- Practice a few times in front of a mirror and/or record your speech. Watch for distracting behavior. Is your posture appropriate, and are you using effective gestures? Audio or video recording a rehearsal is a helpful step. Doing so will allow you to focus on vocal quality. Video recording a rehearsal will also help you pay attention to your body language and eye-contact issues, which are hard to monitor while you practice.

- Time yourself several times while using your finished presentation aids and necessary equipment, if any. You want to get as close as possible to the time limit.

- Practice with a rehearsal audience. Ask family members, friends, or classmates to play the role of audience for you. Ask them to offer feedback on the content of the speech, your delivery, or your strengths and weaknesses. You could even give them a copy of the checklist toward the end of this chapter to guide their thoughts. Remember, they are offering you ways to make your speech better.

- Evaluate what you have learned from the rehearsal audience and from watching and listening to yourself. Change the speech message or your delivery style when necessary. Rehearse the speech again, incorporating these changes. If possible, practice in front of the same rehearsal audience and ask their opinions about the changes.

→ See Chapter 12 (Tab 5) for help with evaluating your speech.

Practice your speech as many times as necessary to feel comfortable with it and your presentation aids. Remember your time limit!

CONFIDENCE BOOSTER

- The more you practice with your delivery outline and presentation aids, the lower your apprehension will be.
- During the speech, avoid apologizing or calling attention to your shortcomings. Your audience may have missed them. Don't dwell on them, or you'll lose your concentration and audience focus.

5
Do a Final "Dress Rehearsal"

The last step in the rehearsal process is to do what actors call a "dress rehearsal." With this rehearsal, you want to simulate as closely as possible the exact event when you will give the speech. So it is important to:

- Rehearse in the space (or a close alternative) where you will give the speech.

- Use the exact delivery outline you will use during the speech. Make sure you number the pages or cards to prevent a mix-up the day of the speech.

- Use the exact presentation aids and necessary equipment.

- Try to rehearse at the exact time to consider potential issues with noise, lighting, temperature, and so on.

- Rehearse standing or sitting as you will during the speech.

- Wear the clothing you plan to wear to see if it is appropriate and makes you feel confident.

- Ask a friend or colleague to watch your dress rehearsal and offer last-minute comments.

- Rehearse until you are as comfortable as possible, but do not wear yourself out. You will need energy for your speech event.

6
Prepare for Questions

Not all speaking situations will have an opportunity for an audience question-and-answer (Q and A) session. Like some impromptu speeches, a Q and A session may happen spontaneously, so be prepared:

- Anticipate questions you might get, and plan answers. Think about and consider questions you hope for—or dread.

- Practice your answers.

- If your topic is particularly complex, prepare a "Facts Sheet" with details that you can consult during the Q and A session.

- Remain calm, confident, and professional with aggressive or difficult questioners.

- Be honest if you do not know the answer. "I don't know" is an acceptable answer if you have demonstrated your knowledge in other ways. Offer to look for an answer and get back to the audience member if the situation allows you to do so.

- Give your speech to a practice audience and have them ask you questions.

How Should You Prepare for the Day of the Speech?

Being prepared and not rushed the day of your speech is essential. You want to focus on being calm and positive. Waiting until the last minute to prepare or getting stressed will only create problems.

Imagine what it is like for Sal the day of his speech. The night before, his friends convinced him to go to a football game rather than rehearse his speech. Sal has a PowerPoint presentation to use during his speech but has not practiced with it in the classroom. He also needs to make photocopies to give to his audience. His speech is at 2:00 in the afternoon tomorrow, so he thinks he will have plenty of time to get those things done. Sal decides to go to the game. The game is close, with a lot of loud cheering and excitement. Sal's team wins, and the guys decide to go out and celebrate.

The next morning, Sal is hoarse from all the yelling and smoke at the pub. He takes some cold medicine and then leaves to make his copies. Overnight, the temperature has dropped, however, and now his car will not start. Two hours later, Sal finds a friend who is willing to take him to campus.

It is now 11:30, and Sal still needs to make sure his presentation works on the class computer and get copies made. Plus, he has a class at 12:00. Sal goes to class and gets the copies made, but it takes longer than he thought because the copy center is busy. Now it is too late to practice in the room. Class starts in a few minutes, and Sal rushes to get there. On the way, he realizes that he is starving. He has forgotten to eat breakfast and lunch. It is too late now.

Sal has set himself up to give a poor speech. He is tired and hungry. His voice is a mess. The cold medicine makes his issues worse because it dries out his throat and messes up his memory. He is running late and has no idea if his presentation aids will work. Sal could have prevented most of these issues if he had just prepared better. Having a life outside of class is important, but never a higher priority than being prepared for your responsibilities on the day of your speech.

Preparing Yourself

THE DAY BEFORE THE SPEECH

- Make sure you are well rehearsed and completely prepared. Don't put off preparation for the day of the speech. Problems can arise that can make your speech day more stressful.

- Be kind to your body and voice. You know you are going to need your voice the next day, so avoid activities that will stress your voice, mind, or body. Get a good night's sleep (eight hours), eat right, keep hydrated, and limit your caffeine and alcohol consumption. Avoid taking drugs such as antihistamines or expectorants before you speak, because they can adversely affect your voice.

- Select and prepare what you will wear.

- If you know there is an event you want to attend the night before your speech, get your speech completely done before you attend the event. Procrastination and speeches do not work well together.

- Practice at least once the day before your speech, so that you can go to sleep that night feeling confident.

- Try to conceive of any problems you might have the next day and prevent them if possible.

- Remind yourself that you can give a successful speech if you are prepared.

THE DAY OF THE SPEECH

- Don't forget to eat. If your body doesn't have the fuel it needs, nervousness may intensify and your memory will decrease. If your stomach is growling loudly, it will distract you and may distract your audience.

- Eat foods that your stomach finds easy to digest and eat well-rounded meals. If your speech is within an hour of a meal, avoid eating foods that can irritate your throat, such as ice cream, milk, and chocolate.

- Get to the speech event early so that you are not rushed.

- Check all necessary equipment and deal with any issues you discover.

- If you will be speaking for a long period of time, you might want to keep water handy.

- Try to be by yourself just before the speech and prepare yourself mentally. Do vocal or physical activities to warm up and lessen your apprehension.

- Look over your notes one more time to make sure they are in the right order.

- Finally, walk to the front of the room with the confidence you should have because you are ready and about to give a well-prepared speech.

Harriet's Speech

Harriet owns a canine sport center and is a member of the American Kennel Club. A local retirement community that caters to retirees with pets has asked her to come speak at their luncheon. Most of the retirees have small dogs, ranging across several breeds and mixed breeds. Harriet decides that an informative speech about how humans domesticated the dog would be interesting. The community's administrator told her that she would be giving the presentation just after the noon meal and should plan to talk about 10 minutes. Harriet did her research and created her preparation outline three days prior to her speech.

REHEARSING HER SPEECH

STEP 1 – Reading Aloud the Preparation Outline:

Harriet simulated giving her speech from the preparation outline. She made sure she would not be interrupted and located a stopwatch to time the speech. The first two times she read it aloud, she did not time it. She was looking for places that needed more detail and making sure she could easily move from one point to another. The next two times she read it aloud, Harriet timed the speech. The first time, it was 6:35; the next, it was 6:15. She was happy with those times, because she still needed to incorporate her visuals and move to a more extemporaneous delivery. Both of those issues would likely lengthen the speech.

#1

INTRODUCTION: (slide)
Approximately 74.8 million dogs owned in the U.S. (slide)
39% of all households own at least one dog. (slide)
You all are special -- 49% of you have a dog that worships you.
I currently run the Bedrock Canine Sport Cent[e]
4 dogs myself.
The history of the domesticated dog!

STEP 2 – Preparing Her Delivery Outline:

Happy with the formal structure of her speech, Harriet turned to creating her delivery outline. She decided not to use a lectern because the gathering was informal, so she put the outline on stiff note cards that would be easy to handle. Harriet noted her slides on the cards.

#2

MAIN POINT:
The domesticated dog originated from the wolf.
According to Christine McGourty (BBC news) — "Origins of Dogs Traced"
• Nearly 15,000 years ago, humans tamed a small pack of
   [wo]lves near China (slide plus sound of wolf calls)
[T]he genetic diversity of East Asian dogs supports this
[or]igin theory.

THE HISTORY OF THE DOMESTICATED DOG

Dogs have had a special bond with humans for 12,000 years.

STEP 3 – Preparing Her Presentation Aids:

Harriet wanted to make her speech more fun by using slides that contained factual information as well as visual and sound cues that might bring the facts to life. She opened with a collage of photos, followed by a series of facts on slides. When possible, she added unique pictures or graphs and sound bites.

STEP 4 – Practicing, Practicing, Practicing:

With everything ready for the final speech, Harriet practiced the speech several times during the next two days. If she had 10 minutes of free time, she would stop and practice, with or without the presentation aids. Three times on one night and twice the night before the event, she practiced the speech with the presentation aids to make sure they were incorporated smoothly into the speech.

STEP 5 – Final Dress Rehearsal:

The last time Harriet practiced (the night before the event), she gave the speech exactly as she planned— and in front of two of the trainers at the sport center. Both trainers thought the retirees would enjoy the presentation. One suggested deleting a slide that seemed unnecessary, as it was a repetitive visual of a a similar kind of dog. Both trainers suggested slowing down and looking less at the slides.

HISTORY OF THE DOMESTICATED DOG – FACT SHEET
Source: *BBC Science and Nature* page for dogs

History
- Dogs are part of the family *Canidae*—which includes wolves, coyotes, and foxes—thought to have evolved 60 million years ago.
- A breed of dog called the Saluki appears on the ancient tombs of Egypt from around 2100 BC and is thought to be the dog mentioned in the Bible. Its body has often been found mummified along with the Egyptian pharaohs in pyramids. The ancient Greeks and Romans developed a number of breeds, including the greyhound, mastiff, and bloodhound. The Romans made sacrifices to the dog-like god Procyon.
- Dalmatians were trained to run along with horse-drawn carriages in the mid-1800s and became known as "carriage dogs."

Life Span
- Ranges from 7 to 18 years, but the average life span is 12 to 14 years.

Works Cited

"Breeds." *American Kennel Club*. AKC. Web. 19 Oct. 2009.

"Dog Facts and Dog Trivia." *Indian Child*. IndianChild.com. Web. 19 Oct. 2009.

Harris, Hannah. "How Dogs Work." *How Stuff Works*. How Stuff Works , 10 Mar. 2008. Web. 19 Oct. 2009.

MacDougall, Elizabeth Blair. *Dumbarton Oaks Colloquium on the History of Landscape Architecture*. Washington: Dumbarton Oaks Trustees for Harvard University, 1987. Print.

McGourty, Christine. "Origins of Dogs Traced." *BBC News World Edition*. BBC, 22 Nov. 2002. Web. 19 Oct. 2009.

"U.S. Pet Ownership Statistics." *The Humane Society of the United States*. The Humane Society, 17 Mar. 2008. Web. 19 Oct. 2009.

STEP 6 – Preparing for Questions:

Harriet has given presentations to retirement communities before and knows the audiences love to ask questions. So she prepared a fact sheet, including her works cited, and planned to answer any questions the audience might have about the sport center. She made copies of the classes offered at the sport center and prepared little "doggie bags" for each pet as a parting gift.

PREPARING FOR THE DAY OF THE SPEECH

The night before the event, Harriet made sure to have everything prepared and got plenty of sleep. She selected a nice pair of khaki pants and her best Sport Center shirt to wear the next day. The day of the event, she ate a healthy breakfast late in the morning so that she could wait to eat lunch after the speech. She arrived at the retirement center before the lunch crowd arrived and set up her projector and tested it. The center provided a wireless lapel microphone, as the room was large and several of the residents had difficulty hearing in the space. Harriet tested the microphone and eagerly awaited the end of the audience's meal, ready to give her presentation.

10

USING PRESENTATION AIDS

Introduction

Sometimes words alone are not enough to convey your message. Imagine describing a praying mantis to someone who has never seen one, without showing a picture. Imagine describing the evolution of Batman over the course of his films without film segments. How would you explain where Serbia is without a map? Or demonstrate how to bake a cake without ingredients and kitchenware?

Think how much easier it is to raise donations for disaster relief when you show pictures of people trying to survive; when you add dramatic music, the emotional power increases. Even dry sales statistics can come to life in a graph.

When a speech is complex, retention is important, or emotions need to be heightened, a presentation aid can support and supplement your speech. This chapter explains your options and shows you how to relate presentation aids to your speech, your audience, and the situation.

Chapter 8: Using Language Successfully	215
Chapter 9: Delivering Your Speech	237

CHAPTER 10 CONTENTS

What Can Presentation Aids Do for Your Speech?	262
What Are the Types of Presentation Aids?	264
1 Actual Items	264
2 Models	265
3 Photographs	266
4 Drawings	267
5 Charts and Tables	268
6 Graphs	269
7 Media	272
How Do You Determine What Presentation Aids You Need to Use?	274
1 Establish Their Purpose	274
2 Select the Best Type	275
3 Consider How to Display Them	275
What Are Common Methods for Displaying Aids?	276
1 Chalkboards and Whiteboards	276
2 Posters	277
3 Handouts	278
4 Flip Charts	279
5 Advanced Technology	280
How Do You Craft an Effective Aid?	282
1 Follow Good Design Principles	282
2 Give Yourself Enough Time to Be Creative	287
How Can You Use Presentation Software?	288
1 Create a Storyboard	289
2 Begin with PowerPoint Basics	290
How Do You Use a Presentation Aid Successfully?	294
Atticus's Speech	296
Tab 4 Review	298

What Can Presentation Aids Do for Your Speech?

Presentation aids are three-dimensional or two-dimensional visual items, video footage, audio recordings, and/or multimedia segments that support and enhance your speech.

These aids can assist you in informing, persuading, or commemorating. They can make it easier for your audience to understand your topic. They can help compel an audience to change their attitudes, values, or beliefs, or to act differently, as the aids can help them see the points for themselves. Presentation aids can intensify a moment of commemoration by energizing multiple senses and emotions.

REINFORCE UNDERSTANDING AND PROMOTE CLARITY

Have you ever heard someone say, "I just don't see it"? Although this statement means that a person doesn't understand something, it hints at how we visualize complex issues, concepts, or processes in order to comprehend them. Illustrating the concepts in your speech with presentation aids helps your listeners visualize and understand them. In addition, providing condensed information (such as key statistics) and examples through presentation aids helps clarify and reinforce the points in your speech.

GRAB ATTENTION AND MAINTAIN INTEREST

The more senses you can kindle in your audience, the more involved, excited, and motivated they will become. Presentation aids can make your information more vivid and usually more dramatic.

ASSIST WITH RETENTION

Your audience will retain more information if you not only *tell* them but also *show* them. Presentation aids organize and emphasize what you believe is important for your audience to remember. Aids are often a useful way to condense or repeat your oral message.

IMPROVE YOUR CREDIBILITY

If your presentation aids are well made, are used appropriately, and do not distract from your message, they will bolster your ethos and professionalism. The right balance is important. Aids that are too flashy or slick will seem superficial or manipulative; and, therefore, you will seem unreliable. Aids that are executed poorly or fail during the speech can also lower your credibility.

HELP YOU CROSS A CULTURAL DIVIDE

Supplementing your words when speaking to a diverse audience can help you connect across cultures. When your languages or experiences differ, presentation aids can assist audience understanding and build empathy. For example, pictures may help if your audience struggles with English. Or enlisting a model to wear a pregnancy body suit may help demonstrate what it is like to be pregnant if, for instance, a speaker is addressing an audience of fathers-to-be.

TIPS: Using Visuals Cross-Culturally

- Limit the number of words and, if possible, use the audience's language.
- Avoid words that might not translate well (technical words, jargon, slang, etc.).
- Avoid images that could be confusing or culturally offensive.
- Consider cultural views of colors. For example, the color red in China symbolizes good luck, but in South Africa, it is the color of mourning.

CONVEY EMOTION

"A picture is worth a thousand words," especially when it comes to emotions. Visual images and audio recordings are effective ways to create an emotional response in your audience. Next time you are watching a movie like one of the classic hits *Jaws, E.T.,* or any of the *Star Wars, Indiana Jones, Harry Potter,* or *Lord of the Rings* films, think about how the soundtrack creates and maintains an emotional feeling. Those songs or brief sound bites serve as presentation aids.

HELP YOU MAINTAIN AN EXTEMPORANEOUS DELIVERY

Proper use of presentation aids forces you to know your speech well enough to venture away from your delivery outline to incorporate and explain the aid. If you use a slideshow, the content of the slides can also serve to jog your memory as you go through the speech. *However, be careful not to make your delivery outline the presentation aid or to read from the slides.* Your presentation aid should jog your memory, not be your memory for you. Keep your aids audience centered and your delivery focused on your audience, not the aid. Practicing multiple times with the actual aids will help you stay audience centered.

CONFIDENCE BOOSTER

Presentation aids can boost your confidence by:

- Helping you internalize your information as you create the aids
- Helping you organize your thoughts
- Serving as a way for you to present your message more professionally
- Giving you the opportunity to change your visual focus and/or physically move during the speech
- Offering you the opportunity to redirect your audience's eyes to something besides you

What Are the Types of Presentation Aids?

1 **Actual Items**

2 **Models**

3 **Photographs**

4 **Drawings**

5 **Charts and Tables**

6 **Graphs**

7 **Media**

1

Actual Items

You can use people, animals, or objects when they are the actual items you are talking about or relate to the topic of your speech and help relay your message. For example, if you are planning to give a demonstration speech on cake decorating, you might decorate cupcakes with different designs for easier transport and display.

Advantages

- Can get your audience's attention
- Can demonstrate, illustrate, exemplify, or emphasize your topic
- Can be simple to add to your speech because you do not need to create them
- Can help the audience visualize persuasive issues
- Can add humor

Disadvantages

- Can be scary or dangerous to your audience or inappropriate for the occasion or location of the speech (e.g., live spiders or snakes, guns, anything with a flame, cats if people are allergic, etc.)
- Can be too small to see or too large to bring
- Can distract the audience from the message

2

Models

Models are three-dimensional representations. Models are usually scaled to size—often smaller than the real thing, such as a model car, but sometimes larger, such as a model of a molecule.

Advantages

- Are great alternatives when you cannot bring the actual items
- Can get your audience's attention
- Can demonstrate, illustrate, exemplify, or emphasize your topic
- Can be simple to add to your speech when you do not need to create them
- Can help you visually compare and contrast

Disadvantages

- Can be hard to locate and expensive
- Can be too small for the entire audience to see
- Can be unpredictable if it has working parts
- Can distract the audience from the message

PRACTICING ETHICS

Do not use dangerous or prohibited presentation aids. If an aid could be harmful to you or your audience, use a model or picture instead. If an aid is illegal or prohibited where you will be giving the speech, do not use it. At best, it will lower your credibility and, at worst, you could be asked to leave, hurt someone, or be arrested.

3
Photographs

Photographs are two-dimensional representations of places, concepts, people, animals, or objects. They can be original photographs, posters of photographic images, or other types of print display.

Advantages
- Can be as effective as an object or model if three-dimensional understanding is not important
- Can condense a lot of material onto one aid
- Can create a sense of authenticity
- Can be easy to use and somewhat economical

- Can help you compare and contrast
- Can appeal to the audience's emotions
- Can help you transport your audience to a distant land or explain an abstract concept

Disadvantages
- Can be hard for the entire audience to see
- Can be less effective than an actual item or model
- Can be overused if they are stock photographs, making them less effective than photographs created for your speech

4
Drawings

Drawings are maps, sketches, diagrams, plans, or other nonphotographic representations of places, concepts, people, animals, or objects. They may show a whole or part of an area, or dissect the parts or workings of something.

Advantages
- Can be very helpful when objects or models are not practical or available
- Can visually demonstrate how something works, operates, or is constructed
- Can sometimes be located ready-made
- Can show detail, processes, details, relationships, or arrangements
- Can be used to emphasize location, geography, or topography (especially maps)

Disadvantages
- Can be hard to locate or create a professional drawing
- Can be hard for the entire audience to see
- Can have too much detail if not created for your speech
- Can lower your credibility if sloppy or too simplistic

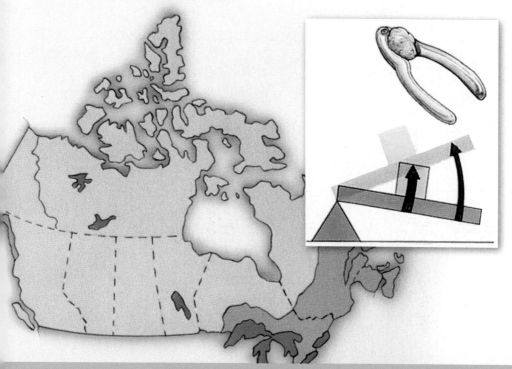

5
Charts and Tables

Charts are visual summaries of complex or large quantities of information. Two common charts are flowcharts and organizational charts. *Flowcharts* (see example below) diagram step-by-step development through a procedure, relationship, or process. *Organizational charts* illustrate the structure or chain of command in an organization. *Tables* consist of numbers or words arranged in rows, columns, or lists.

Advantages
- Can make the complex understandable
- Can summarize a lot of information
- Can show relationships and potential cause-and-effect issues
- Can help an audience think through hypothetical situations (especially charts)
- Can help the audience understand exact numbers or information quickly (especially tables)

Disadvantages
- Can be less memorable than other visuals or ineffective as an attention-grabber
- Can require you to spend a lot of time explaining them
- Can be overwhelming or confusing if too detailed or complex
- Can be hard for the entire audience to see

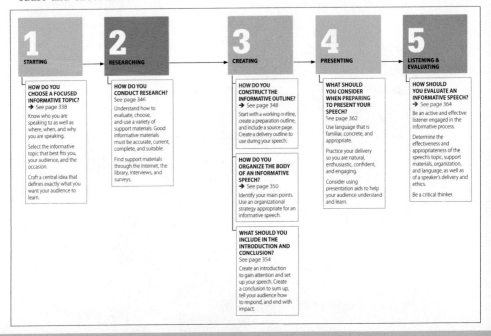

1 STARTING

HOW DO YOU CHOOSE A FOCUSED INFORMATIVE TOPIC?
➔ See page 338
Know who you are speaking to as well as where, when, and why you are speaking.

Select the informative topic that best fits you, your audience, and the occasion.

Craft a central idea that defines exactly what you want your audience to learn.

2 RESEARCHING

HOW DO YOU CONDUCT RESEARCH?
See page 346
Understand how to evaluate, choose, and use a variety of support materials. Good informative materials must be accurate, current, complete, and suitable.

Find support materials through the Internet, the library, interviews, and surveys.

3 CREATING

HOW DO YOU CONSTRUCT THE INFORMATIVE OUTLINE?
➔ See page 348
Start with a working outline, create a preparation outline, and include a source page. Create a delivery outline to use during your speech.

HOW DO YOU ORGANIZE THE BODY OF AN INFORMATIVE SPEECH?
➔ See page 350
Identify your main points. Use an organizational strategy appropriate for an informative speech.

WHAT SHOULD YOU INCLUDE IN THE INTRODUCTION AND CONCLUSION?
See page 354
Create an introduction to gain attention and set up your speech. Create a conclusion to sum up, tell your audience how to respond, and end with impact.

4 PRESENTING

WHAT SHOULD YOU CONSIDER WHEN PREPARING TO PRESENT YOUR SPEECH?
See page 362
Use language that is familiar, concrete, and appropriate.

Practice your delivery so you are natural, enthusiastic, confident, and engaging.

Consider using presentation aids to help your audience understand and learn.

5 LISTENING & EVALUATING

HOW SHOULD YOU EVALUATE AN INFORMATIVE SPEECH?
➔ See page 364
Be an active and effective listener engaged in the informative process.

Determine the effectiveness and appropriateness of the speech's topic, support materials, organization, and language, as well as of a speaker's delivery and ethics.

Be a critical thinker.

6
Graphs

Whereas charts and tables simply organize numbers and words, **graphs** are visual representations of numerical (statistical) information that demonstrate relationships or differences between two or more variables. The main benefits of graphs are:

- They simplify statistical information.
- They add visual interest.
- They can be very informative or persuasive.
- They help you discuss statistical information.
- They help your audience focus on relationships.

There are four common types of graphs: line, bar, pie, and pictograms. The next few pages will briefly introduce you to each type. Making graphs is relatively easy with software like PowerPoint and Excel.

LINE GRAPHS

Line graphs contain numerical points plotted on a horizontal axis for one variable and on the vertical axis for another; you then connect the points to make a line. Be sure to clearly label horizontal and vertical axes so that your audience can see and understand them. See an example at the bottom of this page.

Advantages
- Can simplify complex statistical information
- Can be extremely easy to read if created effectively

Disadvantages
- Can be less effective if you have more than three lines to plot
- Can require a projector

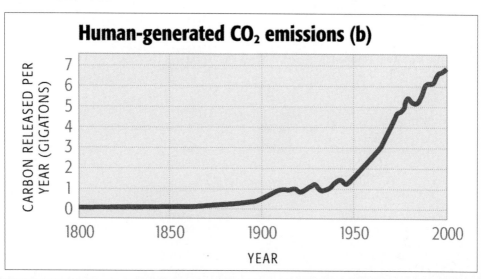

BAR GRAPHS

Bar graphs (also known as bar charts) are visuals consisting of vertical or horizontal bars that represent sets of data. Make sure your horizontal and vertical axes are clearly labeled.

Advantages
- Can be easy for your audience to interpret if created effectively
- Can demonstrate change over time at a glance

Disadvantages
- Can be less effective in black and white
- Can require a projector

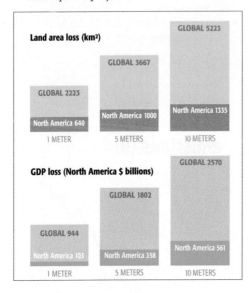

PICTOGRAPHS

Pictographs (also known as pictograms) are bar graphs that use pictures instead of bars. Make sure to label the graph and assign a unit measure to the individual pictorial icons.

Advantages
- Can make statistical information more interesting
- Can be easy for your audience to interpret if created effectively

Disadvantages
- Can take time to locate appropriate pictures or icons to represent your data
- Can be unfamiliar to your audience
- Can be less effective in black and white
- Can require a projector

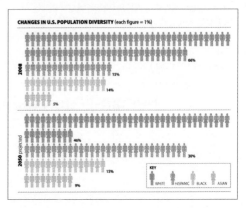

➔ See page 34 for a larger version of this pictograph.

TIP: Finding Icons
These sites offer icons and graphics that might be helpful when creating a pictograph:
www.coolarchive.com
www.freegraphics.com
www.iconbazaar.com

TIP: Showing Time
When creating a line or bar graph and time is a variable, always put time on the horizontal axis.

PIE GRAPHS

Pie graphs (also known as circle graphs or pie charts) are circular graphs with sections representing a percentage of a given quantity. It is best to limit your segments to seven or fewer. You can combine the smallest ones if you have more than seven. Always make sure your pie adds up to exactly 100 percent. Labels should be brief and outside the segments if needed. Pie and bar graphs tend to illustrate the same types of data, but you should use a pie graph when comparing segments of a whole.

Advantages
- Can help your audience quickly visualize the divisions of the whole item you are discussing
- Can effectively graph up to seven variables at once

Disadvantages
- Can be difficult to clearly and visibly label the segments
- Must be in color

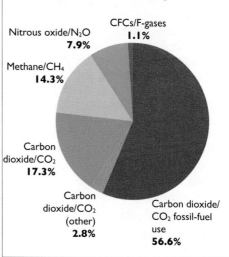

GREENHOUSE-GAS EMISSIONS BY GAS, 2004
CO_2 from fossil-fuel burning and deforestation makes up the bulk of greenhouse-gas emissions.

CFCs/F-gases 1.1%
Nitrous oxide/N_2O 7.9%
Methane/CH_4 14.3%
Carbon dioxide/CO_2 17.3%
Carbon dioxide/CO_2 (other) 2.8%
Carbon dioxide/CO_2 fossil-fuel use 56.6%

When to Use Graphs	Line Graph	Bar Graph	Pictograph	Pie Graph
Informing and persuading	●	●	●	●
Demonstrating change over time or comparing two or more items	●	●	●	
Showing frequency, distribution, and correlations	●	●		
Comparing percentages related to one whole thing				●

7

Media

Sometimes static two- or three-dimensional images are not effective. For example, Whitney is a college basketball player helping conduct a high school basketball camp, and she needs to teach a complex play. She decides to use game footage so that she will be able to slow down, speed up, and pause the video to make sure her audience understands the essence of the play. Such information would be difficult or impossible to present with other types of presentation aids.

Some reasons to consider using media:
- When the topic demands more auditory and visual examples
- When you know it might be difficult to keep your audience's attention
- When you know your message really needs it
- When you have the right equipment and software to make it professional
- When time and money to create the aids are not factors
- When you have practiced enough to make its use seem flawless

When you use mediated presentation aids, you might use video, audio, a combination, or a more complex multimedia format.

VIDEO AND AUDIO

Audio and video clips can be effective presentation aids. **Video clips** are any footage you use from television, movies, or any other type of video. **Audio clips** are recordings of sound only. For example, you might have a recording of the sounds dolphins make, music, an interview, a radio program, or a famous speech.

Advantages
- Can grab attention and make a speech memorable by appealing to your audience through sight, sound, and movement
- Can illustrate a point
- Can be linked to PowerPoint slides
- Can increase your ethos when used properly

Disadvantages
- Can require special production skills
- Can require special equipment that might not be available at your speech event
- Can require a lot of practice with the equipment to smoothly incorporate the video and audio into the speech
- Can be time-consuming
- Should only be used for short durations so that they do not become the speech or compete with the speaker
- Can increase the potential for errors, bad timing, ineffective technology use, and equipment failure

MULTIMEDIA

Multimedia refers to the combination of multiple presentation aids (still images, graphs, text, sound, and video) into one choreographed production.

Advantages

- Can be very creative and appeals to almost all senses
- Can be very professional
- Can increase your ethos when used properly

Disadvantages

- Can be too flashy and steal the stage from your speech's message
- Can be costly and time-consuming to make
- Requires special equipment
- Can require special production skills
- Can be difficult to coordinate—especially in an unfamiliar space
- Should only be used for short durations so that the aids do not become the speech or compete with the speaker
- Can increase the potential for errors, bad timing, ineffective technology use, and equipment failure

PRACTICING ETHICS

Remember to cite the sources for presentation aids that you did not create or the sources of information you put into an aid. For example, "This YouTube video, downloaded July 10, shows…"

It is often wise to put a written reference to a source on a visual you didn't create or collect the content for. This will help you remember an oral citation as well. Place it at the bottom in a font large enough to read and include necessary citation information. Follow your instructor's suggestions.

➜ See pages 284 and 286 for visual citation examples

How Do You Determine What Presentation Aids You Need to Use?

1 **Establish Their Purpose**
2 **Select the Best Type**
3 **Consider How to Display Them**

To determine which presentation aids to use, establish a purpose for each aid; select the best types for you, your audience, and your topic; and consider what options you have to display or produce the aids. You should think about all these elements together, although one might take precedence over another. For example, if you will be speaking to a large audience, a handwritten list of numbers on a flip chart will not do much to support your speech, whereas professionally created graphs can be helpful.

1
Establish Their Purpose

You should never use a presentation aid just because you can or to be glitzy. The important parts of any speech are you and the speech message. Your presentation aids should assist, support, and facilitate your message, not detract from or outshine it. Each aid you use needs a distinct purpose. You can establish the purpose by returning to your preparation outline and considering where in the outline you need to use an aid to:

- Grab attention or maintain interest
- Reinforce understanding and promote clarity
- Appeal to your audience's emotions
- Help the audience remember key issues
- Aid in intercultural communication

> **TIP: Check Your Assignment**
> Consult the requirements for each of your class assignments. Some assignments may require presentation aids, and some may limit or not allow them. Follow the instructor's guidelines.

2
Select the Best Type

You should select the type of presentation aids you use by considering yourself, your topic, your audience, and the situation.

YOU

When considering yourself as a factor, think about the answers to questions such as: What equipment am I comfortable with? What software do I need to create or present the aids? Am I familiar enough with that software to be effective? Which aids would I feel comfortable using? Which types will raise my credibility? Which presentation aids do I have time to create and practice with?

YOUR TOPIC

When considering your topic, think about your speech goal: Is it informative or persuasive? If informative, how can your aids help the audience visualize your message, challenge what the audience already knows, or simplify information? If persuasive, think about how your aids can support an idea, evoke emotions, demonstrate fulfilling a need, call the audience to action, or show audience relevance. Ask yourself: How can each aid move through the speech to reach the conclusion?

YOUR AUDIENCE

When considering your audience, reflect on their relationship with the topic and their ability to access the presentation aid. Ask yourself: What do they need to know about the topic, and which aids would be supportive? Will the information in the speech be difficult for the audience to understand? If so, which aids will best assist their understanding? Are there reasons why all or part of the audience would not be able to access a presentation aid? For example, are there factors that might prevent someone from reading or seeing visuals or hearing video/audio clips?

THE SITUATION

Where, why, and when you are speaking could significantly influence which type of presentation aids you use. For example, many visual aids will not work outside, and even quality audio is challenging. Likewise, many special occasion speeches are given at events where certain presentation aids would seem strange. For example, a PowerPoint presentation might seem inappropriate during a eulogy or wedding toast. However, displaying an object or pictures that relate to the person being eulogized or raising your glass to signal the wedding toast would be acceptable.

3
Consider How to Display Them

Finally, you must consider how the aids will be presented for the audience. Various methods are available to most speakers. Your decision will be determined by what you are comfortable with, the size of the audience, the availability of equipment, what will work in the speech environment, cost, and effectiveness. The next section will explain some options for displaying your presentation aids. Whichever method you select, remember to practice multiple times with that method as you rehearse your speech.

What Are the Common Methods for Displaying Aids?

1 **Chalkboards and Whiteboards**

2 **Posters**

3 **Handouts**

4 **Flip Charts**

5 **Advanced Technology**

1 Chalkboards and Whiteboards

Chalkboards and whiteboards are usually available in classroom settings and provide impromptu surfaces for writing (with chalk or special markers).

Advantages

- Are usually free and easy to use
- Can be used spontaneously
- Can easily be edited or corrected by erasing
- Can have few potential problems
- Can supplement other aids

Disadvantages

- Can be considered low-tech and unprofessional
- Can do little to build ethos
- Can limit your eye contact with the audience
- Require good writing and spelling skills

When to Use Chalkboards and Whiteboards

- For impromptu explanations
- For brainstorming with the audience
- As a backup to other aids

Helpful Hints for Usage

- Use this type of aid sparingly.
- Locate an eraser, some chalk, or a working marker before starting the speech.
- Use upper- and lowercase letters and print legibly.

2
Posters

Posters are hand- or computer-created single-sheet visuals intended to be attached to a wall or displayed on an easel. They typically include text and visual elements but may be entirely visual or entirely textual.

Advantages
- Can grab attention
- Can be useful for condensing information
- Can be professionally prepared (although expensive to print)

Disadvantages
- Are less effective for large audiences
- Can look sloppy if created by hand
- Can be time-consuming and difficult to create

When to Use Posters
- When you do not have or do not trust electronic equipment
- To demonstrate a sequence or change over time by placing each step on a new poster. For example, if you want to demonstrate the evolution of Mickey Mouse from creation to the present day, creating several posters depicting each progression of Mickey could be a way to display how he evolved.
- For small group presentations

Helpful Hints for Usage
- Keep your posters simple, neat, and professional.
- Make them large enough to be seen from the back of the room.
- Proofread your posters or have someone else do it.
- Discreetly number multiple posters to keep track of their order.
- Plan out how to display your posters; never hold them.
- Practice with your posters.

TIP: Posters via PowerPoint
You can create a poster with PowerPoint if you have access to a printer that can print large sheets. However, printing can be costly and is usually not an option for the beginning speaker. In the workplace, this is more common.

To create a poster, use a blank slide and change its size. To do so, click on the Design Tab, select Page Setup, and specify the width and height; most posters are 32"x42", 36"x42", 48"x42", or the maximum, 56"x42".

3
Handouts

Handouts are standard-size printed pages designed to help you distribute new information that will summarize or reinforce your speech message. They typically include text and/or visual elements.

Advantages

- Can be convenient, easy to use, and inexpensive
- Can contain large amounts of information

Disadvantages

- Can be extremely distracting if given to the audience prior to or during the speech
- Can do little to aid your message or build your ethos if given after the speech
- Can be costly if long and/or for a very large audience

When to Use Handouts

- When details are too small to be effective on other types of presentation aids
- When audience retention is crucial
- To reiterate or summarize
- To provide a reading list
- To provide take-home copies of your presentation
- As a backup to other aids

Helpful Hints for Usage

- Under most circumstances, handouts should be given after the speech to prevent them from distracting the audience.
- Only distribute handouts before giving the speech when it is absolutely necessary for your audience to follow you closely. Single-page handouts are best, if possible.
- Never distribute handouts during a speech.
- Include a title, the date, your name, and contact information.
- Make sure they look professionally made.
- Make about 10 percent more copies than you expect to hand out.

TIP: Print Your Presentation

You can print handouts of your PowerPoint presentation directly from the software. Go to the View Tab and select Handout Master to set up the pages. Then click on the Office button in the upper left-hand corner, followed by the Print menu. In the "print what:" box, select "handout."

4
Flip Charts

A flip chart is a large pad, usually of unlined or lined paper, displayed on either a large free standing or small tabletop easel.

Advantages
- Are convenient, easy to use, and inexpensive
- Do not require electricity
- Can be professionally prepared (but then expensive)

Disadvantages
- Do not work well for large groups (best for 10 or fewer audience members)
- Can be sloppy and time-consuming
- Can do little to build your ethos
- Require good writing and spelling skills

When to Use Flip Charts
- To appear spontaneous and involve audience
- For small group presentations

Helpful Hints for Usage
- Practice writing on and using the chart.
- Prepare the pages in advance or pre-write in light pencil.
- The first page should be blank or contain a title.
- Leave every other page blank for "silence" and to avoid having the next aid show through.
- Use no more than five words across and five lines down.
- Write only on the top two-thirds of the page.
- Print legibly; write letters at least three inches tall, and use upper- and lowercase.
- Use black and blue for text and strong primary colors for emphasis or graphs, diagrams, and so on.
- Allow for extra writing time.
- Test your markers.

5

Advanced Technology

CONTEMPORARY MEDIA

Along with the ability to easily transfer information, current media options offer you the ability to display information in ways that were unimaginable to an average person a few decades ago. Rarely will you speak in a professional venue that does not have some type of advanced media technology to assist you in conveying your message. One or more of these devices are in most classrooms, assisting you, your peers, and your instructor in the educational process.

The LCD (liquid crystal display) projector often replaces the television or small monitor and can project large images, from computers or DVD or VCR players, for numerous audience members to all see at once. Document cameras are contemporary overhead projectors with the ability to project opaque pages and objects instead of only transparencies. You might have interactive whiteboards with touch-screen surfaces, allowing you to negotiate the Internet as an audience of 20 or more look on. Digital media players give you easy access to audio or video clips, and video/teleconferencing can bring audiences located around the world to your speech event. Even software packages, like Microsoft's PowerPoint, make presentation aids more polished and integrated into your speech.

Advantages

- Can be more professional-looking to use computer-generated and computer-controlled aids
- Can build speaker ethos
- Can often include Internet access
- Can appeal to multiple senses of the audience members
- Can be seen and heard by larger audiences

Disadvantages

- Can be less effective when you want to create an intimate approach
- Can upstage you
- Can be time-consuming to create the aids
- Can require special knowledge to create or run the aids

TRADITIONAL MEDIA

Although considered less effective and out of date, traditional media devices such as standalone CD players, DVD players, VCRs, overhead projectors, and slide projectors are helpful in some situations. They may be all you have available; the best solution for the size of audience (if it is small); best for the environment; or valuable as a backup plan.

Advantages

- Can be relatively easy to learn to use
- Can back up contemporary media devices
- Can have fewer problems than more-contemporary technologies
- Can be less expensive and, therefore, more commonly available

Disadvantages

- Can be viewed as less-advanced technologies and are therefore not as strong at building ethos
- Can be awkward and more difficult to integrate into a speech than are computer-aided and computer-generated aids

When to Use Advanced Technologies

- When you want aids that are more effective than other printed or handmade display options
- When you are comfortable enough to create an effective aid and can easily present it
- If the equipment is available

Helpful Hints for Usage

- Smoothly integrate the devices into your speech. The technology should not be an obstacle to the audience.
- Don't let the technology upstage you.
- Don't let technology give your speech for you. Your audience expects to hear you, not a long audio/video clip or automated presentation aid.
- Always check the equipment and know its limits. For example, will the room be dark enough for the LCD projector?
- Have a backup plan.
- Keep the presentation simple, neat, and clear. Do not get carried away with bells and whistles.

How Do You Craft an Effective Aid?

1 Follow Good Design Principles
2 Give Yourself Enough Time to Be Creative

1 Follow Good Design Principles

In *Slide:ology: The Art and Science of Creating Great Presentations,* Nancy Duarte writes, "To succeed as a presenter, you must think like a designer."

Communication educators might add that to be a good designer, you must think like an audience-centered communicator, always mindful of your audience. Every decision you make about a presentation aid's design should relay your message better and focus on the audience's needs for understanding that message.

To meet this goal, you must follow good design principles and give yourself enough time to be creative.

Design principles relate to the arrangement and placement of various elements (color, text, line, images, space, etc.) for optimum effect. When you create two-dimensional presentation aids, think about the arrangement and placement of visual elements on the page, poster, or slide. Likewise, when you think about the relationship of all of your aids within a given speech, you need to consider arrangement and placement to allow the aids to nourish your verbal message. There are five design principles you should consider.

TIP: Plan Your Time

Plan your time carefully. You are better off starting early and having time left over to rehearse more—or to relax and feel confident about your preparation—than scrambling at the last minute and creating poor presentation aids.

UNITY

The principle of unity recognizes the need for the elements you use to connect or relate to each other. For example, in Chapter 8, you met Lewis, who was composing a speech about Greece. Here are some aids he might have created for it.

Imagine Greece

Source: Dorling Kindersley

Color unity
Make sure colors work well together and are complementary (opposite on the color wheel), analogous (colors that touch each other on the wheel), or monochromatic (variations of one color, as shown here).

Color harmony
Make sure your color palette is in harmony with the tone of your speech. Here, the blues suggest the waters surrounding Greece.

Country Facts

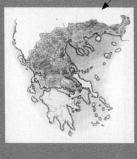

- The country's official name is the Hellenic Republic.

- In area, Greece is roughly the size of Alabama—51,146 square miles.

- Athens is the capital city.

Source: Dorling Kindersley and travel.state.gov

Image unity
Any images should directly relate to the text shown with them and to your verbal message at that moment.

Unity across aids
If you use multiple aids, they should fit together as a unified whole to support your speech. Avoid using unrelated aids or leaving a hole where you need an aid.

PATTERN

The pattern principle recommends that you create a design format and use it consistently. Just like the parallelism trait of effective main points, elements of your presentation aids should mirror each other whenever possible. Reusing patterns will help your audience quickly digest the material because the layout is familiar and not distracting. Keep your pattern simple.

Greece's People

- Population: 11,285,000 (2009 est.)
- The official language is Greek but many people are bilingual.
- The predominant religion is Christianity (Eastern Orthodox).
- Dance is an important cultural art.

Source: Dorling Kindersley, Encyclopedia Britannica Online, and MapsofWorld.com

Backgrounds
Use consistent colors, textures, or images for background.

Fonts
Use the same types, colors, and sizes of fonts with related elements (e.g., format all titles the same).

The Parthenon

- Built in the fifth century BCE
- Measures 101.34 feet wide by 228.14 feet long)
- Constructed of white marble, surrounded by 46 columns
- Contained a nearly 40-foot statue of Athena made of gold, ivory, and wood

Source: Dorling Kindersley

Symbols
Use the same symbols (bullets, checkmarks, etc.) to establish related patterns.

Content
Try to feature similar content for each main point if possible.

BALANCE

Balance deals with the feeling of equilibrium—a feeling of stability, symmetry, and calm. Think of watching a tug-of-war in which one side is obviously bigger and stronger. You immediately feel uneasy about the probable results, whereas, if the sides are balanced, you have a sense of symmetry and feel that the game could go either way. Balance in your aids will enhance your audience's feeling that your speech is balanced and organized. Compare the ineffective aid below with the more effective version.

Ineffective fonts
Avoid using decorative fonts.

Avoid using all caps
These can be hard to read.

Ineffective balance
Scattered arrangement of photos lacks focus.

Balanced fonts
Choose easy-to-read sans serif fonts (such as Tahoma or Arial), and use only one or two.

Readable font size
Use a large enough font size to be seen by everyone in the room—44 point for titles and 24 point to 32 point for other text is one general guideline.

Effective balance
Balance the elements with each other and with the blank space.

EMPHASIS

Emphasis is the highlighter of design. In other words, you can use design elements to help you emphasize what is the most important. See below for some guidelines. Also remember that your complete arsenal of presentation aids for a speech should adhere to the principle of emphasis. Use only aids that are important and that stress the important aspects of your verbal message.

Emphasizing text
Light text against a dark background projects the best and emphasizes the text.

Titles
Use titles for things like lists, graphs, or areas of a poster. Titles emphasize and foreshadow your speech content.

Currency

- Greece's official currency is the euro (symbol €).

- 1 euro equals 100 cents.

- On August 2, 2010, the exchange rate was 1.00 USD – 0.79 EUR.

Source: Worldtravelguide.net and Alamy.com

Emphasizing elements
Bullets, color, images, text size, text structures (underline, bold, or italic), and music are ways to draw the eye or ear to what is important.

RHYTHM

Rhythm has to do with a real or imagined sense of movement. Just as you can create a sense of rhythm with your vocal quality, you can create a visual sense of rhythm by emphasizing movement. Also, the pacing of your presentation aids throughout the speech can establish a rhythmic flow.

Added animation and sound can create rhythm, but be careful that they do not distract from or compete with your speech message. Limit these and use them consistently—and for a meaningful purpose, not simply because they are available. Some easier ways for beginning speakers to use rhythm in aids are text placement and images that contain or suggest movement.

Text placement

Using text or spacing that relates to each other, such as placing titles ands source lines in the same position on each aid, creates one type of rhythm.

Movement

Images that contain movement or move across or around the background can create a sense of rhythm.

TIP: Use an Idea Bank

Use the same idea-bank process you used to narrow your speech topic to focus in on your presentation aids (see Chapter 2). At the beginning of the process, consider anything an option and open your mind to wild ideas. One of your wild ideas just might become the best idea. That's the beauty of the creative process.

2

Give Yourself Enough Time to Be Creative

The time needed to be creative is difficult to predict because of so many variables. For example, can you easily come up with interesting ideas? Are you familiar with how to research and collect ideas? Are you comfortable with the method for producing your aid? The answers to these questions can drastically affect the time it takes to create your aids. For a general idea, Nancy Duarte offers a time frame for creating an hour-long presentation with 30 slides. If you adapt her recommendations to an eight-minute speech with four to six slides, your creation time might be similar to the following timeline:

- **1 to 2 hours** for researching and collecting ideas/information
- **1 hour** to evaluate audience needs and to outline your ideas
- **2+ hours** to create the presentation aids
- **30 minutes to 1 hour** to rehearse with aids

4.5 to 6+ hours total

Keep in mind that this is an estimate and you are the only one who can predict how long it will take. Be honest with yourself. If you don't know how to use the software or tend to spend a lot of time on details, you will need more time. Likewise, if it only takes you 30 minutes to create four slides, are you being creative and supporting your speech the best way you can?

How Can You Use Presentation Software?

1 **Create a Storyboard**
2 **Begin with PowerPoint Basics**

Many presentation software packages are available that can help you create an extremely professional presentation aid incorporating text, images, charts, graphs, sound, and/or video into one presentation. The most common is PowerPoint, which you can use to make posters and handouts as well (see Tip boxes on pages 277 and 278). Although software packages have revolutionized the ability to create professional presentations for almost anyone, they have downsides as well.

- They are overused and often used poorly.
- They can steal the show so much that your speech, which is your main focus, is ignored.
- They can turn the listeners off or destroy your credibility as a speaker.

Learn how to take advantage of presentation software without letting it have power over your speech. Creating computer-generated presentation aids takes time and knowledge. If you have not used such software before, you will need extra time to learn it and use it.

TIP: Software Tutorials

Investing in a good tutorial might be wise if presentation software is something you will use often. Here are some potentially helpful PowerPoint sites.

www.microsoft.com/office/powerpoint/default.asp

office.microsoft.com/en-us/powerpoint/HA101942821033.aspx (This page has a link to a demo on creating a presentation.)

www.iupui.edu/~webtrain/tutorials/powerpoint2000_basics.html#getting_started

www.csun.edu/it/training/guides/#powerpoint

1

Create a Storyboard

Storyboarding is similar to outlining a speech and is the act of sketching out the content and arranging the sequence of your slides. Storyboarding before you open your software is valuable for determining how many slides you will need and their order. A slide's purpose should be to help the audience understand your message better. Your slides should not be just talking points for you to read off of during the speech.

STEPS FOR STORYBOARDING

1. Create each slide by hand on a separate sheet of paper.

2. Include a title slide or an introduction slide. Decide if what you put on that slide reveals or only hints at your topic. Sometimes, mystery is an attention-getter.

3. Think about your main points and try to limit yourself to one slide per main point. You can count slides that build up as one, but limit this type of animation. Do not put your delivery outline on the slides. Give your audience time to read and absorb each slide.

4. Use a slide for the conclusion if helpful or to intensify your WOW statement.

5. Remember to place blank/blackout slides when you need to draw the focus back to you. This form of "white space" will give your audience a break from the visuals and will help them focus on your verbal message.

6. Adhere to effective design principles.

PRACTICING ETHICS

You must observe copyright laws. Students and educators may use original work by another person for a class presentation, but they must follow these rules.

- You may use a very small amount (under a minute) of copyrighted film, video, or animation without permission.

- You may use less than 30 seconds of music or lyrics from one musical piece without permission.

- You can use an entire photograph or illustration, but only a small portion of images from a collection (less than 10 percent of the collection).

- You cannot post that presentation material back to the Web without permission.

- You must display and mention the source, author/creator, title, and date of the material.

- You must display the copyright symbol (©) when necessary.

- Cite all sources of the material in your presentation aids and on your source page.

These rules apply to materials legally downloaded from the Internet or obtained by other legal means. Illegally downloaded materials are never fair use. (See www.utsystem.edu/ogc/intellectualproperty/copypol2.htm for more fair-use information.)

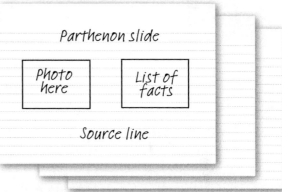

2

Begin with PowerPoint Basics

Although giving a complete tutorial on PowerPoint here is not possible, the following discussion highlights some of the basics you might need to know. Don't be afraid to ask for help from a colleague or someone at a computer center. Many schools have free PowerPoint workshops, and the Internet is another resource. Note that many of the commands and toolbars in PowerPoint resemble those used in Microsoft Word. Make sure you are learning the version of PowerPoint you have on your computer. The examples here are shown in PowerPoint 2007 on a Mac.

Tools

The tabs along the toolbar will allow you to do tasks such as cut and paste, change fonts, add bullets, insert text and images, select a design, check spelling, and view your slide show.

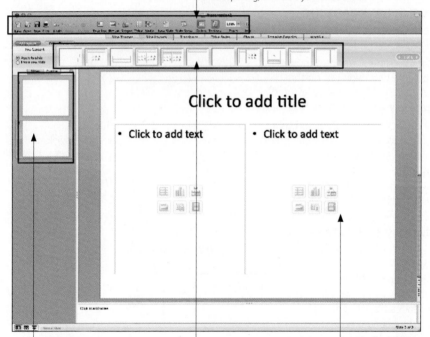

Slide thumbnails

Here you can scroll through mini versions of your slides. Click and drag slides to change order. Click between slides to add one.

Slide layout

This function includes built-in slide layouts as well as a blank slide if you want to build one from the ground up.

Placeholders

Unless you select a blank slide, dotted borders will outline the preset placeholders for inserting images or text.

GETTING STARTED

You have already storyboarded the number of slides and their content. Now it is time to create each one.

- Start with a new slide. You may find it easiest to create a title slide first, before moving on to content slides, to practice with the software's features.
- Select or create a slide theme. Don't pick one that is too busy or distracting.
- Select or create a slide layout. Remember to keep it as simple as possible.
- Using the insert functions, begin inserting your text and/or images.
- Don't forget to periodically save your slide show.

The next pages offer more guidelines for designing your slides.

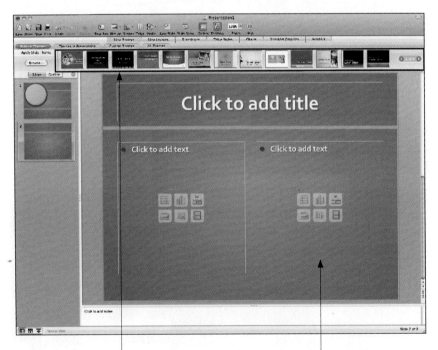

Slide themes

Each of these built-in designs offers a unified theme of colors, fonts, and graphic options.

Color themes

Each built-in design has a default color theme, or you can choose from a variety of other preset color themes. Stick to simple themes.

DESIGNING SLIDES

As you create your slides, follow the design principles outlined on pages 282–287. PowerPoint offers many ways to incorporate text, visuals, video, audio, and animation, but the simpler you keep your aids, the more effective they can be. The main slide elements you need to consider are color, space, text, and images—as well as sound, if used.

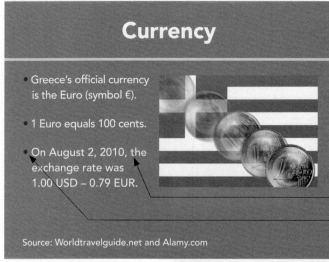

DO use design themes and insert functions to help effectively place your slide content.

DO use consistent, readable fonts, which many pre-built designs include.

DO use simple, pre-built list and bullet designs.

DON'T insert too many graphics or layer them so that they are not visually distinct.

DON'T use decorative or other hard-to-read fonts.

DON'T place text on top of busy photos.

Color

To help maintain the design elements of unity, pattern, and balance, limit your use of color and maintain consistency throughout. Ideally, use one background color or slide theme and two to three font colors, at the most, for titles, text, and emphasis. Use colors appropriate to your subject, audience, and any projected images. Medium colors are usually better than very dark ones.

Space

Using the preset slide layouts will show you how arranging and grouping together similar information and leaving space free of images or text can help you adhere to effective design principles. You do not want your audience to be overwhelmed visually or to feel the slides are out of balance (for example, top- or bottom-heavy). Note how the slide at the bottom of page 292 is completely filled with images and text, making it visually over-stimulating.

Text

Clearly, text will be an important part of your slides. You should use titles and, in some cases, you may include several lines of text in the main part of the slide. Keep text brief and organized so that your audience can read it quickly. Lists and bulleted items work well.

Select fonts that are easy to read. Limit your fonts to no more than two different ones on a single aid, and be consistent through-out the slides. Remember to avoid using all capitals (use both upper- and lowercase). Use italics, underlining, different-colored text, and boldface sparingly and for emphasis only. For the benefit of the audience, titles and subtitles should be in large sizes, such as 36 points or larger for titles and 24 points or larger for text.

Images and Sound

PowerPoint gives you several options for inserting visuals, audio, and video. The first rule for deciding what and if to use inserts in your slides is to ask: How does this item help illustrate, support, or clarify my topic? If you don't have a solid answer to that question, you don't need the image, sound, or video. If the insert passes that test, it must also be:

- Large and clear enough to be seen
- A high-enough resolution to be projected on a large screen
- Clearly related to your topic and ethically appropriate
- Displayed with a title and, if needed, source information
- Smoothly integrated into the presentation

Keep in mind that simpler is often better. For example, the slide on the bottom of page 292 incorporates more visual elements, but the slide above it will be more effective during a speech.

TIPS: Presenting the Slides

- Have a backup plan in case the system fails.
- Check the order of your slides against your delivery outline.
- Know how to display the slides in slide-show view, not the normal view you used as you created them.
- Learn slide-show commands. (For example, when in slide-show mode, press the B key for black out and the W key to return to the visual. This will help you display slides only when you are referring to them in your speech.)
- Rehearse using the slide show (in the speech-event space if possible).
- Make sure you have saved all of the slides, sound clips, and video for transportation to the event.
- Check the equipment the day of the speech.

How Do You Use a Presentation Aid Successfully?

PROOFREAD, PREVIEW, AND PRACTICE

Even before you rehearse with your presentation aids, make sure they work, look good, and are correct. Always proofread your aids for spelling or other errors. Having someone else proofread them is often a good idea to catch details that you might miss because you are so familiar with the aids.

Preview any computer-generated aids in the room where you will give the speech, at or close to the time you will speak, and with the exact equipment if possible. Sunlight can wash out projected images, and some LCD projectors are not very bright. If you encounter such issues, you may need to change color schemes. Make sure the system will accept the medium (flash drive, CD, etc.) your presentation is stored on. Be sure to save all of the files associated with the presentation in the same folder on the medium you will take to the speaking event; a common error is to forget audio or video files. The software you use to create the presentation should be the same version as the one you will use to deliver the presentation.

Practice with all aids you plan to use, including people, objects, models, computer-generated aids, and others. Not knowing how to use an aid or fumbling with it—or the equipment used to project it—will lower your ethos and increase your communication apprehension. You should be comfortable with your aid and any equipment related to it.

CHECK THE EQUIPMENT

Always check that the equipment is present, working, and set how you want it. You do not want to be surprised as you put something on an opaque projector by discovering that you did not turn on the equipment. You will need to pause or talk over the booting-up process, making you seem unprepared. Check the sound level of audio equipment. Even check for chalk, markers, and erasers, if there is any possibility you will use a board for an impromptu explanation.

KNOW WHEN TO DISPLAY AIDS

Display your aids as you need them, and then remove them from sight. The element of surprise helps draw your audience's attention to your topic as you display items and pulls attention back to you as you remove them. Turning the aid around or over, removing it from sight, or going to a blank slide/screen are all simple ways to achieve this.

DON'T PASS THE AIDS AROUND

If you have objects, items, pictures, or handouts, don't pass them around the room. This is distracting, and it is highly unlikely that everyone will get to see passed-around aids within the time frame of your speech. All of your audience needs to see the aid at the time you are speaking about it. If possible, give out all handouts after your speech so that the audience will not be tempted to read them instead of listening to you. If your topic is complex and you think the handouts will help listeners understand as you go, give them to the audience before you begin and incorporate them into the speech. Focus the audience on where you are on the handout.

USE THE TOUCH, TURN, TALK METHOD

The "Touch, Turn, Talk Method" refers to how you should relate to your presentation aid and the audience. The "Touch" stage happens as you point to, direct your eyes toward, move toward, and/or literally touch the aid you are using, drawing the focus completely to the aid. At that moment, you and the audience are attuned to the aid. The "Turn" stage happens as you turn from the aid and regain eye contact with the audience. Then you move into "Talk," where you explain the aid. This method sounds mechanical but should not look that way. The process should be a fluid back and forth between you, the aid, and the audience. You need to acknowledge the aid, return to the audience, and explain the content of the aid. Just displaying an aid or talking directly to the aid, instead of looking at the audience, is not effective.

PREPARE A BACKUP PLAN

Always have a backup plan. Be prepared for it to rain or snow the day of your speech, and have a way to keep your aids dry and safe. Be prepared for equipment to be missing or to fail. More often than not, if a problem arises, you will still need to give the speech, with or without your aids. If you have a plan, you will not be as stressed when something does go wrong, and you will still be able to give your speech effectively.

CHECKLIST for Presentation Aids

❑ Do my aids look professional?

❑ Do they support and enhance my speech?

❑ Are my aids appropriate for the topic, audience, and situation?

❑ Am I ethically representing information with my aids?

❑ Are my aids clear, simple, and understandable?

❑ Did I effectively design the aids?

❑ Do I cite sources in the speech and on the visuals?

❑ Do I effectively incorporate the aids in the speech?

❑ Do I use lead-in and transition devices where necessary?

❑ Do I balance my aids throughout the speech?

Atticus's Speech

Atticus raises birds and, several years ago, adopted a toucan named Zeek. Because toucans are not common birds or pets, Atticus decided to give an informative speech on toucans to a local bird society he belongs to. This group meets monthly to learn about different birds, to discuss breeding issues, and to learn ways to stop illegal and inhumane pet-bird practices. Zeek is a rescued bird, and Atticus wants to show him and other presentation aids during his speech to educate the audience about toucans. Atticus plans to give this speech several more times to others less knowledgeable about birds.

After narrowing his topic, conducting research, and creating his preparation outline, Atticus set out to create presentation aids to support his speech.

THE INTRODUCTION

Atticus grew up in the 1970s, when most kids knew a toucan as a bird looking for Kellogg's Froot Loops cereal. He decided to use a cereal box (object) as an attention-getter, followed by a few photographs of real toucans.

THE BODY OF THE SPEECH

In the body of the speech, Atticus used a topical strategy to cover three main areas about the birds: the physical characteristics of toucans, the variety in the toucan family, and the toucan habitat and diet. Knowing that it is

TOUCAN SIZE

The smallest
Lettered Araçari

The largest
Toco Toucan

important to balance presentational aids throughout his speech, Atticus located these aids at each main point.

When discussing the toucan's physical characteristics, Atticus used a variety of photographs, slides, video segments, and audio clips he found in books and credible sources online. For example, when discussing the different sizes of toucans, he showed a photo of the Lettered Araçari, the smallest, and a photo of the Toco Toucan, the largest.

Because it would be impossible to show all of the 40 different toucans, Toucanets, and Araçari, Atticus selected a variety of different ones to represent the breadth of the toucan family.

Keel-billed Toucan

Chestnut-Eared Araçari

Cuvier's Toucan

Yellow-Eared Toucanet

Atticus demonstrated how different toucans' calls can be by playing audio of the red-necked Araçari and the gold-collared Toucanet, which have distinctly different calls. The Internet Bird Collection Web site had numerous video and audio clips of different birds.

WHERE TOUCANS ARE FOUND

For the section of his speech related to habitat and diet, Atticus used a map highlighting the neotropics of Central and South America, where the birds can be found.

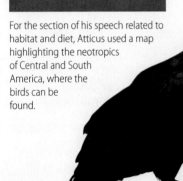

Because Atticus knew the audience members were all bird breeders and advocates, he ended the speech by bringing Zeek out of his covered cage. Zeek is very playful and a great WOW ending. When Atticus gives this speech to other audiences in situations where it might be hazardous for Zeek to make an appearance or Atticus is unsure how the audience might react, he plans to use just a photo of Zeek.

Tab 4: Review

CHAPTER 8 REVIEW QUESTIONS

1. Why is language so important to the public speaker?
2. What are six guidelines for using language effectively? Give an example of each.
3. What are the differences between oral style and written style?
4. What are some ways you can make your language distinctive? Explain.

CHAPTER 9 REVIEW QUESTIONS

1. What elements should you consider in your vocal delivery? Briefly explain each.
2. What elements should you consider in your physical delivery? Briefly explain each.
3. What is the difference between each of the four methods of delivery?
4. What are the main steps for rehearsing an extemporaneous speech?

CHAPTER 10 REVIEW QUESTIONS

1. What are the seven types of presentation aids?
2. What should you consider when determining what aids you need to use? Explain.
3. What are the common methods for displaying an aid?
4. What design principles should you employ when creating an aid?

TERMS TO REMEMBER

Chapter 8
symbolic (216)
arbitrary (216)
denotative meaning (217)
connotative meaning (217)
culture (218)
malapropism (220)
jargon (222)
abbreviation (222)
acronym (222)
clichés (223)
fillers (223)
doublespeak (224)
euphemisms (224)
tropes (231)
schemes (232)

Chapter 9
pitch (238)
monotone (238)
inflection (238)
volume (239)
rate (239)
pause (240)
variety (241)
pronunciation (242)
articulation (243)
enunciation (243)
dialect (243)
appearance (244)
direct eye contact (245)
facial expressions (246)
gestures (246)
emblems (246)
illustrators (246)
movement (247)
posture (247)
extemporaneous speaking (249)
manuscript speaking (250)
memorized speaking (250)
impromptu speaking (251)

Chapter 10
presentation aids (262)
models (265)
photographs (266)
drawings (267)
charts (268)
flowcharts (268)
organizational charts (268)
tables (268)
graphs (269)
line graphs (269)
bar graphs (270)
pictographs (270)
pie graphs (271)
video clips (272)
audio clips (272)
multimedia (273)
design principles (282)

Introduction

"Can you hear me now?"

"Can you hear me now?"

This memorable slogan from a 2002 Verizon commercial emphasizes, in its simplicity, the importance of being heard. If a speaker cannot be heard, the audience cannot listen and the communication process cannot take place.

This chapter focuses on the listening process and how you can help others and yourself become better listeners.

The most basic and powerful way to connect to another person is to listen. Just listen. Perhaps the most important thing we ever give each other is our attention.[1]

RACHEL NAOMI REMEN, M.D.
Clinical Professor of Family and
Community Medicine

CHAPTER 11 CONTENTS

Why Is Listening an Important Skill?	300
1 Your Knowledge Increases	300
2 You Build Better Relationships	301
3 You Fulfill Your Communicative Responsibility	301
What Is the Process of Listening?	302
What Are the Types of Listening?	304
1 Appreciative Listening	304
2 Empathic Listening	304
3 Informative Listening	305
4 Critical Listening	305
What Can Prevent Effective Listening?	306
1 Internal Noise	307
2 External Noise	307
How Can You Help Your Audience Listen More Effectively?	308
1 Know Your Audience	308
2 Grab the Audience's Attention	310
3 Create an Effective Message	310
4 Be Confident	310
5 Control the Environment	311
6 Listen to Your Audience	311
As an Audience Member, How Can You Listen More Effectively?	312
1 Listen Actively	312
2 Listen Critically	313
Elizabeth's Speech	314
CHAPTER 12: Evaluating Speeches	317
Tab 5 Review	332

Why Is Listening an Important Skill?

1 **Your Knowledge Increases**
2 **You Build Better Relationships**
3 **You Fulfill Your Communicative Responsibility**

1

Your Knowledge Increases

Michael is a pre-dental major struggling with his chemistry class. He frequently gets distracted, and his anxiety about understanding the information sometimes causes him to tune out the teacher as he focuses on his notes. Determined to learn the concepts, he decides he needs to listen more carefully to lectures and lab instructions. He starts by sitting in the front of the room, where it is easier to pay attention and prevent his mind from wandering. Also, he begins to participate more in class discussion.

You may have found yourself in a situation like Michael's, whether in a math class when the instructor explained a new equation or at work when your manager explained a new job-related procedure.

Listening allows you to take in, process, and use information. Listening helps you develop your expertise or skill with a subject. It allows you to collect information to make your daily life easier and more enjoyable. Effective listening may prevent you from missing a professional opportunity; it may save you time and money; and it may advance your career. Many accomplished people believe listening is the key to success.

Listening also tells us about ourselves. For example, make a list of what really makes you sit up and listen. What topics can hold your attention for hours? What topics or people do you find easy to listen to? What types of music do you enjoy? The answers to these questions will feature what you value, agree with, or find interesting. Taking an inventory of what you listen to will begin to draw a picture of your self-identity.

2
You Build Better Relationships

Michael's changes in behavior during his chemistry class helped improve his relationship with his instructor. She saw him as a more dedicated student, determined to understand the subject.

Listening allows us to build and maintain healthy relationships with our families, significant others, friends, and coworkers. Just like getting to know yourself, listening to others will help you know what is important to them. Their words will give you clues to their identity.

Through understanding how our identities interlock, you build relationships and strengthen them. Once you choose to maintain a relationship, listening helps you deal with conflict or help the other person cope with or resolve a crisis in his or her life. Listening shows others that you value and care about them.

In a world where you can watch television, use a computer, send text messages and e-mail, or talk on a phone almost anywhere, listening doesn't seem to have a chance. If you often find yourself doing one of these activities and abruptly responding to others with "I'm listening," you are not listening effectively—and that is the message you are sending. Although this type of multitasking is acceptable sometimes, it should not be the norm; and you must know when it is not appropriate.

Good communication is vital in every stage of relationship development. The failure to communicate and listen in an interpersonal relationship will result in a languishing relationship at best and, more likely, an unhappy or negative relationship.

3
You Fulfill Your Communicative Responsibility

If you return to the communication model in the Overview, one of the major reasons scholars view the process as transactional is that the audience actively participates. The act of listening completes the transaction between the speaker and the audience. Each audience member becomes an active participant, not a passive vessel.

Audience members who believe that the speaker is entirely responsible for the effectiveness of the message are falling prey to **passivity syndrome**. For effective communication to occur, the speaker and the audience member are both responsible for completing and understanding the message. When Michael did not understand his instructor, he used nonverbal and verbal communication to signal his confusion and worked to pay closer attention. As a communication participant, Michael met the message head on. His instructor cannot listen or remember a message for him; he must take that responsibility.

Finally, it is your duty to listen actively as a citizen in a democratic society dedicated to the freedom of speech. As journalist Walter Lippmann wrote, "While the right to talk may be the beginning of freedom, the necessity of listening is what makes the right important." In other words, what is said is only as valid as the listener's willingness to listen and ability to comprehend and evaluate what is said. Our duty is to listen and analyze a message, not simply take it as fact or reality regardless of the source.

What Is the Process of Listening?

Understanding the listening process begins with grasping the difference between hearing and listening. As this diagram suggests, **hearing** happens when sound waves strike the eardrum and spark a chain reaction that ends with the brain registering the sound. **Listening** is the conscious learned act of paying attention and assigning meaning to an acoustic message. Hearing is the first step in listening. Unless you are hearing impaired physically or by some artificial means, it is impossible not to hear. In contrast, you must *choose to* listen.

Next, it is important to realize that listening is a process. A process, at its basic level, is the act of inputting something into a series of phases that results in a particular output. To complete the listening process, you must go through at least three phases and up to as many as five. The first three necessary steps are receiving, attending, and understanding. From there, a listener decides to respond and/or commit the message to memory.

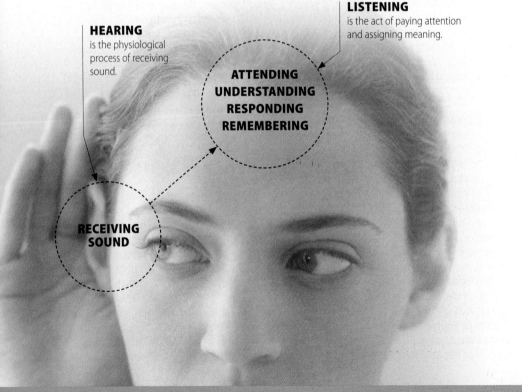

HEARING
is the physiological process of receiving sound.

LISTENING
is the act of paying attention and assigning meaning.

ATTENDING
UNDERSTANDING
RESPONDING
REMEMBERING

RECEIVING SOUND

Receiving is the physiological process of hearing. The outer ear collects the sound waves, sending them to the inner ear, where the ear converts the sound and transmits it to the brain.

Attending is the phase where you make your brain pay attention to a given sound. For example, stop and listen to the sounds around you now. You may be able to hear birds outside, music, people talking next door, or the soft whoosh of air coming from the air conditioner or heater. Now, imagine a person speaking in the middle of this symphony of sound, and pay attention to his or her words. If you are able to do so, you will no longer pay attention to some of those other sounds. It is as if you are not hearing them. The sounds do not go away; you are still hearing them but not attending to them. You have chosen to concentrate (mentally focus) on one sound (the person's voice) and exclude others.

Understanding occurs when you apply meaning to a sound and is where communication really begins. You may hear a message and attend to it, but if you do not understand it, the communication was unsuccessful. If you enter a room where two students from Russia are speaking in their national language, you will hear it, if nothing prevents you from doing so. You may attend to their conversation if they are your friends and you are interested in what they may be discussing. But the understanding will not take place unless you know Russian.

Responding is the phase where you give a formal response to the sounds you have processed. Some communication scholars end the listening process with understanding because communication was either successful or not. However, the communication process is transactional, and most listeners offer one of three different responses or some combination of them.

- *Verbal responses* are spoken or written feedback. Your verbal response might paraphrase the speaker's message, ask for further explanation, or simply answer a speaker's question.

- *Nonverbal responses* are visual cues offered by the listener (such as nodding yes or frowning when confused). They can be effective in their brevity but leave great room for misinterpretation.

- *Silence*, or no perceptible response, can also be a response. The listener may choose not to respond because that seems appropriate, or silence can suggest a problem between the speaker, listener, and/or message. Silence can also signal concentration. You often need other nonverbal cues to interpret silence properly.

Remembering, or retaining what you hear, is the final stage. Good listening skills often make use of a person's short-term and long-term memories. In the short term, you listen carefully for details to help you follow the speech's strategy and/or argument. The memory of those details helps you make sense of the speech in the moment but not necessarily remember it later. In the long term, you may commit a broad understanding of the speech to memory as a means of retaining valuable information or maintaining a change in your attitudes, values, or beliefs.

What Are the Types of Listening?

1 **Appreciative Listening**

2 **Empathic Listening**

3 **Informative Listening**

4 **Critical Listening**

When you engage in the process of listening, you do so to achieve a goal. The four listening goals are to appreciate, empathize, comprehend, and be critical. You will always have one of these goals as your overarching reason for listening. However, listeners often use a combination to achieve that main goal. For example, you may be listening for information but at the same time evaluating it critically for believability. Each of these goals corresponds to a type of listening.

1

Appreciative Listening

Appreciative listening happens when you listen for recreation or enjoyment. Examples of appreciative listening are:

- Listening to a comedy show
- Listening to your favorite band
- Listening to water flowing in a stream and birds singing

Speeches designed with a goal to entertain require this type of listening as well.

2

Empathic Listening

Empathic listening occurs when your purpose is to give the speaker emotional support. Examples here could be:

- A religious leader listening to a congregation member
- A counselor listening to a patient
- A friend listening to another friend in need

This type of listening emphasizes carefully attending to the speaker; supporting the speaker by listening more than responding; and empathizing, or feeling as the other person feels.

3
Informative Listening

You engage in **informative listening** when you want to gain insight or comprehension. This approach to listening emphasizes concentrating on language, ideas, and details as well as remembering the knowledge.

In classes, you use informative listening when you pay attention to your professors. Other places where you might engage in informative listening could be:

- When a friend gives you directions to his new apartment
- At the hardware store as a sales associate tells you how to install tile
- When a doctor gives you medical instructions

In all of these examples, you listen for clarification of the language, you concentrate on the necessary details, and you engage in some sort of activity to help you remember (e.g., taking notes or memorizing).

4
Critical Listening

Critical listening takes place when you listen carefully to a message in order to judge it as acceptable or not. This is the type of listening behavior you use when listening to:

- A presidential debate
- A salesperson trying to sell you a new stereo
- A friend when you are trying to decide if she is telling you the truth

Critical listening is the root of critical thinking. Theorists Brooke Moore and Richard Parker, in their book *Critical Thinking*, define **critical thinking** as "the careful, deliberate determination of whether one should accept, reject, or suspend judgment about a claim [or information] and the degree of confidence with which one accepts or rejects it." Astronomer Carl Sagan called this your "baloney-detection kit." Sagan's suggestion was to "equip yourself with a baloney-detection kit… and be able to tell what is baloney and what is not."

You currently live in a time when informative and persuasive acts bombard you from all sides. They come at you from radio, television, the Internet, T-shirts, and even cereal boxes. You must be able and willing to ask questions such as: Why? Where did that information come from? How old is it? Who benefits from it? Who will get hurt?

PRACTICING ETHICS

Critical listening and critical thinking are such important parts of the communication process that you should almost always engage in a certain level of critical listening and thinking. For example, your main goal for listening to a speaker may be to gather information, but you should never assume information is correct simply because the speaker says so.

What Can Prevent Effective Listening?

1 **Internal Noise**
2 **External Noise**

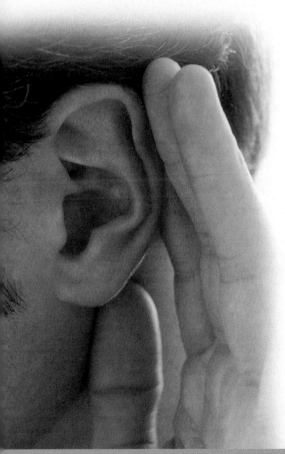

Most people would define noise as unpleasant sounds that might be loud, startling, irritating, or unwelcome. In the process of communicating, **noise** refers to the unwanted barriers that prevent you from listening effectively to the speaker. They can be pleasant or unpleasant things.

For example, you might find the deep, melodious voices of actors James Earl Jones and Morgan Freeman so pleasing that you focus more on the beauty of their voices than their messages. Or you might feel that the harsh, nasal voices of actors Fran Drescher (in character in *The Nanny*) and Gilbert Gottfried (comedian and voice of the AFLAC duck) are so annoying that you stop listening to the words spoken. Either of these vocal qualities could become a barrier and, therefore, noise preventing you from attending to what is important about the message.

Noise is not always connected to the speaker; it can be something like a clock ticking, someone tapping a pencil, distracting thoughts, or hunger. Understanding what can become noise is the first step to preventing it from distracting you. There are two general categories of noise influencing communication.

1
Internal Noise

Internal noise is any barrier to effective listening that originates within the body or mind of the listener. Internal noise can be either a physiological or a psychological barrier.

- **Physiological barriers** are bodily conditions that prevent or constrain your ability to process information.

- **Psychological barriers** are emotional conditions that prevent you from focusing on and absorbing a message. For example, your communication anxiety may prevent you from listening to the speech given just before yours, or your fear of a boss could prevent you from listening to his or her comments. A fight with your best friend or worries over how to make a car payment may preoccupy you. Perspective differences (seeing the message from different points of view) between a teenager and a parent can prevent listening when they do not share the same attitudes, values, beliefs, or expectations.

2
External Noise

External noise is any barrier to effective listening that originates outside of the listener's body and mind. External noise can be either an environmental or a linguistic barrier.

- **Environmental barriers** occur when something within the room or area where the speech is given interrupts your ability to concentrate.

- **Linguistic barriers** happen when the verbal and/or nonverbal messages from the speaker are unfamiliar or misunderstood by the listener.

INTERNAL NOISE		EXTERNAL NOISE	
Physiological Barriers	Psychological Barriers	Environmental Barriers	Linguistic Barriers
Examples	*Examples*	*Examples*	*Examples*
Headache	Boredom	Environmental sounds	Jargon
Lack of sleep	Fear	Smells	Awkward sentence
Pain	Don't-care attitude	Disruptions	structure
Illness	Preoccupation	Bad ventilation	Difficult vocabulary
Hearing or visual	Anger	Room temperature	Unfamiliar or distracting
impairments	Anxiety	Uncomfortable seats	nonverbal delivery
	Frustration	Lighting	Poor organization
	Prejudice	Sight issues	
	Perspective differences		

How Can You Help Your Audience Listen More Effectively?

1 **Know Your Audience**
2 **Grab the Audience's Attention**
3 **Create an Effective Message**
4 **Be Confident**
5 **Control the Environment**
6 **Listen to Your Audience**

1
Know Your Audience

Taking the time to know your audience will help you see what barriers they might have toward you, your topic, or the speaking situation. If you know your audience will have a negative response to either you or your topic, or might have physiological or psychological issues preventing effective listening, often recognizing and addressing these issues up front will help you lessen or alleviate the effects they have.

For example, Elise will be speaking on behalf of the school board to a neighborhood group about making room for a new school that will require the purchase and demolition of many of their homes. This area of town is heavily populated by families whose ancestors immigrated from Germany. Acknowledging how the homeowners might feel and conveying that the board has their best interests in mind is something Elise will need to do at the beginning of her talk. Safety in one's home is a powerful need and would be an equally powerful noise barrier during this interaction.

Likewise, many of the families cannot imagine living anywhere else, and some older members of the community have linguistic barriers that may influence Elise's ability to get her message across. Elise is first-generation German American, so she has some personal insight, but she knows she must do everything possible to analyze who will be in the audience. She needs to think about their age, family history, economic status, and cultural and religious issues that make this move difficult to comprehend.

→ See Chapter 1 (Tab 1) for a detailed discussion on getting to know your audience.

In our increasingly global society, you will likely speak to an audience including individuals from cultures different from yours. Knowing what cultures will be represented in your audience will allow you to help the audience understand your message better. Take the time to learn what you can.

This table offers some suggestions for helping the cross-cultural audience member listen to your speech. However, they can be helpful in any communicative situation.

LENDING A HELPING HAND ACROSS CULTURES

HOW CAN YOU INCREASE EFFECTIVE LISTENING?	EXPLANATION
Get to know other cultures	Try to know what cultures are in your audience and learn about them. Study and interact with other cultures regularly so that you are always sensitive to them. For example, some people from other cultures will nod in agreement to be polite when they do not understand.
Use a comprehensible oral delivery style	Slow down, articulate and pronounce carefully, and use repetition and rephrasing.
Use nonverbal cues	In the United States, smiling demonstrates your enthusiasm, and gesturing could highlight important points. Be careful not to use culturally specific nonverbal cues that might be misread.
Use presentation aids	Presentation aids can help summarize or repeat information that might be difficult to remember or understand through oral delivery alone.
Be realistic and thorough in your message	Take a little longer to discuss complex issues and do not use idioms, jokes, sarcasm, or exaggerations that might be confusing.
Listen to the audience's verbal and nonverbal feedback	Watch for looks of confusion or blank expressions, side discussions that seem to be asking for clarification, shuffling through papers about the speech as if looking for clarification, or significant use of a translation dictionary device as you speak. These are signals that someone is struggling with your message.

2

Grab the Audience's Attention

Just as getting the audience's attention and focusing it on the topic is essential to Elise's speech, it is essential to yours. Otherwise, the audience can miss the first few sentences of your speech. And if you do not have something to "wow" them into staying focused, they may lose more of your speech. Make your attention-grabber the first important thing out of your mouth. Craft one that makes the audience want to listen.

→ See Chapter 7 (Tab 3) for attention-getting ideas.

3

Create an Effective Message

Using appropriate language, a sound organizational strategy, and exceptional supporting materials will help your audience stay connected to your speech. Difficult or obscure language will frustrate them. A poor organizational strategy will confuse them. If the audience feels like your message becomes stagnant at one point, or if you keep circling around to the same thoughts, they will stop trying to follow your message. So a proper organizational strategy is key. Also, presenting unique and compelling information about your topic is one of the best ways to keep your audience listening.

→ See Tab 3 for detailed discussion on organizational strategies and incorporating support materials. Chapter 8 (Tab 4) covers using language successfully.

4

Be Confident

If you have a solid message and have practiced until you are comfortable with the speech, you will demonstrate a high level of confidence. Some audience members have trouble listening to messages delivered with low confidence because their empathy for the speaker overrides their focus on the message's content. Other audience members may not give much weight to the content of a speech when the speaker lacks confidence.

Know your message well and be self-assured, assertive, and bold when you speak. See the Confidence Booster box below for a few things you can do to increase the audience's perception of your confidence level.

→ See Chapter 9 (Tab 4) for more delivery suggestions, and refer to the Confidence Booster boxes throughout this book for ideas on how to increase your confidence.

CONFIDENCE BOOSTER

- Dress for the occasion and for your part in it. Clothes really do make a difference.
- Stand tall.
- Try to minimize nervous behavior. If your hands shake, gesture with them.
- Be interested in your topic.
- Captivate your audience with effective volume, tone, and articulation.
- Maintain eye contact with audience members.

5
Control the Environment

Ironically, the speaking environment is frequently the easiest element to control yet the one most often forgotten or ignored. When you enter into the speaking environment, seize control of it. Follow these simple tips:

- Scout out the space prior to your speech.

- Change aspects that might reduce listening, if you can. Turn up or down the temperature, rearrange the room, fix the lights, or remove any distracting environmental noises if possible. Move a lectern or desk if it is in an awkward place or if you do not plan to use it and it will be in the way. If the room is large and you know your audience might be small, group the seats close to where you will speak, creating a more intimate space.

- If you are using equipment that might emit distracting sounds or lights, such as a slide projector, try to place it where it will create the least amount of distraction.

- Be aware of environmental issues as you speak. If the sun is in someone's eyes, pull the blinds. If a loud noise disrupts your speech, pause until it is over or ask someone in charge to see what they can do to eliminate it. Close doors, windows, or drapes if outside noise and movement become distracting.

Take control and solve the environmental problems when possible.

6
Listen to Your Audience

You must listen to your audience with your eyes and ears as you speak. Watch for verbal or nonverbal behavior that suggests they are confused, bored, or distracted. Remember, they are active participants in the communication process and should try to help you create the best message possible for them to comprehend. For example:

- If someone is nodding off, use his or her name (if you know it) in an example in your speech or walk closer to that area of the room. Just hearing your voice close by may cause the person to perk up.

- When audience members look confused, try asking for questions from the whole group or from individuals. Do not ignore these signals; respond to audience needs if possible.

- Watch for signals from cross-cultural audience members that they may not understand or are having trouble keeping up with you. Try to ask them questions that might determine if they are confused.

- Watch for members squirming in their seats or looking around at other things.

> ### CHECKLIST for Helping Your Audience Listen
> - ❏ What do I know about my audience that might interfere with their ability to listen?
> - ❏ Am I using the best means possible to grab and keep this audience's attention with this topic?
> - ❏ How can my delivery style and confidence level help my audience listen effectively?
> - ❏ How can I control the environment better?
> - ❏ What cues are the audience members sending me, and how can I address them?

As an Audience Member, How Can You Listen More Effectively?

1 **Listen Actively**

2 **Listen Critically**

1

Listen Actively

Listening is a full-time job. The sheer quantity of information you receive each day makes listening a tiresome activity but an even more important one if you are to be an effective consumer of information. A few simple steps will help you be an active participant in the transaction between you and a speaker.

- Give your full attention. Do not watch the cars out the window, daydream, or think about the fight you had with someone before the speech. Help the speaker focus your attention on the topic at hand.

- Listen for the main points.

- Take notes to help you remember.

- Respond to the speech. Giving feedback will help the speaker tailor the message to you and the other audience members. Nonverbal responses, like nodding when you understand or looking confused when you do not, are always helpful. In some cases, the speaker or the situation will signal that you can be more verbally interactive, such as raising your hand or just speaking up to ask a question. Pay attention to what is appropriate.

- Do not fake paying attention.

- Participate in the question-and-answer session after the speech, if one is conducted.

- If you are a cross-cultural listener, work at building your vocabulary and knowledge of idioms/informal expressions. Pay attention to the speaker's body language (posture, gestures, intonation, expression, etc.). Let the speaker know when issues prevent understanding.

2

Listen Critically

As human beings, our ability to think critically is one of the differences that distinguishes us from our furry and feathered friends as well as from machines. When you listen to a speech in a public forum, listening critically is important. Being an effective critical listener takes time and practice. Employing the following tactics will help you develop this skill.

SIGNS YOU ARE A CRITICAL LISTENER/THINKER

- You listen carefully.
- You ask questions—especially the question "Why?" (either mentally asking yourself or, if and when appropriate, directly asking the speaker).
- You explore alternatives.
- You maintain a sense of childlike curiosity—everything is interesting or possible.
- You suspend judgment until more of the details are given.
- You define criteria for making judgments but not at the expense of alternatives.
- You are willing to adjust.
- You are willing to keep an open mind.

You will find active and critical listening easier if you put yourself in the shoes of the person speaking. Just like an effective speaker must consider the audience's traits, an effective listener needs to empathize and identify with the speaker's feelings, thoughts, motives, interests, or attitudes. This act of empathizing and identifying is what theorist and philosopher Kenneth Burke called *identification* in his book *A Rhetoric of Motives*. Identification will prevent you from prematurely judging the speaker or topic, keep you from being resistant to new ideas or speaking styles, and prevent you from overreacting to "hot-button" issues—all of which can be barriers to effective listening and critical thinking. Speaker and listener are co-participants, equals, in the process of communication.

CHECKLIST for Listening More Effectively

❏ Am I giving the speaker my full attention?
❏ Am I actively trying to comprehend the message?
❏ Am I signaling the speaker with the appropriate feedback?
❏ Am I critically listening?

TIP: Taking Good Notes

- If possible, familiarize yourself with the topic before the speech.
- Develop a note-taking shorthand, using symbols or abbreviations such as: i.e. (that is, in other words), & (and), # (number), @ (at), ! (important), ** (remember).
- Prepare your space for note taking.
- Listen for and record main points and pertinent subpoints.
- Use indentations and other similar outlining strategies to distinguish points.
- Use margins for questions or comments you have.
- As soon as possible after the speech, go over your notes and fill in further or summarize.

Elizabeth's Speech

Elizabeth recently earned a business degree and works for a small business consulting firm. Elizabeth's specialty is helping others start up successful small businesses. Her company helps her identify individuals with small business plans, and then she gives that group a series of informative speeches on the process of setting up their businesses. Today, Elizabeth is meeting with a group of 20 potential business owners in a banquet room at a local hotel.

HELPING HER AUDIENCE LISTEN EFFECTIVELY

First, Elizabeth gets to know her audience. Before creating the outline of her presentation, Elizabeth reads over the biographies and business plans submitted by those who will attend her presentation and makes notes about the makeup of the audience.

Armed with this information, Elizabeth realizes she will need to cover some basic business practices and be careful not to use occupation-specific language that might cause a listening barrier.

> *THE PARTICIPANTS*
>
> - *All are women*
> - *Between the ages of 30–40*
> - *All have high school diplomas*
> - *Some have taken local community college courses (Betty, Lynn, Cathy, Jane, Martha, Kelly)*
> - *All but one are first-time business entrepreneurs*
> - *Town—medium size with a college and a lot of growth potential*

CREATING AN EFFECTIVE MESSAGE

Elizabeth decides to grab the participants' attention by opening with statistics demonstrating how effective women are at starting and running small businesses. She will follow these statistics with an extended example of one woman's success. Elizabeth plans to use several such examples throughout the speech to inspire the women, and she will use the chronological strategy to help step them through the process of setting up their businesses.

CONTROLLING THE ENVIRONMENT

The day of the presentation, Elizabeth arrives an hour early to have plenty of time to set up the room. She knew the banquet room would be large for a small group of 20, so she has made a checklist to help her remember what she needs to consider.

> ROOM SETUP
>
> 1. Situate lectern and table for supplies in a good spot (move it all to one end of the big room to make it feel more intimate)
> 2. Set up tables and chairs for participants so that they have writing space
> 3. Check temperature
> 4. Think about sound needs

Once Elizabeth had the room set up, she asked the staff for a microphone. With the high ceilings, she was afraid some of the participants would have trouble hearing. Elizabeth knows that your voice does not carry very far if it can travel up with less resistance; with a high ceiling, her voice would go up, not out to the audience.

HOW HER AUDIENCE LISTENS EFFECTIVELY: CONNIE'S EXPERIENCE

Most of the women in the audience arrive early to get acquainted and to settle comfortably in a seat. Connie, one of the participants, has proposed opening a used bookstore and café in the downtown district of this college town. She is serious about learning as much as she can from Elizabeth, so she is ready to listen for information and, at the same time, to evaluate critically what is valuable and applicable to her situation.

LISTENING ACTIVELY

Connie does not want to be distracted by anything, so she selects a seat in the front row and a little off by herself. She turns off her cell phone and PDA to prevent distractions and prepares her area for effective note taking. As Elizabeth speaks, Connie responds nonverbally as well as asks questions when she needs clarification or more information.

LISTENING CRITICALLY

Connie has attended meetings like this before, only to be disappointed in what they offered. However, Connie decides to give this firm and presenter a chance. Judging Elizabeth and her information before it is presented will not help. Soon after the presentation starts, Connie realizes that this presentation is just what she needs. So she pays careful attention to details, takes notes to help her remember content, and disregards information that does not apply to her small business plan. As her excitement and curiosity build, Connie becomes very involved in Elizabeth's presentation. She cannot believe it is over when Elizabeth signals a conclusion and asks for questions.

TEN STEPS FOR STARTING A BUSINESS
(according to business.gov)

1. Research and plan your business.
2. Get business assistance and training.
3. Choose a business location.
4. Finance your business.
5. Determine the legal structure of your business.
6. Register a business name.
7. Get a tax ID number.
8. Register for state and local taxes.
9. Obtain business licenses and permits.
10. Learn your legal responsibilities as an employer.

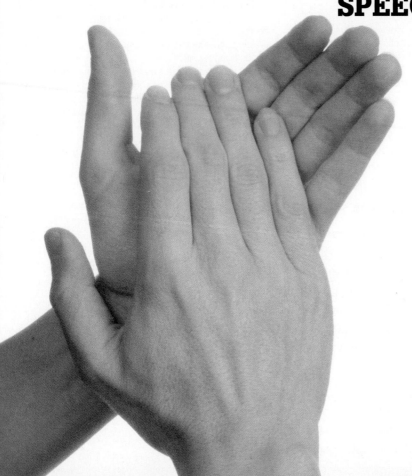

12

EVALUATING SPEECHES

Introduction

Macy is in a speech class at a community college. Although she is able to turn her speaking anxiety into energy and enjoys giving her speeches, what she dreads are the critique sessions that follow. She finds herself ignoring positive comments and fixating on negative ones; in her mind, any suggestion for improvement is framed as a failure. Macy needs to learn how to use critiques constructively.

For a beginning speaker, that's hard to do. But this chapter will help you and Macy become effective participants in the process of evaluating public speaking.

Whether you are sitting beside a pond talking to a friend or speaking in an audi-torium to 300 people, your communicative act is scripted for that audience and framed in a certain context or culture, with participants motivated by different needs, all creating their own meanings. Once two or more people engage in a communicative act, their need to make meaning of the message also requires them to engage in evaluation, as both speaker and audience. This process begins with effective listening (see Chapter 11) and has its heart in the assessment of the communicative act. Whether communicating with our best friends or a large audience, we base the differences in these evaluations on where the act falls on the continuum between the personal (informal evaluation) and the public (formal evaluation).

Whether we are communicating interpersonally or publicly, rules, standards, language, and culture guide us if we are to make sense. Our job as speakers is to welcome and grow with evaluation. Our job as listeners is to offer constructive criticism to help with that growth.

CHAPTER 11: Listening   299

CHAPTER 12 CONTENTS

Why Is Evaluation Important to a Speech?   318
1 Evaluation Is a "Good Thing"   318
2 Evaluation Teaches Critical Thinking Skills   320
3 Evaluation Builds Your Confidence   321
4 Evaluation Makes You a Better Communicator   321

How Might Evaluations Be Conducted?   322
1 Oral Evaluations   323
2 Written Evaluations   323

What Should You Consider When Evaluating Speeches?   324
1 The Speech Message   324
2 The Speaker's Presentation   324

Who Evaluates Your Speech?   326
1 You   326
2 The Audience   327
3 The Instructor   328
4 Your Classroom Peers   328

Kyle's Speech   330

Tab 5 Review   332

Why Is Evaluation Important to a Speech?

1 **Evaluation Is a "Good Thing"**

2 **Evaluation Teaches Critical Thinking Skills**

3 **Evaluation Builds Your Confidence**

4 **Evaluation Makes You a Better Communicator**

1

Evaluation Is a "Good Thing"

Evaluation is a good thing!
Evaluation is a good thing!

Keep repeating this as your new mantra. Because, believe it or not, this statement is true, and the earlier you adopt it as your mantra for most things you do in life, the better you will do those things.

Like Macy in the introduction, you may be skeptical of this simple sentence because you view criticism or evaluation as a demoralizing, negative experience. You may see it as finding fault, censuring, or disapproving. But constructive evaluation can be a very positive experience.

Do you remember the discussion in Chapter 8 (Tab 4) demonstrating how language helps us denotatively and connotatively create and give meaning to our lives and experiences? Well, that works with evaluation as well. So, changing a negative connotation of evaluation allows a positive connotation to develop.

CHECKLIST for Effective Evaluation

❏ Did I describe for the speaker what I saw and heard?

❏ Did I offer an evaluation of whether the speech was effective or not?

❏ Did I explain my personal feeling on why it was effective or not?

❏ Did I support the evaluation with a rationale or related norm?

At its basic level, **evaluation** is description grounded in a justified judgment. In other words, evaluation is simply someone telling what he or she saw and heard, grounded in "why."

In their book *Performance Studies: The Interpretation of Aesthetic Texts*, Ron Pelias and Tracy Stephenson Shaffer break down the process of evaluation as *description*, *judgment*, *justification*, and *rationale*. Pelias and Shaffer are performance-studies scholars, and their discussion focuses on the evaluation of staged artistic performances; but because public speaking is a public event, their discussion applies here as well. Pelias and Shaffer argue that effective evaluation involves accurately describing a speech, fairly judging its worth, and logically justifying your view of it based on rational norms and reasons. For example:

DESCRIPTION
"When your attention-getting device took us to the edge of the canyon and described the air…"

Description answers: What did I see and hear?

JUDGMENT
"I really liked that."

Judgment answers: Was it good or not?

JUSTIFICATION
"The moment was so real, it gave me goose bumps. I was pulled into the speech, and I felt like I was there by the canyon."

Justification answers: Why was it good or not?

RATIONALE
"One of the major functions of the introduction is to grab the audience's attention and pull them into the speech. You achieved that goal by using emotive language and a great extended narrative."

Rationale answers: What is the logic or norm behind my justification?

Note that nothing in the examples above talks about fault, censorship, or disapproval. Evaluation is about describing what you see, making a judgment about how you feel about it, and then offering a sensible justification for what works or needs improvement. (Use the checklist on page 318 as a reminder.) Improvement does not mean tearing down or destroying; it means elevating to the next level of worth. If something about your speech is not quite working, then the message you intend to send may be misinterpreted or not received at all. Evaluation can help you adjust your speeches so that your messages are successful.

Nothing we do is perfect, and we can always strive to improve. When given appropriately and constructively, evaluation fosters growth and progress along the lifelong path to developing the great speaker and thinker who resides within you. View your speech as a diamond in the rough and evaluation as helping you carve a way to the beauty. Embrace evaluation; do not fear it. Evaluation is a good thing!

2

Evaluation Teaches Critical Thinking Skills

Think a moment about these questions.

- Are you being too trusting?
- Is that really the best buy?
- Can you learn from history?
- Are you thinking creatively?
- Can you think outside of the box?

These are all questions that force us to think about our mindset and that of others. Such questions are designed to make us creators and participants in our own lives rather than passive vessels.

Imagine if Alexander Graham Bell had not wondered if there was a way to send our voices across vast spaces or if he had given up after the first experiments failed. You might still be sending messages only by mail or telegraph, and cell phones would not even be in our vocabulary, much less in our pockets. Imagine if your grandmother had never played around with her recipes to make them better. You would not have those special cookies or cakes to eat.

Critical thinking is important in our lives, and we must always strive to be better thinkers. Chapter 11 first introduced you to critical thinking as it relates to critical listening; here you should note that critical thinking is the mechanism for evaluation.

PRACTICING ETHICS

A good critical thinker should also be an honorable one. Don't use your critical thinking skills to mislead, exploit, deceive, confuse, confound, aggravate, discourage, or harm. Great critical thinkers practice their skills with civility.

As the detective Sherlock Holmes says in *The Hound of the Baskervilles*, "The world is full of obvious things which nobody by any chance ever observes." Holmes understands that chance observation teaches nothing and often passes by us. When you evaluate another speaker, your own speech, or a listener's evaluation of your speech, you are engaging and honing your critical thinking skills—observing detail and making a reasoned judgment about that detail.

Critical thinkers are always, like Holmes, seeking the answers to these questions: Who? What? When? Where? Why? To whom?

Imagine if Macy gives a speech arguing that an electric toothbrush is better than a regular brush and she says:

Research shows that you will get better dental checkups if you use an electric toothbrush.

This statement may be true, but you as the listener should ask questions like:

Who conducted and funded the research? Who is reporting the research Macy quotes? Are there any studies refuting this?

Asking these questions allows you to seek alternative viewpoints and may give you reason to change your own.

Critical thinking skills will help you employ clear and successful reasoning. If you are a listener in the process of communication, critical thinking will help you create and apply criteria in a fair and clear manner. These are skills you will use in your personal and your professional life, to make both mundane decisions and critical ones.

3
Evaluation Builds Your Confidence

Effective evaluation will build your confidence if you let it. Effective evaluation is not only about what needs to be improved; it also focuses on the successes.

As individuals, we are often hardest on ourselves and see only the negative. If evaluators listen carefully and do their job completely, they will describe the complete picture of your speech. Their evaluations will enrich your speech experience so that your next speech will be better and your confidence higher. Knowing what worked and what needs to be improved, and then taking the steps to work on those issues, will build your view of yourself as a good speaker. For example, Macy might respond negatively if someone gave her this response:

> **Your evidence and logic were great. However, you need to work on keeping my attention during the detailed explanations and watch moving around aimlessly too much.**

Yet this is really a nice comment if she listens carefully to it. First, having solid evidence and logic is one of the hardest things to do and this listener has just stated that Macy excelled in those areas. She should be very proud of that. Secondly, working on using language and delivery techniques to keep the audience attention during detailed explanations might take a little work to fix, but these are areas even the beginning speaker can improve on quickly. Some of the new delivery techniques employed to keep the audience's attention might even keep Macy from moving around so much.

4
Evaluation Makes You a Better Communicator

No matter whether you are the one receiving the evaluation or giving it, participating in the act of evaluating will make you a better communicator. Most people learn better by watching and doing. The more you watch other speakers to learn where they succeed or need improvement—and then apply that knowledge to your own speeches—the more you will elevate your own skills.

So watch and listen to other speeches for ideas. As you observe a speech, ask yourself questions like these:

- What type of support materials stood out as the most effective in this speech?
- What language choices worked well?
- What about this person's delivery was effective?
- What made the speaker appear extremely confident?
- How did the speaker use space?
- How did the speaker incorporate audience feedback?
- What "tricks of the trade" did the speaker use to keep your attention?

The list of questions you could ask is almost endless, and the skills and concepts you are learning throughout this book will guide you to what to look for in a successful speech. As you grow as a speaker as well as an audience member, you will ask better, more detailed, questions. You will notice the nuances of great communication.

How Might Evaluations Be Conducted?

1 **Oral Evaluations**
2 **Written Evaluations**

Evaluations in the public speaking classroom focus on making you and your classmates better speakers. In a public forum, they focus more on the effectiveness of your message.

Although being a good speaker and delivering an effective message are interrelated, the purpose for giving the speech changes. On the public stage, you are not speaking as a means to be a better speaker but as a means to pass on a message.

Given this difference in purpose, the evaluations in your classroom will probably be different from ones you experience in the public setting. Even from instructor to instructor, class to class, or assignment to assignment, the evaluations you receive and give may differ. Macy's speech instructor, for example, has three individual students conduct detailed oral and written evaluations for each speaker. Her instructor leads the oral discussion after the speech and attaches a written evaluation to the graded outline when he returns it to Macy. In another class, the instructor is the only one who gives a written evaluation and the whole class participates in the oral one.

So, as you read the remainder of this chapter, keep in mind your instructor's view of evaluation and what he or she considers helpful. There are multiple ways and devices to evaluate speeches, and evaluators may use two basic methods, singly or in combination, for delivering an evaluation.

TIP: Job Evaluations

In your professional life, you will receive evaluations (reviews) of your work and work behavior. Much of what you learn here about evaluating a speech or receiving an evaluation can help you negotiate job reviews as well.

→ See pages 488–489 in Chapter 17 (Tab 9) for more on job-related reviews.

1
Oral Evaluations

Oral evaluations are brief overviews, delivered in oral form, describing what the evaluator saw and felt about the speech.

Oral evaluations may come either after each individual speech or at the end of a session of speeches. If given right after each speech, an oral evaluation focuses on the effectiveness and need for improvement for each individual while the speech is still fresh in the minds of the speaker and the audience members.

Giving the oral evaluation at the end of a group of speeches can help depersonalize the evaluation process by focusing on general feedback that can be helpful to the entire group. At this point, the individual speakers are usually seated among the other class members or speakers and physically become a part of the group, taking the focus off each individual. Some time has passed since they gave their speeches and their nervousness is usually diminished, making the evaluations less intense. Also, collective evaluation tends to focus more on the text of the speeches rather than on the speaker. This form of oral evaluation can be very effective if communication apprehension is an issue.

Formal oral evaluation of a speech in a public forum is rare. However, if a question-and-answer session follows, the speaker can often get a feel for how effective the speech was, based on the audience's questions.

If you want to grow as a speaker, asking someone you know in the audience to give you feedback is always smart. Growth and evaluation should be a lifelong process for the public speaker.

2
Written Evaluations

Written evaluations are assessments given in written form, which tend to contain more detailed descriptions and suggestions.

The evaluator creating a written evaluation should follow the process of description, judgment, justification, and rationale. Some written evaluations can be checklist-style evaluations, others are detailed narrative evaluations with concrete examples, and still others are a combination of the two. The speaker may receive the evaluation just minutes after the speech or days later, depending on how the evaluator creates the written evaluation or how detailed it may be.

Use the written evaluations to elevate your subsequent speech to the next level of effectiveness, and, if possible, discuss the evaluation with the evaluator. Try to understand clearly what she or he is trying to tell you. Translating the evaluation of an oral act into written words can be difficult, and sometimes it is easier to discuss evaluations.

➔ See page 325 for one example of a checklist that could be used as a written evaluation.

CONFIDENCE BOOSTER
Beginning speakers tend to focus their listening on what they consider "negative comments." Listen carefully to the whole evaluation. Assess what is important for you to work on in your next speech, and celebrate what was a success. Realize that striving for excellence in public speaking is an exciting, continually evolving process.

What Should You Consider When Evaluating Speeches?

1 The Speech Message

2 The Speaker's Presentation

Unless you are competing or debating with someone else, most evaluators base their evaluations on established standards (often called a *criterion-based evaluation*). This form of evaluation assesses speakers' abilities to meet set standards and does not compare them to others.

In the classroom, your instructor will explain the standards she or he deems important to the class objectives or the assignment. You can categorize most, if not all, of those standards under one of two headings: the speech message or the speaker's presentation.

1

The Speech Message

Evaluation standards related to the speech message focus on the effectiveness of the topic selection, research, and the creation of the message. These standards correspond to the discussions in Tabs 1 through 3 of this book and to the first four sections (topic, introduction, body, and conclusion) in the brief listing of potential standards on the next page.

2

The Speaker's Presentation

Evaluation standards related to the speaker's presentation spotlight successful uses of language, delivery techniques, and presentation aids. These standards correspond to the discussion in Tab 4 and to the last section (presentation) of the list on the next page.

Remember, this form is only one sample; your instructor will use an evaluation that corresponds to your assignments.

TOPIC
- ❑ Speech accomplished purpose (to inform, to persuade, or to accentuate)
- ❑ Topic appropriate to speaker, audience, and occasion
- ❑ Interesting topic

The speech message

INTRODUCTION
- ❑ Gained attention and interest
- ❑ Established credibility
- ❑ Indicated relevance to audience
- ❑ Declared central idea
- ❑ Previewed speech

BODY
- ❑ Main points clear and obvious to the audience
- ❑ Points followed an appropriate organizational strategy
- ❑ Main points appropriately researched and supported
- ❑ Main points supported with appropriate presentation aids when necessary
- ❑ Oral citations included throughout speech
- ❑ Linked parts of speech

CONCLUSION
- ❑ Contained a summary statement
- ❑ Offered an audience response statement
- ❑ Effectively came to closure (WOW statement)

PRESENTATION
- ❑ Language was clear, concise, and appropriate
- ❑ Gestures/body movements were effective
- ❑ Consistent and effective eye contact
- ❑ Used vocal variety/emphasis/volume/rate
- ❑ Used appropriate delivery style
- ❑ Spoke with enthusiasm
- ❑ Spoke with conviction and sincerity
- ❑ Good use of delivery outline
- ❑ Presentation aids appropriate to speech topic (if applicable)
- ❑ Used presentation aids throughout entire speech (if applicable)
- ❑ Used professional presentation aids (if applicable)
- ❑ Speech met time requirements

The speaker's presentation

Who Evaluates Your Speech?

1 **You**

2 **The Audience**

3 **The Instructor**

4 **Your Classroom Peers**

1

You

Good evaluation begins with you, and you are already doing it as you create your speech. Tabs 1 through 4 of this book teach you how to make decisions along the path to creating a speech based on what works for you, your audience, and the speech situation. That is a form of evaluation.

However, your self-evaluation should not stop at the moment you begin or end your speech. As a speaker interested in effective communication, you should be reflexive after the speech as well. **Reflexivity** happens when you take a moment to consider yourself in relation to the speech and vice versa. In other words, how did your actions or discussion in the speech affect the speech event, and how did the speech event affect your actions? What were the positive outcomes? What can be improved? How do you plan to address areas needing improvement before your next speech?

Your instructor may formally require you to turn in a written self-evaluation as part of the class experience. With or without the class requirement, you should always self-evaluate your performance and effectiveness as a speaker.

2
The Audience

When an audience actively participates in your speech, they offer you feedback that can help you adjust your speech. So, in some sense, all audiences are offering you evaluation as you engage them in communication during your speech. They nod their heads in agreement; they lean forward when you draw them into the speech; they ask questions for clarification; and they sometimes struggle to stay focused or to understand a complex subject. These nonverbal and verbal responses are all clues to how effective you are being as the speaker.

Formally, someone like a teacher or boss may ask an audience to evaluate your speech afterwards. In most public settings, the evaluations are usually written comments that come from evaluation forms the audience fills out after the speech. These evaluations tend to be broad and focus more on the subject rather than the speaker, as this example demonstrates.

Session 1: New Documentation Policy
Presenters: Brian Bourke and Adelpha Kostas

Please complete a questionnaire after each session and return them to the drop box outside of the Human Resources office. Thank you for your input.

1. What information was the most beneficial?

2. How would you improve this session?

3. What benefits or problems do you see with implementing this new policy?

Other comments:

These evaluations sometimes offer details that will help you become a better speaker, but you might find that asking a few people in the audience to give you specific suggestions to improve your speech is even more beneficial. It is never a bad idea to ask, "What can I do next time to make this presentation even more effective?"

In the public speaking classroom, your teacher might ask the other students to evaluate your speech, which can be very different from a public audience evaluation. The following pages will discuss this type of evaluation under the heading "Your Classroom Peers."

3
The Instructor

If you are in a speech class, as in any class, your instructor will evaluate you. In the public speaking class, evaluation is an essential part of the learning process. Most instructors use both oral and written evaluations to reinforce learning and the main principles taught in the class. When and how they evaluate, as well as the format they choose, can vary widely. Instructors will select the form that best represents their goals for students, their teaching style, and, their teaching philosophy.

Keep in mind that your instructor is evaluating you within the frame of the class, and, just like the creative process, evaluation is not a static process. As the class progresses, the evaluations may become more detailed and expectations may increase. You should use each evaluation as a tool for improving your next speech. During the evaluation, ask questions of the evaluators and make comments. Actively engage in the evaluation process. Do not just glance at the evaluation once and forget it. Study the comments prior to creating your next speech and during the rehearsal stage of that speech. Let the previous evaluations be a guide to making that subsequent speech the best it can be.

REVIEW CHECKLIST for Effective Listening

❏ Am I giving the speaker my full attention?
❏ Am I actively trying to comprehend the message?
❏ Am I signaling the speaker with the appropriate feedback?
❏ Am I critically listening?

4
Your Classroom Peers

In the public speaking classroom, students will often evaluate speeches given by others in the class. Depending on your instructor's teaching practices, peer evaluation can be oral and/or written.

You do not need to be an expert in public speaking before you can offer a useful evaluation. However, the more you give speeches and evaluate others, the better and more helpful your evaluations will be.

- Your instructor will help you focus your evaluations.
- Reread the previous section on "What Should You Consider When Evaluating Speeches?" before each evaluation session to help you focus on what is important.
- Listen carefully to the speaker. Actively listen as if this is the first time you have heard him or her speak. Use the checklist on this page to review effective listening skills.
- Make notes on several things the speaker is doing well and what could be changed to have a stronger impact.
- Offer your feedback in the spirit of helping the speaker improve.
- Treat others the way you would like to be treated, and offer others the type of feedback that you would like to receive to help you improve.
- Construct your evaluations to offer a description of what you saw and heard, a judgment of what is effective or not, a justification for the judgment, and the rationale behind the judgment.

HOW CAN YOU EVALUATE A SPEECH?	EXPLANATION	EXAMPLES
Offer constructive feedback	Instead of just offering a quick, unexplained response, include specifics. Answer the question "Why?"	INCORRECT: "It was good." CORRECT: "It was a good persuasive speech. The range of supporting evidence and reliability was really convincing."
Be positive first	Look for positive elements and offer them first to frame your evaluation in an encouraging way. If you listen effectively, you will note something positive about the speech.	INCORRECT: "You had more than 45 'ums' in your speech." CORRECT: "Wow, this was a unique topic. I've read about victory gardens but didn't realize how important they were during the war. To improve your effectiveness, you might want to work on eliminating the vocal filler um. You had a lot of these, and they became distracting."
Always offer improvement tips	No speech is perfect. Always give speakers advice on what they might do to be even better next time.	"I loved your use of presentation aids during the first half of the speech. It might be nice to carry that throughout the full speech by adding a few aids in the second half."
Avoid attacks	Blunt negative responses about the speech are not helpful. Remember to describe, judge, justify, and rationalize your response.	INCORRECT: "This was a dumb topic for this audience." CORRECT: "As a college student, I had a bit of trouble staying with your topic of banning school uniforms in high schools because I am older. Is there a way to make this topic more appropriate to this audience?"
Avoid demeaning comments	Humiliating the speaker will increase apprehension and be counterproductive. Again, remember to describe, judge, justify, and rationalize your response.	INCORRECT: "Your delivery bugged me." CORRECT: "You tend to read your speech, which makes you sound a bit monotone and rhythmic. Because exact wording really isn't necessary with this topic, it would be more effective to speak extemporaneously."
Be objective	Evaluation is hard work, and personal feelings can cloud the goal. If you have issues with the topic or speaker or think either is "cool," do not base your evaluation on unrelated or superficial feelings.	INCORRECT: "You're so funny!" CORRECT: "This speech was very funny, and I loved it. I was really entertained. However, the purpose was to persuade me. I got caught up in the funny parts and forgot what you wanted me to do."

Kyle's Speech

Kyle is a first-year student enrolled in an Introduction to Public Speaking class. His instructor assigned the class a nine-minute persuasive speech for the final presentation. Kyle has researched, written, and practiced his speech about why students should be cautious when applying for and using credit cards. On the day of his speech, Kyle is looking forward to completing this last assignment and hearing what others have to say about it.

THE IMPORTANCE OF EVALUATION

At the beginning of the semester, Kyle dreaded listening to his instructor and peers evaluate his speech. However, throughout the semester, he has grown to view their evaluations as valuable. He sees the process as a means to make his speeches better, his delivery stronger, and his confidence higher. Participating in his own evaluations and the evaluations of others has improved his critical thinking and listening skills and has taught him to be reflexive about his own speeches.

THE ORAL EVALUATION

Kyle's instructor, Ms. Warren, uses both oral and written evaluations. Immediately after his speech, she asks the class what parts of Kyle's speech were effective. She reminds them to consider:

- Topic choice and focus
- The introduction
- The body of the speech
- The conclusion
- The presentation

SOME OF KYLE'S PEERS MAKE THESE ORAL COMMENTS

NATHAN

"The statistics were the most powerful argument for your claim. I was blown away. I mean, the logical side of your brain knows to be cautious, but until you see those numbers right in front of you, it doesn't seem so bad to get several cards and use them. Seeing those statistics from a reliable source changes all of that for me. Plus, your slides were easy to read and really helped explain all those numbers. Wow, I never want to use or take out another card ... but I guess that's the point."

SORAYA

"I agree with Nathan and I think it was a good speech, but I found myself distracted when you spoke about the slides. They had great information and looked nice, but you talked to the screen more than you did to us. I think if you had rehearsed with them more or forced yourself to turn out and look at the audience instead of the slides, you would have really impressed us."

MILOS

"Even though people from my country don't use credit cards like this, and I don't have any, you made me stop and think about other things I might be doing that might affect my financial future. And then I thought, maybe looking at countries like mine and their credit habits might offer evidence to even further strengthen your claim. I don't know—that information may be hard to find. Just a thought."

MS. WARREN WRAPS UP HER EVALUATION WITH THESE COMMENTS

I liked your use of two well-known advertisement slogans, one as the attention-getter ("There are some things money can't buy. For everything else, there's MasterCard.") and one as the WOW statement at the end ("Having the time of your life—PRICELESS!") Very creative, and it catches our attention because of its familiarity.

I am concerned that the speech seems more informative than persuasive because of its "how-to" focus on the "dos and don'ts" of using a credit card.

Seeing her point, Kyle asks for advice on how to make it more persuasive.

Try a problem–solution strategy and spend more time defining the problem. Then your "dos and don'ts" of using a credit card become the solution to the problem.

THE WRITTEN EVALUATION

During the class period following Kyle's presentation, Ms. Warren gives Kyle her written evaluation and the written evaluations from his peers. These evaluations give Kyle more things to consider and demonstrate how some of the areas for improvement were noticeable during the speech. For example, several evaluators discussed that his vocal quality seemed too fast, choppy, and monotone. These are all qualities that often stem from reading too much. Here is part of the presentation section of Ms. Warren's evaluation.

PRESENTATION	COMMENTS
Language was clear, concise, and appropriate	Very!
Gestures/body movements were effective	Good—be careful not to play with pen
Consistent and effective eye contact	Long moments of looking at notes and slides
Used vocal variety/emphasis/volume/rate	Good volume—watch being monotone, fast, and choppy
Used appropriate delivery style	Yes, extemporaneous
Spoke with enthusiasm	Good! Just relax a bit more—you seemed a bit stiff
Spoke with conviction and sincerity	Yes
Good use of delivery outline	Seemed to refer to it a lot—practice more

Tab 5: Review

CHAPTER 11 REVIEW QUESTIONS

1. Why is effective listening important?
2. Explain the listening process. Include in your answer the steps of the process and how listening differs from hearing.
3. What are the four types of listening? Briefly explain each.
4. What is noise? Include in your answer a brief explanation of the types and barriers.
5. What can you do to help your audience be more effective listeners?
6. What can you do to be a more effective listener?

CHAPTER 12 REVIEW QUESTIONS

1. Why is evaluation important to you and your speech?
2. Explain and give a brief example of an evaluation as it moves through the evaluation process (description, judgment, justification, rationale).
3. What should you consider when evaluating a speech?

TERMS TO REMEMBER

Chapter 11
passivity syndrome (301)
hearing (302)
listening (302)
receiving (303)
attending (303)
understanding (303)
responding (303)
remembering (303)
appreciative listening (304)
empathic listening (304)
informative listening (305)
critical listening (305)
critical thinking (305)
noise (306)
internal noise (307)
physiological barriers (307)
psychological barriers (307)
external noise (307)
environmental barriers (307)
linguistic barriers (307)

Chapter 12
evaluation (319)
description (319)
judgment (319)
justification (319)
rationale (319)
oral evaluations (323)
written evaluations (323)
reflexivity (326)

Introduction

From the interpersonal to the public, informative speaking permeates our daily lives. Throughout the course of your life, you will give numerous informative speeches of all types.

For example, you might need to tell a friend how to fix the carburetor on an old John Deere tractor, how to groom a dog, or how to plant a garden. You might need to explain the components of a computer or digital camera. If you have children in your life, you will need to teach them things like how to tie their shoes, brush their teeth, fold their shirts, safely use a stove, or the importance of family traditions.

In your public and professional lives, you will need to understand how to pass on information effectively if you want to be successful. No matter if you are an auto mechanic, truck driver, doctor, teacher, accountant, forensic scientist, or nanny, you will need to use your informative skills daily.

Through informative speaking, we pass on knowledge, create our cultures, and survive. The better we are at informative communication, the better our lives will be.

The first five tabs in this book outline the steps in the process of creating a successful speech. The next four will help you see how to use this process or parts of it for specific types of speeches and speaking situations.

In this chapter, you will use the public speaking process to build an informative speech.

CHAPTER 13 CONTENTS

What Is the Creative Process for Informative Speaking?	334
What Is Informative Speaking?	336
How Do You Choose a Focused Informative Topic?	338
1 Get to Know the Audience and Situation	338
2 Create an Informative Idea Bank	340
3 Select and Narrow Your Informative Topic	341
4 Determine the Best Type of Informative Speech	342
5 Identify Your Specific Purpose	343
6 Identify Your Central Idea	344
7 Create a Working Outline	345
How Do You Conduct Research?	346
How Do You Construct the Informative Outline?	348
How Do You Organize the Body of an Informative Speech?	350
1 Recognize Your Organizational Strategy	350
2 Commit to a Strategy	350
3 Construct Main Points	352
4 Organize Support Materials	353
What Should You Include in the Introduction and Conclusion?	354
What Should You Consider When Preparing to Present Your Speech?	362
1 Language	362
2 Delivery	363
3 Presentation Aids	363
How Should You Evaluate an Informative Speech?	364
1 Listen Effectively	364
2 Evaluate the Speech Message	364
3 Evaluate the Presentation	365
Laura's Speech	366
Tab 6 Review	368

What Is the Creative Process for Informative Speaking?

Passing information on to other individuals through speech requires you to be logical and purposeful. This chart briefly outlines the five basic activities you will use to create an effective informative speech. Allow yourself to move creatively back and forth between each activity as you fashion your speech to pass on information.

1 STARTING

HOW DO YOU CHOOSE A FOCUSED INFORMATIVE TOPIC?
→ See page 338

Know who you are speaking to as well as where, when, and why you are speaking.

Select the informative topic that best fits you, your audience, and the occasion.

Craft a central idea that defines exactly what you want your audience to learn.

2 RESEARCHING

HOW DO YOU CONDUCT RESEARCH?
→ See page 346

Understand how to evaluate, choose, and use a variety of support materials. Good informative materials must be accurate, current, complete, and suitable.

Find support materials through the Internet, the library, interviews, and surveys.

3
CREATING

HOW DO YOU CONSTRUCT THE INFORMATIVE OUTLINE?
→ See page 348

Start with a working outline, create a preparation outline, and include a source page. Create a delivery outline to use during your speech.

HOW DO YOU ORGANIZE THE BODY OF AN INFORMATIVE SPEECH?
→ See page 350

Identify your main points. Use an organizational strategy appropriate for an informative speech.

WHAT SHOULD YOU INCLUDE IN THE INTRODUCTION AND CONCLUSION?
→ See page 354

Create an introduction to gain attention and set up your speech. Create a conclusion to sum up, tell your audience how to respond, and end with impact.

4
PRESENTING

WHAT SHOULD YOU CONSIDER WHEN PREPARING TO PRESENT YOUR SPEECH?
→ See page 362

Use language that is familiar, concrete, and appropriate.

Practice your delivery so that you are natural, enthusiastic, confident, and engaging.

Consider using presentation aids to help your audience understand and learn.

5
LISTENING & EVALUATING

HOW SHOULD YOU EVALUATE AN INFORMATIVE SPEECH?
→ See page 364

Be an active and effective listener engaged in the informative process.

Determine the effectiveness and appropriateness of the speech's topic, support materials, organization, and language, as well as the speaker's delivery and ethics.

Be a critical thinker.

CONFIDENCE BOOSTER
Tabs 1 through 5 have prepared you for this process. This chapter will take you step-by-step through the process as it relates to the informative speech. Remember the Jesse Jackson quotation from the Overview. You can conceive a great speech a step at a time. You can believe in yourself. You can achieve it. Relax and be confident that you can create a successful informative speech.

What Is Informative Speaking?

At its essence, speaking to inform is the act of *giving*. **Informative speaking** gives your audience *completely new* knowledge, skills, or understanding about your topic or increases their *current* knowledge, skills, or understanding.

The gift you give can range from a topic that seems indefinable, like the origin of life, to a practical topic like changing a tire. Whether you are the CEO of a large corporation, a local automotive salesperson, or a parent involved in the community's educational system, informative speaking is the bread and butter of our daily communication. We are constantly asked to describe, explain, demonstrate, or report on almost every aspect of our lives.

PRACTICING ETHICS

The main benchmarks of great informative speaking are accuracy, unity, and inclusiveness. Ethically, these benchmarks translate into being:

- Truthful and reliable when selecting support materials
- Complete in your coverage of the topic, not simply relying on personal knowledge
- Organized enough to demonstrate how things "fit together" in the speech
- Evenhanded and unbiased when offering information
- Responsible in selecting an appropriate and legal topic for you, your audience, and the situation

You can categorize most informative speeches as speeches to describe, explain, or instruct. A *speech to describe* usually describes an object, a person, an animal, a place, or an event. A *speech to explain* clarifies a concept or issue. A *speech to instruct* teaches or demonstrates a process. Normally, the topic—or what your audience needs to know about the topic—determines the type.

In some speaking situations, you might be required to give an informative *speech to report,* which is an oral report or briefing. You will most often give this type of speech when you are part of a group or organization, including the workplace, and need to report on the progress of something.

→ See Chapter 17 (Tab 9) for more information on a speech to report.

The following table lists each type of informative speech, its corresponding topic labels, and examples of a speech topic for each.

TYPE OF INFORMATIVE SPEECH	TOPIC LABEL	SAMPLE SPEECH TOPICS
TO DESCRIBE	Object	To describe the features of an iPod touch
	Person	To describe the life and music of Odetta
	Animal	To describe the life cycle of the butterfly
	Place	To describe the Great Coral Reef
	Event	To describe what happens at the opening of the Olympics
TO EXPLAIN	Concept	To explain basic principles of Islam
	Issue	To explain current concerns surrounding same-sex marriage
TO INSTRUCT	Process	To instruct about (demonstrate) creative ways to wrap a gift
TO REPORT	Oral report or briefing	To report recent findings related to student parking needs on campus

How Do You Choose a Focused Informative Topic?

1 **Get to Know the Audience and Situation**

2 **Create an Informative Idea Bank**

3 **Select and Narrow Your Informative Topic**

4 **Determine the Best Type of Informative Speech**

5 **Identify Your Specific Purpose**

6 **Identify Your Central Idea**

7 **Create a Working Outline**

1

Get to Know the Audience and Situation

Selecting an effective speech topic is critical for success. If your topic is not appropriate to your audience and situation, you face an uphill struggle to engage your audience. Take time to learn about your audience and situation, whether you are speaking to your class or at a formal or professional function. Doing so will also help you determine what type of informative speech (to describe, explain, instruct, or report) to create.

For example, if you work for a research lab and must present findings to the board of the company funding your research, you would give a speech to report. However, you might give the same information in a different format, a speech to explain, at a conference related to your field. The board members might be novices, and your peers at the conference might be experts; therefore, your speech's content, language, and delivery would change.

Here are some reminders for how to learn about your audience and situation:

- Review what you already know about the audience and situation, and brainstorm with others who might have insight.

- Interview someone who can tell you about the audience and situation.

- Survey potential audience members.

- Do a little research. For example, searching online can be helpful when you want to learn about an organization and its membership.

→ Chapter 1 (Tab 1) discusses in detail how to analyze your audience and the situation.

THE AUDIENCE

Determine who is in your audience and understand what they know, what they do not know, and, perhaps more importantly, what they need to know about your potential topic.

Other information you should seek relates to your audience's personal traits (age, race, income, etc.), psychological traits (needs), and social traits (group affiliations, etc.). Understanding these traits will help you appreciate and recognize your audience's identity.

You can then use that information to determine the type of informative speech you need to give, what an appropriate topic would be, and the detail you need to include for their knowledge level. Even your language and delivery choices can vary based on the audience's knowledge and expectations.

Use the review checklist below to help you analyze your audience.

THE SITUATION

Information you should know about your speaking situation includes details about the place where you will give your speech, the time, and the occasion. The situation may determine the type of speech or focus you should give or what your delivery style should be. Some topics will not work well in certain environments, within a given speech time limit, or for a given occasion.

For example, if you are asked to give a speech demonstrating a craft to a group of Girl Scouts at a local park in an outdoor shelter, you would avoid selecting a craft that might have a lot of small details that would be difficult to see or small or lightweight parts that might blow in the wind. Anything too complex might be difficult to teach with all the outdoor distractions.

Use the review checklist below to help you analyze your situation.

REVIEW CHECKLIST for Audience Analysis

❏ What is the average age, gender, occupation, income, education level, and/or household type of my audience?

❏ Are there additional characteristics to consider, such as nationality or disabilities?

❏ What are my audience's needs and knowledge level?

❏ What might they know about potential topics? How does that influence my topic or the type of informative speech I need to give?

REVIEW CHECKLIST for Situation Analysis

❏ Why is the audience here?

❏ What is my relationship with the event?

❏ How much time will I have to speak?

❏ What are the details (location, time, other speakers, occasion, etc.) of the event?

❏ What are the audience's expectations because of the occasion?

❏ How do these factors influence my topic or type of informative speech?

2

Create an Informative Idea Bank

An informative idea bank consists of a list of broad ideas that you could describe, explain, or demonstrate. This bank should contain words and phrases that come to mind when you consider your personal history, the audience, and their needs, as well as when and where you are giving the speech. Remember to consider anything a potential topic at this point. Look around and let your mind free-associate.

If you have trouble getting started, look through magazines or local papers, browse the Internet for ideas, or just walk through a store, such as a hardware or specialty store, for unique ideas. Even looking around your room or house might help you get started. Almost anything you own has a story about it or a history. For example, what's the history of the Coke bottle shape? How was bubble gum invented? How can you make a pie out of the breakfast drink Tang?

CREATING AN IDEA BANK

1. Use a sheet of paper—free-associating can be difficult on a computer.

2. Evaluate your speech assignment or speaking event for clues.

3. Make a list of potential topics that lean toward a specific purpose to inform—any topic you can explain, describe, or demonstrate. Your assignment may not allow you to do all three, but you can delete topics later if they do not work. Below is one example of an informative idea bank.

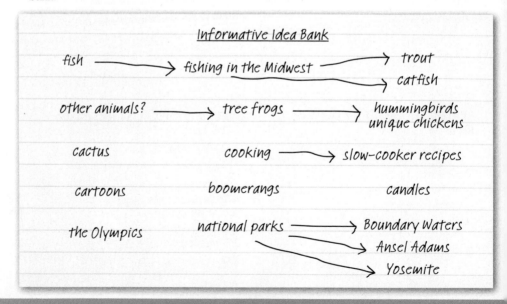

Informative Idea Bank

fish ⟶ fishing in the Midwest ⟶ trout
catfish

other animals? ⟶ tree frogs ⟶ hummingbirds
unique chickens

cactus   cooking ⟶ slow-cooker recipes

cartoons   boomerangs   candles

the Olympics   national parks ⟶ Boundary Waters
Ansel Adams
Yosemite

3

Select and Narrow Your Informative Topic

You can now focus in on the broad topic that best fits you, your audience, and the situation. Use the following questions to narrow your idea bank. Cross off topics that do not fit these criteria.

- Which topics suggest an informative general purpose and fit your assignment?
- Which topics are you comfortable speaking about?
- Which topics are appropriate for the situation and audience?
- Which topics might give completely new knowledge to your audience?
- Which topics would listeners like to know more about?

Suppose you created the idea bank on the previous page for class. Below, you narrow your selections, crossing off topics you think your audience may not enjoy. You focus on national parks, as many people like to travel, but "parks" is too broad. You've already begun narrowing the topic with free associations of Boundary Waters, Ansel Adams, and Yosemite. As your college is near the Boundary Waters and Ansel Adams is only peripherally related to parks, you choose Yosemite.

This topic is still broad, but you can narrow it further later. For now, do some preliminary research to see if you can find quality information on the topic. If researching it seems difficult, you may want to revisit your idea bank for another topic or change the angle of this one.

➔ See Chapter 2 (Tab 1) if you need more help selecting and narrowing a topic.

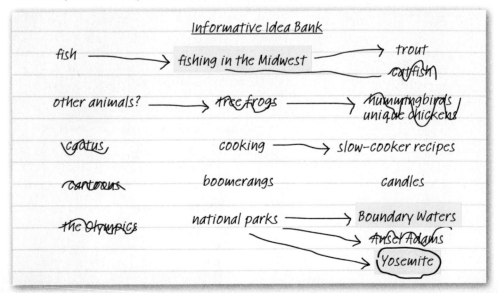

4

Determine the Best Type of Informative Speech

Earlier in this chapter, you learned that there are different types of informative speeches. Sometimes, simply labeling your topic as an object, person, animal, place, event, concept, issue, or process is enough to determine the type of speech you will create. For example, your Yosemite topic clearly fits as a speech to describe (see chart below).

If you do not yet have an angle for your topic, consider what your audience needs to know. For example, if your topic is baseball gloves and your audience consists of players, they probably know how to take care of a glove. So a process speech on cleaning a glove might not interest them unless you have unique information. However, they may not know how a glove is made (a different process topic) or the history of the glove (an object topic).

Use the chart below to help determine the appropriate type of informative speech for your topic. Correctly identifying your type of informative speech will help you settle on a suitable organizational strategy later.

TYPE OF INFORMATIVE SPEECH	TOPIC LABEL	SAMPLE SPEECH TOPICS
TO DESCRIBE	Object	To describe the features of a Wii
	Person	To describe the political life of Alexander Haig
	Animal	To describe red-tailed hawks
	Place	To describe Mount Vernon
	Event	To describe what happens at Balloon Fest
TO EXPLAIN	Concept	To explain basic principles of cognitive dissonance
	Issue	To explain current concerns surrounding immigration reform
TO INSTRUCT	Process	To instruct about (demonstrate) how to properly clean a pearl

> **TIP: Time Limits**
> Classroom speeches usually have a time limit of 3 to 10 minutes, which is not much time for a broad topic. Therefore, you need to know precisely what you intend to cover in the speech. Narrow your topic for the time you have.

5
Identify Your Specific Purpose

A good specific purpose begins to shape your speech topic into a more manageable size. The specific purpose is a single statement merging together your general purpose, your audience, and your objective for the speech.

For your Yosemite topic, you know your general purpose is to inform.

TOPIC

Yosemite National Park

GENERAL PURPOSE

To inform

Merging your general purpose with your audience and objective, your specific purpose would look like this:

SPECIFIC PURPOSE

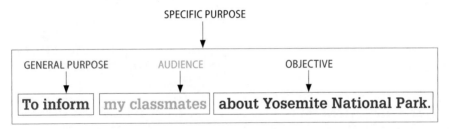

GENERAL PURPOSE

To inform

AUDIENCE

my classmates

OBJECTIVE

about Yosemite National Park.

This specific purpose will help you keep your general purpose (to inform) and your audience (college students) connected to the objective of your speech (telling about Yosemite National Park). From this point on, anything you include in the speech should inform a college-student audience with little knowledge of the park.

→ See Chapter 2 (Tab 1) if you need more help identifying your specific purpose.

REVIEW CHECKLIST for Evaluating an Informative Specific Purpose

❑ Does my specific purpose contain my general purpose, my audience reference, and my objective?

❑ Is my specific purpose an infinitive statement beginning with "to inform"?

❑ Is it a statement, not a question?

❑ Is it clear and concise, with only one speech topic?

❑ Does it relate well to me, the audience, and the situation?

6
Identify Your Central Idea

Now you are ready to formulate your central idea (also called a thesis statement), or the concise one-sentence summary or preview of exactly what you want to say in your informative speech. This is the course you will take to achieve the objective of your specific purpose.

Below are two possible examples of how the specific purpose of your Yosemite speech can become a central idea. The objective of the specific purpose is shown in blue.

If Your Specific Purpose Is...

To inform my classmates **about Yosemite National Park.**

Your Central Idea Could Be...

Yosemite National Park is more than a park; it is an experience that can change people.

or

Yosemite National Park is more than a park; it is an experience that can change people through its adventures, its waterfalls, and the great Half Dome.

Both could be acceptable. Some speech instructors like the simpler form of the first, and others like the central idea to reflect your main points, as the second example does. For some speeches, it might be difficult to establish the exact main ideas prior to doing research. You can always refine that part of the central idea as you begin to create your preparation outline.

→ See Chapter 2 (Tab 1) if you need more help formulating your central idea.

TIP: Build on Your Central Idea

As you build your speech, you should always return to your central idea and use it as a test for how appropriate your support materials are to the speech. Always ask: Does this material directly relate to my speech objective? Will my audience see my reason for including this material as support for a main point? How can I clearly show them?

REVIEW CHECKLIST for Evaluating an Informative Central Idea

❏ Is my central idea informative in nature?
❏ Is my central idea written as a complete sentence?
❏ Is it a statement, not a question?
❏ Does the statement use clear and concise language?
❏ Does my central idea focus on one speech topic?
❏ Can I cover this central idea in the time allotted?
❏ Is this informative central idea worth my audience's time?

7
Create a Working Outline

At this stage, you should take a few minutes to map out a working outline to guide your research. A working outline is a rough (often handwritten) outline or road map for your final speech. This process will help you see connections and develop your goal. As you collect support materials for your speech, add what you find to this working outline. This will help you see where you need more information or when you need to change something.

Your working main points might be questions you think need to be answered or simply phrases that relate to subtopics. As with your central idea, your main points will continue to evolve and become more defined as you create your speech. They may change significantly because, in the preparation outline stage of creating your speech, you want your main points to be concise and complete declarative sentences, not questions.

→ Chapter 5 (Tab 3) explains the benefits of a working outline and the elements of a preparation outline.

TOPIC: Yosemite National Park

GENERAL PURPOSE: To inform

SPECIFIC PURPOSE: To inform my classmates about Yosemite National Park.

CENTRAL IDEA: Yosemite National Park is more than a park; it is an experience that can change people through its adventures, its waterfalls, and the great Half Dome.

I. What adventures are available at Yosemite?
II. What is important to know about the waterfalls?
III. What is important to know about Half Dome?

Remember, you may use questions for the main points in your working outline, but you should use declarative sentences in your preparation outline.

REVIEW CHECKLIST for Working Main Points
❑ Does each main point cover only one key idea?
❑ Are my main points similarly constructed (are they parallel)?
❑ Am I roughly balancing the time spent on each point?
❑ Do my main points relate back to my central idea?

How Do You Conduct Research?

The key to any good speech is a variety of acceptable support materials. Keep your eyes open for different possibilities, and do not rely on only one research tool (for example, only the Internet). Think about your audience and their relationship with your topic to help you select appropriate materials.

Most informative speeches will rely heavily on facts, definitions, testimony, and examples. Although you might use statistics, they should be used only to explain or describe, not to persuade.

When you are researching an informative speech, you want to find materials that will make your audience want to listen and learn. The best ways to do that are:

- Select materials that have a language level appropriate for your audience.

- Find materials that will interest your audience because they are relevant, unique, current, and easy to understand.

- If the topic is complex, make sure you use materials from multiple perspectives and means. Everyone learns differently.

You should always leave the Internet, library, or other research venue with everything you need to support your speech and to cite the materials correctly. Some instructors suggest that you need to collect four times the amount of support materials that you think will go into the speech. That way, you always have enough to select from. There is no more frustrating waste of time than needing to return to the library at the last minute to get more materials or to find a publication date or page number.

Web sites, books, newspapers, magazines, newsletters, journals, government resources, reference works, and firsthand personal knowledge are all effective sources of support materials for an informative speech. The Internet, library, interviews, and even surveys can offer a wealth of information. Government pamphlets and Web sites are often a good resource for speech topics that demonstrate or instruct.

If your topic directly relates to a local business, the staff there might be able to supply materials. For example, even if you do not live in the area of Yosemite National Park, most cities have travel agencies that will have information on Yosemite. If a national park is located near you, someone there might be able to help you locate information. You could also search newspapers near Yosemite or contact the park directly via phone or e-mail. Be creative when considering possible locations for quality support materials. Ask yourself:

- Where could I look on the Internet to find support materials?
- What newspapers or magazines could I search?
- What could I use from almanacs, books of quotations, and other reference works?
- Whom could I interview?
- What government agencies could offer current information and statistics?
- What local businesses, organizations, or attractions could offer information?
- What suggestions does my local librarian have for locating materials?

→ See Tab 2 if you need help with research.

REMEMBER
To test your support materials, you should make sure they are:
- Accurate
- Current
- Complete
- Trustworthy
- Suitable

REVIEW CHECKLIST for Informative Support Materials
❑ Will my support materials make my audience want to listen and learn?
❑ Will my support materials help my audience learn something new?
❑ If my topic is difficult, do I have multiple ways of approaching the topic?
❑ Are the support materials unique for my audience?
❑ Do I have a variety of types from various sources?
❑ Are the materials current and complete?
❑ Are the sources credible?
❑ Did I take good notes so that my information is correct with complete citation information?

How Do You Construct the Informative Outline?

Next, you need to organize your thoughts. For an informative speech, sound organization is critical if you want your audience to learn and remember. Outlining is the only way to tighten up your organization.

Most instructors will ask you to complete a preparation outline (also called a full-sentence or formal outline). This outline is highly structured, includes complete sentences, and typically ends with a source page. Your instructor may ask you to turn in a copy of the preparation outline as a valuable diagnostic tool. Later in this chapter, you will create your delivery outline for rehearsal and for presenting the speech.

Preparation outlines should adhere to several traits, which are discussed in Chapter 5, but you can use the review checklist below and the template on the next page to help you create your outline. Be sure to link parts of your speech together with a transition, a signpost, an internal preview, or an internal review.

The following sections on organizing the speech body and creating an introduction and conclusion will help you further develop your preparartion outline. Remember, this process is not linear and referring back and forth between sections in this chapter will help you achieve your goal.

➜ See Chapter 5 (Tab 3) if you need more help with outlining or with creating links.

> ## REVIEW CHECKLIST for Creating an Outline
> ❏ Am I using full sentences?
> ❏ Am I introducing only one point per outline symbol?
> ❏ Are my main points parallel and do they coordinate?
> ❏ Do my main points relate to my central idea?
> ❏ Do my subpoints relate to the point they follow?

Follow either the format shown below or one that your instructor suggests.

Student name   Class
Date   Instructor name

Topic: Yosemite National Park
General purpose: To inform
Specific purpose: To inform my classmates about Yosemite National Park.
Central idea: Yosemite National Park is more than a park; it is an
                    experience that can change people through its
                    adventures, its waterfalls, and the great Half Dome.   ◄

INTRODUCTION
    Attention-getter
    Credibility material
    Relevance to audience
    Preview of speech

(Link from introduction to first main point)

BODY
    I.   Yosemite's adventures are for all ages and cultures with varied
         interests.   ◄
         A. Subpoint
         B. Subpoint
             1. Subpoint of B
             2. Subpoint of B
             3. Subpoint of B

(Link between first and second main points)

    II. Second main point
         A. Subpoint
         B. Subpoint
             1. Subpoint of B
             2. Subpoint of B
         C. Subpoint

(Link: If you continue your hike past the Vernal and Nevada Falls, you   ◄
    will reach what is possibly the most photographed place in the
    park—Half Dome.)

    III. Third main point
         A. Subpoint
             1. Subpoint of A
                 a. Subpoint of 1
                 b. Subpoint of 1
             2. Subpoint of A
         B. Subpoint
         C. Subpoint

(Link to conclusion)

CONCLUSION ◄
    Summary statement
    Audience response statement
    WOW statement

                Works Cited (or References)

This example shows how you would begin to use the template to create your Yosemite speech.

Begin filling in main points as you have them written. Use only one sentence per each outline symbol, whether it is a main point or a subpoint. You must have two or more subpoints.

Be sure to formally write out your links. In an informative speech, the links help your audience group information for better understanding and retention.

The introduction and conclusion are extremely important to the effectiveness of your speech. Spend time on them. A section later in this chapter will help you.

How Do You Organize the Body of an Informative Speech?

1 **Recognize Your Organizational Strategy**

2 **Commit to a Strategy**

3 **Construct Main Points**

4 **Organize Support Materials**

1

Recognize Your Organizational Strategy

Informative speeches can utilize a chronological, topical, spatial, order of intensity, comparative, problem–solution, or causal strategy. Knowing which types of informative speech these strategies fit with most comfortably should begin to help you recognize which strategy you want. Use the chart on the next page as a guide.

For example, in your Yosemite speech, you want to talk about park adventures, the waterfalls, and Half Dome. These are natural subtopics, which lend themselves well to the topical strategy.

2

Commit to a Strategy

The lines between objects, people, animals, places, events, concepts, issues, and processes can blur. Often it is difficult to speak about a process without defining some objects or to speak about people without placing them at events. Who could talk about the 1960s singer Janis Joplin without placing her at the Monterey Jazz Festival or Woodstock? To understand her and her music, you must talk about those events in music history. Therefore, many topics can fit into one or more strategies. The important thing is that you select one and stay with it.

➔ See Chapter 6 (Tab 3) if you need help selecting an organizational strategy.

The best way to stay committed to a strategy is to choose one as you begin to construct your main points and think about what you need to tell your audience. Again, this process is not linear. You cannot finalize main points before selecting the strategy; and some strategies will not work for certain speech goals because you cannot create or support the main points necessary to use that strategy.

STRATEGY	WHAT TYPES OF INFORMATIVE SPEECH DOES IT FIT?	WHEN MIGHT YOU USE IT?	SAMPLE SPEECH TOPICS
Chronological	To describe To instruct	When giving a speech related to time, history, or you need to teach a sequence/process	• To describe the history of Savannah, Georgia • To instruct on the proper way to wax skis
Topical	To describe To explain	With any informative speech that has natural, inherent subtopics	• To describe different types of butterflies in the West • To explain basic principles of color theory
Spatial	To describe	To describe a place, event, or object based on its relationship to space	• To describe a film festival based on the different venues around town • To describe the human tooth from the inside out
Comparative	To describe To explain	To compare a complex topic to something your audience knows better	• To explain Islam by comparing it to Christianity
Order of intensity	To describe To explain To instruct	When arranging from least to most, easy to difficult, or neutral to intense to help describe, explain, or demonstrate	• To describe tea roses by fragrance, from neutral to intense • To demonstrate exercises to tighten your stomach muscles, from easiest to most difficult
Problem–solution	To explain To report	When a solution has been implemented and you need to explain why	• To explain next year's tuition increase
Causal	To describe To explain	To describe or explain something based on how it is caused (or the reverse)	• To explain how second-hand smoke causes asthma

3

Construct Main Points

If you return to your working outline, you can see the basis of your main points in the questions you wrote. However, final main points cannot be questions, so these need some work.

TOPIC: Yosemite National Park

GENERAL PURPOSE: To inform

SPECIFIC PURPOSE: To inform my classmates about Yosemite National Park.

CENTRAL IDEA: Yosemite National Park is more than a park; it is an experience that can change people through its adventures, its waterfalls, and the great Half Dome.

I. What adventures are available at Yosemite?
II. What is important to know about the waterfalls?
III. What is important to know about Half Dome?

Form is incorrect for a preparation outline

Main points need to be complete declarative sentences, written in a parallel structure, and balanced with each other. The working main points above could be rewritten as:

I. **Yosemite's adventures are for all ages and cultures with varied interests.**

II. **Yosemite has several magnificent waterfalls, many of which are America's tallest.**

III. **Yosemite's most famous icon is Half Dome.**

These three declarative sentences are parallel and roughly balanced in terms of the time and attention you will spend on each. You have your main points and can now move on to organizing your support materials.

→ See Chapter 6 (Tab 3) if you need help with constructing main points.

TIP: Main Points
Remember, most classroom speeches are too short for more than five solid points. Two to three main points are most common in the average classroom speech.

4

Organize Support Materials

Proper outlining requires you to demonstrate how your subpoints containing the support materials are subordinate to your main points and to any subpoints that precede them. For example, if you have your first main point of the Yosemite speech and have located appropriate support materials, you will be able to add the next level of the outline.

I. **Yosemite's adventures are for all ages and cultures with varied interests.**
   - A. **You can take it easy watching for wildlife like the black bear, bobcat, white-headed woodpecker, or mountain goat.**
   - B. **Physical activities you could engage in include hiking, rock climbing, swimming, horseback riding, camping, and white-water rafting.**
   - C. **Nightlife activities include stargazing at a vast, open sky or even having a cocktail at the Iron Door Saloon.**

Indenting the three subpoints demonstrates that they must relate back to the first main point

As you add the next level of support material detail, your outline will start to fill out even more. Here is how subpoint A might look with its developing subordinate points.

I. **Yosemite's adventures are for all ages and cultures with varied interests.**
   - A. **You can take it easy watching for wildlife like the black bear, bobcat, white-headed woodpecker, or mountain goat.**
     1. **There are more than 250 species of animals in Yosemite.**
     2. **The wide range of species is mostly due to the diverse habitats that have not been degraded by human activity.**
     3. **Yosemite covers nearly 1,200 square miles.**
   - B. **Physical activities you could engage in include hiking, rock climbing, swimming, horseback riding, camping, and white-water rafting.**

How you organize the material under each point or subpoint depends on the strategy you are using and/or what you see as the best order. For example, the Yosemite speech can use a topical strategy at all levels of the outline, so it is really up to you to decide which point comes first. If you were giving a speech chronologically, the strategy would force you to organize based on time or steps.

> **TIP: Informing**
> - Don't assume that the audience has knowledge of your topic. Explain terms and concepts.
> - Use clear, concrete language that your audience will understand.
> - Be interesting and logical.
> - Appeal to different learning styles.

What Should You Include in the Introduction and Conclusion?

Like a good movie, a speech should grab the audience's attention at the beginning and end by gradually leading up to a WOW moment. The introduction and conclusion of your speech can make or break its success. So spend some quality time crafting both, and use some of your best support materials to make them sing.

LAUNCH YOUR SPEECH

Don't forget the importance of literally *launching* into your speech. Your introduction should be one of the most exciting, moving, and interesting moments of your speech. An introduction for an informative speech should "pitch" your speech to your audience. It should tell them why they need to learn more about your topic or at least amuse them in some creative way about the topic.

REMEMBER
The introduction should be less than 15 percent of your total speech time.

END YOUR SPEECH

The conclusion of a speech is almost the reverse of the introduction, minus the need to demonstrate your credibility (your speech should do that). The informative speech conclusion should leave your audience hungry for more knowledge about your topic. Your ultimate goal is to inspire them so much that they go out on their own to find more information about the topic.

REMEMBER
The conclusion should be less than 5 percent of your total speech time.

→ See Chapter 7 (Tab 3) for more details on writing introductions and conclusions.

INTRODUCTION

This should be one of the "wow" moments in your speech

ATTENTION-GETTER: Several years ago, when I was about to embark on a serious life change and move half a world away from where I had lived since 18, I went to a place, a location, a mystical spot that had a healing and peaceful effect on me. I had to say "good-bye and thank you." Michele, my friend, and I had made it to the top of Half Dome in Yosemite National Park, and I felt like I was on top of the world! I was near heaven—almost close enough to reach out and touch it. I knew I would never forget this moment as a strange but oddly familiar feeling came over me. I had never felt so independent and free, nor had as much confidence in myself. I knew from then on that if I put my mind to it and had faith in myself, I could achieve anything.

State why you should give this speech

CREDIBILITY MATERIAL: When I moved to Atwater, California, my grandmother told me that I must visit Yosemite. "It is awesome," she said. My teenage mind thought, "Yeah, right! As if nature could be all that exciting." In the end, I became a regular customer of this adventure, peacefulness, and beauty, making the 45-minute drive to Yosemite often.

Give them a reason to listen

RELEVANCE TO AUDIENCE: Yosemite has a similar effect on almost all visitors. Conservationist and Sierra Club founder John Muir stated it well in *Our National Parks* when he said, "Climb the mountains and get their good tidings. Nature's peace will flow into you as sunshine flows into trees. The winds will blow their own freshness into you, and the storms their energy, while cares will drop off like autumn leaves."

Give them a road map to your speech

PREVIEW OF SPEECH: Although my words and pictures could not do Yosemite justice, I hope to give you an idea of how wonderful it is by taking a glimpse at some general adventures the park has to offer, its waterfalls, and the awe-inspiring Half Dome.

CONCLUSION

What should your audience remember?

SUMMARY STATEMENT: Sadly, my speech has only given you a small piece of Yosemite, and it is ever changing with the seasons. In the winter, it is a vast wonderland of white beauty that is just indescribable. In the fall, the colors explode all around you. It is no wonder that John Muir spent so many years there and worked so hard to protect and defend it. And it is no wonder that Ansel Adams, the world-famous photographer, spent many years there photographing landscapes.

What do you want them to do with that information?

AUDIENCE RESPONSE STATEMENT: If you think national parks are only for family vacations and retirement visits, then you are seriously mistaken and will miss out on so much that you could experience and benefit from. Yosemite is a place to visit when you are young and healthy and can do all the physical adventures it has to offer.

Dazzle them one more time

WOW STATEMENT: Yosemite healed my soul. It taught me what is important in life and that we can miss so much beauty. Until I did the research for this speech, I didn't realize that I was feeling the same motivations as John Muir and Ansel Adams a century before me. Don't you want to experience the same?

PREPARATION OUTLINE FOR AN INFORMATIVE SPEECH

Your name   Class

Date   Instructor's name

Topic: Yosemite National Park

General purpose: To inform

Specific purpose: To inform my classmates about Yosemite National Park.

Central idea: Yosemite National Park is more than a park; it is an experience that can change people through its adventures, its waterfalls, and the great Half Dome.

INTRODUCTION

Attention-getter: Several years ago, when I was about to embark on a serious life change and move half a world away from where I had lived since 18, I went to a place, a location, a mystical spot that had a healing and peaceful effect on me. I had to say "good-bye and thank you." Michele, my friend, and I had made it to the top of Half Dome in Yosemite National Park, and I felt like I was on top of the world! I was near heaven—almost close enough to reach out and touch it. I knew I would never forget this moment as a strange but oddly familiar feeling came over me. I had never felt so independent and free, nor had as much confidence in myself. I knew from then on that if I put my mind to it and had faith in myself, I could achieve anything.

Credibility material: When I moved to Atwater, California, my grandmother told me that I must visit Yosemite. "It is awesome," she said. My teenage mind thought, "Yeah, right! As if nature could be all that exciting." In the end, I became a regular customer of this adventure, peacefulness, and beauty, making the 45-minute drive to Yosemite often.

This outline is only one example. Be sure to follow your instructor's guidelines.

Using descriptive language and emotional appeal can grab your listeners' interest.

Relevance to audience: Yosemite has a similar effect on almost all visitors. Conservationist and Sierra Club founder John Muir stated it well in *Our National Parks* when he said, "Climb the mountains and get their good tidings. Nature's peace will flow into you as sunshine flows into trees. The winds will blow their own freshness into you, and the storms their energy, while cares will drop off like autumn leaves."

An engaging quotation can provide expert testimony and effective emotive language, to help build your ethos.

Preview of speech: Although my words and pictures could not do Yosemite justice, I hope to give you an idea of how wonderful it is by taking a glimpse at some general adventures the park has to offer, its waterfalls, and the awe-inspiring Half Dome.

(**Link:** Let's begin with some general attractions at the park.)

BODY

I.   Yosemite's adventures are for all ages and cultures with varied interests.

    A.   You can take it easy watching for wildlife like the black bear, bobcat, white-headed woodpecker, or mountain goat.

        1.   According to the National Park Service's Web page for Yosemite, there are more than 250 species of animals in Yosemite.

        2.   The wide range of species is mostly due to the diverse habitats that have not been degraded by human activity.

        3.   John William Uhler, on the Web page "Yosemite National Park," states that Yosemite embraces nearly 1,200 square miles and ranges from 2,000 feet in altitude to over 13,000 feet above sea level.

Including your oral citations on the outline will help you remember them during the speech and prevent you from committing plagiarism.

    B.   Physical activities you could engage in include hiking, rock climbing, swimming, horseback riding, camping, and white-water rafting.

        1.   White-water rafting takes place on the ferocious Merced River during the spring and early summer months, when snow from atop the mountains is melting into the river.

2. Although the waters are ferocious, there are rafting trips available for beginners and advanced levels.

C. Nightlife activities include stargazing at a vast, open sky or even having a cocktail at the Iron Door Saloon.

(**Link:** When you are exhausted, you can relax and take in the breathtaking beauty of the world-famous waterfalls.)

II. Yosemite has several magnificent waterfalls, many of which are America's tallest.

A. May and June are the best months to visit most of the falls.

B. There are hundreds of waterfalls in the park, but they begin to disappear in July as the last of the snow melts from atop the mountains.

C. The most popular are Yosemite Falls, Bridalveil Fall, Vernal Fall, and Nevada Fall.

1. The roaring and crashing of the water is so loud when you get close that you can't hear someone talking right next to you.

2. It is overwhelming and makes you feel small.

3. It made me realize that my problems were even smaller.

4. As Paul Whitfield states in *The Rough Guide to Yosemite National Park*, Yosemite Falls is the highest in North America at 2,425 feet.

   a. Yosemite Falls is actually two falls—Upper Yosemite Fall and Lower Yosemite Fall.

   b. A steady breeze blows from the base of the lower fall due to the force of the air drawn down with the water and creates a steady spray.

   c. During a full moon in the spring and early summer, the spray creates "moonbows" at the base of the falls.

Interesting detailed facts and statistics support the main point about waterfalls.

5. The Bridalveil Fall is a mere 620 feet, notes Whitfield.
   a. The National Park Service's Web page states that this is "often the first waterfall visitors see when entering the valley."
   b. In the spring, it is huge, but the rest of the year, it has its characteristic light, swaying flow that gives it its name.
   c. You can walk to the base up a steep trail.
6. Vernal Fall is 317 feet, according to Whitfield.
   a. This fall is still active in September and October, with peak flow in late May.
   b. This fall is not visible from the main valley, but you can see it from the Happy Isles Trail.
   c. The National Park Service notes that when the road is open, a wheelchair-accessible trail is available.
7. Nevada Fall is 594 feet.
   a. This fall is active in September and October as well, with peak flow in late May.
   b. This fall is not visible from the main valley, but you can see it from the Happy Isles Trail.
   c. When the road is open, a wheelchair-accessible trail is available, according to the National Park Service.

(**Link:** If you continue your hike past the Vernal and Nevada Falls, you will reach what is possibly the most photographed place in the park—Half Dome.)

III. Yosemite's most famous icon is Half Dome.
   A. According to the National Park Service, Half Dome rises to 5,000 feet above the Yosemite Valley and 8,800 feet above sea level.

Include your links in the outline, and use them where you need to guide your audience to the next thought (usually between parts of the speech and the main points).

B. Getting to the top of Half Dome is a 17-mile hike that takes nine to 12 hours to complete, round trip.
    1. You must complete the trip in one day.
    2. You do not still want to be on the mountain after dark.
C. The last 400 vertical feet is at an angle of 60 degrees that requires the use of steel cables and wooden two-by-fours to reach the summit.
D. If you have forgotten gloves, which we did, there are usually some stuffed under a rock at the base of the cables, left by fellow hikers and rangers.
E. Before climbing this last leg, be sure to heed the warning engraved on the steel sign that's embedded into the side of the granite mountain: "DO NOT ASCEND TO THE TOP OF HALF DOME IF THUNDERCLOUDS ARE VISIBLE ANYWHERE IN THE SKY. HALF DOME HAS BEEN STRUCK BY LIGHTNING IN EVERY MONTH OF THE YEAR."
    1. When we began to climb, the sky was a beautiful crystal-clear blue.
    2. After 15 minutes on top, in the midst of taking in the magnificence and feeling on top of the world, black clouds rolled in from out of nowhere.
    3. The 20 or so people on top of Half Dome were then all trying to get down at once and in a hurry, because both the peak and the steel cables attract lightning.
    4. We made it down fine by staying calm, but we were sad that we had to cut the summit visit so short after that long journey.

CONCLUSION

Summary statement: Sadly, my speech has only given you a small piece of Yosemite, and it is ever changing with the seasons. In the winter, it is

> Personal testimony with a hint of emotional drama can build up to your conclusion.

> Signal the conclusion with language and vocal delivery.

a vast wonderland of white beauty that is just indescribable. In the fall, the colors explode all around you. It is no wonder that John Muir spent so many years there and worked so hard to protect and defend it. And it is no wonder that Ansel Adams, the world-famous photographer, spent many years there photographing landscapes.

Audience response statement: If you think national parks are only for family vacations and retirement visits, then you are seriously mistaken and will miss out on so much that you could experience and benefit from. Yosemite is a place to visit when you are young and healthy and can do all the physical adventures it has to offer.

WOW statement: Yosemite healed my soul. It taught me what is important in life and that we can miss so much beauty. Until I did the research for this speech, I didn't realize that I was feeling the same motivations as John Muir and Ansel Adams a century before me. Don't you want to experience the same?

> Evoke or give expert testimony whenever you can to build ethos.

References

DNC Parks & Resorts at Yosemite, Inc. (2010, June 3). Yosemite National Park. Retrieved from http://yosemitepark.com

Muir, J. (1901). *Our national parks*. New York, NY: Houghton Mifflin.

Uhler, J. W. (2007). Yosemite National Park. Retrieved from http://yosemite.national-park.com

U.S. Department of the Interior, National Park Service. (2008, December 8). Yosemite National Park. Retrieved from http://www.nps.gov/yose

Whitfield, P. (2008). *The rough guide to Yosemite National Park* (3rd ed.). New York, NY: Rough Guides.

Yosemite Association. (2010, April). Visit Yosemite National Park and the Sierra Nevada. Retrieved from http://yosemite.org

> Include only sources cited in the speech and format them according to an acceptable style manual (APA style is shown).

What Should You Consider When Preparing to Present Your Speech?

1 **Language**
2 **Delivery**
3 **Presentation Aids**

You have finally made it to where you can put your speech on its feet. This step is very important and the one most beginning speakers tend to ignore or shorten. Remember to practice, practice, and practice your speech just as you plan to give it. The more you put your speech on the tip of your tongue and in your body, the better it will flow and feel.

1

Language

Because you are always considering your audience, your situation, and yourself throughout the process of creating your speech, you have been working on language already. However, as you move to the delivery stage, you need to pay special attention to the final language choices you make. Effective language in an informative speech will assist in the learning process by being simple and clear, yet unique enough to be educational. The main rules to follow for language are:

- Remember that language creates meaning and can be culturally specific. You may have one definition for a word while your audience may have another.

- Avoid jargon, acronyms, and unfamiliar references. If you need to use them, explain them in your speech.

- Use vivid and evocative language (language that creates a picture). Some people learn better when they can visualize ideas and concepts.

- Use language devices such as repetition to help your audience learn and remember.

You language should be accurate, appropriate, conversational (using an oral style), and distinctive.

→ See Chapter 8 (Tab 4) for detailed help with using effective language.

2

Delivery

Now you need to rehearse the speech several times to make it sound natural and conversational, while still adhering to the organization of your preparation outline. But you must give the speech from a delivery outline, which you will now create.

First, practice the speech a few times from the preparation outline. Think about parts you know well, and cut them from the outline. Practice and eliminate more until you only have words, phrases, and quotations you need to read for accuracy. Put this resulting outline on note cards or other easy-to-handle materials to use during your speech. This process of whittling down the preparation to the delivery outline will help you learn the speech but not memorize it.

Mark delivery notes where you need them. Practice several more times with the delivery outline, paying attention to your voice one time, your body the next, and then all together. Vary your volume, pitch, rate, and pauses, and use correct pronunciation and articulation. Be aware of your appearance, eye contact, facial expressions, gestures, movement, and posture. Practice ways to use your voice and body to stress important information and to aid audience retention. Most of all, your voice and body should convey your positive enthusiasm for the topic. If you seem bored giving your speech, your audience will be bored, too.

➔ See Chapter 5 (Tab 3) for help creating a delivery outline and Chapter 9 (Tab 4) for help with your delivery.

3

Presentation Aids

Presentation aids are not necessary in every speech, but they can be very beneficial to an informative speech. Different people learn from different methods—by doing, seeing, listening, or a combination of these. In the informative speech, a presentation aid can help:

- Build redundancy, which will help your audience remember information.
- Gain and keep your audience's attention.
- Summarize large portions of information.
- Build your credibility.

When you use presentation aids, they should look professional but simple, be used throughout the speech, and be used effectively and appropriately. Practice repeatedly with them to make sure they work and are incorporated smoothly into the speech. You should always have a backup plan for equipment or aids that could potentially not work on the day of your speech.

➔ See Chapter 10 (Tab 4) for help with presentation aids.

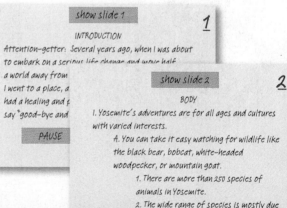

How Should You Evaluate an Informative Speech?

1 Listen Effectively
2 Evaluate the Speech Message
3 Evaluate the Presentation

1
Listen Effectively

Whether you are the speaker or an audience member, listening is crucial if the information in a speech is to be understood and retained.

If you are the speaker, think about how you can help your audience understand and retain information, and pay attention to their feedback during your speech. Many of the language, delivery, and presentational techniques mentioned in the previous section will help them listen effectively and want to listen. Be willing to adapt or adjust.

If you are an audience member, strive to make sense of and remember the information. Take notes if appropriate. Offer the speaker appropriate feedback during the speech. Listen critically by evaluating the information. Do you understand it? Is it believable? Is it complete?

2
Evaluate the Speech Message

The informative speech should never lose sight of the informative goal: to give the audience new knowledge, skill, or understanding relating to the speech topic or to increase current knowledge, skill, or understanding. Evaluate the message for clarity, accuracy, and organization. Does the speech inform (and not persuade)? Is it interesting? Does it relate to audience needs? Does it neither overestimate nor underestimate the audience's knowledge? Evaluate the appropriateness of the topic, the quality of support materials, and the citation of sources.

3

Evaluate the Presentation

Even a solid speech message cannot stand on its own without an effective presentation. Evaluating yourself and other speakers will help you improve your own techniques. Because effective techniques tend to go unnoticed, you need to keep a critical eye out for what works and what does not. Successful speakers emulate vocal and physical traits that are comfortable to them and that inspire their audience to listen and remember. They are prepared, energetic, natural, and audience-centered and present information honestly and ethically.

→ See Tab 5 if you need help with listening critically to and evaluating speeches.

Use this checklist, or guidelines provided by your instructor, to evaluate informative speeches. This list can also help guide you as you create and practice a speech.

CHECKLIST FOR EVALUATING THE INFORMATIVE SPEECH

TOPIC
.... Speech accomplished purpose to inform
.... Topic appropriate to speaker, audience, and occasion
.... Interesting topic

INTRODUCTION
.... Gained attention and interest
.... Established credibility
.... Indicated relevance to audience
.... Declared central idea
.... Previewed speech

BODY
.... Main points clear and obvious to the audience
.... Points followed an appropriate organizational strategy
.... Main points appropriately researched and supported
.... Main points supported with appropriate presentation aids when necessary
.... Oral citations included throughout speech
.... Linked parts of speech

CONCLUSION
.... Contained a summary statement
.... Offered an audience response statement
.... Effectively came to closure (WOW statement)

PRESENTATION
.... Language was clear, concise, and appropriate
.... Gestures/body movements were effective
.... Consistent and effective eye contact
.... Used vocal variety/emphasis/volume/rate
.... Used appropriate delivery style
.... Spoke with enthusiasm
.... Spoke with conviction and sincerity
.... Good use of delivery outline
.... Presentation aids appropriate to speech topic (if applicable)
.... Used presentation aids throughout entire speech (if applicable)
.... Used professional presentation aids (if applicable)
.... Speech met time requirements

Laura's Speech

Laura has decided to give an informative speech about trout. Spring break is around the corner, and Laura lives in northwestern Arkansas, where many of the rivers offer some of the nation's best trout-fishing opportunities. She listed trout in her idea bank because she trout fishes several times a year.

FINDING THE BEST TOPIC FOR HER AUDIENCE

Laura attends college in the Midwest, close to Arkansas, but she is not in an area with many trout rivers. She surveyed her audience about their knowledge of fishing in general and discovered that most have some fishing knowledge and are very open to a fishing trip. Few of her classmates knew there were different types of trout or how to fish for trout.

DECIDING ON THE CENTRAL IDEA

Because her classmates didn't have a general knowledge of trout, Laura decided to focus on teaching them about the different kinds.

> TOPIC: Trout
>
> GENERAL PURPOSE: To inform
>
> SPECIFIC PURPOSE: I want to inform my classmates about trout in the Midwest.
>
> CENTRAL IDEA: The cool waters of many Midwestern states offer today's fishers an exciting opportunity to catch a variety of trout that differ in appearance, habitat, and population.

CONSTRUCTING HER MAIN POINTS

With this central idea, Laura could construct her main points around the types of trout (brook, brown, cutthroat, and rainbow), or her main points could be types of trout, habitat, and population. Laura decided to use the four types of trout so that she won't be jumping between the types under the other two categories. She organized the speech topically be-cause trout is a living thing. Laura ordered the main points by largest population to smallest to mirror the Midwest trout-population trends and because population is a major emphasis in her central idea.

> I. FIRST MAIN POINT: What are the unique characteristics of a rainbow trout?
>
> II. SECOND MAIN POINT: What are the unique characteristics of a brown trout?
>
> III. THIRD MAIN POINT: What are the unique characteristics of a cutthroat trout?
>
> IV. FOURTH MAIN POINT: What are the unique characteristics of a brook trout?

LAURA'S OUTLINES

After conducting research on the Internet and at her local library, Laura created her preparation outline and then transferred her delivery outline to note cards. Laura put only enough on the cards to jog her memory. She also included her delivery and presentation-aid notes. Laura practiced several times before her speech date.

Topic: Trout

General Purpose: To inform

Specific Purpose: I want to inform my classmates about trout in the Midwest.

Central Idea: The cool waters of many Midwestern states offer today's fishers an exciting opportunity to catch a variety of trout that differ in appearance, habitat, and population.

INTRODUCTION

Attention-getter: Imagine the cool, crisp air on your skin as the fog rolls down the river and the sun peeps up over the trees. It is June, but the air feels cool like early May, coming off the cold river water just below the dam. You hear no industrial sounds—just the trickling of water over rock and the local wildlife calling the morning into being. A quick repetition of a jerk at the end of the fishing pole you hold breaks the calm and startles you into action. You respond with one quick jerk and begin ... in seconds, you release a colorful s. This is trout-fishing heaven. tart many a morning in the spring

---

ATTENTION-GETTER: Imagine the cool, crisp air on your skin.... This is trout-fishing heaven

CREDIBILITY: 10 years on the Wh

RELEVANCE TO AUDIENCE: live i

some of the best trout

PREVIEW: rainbow, brown, cutt

(LINK: So let's begin by looking

different trout can be.)

slide

1

BODY:

I. Rainbow—According to Arkansas Sport

  A. Looks

    1. colorful pink-and-red stripe

    2. black dots on the back, dorsal, and tail fins

    3. slightly forked tail

    4. up to 32 lbs, rarely make it over 5 lbs.

  B. eat—insects, crustaceans, and fish

    runners on hook

slide

2

  D. Habitat

    1. Web site Fly Fishing Gear, found only in the western coastal rivers of the U.S.

      a. Today—throughout United States,

3

Tab 6: Review

CHAPTER 13 REVIEW QUESTIONS

1. What is informative speaking?

2. What are the four types of informative speeches? Explain each.

3. How do you determine the best type of informative speech to use?

4. Write three effective informative central ideas for your speech class. Explain why they are effective.

5. When conducting research for an informative speech, what should you consider when selecting effective support materials?

6. What organizational strategies work well with informative speaking?

7. Give examples of informative speeches using order of intensity, problem–solution, and causal strategies. How would they differ from a persuasive speech using these strategies?

TERMS TO REMEMBER

Chapter 13
informative speaking (336)
speech to describe (337)
speech to explain (337)
speech to instruct (337)
speech to report (337)

Introduction

Suppose your friend Molly, a runner, buys a special brand of running shoes, and you feel persuaded to buy the same brand because of her choice. Or, what if you see a commercial for a new sports drink, and you decide to give it a try? According to some definitions of persuasion, both of these scenarios could describe persuasive acts; with other definitions, only one might be considered persuasion. Some communication scholars would not call your shoe purchase—based on Molly's brand choice—a result of persuasion, while they might call the sports drink commercial persuasive. This chapter will explain why.

Chapter 14 introduces you to what constitutes persuasion, what techniques you use to persuade, and how to construct an argument. Chapter 15 will help you create your persuasive speech.

CHAPTER 14 CONTENTS

What Is Persuasive Speaking?	370
What Should a Persuasive Speech Do?	372
1 Narrow Listeners' Options	372
2 Seek a Response	372
3 Support a Proposition of Fact, Value, or Policy	373
4 Rely on Varied and Valid Support Materials	374
5 Use Highly Structured Organization	374
6 Use Different Types of Appeals	374
7 Highlight Emotive and Stylisic Language	375
8 Emphasize Powerful and Direct Delivery	375
9 Acknowledge the Audience's Freedom to Decide	375
What Are the Traditional Appeals Used to Persuade?	376
1 Appeal to Pathos	376
2 Appeal to Mythos	377
3 Appeal to Ethos	378
4 Appeal to Logos	379
What Are the Modern Appeals Used to Persuade?	380
1 Appeal to Need	380
2 Appeal to Harmony	382
3 Appeal to Gain	383
4 Appeal to Commitment	383
What Are the Parts of an Argument?	384
1 Claim	385
2 Evidence	385
3 Warrants	386
What Are the Different Types of Arguments?	388
1 Argument by Deduction	388
2 Argument by Induction	390
3 Argument by Analogy	391
4 Argument by Cause	391
5 Argument by Authority	391
What Are Faulty Arguments?	392
1 Hasty Generalization	393
2 Faulty Use of Authority	393
3 Post Hoc Ergo Propter Hoc	394
4 False Analogy	394
5 Ad Hominem	395
6 Either-Or Fallacy	396
7 Slippery Slope	396
8 Begging the Question	396
9 Straw Man	397
10 Ad Ignorantiam	397
11 Non Sequitur	398
12 Appeal to Tradition	398
13 Ad Populum	399
14 Faulty Emotional Appeals	399
Shimin's Speech	400
CHAPTER 15: The Persuasive Speech	403
Tab 7: Review	442

What Is Persuasive Speaking?

Persuasion is a deliberate attempt by the speaker to create, reinforce, or change the attitudes, beliefs, values, and/or behaviors of the listener. Considering this definition in smaller parts will help you understand the complexities of persuasion.

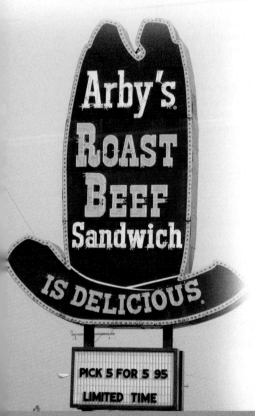

A DELIBERATE ATTEMPT...

This portion of the definition connects back to our earlier discussion of the process of communication. If you remember the communication model, you know that the act of communication grounds its beginning in the speaker and the speaker's deliberate attempt to send a message to the audience. The speaker is responsible for initiating the message.

→ See pages 14–15 in the Overview (Tab 1) for the explanation of the process of communication.

For a communicative act to be persuasive, the speaker's intent or general purpose must be to persuade. Remember Molly, who bought the new pair of shoes? Her act of purchasing a new pair of running shoes is not a *deliberate* attempt to persuade you, as her friend, to do the same. You may use Molly's purchase as evidence to support your decision to buy the shoes, but that is not due to persuasion on the part of Molly.

If Molly were to give a speech arguing that this chosen style of running shoe is the best for cross-country running, she would be engaging in the act of persuasion. Likewise, the sports drink commercial referenced in the introduction is persuasion, as it is a deliberate attempt to convince you to buy the product.

... TO CREATE, REINFORCE, OR CHANGE ATTITUDES, BELIEFS, VALUES, AND/OR BEHAVIORS

In Chapter 1, you learned that attitudes, beliefs, and values make up your audience's identity. Along with the behaviors your audience members engage in, these audience attributes are what you deliberately plan to create, reinforce, or change when you persuade. Let's review each.

- *Attitudes* are learned and persistent psychological responses, predispositions, or inclinations to act one way or feel a given way toward something, according to Martin Fishbein and Icek Ajzen in their book *Belief, Attitude, Intention, and Behavior: An Introduction to Theory and Research*. For example, you may not like the color pink and, therefore, do not respond favorably to anything that is pink. There is nothing wrong with the color, you just do not care for it. Attitudes are often, but not always, the easiest to change.

- *Beliefs* are anything people have learned to accept as plausible based on interpretation and judgment. According to Ann Bainbridge Frymier and Marjorie Keeshan Nadler in *Persuasion: Integrating Theory, Research, and Practice*, you create a belief when you connect the object of your belief to an attribute. For instance, you believe water (object) is wet (attribute). These beliefs tend to be peripheral, or less important, to the person holding them, because they are less related to the person's sense of self and identity in the world. They can be, although not always, more unstable or changeable than values. For example, you may believe that red high-tops are cool today and not a month from now.

- *Values* (also called *core beliefs*) are enduring principles related to worth or what a person sees as right or wrong, important or unimportant. Frymier and Nadler indicate that values are closely linked to the core of our personalities and self-identities. Values are hard to change, and they support our attitudes and beliefs. For example, you may value a conservative ideology, higher education, or the Christian faith.

- *Behaviors* are unconcealed actions or reactions people have, often in response to some sort of stimuli. The ways people behave generally relate to their attitudes, beliefs, and values.

When an audience does not have the knowledge to hold a set attitude, belief, or value, or to understand why to behave a particular way, you persuade the audience to *create* or *adopt* the attitude, belief, value, or behavior you are advocating.

If the audience already agrees with you, you *reinforce* that attitude, belief, value, or behavior.

At other times, you help your audience *change* existing attitudes, beliefs, values, and behaviors.

PRACTICING ETHICS
Persuasion is a complex process and a powerful practice that you must not take lightly. You must use the highest ethical standards when your intent is to persuade someone to think or act in a proposed way.

What Should a Persuasive Speech Do?

1 Narrow Listeners' Options

2 Seek a Response

3 Support a Proposition of Fact, Value, or Policy

4 Rely on Varied and Valid Support Materials

5 Use Highly Structured Organization

6 Use Different Types of Appeals

7 Highlight Emotive and Stylistic Language

8 Emphasize Powerful and Direct Delivery

9 Acknowledge the Audience's Freedom to Decide

1

Narrow Listeners' Options

Chapter 13 shows you that informative speaking is like giving a gift to your listeners. Persuasive speaking is like offering guidance to your listeners when they have several options to choose from and need your help to determine which is the best one. The job of the ethical persuasive speaker is to determine the best and safest option, support that decision logically, and offer information to the audience in a manner that allows them to make a wise decision. Persuasive speaking helps an audience limit their options and make a wise choice.

2

Seek a Response

In the persuasive speech, you have an audience response in mind. That audience response determines which of the three types of persuasive speeches you will give.

- When you want to create a new or change an existing attitude, belief, value, or behavior for your audience, you are creating a persuasive speech to *convince*.
- When you overcome apathy in your audience or reinforce an existing attitude, belief, value, or behavior, you are creating a persuasive speech to *stimulate*.
- When you ask your audience to take action, you are giving a speech to *actuate*.

3

Support a Proposition of Fact, Value, or Policy

When you create a persuasive speech, you have an overarching argument (the body of the speech) that supports the assertion you are making in your central idea. The assertion you are making in your central idea is a proposition of fact, value, or policy.

For example, if your central idea is:

Foods marked organic are not necessarily healthier than conventional foods.

The proposition you are supporting with this central idea is:

Organic foods are not healthier than conventional foods.

And once you have identified your proposition, you can determine if it is a proposition of fact, value, or policy. Let's look at each category:

- *Proposition of fact:* Answers "What is accurate or not?" For example:

   SUVs are safe.

   Lee Harvey Oswald was part of a conspiracy to assassinate President John F. Kennedy.

   Genetically altered vegetables are not healthy.

- *Proposition of value:* Answers "What has worth or importance? What is good, wise, ethical, or beautiful?" For example:

   Funding NASA programs is a good use of tax dollars.

   Downloading or sharing music without payment or permission from the copyright holder is unethical.

   It is irresponsible to text message while driving.

- *Proposition of policy:* Answers "What procedures, plans, or courses of action need to be terminated and/or implemented?" This type of proposition can ask the audience to immediately act (To persuade my audience to volunteer to clean the city) or to simply agree (To persuade my audience that the city should outlaw smoking in public buildings). Other propositions of policy include:

   All homeowners should be required to recycle.

   The City of Jonestown should not implement a tax on pet owners.

   The recreation center should be open 24 hours a day.

   The state needs stiffer laws related to child abuse crimes.

In your organic foods speech, your proposition looks at the *accuracy* of the assertion that organic foods are not necessarily healthier than conventional foods. Therefore, your central idea seeks to support a *proposition of fact*.

Knowing the type of proposition your central idea supports will help you select an organizational strategy for creating the body of the speech, which will be made up of smaller arguments. These arguments will ultimately sustain your central idea—for instance, that organic is not necessarily healthier than conventional.

4
Rely on Varied and Valid Support Materials

Think about the last time someone misled you, either accidentally or intentionally, into thinking or doing something that you might not have if you had known all the facts. Most of the time when a deception of this type occurs, it is because someone did not make sure you were given accurate, complete, current, or trustworthy information. The outcome of this act could at worst be dangerous and at least negatively influence your relationship with the deceptive person for a very long time.

As the person crafting a persuasive message, you have a responsibility and a duty to prevent either accidental or intentional deception, and just "saying so" does not prove a point. You must use quality material such as testimony (mostly expert), statistics, comparisons, brief and detailed examples, and narration to support your points. Valid support materials are accurate, current, complete, trustworthy, suitable, and from ethical sources.

➔ See Tab 2 for how to find and test support materials.

CONFIDENCE BOOSTER

A variety of quality, persuasive support materials is a must for effective persuasion. Knowing you have quality support materials will help you have confidence in your speech as well.

5
Use Highly Structured Organization

Your audience needs to follow every detail of the argument you are presenting, so your organization must be appropriate to the topic and precise down to the smallest detail. There are organizational strategies that are only appropriate for persuasive speaking, and some strategies will be better for certain topics. Once you have the overarching strategy for the speech (such as a problem–solution strategy), you need to think about how to arrange your arguments. If you want to have a successful persuasive speech, you must choose your organizational strategy carefully and arrange your support materials into effective arguments for the entire speech.

➔ See Chapters 5 and 6 (Tab 3) for detailed discussion on how to organize your speech.

➔ See "What Are the Different Types of Arguments?" on page 388 for how to arrange your arguments effectively.

6
Use Different Types of Appeals

Appeals (also called *proofs*) are the means by which you prove or establish the argument you are making. Because human beings often rationalize before they act or change, you must use a variety of appeals to persuade them. Appeals can be categorized as either *traditional* or *modern*.

➔ See "What Are the Traditional Appeals Used to Persuade?" and "What Are the Modern Appeals Used to Persuade?" on pages 376 and 380 for an extended discussion of appeals.

7

Highlight Emotive and Stylistic Language

As with all speeches, selecting the most effective language for a persuasive speech is very important. In persuasive speeches, using emotive and stylistic language helps your audience members follow your arguments, remember them, and be emotionally moved. Good persuasive speakers are extremely careful to follow the guidelines for language usage common to all speeches. For example, think about how you might use language devices like "therefore" and "as a result of" to signal clearly the bridge between two steps in an argument or how you can use language ethically to stir the emotions of your audience.

➔ See Chapter 8 (Tab 4) for how to use language successfully.

8

Emphasize Powerful and Direct Delivery

If you want to persuade an audience to agree with you, your delivery must be powerful and direct. Your voice and body language should suggest a high level of confidence and trust. You want an enthusiastic and varying vocal quality as well as good eye contact. Your posture should be lively and energetic. Your voice and body should be saying, "I believe what I am saying with my heart and soul. Isn't this exciting!"

➔ See Chapter 9 (Tab 4) for help with your speech delivery.

9

Acknowledge the Audience's Freedom to Decide

Imagine if you were forced to hold a belief you knew was not plausible, support a value that you did not agree with, or act in a way that went against everything you stand for. Good and ethical persuasion is a democracy. In other words, when a speaker engages in a good and ethical persuasive act, she or he allows and recognizes that anyone involved in that act is a free and equal participant in the decision-making process.

As the saying goes, "Life is full of choices," and your audience has the ultimate right to make whatever choices they wish. Forcing a choice or disrespecting someone for not selecting the choice you care about is not appropriate or ethical. Your job as a persuasive speaker is to present the best arguments possible so that the audience can make the best decision possible.

PRACTICING ETHICS
Persuasion is not coercion! *Coercion* is forcing somebody, via threats or intimidation, to do something against his or her will. Persuasion gives the person the necessary knowledge to change or act differently via her or his own free will.

What Are the Traditional Appeals Used to Persuade?

1 **Appeal to Pathos**
2 **Appeal to Mythos**
3 **Appeal to Ethos**
4 **Appeal to Logos**

In the fourth century BCE, Aristotle wrote in his *Rhetoric* about persuasion. Aristotle determined that you persuade others by three main appeals (pathos, ethos, and logos), and even a fourth one (mythos) under certain circumstances. Aristotle was so insightful when he came up with this system for understanding persuasion that it still applies today. Although he favored logos, Aristotle realized that the best persuasive speech uses some combination of the four.

1

Appeal to Pathos

An appeal to *pathos* deals with the listener's emotions. In other words, you can use your audience's sympathy and imagination to affect their attitudes, values, beliefs, or behaviors.

Eliciting your audience's emotions is a conjuring process and not a command! You must use vivid description and emotive language to stir your audience's sense of emotions such as fear, sympathy, empathy, happiness, or anger.

You see this type of appeal often in the media. The January 12, 2010, earthquake that devastated Haiti offered many opportunities for the news media and relief organizations to appeal to the world's emotions through video and photos of the people of Haiti. In the months after the quake, many news stories and appeals for money included pictures of women, men, and children covered in dust, being pulled from the rubble. Appeal to human emotion is often an effective way to advance a cause. Vivid description, especially by trusted experts who have firsthand knowledge, can be very moving.

> **PRACTICING ETHICS**
> Appeals to emotions should always be used in conjunction with a variety of other types of appeals. For the best effect, pair appeals of pathos with logos.

Imagine giving a speech to persuade your audience to donate to Haitian relief and using this quotation from the Web site for the International Committee of the Red Cross (www.icrc.org), immediately before calling for an audience response.

> According to Riccardo Conti, the ICRC's head of the delegation in Haiti, "Amid the crying and wailing, people are spending the night outside. People are trying to comfort each other. What you are hearing in the street are the prayers of thanks of those who surivived." These Haitians survived the quake and now it is time for us to help them survive the aftermath.

Although it may seem unethical to play with your audience's emotions, philosophers and rhetoricians from Aristotle to George Campbell and Richard Whately have argued that logic alone may not be enough to get people to act. Appeals to emotions should rarely be used alone; but depending on the topic and your audience's relationship with that topic, you may need emotional appeals to put your audience in the right mood to accept your logical argument, or you might need the logical argument to frame the appeal to their emotions.

Examples and narratives (stories) are often the most effective support materials for appealing emotionally. When you give speeches to persuade your audience to donate time or money to help a cause, you can humanize the cause for the audience members by using extended examples (mini stories) about the people they will help.

2
Appeal to Mythos

The appeal to mythos is often fueled by emotion and not always viewed as a noteworthy appeal. *Mythos* relates to a sense of one's history in the larger culture and the need to be a member of that culture. For example, our sense of what it means to be a woman or man evolves from a community-accepted understanding of what is valued in women and men.

Other aspects of our cultural identity have a mythic appeal as well. In the United States, patriotism, nationalism, faith, pride, and valor are strong traditions and values. For example, you could appeal to mythos in a speech advocating buying American:

> In conclusion, we have seen that American-made products tend to be safer because we have stricter regulations and that buying them keeps our people employed and puts money back into local economies. So, be an American—buy American!

Most cultures create and perpetuate their mythic identity in the stories they weave into legends, folktales, music, and poetry. When you appeal to mythos in a speech, you often use narratives (stories) to create a strong sense of cultural identity, which, in turn, moves your audience to a change in belief, attitude, value, or behavior. For instance, you might use mythos in a speech about increasing taxes to fund local schools:

> Determination and knowledge are what built this great country, and we need to support our country by supporting our schools.

A downside to mythos is that it can promote *ethnocentrism*, or the notion that one's culture or viewpoint is superior to that of others.

3

Appeal to Ethos

Ethos is the credibility inspired by the speaker's character, or what Aristotle called *moral character*. You can have a strong argument and emotional appeal, but if the audience questions your character, you will have trouble persuading them.

The key to using your credibility effectively is to realize that it resides in *how your audience views you* and not in how you view yourself. You may have the best of intentions, but if your audience doesn't trust you, your credibility and persuasive ability will be low. Aristotle claimed that the speaker's credibility evolved from *competency* and *character*. In modern times, a third trait, *charisma*, has been recognized.

- *Competency* is the audience's perception of how knowledgeable you are about your topic. The more knowledgeable you appear, the greater the likelihood of persuading your audience. Mentioning your related experience/education, citing a variety of support materials from credible sources, and presenting a polished speech will help demonstrate your competency.

- *Character* is the audience's perception of your intentions and of the concern you have for the audience. Do they see you as trustworthy, objective, honest, and similar to them? Finding ways to connect with the audience, demonstrating that you have investigated alternatives and oppositions to your positions, and emphasizing your concern for the audience rather than just for yourself will build your character.

- *Charisma* is the audience's perception of your personality. Do they see you as energetic, friendly, approachable, and vocally

as well as physically pleasing? Be confident and assertive in a positive manner. Use language and gestures to demonstrate your dynamic personality and excitement about the topic.

Your ethos progresses through three levels:

- The *initial level* of ethos is the credibility your audience perceives in you before your speech starts. The audience may have preconceived feelings about you that give you either high or low credibility. They may not know you at all, which might make them apathetic, or they may assign you a level of credibility by how you are introduced, who introduces you, or the reason for the speaking event.

- The *derived level* of ethos is the credibility your audience assigns you during your speech based on the content and effectiveness of the speech.

- The *terminal level* of ethos is your credibility with your audience after you have finished your speech. Your ability to handle questions after the speech, your exiting behavior, and any follow-up comments you make after the end of your speech can influence the level of credibility your audience assigns you.

The appeal to ethos also includes the ethos of your sources. You audience must view your sources within the speech as accurate, recent, and without bias. You must identify your sources and demonstrate why they are trustworthy.

→ See Tab 4 for discussion of source credibility and citations.

4
Appeal to Logos

The human ability to use logic can be a powerful persuasive tool. When you appeal to logic, or *logos*, in a speech, you appeal to the listener's ability to reason through statistics, facts, and expert testimony to reach a conclusion. Therefore, you engage in *reasoning*—the rational thinking humans do to reach conclusions or to justify beliefs or acts. You build arguments to influence your audience's beliefs, values, attitudes, and behaviors. The rest of this chapter will explain arguments in more detail, but here is the basic format of an argument:

1. Make a statement.
2. Offer support materials related to the statement as evidence.
3. Draw your conclusion.

For example, Katie is a student in a state that is considering a ban on cell phone use while driving. Katie, whose best friend died in a crash while using her phone, will argue in her speech for supporting the ban. She creates her first argument using this basic format.

STATEMENT:	Cell phone use while driving is pervasive.
EVIDENCE:	As of October 2008, 266 million people in the United States subscribed to some form of wireless communication, including cell phones. This is up from 4.3 million in 1990 (Insurance Information Institute, 2008).
EVIDENCE:	In 2006, a study reported that at any moment during the day, 8 percent of all drivers are on their cell phones (Siegel).
CONCLUSION:	Given the number of people subscribing to cell phones and the number of drivers using them, it would be difficult to drive anywhere and not meet someone using a cell phone.

Katie's next argument uses this same format and continues to support her overall purpose.

STATEMENT:	Cell phone use while driving is dangerous.
EVIDENCE:	A National Highway Traffic Safety Administration study showed that 80 percent of crashes and 65 percent of near crashes involve driver inattention three seconds before the event, with the most common distraction being cell phones (Insurance Information Institute, 2008).
EVIDENCE:	Conversations using a cell phone demand greater continuous concentration from the driver, diverting attention away from the road (Insurance Information Institute, 2008).
EVIDENCE:	A 2005 Australian study showed that crashes were four times more likely while drivers were talking on cell phones and for 10 minutes after the phone call than when a cell phone was not used (Healy, 2008).
CONCLUSION:	Numerous studies suggest that cell phone usage while driving is dangerous.

This material is only a part of Katie's speech, but you can begin to see how she logically leads her audience to the same conclusions she has reached.

What Are the Modern Appeals Used to Persuade?

1 **Appeal to Need**

2 **Appeal to Harmony**

3 **Appeal to Gain**

4 **Appeal to Commitment**

Although much of how you persuade relies on the classical appeals of logic, credibility, emotions, and cultural identity, the modern speaker can use other types of motivational appeals. Modern theorists argue that motivation to change can be grounded less in the logical and more in the psychological. In other words, people are motivated by such psychological appeals as meeting their needs, creating a sense of harmony, gaining something, or acting out of commitment.

1

Appeal to Need

This modern method of persuasion recognizes that your audience members have needs they see as important and necessary to fulfill. Demonstrating, when possible, how your topic will help your audience fulfill a need can be an effective motivator.

In Chapter 1, you learned about Abraham Maslow's *hierarchy of needs* theory, which states that humans have a set of needs that must be met. These fit into five hierarchical categories, beginning with *physiological needs* and then progressing up to *safety, social, self-esteem*, and *self-actualization needs*. They are hierarchical in that you must meet the lower, more basic needs before you can progress up to the higher ones.

Appealing to your audience's needs makes for an effective persuasive speech. With this type of appeal, you collect and arrange support materials to demonstrate that what you are suggesting in your speech fulfills a need of the audience members.

Described by Alan Monroe in *Principles and Types of Speech*, Monroe's motivated sequence is a classic organizational strategy using an appeal to need (see Chapter 6, page 182). In the second, third, and fourth stages of the sequence, you thoughtfully and intentionally demonstrate to your audience that they have a need; propose a solution to them that will satisfy the need; and then help them visualize the benefits. This appeal relies on you knowing the audience's needs and paying attention to the hierarchy. For example, trying to convince a group of recently unemployed autoworkers to contribute to a 401K retirement fund will not be effective, because they have other important financial needs.

THE HIERARCHY OF NEEDS

Self-actualization needs relate to the need to reach your highest goal or potential.

Self-esteem needs relate to the need for respect or being viewed by others as important, which leads to feeling good about oneself.

Social needs relate to the need to belong or to be in lasting relationships, such as intimate partnerships, friendships, families, and social groups.

Safety needs are needs for overall security and protection, such as a sense of safety in your home, relationships, or shelter.

Physiological needs are needs for food, water, air, general comfort, and sex.

SELF-ACTUALIZATION NEEDS

SELF-ESTEEM NEEDS

SOCIAL NEEDS

SAFETY NEEDS

PHYSIOLOGICAL NEEDS

MONROE'S MOTIVATED SEQUENCE

ATTENTION STAGE
You direct your audience's attention toward you and your topic.

NEED STAGE
You demonstrate to your audience that they have one of the needs in the hierarchy.

SATISFACTION STAGE
You propose a solution to meet the need.

VISUALIZATION STAGE
You help the audience visualize the benefits of the solution.

ACTION STAGE
You tell the audience what they must do to adopt the solution and achieve satisfaction.

→ See Chapter 6 (Tab 3) and Chapter 15 (Tab 7) for more on using Monroe's motivated sequence to structure a persuasive speech.

2

Appeal to Harmony

In his book *A Theory of Cognitive Dissonance*, Leon Festinger introduced **Cognitive Dissonance Theory,** which emphasizes the human need to be in a harmonious state (consonant state). However, sometimes, there are conflicting attitudes, values, beliefs, ideas, or behaviors that cause an inharmonious feeling (dissonant state).

For example, think about how you feel when you eat really good pizza or chocolate cake. Part of your mind is happy with the taste of the food and eating it all, but another part of your conscious is reminding you that eating a lot of pizza or cake is not healthy. You end up feeling guilty, or in a dissonant state of wanting more of the good food but torn about the amount of calories and/or fat. Once there, you rationalize your way to a harmonious state by either convincing yourself that eating a lot of pizza or cake is okay because you will diet tomorrow or stopping because your healthy side wins out.

People are driven to reduce a dissonant feeling, and as a speaker, you can use that drive to motivate your audience to agree with you. For example, if you were giving a speech to an audience you know believes in the greenhouse effect, you might convince them to reduce their carbon footprint by creating a dissonant feeling in them. One way to do that would be to show them how big their carbon footprint is and how it directly relates to environmental destruction.

Creating an uncomfortable feeling in your audience can be unpredictable, especially if their beliefs in what you are discussing are deeply seated. Just because you create dissonance does not mean your audience will automatically accept your solution. They may find a way to discredit you or your sources, they may stop listening, or they may simply hear what they want to hear by tuning in only to parts of your message. When an audience has deeply held feelings about your topic, you might choose not to create dissonance for them.

3
Appeal to Gain

When you appeal to gain, you are recognizing that most people weigh or evaluate their actions based on what the actions might cost them. In *Belief, Attitude, Intention, and Behavior*, Martin Fishbein and Icek Ajzen formulated a theory that helps you understand how this appeal works. Their theory, the **Expectancy-Outcome Values Theory**, suggests that people will evaluate the cost, benefit, or value related to making a change in an attitude, value, belief, or behavior to decide if it is worthwhile or not. People in a situation like this will ask questions such as:

- Is this a good or bad idea?
- Will my family, friends, or colleagues approve or disapprove?
- If they disapprove, what are the ramifications?
- Are those ramifications worth it?
- Will my family, friends, or colleagues think better of me if I do this?

People will try to determine what they will gain or lose by changing. During a persuasive speech, if you can demonstrate to your audience that what you are asking to change or do will be a gain and not a loss, you may be able to motivate them to agree.

For example, if you are trying to convince a group of college students that they should engage in community service or sign up for an internship because future potential employers like to see these activities on résumés, you are appealing to the students' need to gain more than the time it will take to participate in the service or internship.

4
Appeal to Commitment

Another appeal recognizes how audience members might react to your message depending upon their relationship with the topic. The **Elaboration Likelihood Model**, presented by Richard Petty and John Cacioppo in *Communication and Persuasion*, suggests that people process persuasive messages based on their commitment or involvement. The model argues that people will process your message by one of two ways: central processing or peripheral processing.

Audience members who are motivated and want to think critically about your topic are engaging in *central processing*. Those who see your message as irrelevant, uninteresting, or too complex will not pay close enough attention to be critical and are engaging in *peripheral processing*.

Think about how you listen in a class you do not find interesting. Then think about how you listen in your favorite class. Your level of commitment and involvement makes you process those courses differently. In the less interesting course, your listening may be shallow—just enough to get the facts to pass the test. In your favorite course, you may take notes, read before class, and participate in discussion. You are excited about the course.

As a speaker, you can use this knowledge to create a message relevant to the majority of your audience's interests. The challenge with this type of appeal is that you need to know your audience and what they will process centrally. This heightens the significance of conducting effective audience analysis.

→ See Chapter 1 (Tab 1) for more information about audience analysis.

What Are the Parts of an Argument?

1 **Claim**

2 **Evidence**

3 **Warrants**

An ***argument*** is a reason or a series of reasons you give to support an assertion. Arguments have three parts: a claim, evidence, and warrants.

One way to understand an argument is to think of it as a bridge that you need to build so that you can convince an audience to cross to the other side of a vast river. The claim or conclusion of your argument is like the road-bed of the bridge. The evidence is the material making up the piers, which holds the roadbed in place; and the fact that the piers are made of concrete and metal is the warrant that makes the audience believe it is safe to cross. If your audience does not see the bridge as strong, they will not cross the bridge.

Let's look at each part of an argument in more detail.

1
Claim

Earlier you learned that all persuasive speeches support a proposition of fact, value, or policy and that your central idea summarizes or previews what you specifically want to assert. Now you can start to see how arguments work. When you make a smaller argument within the body of the speech, you will have a claim that acts just as your central idea does for the whole speech. The *claim* of an argument is the assertion you are making and will be a claim of fact, value, or policy. Each claim should be a single, concise sentence. For example:

CLAIM OF FACT: People who wear seat belts tend to take better care of their health.

CLAIM OF FACT: Too much fluoride in our drinking water can be dangerous.

CLAIM OF VALUE: Owning a gun is wrong.

CLAIM OF VALUE: You should always adopt an animal from a shelter.

CLAIM OF POLICY: All public buildings should be smoke-free.

CLAIM OF POLICY: The city should change the current city ordinance to allow citizens to own a small flock of hens within the city limits.

Rarely, if ever, can you prove that a claim is 100 percent correct. Claims can be qualified as "possible," "probable," or "beyond doubt." If the qualification assigned to the claim has solid reasoning and enough evidence to support it at the level you are arguing, then the claim is sound and your audience is more likely to believe it. Clearly, if you wish to argue "beyond doubt," your reasoning and evidence have to be strong.

2
Evidence

When you make a claim, you have to support it. Here you ask, "What proof do I have to support this claim?" In this step, the support materials you have gathered become *evidence*, or the information that proves your claim. Evidence comes in the form of examples, facts, definitions, testimony, and statistics.

Let's say your speech is on the change-of-policy claim about chickens:

CLAIM OF POLICY: The city should change the current city ordinance to allow citizens to own a small flock of hens within the city limits.

To support your claim, you consult books like *Keep Chickens! Tending Small Flocks in Cities, Suburbs, and Other Small Spaces* by Barbara Kilarski and *Chickens in Your Backyard: A Beginner's Guide* by Rick and Gail Luttmann, and you discover the following potential evidence:

- Chickens and their eggs are great sources of protein.

- Naturally raised chickens and eggs have a better nutrient value than factory-farmed chickens.

- Chickens can reduce solid waste by eating table scraps.

- During hard economic times, raising your own chickens can be cheaper than buying the meat and eggs from a grocery store.

- Raising your own food puts you in control of what goes into your body.

- The practice of raising chickens in our backyards is more humane than supporting corporate chicken farms.

3
Warrants

Just presenting evidence will not necessarily demonstrate that your claim is accurate. British philosopher Stephen Toulmin, in his book *The Uses of Argument*, suggests that you also need **warrants**, or assumptions that act as links between the evidence and the claim. This step is where you help your audience draw a conclusion about your claim and the evidence provided.

EVIDENCE
What information do you have to support your claim?

WARRANT
How do you justify moving from this evidence to the claim?

CLAIM
What exactly is your assertion or stance?

Staying with your topic about urban chickens, if you take two bits of information—one about the health benefits of chicken in general and one that naturally raised chickens tend to be more nutritious than chickens raised on factory farms—you could support your claim like this:

EVIDENCE
Chicken is a great source of protein. Naturally raised chickens have a better nutrient value than those raised on factory farms.

WARRANT
Anyone raising his or her own chickens has access to a more nutrient-enriched form of protein.

CLAIM
Local citizens should be allowed to raise chickens.

There are three types of warrants: *authoritative, motivational,* and *substantive.* Here is another example, related to the need for calcium in most men's diets, to demonstrate the three types of warrants.

1.
Authoritative warrants link the evidence to the claim by assuming that the claim is accurate based on the credibility of the source of the support materials. For example, look at this outline of an argument:

EVIDENCE:
Doctors at the Mayo Clinic say calcium is necessary for men.

WARRANT:
The Mayo Clinic doctors are viewed as an extremely reliable source.

CLAIM:
Men need calcium.

2.
Motivational warrants link the evidence to the claim based on the speaker's and audience's needs and values. For example:

EVIDENCE:
Men need calcium to prevent brittle-bone issues late in life.

WARRANT:
Men's happiness and quality of life in later years is dependent on healthy bones.

CLAIM:
Men need calcium.

3.
Substantive warrants link the evidence to the claim based on the reliability of the support materials. In other words, are there enough examples and/or data to be convincing? Are the support materials representative?

EVIDENCE:
Several studies have found that many men are getting insufficient levels of calcium and suggest that this deficiency is beginning to negatively influence their bodies and lives later in life.

WARRANT:
Enough evidence exists to support the fact that some men are not getting enough calcium and that this can have serious effects.

CLAIM:
Men need calcium.

Warrants can be expressed or unexpressed, but in order for your argument to work, your audience must either intuitively understand or be shown the connection.

CHECKLIST for Creating an Argument
❏ Is my claim a concise, declarative sentence?
❏ Do I have enough quality evidence to support my claim?
❏ What are my warrants or justifications for moving from the evidence to the claim?

What Are the Different Types of Arguments?

1 Argument by Deduction

2 Argument by Induction

3 Argument by Analogy

4 Argument by Cause

5 Argument by Authority

The differences between types of arguments relates to how they are constructed after you create your claim. Remember, a claim is a concise sentence stating what you want to prove. For example:

All dolphins, whales, and porpoises are mammals.

Once you know what you want your audience to accept, you need to decide what type of argument you want to construct. There are five types of arguments.

1

Argument by Deduction

Argument by deduction constructs a series of general statements (known as *premises*) that together prove the claim/conclusion correct.

When arguing by deduction, you can use one of two formats: a *syllogism* or an *enthymeme*. The **syllogism** is the classical form of deductive reasoning with this structure.

MAJOR PREMISE
All mammals feed their young milk via mammary glands located on the female of the species.

— Includes a generally accepted statement

MINOR PREMISE
All female dolphins, whales, and porpoises feed their young milk produced by mammary glands on the female.

— Includes a specific observation

CONCLUSION
Therefore, all dolphins, whales, and porpoises are mammals.

— Includes a statement that ties the major and minor premises together

When you use deductive arguments in a speech, you will not usually be so methodical in how you phrase the argument. This same syllogism might be presented as:

According to scientists, there are several characteristics that define mammals, but the most significant is how they feed their young. All mammals have the ability to feed their young through mammary glands located on the body of the female of the species. Dolphins, whales, and porpoises all have this unique ability to allow their offspring to suckle. We consider dolphins, whales, and porpoises to be marine mammals.

MAJOR PREMISE

MINOR PREMISE

CONCLUSION

Sometimes, one of your premises will be obvious or common knowledge and you will not need to state it; this type of truncated syllogism is an **enthymeme**. In the example below, you would drop the obvious minor premise—that Fred is a human—and jump to the conclusion.

MAJOR PREMISE
All humans are mortal.

CONCLUSION
Therefore, Fred is mortal.

Deductive reasoning must present a sound argument. To be sound, the major and minor premises as well as the conclusion must be factual; if they are not, the result is a *faulty syllogism*. For example:

MAJOR PREMISE
All environmentalists are vegetarians.

MINOR PREMISE
Yeon is an environmentalist.

CONCLUSION
Therefore, Yeon is a vegetarian.

FAULTY SYLLOGISM

The major premise here is false because many environmentalists are not vegetarians. Yeon may be an environmentalist, but that does not necessarily mean Yeon is a vegetarian. Likewise, Yeon may be an environmentalist and a vegetarian, but being a vegetarian may have nothing to do with being an environmentalist. To make a sound deductive argument, you want to ask: "Can I prove the major and minor premises are true? Is the conclusion reasonable, given the two premises?"

2

Argument by Induction

Whereas deduction deals with certainty, induction predicts probability. When you construct an **argument by induction**, you will argue from specific cases to a general statement suggesting something to be likely based on the specific cases. We often use this type of reasoning in our everyday lives.

For example, if you buy a box of assorted chocolates and you eat three or four pieces in the box only to discover they are stale, you do not keep eating and assume the next one will not be stale. Instead, you reason that if the first three or four pieces (the specific) are stale, the whole box (the general) is stale. If you check out gas prices at 9 or 10 gas stations in your city and they are all $2.79, you reason that gas in your town will probably cost $2.79 everywhere.

The reliability of these claims resides in the quantity and quality of the specific cases. The same is true for a speech using argument by induction. The induction can be based on examples, statistics, facts, or testimony.

This diagram demonstrates how you might reason through specific cases to support the claim "ZZtravel.com is the cheapest and best place to book spring-break trips."

SPECIFIC CASE #1
Student A purchased airline tickets and hotel reservations to Cancun from ZZtravel.com because the service was the cheapest.

↓

SPECIFIC CASE #2
Student B rented a car and made hotel reservations for a trip to Orlando from the same online service because it was the cheapest she could locate.

↓

SPECIFIC CASE #3
Student C purchased airline tickets to make a trip back home to Oregon from the same online service because it was the cheapest.

↓

SPECIFIC CASE #4
Student D purchased airline tickets and a Eurail pass for a trip to Germany from the same online service because it was the cheapest he found.

↓

CLAIM
ZZtravel.com has the best rates for a variety of travel needs and destinations.

TIP: Inductive Arguments
Inductive arguments are useful when you know your audience is against what you are about to claim.

3
Argument by Analogy

When you create an **argument by analogy**, you conclude that something will be accurate for one case if it is true for another similar case. In other words, if it is true for A, it is true for B because they are so similar.

For example, many people who argue for a universal health care plan in the United States do so by making a comparison to Canada. Their claim based on an argument of analogy might be something like this:

> Because the United States and Canada are so similar and a universal plan works in Canada, then universal health care will work in the United States.

As in this example, you will most often use an argument by analogy when giving a persuasive speech on a proposition of policy.

As discussed in Chapter 4, there are two types of analogies: literal and figurative. An argument based on literal analogies (the comparison of two similar things) works the best. Rarely will a figurative analogy (a metaphorical comparison of dissimilar things) prove a claim, and most of the time, a figurative analogy ends in faulty reasoning.

4
Argument by Cause

Argument by cause attempts to demonstrate a relationship between two events or factors in which one of the events or factors causes the other. This form of reasoning may take an effect-to-cause or cause-to-effect form. Here are two claims suggesting this type of argument.

> **The increase in violence in our public schools is the effect of increased violence in the entertainment world.** — EFFECT-TO-CAUSE

> **Procrastinating on your assignments will cause you to get lower grades.** — CAUSE-TO-EFFECT

5
Argument by Authority

Argument by authority locates its power in the ethos of the testimony of others you might use to support your claim. When you use this type of argument, you collect testimony from individuals the audience will perceive as experts on the topic.

Argument by authority works only if the audience perceives the experts as credible and unbiased. For example, if you wanted to support the claim that stoplight cameras decrease accidents and save lives, you might consider quoting the chiefs of police in towns and cities already using these devices. For maximum effect, you should quote your sources directly, and you should always give their credentials.

What Are Faulty Arguments?

1 **Hasty Generalization**

2 **Faulty Use of Authority**

3 **Post Hoc Ergo Propter Hoc**

4 **False Analogy**

5 **Ad Hominem**

6 **Either-Or Fallacy**

7 **Slippery Slope**

8 **Begging the Question**

9 **Straw Man**

10 **Ad Ignorantiam**

11 **Non Sequitur**

12 **Appeal to Tradition**

13 **Ad Populum**

14 **Faulty Emotional Appeals**

When a speaker creates an argument, she or he can unintentionally or intentionally create a faulty argument known as a **fallacy.**

As a speaker and as an audience member, it is important for you to be able to recognize when an argument falls apart or does not make sense, making it a bad argument.

There are numerous fallacies, but the following are some of the most common. Edward Corbett and Robert Connors in *Classical Rhetoric for the Modern Student* and Steven Toulmin, Richard Rieke, and Allan Janik in *An Introduction to Reasoning* offer more detailed discussions of these and additional fallacies.

PRACTICING ETHICS

Using a fallacy to persuade is unethical. You should never do so intentionally, and you should work to prevent fallacies from occurring in your speech by mistake.

1

Hasty Generalization

WHAT IS IT?

A *hasty generalization* occurs when you use faulty inductive reasoning (specific cases to the general claim). You commit this fallacy when you have an insufficient amount of valid support materials (examples, statistics, etc.) to draw a conclusion about the general based on those support materials. You jump to your point too quickly or without substance, and your audience doesn't believe it. Your claim may be true in the end, but you have to prove it.

EXAMPLES
"I have had three major problems with my new car. This brand of car is worthless."

"My grandmother became addicted to gambling. Gambling should be banned because it is addictive."

HOW CAN YOU AVOID IT?

Using a significant number of current and quality cases to argue from the specific to a general statement will prevent this type of fallacy.

OTHER NAMES OR RELATED TYPES

Leaping to a conclusion, hasty induction, law of small numbers, unrepresentative sample, fallacy of insufficient statistics or sample, and *secundum quid*

2

Faulty Use of Authority

WHAT IS IT?

A *faulty use of authority* occurs when you use information or testimony from someone who is not a legitimate authority on the subject. The source's lack of authority may have several origins.

- The source has insufficient expertise.
- The source is not an expert in the area under discussion.
- The area of expertise is not a legitimate discipline or area.
- Most other experts disagree with this expert.
- The expert is biased for some reason.
- The speaker does not identify the source's qualifications.

EXAMPLES
We see this type of fallacy a lot in advertisements. For instance, an actor or athlete endorsing a product as the best can be faulty use of authority because they are frequently not experts on that product. In introductory speech classes, beginning speakers often use testimony from individuals who are not experts but are convenient. For example: "My roommate agrees that the tuition increase is too high."

HOW CAN YOU AVOID IT?

If you wish to use expert testimony to support a claim, make sure the person is a recognized expert related to the topic, and note her or his expertise during the speech.

OTHER NAMES OR RELATED TYPES

Fallacious appeal to authority, misuse of authority, irrelevant authority, questionable or inappropriate authority, and *ad verecundiam*

3
Post Hoc Ergo Propter Hoc
WHAT IS IT?

Post hoc ergo propter hoc is Latin for "after this, therefore because of this." This fallacy occurs with causal reasoning when you assume that because one event comes after another, the first event must be the cause of the second. This fallacy is fairly common, because causal reasoning often does have some relationship to the sequence of things.

However, sequence alone is not enough to support the claim, and in some cases, there is no relationship. For example, is there any real causal relationship between eating black-eyed peas on New Year's Day and having good luck the rest of the year? No, but many southern mothers have managed to (and still do) convince their families to eat this hearty and cheap meal on that day. As you can imagine most of our superstitious practices evolve from this type of reasoning.

> EXAMPLE
> "People consume a lot of ice cream in the summer months. Crime in many cities rises during the summer. Ice cream consumption must increase crime." (More likely the hot weather and the closing of schools are what influence crime levels.)

HOW CAN YOU AVOID IT?

Spend the necessary time during your speech to help your audience see how the two events relate and could potentially influence each other, and then determine a sequence of events. Which came first, and could the first one cause the second?

OTHER NAMES OR RELATED TYPES

Post hoc, false cause, and questionable cause

4
False Analogy
WHAT IS IT?

In the earlier section on argument by analogy, you learned that a literal analogy is the only type of analogy that has real persuasive powers. Given that notion, a *false analogy* occurs when the two things being compared are not similar or are dissimilar in some radical and/or important way related to the claim.

> EXAMPLE
> Comparing campus life on a small liberal arts campus to that of a large state-university campus, when trying to argue that they are really the same experience, is a false analogy.

HOW CAN YOU AVOID IT?

When you set up an analogy, make sure the two things being compared are similar at least in the characteristics important to your claim. Consider how they are dissimilar, and make sure those characteristics are not significant.

OTHER NAMES OR RELATED TYPES

Faulty analogy, weak analogy, and questionable analogy

5

Ad Hominem

WHAT IS IT?

Ad hominem is Latin for "to or against the person." Speakers often use this fallacy to divert the audience's attention from the real issue by attacking the person who is associated with a claim presenting a counterargument or by challenging the speaker's claim. This type of fallacy happens most often in debates, campaigns, or when using the refutational strategy. *Ad hominem* is different from questioning a person's credibility; it is an outright attack of the person and often involves name-calling. It distracts the audience and/or incites an aggressive emotional response that prevents them from engaging in logical reasoning. There are different types of *ad hominem* fallacies. Here are a few of the most common:

- *Ad hominem* abusive: Belittling or insulting your challenger

- Circumstantial *ad hominem*: Suggesting that a person making a claim is doing so only out of self-interest

- Guilt by association: Simply rejecting a claim because you dislike the people supporting the claim

- Inverse *ad hominem*: Praising a source to prove a claim is true: "She never tells a lie. It must be true."

EXAMPLES

"Who are you to question my educational policy? You don't even have children in our school system."

"That candidate would be a bad president. The Woman's International League for Peace and Freedom and the National Organization of Women support him."

HOW CAN YOU AVOID IT?

Focusing your argument on the issues being discussed and not the people discussing them will prevent this type of fallacy. When you do discuss the people, only consider issues and traits related to the speech topic or claim.

OTHER NAMES OR RELATED TYPES

Attack the person, *ad hominem* abusive, circumstantial *ad hominem*, guilt by association, and inverse *ad hominem*

6
Either-Or Fallacy
WHAT IS IT?

The *either-or fallacy* occurs when an argument considers only two alternatives when in fact there are more options. The speaker fails to consider the range of options and tends to think in extremes. This fallacy can even occur when more than two choices are considered but the speaker still fails to offer other extremely viable options (called *false choice* or *fallacy of exhaustive hypotheses*). This type of fallacy occurs often in arguments for changing a policy or offering a solution.

EXAMPLES
"You are either for prayer in schools or you are an atheist."

In his 1968 presidential campaign, Eldridge Cleaver created this type of fallacy when he expressed the now-famous words "you're either part of the solution or part of the problem." Cleaver did it intentionally to force a choice among voters.

HOW CAN YOU AVOID IT?

The best solution is to never set up an either-or argument and to be as inclusive as possible when offering options.

OTHER NAMES OR RELATED TYPES

Black-and-white thinking, false dichotomy, false dilemma, fallacy of false choice, and fallacy of exhaustive hypotheses

7
Slippery Slope
WHAT IS IT?

The *slippery slope fallacy* occurs when you argue that a relatively small event or step sets off a chain reaction to disaster.

EXAMPLES
"If you drop out of school, you will end up in jail."

"If you allow for an increase in state taxes, the government will just want more and more."

HOW CAN YOU AVOID IT?

Always consider the middle ground as a potential end result, and do not be overly dramatic.

OTHER NAMES OR RELATED TYPES

The camel's nose and the thin end of a wedge

8
Begging the Question
WHAT IS IT?

Begging the question happens when you use deductive reasoning incorrectly by implicitly or explicitly assuming the conclusion of the argument in one of the premises.

EXAMPLES
"Women should not be allowed to join men's sports teams. These teams are for men only."

"The belief in God is universal. After all, everyone believes in God."

HOW CAN YOU AVOID IT?

Make sure that your premises lead to your claim and that the claim is independent of the premises.

OTHER NAMES OR RELATED TYPES

Circular reasoning and *petitio principia*

9
Straw Man
WHAT IS IT?
You commit a *straw man fallacy* when you ignore a person's actual position and substitute a weaker, distorted, exaggerated, or misrepresented version of his/her claim. Their claim is wrong or flimsy because you make it that way.

> EXAMPLE
> **"Some senators are pushing to cut funding and troops for the current war. I can't understand why they want to leave us defenseless and our current troops on the front lines exposed."**

HOW CAN YOU AVOID IT?
To prevent this type of fallacy, always refute and state the other person's arguments as presented.

OTHER NAMES OR RELATED TYPES
Argument to logic and *argumentum ad logicam*

10
Ad Ignorantiam
WHAT IS IT?
Ad ignorantiam is Latin for "arguing from ignorance." You commit this type of fallacy when you argue that no one can prove that a claim is false because no one has proven it true, or that a claim is true because no one has proven it false.

> EXAMPLES
> **"No one has proven that UFOs exist. Therefore, they don't exist."**
>
> **"No one has ever found an alive or dead Loch Ness monster. Therefore, it is not real."**
>
> **"No one has proven that there was life on Mars. Therefore, there wasn't."**

HOW CAN YOU AVOID IT?
Appeal to ignorance never works, so use examples, facts, statistics, definitions, and testimony to support your claim.

OTHER NAMES OR RELATED TYPES
Appeal to ignorance, argument by lack of imagination, and argument by negative evidence

11
Non Sequitur

WHAT IS IT?

Non sequitur is Latin for "it does not follow." In this type of fallacy, the conclusion of a deductive argument may be true or false, but it is a fallacy because the conclusion does not connect to the premises. Often with this type of fallacy, your audience has the urge to say "What?" after the argument because it doesn't follow.

EXAMPLES
"Stephanie drives a large truck, so she must own cattle."

"If there was an adolescent present when the money was stolen, he/she most likely did it."

HOW CAN YOU AVOID IT?

Making sure every step of your argument leads to the next and connects to the final claim will prevent this logic fallacy.

OTHER NAMES OR RELATED TYPES

It does not follow, irrelevant reason, and fallacy of consequent

12
Appeal to Tradition

WHAT IS IT?

Appeal to tradition occurs when you assume that something is best or correct because it is older, it is traditional, or it has "always been that way."

EXAMPLES
"Of course this detergent is best. This formula hasn't changed for 40 years."

"My grandfather bought a Ford, my father bought a Ford, so Ford must be best."

HOW CAN YOU AVOID IT?

Base your claims on solid forms of evidence such as facts, statistics, and testimony, and use tradition only to supplement that evidence.

OTHER NAMES OR RELATED TYPES

Appeal to the old, appeal to the past, and appeal to age

TIP: Fallacies

Faulty arguments (fallacies) occur when you use evidence incorrectly or your interpretation of the evidence is incorrect. Always check how you are using and interpreting your evidence for each type of argument.

13

Ad Populum

WHAT IS IT?

Ad populum is Latin for "to the people." This type of fallacy distracts the audience's attention from examining a claim by arguing that the claim must be accurate because many believe it to be accurate. This fallacy is similar to the faulty use of authority and the appeal to tradition.

> **EXAMPLES**
> "Lots of people text while driving and don't wreck. As long as I am careful, nothing will happen."
>
> "Most people in St. Louis voted for candidate A; the state of Missouri must be for candidate A."
>
> "Brand X is the most popular brand of LCD televisions. It must be the best."

HOW CAN YOU AVOID IT?

You can use popular opinion to help support a claim, but you should never rely on it completely. Use popular opinion to supplement other forms of evidence.

OTHER NAMES OR RELATED TYPES

Bandwagon fallacy, appeal to the masses, appeal to belief, argument by consensus, and appeal to the majority of people

14

Faulty Emotional Appeals

WHAT IS IT?

Although appealing to emotion is a legitimate form of appeal, it can become a fallacy when a speaker uses only emotional appeal or unethically manipulates an audience's emotions to get them to accept a claim. Unethical manipulation often evokes irrelevant emotions and draws attention away from logic or conceals something. *Faulty emotional appeals* may manipulate a variety of emotions such as fear, wishful thinking, spite, and flattery.

> **EXAMPLE**
> A speech inducing fear that eating pork could transmit the H1N1 virus, rather than looking at the evidence that suggests transmission from pig to human is rare and the 2009 virus is a mutation, would be a faulty appeal to fear.

HOW CAN YOU AVOID IT?

To prevent this type of fallacy, use emotional appeal in conjunction with other forms of appeal. Extreme cases of faulty emotional appeal are highly unethical. A speaker who stirs up his or her audience's feelings by strong provocation is a demagogue. For example, Adolf Hitler was a **demagogue**. He preyed on the fears of the people in an attempt to take over Europe. Use emotional appeals wisely and sparingly.

OTHER NAMES OR RELATED TYPES

Appeal to emotions

Shimin's Speech

Shimin is from Singapore but has been in the United States attending school for several years. In an environmental class, she recently became aware of the staggering volume of plastic pollution in the United States alone. Although her country pushes the notion of recycling and is a very clean-conscious society, recycling is not practiced much in Singapore. In her home country, Shimin lived on the ninth floor of an apartment building, and tenants simply threw all their trash together, down a chute to the basement; out of sight, out of mind.

After her environmental class ended, Shimin joined the "Clean Up Your City" coalition in her college town. Now, she needs to give a speech about recycling to fellow students who live off campus. Shimin is concerned about the amount of plastics college students consume.

WORKING OUTLINE

Shimin focused her speech topic on plastics and created the following working outline.

TOPIC:
Plastic pollution

GENERAL PURPOSE:
To persuade

SPECIFIC PURPOSE:
To persuade college students to reduce their plastics consumption.

CENTRAL IDEA:
The amount of plastics created and thrown away daily has become a serious problem globally, but a few simple steps on our part will help lower the plastics impact on our environment and our futures.

MAIN POINT # 1: What is plastic?

MAIN POINT # 2: How do we use it?

MAIN POINT # 3: How is it influencing our environment?

MAIN POINT # 4: What is the solution?

APPEALING TO HER AUDIENCE

Once Shimin collected a significant amount of support materials, she sat down to think about how she would construct a series of arguments to support her central idea. She had already decided that the overall organizational strategy would be a problem–solution format. Now, she needed to think about how to arrange her support evidence to create arguments and what types of appeals she would use.

TRADITIONAL APPEALS

Logos: Because she was using the problem–solution strategy, she would need to demonstrate logically that plastics are a major problem. Shimin had great information showing how most of the plastics in the United States come from raw material rather than recycled material, thus creating a greater dependence on crude oil or natural gas because they are major components of plastics. Likewise, she had statistics, examples, and visuals showing how plastics do not decompose and often end up in our waterways.

Pathos: Shimin knew that several of the photos and video clips she had were great emotional-appeal devices. Seeing birds and sea creatures tangled in plastic string and nets or albatross carcasses with exposed belly contents full of human-made trash (mostly plastic) would move anyone. But she would need to back that appeal with others to make the change long lasting.

Ethos: Shimin does not consider herself an expert on plastics or recycling, but she is living proof that you can change for the better. Coming from Singapore, where she did not recycle anything, to being an active member of a community coalition illustrates conviction. Shimin recycles so much that she has only one small bag of trash every two weeks. Plus, she has educated herself about plastics and plans to cite many current and reliable sources during the speech.

Mythos: At first, she thought this one would be difficult, but even here she found a way to use the appeal in the solution portion of the speech. Because she will be speaking mainly to U.S. students, she could connect making changes in their use of plastic to a civic responsibility for preserving their beautiful country and wildlife. The United States could become the leader in this endeavor.

MODERN APPEALS

Appeal to Need and Harmony: Although Shimin could make the argument that the audience needed to conserve plastics to preserve their needs for food and safety, she did not feel like that was a strong argument for an audience of young college students. As for harmony, Shimin could create dissonance in her audience about their use of plastics, but it might backfire on her because they consume a lot of plastic.

Appeal to Gain and Commitment: She might be able to convince her audience that they would gain the respect of others, but that alone did not seem enough to make them change their behaviors. However, Shimin noticed that a lot of her peers were supportive of recycling in general, which she might be able to draw on to get them behind recycling, reducing, reusing, and refusing plastics.

SHIMIN'S FINAL DECISION

—Use all of the traditional appeals throughout.

— Arguments by induction and authority are most appropriate.

At the end of Chapter 15, you will see more details about how Shimin creates her speech.

15

THE PERSUASIVE SPEECH

Introduction

Jade is enrolled in an Introduction to Public Speaking class, and her next speech is due in a few weeks. The assignment states:

> The general purpose of this speech is to persuade. The topic of your speech should be a noteworthy current issue with meaning for and the potential to influence the lives of your audience. To meet this goal, you must analyze your classmates and select a topic that they connect with enough so that you might create, reinforce, or change their attitudes, beliefs, values, and/or bring them to action.
>
> The time limit is nine minutes. At least three sources are required for this speech (you will most likely need more to do an effective job). You must hand in a printed copy of the preparation outline as your ticket to the lectern the day of your speech. Remember to be natural, enthusiastic, engaging, confident, and sure. Use effective vocal qualities and body language.

Jade is a bit concerned about the complexity of creating a persuasive speech and finding the right topic. She is excited about engaging her classmates in a sort of debate about a current topic. She remembers something her instructor said: "The complexity of creating a persuasive speech may be a daunting chore at first, but taking it one step at a time will make it a doable task."

This chapter will help you and Jade walk through the process of creating a persuasive speech. This process is not fundamentally different from that of any other type of speech. So relax and enjoy the energy and impact you can have with persuasion.

CHAPTER 14: Tools for Persuading 369

CHAPTER 15 CONTENTS

What Is the Creative Process for Persuasive Speaking? 404

How Do You Choose a Focused Persuasive Topic? 406
1 Get to Know the Audience and Situation 406
2 Create a Persuasive Idea Bank 408
3 Select and Narrow Your Persuasive Topic 410
4 Determine the Best Type of Persuasive Speech 412
5 Identify Your Specific Purpose 414
6 Identify Your Central Idea 415
7 Create a Working Outline 416

How Do You Conduct Research? 418

How Do You Construct the Persuasive Outline? 420

How Do You Organize the Body of a Persuasive Speech? 422
1 Recognize Your Organizational Strategy 422
2 Commit to a Strategy 423
3 Construct Main Points 424
4 Organize Support Materials into Arguments 425

What Should You Include in the Introduction and Conclusion? 426

What Should You Consider When Preparing to Present Your Speech? 436
1 Language 436
2 Delivery 436
3 Presentation Aids 437

How Should You Evaluate a Persuasive Speech? 438
1 Listen Effectively 438
2 Evaluate the Speech Message 438
3 Evaluate the Presentation 439

Shimin's Speech 440

Tab 7 Review 442

What Is the Creative Process for Persuasive Speaking?

Influencing others through a speech is a remarkable task requiring you to be diligent and ethical in some ways that differ slightly from those of informative speaking. This chart briefly outlines the five basic activities you will use to create an effective persuasive speech. Remember, being creative is not a linear process, so move back and forth between each activity as you mold your speech.

1 STARTING

HOW DO YOU CHOOSE A FOCUSED PERSUASIVE TOPIC?
→ See page 406

Know who you are speaking to as well as where, when, and why you are speaking.

Select the persuasive topic that best fits you, your audience, and the occasion. Craft a central idea that defines what you want to persuade the audience of, keeping in mind the audience's relationship to the topic.

2 RESEARCHING

HOW DO YOU CONDUCT RESEARCH?
→ See page 418

Understand how to evaluate, choose, and use a variety of support materials. Good persuasion requires a wide variety of accurate, current, complete, and suitable materials.

Find support materials through the Internet, the library, interviews, and surveys.

3

CREATING

HOW DO YOU CONTRUCT THE PERSUASIVE OUTLINE?
→ See page 420

Start with a working outline, create a preparation outline, and include a source page. Create a delivery outline.

HOW DO YOU ORGANIZE THE BODY OF A PERSUASIVE SPEECH?
→ See page 422

Identify your main points. Use an organizational strategy appropriate for a persuasive speech, and carefully construct your arguments.

WHAT SHOULD YOU INCLUDE IN THE INTRODUCTION AND CONCLUSION?
→ See page 426

Gain the audience's attention and set up your speech in the introduction. Sum up, suggest an audience response, and end with impact in the conclusion.

4

PRESENTING

WHAT SHOULD YOU CONSIDER WHEN PREPARING TO PRESENT YOUR SPEECH?
→ See page 436

Use language that is familiar, concrete, and appropriate. Use vivid language and unique speech devices to appeal to your audience logically and emotionally.

Practice your delivery so that you are natural, enthusiastic, confident, and engaging.

Consider using presentation aids to help your audience understand evidence and follow arguments.

5

LISTENING & EVALUATING

HOW SHOULD YOU EVALUATE A PERSUASIVE SPEECH?
→ See page 438

Be an active and effective listener who can overcome barriers to listening and who shares responsibility in the persuasive process.

Determine the effectiveness and appropriateness of a speech's topic, support materials, organization, and language, as well as the speaker's delivery and ethics.

Be a critical thinker.

How Do You Choose a Focused Persuasive Topic?

1 **Get to Know the Audience and Situation**

2 **Create a Persuasive Idea Bank**

3 **Select and Narrow Your Persuasive Topic**

4 **Determine the Best Type of Persuasive Speech**

5 **Identify Your Specific Purpose**

6 **Identify Your Central Idea**

7 **Create a Working Outline**

1

Get to Know the Audience and Situation

You already understand that it is important to know your audience and the speaking situation before you even begin to narrow in on a speech topic. Taking the time to know your audience and the situation is even more significant with the persuasive speech.

Think about what you are about to do. You are going to attempt to change, influence, or reinforce the attitudes, beliefs, values, and/or behaviors of an audience. That is a major task, and if you do not know where your audience stands on your topic or how the situation will influence them or what their needs are, you cannot expect to persuade them.

There are several methods you can use to get to know the audience and situation.

- Stop and think about what you already know about the audience and situation. Brainstorm with others who might have ideas or insight.

- Interview someone who can tell you about the audience and situation.

- Survey members or potential members of the audience to gain knowledge.

- Do a little research or simple detective work. For example, the Internet can be extremely helpful when you want to find information about an organization and its membership.

→ See Chapter 1 (Tab 1) for more on how to analyze your audience and the situation.

THE AUDIENCE

The information to know about the audience relates to their personal traits (age, race, income, etc.), psychological traits (needs), and their social traits (group affiliations, etc.). Understanding these traits will help you appreciate and recognize your audience's identity, giving you insight into their attitudes, values, and beliefs. This insight, gained through audience analysis, will often reveal whether or not the audience already has a viewpoint related to your potential topics. Later in this chapter, you will continue to focus and craft your speech even more with your audience in mind by targeting the group you aim to appeal to the most.

→ See the section "Determine the Best Type of Persuasive Speech" on page 412 for more information on target audiences.

THE SITUATION

What you need to know about the situation includes the details of the place where you will give your speech, the time, and the occasion. Some topics will not work well in certain environments, with certain time constraints, or for a specific occasion. For example: What if you are outside during the speech but need to use a slide show? What if you only have five minutes to speak? Or what if you are speaking at a Martin Luther King, Jr, Day celebration? All of these elements will influence and guide your topic decisions.

Remember Jade from the introduction to this chapter? Well, it is the end of the semester, and she is giving one of the last speeches in the class. She knows many of her audience members from outside of class and feels confident that she knows enough about the others just from interaction in the class. Before she started to think about a topic, she wrote down some basic thoughts about the audience and situation. This information should help her narrow in on a topic.

MY AUDIENCE AND THE SITUATION:

- 18 students and 1 female instructor
- 8 men and 10 women
- Age range 18 to 40ish—mostly 18–20
- 10 Caucasians (not sure of all of their ethnicities), 4 African Americans, 3 Koreans, 1 South African
- 11 of the students live on campus
- From previous discussion, the majority seems to lean toward the liberal side
- Most of the U.S. students are from a 100-mile radius of campus
- Class is at 12:30 on Tuesday/Thursday
- My speech will be given between Thanksgiving and Christmas

2

Create a Persuasive Idea Bank

You know your general purpose is to persuade, so you need to create an idea bank full of topics that are debatable—in other words, there are two or more different opinions people may hold about each topic. This bank can contain words only, but phrases may be more beneficial because they allow you to consider some of the multiple points of view.

Beginning speakers often have trouble getting started because they want to pinpoint the perfect "be all, end all" topic right from the beginning. Relax, consider a wide variety of topics at first, and let your mind wander.

Databases like CQ (Congressional Quarterly) Researcher, CQ Weekly, and Opposing Viewpoints Resource Center, or newspapers and magazines like the *New York Times*, your local newspaper, *Time* Magazine, and *The Week* are all great places to locate current persuasive topics.

As you scroll through the databases or flip through the pages of printed material, note topics that seem interesting. Let your brain free-associate other ideas.

In the CQ Researcher database, a Pro/Con link connects to an alphabetical list of persuasive topics.

Sections like Current Report, Recent Reports, and In the News can offer current, debatable topics.

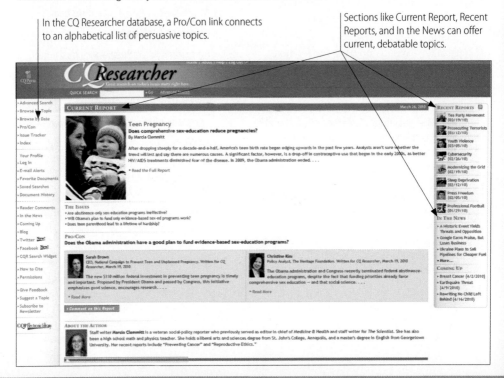

BUILDING AN IDEA BANK

1. Start with a clean sheet of paper.

2. Evaluate your speech assignment or speaking event for clues.

3. Make a list of potential topics. Make sure they are debatable and topics you can be passionate about. Include as many as you can for now; eliminate later.

→ See Chapter 2 (Tab 1) for more information on creating an idea bank.

Jade decided to go to the Opposing Viewpoints Resource Center database on her library Web site and to look through the local city newspaper. She created this idea bank for her speech class assignment:

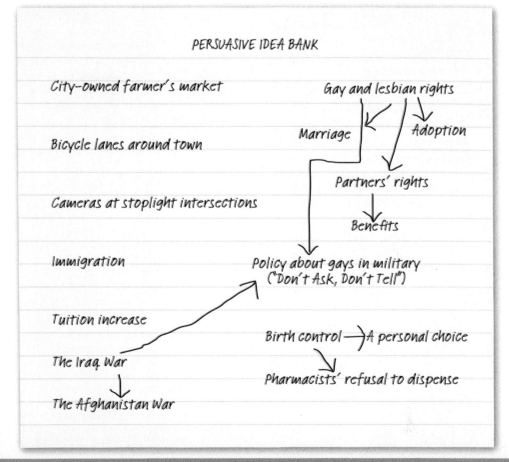

PERSUASIVE IDEA BANK

City-owned farmer's market

Bicycle lanes around town

Cameras at stoplight intersections

Immigration

Tuition increase

The Iraq War

The Afghanistan War

Gay and lesbian rights

Marriage   Adoption

Partners' rights

Benefits

Policy about gays in military
("Don't Ask, Don't Tell")

Birth control → A personal choice

Pharmacists' refusal to dispense

3

Select and Narrow Your Persuasive Topic

Once you have a list of broad topics and some that begin to narrow toward a viewpoint, you may still not know which is best for you, your audience, and the situation. The following questions should help you eliminate some topics, narrow the scope of others, and focus on what might be the best one.

- Are there topics that are just not persuasive enough? Is there any way to make them persuasive?
- Which topics are best for me?
- Which topics fit the speech assignment?
- Which topics are best for the situation?
- Which topics are best or appropriate for the audience?

Will the audience be neutral, negative, or positive? How does this impact my focus? Is the audience just too neutral or negative about the topic? Will they have an extreme reaction?

→ See Chapter 2 (Tab 1) and Chapter 14 (Tab 7) for more questions to help you narrow your topic.

Before you commit to a topic, it is smart to do some preliminary research to see if you can find current quality information on the topic. If locating information is difficult, talk with a research librarian if possible. If he or she agrees that you will have trouble finding information, you may want to select another topic or change the viewpoint of the one you are researching.

→ Tab 2 gives detailed guidance on researching.

Being a local resident and interested in equal rights, Jade was excited about almost every topic in her bank. So, she began to systematically consider the topics and to eliminate the ones that did not seem to be the best choices.

Jade realized that she did not know much about the proposal to install cameras at intersections, so she crossed it off.

Other students in Jade's class had recently given speeches relating to immigration, tuition, and war issues, so Jade thought her audience might not listen to another speech on any of these topics. She decided to eliminate them and focus on topics that hadn't come up in class yet.

Because most of her audience did not live off campus, Jade eliminated the local city topics.

The adoption topic didn't seem to relate enough to her classmates' interests.

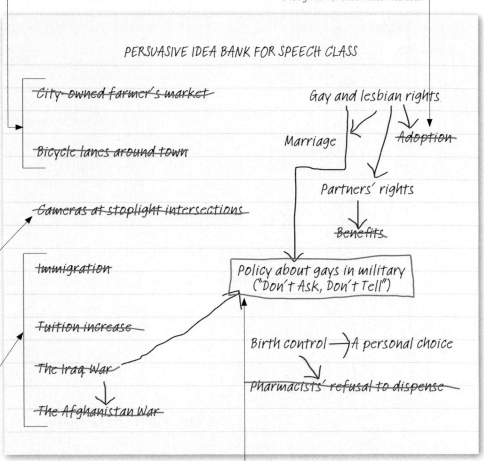

PERSUASIVE IDEA BANK FOR SPEECH CLASS

~~City-owned farmer's market~~

~~Bicycle lanes around town~~

~~Cameras at stoplight intersections~~

~~Immigration~~

~~Tuition increase~~

~~The Iraq War~~

~~The Afghanistan War~~

Gay and lesbian rights

Marriage   ~~Adoption~~

Partners' rights

~~Benefits~~

Policy about gays in military ("Don't Ask, Don't Tell")

Birth control → A personal choice

~~Pharmacists' refusal to dispense~~

Jade decided to go with the topic about gays in the military, or the "Don't Ask, Don't Tell" policy. She thought her classmates could connect with this topic and that it fit the assignment well.

4

Determine the Best Type of Persuasive Speech

A persuasive speech is a speech to convince, stimulate, or actuate. To determine the best type of persuasive speech, consider the response you want from your audience.

TYPE OF PERSUASIVE SPEECH	DESIRED AUDIENCE RESPONSE	EXAMPLES
TO CONVINCE	To convince my audience to change their attitudes, values, or beliefs	• A speech arguing that the current U.S. military plan in Afghanistan will help reduce terrorism, presented to an audience skeptical about these wars • A speech arguing that outsourcing harms the U.S. economy, presented to a group of CEOs
TO STIMULATE	To stimulate the attitudes, values, or beliefs my audience already holds	• A speech arguing that it is important for the United States to help rebuild Haiti, presented to members of the Red Cross • A speech arguing that animal theme parks are cruel, presented to an animal rights group
TO ACTUATE	To move my audience to action	• A speech arguing to vote for medical marijuana use, at a rally supporting a medical marijuana initiative • A speech arguing to boycott restaurants that allow smoking, at a meeting of Citizens for a Smoke-Free City

When you consider your type of persuasive speech and how it relates to your audience, you must contemplate the characteristics of your target audience. The **target audience** is the primary group of people you are aiming to appeal to. You cannot appeal to everyone in the audience, but you can appeal to a portion of them and, hopefully, the majority. This aim requires that you reflect again on your audience analysis.

REVIEW CHECKLIST for Audience Analysis

❏ Who are the members of my audience?

❏ How do they feel about my topic?

❏ What is their relationship to my topic?

❏ Will I primarily be creating, reinforcing, or changing attitudes, values, or beliefs?

Muzafer Sherif and Carl Hovland, in their book *Social Judgment,* explain why it is important to know where your audience stands in relationship to a given topic. Sherif and Hovland's social judgment theory tries to help you predict which way your audience will go with your speech's viewpoint. For example, will your audience agree that the "greenhouse effect" exists or not?

The **social judgment theory** states that your persuasion will be easier, tolerated more, and potentially longer lasting if your audience can tie in what you are persuading about to what they find most acceptable, or what are called their **attitudinal anchors.**

For example, if your audience is primarily conservative, they will more likely favor conservative ideas; a liberal audience, more likely liberal ideas. If your audience is primarily composed of female athletes, they will more likely support Title IX, which paved the way for equality in men's and women's athletics; male athletes can be less supportive, out of fear that it will reduce funding for male-dominated sports.

You need to analyze your audience, predict their attitudinal anchors, and create your target audience. From there, you can determine the best type of persuasive speech. When using this theory, be careful not to negatively stereotype, but instead use it as a means of potentially predicting a reaction.

Jade, for example, remembered that her audience's age (mostly early 20s) suggests that they might have traits like most millennials, making them potentially open to diversity issues. Plus, when the class discussed an earlier speech on gay marriage, most of the class was supportive of civil marriage. However, in the past, two or three students seemed to lean toward very conservative and religiously based viewpoints. Since focusing in on this topic, Jade also remembered that almost all of the students have ties to the military. Because she does not know for sure how they feel about this topic and she wants them to support changing a policy, she will give a speech to *convince.*

SOCIAL JUDGMENT THEORY

THE AUDIENCE WILL AGREE

ATTITUDINAL ANCHORS DETERMINING REACTION

THE AUDIENCE WILL DISAGREE

THE AUDIENCE WILL NOT BE SURE OF A RESPONSE

5
Identify Your Specific Purpose

If you remember the discussion in Chapter 2 about the specific purpose, you will remember that it is a single statement combining your general purpose, your audience, and your objective. Let's return to Jade's speech to see how she created her specific purpose.

You already know that Jade's topic is the military's "Don't Ask, Don't Tell" policy. Jade's assignment requires that she do a persuasive speech, and she knows that she personally wants to eliminate the policy. Given this information and the focus of her target audience, Jade decides to go with a claim of policy speech targeting an audience that would be willing to accept, or at least consider, a change to the "Don't Ask, Don't Tell" policy. As she wrote her specific purpose, she remembered that it should include the general purpose, her audience, and her objective in giving the speech.

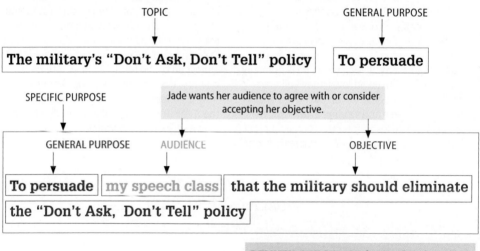

TOPIC

The military's "Don't Ask, Don't Tell" policy

GENERAL PURPOSE

To persuade

SPECIFIC PURPOSE

Jade wants her audience to agree with or consider accepting her objective.

GENERAL PURPOSE   AUDIENCE   OBJECTIVE

To persuade | my speech class | that the military should eliminate the "Don't Ask, Don't Tell" policy

REVIEW CHECKLIST for Evaluating a Persuasive Specific Purpose

❑ Does my specific purpose contain my general purpose, an audience reference, and my objective?

❑ Is my specific purpose an infinitive statement beginning with "to persuade"?

❑ Is it a statement, not a question?

❑ Is it clear and concise, with only one speech topic?

❑ Does it relate well to me, the audience, and the situation?

6
Identify Your Central Idea

When you construct the central idea for a persuasive speech, you are constructing one concise sentence that states the core claim you want to make. It may also hint at your speech's main points. The central idea evolves from the objective in your specific purpose and relates to what you know about your audience. Jade's looked like this:

If Jade's Specific Purpose Is...	Jade's Central Idea Could Be...
To persuade my speech class that the military should eliminate the "Don't Ask, Don't Tell" policy.	As citizens of a democratic society, we need to support the elimination of the "Don't Ask, Don't Tell" policy.

At this point, it should be easy to see the overarching proposition that your speech—and Jade's speech—is trying to answer. Remember, all persuasive speeches support a proposition of fact, value, or policy. Jade's speech seeks to support a proposition of policy.

OVERARCHING PROPOSITION	GUIDING QUESTIONS	EXAMPLES OF PERSUASIVE CLAIMS
Proposition of fact	What is accurate or not? What will happen or not?	The military plan in Afghanistan will bring down terrorism.
Proposition of value	What has worth or importance? What is good, wise, ethical, or beautiful?	Animal theme parks are cruel.
Proposition of policy	What procedures, plans, or course of action needs to be terminated or implemented? (This question can ask the audience to just agree or to act.)	The "Don't Ask, Don't Tell" policy should be eliminated.

→ See Chapter 2 (Tab 1) for more on focusing your speech topic.

REVIEW CHECKLIST for Evaluating a Persuasive Central Idea

❏ Is the central idea persuasive in nature?
❏ Does my central idea focus on one speech topic?
❏ Is it a statement, not a question?
❏ Is it clear and concise?

❏ Can I do this in the time allotted?
❏ Is it unique?
❏ Is it worth persuading the audience of and worth the audience's time?

7

Create a Working Outline

Before embarking on research, it is helpful to create a working outline to guide you. Briefly write out what you have composed so far, and think about working main points, or early drafts of potential main points.

At this stage, your working main points might be questions you think need to be answered, or they could simply be phrases that relate to subtopics. As you create your speech, your main points—and even your central idea—will continue to evolve. All may change significantly as you narrow and focus your topic. Later, when you get to your preparation outline stage, you want your main points to be concise and complete declarative sentences. Your preparation outline's main points should never be in the form of questions.

Your central idea might hint at possible main points even though you have not yet researched your topic completely or chosen an organizational strategy. Also, the preliminary research you did on your topic should offer some insight into what you need to consider.

Jade's central idea did not offer insight into her main points. However, her own curiosity about the history and details of the policy inspired two good points to cover. When she conducted the preliminary research on her topic, she noticed discussions about how the policy has been used and the problems it presents. She created four working main points (see next page) that would eventually lead to her final main points and potential strategy.

REVIEW CHECKLIST for Working Main Points

❏ Does each main point cover only one key idea?

❏ Are my main points similarly constructed (are they parallel)?

❏ Am I roughly balancing the time spent on each point?

❏ Do my main points relate back to my central idea?

Working outline for "Don't Ask, Don't Tell" speech

TOPIC:
The military's "Don't Ask, Don't Tell" policy

GENERAL PURPOSE:
To persuade

SPECIFIC PURPOSE:
To persuade my speech class that the military should eliminate the "Don't Ask, Don't Tell" policy.

CENTRAL IDEA:
As citizens of a democratic society, we need to support the elimination of the "Don't Ask, Don't Tell" policy.

I. What is the history of gays in the military?

II. What does the "Don't Ask, Don't Tell" policy stipulate?

III. How has the policy been used?

IV. What are the problems with the policy?

Remember, you may use questions for the main points in the working outline but should use declarative sentences for your main points in the preparation outline.

How Do You Conduct Research?

Depending on your topic, your central idea, and the arguments you are using to support your claim, different types of support materials will be more effective than others. As with any speech, a variety is important. You can use:

- Facts
- Definitions
- Testimony: personal, lay, and expert
- Examples: brief, extended, and hypothetical
- Statistics: descriptive and inferential

Good persuasion will require most of these.

For your arguments to be strong, effective, and ethical, your support materials must be:

- *Accurate:* Are your support materials verifiable? Are you using the information as it was originally intended (not twisting it for effect)?
- *Current:* Is the information the most current (up to the time of the speech, if possible)?
- *Complete:* Do you have enough material to make your argument? Does it give a complete picture? Did you consider all alternatives, including opposing ones?
- *Trustworthy:* Can you trust the evidence and the source? Can they be verified? Are they unbiased? If they came from the Internet, where anyone can create a site and information can easily be changed, are they correct?
- *Suitable:* Is your material appropriate for this topic, audience, or occasion?

→ See Tab 2 if you need help with research.

To create an effective persuasive speech, research as many angles as possible. Most debatable topics have more than two issues, solutions, or viewpoints. Your job is to understand as much as you can about them and present the viewpoint or solution you think is best. Complex topics require good detective work, and you will not find all the answers in one place.

WHERE CAN YOU LOCATE MATERIALS?	WHAT CAN IT OFFER THE PERSUASIVE SPEECH?
The **Internet** offers: Search engines, personal Web sites, commercial Web sites, nonprofit organization Web sites, blogs, government Web sites, and reference work Web sites. Plus, you can often access libraries via the Internet.	• Search engines help you sort through a large amount of information. • The Internet gives you access to a lot of topic-related material that can be very current or be an archive for older but important material. For example, Jade found that many of the government reports related to her topic dated back to the Clinton era. • You can often locate some of the most current statistics on the Web, and many professional organizations (expert testimony) are present there. Jade even found a recording of a National Public Radio interview with the author of one of her sources.
Libraries offer: Library catalogs, databases, books, newspapers, magazines, newsletters, journals, special collections or rare books, government resources, and reference works.	• Although some items you locate in the library can be found on the Internet as well, the library item can often be viewed in its original form for verification. Make sure you let your audience know where you verified the information supporting your claims. For example, Jade found a lot of references to a book (*Unfriendly Fire*) but needed the actual book to verify quotations. • Even though databases are electronic, you often need to go through a library to access their contents. • There are still numerous items in a library that you cannot locate on the Internet.
Interviews	• Interviews can give you access to testimony that is often not available in print—especially expert testimony, which can significantly support a claim.
Surveys	• Surveys help you collect information from a large population. • Survey data can help you gauge the current reactions or beliefs of a group.

REMEMBER

Taking good notes is key to collecting effective, accurate support materials. Remember to:
• Prepare to research—think about the options out there and what you might need.
• Use a consistent note-taking system—don't forget to include citation information.
• Know your appropriate style manual or where to consult one if you need it.

How Do You Construct the Persuasive Outline?

Constructing an effective preparation outline is imperative if you want to create a persuasive speech that your audience can follow, that you can follow as you speak, and that can persuade others. At this stage in the process, you want to create a preparation outline consisting of an introduction, a body, a conclusion, and a source page.

Later sections in this chapter will help you with the parts of an outline and how to organize each. For now, remember that a successful preparation outline will:

- Record the topic, specific purpose, and central idea
- Use full sentences
- Cover only one issue at a time
- Develop the introduction and conclusion
- Use correct outline format
- Use balanced main points
- Employ subordination
- Plan out formal links
- Use proper citations

Your outline should follow either a format similar to the one on the next page or a format your instructor suggests.

→ See Tab 3 for an extended discussion of how to construct an outline.

Student name   Class
Date   Instructor name

Topic: The military's "Don't Ask, Don't Tell" policy
General purpose: To persuade
Specific purpose: To persuade my speech class that the military should
                      eliminate the "Don't Ask, Don't Tell" policy.
Central idea: As citizens of a democratic society, we need to support ◄——
                      the elimination of the "Don't Ask, Don't Tell" policy.

Jade begins working on her outline by filling in this template.

INTRODUCTION
    Attention-getter
    Credibility material
    Relevance to audience
    Preview of speech

(Link from introduction to first main point)

BODY
    I.   The U.S. military's ban on gays has a long, negative history. ◄——
         A. Subpoint
         B. Subpoint
             1. Subpoint of B
             2. Subpoint of B
             3. Subpoint of B

Jade begins to fill in her main points, making sure they are full, declarative sentences and cover only one idea at a time. She will make sure to have only one sentence per outline symbol and fill in the support material.

(Link between first and second main points)

    II. Second main point
         A. Subpoint
         B. Subpoint
             1. Subpoint of B
             2. Subpoint of B
         C. Subpoint

(Link between second and third main points)

    III. Third main point
         A. Subpoint
             1. Subpoint of A ◄——
                 a. Subpoint of 1
                 b. Subpoint of 1
             2. Subpoint of A
         B. Subpoint
         C. Subpoint

Jade doesn't know yet how many subpoints each of her main points will have. For now, she leaves a variety of subpoint placeholders in her outline.

(Link between third and fourth main points)

    IV. Fourth main point ◄——
         A. Subpoint
             1. Subpoint of A
                 a. Subpoint of 1
                 b. Subpoint of 1
             2. Subpoint of A
         B. Subpoint
         C. Subpoint

(Link to conclusion)

CONCLUSION
    Summary statement
    Audience response statement
    WOW statement:
                        Works Cited

Although Jade started with a template that only showed three main points, her speech will have four. She includes a place for the fourth point in her outline.

How Do You Organize the Body of a Persuasive Speech?

1 **Recognize Your Organizational Strategy**

2 **Commit to a Strategy**

3 **Construct Main Points**

4 **Organize Support Materials into Arguments**

1

Recognize Your Organizational Strategy

Many beginning speakers look to chronological and topical strategies for persuasive speeches, but although these tend to be easier to construct, they are not the best choices. Some instructors prohibit their use for a persuasive speech, in favor of more effective strategies. Also, because the refutation strategy is typically used in a situation such as a debate or a court case, you will rarely use it for a class speech. The common persuasive strategies are:

- Causal: ordered by cause-to-effect or effect-to-cause
- Order of intensity: ordered by rising to a climax or the reverse
- Comparative: ordered by contrasting two or more things
- Problem–solution: ordered by demonstrating and solving a problem
- Monroe's motivated sequence: ordered by demonstrating and solving a need

To select the right strategy, think about your speech type, overarching proposition, general purpose, topic, and audience. Your central idea can offer clues. For example, suppose your central idea is:

Recycling is a great solution to solid waste disposal problems because it decreases landfill usage, conserves natural resources, and saves money.

Guided by the first part of this sentence, you might use the problem–solution strategy to highlight the problem of solid waste disposal and the solution of recycling.

2
Commit to a Strategy

Committing to a strategy begins with selecting the best one, but the act of commitment also requires you to strictly adhere to that strategy. As a beginning speaker, it is easy to stray from your point or randomly connect thoughts together. Select your strategy and write your main points so that they stick to the strategy. Periodically, you should return to Chapter 6, where the strategies are explained in detail, and make sure you are following yours.

WHAT FACTORS SHOULD YOU CONSIDER WHEN SELECTING A STRATEGY?	STRATEGIES
Speech to stimulate	
Audience viewpoint needs reinforcement	Order of intensity, topical, chronological, Monroe's motivated sequence, or problem–solution
Speech to convince	
Audience is apathetic or uninformed and needs to create a viewpoint	Chronological, topical, problem–solution, comparative, Monroe's motivated sequence, refutation, or causal
Audience viewpoint needs to change because they disagree or are conflicted	Refutation, comparative, problem–solution, or causal
Speech to actuate	
Audience needs motivation to act.	Most of the strategies work for this type, but Monroe's motivated sequence is often the best
Overarching proposition for your speech	
Proposition of fact	Chronological, topical, or order of intensity
Proposition of value	Comparative, topical, or order of intensity
Proposition of policy	Topical, problem–solution, comparative, causal, refutation, or Monroe's motivated sequence

Jade selected and committed to the problem–solution strategy. She will spend most of her speech outlining the problems she feels are most important to proving that the policy needs to be changed, and then she will offer her simple solution in the conclusion—to lift the ban.

→ See Chapter 6 (Tab 3) for a detailed explanation of these strategies.

REVIEW CHECKLIST for Selecting an Organizational Strategy

❑ Am I using a strategy that will work for my general purpose to persuade?

❑ Does my topic suggest a strategy? For example, if my specific purpose calls for my audience to accept a defined result, could the problem–solution strategy be best?

❑ What is my audience's relationship with the viewpoint of my speech? For example, if they will be hostile toward the speech, would the refutation strategy be best?

3

Construct Main Points

Depending on how you constructed your central idea or which strategy you selected, one or both of these might hint at the main points you will need to cover in the speech. If your central idea has evolved since the working outline, study it again for three or four possible subtopics and/or think about the strategy you want to use and how it might influence your main points. Strategies like Monroe's motivated sequence have certain steps that become main points and determine the focus of those main points.

Let's look again at the central idea about recycling:

Recycling is a great solution to solid waste disposal problems because it decreases landfill usage, conserves natural resources, and saves money.

You know from earlier discussion that a problem–solution strategy is a good one for this central idea. From the central idea, you should figure out what the problem and the solution are. Once you discover those, you are ready to craft your main points. They might look like this:

I. **Solid waste disposal is an environmental and economic problem.**

II. **Recycling is a great solution because it decreases landfill usage, conserves natural resources, and saves money.**

A problem–solution strategy with two main points works well with this central idea.

If your central idea or strategy does not help determine main points, make a list of what you want to convey in the speech, group items that relate to each other, and create main points from those groups. You will not have time to cover everything related to your topic, so select the three or four most important ideas. To create effective main points, follow these guidelines:

- Use full sentences to focus your main points into complete thoughts.
- Introduce only one idea in each main point.
- Write your main points in parallel form.
- Use declarative sentences.
- Adhere to coordination.

→ See Chapter 6 (Tab 3) for a detailed explanation of these guidelines.

Although Jade's central idea did not suggest exact main points, her continued research helped her focus. Her working outline questions pointed to problems with the ban and hinted at lifting the ban as the best solution. Her working main points evolved into these main points:

I. **The U.S. military's ban on gays has a long, negative history.**

II. **The U.S. military had several false, unnecessary reasons for implementing the ban.**

III. **The U.S. military's ban has cost us a lot.**

IV. **The U.S. military has several allies that have lifted their ban on gays with no significant problems.**

Unlike the recycling speech, Jade's speech has three main points presenting the problem and a fourth one that sets up the solution.

4

Organize Support Materials into Arguments

In the persuasive speech, your arguments will become the subpoints supporting your main points, so it is time to decide which appeals you want to use, the type of arguments that best fit your speech, and how to arrange the arguments.

Chapter 14 offers you guidance on choosing appeals and types of arguments, but ultimately, you will make these decisions based on what you want to accomplish with the speech, your audience's relationship to the speech, and the needs of the organizational strategy.

Jade decided to use an appeal to mythos in her introduction to establish her own credibility as a member of a patriotic family. Jade also put this appeal early on in her speech to arouse the audience's sense that patriotism is good but is separate from the issue about the "Don't Ask, Don't Tell" policy. She wanted to make sure the audience could see her as patriotic but against the policy. During the body of her speech, Jade plans to use inductive reasoning because she has a lot of facts, statistics, examples, and testimony demonstrating that the policy is more harmful than good.

When you have the arguments you want to use, you then need to decide how to arrange them, or put them in a logical order. As you know from Chapter 14, there are many ways to organize your arguments. Jade will order her arguments chronologically because most are related to past practices and decisions; this stresses the historical nature of the topic.

Two additional models can help you decide how to arrange arguments in your persuasive speech:

- The ***primacy model*** suggests that you should put your strongest arguments first in the body of the speech. The idea grounding this theory is that you are more likely to persuade if you win over your audience early. This method is best if your audience opposes your viewpoint.

- The ***recency model*** is the reverse of primacy. Here, you begin with the weakest argument and end with the strongest. Metaphorically, this is like most Fourth of July fireworks shows, where they set off the small fireworks first and end with the grand finale. If your audience is unfamiliar with your topic, is apathetic, or already agrees with you, this method is best.

There is no one set way to approach creating arguments, and the more you do it, the better you will get. Brainstorming with your peers or instructor will help.

What Should You Include in the Introduction and Conclusion?

Even though the body of a persuasive speech takes a bit more time and thought to develop, you still must create a strong introduction and conclusion. If you do not have your audience's focused attention, they will miss important information in the body of the speech. If you do not help them remember your speech, tell them how to respond, and dazzle them one more time, your ending can undo everything you have previously said.

You are almost done creating your speech, so spend just a bit more time creating an effective introduction and conclusion.

LAUNCH YOUR SPEECH

Keep your introduction stimulating, poignant, and fascinating. An introduction for a persuasive speech should focus your audience's attention toward what you intend to claim about your topic. Remember, your audience will tend to wander off subject if you let them. So, don't take too long to get to your point.

→ Some of Jade's introduction is excerpted on the facing page. See the preparation outline on the following pages for her complete introduction.

YOUR SPEECH'S FINALE

The persuasive speech's conclusion should leave your audience knowing your viewpoint and give them one more push to accept it or be influenced by it. Keep your specific purpose in mind as you construct the conclusion.

INTRODUCTION

This should be one of the "wow" moments in your speech.

ATTENTION-GETTER: The U.S. military has long been known as a force to be reckoned with. The U.S. military has often stepped up to protect this great land we call home or stepped out to save the day for many other countries, many times. We have been taught to treat our veterans with respect and reverence. We put magnets on our cars to support our troops and have a holiday with parades and ceremonies to honor the sacrifices that servicemen and servicewomen have made for people they do not even know, and a country they are willing to die for.

State why you should give this speech.

CREDIBILITY MATERIAL: I had a great-grandfather who fought in World War I, and both of my grandfathers fought in World War II. My mother and father met when he was an airman and she a nurse in the Vietnam War. My father was a career airman and my brother, who is currently in Iraq, wants to make it a career as well. The military is deeply seated in my family. My family is proud of its military history. I am proud of my family's military history.

Give them a reason to listen.

RELEVANCE TO AUDIENCE: From previous conversations we have had in this class, I know many of you have a connection to the military, be it a family member or friend who served in the past or one who is currently serving in Iraq or Afghanistan. In many cases, the military has been a positive experience and helped our family members and friends through difficult times, such as getting a job to take care of family or getting a college education or other training. . . .

Give them a road map to your speech.

PREVIEW OF SPEECH: However, there is part of this equation that I am not proud of. . . . Today, I want to persuade you that as citizens of a democratic society, we need to support the elimination of the "Don't Ask, Don't Tell" policy. In the next few minutes, we will look at the history of the ban, the reasons for the ban, what the ban costs us, and what our allies do. I will demonstrate why this policy is such a problem and offer support for what I see as the best solution.

CONCLUSION

What should your audience remember?

AUDIENCE RESPONSE STATEMENT: In conclusion, I offer no fancy solution. It is simple. The United States needs to lift this ban.

What do you want them to do with that information?

SUMMARY STATEMENT: Research has shown that gays in the military are not a threat to our security. Research has shown that gays in the military are not a threat to "privacy, cohesion, and effectiveness" (Frank, *Unfriendly Fire* 113). If nothing else, the ban is too costly and unfair. Even polls demonstrate that a sizeable majority of American citizens are ready to make this wrong a right.

Dazzle them one more time.

WOW STATEMENT: U.S. Congressman Barney Frank said it best: "Saying we can't have gay people in the military because heterosexuals won't like them, regardless of how they behave, is like saying we can't have black people around because white people won't like them. That was wrong and this is wrong" (Frank, *Unfriendly Fire* 61). Let's get rid of "Don't Ask, Don't Tell" and replace it with "Don't Discriminate, Don't Turn Away."

PREPARATION OUTLINE FOR A PERSUASIVE SPEECH

Jade Hunter   COMM 110
November 17, 2009   Dr. Davis

Topic: The military's "Don't Ask, Don't Tell" policy

General purpose: To persuade

Specific purpose: To persuade my speech class that the military should eliminate the "Don't Ask, Don't Tell" policy.

Central idea: As citizens of a democratic society, we need to support the elimination of the "Don't Ask, Don't Tell" policy.

INTRODUCTION

Attention-getter: The U.S. military has long been known as a force to be reckoned with. The U.S. military has often stepped up to protect this great land we call home or stepped out to save the day for many other countries, many times. We have been taught to treat our veterans with respect and reverence. We put magnets on our cars to support our troops and have a holiday with parades and ceremonies to honor the sacrifices that servicemen and servicewomen have made for people they do not even know, and a country they are willing to die for.

> Jade evokes an appeal to mythos by discussing respecting veterans as a civic duty.

Credibility material: I had a great-grandfather who fought in World War I, and both of my grandfathers fought in World War II. My mother and father met when he was an airman and she a nurse in the Vietnam War. My father was a career airman and my brother, who is currently in Iraq, wants to make it a career as well. The military is deeply seated in my family. My family is proud of its military history. I am proud of my family's military history.

> She uses repetition for emphasis and to build emotional appeal.

Relevance to audience: From previous conversations we have had in this class, I know many of you have a connection to the military, be it a family member or friend who served in the past or one who is currently serving in Iraq or Afghanistan. In many cases, the military has been a positive experience and helped our family members and friends through difficult times, such as getting a job to take care of family or getting a college education or other training. Some have even made a career out of the military, meeting the standards of excellence, following the rules, and giving decades of their lives to service.

> Here, Jade appeals to the importance of the military, fulfilling an audience need.

Preview of speech: However, there is part of this equation that I am not proud of. I am not proud that there are men and women who do meet the standards, who do follow the rules, and who are putting their lives on the line for this country or have already given decades of their lives in service, but who were or may be discharged with no thank you, no privileges, no financial security in their later years, or no funding for an education because of an archaic law. That law is the basis of the current "Don't Ask, Don't Tell" policy preventing openly gay individuals from entering or continuing service in the military. Today, I want to persuade you that as citizens of a democratic society, we need to support the elimination of the "Don't Ask, Don't Tell" policy. In the next few minutes, we will look at the history of the ban, the reasons for the ban, what the ban costs us, and what our allies do. I will demonstrate why this policy is such a problem and offer support for what I see as the best solution.

(**Link:** First, let's look at the problems associated with the gay ban in the military.)

BODY

I.   The U.S. military ban on gays has a long, negative history.
   A.   Nathaniel Frank, in *Unfriendly Fire: How the Gay Ban Undermines the Military and Weakens America*, historically traces the military's homosexual intolerance to World War I.
      1.   In 1917, the military revised the Articles of War, making the act of sodomy, when committed as part of an assault, a military crime.
      2.   Three years later, a second revision "made consensual sodomy a crime in the military" (5).
      3.   However, this policy became the basis for the Navy, too, in "shocking" and "indefensible" investigation tactics to rid the Navy of unwanted sexual perversion—homosexuals (5).
         a.   Chief Machinist's Mate Ervin Arnold stated that he could spot "degenerates" a mile away by their clothing, walk, and effeminate manner.
         b.   The U.S. Senate eventually censured the Navy.
   B.   According to a 1947 *Newsweek* article republished in the book *Gay Rights*, the recruitment practice of asking "Are you a homosexual?" started during World War II (Burns 25).
      1.   If the recruit answered "yes," the recruit was usually referred to a psychiatric center.
      2.   This was a period of time in our history when being gay was viewed as abnormal and dangerously associated to communism (Burns 25).

Jade uses inductive reasoning with specific case support in A and B to sustain her first main point.

3. According to Frank, in 1949, the Department of Defense created a single policy throughout the branches of the military.
   a. "The new regulation stated: 'Homosexual personnel, irrespective of sex, should not be permitted to serve in any branch of the Armed Forces in any capacity, and prompt separation of known homosexuals . . . is mandatory'" (Frank, *Unfriendly Fire* 9).
   b. Each branch was asked to give homosexuality indoctrination lectures to ferret out the gays (9).
4. In 1950, Congress created the Uniform Code of Military Justice and made "unnatural carnal copulation" between heterosexuals or homosexuals in the armed forces punishable by five years of hard labor and dishonorable discharge without pay (9–10).
5. In 1981, the Carter administration created a ban on gays and lesbians in uniform by stating that "homosexuality is incompatible with military service" (10).
6. Another article in the book *Gay Rights*, entitled "The Military's 'Don't Ask, Don't Tell' Policy Cannot Be Justified" and written by Rhonda Evans, states that when Bill Clinton ran for president in 1992, part of his platform was to repeal the ban on gays in the military, allowing them to serve without fear (Burns 149).
   a. A total repeal was not supported, and the compromise was the "Don't Ask, Don't Tell" policy, which is a compilation of regulations, directives, and a federal law.
   b. The Department of Defense issued a directive in 1994, stating: The Department of Defense has long held that, as a general rule, homosexuality is incompatible with military service because it interferes with the factors critical to combat effectiveness, including unit morale, unit cohesion, and individual privacy. Nevertheless, the Department of Defense also recognizes that individuals with a homosexual orientation have served with distinction in the armed services of the United States. Therefore, it is the policy of the Department of Defense to judge the suitability of persons to serve in the armed forces on the basis of their conduct. Homosexual conduct will be grounds for separation from the military services. Sexual orientation is considered a personal and private matter, and

When directly quoting, Jade puts the material in quotation marks or indents it further (see subpoint 6b).

This subpoint appears to break the "only one issue/sentence to an outline component" rule. However, Jade is simply incorporating a lengthy quotation. Follow your instructor's guidelines for how to do this.

homosexual orientation is not a bar to service entry or continued service unless manifested by homosexual conduct (Burns 150).

   c. However, by the time the directive was implemented, Congress passed its own legislation weakening the distinction between conduct and the status of being gay by setting the grounds for "discharge as engaging in, attempting to engage in homosexual acts off-duty or not" (Burns 151).

   d. The Pentagon's policy includes the "don't ask" provision, but the law passed by Congress does not (Frank, *Unfriendly Fire* xii).

   e. Furthermore, personnel can be "outed" by someone else.

   f. According to Frank, "the government's conclusion was that banning open gays from the military is necessary to preserve privacy, cohesion, and effectiveness" (*Unfriendly Fire* 113).

   g. Even 44 percent of Americans in 1993 were against gays in the military (Dropp and Cohen).

(**Link:** Now that we have a historical context for the ban, let's look at why this ban is a problem.)

II.   The U.S. military had several false, unnecessary reasons for implementing ◄ the ban.

   A. In *Unfriendly Fire*, Frank discusses several studies suggesting that gays pose no more risk to the military than do heterosexuals.

      1. In 1957, the secretary of the Navy appointed a panel to investigate the ban.

         a. The results of this investigation are known as the Crittenden report.

         b. The researchers found that homosexuality posed no greater security risk and that certain heterosexual relations were considered more threatening (118).

      2. The 1993 Rand study, commissioned by then-Secretary of Defense Les Aspin, involved 75 social scientists who "analyzed the policies of other countries' military, and the police and fire departments of six U.S. cities" ("Changing").

         a. The researchers studied all kinds of different data on group cohesion, sexual harassment, leadership, health concerns, and public opinion.

Again, Jade uses inductive reasoning in this second main point.

Even though these are in chronological order, Jade uses the theory of recency here as well by spending more time on 2, which is the better of the two arguments.

    b. Frank states that the Rand report cost the taxpayers $1.3 million but barely made it out of the Rand office because it concluded that the gay ban could be lifted with little effect.

    c. On the Rand Web site, rand.org, you can find a more detailed summary of the findings, but I find three of their seven main findings interesting.

       i. Acknowledged homosexuals very seldom challenge the norms or customs of the organization.

       ii. Anti-homosexual sentiment does not disappear but is more moderate than expected.

       iii. Effectiveness of the organization had not been diminished ("Changing").

B. Even public opinion polls strongly suggest that Americans no longer think the ban is necessary.

    1. In their *Washington Post* article "Acceptance of Gay People in Military Grows Dramatically," Kyle Dropp and Jon Cohen report that 75 percent of Americans support dropping the ban.

    2. That is up from 62 percent in 2001 and 44 percent in 1993, when President Clinton first tried to end the ban.

(**Link:** From only these two studies and one poll, we are starting to see that the reasons for having the ban are not necessarily valid. But that is not enough; let's turn to discovering how this ban greatly costs the United States.)

III. The U.S. military's ban has cost us a lot. ◄

A. More than 35,000 people have been discharged because of the policy from 1994 to 2007 (Frank, *Unfriendly Fire* 169).

B. As Frank puts it so poignantly, "This translates to a cost of $364 million, or 2,500 loaded, armored Humvees that could have been sent overseas" (*Unfriendly Fire* 169).

C. "Who are these discharged soldiers?" is another cost-oriented way to look at this.

    1. The loss of any well-qualified soldier is costly no matter what their specialty is; but, according to Frank's interpretation of reports from the Government Accountability Office and other sources, 757 of these people were in "critical operations" (*Unfriendly Fire* 220).

Jade makes sure that she gives enough information to direct her audience to this Internet source.

Again, Jade uses inductive reasoning. This consistency will help her audience follow the logic she is using.

a. "These included voice interceptors, interrogators, translators, explosive ordnance disposal specialists, signal intelligence analysts, and missile and cryptologic technicians" (Frank, *Unfriendly Fire* 220).

b. Now, as Frank suggests in his book, there is no magic bullet for fighting radical Islamic violence (*Unfriendly Fire* 220).

c. However, it does seem important that we keep people who can speak the language (Arabic).

d. For example: On September 10, 2001, the National Security Agency intercepted two very brief messages in Arabic.
   i. "Tomorrow is zero hour."
   ii. "The match is about to begin" (*Unfriendly Fire* 215; Grace).

e. These messages were not translated until September 12, 2001.

f. Although not enough information was intercepted to predict 9/11, it does give you pause to think: What if there was enough and these were translated a day late?

g. From 1994 to 2005, at least 54 Arabic speakers with the high level of training that the military requires have been fired because of the "Don't Ask, Don't Tell" policy (*Unfriendly Fire* 220).

Jade employs an appeal to need (safety) in subpoints a to g.

2. Lt. Col. Victor Fehrenbach's story was published by *Stars and Stripes*, an independent news source for the U.S. military community (Shane).

a. For 18 years, he was an F-15 pilot and had such achievements as serving in Kosovo, Iraq, and Afghanistan.

b. In May 2009, he was grounded, and he now stands to lose his military pension two years before his retirement because his sexuality was discovered.

This story appeals to emotions and mythos.

(Link: So, is there a solution to the ban? Well, let's look at what our allies do.)

IV. The U.S. military has several allies that have lifted their bans on gays with no significant problems.

A. According to Frank in his book and a commentary on CNNPolitics.com, 24 foreign countries, close allies to the United States—including Britain, Canada, and Australia—have lifted their bans on gays with no significant problems (Frank, "Allow"; *Unfriendly Fire* 137).

Arguing by analogy, Jade uses Frank's information to compare the United States to some allies.

1. Australia and Canada lifted their bans in 1992 (Frank, *Unfriendly Fire* 137).
2. In 2000, Britain lifted ban (148).

B. Research conducted in Britain, Israel, Canada, and Australia by the Palm Center at the University of California, Santa Barbara, found that persons or professional organizations related to the issue had not observed "any impact or any effect at all that undermined military performance, readiness, or cohesion, nothing that led to recruitment problems, or increased HIV health issues among the troops" (*Unfriendly Fire* 148).

1. The Palm Center reports that in Australia, complaints regarding sexual orientation issues comprise less than 5 percent of the total complaints received of incidents related to sexual harassment, bullying, and other forms of sexual misconduct ("The Effects").
2. During the year after the lift, "there was 'not a single . . . case of resignation, harassment or violence because of the change in policy,' the center says. 'The issue . . . has all but disappeared from public and internal military debates' in Canada'" (Price).
3. "In 1995, two-thirds of the men in Britain's all-volunteer armed forces said they would not be willing to serve if the gay ban were lifted. The gay ban ended in January 2000, and a grand total of three people actually resigned. With recruitment levels 'buoyant,' the policy change is 'hailed as a solid achievement' by the Ministry of Defense" (Price).
4. So impressed by these results, in 2006, Britain's Royal Air Force hired the Stonewall Group, a homosexual advocate alliance, to attract more gay and lesbian recruits.
5. Also, they enacted a policy that provided equal survivor benefits to same-sex partners (Frank, *Unfriendly Fire* 149).
6. As political scientist and director of the Center for the Study of Sexual Minorities in the Military at the University of California, Santa Barbara, Aaron Belkin states about lifting the ban in these countries: "It has no effect on unit cohesion. It has no effect on military performance. It has no effect on recruitment. It has no effect on any of the indicators of military capability" (Price).

(**Link:** If countries similar to the United States, such as Britain, Canada, and Australia—countries we already fight side by side with—lifted the ban with no problems, so could the United States.)

Jade uses effective statistics in this section.

CONCLUSION

Audience response statement: Therefore, I offer no fancy solution. It is simple. The United States needs to lift this ban.

Summary statement: Research has shown that gays in the military are not a threat to our security. Research has shown that gays in the military are not a threat to "privacy, cohesion, and effectiveness" (Frank, *Unfriendly Fire* 113). If nothing else, the ban is too costly and unfair. Even polls demonstrate that a sizeable majority of American citizens are ready to make this wrong a right.

WOW statement: U.S. Congressman Barney Frank said it best: "Saying we can't have gay people in the military because heterosexuals won't like them, regardless of how they behave, is like saying we can't have black people around because white people won't like them. That was wrong and this is wrong" (Frank, *Unfriendly Fire* 61). Let's get rid of "Don't Ask, Don't Tell" and replace it with "Don't Discriminate, Don't Turn Away."

Works Cited

Burns, Kate, ed. *Gay Rights*. Detroit: Thomson Gale, 2006. Print.

"Changing the Policy toward Homosexuals in the U.S. Military." *Rand: Objective Analysis. Effective Solutions*. Rand, 2000. Web. 25 Nov. 2009.

Dropp, Kyle and Jon Cohen. "Acceptance of Gay People in Military Grows Dramatically." *Washington Post*. Washington Post, 19 July 2008. Web. 25 Nov. 2009.

"The Effects of Including Gay and Lesbian Soldiers in the Australian Defense Forces: Appraising the Evidence." *Palm Center: Blueprints for Sound Public Policy*. Palm Center, 1 Sept. 2000. Web. 25 Nov. 2009.

Frank, Nathaniel. "Allow Gays to Serve Openly in Military." *CNNPolitics*. Cable Network News, 16 Apr. 2009. Web. 25 Nov. 2009.

—. *Unfriendly Fire: How the Gay Ban Undermines the Military and Weakens America*. New York: St. Martin's, 2009. Print.

Grace, France. "9/10 Message: 'Tomorrow Is Zero Hour.'" *CBSNEWS*. CBS Worldwide, 20 June 2002. Web. 25 Nov. 2009.

Price, Deb. "Gays in Military Succeeds Abroad." *The Detroit News*. 19 Feb. 2001. Palm Center, 2009. Web. 25 Nov. 2009.

Shane, Leo. "Pilot Facing Discharge under 'Don't Ask, Don't Tell' Policy." *Stars and Stripes*. Stars and Stripes, 23 May 2009, Mideast ed. Web. 25 Nov. 2009.

Jade returns to the appeal to mythos she first employed in the introduction—belonging to a democratic society and respecting veterans.

Jade follows the proper MLA citation style for the "Works Cited" section.

What Should You Consider When Preparing to Present Your Speech?

1 Language
2 Delivery
3 Presentation Aids

1
Language

Effective language is a must if you intend to persuade. Emotive and stylistic language helps your audience follow your arguments, remember them, and be emotionally moved. Remember, language is grounded in culture, is extremely powerful, and creates meaning. Select your language carefully and purposefully by being:

- Accurate—correct, familiar, and concrete
- Appropriate—suitable to you, your audience, and the situation
- Verbal—conversational language, sentence structure, and delivery aspects
- Distinctive—vivid language and unique speech devices

→ Chapter 8 (Tab 4) covers language usage.

2
Delivery

Practice your speech. Because most speeches are delivered extemporaneously, you will need a delivery outline containing just enough words, phrases, and delivery notes to jog your memory. Practice from the preparation outline the first few times, but then use the delivery outline. Your delivery should be powerful, direct, and enthusiastic, to suggest a high level of confidence and trust. Rehearse your speech until you can get through it several times without major errors or glitches. Also, prepare yourself the day of the speech by dressing appropriately, checking the space/sound, and practicing the speech one last time as you will give it.

→ See Chapter 9 (Tab 4) for more delivery hints.

3

Presentation Aids

There are multiple types of presentation aids you can use to support your speech (three-dimensional, two-dimensional, computer-generated, or audiovisual). Presentation aids are often necessary for a persuasive speech, to help your audience understand facts and figures or to follow the logic of an argument. Keep in mind that aids should support your speech and not be added on just because you can make them. Your presentation aids should be:

- High-quality
- Easy to see
- Simple
- Safe and appropriate

Jade planned a slideshow for her speech. During the introduction, she used photos and brief video to reinforce military and country pride. During the body of the speech, she used slides with tables, quotations, or photos. Near the end, her slideshow remained on a photo of Lt. Col. Fehrenbach until her last sentence, when she advanced to a slide with the American flag while saying her ending phrase, "Don't Discriminate, Don't Turn Away!"

Jade prepared her delivery outline, marked her delivery notes on it, and practiced her speech several times. Jade was excited and ready to give her speech.

➜ Chapter 10 (Tab 4) offers details on creating presentation aids for your speech.

Attention-getter: (*slide*)   # 1
The U.S. military has long been known as a force to be reckoned with. . .

Credibility material: Great-grandfather in World War I. . . grandfathers fought in World War II, . . . mother and father in the Vietnam War. My brother. My family is proud. I am proud.   (*slide*)

Relevance to audience: Connect to their family member or friend
(*slide*)

Preview of speech: The history of the ban
The reasons for the ban
What the ban costs us
What our allies do

(Link: First, let's look at the history of the gay ban in th

I.   The military ban on gays has a long, negative history.   # 2
A. Frank -- *Unfriendly Fire* historically traces homosexual intolerance to WWI.
(*slide*)

    1. In 1917--Articles of War making the act of sodomy . . .
    2. 3 years later, revision "made consensual sodomy a crime in the military"
    3. Navy response
       a. Chief Machinist's Mate Ervin Arnold stated that he could spot "degenerates" a mile away by their clothing, walk, and effeminate manner.
       b. The U.S. Senate censured.
B. According to a 1947 *Newsweek* article in the book *Gay Rights*, the recruitment practice of asking," Are you a homosexual?" started during WWII.   (*slide*)

REMEMBER

Always practice with your presentation aids, and make sure they are working and ready to use before your speech event starts.

How Should You Evaluate a Persuasive Speech?

1 **Listen Effectively**

2 **Evaluate the Speech Message**

3 **Evaluate the Presentation**

PRACTICING ETHICS

As a member of a democratic society and a society that bombards you with multiple messages daily, you must be willing to ask the hard questions to ensure your safety and the safety of others: Is this true? Who stands to gain? Are these sources unbiased? This is true whether you are a speaker or an audience member—or a media consumer.

1

Listen Effectively

As the transactional model of communication indicates, speaker and audience are equally responsible for engaging in the process of communicating. Listening is essential to fulfill that responsibility. As a speaker, you need to work at helping your audience listen effectively; and as an audience member, it is your responsibility to listen actively and critically. When persuasion is the goal, critical listening is even more important.

For example, suppose you already agree with Jade that the gay ban should be removed. However, nothing is ever that simple. Have you and Jade considered whether the cost of reversing the policy during two wars is too great? Or is that question irrelevant given the discrimination factor? If you were for the ban going into Jade's speech, did you suspend judgment to consider the facts she presented?

2

Evaluate the Speech Message

As you can tell by the focus of this chapter, Chapter 14, and the majority of Tabs 1 through 5, crafting an effective message is critical to a persuasive speech. You must use an effective persuasive organizational strategy, use enough correct evidence to support arguments, employ the right proofs for your audience, and call for a proposed change or action to persuade successfully. As someone evaluating a persuasive speech, you should pay close attention and listen critically for each of these aspects.

3

Evaluate the Presentation

During the presentation, evaluate verbal and nonverbal characteristics. Successful delivery techniques rarely draw attention to themselves but help the audience stay interested in the speech while the speaker (you or another) builds ethos. Persuading an audience is difficult and will not happen if the speaker does not think about voice, gestures, and enthusiasm, or use an appropriate delivery style or presentation aids. If Jade's enthusiasm is low and her audience members are not sure how they feel about the military policy or do not agree with eliminating it, she will not convince them.

→ See Tab 5 for more about listening to and evaluating a speech.

This checklist, or guidelines provided by your instructor, will help you evaluate persuasive speeches.

CHECKLIST FOR EVALUATING THE PERSUASIVE SPEECH

TOPIC
.... Speech accomplished purpose to persuade
.... Topic appropriate to speaker, audience, and occasion
.... Interesting topic

INTRODUCTION
.... Gained attention and interest
.... Established credibility
.... Indicated relevance to audience
.... Declared central idea
.... Previewed speech

BODY
.... Main points clear and obvious to the audience
.... Points follow an appropriate organizational strategy
.... Main points appropriately researched and supported
.... Used effective proofs/arguments
.... Main points supported with appropriate presentation aids when necessary
.... Oral citations included throughout speech
.... Linked parts of speech

CONCLUSION
.... Contained a summary statement
.... Offered an audience response statement
.... Effectively comes to closure (WOW statement)

PRESENTATION
.... Language was clear, concise, and appropriate
.... Gestures/body movements were effective
.... Consistent and effective eye contact
.... Used vocal variety/emphasis/volume/rate
.... Used appropriate delivery style
.... Spoke with enthusiasm
.... Spoke with conviction and sincerity
.... Good use of delivery outline
.... Presentation aids appropriate to speech topic (if applicable)
.... Used presentation aids throughout entire speech (if applicable)
.... Used professional presentation aids (if applicable)
.... Speech met time requirements

Shimin's Speech

You met Shimin at the end of the last chapter and know she wants to persuade college students to reduce their plastics consumption. Shimin will give her speech at a Saturday workshop held once a month to bring off-campus students together to build community and to show them how to be better consumers and citizens. Shimin has been a part of the group for some time, so she knows many of her audience members, making her audience analysis relatively easy. Shimin developed this working outline.

Topic: Plastic pollution

General purpose: To persuade

Specific purpose: To persuade college students to reduce their plastics consumption.

Central idea: The amount of plastics created and thrown away daily has become a serious problem globally, but a few simple steps on our part will help lower the plastics impact on our environment and our futures.

Main Point # 1: What is plastic?

Main Point # 2: How do we use it?

Main Point # 3: How is it influencing our environment?

Main Point # 4: What is the solution?

The problem

I. *Plastics are made from problematic raw materials.*

II. *Plastics cause major environmental issues.*

III. *There are alternative forms of plastics and materials.*

IV. *There are alternative ways we can think about using plastics.*

CONSTRUCTING HER MAIN POINTS

After conducting her research on the Internet and at the local libraries and then interviewing a professor who specializes in waste management, Shimin was ready to construct her main points. Shimin selected the problem–solution strategy for her speech and created her main points to fit that strategy.

The solution

SHIMIN'S OUTLINES

After refining her central idea, and with her research, main points, and strategy in place, Shimin created her preparation outline first and then her delivery outline. After creating her presentation aids, she practiced the speech several times, including twice in the space where she would give the speech.

Topic: Plastic pollution

General purpose: To persuade

Specific purpose: To persuade college students to reduce their plastics consumption.

Central idea: As citizens concerned about our futures and the future of our planet, we need to be aware of the amount of plastics in our lives and support ways to reduce its usage.

INTRODUCTION

Attention-getter: The nonbiodegradable nature of plastic and our mass consumption can be seen in artworks by Chris Jordan. Jordan, a U.S.-based photographer and artist, used plastic bottles and cups to show our unconscious behavior of consumerism.

Credibility material: I came in contact with the concept of recycling a long time ago but made no effort to do much about it. Recycling is preached but seldom put into practice in Asia. I stayed on the ninth story of an apartment building, and trash was usually unsorted and thrown down the rubbish chu[...]
is renowned for being a clean city, probably bec[...]
day—clearing the rubbish, making trash out of [...]
about the garbage patch swirling around in the [...]
this issue and be aware of my impact on the env[...]

Relevance to audience: Do you know how mu[...]
day where you do not use plastic? I cannot, and [...]
use it too much.

Preview of speech: Our reliance on plastics, ho[...]
and how we dispose of them, are impacting our [...]
with plastic pollution. Today, I would like to pers[...]
plastic use and to support alternatives to plastic by hig[...]
offering you the solutions.

(**Link:** Let's start with the problems.)

BODY

I. Plastics are made from problematic materials.
   1. The raw materials for plastics are usually made fr[...]
      A. In the United States, 70 percent of plastics are [...]
      B. For plastic bottles, 10 percent or less are from re[...]
         from PET derived from raw materials.
      C. The production of plastic is heavily dependent on fossil fuels, which are limited

---

> **# 1**
>
> INTRODUCTION
>
> **The nonbiodegradable nature of plastic and our mass consumption can be seen in artworks by Chris Jordan. Jordan, U.S.-based photographer and artist, used plastic bottles and cups to show our unconscious behavior of consumerism.   (3 slides)

> **# 2**
>
> **I came in contact with the concept of recycling a long time ago but made no effort to do much about it. . . .
>
> **Do you know how much plastic you use? Can you imagine a day when you do not use plastic? I cannot, and that is the problem. We—you and I— use it too much.

Tab 7: Review

CHAPTER 14 REVIEW QUESTIONS

1. Define persuasion and explain how attitudes, beliefs, values, and behaviors relate to the persuasive process.
2. What should a persuasive speech do?
3. List and explain the traditional and modern forms of appeal.
4. Explain the three traits and the three levels of ethos.
5. What are the parts of an argument? Explain how they work to form an argument.
6. Briefly explain the three types of warrants.
7. List and explain the five types of arguments.
8. What are faulty arguments? Select 3 of the 14 discussed in the chapter and explain them. Include an example in your explanation.

CHAPTER 15 REVIEW QUESTIONS

1. Explain the three types of persuasive speeches. Include an example in your explanation.
2. What is the social judgment theory, and how does it relate to selecting a persuasive topic?
3. What factors should you consider when selecting an organizational strategy for a persuasive speech?
4. Explain how the primacy and recency models can help you organize an argument.

TERMS TO REMEMBER

Chapter 14
persuasion (370)
proposition of fact (373)
proposition of value (373)
proposition of policy (373)
appeals (374)
coercion (375)
ethnocentrism (377)
Cognitive Dissonance Theory (382)
Expectancy-Outcome Values Theory (383)
Elaboration Likelihood Model (383)
argument (384)
claim (385)
evidence (385)
warrants (386)
argument by deduction (388)
syllogism (388)
enthymeme (389)
argument by induction (390)
argument by analogy (391)
argument by cause (391)
argument by authority (391)
fallacy (392)

Chapter 15
target audience (412)
social judgment theory (413)
attitudinal anchors (413)
primacy model (425)
recency model (425)

Introduction

Garrett has been best friends with Joe since grade school. In high school they played basketball on the same team, hunted quail, and took road trips together; in college they were roommates. When Joe began dating Stephanie, Garrett was happy his friend had found a great match.

Several months ago, Joe asked Stephanie to marry him and asked Garrett to be his best man. When Garrett told his dad, his father noted that Garrett would be expected to give a toast at the wedding reception. Wanting to do his best for Joe and Stephanie's event, Garrett gave his toast a lot of thought before the wedding.

First, he jotted down a few thoughts. His notes included how important Joe and, now, Stephanie are to him and a few stories that might make the toast fun or interesting. Because many of the audience members will not know him, Garrett decided to begin by briefly defining his relationship to Joe. Garrett then selected one favorite story and carefully crafted a toast that would honor the newlyweds. He practiced it several times in front of his dad to make sure it seemed from the heart and would flow well.

This chapter will help you give speeches in situations like Garrett's. During your lifetime, you may find yourself giving a wedding toast, commemorating someone's life work, or paying tribute to a friend. These are special occasion speeches, and much of what you have read in previous chapters will help you here as well. This chapter will offer additional insights about speaking at special events.

CHAPTER 16 CONTENTS

What Is the Creative Process for Special Occasion Speaking?	444
What Are Special Occasion Speeches?	446
1 Speeches to Celebrate	447
2 Speeches to Commemorate	447
3 Speeches to Inspire	447
4 Speeches to Entertain	447
How Do You Write a Special Occasion Speech?	448
1 Determine the Purpose of the Occasion	449
2 Clarify the Type of Special Occasion Speech	450
3 Analyze the Audience	451
4 Focus on a Central Idea	451
5 Research Your Speech	452
6 Create Your Outline	452
7 Practice the Speech	453
8 Evaluate the Special Occasion Speech	453
What Are the Types of Special Occasion Speeches?	454
1 Eulogy or Tribute	454
2 Speech of Introduction	456
3 Toast or Roast	457
4 Speech of Award Presentation	458
5 Speech of Award Acceptance	459
6 After-dinner Speech	460
7 Speech of Inspiration	464
Jeremy's Speech	468
Tab 8 Review	470

What Is the Creative Process for Special Occasion Speaking?

Speeches for special occasions are some of the most creative you will ever present. They bring public speaking into your daily life to celebrate, commemorate, inspire, and amuse audiences during extraordinary times. This chart briefly outlines the five basic activities you will use to create an effective special occasion speech. Remember, being creative is not a linear process, so move back and forth between each activity as you mold your speech.

1 STARTING

DETERMINE THE PURPOSE AND TYPE OF SPEECH
➜ See pages 449–450

Know your audience as well as where, when, and why you are speaking. Select the topic that best fits you, your audience, and the occasion. Let the special occasion determine which type you should give.

ANALYZE THE AUDIENCE
➜ See page 451

Get to know who will be in the audience. Special occasion speeches can be culturally specific and tied to a particular audience.

FOCUS ON A CENTRAL IDEA
➜ See page 451

State in one sentence what you want the overall theme or message to be.

2 RESEARCHING

RESEARCH YOUR SPEECH
➜ See page 452

Research for accurate, current, complete, and suitable materials about your audience, topic, and special occasion.

Because of the personal nature of most special occasion speeches, you might locate much of your speech material from your own personal experience and relationship with the people, place, or event being celebrated.

3 CREATING

CREATE YOUR OUTLINE
→ See page 452

Create a preparation outline so that you are sure to have an introduction, body, and conclusion.

Use an organizational strategy appropriate to the special occasion speech.

Create a delivery outline if appropriate.

4 PRESENTING

PRACTICE YOUR SPEECH
→ See page 453

Use language that is familiar, concrete, and appropriate.

Practice your delivery so that you are natural, enthusiastic, confident, and engaging.

Use presentation aids *only* when appropriate and effective for the specific occasion.

5 LISTENING & EVALUATING

EVALUATE THE SPECIAL OCCASION SPEECH
→ See page 453

Determine the speech's effectiveness and appropriateness for the occasion and the audience.

Be an active and effective listener when helping someone with a speech.

What Are Special Occasion Speeches?

1 **Speeches to Celebrate**

2 **Speeches to Commemorate**

3 **Speeches to Inspire**

4 **Speeches to Entertain**

A ***special occasion speech*** has the general purpose to celebrate, commemorate, inspire, or entertain. The speaker's intent is to mark the occasion by making it a time to rejoice, honor, arouse, or amuse.

The special occasion is unique in that it often seems like you are bringing public speaking into the home or heart. The special occasion speech intertwines public speaking with your personal life, as the opening toast example demonstrates. Although you could be asked to give a special occasion speech because of who you are professionally, some aspect of the special occasion speech is usually tied to the daily lives of the speaker and/or the audience.

Special occasion speeches accentuate the extraordinary events in life, marking rites of passage, celebrating new beginnings, paying tribute to those you admire or love, and sometimes even entertaining your audience.

> *Let us celebrate the occasion with wine and sweet words.*[1]
>
> PLAUTUS

1
Speeches to Celebrate

Speeches to celebrate will honor or highlight a person, group, institution, place, or event. You may give a speech to celebrate at such events as weddings, anniversaries, retirements, banquets, welcome sessions, and birthdays. The speaker should praise the subject(s) of the special occasion and adhere to the expected customs of the group hosting the event. The tone of your speech should emulate the personality of the person, group, institution, place, or event being celebrated.

2
Speeches to Commemorate

Speeches to commemorate pay tribute to or remember a person, group, institution, place, or event. Unlike the speech to celebrate, which honors the event of the moment (an eleventh birthday), speeches to commemorate reside more in the past, or future, such as a speech marking the eighth anniversary of the September 11 attacks or the death of Senator Ted Kennedy. In both of these examples, the events really being remembered are September 11, 2001, and the past life of Senator Kennedy. The focus of the speech to commemorate can touch thousands or be closer to home, as with the death of a local police officer or a family member. This type of speech should reflect the personality of the person or the tone of the group, institution, place, or event being commemorated, and it should consider the needs of the audience as well as the cultural expectations of the speaking event.

3
Speeches to Inspire

Speeches to inspire are created to motivate, stir, encourage, or arouse the audience. Commencement speeches, keynote addresses, inaugural speeches, sermons, and daily devotionals are often examples of speeches to inspire. Inspirational speeches may reflect the personality and professional status of the speaker, but the main considerations are the needs of the audience and the expectations of the speaking event.

4
Speeches to Entertain

Speeches to entertain all have the general goal to amuse, delight, and engage the audience for the purpose of enjoyment, with a bit of wisdom or tribute thrown in depending on the special occasion. Speeches given at banquets, award dinners, and roasts are often speeches to entertain. The speeches are expected to be cheery, playful, light, and usually optimistic but may have an underlying serious message that can be informative or persuasive.

PRACTICING ETHICS
Special occasion speeches are very culturally specific and embedded. Make yourself aware of protocol and cultural expectations. Be audience centered.

How Do You Write a Special Occasion Speech?

1 **Determine the Purpose of the Occasion**

2 **Clarify the Type of Special Occasion Speech**

3 **Analyze the Audience**

4 **Focus on a Central Idea**

5 **Research Your Speech**

6 **Create Your Outline**

7 **Practice the Speech**

8 **Evaluate the Special Occasion Speech**

You can tackle the creation of a special occasion speech much like you would an informative or persuasive speech. In actuality, a special occasion speech is an informative speech, a persuasive speech, or a little of both in one.

The primary difference is that this speech is determined by the occasion more than almost anything else and changes where you start in the creative process. With most speeches, you first focus on understanding your audience. With the special occasion speech, you start by determining your purpose and the type of special occasion speech you are expected to give. Once you have those considerations in mind, you can turn your attention to the audience and their cultural expectations for the event.

The following pages explain the basic process. The section "What Are the Types of Special Occasion Speeches?" (page 454) will offer you more suggestions for each type of special occasion speech.

1

Determine the Purpose of the Occasion

When you are invited to deliver a special occasion speech, use that opportunity to ask about the purpose of the occasion. If the person inviting you is not able to answer your questions, seek out someone directly related to the occasion to help you focus your speech. You should ask:

What is the purpose of the overall event (meeting, conference, or ceremony)?

This general question gets at the purpose—or the overall reason—why the audience has gathered. For example, the audience may be attending the annual convention of the National Association for the Advancement of Colored People (NAACP). Knowing the focus or theme of the event can help you determine your topic. Even learning when your speaking event will happen (e.g., the last night of a long conference) can influence your choices.

What is the purpose of the specific event where I will speak?

For example, you could be asked to give a speech at an awards banquet during the convention. You need to understand the purpose for the larger convention event as well as the focus of the awards banquet.

What are the requirements of the event?

Does the event or its audience come with specific expectations or wishes?

Do you have an idea of what you would like my speech to achieve?

Talk to the event representative about the general purpose of your speech—should it celebrate, commemorate, inspire, or entertain?—or ask if there are specific areas you should cover.

Who will be in the audience?

You want to know general characteristics, special needs, and how many at the minimum.

You still need to know a few things that might influence your speech or that you might need to prepare for. You should also ask:

Will someone introduce me?

If so, try to discuss with the person introducing you what he or she might say. You will not want to repeat the introduction, and you might be able to help him or her focus the introduction.

Where will I speak?

Try to get an idea of the location's atmosphere. How big is the space? Will there be a lectern and/or microphone?

Will there be other speakers? Where am I in the order of speakers?

You may want to coordinate your speeches so that they reflect the same theme or mood but do not cover the same information. Be willing and ready to adjust your speech, if necessary, to fit with the speeches of others.

How long should I speak?

Most special occasion speeches are short, but you need to know what the event organizers expect.

→ See Chapter 1 (Tab 1) for more on how to analyze the situation.

2

Clarify the Type of Special Occasion Speech

As suggested in the last section, the person inviting you will often suggest or hint at the general purpose of your speech or a particular type of special occasion. For example, "We want you to help us celebrate our grand opening" or "Would you be willing to give the eulogy?" Ultimately, you want to determine if you should give a speech to celebrate, commemorate, inspire, or entertain, and also the specific type of special occasion speech. In general, the type of speech you give will match up to one of the following general purposes.

TYPE OF SPEECH	GENERAL PURPOSE
Toast or roast	Speech to celebrate
Introduction	
Award presentation or acceptance	
Eulogy or tribute	Speech to commemorate
Speeches of inspiration, such as sermons, commencement addresses, or motivational talks	Speech to inspire
After-dinner speech	Speech to entertain

Although the lines between these types of general purposes seem to blur, you will only have one purpose for each type of speech. For example, a eulogy is a speech to commemorate but can be an uplifting speech praising or celebrating a life. Your general purpose is to commemorate; your speech's tone is celebratory.

> **TIP: Clarifying the Speech Type**
> You should pay attention to how the person offering you the invitation to speak talks about the speech event. Their description of the event or topic might give you clues to the type of speech expected.

3

Analyze the Audience

As with any speech, you need to understand your audience's beliefs, values, and attitudes by investigating their personal, psychological, and social traits. For example, if you are asked to give a eulogy at a Catholic wake and you are not Catholic, the audience's expectations could be radically different from yours. You need to know who your audience is for even the shortest speech to be effective.

The person inviting you to speak can have insight, and talking with audience members before the event can offer you information. Researching the general demographics of groups represented in the audience can also be helpful. For example, a college commencement speech included this:

> When I asked the university's staff to tell me a bit about you, they told me that 65 percent of the students graduating today are African American, 20 percent are in the military or dependents of military personnel, 65 percent are female, and the average age is 31. As I read these stats, I remembered that . . . most low-income and first-generation students, as well as students of color, are less likely to attend four-year institutions and persist through degree completion.

> Do you know how many U.S. residents hold a bachelor's degree as of 2009? According to the Census Bureau, only 30 percent. Today, you will increase that number—you should be proud!!! If you are black, that number drops to 19 percent, and 13 percent if you are Hispanic. Today, you will increase those numbers—you should be proud. . . .

This speaker merged information she gathered from the college staff with facts and statistics to inspire her audience.

4

Focus on a Central Idea

Central ideas for longer special occasion speeches, such as a keynote address or nomination speech, will be similar to those of informative or persuasive speeches. Shorter special occasion speeches, such as toasts or award acceptance speeches, will focus more on a theme. For example, if you return to Garrett's wedding toast, his central idea is:

> **Special people deserve special people in their lives.**

Although this central idea does not tell you exactly what Garrett will say, it establishes a theme. With this central idea, Garrett is ready to brainstorm for the main points he wants to make and to craft the toast.

If you are giving a longer special occasion speech and have your central idea, take the time to draft working main points and a working outline to guide your research.

Later in this chapter are specific suggestions for what to include in each type of special occasion speech. For now, you might use these questions as you draft potential main points:

- What were the first ideas that came to mind when you were invited to give the speech?

- If you were invited because of your expertise or profession, how might that focus your content?

- What might the audience know about you that would help you focus?

- If you had to select three things for your audience to remember, consider, believe, or enjoy, what would they be?

→ See Chapter 2 (Tab 1) for how to craft a central idea.

5
Research Your Speech

Depending on the type of special occasion speech you are giving, your research may be more personally reflective (from within your own experience) or you may need to do more formal research. For a wedding toast, you will use your own knowledge and experience of the couple, but for an award presentation, you might need to research the history of the award and the recipient. Some speeches to inspire, such as a commencement speech, can require a lot of research, depending on the main points covered.

Here are some specific questions that might guide your research.

- Are there special issues related to the occasion that require detailed understanding of a person, group, institution, place, or event? What do you need to know and tell your audience about this person, group, institution, place, or event?

- What types of materials (quotations, statistics, facts, etc.) might you need to locate related to your *topic* to celebrate, commemorate, inspire, or entertain this audience?

- What types of materials (quotations, statistics, facts, etc.) related to your *audience* might you need to help them celebrate, commemorate, be inspired, or be entertained?

→ See Tab 2 for more on how to conduct research.

6
Create Your Outline

Outlining is as important to the special occasion speech as it is to the informative or persuasive speech, to help you avoid rambling or forgetting important parts.

Even the shortest special occasion speech will include an introduction, a body, and a conclusion. However, you may condense the parts into one, two, or three sentences. Use links to connect key points and to lead your audience through the speech. The chronological, topical, spatial, order of intensity, and comparative strategies are most common in special occasion speeches.

INTRODUCTION
Attention-getter
Credibility material
Relevance to audience
Preview of speech

Short speeches may incorporate all of these in one sentence.

BODY
  I. First main point
  II. Second main point
  III. Third main point

Very short speeches may have only one main point.

CONCLUSION
Summary statement
Audience response
  statement
WOW Statement

Should reflect the mood of your audience and speech.

For long speeches, create a delivery outline. Deliver shorter speeches, such as a toast, without notes—although you might review an outline privately beforehand.

→ See Tab 3 for how to outline, organize the speech body, and construct introductions and conclusions.

7
Practice the Speech

Most special occasion speeches will be delivered extemporaneously. More formal and longer speeches, such as commencement or keynote addresses, might be delivered from a manuscript, as time and details are usually important considerations. Also, they are often printed in full manuscript form in the proceedings of the event or posted on a Web site.

But most special occasion speeches, because they are a part of everyday life, need to come from the heart rather than a piece of paper. Can you imagine someone reading a wedding toast from a manuscript? On the other hand, can you imagine someone introducing a speaker without thinking and practicing what he or she specifically needs to say about the speaker? Both scenarios could be disastrous and show why outlining and rehearsing your speech is so important.

Here are some helpful hints for practicing the special occasion speech.

- Rehearse the entire speech several times.
- Practice in front of an audience—preferably someone who will be at the event and understands the audience.
- If your speech is lighthearted or leans to the humorous, practice it with someone who will be honest about whether you achieve those goals.
- Almost constant eye contact is crucial for the special occasion speech.

8
Evaluate the Special Occasion Speech

Unless you are giving special occasion speeches as part of a class assignment, they are rarely formally evaluated. However, you still want to make sure you have covered the necessary parts, used an appropriate organizational strategy, and crafted a speech appropriate to the audience, topic, and occasion.

Poorly crafted special occasion speeches can hurt your interpersonal relationships or adversely affect your professional career if given in a situation related to your job. So remember: carefully and ethically craft these speeches as you would an informative or persuasive speech.

If you are helping someone else craft a special occasion speech, be sensitive to the special needs of the occasion and honest with the speaker. If something does not work for you in rehearsal, it will most likely not work during the actual speech.

CHECKLIST for Evaluating a Special Occasion Speech

❏ Does my introduction include an attention-getter, credibility material, statement of relevance, and preview?

❏ Does the body of my speech have an appropriate organizational strategy and supported main points?

❏ Is my language clear, vivid, and appropriate?

❏ Does my conclusion include a summary, an audience reaction statement, and a WOW ending?

❏ Is the length of my speech appropriate?

❏ Is my delivery dynamic and enthusiastic? If appropriate, am I delivering the speech extemporaneously? Do I maintain almost constant eye contact?

What Are the Types of Special Occasion Speeches?

1 **Eulogy or Tribute**

2 **Speech of Introduction**

3 **Toast or Roast**

4 **Speech of Award Presentation**

5 **Speech of Award Acceptance**

6 **After-dinner Speech**

7 **Speech of Inspiration**

1

Eulogy or Tribute

The word *eulogy* derives from the Greek word *eulogia,* meaning "praise" or "good word," and is a speech presented after a person's death. A eulogy is given at ceremonies, like funerals, marking the death of an individual. You may be asked to eulogize or commemorate the life of a family member, friend, or close colleague.

A *tribute* commemorates lives or accomplishments of people, groups, institutions, or events. A tribute can be given with the recipient present or posthumously (after death). Tributes may be given at such events as award ceremonies, banquets, and retirement dinners.

SPECIAL GUIDELINES

- Your focus should be to commemorate and celebrate the life of the honoree.

- Although eulogies and tributes should be brief (under 10 minutes), determine what is expected.

- For a eulogy, your purpose is to celebrate the deceased and to comfort the living. Pay attention to the needs of the audience.
  - Stay in control of your emotions.
  - Refer to the family or close friends and colleagues.
  - Focus on the person, not how he or she died.
  - Be positive, but genuine, about the deceased.

- For a tribute, remember that your purpose is to honor the achievements of a person, group, institution, or event.
  - Vividly describe the accomplishments without overstating the facts.
  - Be genuine and informative.
  - Use those achievements to inspire and educate the other members of the audience.

EXAMPLE

On August 28, 2009, Senator Chris Dodd eulogized Senator Edward M. Kennedy at a memorial service at the John F. Kennedy Library in Boston. The eulogy first addresses the members of the audience and frames the speech as a celebration of an American story and a great friendship.

> Tonight, we gather to celebrate the incredible American story of a man who made so many other American stories possible, my friend Teddy Kennedy. Generations of historians will chronicle his prolific efforts on behalf of others. I will leave that to them. Tonight, I just want to share some thoughts about my friend. And what a friend he has been—a friend of unbridled empathy, optimism, and full-throated joy. Examples of his friendship are legion.

> Many years ago, a close friend of mine passed away. Teddy didn't know him. I was asked to say a few words at the funeral. As long as I live, I will never forget that, as I stood at the pulpit and looked out over the gathering, there was Teddy, sitting in the back of the church. He wasn't there for my friend. He was there for me, at my time of loss. That was what it was like to have Teddy in your corner.

Throughout the speech, Senator Dodd uses stories, humor, and quotations to evoke the character of Senator Kennedy.

> In 1994, he was in the political fight of his life against Mitt Romney. Before the first debate, held in Boston's historic Faneuil Hall, I was with Teddy and his team and, along with everyone else, offering him advice. "Teddy," I cautioned, "we Irish always talk too fast. Even if you know the answer to a question, you have to pause, slow down, and appear thoughtful." Out he went, and, of course, the first question was something like this: "Senator, you've served the Commonwealth of Massachusetts for nearly 35 years in the United States Senate. Explain, then, why this race is so close."

> Teddy paused. And paused. And paused. Five seconds. Ten seconds. Finally, after what seemed like an eternity, he answered.

> After the debate, I said, "Good Lord, Teddy, I didn't mean pause that long after the first question! What were you thinking about?" He looked at me and replied, "I was thinking—that's a damn good question! Why IS this race so close?"

Senator Dodd ends the speech with an inspirational call to keep Senator Kennedy's legacy alive.

> We will remember him as a man who understood better than most that America is a place of incredible opportunity, hope, and redemption. He labored tirelessly to make those dreams a reality for everyone. Those dreams, the ones he spoke of throughout his life, live on like the eternal flame that marks President Kennedy's grave, the flame that Teddy and Bobby lit 46 years ago. And in all the years I knew and loved him, that eternal flame has never failed to burn brightly in Teddy's eyes. Now, as he re-joins his brothers on the hillside in Arlington, may the light from that flame continue to illuminate our path forward.

To read the complete eulogy, visit http://dodd.senate.gov/?q=node/5172.

2
Speech of Introduction

A **speech of introduction** presents an
event's next or main speaker to the audience.
This type of speech might also set out to
welcome the audience; establish the tone,
mood, or climate of the event; and/or build a
level of excitement.

SPECIAL GUIDELINES

- Research the background of the speaker
  so that you can give a brief overview of
  his or her accomplishments and credentials. Review the speaker's résumé if you
  can. You might also talk with the event
  organizer or conduct a mini-interview
  with the speaker prior to the introduction. Do not wait until the last minute to
  research. You need time to prepare, and
  the speaker needs the time before the
  speech to get ready as well.

- Briefly preview the speaker's title and
  topic if appropriate. You should work this
  out ahead of time with the speaker. Do
  not give your own speech on the topic.

- Introductions should be short. The
  audience has come to hear the featured
  speaker.

- Your final words should ask the audience
  to welcome the speaker and include his
  or her name. For example, "Please join
  me in welcoming the CEO of AirBound,
  Joyce English."

EXAMPLE

The great screen and stage star Rosalind
Russell once said, "Acting is like standing
up naked and turning around very slowly."
Luckily, if that is true, our next speaker isn't
afraid of baring it all for his craft. It is my
honor tonight to introduce a man who has
graced our stage and hearts for years. He was
here the day they placed the first coat of paint
on the stage floor and opened the box office
for our first production of *Hamlet*, where he
had the leading role. He has acted in 35 main
stage productions, 15 reading-hour productions, and directed 18 plays over the years.
Tonight, he is going to celebrate the history of
the 18th Street Playhouse. He not only knows
our history, he is our history. Please join me
in giving a warm welcome to our founder,
Leonardo Garrick.

This speaker started with a quotation as an
attention-getter and humorous transition
to the featured speaker. She then gives a
brief preview of the accomplishments and
connection to this audience before giving his
title and name.

CONFIDENCE BOOSTER

Most special occasion speeches relate to affirmative
topics, and their audiences usually want to listen.
Even eulogies are positive in that they affirm the life
of someone special to the audience, and you wouldn't
be giving the eulogy if you weren't a positive part of
that experience. Use that affirmative spirit to override
your nervousness or lack of confidence. Decide
beforehand to make your speech a powerful and
positive experience for you and your audience.

3
Toast or Roast

A ***toast*** is a ritual expressing honor or goodwill to a person, group, institution, or event, punctuated by taking a drink. You may offer a toast at events such as New Year's Eve, weddings, births, housewarmings, graduation dinners, and retirement parties. A ***roast*** is a humorous tribute to a person. The event and the speech are both called a roast. The protocol involves a series of speakers, all joking or poking fun at the honoree, often with a few heartwarming moments.

SPECIAL GUIDELINES

- Reflect the tone and purpose of the event.
- Speak mostly about the honoree.
- Be positive, appropriate, and gracious.
- Mix your humor with heartfelt meaning.
- Know the protocol for the event (e.g., wedding toasts usually follow an order—father of the bride or host of the reception, best man, maid of honor, and groom).
- Be brief and adhere to your time limit, especially at a roast. A toast should be three to five minutes or less.
- Praise, honor, and compliment. It is the honoree's day to shine and be happy.
- Tailor remarks to mirror the values, beliefs, and attitudes of the honoree and those close to him or her. Anything you say will be recorded in their memories and potentially on video.
- Stand, if possible, when you offer a toast or roast.

EXAMPLE

Garrett, the best man you met in the chapter's introduction, wrote this toast.

> May I have your attention, please? Wow, what an amazing day and celebration. For those who don't know me, I'm Garrett Cooper, Joe's shadow. We met in grade school and will leave this life as best friends. We have played ball, chased after quail, and hitchhiked across this great land together.
>
> On one of our trips, I learned a lot about how calm, cool, and trainable Joe could be. We were camping out under the stars in Washington state when we awoke to a large female moose straddling Joe's body, literally, and staring straight into his eyes. I'm there in my sleeping bag, wondering what her breath smells like and if she will bite or lick his face. Joe had to be wondering what her plans were for him in that compromising position. He didn't move. I didn't move. She checked us out for what seemed like an eternity and sauntered off eventually. We learned that day to stay calm and cool and let the ladies have their way. Stephanie, you owe that moose a lot.
>
> Joe, you better be glad you saw Stephanie first. She is one special catch and deserves the best. Too bad for her, she saw you first. No, seriously, I wish you two many years of happiness and a lifetime of joy. Special people deserve special people in their lives. Today, two very special people begin a lifetime of happiness and joy together. Congratulations, Joe and Stephanie! (*toast*)

TIP: Responding from the Audience

As an audience member to a toast, if you pick up your glass at the beginning of the toast, don't put it down until the end. You should always raise your glass and sip some liquid, or you will appear impolite or seem to suggest that you don't agree with the toast.

4

Speech of Award Presentation

You will give a **speech of award presentation** when you are asked or are in a position to be the individual announcing the recipient(s) of an award, prize, or honor. This type of speech may be given at an award ceremony, banquet, party, business meeting, convention session, or the end of a long gathering for a particular purpose (e.g., a retreat).

SPECIAL GUIDELINES

- You should either set or mirror the tone of the proceedings.
- If it is not obvious to the audience, explain who you are and why you are giving the award. This should be very brief, because the award is not about you.
- Explain the significance of the award.
- Compliment and recognize all of the nominees as a group.
- Highlight the achievements of the recipient(s) or explain why the individual or group is receiving the award.
- Be brief—no longer than five minutes and usually much shorter.
- If possible, physically hand the award to the recipient. In Western culture, it is common to hand the award with the left hand and shake hands with the right. Be sure to investigate, ask someone, or pay attention to others' behavior to determine the proper cultural procedure for shaking hands, as it can vary. Practice this maneuver so that it is not awkward.

EXAMPLE

It is my honor and privilege to present the fifth annual St. Vincent Award. Ester St. Vincent worked in our elementary schools for more than 40 years. Outside the classroom, she dedicated much of her life to civic duty. She was a volunteer at the local soup kitchen and the hospital, taught adults to read, and took in countless animals until they could make it on their own. She led the cry to save this town after a major flood.

This award was established in 2006, to honor this extraordinary citizen. Each year, we give the award to a local community member who carries on Ms. St. Vincent's spirit, sense of civility, and duty.

This year, we had several outstanding nominees, making the decision a tough one; we honor you all. However, after great scrutiny, one obvious candidate began to emerge. This year's recipient grew up here, works as a nurse practitioner in our community, volunteers to maintain the city gardens, helps give medical care to the homeless, and has organized several successful fundraisers.

The 2011 recipient of the St. Vincent Award is Eliana Lee.

Notice how this speaker briefly explains the award, praises those candidates who did not receive it, and quickly highlights the important achievements of the award recipient just before announcing her name. This speech is to the point and builds the intensity of the moment.

5

Speech of Award Acceptance

A *speech of award acceptance* is the response you give when receiving an award, prize, or honor. You may give this type of speech after receiving an award or honor, or at an event marking a significant achievement in your life (e.g., a retirement reception, sports event, or contest).

SPECIAL GUIDELINES

- Be prepared if you know you will or might receive an award. The audience usually expects to hear from you.

- Be respectful of the event and give your speech from the heart. Unless the award ceremony is intended to entertain rather than to honor, you should respect the organizers' purpose to honor you. Be humble.

- Be appropriate to the event.

- Thank the person or group giving you the honor.

- Thank those close to you and/or those who have contributed greatly to your success. Limit this list to the most significant people, and avoid a long list (three to five works best).

- Show a little emotion or pride.

- Make the award meaningful for your audience or appeal to their emotions. For example, dedicate your award to someone or something appropriate to the occasion.

- Know when to stop. Do not go on and on. Be as brief as possible (usually three to five minutes). Pay attention to your audience.

EXAMPLE

Thank you, Mayor Craig, for your kind words and endless support. I would also like to thank the award committee and the other nominees. I am truly humbled by your recognition and company. Giving back to this community is my life and passion. Growing up here, I have loved this small town and its people—the people who made me who I am today. It took people like Ms. St. Vincent and my family to show me that I could be whatever I wanted, and I thank them for pushing and lifting me. They inspired me to do the same for others.

Almost every day when I would walk home from school or my dad's store, Ms. St. V, as we called her, would be on her way to help a cause. Or she would call me over to help take care of baby rabbits, a doe, or other animals someone had brought her to rehabilitate. When my dad's store was wiped out by the flood, she was the first one there with a mop and bucket to help. No cause was too small or too large in Ms. St. V's eyes. Her motto was "Keep movin' forward and smile!" Thank you for this honor.

Here, the recipient of the award begins by thanking the appropriate people and graciously dedicates the speech to make a point about helping others.

6
After-dinner Speech

Despite the name, an **after-dinner speech** can be given any time you need to give a speech with the general purpose to entertain but with a relevant message. Most after-dinner speeches are lighthearted but contain a more serious element buried in the entertaining parts. This type of speech can occur before, during, or after meal gatherings; at professional and civic meetings; at events opening or closing campaigns; or at end-of-the-year events. After-dinner speeches tend to be longer than other special occasion speeches and are usually specific to the audience and/or the occasion.

SPECIAL GUIDELINES

- Start preparing the speech early. An after-dinner speech is one of the more difficult speeches to create, because you are trying to entertain and deliver a relevant message at the same time.

- Tailor the speech to the occasion and the audience. Do not simply pull a canned speech out of your repertoire.

- Be appropriate. Do not offend. Analyze your audience and situation to learn what might be appropriate or expected.

- Be focused and structured. You still need an introduction, a body, and a conclusion. Decide if the relevant message is meant to inform or to persuade your audience.

- Be creative but avoid doing stand-up. You were asked to do a speech, not a comedy routine, and that is the expectation. Likewise, you probably are not a professional comedian, and although it might look simple, stand-up

comedy takes years to perfect. You can still use humor in a structured, well-organized, and purposeful speech—just avoid making the speech all about being comical.

- Be dynamic and cheerful. Your delivery should be extremely upbeat. If you aren't excited and having fun, the audience won't be either. Use a lot of eye contact and speak extemporaneously.

- Some presentation aids (e.g., video, images/pictures, or items) can help make the speech entertaining.

- Know your time limit and stick to it. Your audience will not expect a long speech. This type of speech can be as short as two to three minutes or as long as 10 to 15 minutes.

- Practice. When you are being creative and entertaining, effective timing and delivery are musts. Always rehearse this type of speech in front of an audience for feedback, and editing hints.

PRACTICING ETHICS

- When your goal is to entertain, avoid using language, jokes, or examples that are potentially insensitive to religion, race, gender, ethnicity, sexual orientation, age, or even political persuasion. Such references will destroy your credibility, will offend your audience, and may provoke an undesired response.
- Do not make your audience feel alienated or uncomfortable for any reason.

EXAMPLE

To see the essence of an after-dinner speech, you need to hear or read the whole speech. This example is a full manuscript of a student speech given by Brendan. He gave the speech extemporaneously for a student organization.

I have a confession to make. I joined the Asian Business Students Association at my school last week, and I'm kind of intimidated. First of all, they call themselves The Asians. You know, like The Gays or The Homeless. And second, not to be a racist or anything, but they're all really Asian-y and I'm really... not-y. My first event with the organization was this penny-toss fund-raiser, which is one of those games where you throw a penny into a tub and then you win a prize. It's for charity. We raised a lot of pennies, and we had more visitors than The Hispanics (our rivals, who are all about the Ben-jamins!). And as I began to truly revel in my racial identity, I started counting all the money we had raised from the penny toss. $2.67?! What the Asian-loving hell?! These pennies are useless! We should just get rid of them! So I decided to join the Citizens for Retiring the Penny, or Crips, who state on their Web site: "Dealing with pennies on a day-to-day basis costs U.S. citizens approximately $10 billion a year." And as Jay Sean—featuring Lil' Wayne—puts it, because we're all feeling "down like the economy," everyone should get up out of their seats and demand change! Not convinced? Just you wait. Because in this current depressed economy, that kind of money could be just the Prozac we need, which is why we must get rid of the physical penny in the United States monetary system. But Brendan! What did this brilliant copper Lincoln face ever do to you?! Nothing—which is exactly my point. To find out how to get rid of this meddlesome metal sum, we will coin some problems, mint some causes, and loaf for some solutions! Mnahh, and you thought this speech was going to be about race. In all seriousness, getting rid of the penny is a necessity. It just makes cents! Ooh, hope that one doesn't cost me. Ahahaha!

After the fail of the penny toss, The Asians gave up on fund-raising and started doing what Asians do best: Calculus! And Geometry! And Rudimentary English! What a problem! And there are two more problems that come with pennies: increased issues with our economy, and wasting precious and shiny resources.

Initially, with the existence of the penny, we are furthering the poor state of the economy, because it costs more than a pretty penny to produce it. Little known fact: Producing the penny actually costs more than it's worth.

Using a problem–solution strategy of sorts, Brendan begins to outline his relevant message by highlighting the problems.

Even though this is a speech to mainly entertain, Brendan still uses sources to support his relevant message—building his case and ethos.

BELIEVE it! *Parade* Magazine shared on April 5, 2009, that in 2008, "It cost the U.S. Mint 1.5 cents to create each penny." And according to NPR on December 16, 2009, having the penny adds up to almost "an annual loss of $54 million." Fifty million for coins that chill in our couch or sit at the bottom of wishing wells?! (*Toss penny*.) "I wish my daddy had a job!" Exactly. And $54 million can pay for a lot of salaries for *a lot* of jobs. And maybe that means my dad will get a job again. Seriously, I'm so hungry. Oh so hungry.

Next, we waste our resources producing pennies. The most obvious resource wasted is the metal that goes into making pennies. And guess what? That metal isn't even copper! It's zinc, the tawdry harlot of the alloys. Even their metallic makeup is lies! Whatever happened to Old Honest Abe?! The consulting company PSFK quotes Harvard economist Gregory Mankiw on its Web site on June 9, 2009, who said "The purpose of the monetary system is to facilitate exchange, but... the penny no longer serves that purpose." My peeps, pennies just aren't worth it! With the elimination of the physical penny, we could save the amount of time it would take to deal with pennies in everyday transactions, and save the metal for more pressing matters. Check it—metal is everywhere, so why waste it? Man, that's heavy. Heavy metal....

Again, he uses many sources to build his case and ethos.

Initially, metal prices have been skyrocketing over time. This has to do with the fact that the penny made the Hannah Montana-esque switch-eroo from copper to zinc. NPR reports on November 29, 2009, that "The percentage of penny that is copper [is now just] 2.5%, [while zinc is] 97.5%." Socyberty (that means society and cyber) also elucidates (that means shows us) on November 30, 2009, that "A penny hasn't been worth the metal it's made from for over six years at least." On top of that, the London *Guardian* shares on June 24, 2009, that "Metal prices are moving higher... as the dollar weakens." (*Toss a dollar*.) You're dead to me. With the increasing cost of metal, it is now costing the United States government more money to produce something that is offering less value to our monetary system, perpetuating the downfall of the economy for no real reason at all. Hoobastank taught me that the reason is you, but really, it's the government.

Next! The economy sucks. The *Wall Street Journal* explains on March 18, 2010, that consumer saving on a small scale, also known as penny-pinching, leads to the economy hurting. And in an article in the *Socialite Life* of January 9, 2009, entitled "Taylor Swift Realizes Our Economy Sucks," Swift says "Ew! A poor person! OMG, they're everywhere!!!" Too true, Ms. Swift, much like your pitch. But penny pinching is being treated as though it's the answer to our economic problems. As Fox News elaborates on October 8, 2009, by quoting author Danny Kofke, "Saving money on little things can lead to better financial habits." But penny pinching isn't getting us anywhere. We have to turn our penny-pinching behavior into nickel- and quarter-pinching behavior.

So there's really only one real solution: Nickels! And that's change that we can believe in! Ahh! So much change! Too bad it's all in pennies. Let's fix it in two ways!

He offers his solution.

First off, the government needs to stop producing pennies and mandate that the physical penny no longer exists. Now, I know it sounds farfetched, but this is how it would work: We would get rid of the physical penny with cash without getting rid of one-cent denominations. In dealing with cash, we'd simply round up or round down to the nearest $.05! It's brilliant! And we've done it before! Spend a Confederate dollar recently? Or a $2 bill? Or a seashell? And it works—countries like Australia and the Czech Republic have wildly successful economies without the penny. Intuition states that everyone would round up and that we'd end up spending more money—but back in 2006, Professor of Economics at Wake Forest University Robert Whaples analyzed approximately 200,000 transactions to show that with a system of rounding, "customers basically broke even." Major opponents of retiring the penny come from Illinois, and I recognize that Lincoln is from Illinois, but I want to clear something up. He's also on the $5 bill. Pssst! That's worth 500 pennies!

Next, we have to do something with the pennies that still exist! With the U.S. Mint estimating that there are between 140 and 200 billion pennies in circulation, that's a whole lot of metal! And what can we do with all of that metal? Simple! Zinc is used in ridiculous amounts of things, from medicine to rubbers to batteries. We need to recycle all of the pennies that we have and recirculate them in the form of different resources. And if you don't want to turn the pennies back into zinc, make stuff out of them! Like jewelry! And clothing! (*Show penny vest*.) This only cost me $4.72! What a bargain! Take the 140–200 billion pennies sitting in your penny jars and that's a huge influx of metal going back into our resources. And that's something that you can take to the bank. Lit'rally!

Brendan ends by returning to the opening story and humor.

After I spent the day with The Asians, I learned that pennies are terrible for fund-raisers—so now I just use them for magic tricks! Wanna see? (*Magic trick*.) Today, we looked at the problems with pennies still exist-ing in our monetary system; next, why the penny plagues our wallets; and finally, learned some ways to get rid of the penny once and for all! So just remember the next time you get some change: It's 20 dime, not 20.01 cent. And that one was money.

7

Speech of Inspiration

A **speech of inspiration** strives to fulfill a general purpose to motivate, encourage, move, or arouse an audience in a positive manner. Religious sermons, commencement addresses, motivational talks in the workplace or locker room, and nomination speeches at rallies, as well as keynote and welcoming addresses at conventions, are all speeches of inspiration. These speeches aim to awaken an audience's feelings, such as pride, perseverance, spirituality, and the search for excellence. The effectiveness of this type of speech is rooted in the speaker's ethos and appeal to audience pathos. Vivid language and storytelling are often key, as demonstrated in this devotional given by the Rev. John Yonker.

> An old story tells about a teacher who held up a sheet of clean, white paper. "What do you see?" he asked the children. "A piece of paper," they told him. He then took a pen and drew a small black dot on the paper. "Now, what do you see?" he asked. "A dot," they all responded. "A dot?" he asked. "Why do you see the dot and not the rest of the paper?"

> Sometimes, life goes the same way. With each new sunrise, God gives us a clean sheet of paper, but we often let some small incident ruin it for us. A disagreement, a lost earring, an unkind word, a disruptive phone call—these trivialities become the dot we concentrate on instead of the rest of the paper.

> This is John Yonker at First Christian Church, reminding you to hang onto your perspective. Don't let one tiny ink spot blind you to a whole sheet of white paper!

SPECIAL GUIDELINES

- Select a topic, theme, or subject that reflects the expectations, mood, and tone of the speaking event.
- Know your audience and what would inspire them.
- Talk about something that inspires you. If you are not inspired, your audience will not be either. Let your passion be inspirational.
- Appeal to your audience's pathos via stories (especially true ones), extended examples, or anecdotes. Use strong examples of what is or could be.
- Use vivid language, repetition, alliteration, metaphor, and other speech devices, and focus on connotative (emotional) usage.

  → See Chapter 8 for more on effective language usage.

- Draw on the power of inspirational people by quoting them at key moments.
- Use a vocal flow and rhythm that builds in intensity. Rally the audience's emotions with your delivery style. Be very dynamic.
- End with a significant WOW moment.

EXAMPLE

This speech was given at a ceremony just before a college graduation. Kyra, the student speaker, was elected by her peers to speak at this symbolic ceremony marking the passage from member of the senior class to alumna of the institution.

Kyra draws attention to a large portion of the audience.

Let me begin by welcoming all of you to this wonderful tradition. I would especially like to welcome and thank those of you in the audience who supported us over the last few years. Without our parents, partners, professors, friends, and the administrative staff, this journey would not have been possible or, for that matter, as much fun. If it is not too presumptuous of me to speak for all of the seniors, I would like to thank all of you from the bottom of our hearts for your support and the sacrifices you have made so this event could happen. It is a glorious day and one that I—no, we—will remember for years to come.

As many of you know, I have been very involved in theatre during the last four years. As a member of the Elysium Players, I took my job of bringing theatre to life again on this campus very seriously. So today, as we prepare to celebrate our years of hard work and education, it seems only fitting that I take a few moments to share with you five life lessons I have learned from theatre and that I hope will guide your future personal and professional lives.

She signals there will be five points in her speech.

Lesson Number One—Passion

Agnes George de Mille, actor, dancer, and niece to the great Cecil B. de Mille, once said, "It takes great passion and great energy to do anything creative, especially in theatre. You have to care so much you can't sleep, you can't eat, you can't talk to people. It's got to be just right. You can't do it without passion." To excel in theatre, you must love it; because, if you don't, you won't be successful in it. You have to be willing to memorize pages and pages of text, which you will forget as soon as the show is over. You have to make it through the long, tiring rehearsals night after night for over three months straight. And, you WILL but you definitely don't want to come back to the next rehearsal after spending a whole evening believing that at any moment the bats living in Launer Auditorium are going to attack. I can say from much experience that if you don't love theatre, the Launer bats will scare you away. In essence, the show can't go on without passion. Your future is the same. You must love life and be passionate about living it. If you live apathetically, never taking a stand, never pushing yourself, you won't enjoy living it and you won't succeed at even the small things. You must live your life with a passion strong enough to see past the mundane, the exhaustion of hard work, and the scary little unknown things. YOU MUST BE PASSIONATE!

Lesson Number Two—The Ensemble

As Kenneth Haigh once said, "You need three things in the theatre—the play, the actor[s], the audience—each must give something." All the parts of the play must work together in unison to make a successful production. This unity or working together is what we define as an ensemble or a group of complementary parts that contribute to a single effect. In life, whether we are teachers, athletes, businessmen and women, lawyers, doctors, partners, or parents, we all have something to give and a role to play. That role cannot simply stand alone as a solo act; it must work toward achieving unity, balance, and technique. We must recognize that our roles touch, create, and compliment the lives of those around us—our students, patients, clients, customers, loved ones, and children. The quality of our role balances and elevates theirs. We must remember to work together and not against each other, because life is an ensemble with the people we care about the most.

Lesson Number Three—A Supporting Role

Believe it or not, you don't always have to be center stage. There are times when you must choose to play a supportive role. Ninety-eight percent of what goes on in theatre productions happens before the audience even enters the auditorium: late-night rehearsals, set design and production, advertising, and costuming (just to name a few), and although the star actor of the show may be a vital part, the show wouldn't go on without the rest. In life, we must know when to step back in the shadows and live life because we love it, and not because we want formal recognition for what we are doing. We must help others receive the recognition they deserve, and support them as they endure challenging and exciting times, just as so many have done for us during our four-year journey to this day. And, possibly the most important, we must learn to support others and lift up those who lag a bit behind.

Lesson Number Four—"Criticism Is a Good Thang"

I will admit I still struggle with this lesson. A very wise professor and director once told me (actually told me and all the other Elysium players a few

To draw attention to a new lesson, Kyra uses a famous quotation.

Kyra ends each lesson with an inspirational challenge.

hundred times), "criticism is growth." And although none of us likes to hear that we aren't doing everything perfectly as we see it, she is right. A play looks very different from the point of view of the director or the audience, and actors on stage are often stuck in the small scene they are creating instead of seeing the whole picture. A performance is only as good as the image the actors create in the minds of others—not just within their own mind. We are not always perfect and can't always see things from the other perspective. Therefore, criticism is growth. Although at times it can be hard to swallow, criticism will only make us stronger and better if we choose to listen. We also need to be aware of ourselves as critics, that we offer criticism to those we care about not in an effort to break them down but rather to build them up—to feed their potential for growth. "Criticism is a good thang!"

Lesson Number Five—Stretch

Moving into the last point, Kyra draws the speech back to the moment by referencing Rogers Gates, which are just behind her during the speech.

Four years ago when I first walked through Rogers Gates, if someone had told me that if I stayed here I would someday be sitting center stage in Launer singing "Happy Birthday" to myself in a horrible southern accent in front of an audience of my peers, I would have laughed and then turned and run back to Colorado. Well, I did that 3 weeks ago. An actor can't grow on stage if she or he is not willing to stretch. And I firmly believe we can't grow in life if we aren't willing to step out of our comfort zones. The College, believe it or not just after finals week, has become a comfortable space for us and it is time to move on. I feel both excited and apprehensive of that move. However, I believe that it is time to brave the future. As Alan Alda once said, "Be brave enough to live life creatively. The creative is the place where no one else has ever been. You have to leave the city of your comfort and go into the wilderness of your intuition. You can't get there by bus, only hard work and risk and by not quite knowing what you're doing. What you'll discover will be wonderful. What you'll discover will be yourself."

She follows the theatre metaphor through to the end of her speech and incorporates strong quotations in the last few seconds.

   As I close, I challenge you, as we enter the next phase of our lives, to live your life creatively. Step out, take risks, and force yourself to grow in ways you never imagined. Aristotle claimed happiness could be found in choosing well. I say, if theatre has taught us anything, it has taught us that happiness can be found in choosing creatively. Be bold. Discover yourself by living a life that is passionate, part of the ensemble, filled with supporting roles, healthy criticism, and stretching outside of the comfort zone! Live a life of theatre.

Jeremy's Speech

Jeremy is the student president at his college and has been asked to give a brief speech to commemorate the groundbreaking ceremony for a new student commons building. He will be one of seven speakers at the outdoor event. The event coordinator suggested he speak for only two to three minutes and focus on how important the building is to the students.

FOCUSING HIS SPEECH

The groundbreaking ceremony was scheduled to be held during the weekend-long homecoming activities, so Jeremy knew there would be many students, new and old, in the audience. He knew there were several students, like himself, who would graduate before the building opened but were excited about its potential. So he decided to write and craft his language to inspire pride and anticipation for something that would be a great addition to the college and student life. Jeremy wanted the overall central idea or theme to be:

> "This is the beginning of a special place for students."

RESEARCHING HIS CONTENT

During the four years Jeremy served as a member of the student committee helping with the building's design, he took notes and collected information about what the student body needed in a new commons. He glanced through the notes and surveys to create a list of what this new space would offer the students.

From there, he crafted his speech to reflect how the new building would meet these needs.

> "This is the beginning of a special place for students."
>
> 1) a place that is open and relaxed
> 2) rooms for studying
> 3) game and TV rooms
> 4) a student lounge
> 5) coffee shop
> 6) meeting rooms
> 7) lots of soft furniture

Because Jeremy was speaking at a news-televised event with the college president, a local senator, and the major donors for the student commons, timing and proper wording were extremely important. So, he delivered his speech from this manuscript.

New Student Commons Groundbreaking

Jeremy grabs the audience's attention by briefly recognizing the audience and key people involved in the ceremony.

▶ Thank you, President Brock. I appreciate the kind words. I would like to extend a heartfelt welcome to all of you and especially to Mr. and Mrs. Adams—without your generosity, we would not be here today.

This is the beginning. The beginning of a building designed specifically for us, the students. It is:

Here, he uses repetition of sentence structure and slightly emotive language to build intensity and excitement.

- A building that will provide a space away from structured classrooms and library rules.
- A place for interaction, inspiration, and reflection.
- A safe haven where study groups will meet and friends will unwind together over a cup of coffee.
- A social rendezvous where we can let our hair down and be ourselves.
- A meeting place where important decisions will be made by students and for students to cultivate the finest opportunities and experiences possible.
- A quiet place to relax after a hard day with the books.

It has been my honor and privilege to serve on the New Student Commons Design Committee for almost four years now. When the brainstorming process first began, I never thought this day would come so quickly—that I would be able to stand before you and break this very ground for the purpose of adding the newest member of the Bass Commons family. Yet here we are.

In the conclusion, Jeremy returns to his "New Beginning" theme, which frames the speech.

▶ This is the beginning—the beginning of a building designed specifically for us, the students. This building will become a place we call our own. Home.

Tab 8: Review

CHAPTER 16 REVIEW QUESTIONS

1. What is a special occasion speech? Include in your answer an explanation for each of the four general purposes of a special occasion speech.

2. What should you consider when determining the purpose of the special occasion speech?

3. How do you research for a special occasion speech?

4. What are some helpful hints for practicing a special occasion speech?

TERMS TO REMEMBER

Chapter 16
special occasion speech (446)
speeches to celebrate (447)
speeches to commemorate (447)
speeches to inspire (447)
speeches to entertain (447)
eulogy (454)
tribute (454)
speech of introduction (456)
toast (457)
roast (457)
speech of award presentation (458)
speech of award acceptance (459)
after-dinner speech (460)
speech of inspiration (464)

Introduction

So far, this book has focused on public speaking as prepared, thoughtful communication with the intent to inform a larger audience, influence them, or accentuate a special occasion. On-the-job speaking involves much of the same dedication and preparation to achieve the communicative goal and to build continually the speaker/employee's ethos.

Think about a meeting you have attended, either at work or at other places in the community and school, where the person in charge of the meeting—let's call him John—is not prepared or does not keep the group on task. John has no agenda, has not considered what is important for this meeting, and wastes a lot of time on unimportant issues. These moments are frustrating at best and detrimental to completing the tasks at the worst. You leave the meeting with little respect for John and wish for someone else to take over in the future. If John's behavior continues, you may become very discouraged about your job.

Now, imagine that you are John's supervisor. You will need to advise John about the issues in his review, and it may be difficult to recommend him for promotion or significant pay raise until he improves.

This chapter will help you see that the process and guidelines for creating an informative or persuasive speech can help with everyday, on-the-job speaking.

In business, communication is everything.[1]

ROBERT KENT
former dean of Harvard Business School

CHAPTER 17 CONTENTS

How Will Public Speaking Help You in Your Profession?	472
How Do You Create a Business Presentation?	474
1 Starting	475
2 Researching	476
3 Creating	477
4 Presenting	478
5 Evaluating	479
How Do You Effectively Communicate in a Meeting?	480
1 Lead	480
2 Participate	481
How Do You Effectively Communicate in an Interview?	482
1 Prepare to Conduct an Interview	482
2 Prepare to Be Interviewed	484
How Do You Effectively Communicate in a Review?	488
Dylece's Interview	490
Chapter 18: Speaking in Small Groups	493
Tab 9 Review	506

How Will Public Speaking Help You in Your Profession?

Your professional success depends on effective communication within the organization where you work and with those individuals or groups your organization serves. The ability to listen and to communicate well in speaking and writing are the skills most often mentioned by employers as crucial and almost always noted in job advertisements. Understanding and practicing good public speaking skills will:

- Help you spread your professional knowledge and promote your ideas.

- Aid in sustaining a positive and professional image for you at work.

- Develop your skills as a team player.

- Improve your chances of receiving raises, bonuses, and other benefits for a job well done.

- Help you be more promotable into managerial positions.

- Bolster your abilities to carry out managerial functions such as collecting and conveying information, making your own decisions or persuading others, communicating complex ideas, and promoting a congenial workplace environment.

- Help you negotiate an increasingly global economy and intercultural workforce.

- Improve the overall effectiveness of your organization and the product or service it provides—poor communication costs time and money.

> **TIP: Applying Public Speaking Skills**
> Even though the focus of this book is oral communication, you can apply many of the skills learned here to written forms of communication. For example, formal working outlines are much like meeting agendas.

Back in the Overview of this book, you learned that to be a successful public speaker you must:

- Be audience centered.
- Select appropriate topics.
- Be knowledgeable.
- Use appropriate verbal and nonverbal behavior.
- Use appropriate appeals.
- Be creative but organized.
- Select appropriate delivery styles.
- Practice.
- Boost your confidence.

If you return to John and his problem with conducting meetings, you might be able to see the root of his problem as an inability to apply or recognize the importance of these characteristics.

For example, without an agenda or sense of purpose, John is not adequately prepared or organized for the meeting. He allows the meeting to get off topic and might even ignore audience/committee members' feedback that suggests they are frustrated or annoyed with the progress of the meeting. John's delivery could be too informal, signaling that the meeting is unimportant. Or he simply may not be confident or knowledgeable enough to focus the meeting and its agenda. Maybe John is new at leading meetings and just needs more instruction or practice. In essence, you and your colleagues must be able to exchange information, plan, hire, motivate each other, work efficiently together, and persuade.

Every time you give some type of presentation or engage in professional communication, you are creating and molding your professional image. Impressions do count and they are grounded in your ability to communicate well.

Communicating with others interpersonally, in small or large groups, will always be a part of any career you choose. Trying to offer guidance and suggestions for every communicative situation you find yourself in would be impossible. However, being audience centered, focusing on a topic that is well researched, crafting an effective message, and using an appropriate delivery will help you in situations ranging from talking to your manager to being the boss of an international corporation.

The rest of this chapter will focus on four of the most common forms of on-the-job communication. They are business presentations, meetings, interviews, and reviews. Chapter 18 will discuss small group communication, which can occur on the job, in school, or in your personal or civic life.

PRACTICING ETHICS

When you consider being an ethical and successful public speaker on the job, you must:

- Be open to differences.
- Select and use reliable evidence, logic, and reasoning.
- Be sensitive to the power of language.
- Be dedicated and thorough in citing sources.
- Accept responsibility for your communication in the short term and the long term.
- Support and endorse freedom of expression.

How Do You Create a Business Presentation?

1 **Starting**
2 **Researching**
3 **Creating**
4 **Presenting**
5 **Evaluating**

Most of the time, business presentations will be either reports or recommendations.

REPORTS

Oral *reports* are forms of informative speaking designed to present business-related information to others. What you report on is tied to your profession or expertise, but some general topics might be to:

- Account for resource usage such as supplies, hours, and employees.
- Update coworkers or other departments on project progress or concerns.
- Announce findings.
- Offer professional insight and expertise.
- Introduce new information, products, or potential purchases.

RECOMMENDATIONS

Recommendations are proposals arguing for a belief or course of action and, therefore, are a form of on-the-job persuasion. This presentation often asks the audience to:

- Approve of your proposal.
- Adopt your ideas or solutions.
- Buy your product or services.

The process for creating a public speech works for a business presentation with minor changes. For example, what you need to know about your audience becomes more focused and related to the professional setting. Remember to consider each of the five basic activities of the creative process.

1
Starting

When reporting information or making recommendations in the workplace, forgetting to consider who will be present is one of the most common mistakes. You still need to think about the personal beliefs, values, attitudes, and needs audience members might have in relationship to your topic and the workplace.

For example, you may have a potentially negative or hostile audience if you are a director presenting information about your area within the company and several other directors—who have concerns that your area is getting too much of the company's resources—are present. Or, if the company president is attending, you should be future-oriented for the betterment of the company. Getting to know your audience is as important in on-the-job speaking as in any other situation. You should seek to answer:

- Who will attend? Will any guests or key players in the organization (such as the president, a client, or an outside vendor) attend?

- What level of knowledge and understanding will the audience have about your topic? If key players are present, is their level of knowledge or understanding different?

- Given the knowledge and understanding your audience has, what types of questions or concerns are they likely to have?

- If you are making a recommendation, is there anyone in the audience that you could enlist as an advocate to help support your viewpoint?

- Given your knowledge of the audience members, what do you want them to understand, remember, or do?

- How might the speaking situation influence your message and/or the audience? What is the occasion, time of day, and place? What is the current climate within the workplace?

Once you have an idea of the audience, the depth of the topic, and the situation, you need to create a specific purpose and central idea just as you would for an informative or persuasive speech. Some examples might be:

SPECIFIC PURPOSE:	CENTRAL IDEA:
To inform the board of directors about the efficiency of the Technology Help Desk.	The Technology Help Desk has seen a significant increase in efficiency during the last 12 months.

SPECIFIC PURPOSE:	CENTRAL IDEA:
To persuade the board of directors to invest in new software to track accounting transactions.	Accounting software by Account Now will decrease human error, speed up transactions, and create necessary tracking information for yearly audits.

→ See Tab 1 if you need help with audience or situation analysis, a specific purpose, or a central idea.

REVIEW CHECKLIST for Specific Purpose and Central Idea

- ❏ Does my specific purpose contain my general purpose, my audience reference, and my objective?
- ❏ Does my central idea focus on one topic?
- ❏ Is my central idea a complete declarative sentence?
- ❏ Are both clear and concise? Do they relate to the audience and situation?

2

Researching

Researching for a business report or recommendation may involve some of the same support materials and options for locating such materials as the more traditional public speech (the Internet, the library, interviews, or surveys).

However, presentations in the workplace often require that you do more in-house research, such as collecting pertinent information from peers or those who report to you, asking for statistics or facts from other departments or vendors (someone who supplies a service or product to your organization), or collecting corporate-created documentation.

These types of support materials may even need to be created for your specific presentation. Most organizations have in-house procedures and forms required for the generation of statistics and facts. Your manager will often know the proper protocol or who to contact. Some organizations have places on their Web sites dedicated to forms and directions for such requests.

When making a recommendation, you should demonstrate how your suggestion is good for the entire organization and not just your department or area. If the recommendation involves change, be prepared to help your audience see how the change is in their best interest. Change is scary for most people, so try to anticipate objections and research/prepare a rebuttal for each one. Finally, research any recent issues that could positively or negatively influence your recommendation. Recognize those issues in your presentation and try to highlight or eliminate them as a variable in accepting your recommendation.

The key to on-the-job research is to start early. You might need to rely on someone else's schedule, and you should follow the same principles and guidelines outlined for selecting, testing, and locating support materials.

→ See Tab 2 for detailed help with researching.

CHECKLIST for Researching a Business Speech

❏ What sources outside of workplace ones can I use to support my speech? What could local libraries, Internet sources, and interviews offer me? What government agency (city, state, or federal) could be helpful?

❏ What in-house documentation could offer support for my speech?

❏ Would it be helpful to interview managers or staff directly related to my area and other areas in the company?

❏ What recent issues could positively or negatively influence my speech, both inside and outside the company?

PRACTICING ETHICS

When making recommendations, you should hold yourself to the same ethical considerations you use when trying to persuade others.
- Do not hide or omit relevant information.
- Do not manipulate information to make it appear better than it is.
- Use ethical sources and cite them appropriately.

3
Creating

Sketch out a working outline to help you visualize the materials you need to collect and help you focus. The majority of workplace presentations are usually shorter than 20 minutes. Three main points work best for this time frame, but your topic or organizational strategy might suggest a different number of points. Just keep in mind your time constraint.

Once you have collected your support materials, create the preparation outline. The chronological, topical, or spatial strategies are used most often in reports.

CHRONOLOGICAL:
The lab's budget from the past three years, current year, and the projections for the next three years demonstrates effective resource allocation.

TOPICAL:
Our current expenditures for employee benefits are divided between health, disability, and retirement.

SPATIAL:
The new conveyor system is most efficient during the creation, the assembly, and the packaging sectors.

Causal, comparative, or problem–solution strategies are most common for recommendations.

CAUSAL:
Poor response time, ineffective equipment, and inferior materials account for low consumer satisfaction.

COMPARATIVE:
Our current inventory tracking software is better than TrackWright's.

PROBLEM–SOLUTION:
Investing more money in bonuses, benefits, and employee education will improve employee retention.

Other strategies may work as well for either your report or recommendation. For example, Monroe's motivated sequence works well in an effective sales presentation.

Remember to use links between each part of your presentation to guide your listeners. The introduction and conclusion to your report or recommendation should have the same functional parts as any speech. In an on-the-job presentation, you are likely to use startling statements, narration or anecdotes, questions, and quotations as your attention-getting devices or WOW statements.

→ See Chapters 5, 6, and 7 (Tab 3) for more help with creating your outlines.

4

Presenting

The type of language you use should be appropriate to you, your audience, and the occasion. No matter what your profession is, your workplace will have a certain level of professional language and you should strive to meet it—or to be just a bit better.

For the most part, you want to use formal language when speaking on the job. When using formal language, be careful not to take shortcuts such as using contractions (*y'all*), colloquialisms (*all y'all*), slang (*dude*), acronyms, abbreviations, or jargon. Such language can appear to be sloppy, lazy, or confusing at best. Interculturally, informal language can be confusing and misunderstood.

Most often you will present your reports and recommendations extemporaneously. Your delivery should be enthusiastic. Good eye contact, especially with key people, is important to build the credibility of your message and your ethos.

If you are planning to use a presentation aid, rehearse with it. You should:

- Have multiple backups (e.g., your PowerPoint presentation on the computer and a jump drive in the event the computer must be replaced).

- Have extra equipment if possible. A spare bulb for the projector can save valuable time. Check the equipment early to have extra time to solve issues.

- Know the technical assistance personnel and contact numbers. Have a phone available.

- Create handouts or paper copies of your slide presentation. If something major goes wrong and there is no time to fix it, you can distribute the handouts to your audience. For general use after your presentation, you could make your slides available on a Web site. Be sure to include the URL in your presentation.

- If a Web site is an important part of your presentation, figure out what you will do if the site suddenly is not available or goes out partway through your presentation. Be prepared for anything.

You might need to give your report via speakerphone or videoconferencing equipment, so know how to use it and know your organization's etiquette for these procedures. You should:

- Make sure someone has tested all the connections just prior to the meeting.

- Make sure phone numbers are correct if conducting a phone conference.

- Ask everyone at the remote sites if they can adequately hear and/or see.

5

Evaluating

As the speaker or an audience member, try to listen critically, not defensively. Because business presentations are connected to your profession and livelihood, you can quickly become defensive. Withhold judgment until you have heard the entire message. As a speaker, think about the knowledge, expertise, and perspective your audience members bring to the presentation and listen to their suggestions.

After each presentation, seek out someone in the audience who can mentor you as a professional speaker. Ask him or her to evaluate your effectiveness. If you are an audience member and have praise or concerns for a fellow employee's speaking abilities or delivery methods, offer constructive evaluation.

Sometimes, businesses will ask you to complete a formal written evaluation of a report or recommendation. These evaluations tend to be general and focused on content.

→ See Chapter 11 (Tab 5) for detailed help with listening critically.

→ See Chapter 12 (Tab 5) for more on evaluating your and others' presentations.

CHECKLIST for Shaping a Business Presentation

❑ How might my topic influence the professional lives of my audience? How could that interfere with or support my message?

❑ What can I use to grab their attention?

❑ How might the workplace environment interfere with or support my message?

❑ What is an appropriate delivery style for this particular situation? How can I improve on my confidence level to help the audience listen better?

❑ During the presentation, what cues are the audience members sending me, and how can I address or use them beneficially?

CHECKLIST for Listening in the Workplace

❑ Am I giving the speaker my full attention? Did I turn off electronic devices that might distract me? Did I put away work or papers that might distract me?

❑ Am I actively listening to the content of the message?

❑ Am I critically listening to the content?

❑ If the topic is sensitive for me, am I being careful not to become defensive? Am I listening to the content rather than crafting a defensive response?

❑ Am I appropriately and effectively giving feedback to the speaker?

Building Improvement Session, Thursday 12:00–2:00 pm

1. Did you find the content of this session helpful? If so, what was particularly useful about it for you?

2. What did you find less helpful about the content of the session? What would you like more information on?

3. Was the presentation effective?

4. Were the audiovisual aids and handouts effective?

How Do You Effectively Communicate in a Meeting?

1 Lead

2 Participate

In many jobs, meetings can be a significant part of your regular activities whether you are a leader or participant. Meetings are a specific form of communicative interaction that can have different goals, such as sharing information, brainstorming ideas, making decisions, creating materials, or motivating employees. Some meetings are formal, conducted under strict rules, ethics, and customs. Usually formal meetings best fit civic organizations, clubs, and government. Informal meetings are more common in the workplace but should adhere to rules, ethics, and customs appropriate to the work environment.

1

Lead

If you are leading the meeting, these guidelines will help you conduct an effective and productive meeting.

- Have a purpose and share it. Holding an unnecessary, undefined meeting wastes time and lowers morale.

- Create an agenda and send a copy to each attendee. An agenda is a written document outlining the meeting's goal and what will happen during the meeting, item by item. Depending on your workplace norms or what works best for you as a leader, your agenda could simply list each item to be considered during the meeting or it could be very detailed. Detailed agendas often list how each item will be considered (for information, for discussion, or for action), who is presenting the item, and how much time will be spent on each item. In either case, you want your information to be specific enough that participants can prepare accordingly. Include the date, time, and location of the meeting.

- If the meeting was called suddenly and you have no time for an advance agenda, quickly type one to be distributed at the beginning of the meeting or take a few minutes to outline orally what will be considered.

- If you will call on someone to speak, make sure he or she is aware of when and for how long. Give the person enough notice to prepare.

- Set beginning and ending times for the meeting, and share this information with participants in advance. Make sure you have a visible clock or watch during the meeting.

- Select a room large enough to accommodate known participants and maybe a few extra, in case a participant invites someone else. Make sure all necessary equipment is present and working before the start of the meeting.

- Start your meetings on time and end when you said you would, even if you are not finished.

- Arrive a few minutes early and chat with participants. By doing so, you personalize your relationship with the group and give them time to "talk off-topic" about things that might otherwise come up during the meeting.

- Turn off your pager, PDA, unnecessary computers, and/or cell phone, and close the door to minimize interruptions. Doing so in front of the participants can be a subtle hint that they should do the same.

- Conduct introductions if new participants or guests are present.

- Keep control of the meeting. Do not let a participant take it over or monopolize the time. Limit the amount of time someone can speak, and try to engage all participants. Be energetic and focused.

- Save enough time at the end of the meeting to summarize what transpired, divide up responsibilities or tasks, ask if there are any questions, and thank the participants for their input.

- If needed, arrange a time and date for the next meeting.

2
Participate

Participants share the responsibility of using meeting time wisely and productively. As a participant, you should:

- Respond quickly when asked to participate in a meeting. You may be important to an agenda item, and the meeting may need to be rescheduled if you cannot attend.

- Read the agenda as soon as you get it, to see what you need to prepare. Anticipate how you might respond to questions about each item, and do your research.

- During the meeting, focus on the agenda items and keep your discussion to a minimum. Allow others to participate and try not to interrupt. Be enthusiastic.

- Ask questions when appropriate, and write down your follow-up responsibilities.

→ See Chapter 18 (Tab 9) for additional information on leading and participating in small group situations, such as meetings.

How Do You Effectively Communicate in an Interview?

1 Prepare to Conduct an Interview
2 Prepare to Be Interviewed

Whether you are the interviewer or the interviewee, conducting and giving a successful job interview is difficult work that is important to the future of a business and your career. Interviewing in the digital age has become even more complicated. Interviews can now be (and often are) conducted by phone, computer, or videoconferencing.

1
Prepare to Conduct an Interview

One of the best ways to learn how to conduct an interview is to observe someone else, who is good at interviewing conduct an interview. If you know you will be in a position to interview candidates, try to observe senior employees as they interview others. You should pay attention to the questions that seem to elicit a genuine response and the overall feeling of the interview.

Some interviewers are very aggressive and try to deliberately put the interviewee in a stressful situation to gauge how the interviewee handles it. Still others will ask questions designed to elicit a behavioral response. "What would you do if . . . ?" If your human resources (HR) office offers sessions on how to conduct interviews, attend them.

You're only as good as the people you hire.[2]

RAY KROC
founder of McDonald's

Overall, here are some general guidelines.

1. Meet with your HR personnel to determine what you can and cannot ask during an interview. It is illegal to ask about age, marital status, children, childcare arrangements, religion, gender preferences, citizenship, where a person lives and with whom, clubs or social organization membership, arrest record, or how someone was discharged from the military. Requesting personal information (such as height, weight, and/or disabilities) is prohibited as well. However, you can ask if a person is able to do a specific task or test them in some cases. You should ask your HR office if testing is acceptable.

2. Closely review the candidate's cover letter, résumé, and any other material. Research the candidate's past employment and positions. Make note of how long the candidate has held previous and similar positions, if she or he was promoted and how often, and any other indications of job successes, failures, or concerns. You might ask them to explain any positive or negative issues.

3. Set up a time and location. Allow 45 to 60 minutes for each interview, and select a location that is comfortable and quiet (no phones). Do not let the location intimidate the candidate unless that is your intent. Tell the candidate what she or he should bring, if anything. You might ask for a list of references, a writing sample, or a copy of their résumé if that was not a part of their application materials.

4. Construct a list of questions you want and need to ask. Using a set of standard questions asked of all of the candidates may be the best way to ensure a fair selection process. You may need to clear these questions with HR. Try to begin with easier questions to ease the candidate into the process. For example, "Tell me about yourself." Most people can and are willing to talk about themselves. Then move to more-complex questions like:

   Why do you feel you are a good candidate for this position?

   What have you done in the past that you feel has helped you to prepare for this position?

   Tell me about a time you felt you went above and beyond the call of duty at work.

5. Observe the candidate closely. Is the candidate dressed appropriately? Well-groomed? Does he or she look you in the eye and shake your hand firmly? Is the candidate energetic and enthusiastic?

6. When listening to the candidate's questions, pay attention to content and how comfortable or uncomfortable he or she was in answering. Does the response sound generic and/or overly prepared?

7. When specific job qualifications are important, you might set up a numeric ranking system for those qualifications and total the scores for each candidate. However, do not rely on this system alone.

8. Think about how the candidate's personality will fit in with other employees and the goal of the business.

9. Check references and/or conduct background checks if required.

10. If possible, have several members at your organization interview the candidate.

2

Prepare to Be Interviewed

Alex is graduating from college in a few months and is concerned about interviewing. He worked for his Dad's landscape business throughout most of high school and college. The only time he has been interviewed was for an on-campus job, and the hiring professor already knew him and asked few questions. So, Alex has not had the opportunity to create a résumé or take part in a formal interview. He is not sure how to begin the process or where to find information.

Like Alex, if you truly want a job, you have to work at it. You may be required to take several tests, participate in many interviews, and/or provide sample work—all to help you stand out from the rest as the right candidate. Trying to find the right job can be as time-consuming as a full-time job and takes dedication. Even getting an interview requires that you dedicate time and care to your application. You should always type, proofread, and update any material you send as part of your application. Tailor the material to the specific job and hiring organization.

THE APPLICATION

Although filling out and creating your application package is not directly related to oral communication, it is the first step to getting the job interview. Many of the skills you have discovered in this book can apply to the application process as well. You want to build strong ethos from the beginning and succinctly sell yourself as the best candidate. If your application is messy, incomplete, or too general, the reader will view you as a poor applicant. Here is a quick checklist to help you with the application process.

TIP: Finding Help with Interviewing

While you are still connected with a college or university, use the available resources created to help you with landing your first job.

- If your institution has a Career Center, ask them for help with the application process, creating a résumé, and/or setting up a mock interview session.
- Look for examples and guidance from Internet sources or at your local libraries.
- Attend any special sessions at your institution designed to help you succeed, such as how to handle yourself at a business dinner or recognize illegal interview questions. Sessions like this can offer practical advice.
- Take classes designed to assist you. Often a major will have one class designed for mentoring you as you move out into your field, and some communication or business courses are created for this very purpose.

CHECKLIST for Your Application

- ❏ Did I tailor my letter, résumé, and/or application to the specific job, requirements, and organization?
- ❏ Did I type and proofread my letter, résumé, and/or application? (Have someone else check it as well.)
- ❏ Did I update my résumé and reference list? (Always ask permission to list someone as a reference, and give him or her a copy of the job description and your current résumé.)

BEFORE THE INTERVIEW

Once you have an interview scheduled, prepare for it much like you would for a speech. An interview is like an informative and persuasive speech rolled into one. You want to tell (inform) the potential employers about you and persuade them to hire you. You need to research the audience and the topic (the hiring organization and you); create and craft what you want to cover in the interview; think about how you will present yourself; and evaluate the effectiveness of the interview. Much of the information from Tabs 1–5 of this book will assist you, and the table below gives additional tactics.

PREPARING BEFORE THE DAY OF YOUR INTERVIEW

WHAT SHOULD YOU DO?	HOW CAN YOU DO IT?
Research the job.	• Search on the Internet or at the library for information related to the job. • Interview someone with insight into the specifics of such a job. If interviewing someone as research, ask him/her to suggest questions you should ask of the potential employer. • Try to find information about salaries in your area, specific duties of the job, potential for advancement, etc.
Research the hiring organization.	• Check news articles, press releases, the organization's Web site, annual reports, trade journals, and other specialized publications. • Talk to someone with ties to the organization, if appropriate and possible. • Try to get a feel for the company's focus, hiring practices, growth, and employee satisfaction.
Prepare an introduction of yourself and a closing statement.	• Often, the first request you will get is "Tell me a bit about yourself." Think about some professional and personal traits and experiences you have that might interest the interviewer. • Review your résumé so that you are very familiar with the content and layout.
Research and prepare for questions you may be asked.	• Look up standard interview questions in books, magazines, and online. • Craft and practice your answers to them.

Prepare questions to ask the interviewer(s).	• Use the information you gathered when researching the job and the hiring organization and create some questions. Search online for help. Type in "questions to ask employers during interview" or something similar.
	• Some examples:
	    What are the organization's future plans for growth?
	    Are there training or educational opportunities with this position?
	    What are the normal promotion steps for this position?

Be very familiar with your application material.	• Read over ALL your application material several times. • If any issues in the material might cause concerns for an employer, prepare a response to those potential concerns. • Think about how the materials show that you are the best candidate for the position. Prepare to cover any issues you think are particularly important.

THE INTERVIEW DAY

On the day of the interview, you want to do some last-minute research to see if anything has changed related to the organization where you will interview. You can do this by checking the organization's Web site, the local newspaper, or other possible local sources. If you discover something that raises a question for you about the organization, mention or ask your interviewer about the developments during the interview if possible and appropriate. Here are a few pointers for getting yourself ready.

Dressing for Success

Dress for the interview and the particular job. Try to discover the organization's approved dress code and dress slightly more formally than the code for the organization or position.

In most interviews today, men should wear traditional business attire (dark, conservative suits, white, long-sleeved shirts, and silk ties that are not flashy). Women should wear a conservative (dark is best) suit or dress and avoid distracting jewelry or makeup. Both men and women should remove unusual body piercings or other distracting ornamentation and perfumes/colognes/lotions. You should be well groomed and your clothes pressed. You want to be memorable as a potential asset, not stick out for the wrong reasons.

Getting to the Interview

Plan your arrival, including how to get to the location. You want to arrive early enough that you can sit somewhere quietly and look over your notes one last time. Being late to an interview is unacceptable for almost any reason. Be on time.

Before entering the building, switch off your digital watch, cell phone, PDA, and/or pager—anything that could make noise. Never use one of these devices or take a call or message during an interview. It is a sure way to lose the job.

Being Interviewed

Give a good firm handshake and make direct eye contact with the interviewer(s); first impressions begin there, and they are hard to reverse. Try to chat for a few seconds to seem personable and to calm your nerves.

When answering questions:

- Be confident.
- Show enthusiasm.
- Make eye contact.
- Articulate your words.
- Use formal language but be conversational.
- Watch for and respond appropriately to nonverbal cues.
- Ask questions at the appropriate times.
- Try to find just the right vocal speed. You do not want to rush or be too hesitant.
- Construct answers that are more than one word or sentence but not too long.
- Never make up information or lie. If you don't know something, say so—though also be careful not to do that too much. If you find that you need to say so a lot, you weren't prepared.

End with an enthusiastic conclusion. Ask when you might hear something, and give a firm handshake and thank-you as you leave.

Redirecting Illegal Questions

Due to federal and state laws, prospective employers are prohibited from asking certain questions that are not related to the job you are applying for. Most questions that relate to personal information are illegal. Therefore, the interviewer should not ask questions related to your marital status, race, ethnicity, gender, religion, disabilities, country of origin, sexual preferences, age, or arrest record.

Interviewers may accidentally or intentionally ask an illegal question, nonetheless. If the interviewer is asking illegal questions, you will need to decide if this is a legal matter that needs to be pursued or if this is simply not the job for you. However, during the interview, you should try to steer the question back to your qualifications for the job. The table below offers some response options.

After the Interview

Send a thank-you e-mail or note the day after the interview.

Evaluate your feelings about your performance and the interview process. Think about the content of your responses, your delivery, and the effectiveness of the materials you submitted as your application. Evaluate them as you would a speech.

➔ Refer to the speech evaluation guidelines in Chapter 12 (Tab 5) if needed.

If you do not get the job and you think it is appropriate, ask the interviewer if he or she would offer you suggestions on how to improve your skills or tell you what was the deciding factor in not getting the job. Be careful not to make this a defensive question. Frame it as a growth moment for you.

Make a list of things you want to change or work on before your next interview. Practice interviewing with someone else. Try to interview as much as possible to continue improving.

ILLEGAL QUESTION	EFFECTIVE RESPONSE
Are you a U.S. citizen?	"I am authorized to work in the United States."
How will you deal with children (or your spouse) and business travel?	"I can meet the needs of my travel and work schedule." "I have nothing in my personal life that would prevent me from doing a good job or would compromise the organization." Try to follow with a positive, related question, such as: "I have always had beneficial experiences traveling for business and training at my previous job. What kind of traveling would the job require?"

How Do You Effectively Communicate in a Review?

Reviews (or performance appraisals) are part of a process to assess and discuss employee work performance. They are usually conducted by the employee's supervisor or manager and can include human resources staff. Like the evaluation process discussed in Chapter 12, reviews seek to recognize strengths and accomplishments as well as to identify areas needing improvement and offer suggestions. This process usually occurs annually but can be sooner for various reasons. The process usually includes some type of standard evaluation sheet and an oral discussion of the employee's performance. A good evaluation should describe the work behavior, judge its worth, and logically justify that view based on rational norms.

➜ See Chapter 12 (Tab 5) for more on how to evaluate.

RECEIVING REVIEWS

Even when you have had a great year at work, the review process can seem a bit nerve-racking. So meet the evaluation process head-on with a commitment to do an even better job next year. Listen critically, not emotionally, to what the evaluator is suggesting. Do not let other employees influence your response to the evaluation process. Be confident that if you do a good job, it will be reflected in the evaluation. Read through the next section on giving reviews, for more insights into the process.

REMEMBER
Try to remember what Chapter 12 suggests about the positive aspects of evaluation.
- Evaluation is a "good thing."
- Evaluation teaches critical thinking.
- Evaluation builds your confidence.
- Evaluation makes you better.

GIVING REVIEWS

If you are a manager, evaluating your employees is one of your most crucial and significant tasks. Your evaluation can, and often should, influence an employee's morale, retention, and the rewards he or she will receive. Here are a few suggestions:

- Locate a standard evaluation form. Your organization may have one that you must use and is consistent with all areas of the organization. If not, you can make one by researching what others use or collecting examples from the Internet and other written sources. Make sure you include a place for your signature, the employee's signature, and the date you discussed the evaluation. You might include a section where the employee can add two or three goals for the coming year.

- Employees should never be surprised by your reviews if you have given them feedback throughout the year. As a manager or supervisor, you should consistently mentor and advise those who report to you. This review process should simply be a summary of your periodic conversations with each employee.

- If the evaluation form allows for explanation, provide details. The employee will be better able to improve or maintain a good work ethic if he or she understands the issues.

- On the written form, try to start with the good and follow with suggestions for improvement. Find a location for the oral review that is not threatening (unless, in extreme cases, that is necessary). Be confident in your evaluation but not authoritarian. Using a friendly and conversational approach recognizes this is often a difficult process for employees.

- Ask if the employee understands the evaluation or has any concerns with it. Try to come to a consensus on the value of the suggestions. Before ending the evaluation, both of you should sign and date the forms. Make a copy for the employee.

CONFIDENCE BOOSTER

The great football coach Vince Lombardi once said, "Confidence is contagious. So is the lack of confidence." So surround yourself with colleagues who are confident and positive in their jobs. Demonstrate confidence in what you do—it will lift others and come back to you.

EMPLOYEE PERFORMANCE EVALUATION

Employee Name: _____

Department: _____   Position: _____

Evaluation Purpose: _____   Evaluation Date: _____
_____ Annual _____   New Employee _____ Other _____

Position Knowledge
Consider ability to apply knowledge to daily activities:

☐ Below expectations   ☐ Marginal expectations   ☐ Meets expectations   ☐ Frequently exceeds expectations   ☐ Consistently

Comments: _____

Dylece's Interview

Dylece has a Bachelor of Science degree in business administration and is applying for her first position after college. Dylece has applied to several banks and financial institutions and has an interview with Commerce Bank. She has received a call from Human Resources at the bank and been told that she will meet with several bank employees for her interview. The major portion of the interview will be with Mr. Seth Mason, Senior Credit Manager.

PREPARING TO BE INTERVIEWED

Before thinking about questions she will ask, Dylece asked one of her professors about how to research the bank. Dr. Campbell recommended that she check Commerce Bank's performance ratings on Moody's and Standard & Poor's to see how the company compares to averages in the banking industry. Also, checking out the bank Web site could be very helpful. Dr. Campbell told Dylece that if the bank is publicly traded, it should have its investor information somewhere on the home page. Dr. Campbell also offered some advice on questions she should ask.

When Dylece checked out Commerce's Web site, she found useful information, including a press release indicating that Commerce is number three on the *Forbes* Magazine list of best banks in the United States.

Armed with the advice from Dr. Campbell and the information she gathered, Dylece created her list of questions.

Dylece selected a professional suit to wear and made extra copies of her résumé. She left early for the interview and read over her application material one more time in the car before entering the bank.

Commerce Bank Interview

Monday, April 5, 2010, at 9:30 a.m.

Contact person: Ms. Sally O'Dell, Human Resources Director

Main Interviewer: Mr. Seth Mason, Senior Credit Manager

My Questions:

1. I noticed Forbes ranked Commerce as the third-best bank in the United States in January. That is a huge accomplishment, especially during an economic recession. What steps did the bank take to achieve this? What strategies are you using to stay there?

2. Does the Bank invest in its people? What types of training and development do you offer your employees?

3. What is the corporate culture like?

4. What is your employee retention rate? Explain why it is high or low?

5. What potential is there for moving up in the organization?

PREPARING TO CONDUCT THE INTERVIEW

Seth Mason has just been promoted to a senior management position, so he is somewhat inexperienced at conducting interviews. However, he has been a part of several interviews conducted by a committee. First, he asked the HR office for rules, regulations, or guidelines. Then, he wrote out several questions and notes relating to Dylece's application materials and describing the duties related to the particular job Dylece applied for.

Commercial Financial Analyst Interview

Interviewee: Ms. Dylece Williams
Interview appointment: April 5, 2010 – 9:30 a.m.

Questions:

1. Tell me a bit about yourself.
2. You were really active in college. What did you like the best about your college experience?
3. What skill set do you bring to the bank?
4. Where do you see yourself in five years? Ten years? How do you plan to get there?
5. Provide an example of how you would put your customers first.
6. Provide an example of how you work or could work in a team environment.
7. We always strive to produce quality results in a timely fashion for our customers. How do you handle multiple tasks at once and increased responsibility? Can you provide an example?
8. How would you handle a deadline-oriented environment? How is your attention to detail? Provide an example.
9. What do you consider to be your best accomplishment so far?
10. You résumé suggests you have many different interests and hobbies. Why do you want to work in the banking industry?

Commercial Financial Analyst Duties:

- Analyze borrower financial information and calculate lending terms
- Analyze companies' lending risks
- Calculate debt service coverage and determine repayment terms for fixed and floating loans and leases

Seth created a standard list of questions that he planned to ask each interviewee.

Seth wanted Dylece to be comfortable, so he decided to conduct the interview in a more informal seating area in his office. Right before her interview time, Seth read over her application material and his questions one more time.

18

SPEAKING IN SMALL GROUPS

Introduction

It will be a rare occasion when you are not working in a small group. Think about a holiday, like Christmas Day, when you work with family members to fix a special meal; you are working in a small group situation. When you play football, basketball, softball, baseball, or soccer, you are working in a small group. Religious and social club meetings, as well as some class assignments, require you to interact with others in a small group.

Once you enter the workforce, many of your daily activities will be in small group settings. Engineers creating a more fuel-efficient car; doctors, nurses, and technicians working in the emergency or operating rooms; police officers working in the same precinct; and almost anyone employed must work together with others to provide products and services. Even if you work from home, you have to interact by phone and/or online, and you will participate in and schedule these virtual meetings with others.

Speaking in small groups is a complex process. You need to effectively communicate as the group works toward its goal, and often you will also communicate the group's findings in a more formal presentation format. Much of what you have learned previously in this book will help you with both of these tasks.

Applying your public speaking skills to the small group setting begins with knowing how groups work. Therefore, this chapter will help you understand what effective roles and behaviors you can use and how you can successfully solve problems in small group situations. The last section offers ideas for presenting small group findings when necessary.

CHAPTER 17: On-the-Job Speaking   471

CHAPTER 18 CONTENTS

What Is a Small Group?   494

What Roles Can You Play in a Small Group?   496
    1 Leader   496
    2 Member   498

How Do Groups Make Decisions or Solve Problems?   500

How Do Groups Present Their Findings?   502
    1 Determine the Format   502
    2 Create the Presentation   503
    3 Give the Presentation   503
    4 Listen and Evaluate   503

Ramón's Group   504

Tab 9 Review   506

What Is a Small Group?

Determining an exact definition of a *small group* is difficult because the term *small* is so ambiguous. Small could be two, 20, or more, depending on what you are comparing it to. However, some parameters can help you define what constitutes small group communication.

First, what number of people constitutes a small group? *Two* people communicating with each other is called a *dyad*. According to Katherine Adams and Gloria Galanes in *Communicating in Groups,* dyads function differently because they immediately cease to exist if one person leaves the dyad, and they do not have multiple communication networks or leadership hierarchies. Therefore, a **small group** must include at least three or more people. The upper number is more complicated. Indeed, if you asked several communication scholars for a limit, most would say it falls somewhere between 7 and 20, with the majority in the range of 7 to 12 communicators.

What communication scholars can agree on is defining small group communication based on how the process works. **Small group communication** occurs when three or more people unite over time for a common purpose, feel a sense of belongingness, and have the ability to influence each other and the outcome. Most often, these people come together in face-to-face interaction, but today, virtual groups are possible. **Virtual small groups** function much like other small groups, only they may never or rarely meet face-to-face.

SMALL GROUP TYPES

Small groups can be either social or working groups. **Social groups** form when individuals come together informally for the purpose of socializing. These groups may use an activity, what appears to be a major goal, as a means for gathering and interacting. For example, a group of friends may meet once a month as a Gourmet Club, fixing meals and swapping recipes. The goal is to socialize and the gourmet theme is the means.

Working groups are more formal and are created to work on a specific task. A study group you form for a particular class is a working group.

The table below describes the different types of working groups you might encounter in your personal and professional lives.

SMALL GROUP DEVELOPMENT

According to Bruce Tuckman in "Stages of Small Group Development Revisited," when small groups form, they go through five phases.

- **Forming:** The group creates its identity, seeks guidance and direction from the leader, and determines membership and roles.

- **Storming:** The group starts focusing on its goal and may become complex as power and relationship issues emerge.

- **Norming:** Occurs after the conflict of the storming phase is expressed and addressed. The members begin to outline necessary tasks and assignments to achieve their goal.

- **Performing:** The "real work" phase where the group conducts the work necessary to make a decision or solve a problem.

- **Terminating/Reforming:** The end point for the entire group. The group is done with that task and either disbands or reforms with a new goal.

TYPE OF BUSINESS OR CIVIC WORKING GROUP	WHAT IS IT?
Decision-making group	A group that draws conclusions and decides policies for action
Problem-solving group	A group united to solve a particular problem
Focus group	A group that addresses an issue and searches for the best solution
Brainstorming team	A group charged with generating ideas but not evaluating them
Project team	A group consisting of members with the necessary expertise to perform all the activities required to create and produce a product, service, etc.
Advisory group	A group of experts who offer skilled advice to an individual or group that needs to make a decision
Quality assurance group	A group that works to improve the quality of an organization's products, services, etc.

What Roles Can You Play in a Small Group?

1 Leader

2 Member

When a small group is formed, you will either play the role of leader or member. A leader is sometimes called a chairperson (or chair). As a member of the group, your role will be further defined as the group moves through the development phases.

1

Leader

During small group communication, a *leader* is a person who guides the group toward its goal. The tools for analyzing and researching a speech's audience, situation, and topic will help when leading a group. For example, leaders need to analyze a group's membership to determine strengths and weaknesses. Leaders will also analyze the situation surrounding the group's task and the broader audience that its decisions will affect. Developing a specific purpose and central idea that encapsulate the group's goal will focus group activities.

In some groups, although rarely in a working group, you may not have a leader. This absence of leadership usually evolves and works best when each member has equal influence and status or in groups like advisory groups or focus groups. There are three general types of leaders, based on how the leader is selected for the position.

TYPE OF LEADER	HOW IS THIS LEADER CHOSEN?
Implied leader	When other group members defer to a member because of her or his rank, expertise, or other characteristics
Designated leader	By election or appointment when the group is formed
Emergent leader	During the early stages of the group's formation, a member evolves as the leader

→ See Tab 1 for help with audience or situational analysis and focusing a topic.

LEADERSHIP STYLES

Leadership style refers to how a leader chooses to lead or influence the group. The leader may select the style based on what he or she is comfortable with or what is necessary with the group members and situation.

The three leadership styles are:

Authoritarian leaders (also called *autocratic*) assume and maintain control over the group. Such leaders tell their groups what needs to be done, and how, and ask for minimal advice from the members. Although authoritarian leaders can be demanding and controlling, they are effective in situations where the solution to a problem is obvious and simply needs to be carried out; when time is short; when members are new to the workplace or situation; or in times of crisis or disaster. This style is not a license to degrade, abuse, or threaten, and it requires a wise use of power.

Democratic leaders (also called *participative*) involve group members in decision-making and/or creative processes. This leaders guide the discussion and offer insight. Here, either the group makes the final decision or the leader maintains control over the final decision. This leadership style works best when you need the knowledge and expertise of others.

Laissez-faire leaders (also called *delegative* or *free-reign*) give group members complete freedom with the process necessary to reach the goal. However, the leader is still responsible for the the final decisions. This style of leadership works best when members are capable of analyzing the situation and doing something about it. However, the laissez-faire style is often misused, leaving the group confused and frustrated.

TASKS OF A LEADER

The main responsibility of a leader is to facilitate and manage the types of communication (procedural, task, and maintenance) required to reach a group's goal.

Procedural communication includes the routine interactions necessary for group functions, such as:

- Establishing the places, dates, and times the group will meet.
- Setting and distributing the agenda.
- Finding a room, setting up equipment, and taking care of personal needs (water, coffee, comfortable space, etc.).
- Preparing and distributing materials.
- Taking notes or minutes or appointing someone else to do so.
- Summarizing at the end of each meeting.

Task communication includes the necessary interactions during the group meetings to keep the group on task to reach its goal. These interactions include:

- Helping the group with decision-making or problem-solving processes.
- Helping research and collect information.
- Pushing the group to consider all options.
- Assigning tasks to each member.
- Helping the group reach a consensus.

Maintenance communication activities involve creating and maintaining effective interpersonal relationships within the group:

- Controlling conflict and bad behavior.
- Determining if members are fulfilling their tasks.
- Creating and maintaining a supportive environment.

2
Member

Usually, you will assume the responsibility of group member. Although the situation will dictate the number of group members, many communication scholars suggest that the most effective groups have seven to nine members and a leader. With too few members, you might not have the necessary knowledge base; too many members will impede the decision-making process. In a classroom setting, groups of four or five seem to work well.

As a member, you will bring your expertise to the group, be given special tasks to complete, and take on certain membership roles. Members can use audience and situational analysis to examine who and what will be affected by a group's decisions and to conduct research to guide those decisions. Outlining can help organize ideas.

Positive member roles are clustered as either group task or group interaction roles. If you take on a **group task role**, your behavior will assist the group at completing tasks and the group goal. A **group interaction role** helps create and maintain a positive climate and interpersonal relationships.

Not all group member roles are positive, however. A member (or members) of the group might play a **self-centered role** by focusing on his or her own needs.

Adapted from Thomas E. Harris and John C. Sherblom's text *Small Group and Team Communication*, the table on page 499 outlines the various roles members may play in a group.

➜ See Tab 1 for help with analysis, Tab 2 for research guidance, and Tab 3 for outlining ideas.

CONFIDENCE BOOSTER

Rarely will you find yourself as a member of a group without having a good reason to be involved in that group. Take pride in being asked or elected to join a group and try to overcome your apprehensions. The effectiveness of the group depends on participation from everyone. If you are very concerned about openly participating, gradually participate by offering to take notes or be the one who encourages others to speak. Offer supportive nonverbal cues and/or statements. Eventually, you will find yourself contributing.

PRACTICING ETHICS

To be a productive and ethical member of a small group, you must act in a responsible way. Recognize and dedicate yourself to the 5-C principles of small group membership to become a productive and ethical participant.

Commitment:
Be willing to give the group your complete attention and align your personal goals with the group's goal. Do not impair or destroy the group goal by manipulating others for a personal goal.

Confidential:
Often, sensitive issues are discussed by groups, so be respectful of privacy and personal conversation. Only share group discussions outside of the small group when appropriate.

Coalesce:
Allow the group members to come together and work *with*—rather than against—each other. Avoid interpersonal conflicts by being civil, courteous, respectful, and inclusive. Encourage all to contribute.

Contribute:
Use your talent for the betterment of the group and complete your tasks. An effective group requires EVERY member to be responsible.

Concentrate:
Stay on task and focus on the group goal. Do not hijack the discussion.

GROUP TASK ROLES (Positive)	**Initiator** proposes and prods the group for new ideas, goals, plans, activities, etc.
	Elaborator asks for clarification, expands on ideas or suggestions, and develops thoughts.
	Coordinator puts ideas together, organizes, and promotes cooperation.
	Summarizer pulls work and ideas together and makes connections to previous work and discussion.
	Recorder takes good notes on the proceedings, prepares minutes, or creates reports.
	Evaluator thinks critically and offers effective analysis of ideas.
	Information giver or seeker researches for data, facts, and other materials related to the goal of the group.
	Opinion giver draws conclusions about group actions or discussion based on his or her beliefs, values, interpretations, and judgments.
	Clarifier asks for more details to make the group's discussion less ambiguous.
	Consensus-taker asks how the group feels about issues, discussions, or actions.
	Agenda-setter suggests a path or procedure to take or how to make a decision.
GROUP INTERACTION ROLES (Positive)	**Encourager** reinforces group cohesiveness by recognizing and openly appreciating contributions.
	Supporter tends to follow the lead of other members by supporting and agreeing with others' proposals or ideas.
	Harmonizer works to relieve tension by mediating, compromising, or offering new suggestions.
	Gatekeeper allows all members to have a say in the process.
	Observer focuses on observing and commenting on the process the group is taking.
	Standard-setter helps set and enforce standards, rules, and norms.
	Tension-reliever works at making members feel at ease with each other by encouraging informality, using humor, and/or developing a group spirit.
SELF-CENTERED ROLES (Negative)	**Blocker** blocks progress by *constantly* objecting, repeatedly bringing up old issues, and refusing to accept or support a group decision.
	Attacker prevents effective collaboration by harshly criticizing and threatening others.
	Avoider does not contribute, refuses to deal with conflict, hides emotions, and cannot take a stance.
	Dominator dominates, interrupts, and refuses to listen to other options or opinions.
	Attention-seeker is always boasting and calling attention to herself/himself or engages in games or humor for attention.
	Joker engages in games and humor that distract group work.
	Special-interest pleader pleads for his or her own subgroup or special interest at the expense of group time and resources.

How Do Groups Make Decisions or Solve Problems?

Often groups are brought together to make a decision or to solve a problem. Even a class's small group assignments frequently complete one of these tasks. Numerous decision-making methods are available and many are variations of reflective thinking, first proposed by philosopher John Dewey (1910).

Thomas E. Harris and John C. Sherblom outline one of these variations, called the ***DECIDE model,*** for decision making and problem solving. Their unique approach makes it easy to remember the steps, and with slight modifications, DECIDE resembles the creative process for any type of public speaking. The table on page 501 explains each step.

1
STARTING

2
RESEARCHING

3
CREATING

4
PRESENTING
→ See pages 502–503

5
LISTENING &
EVALUATING

THE DECIDE MODEL

THE STEPS	WHAT NEEDS TO BE ESTABLISHED	EXAMPLES
► Define the goal and problem	For whom is it a problem? What is the problem? Why, when, where, and how is it a problem?	The 5,000 jobs lost last year are a concern for the city, industry, housing market, and taxpayers, as it demonstrates a loss in growth and potential.
► Examine issues preventing goal success	What is causing the problem and how severe is it? To reach your goal, what would be satisfactory, realistic, or achievable?	Closing of major industries and lost jobs in higher education and the medical field seem to be the sources of the problem. This job loss is 50 percent more than 2008. Our goal is to reduce the number of jobs lost by 25 percent (still above 2008).
► Consider alternatives	What are the standards for solving the problem? What are potential solutions?	Potential solutions are to rally for more state funding of higher education and medicine or to work at attracting new businesses.
► Initiate a decision	Which solution is the best according to the group?	Because the state budget is being drastically cut, rallying for more state funds seems useless. Therefore, we should work to bring more new businesses to town.
► Develop a plan	How will you implement the solution?	We will create tax decrease incentives, build assistance programs, and step up public relations activities to attract growing industries.
► Evaluate the results	Did the solution work? Was it too costly?	Although somewhat costly initially to the city and still high, the lost-job rate did drop 15 percent, which was better than for any other city in the state.

PRACTICING ETHICS

Avoid groupthink. *Groupthink* is the willingness to conform to what the group thinks at the moment rather than to critically think about the issue and potentially come to a better conclusion. According to Adams and Galanes, thoroughly exploring the problem, encouraging "anything goes" brainstorming, establishing norms for evaluating conclusions, preventing leaders from stating preferences too early, and inviting outside input will help prevent groupthink.

How Do Groups Present Their Findings?

1 **Determine the Format**

2 **Create the Presentation**

3 **Give the Presentation**

4 **Listen and Evaluate**

Once a group comes to a decision, the members may need to present their findings or decisions to a larger audience. To present findings, the group must decide on the format, create the presentation, give the presentation, listen and watch for the audience's feedback, and evaluate the presentation.

1

Determine the Format

There are five small group presentation formats.

Group oral report:
A speech reporting the findings, conclusions, and decisions of the group and given by the group leader or someone selected from the group to do so. A question and answer session may follow.

Forum:
An interactive session between the audience and the small group. Here, the audience members play a more active role by offering their comments as well as asking questions. A forum may follow a symposium or prepared speech. Forums require significant knowledge of the topic.

Symposium:
A series of short reports by each group member, presented to an audience. Each report is coordinated to prevent duplication of information. A moderator introduces and connects each speech and summarizes after all are given. There may be a question and answer session.

Colloquium:
A public discussion between the group members in front of a public audience. The members usually have divergent views, a moderator facilitates, and the audience may participate in a question and answer session.

Panel discussion:
Usually led by a moderator or chairperson, this format is designed to give information about an issue, problem, or recommendation.

2
Create the Presentation

- Determine the goal and central idea of the presentation. As with an informative or persuasive speech, this step requires analyzing your audience and the situation as well as narrowing your topic. Make sure each group member understands and supports the goal and focus of the presentation.

→ See Chapter 2 (Tab 1) for help with focusing a central idea.

- Adhere to your presentation format.
- Assign individual tasks. If you agree to do something, do it.
- Create preparation and delivery outlines for each member. Also, think about electing someone to serve as moderator to help connect the individual parts, giving the presentation a solid structure. Moderators should also try to facilitate interaction between the presenters and the audience.

→ See Tab 3 for more on creating outlines.

- Use language appropriate to the audience and situation. Define any specialized terms.

CHECKLIST for Creating Group Presentations

❏ Has my group determined the goal?

❏ Does each member have an assigned task?

❏ Did we create preparation and delivery outlines?

❏ Do we have a moderator?

❏ Have we created necessary presentation aids? Are they consistent?

❏ Have we rehearsed enough to feel confident?

3
Give the Presentation

- Create necessary presentation aids. If each member creates his or her own, try to coordinate them.
- Rehearse as a group several times. Working with each other and using the presentation aids will uncover any trouble spots. Time your presentation to ensure that you are within the limit. Panels and forums are usually extemporaneous or impromptu. Symposiums and oral reports may be delivered extemporaneously, from a manuscript, or from memory.
- Dress for the occasion.
- Use technology if appropriate and available.

→ Refer to Tab 4 for help with language, delivery, or presentation aids.

4
Listen and Evaluate

- Listen/watch for verbal and nonverbal feedback from your audience and respond.
- Be ready to take and answer questions.
- Evaluate the presentation for its effectiveness.

→ See Tab 5 for guidance on listening and evaluating.

CONFIDENCE BOOSTER

Rehearsing with your group will build confidence, so encourage the group to practice several times. Incorporate ways to interact with your presentation aids or other group members to lessen your apprehension.

Ramón's Group

Ramón works for a small company named Re-Play that creates playground equipment and surfaces. The company president appointed Ramón as leader of a brainstorming team assigned the task of discovering new, usable forms of recycled materials and new products. Ramón's first task is to select the team members. Because the brainstorming group is charged with coming up with new materials and products, Ramón wants to bring together coworkers from various divisions within the company.

2011 Re-Play Innovation Team (RIT)
Ramón Gómez, Leader

Members:
Phoebe Snow, Design Team
Lars Jenkins, Material Resource Department
Star Williams, Material Resource Department
Mia Baker, Quality and Safety Assurance
Max Howell, Production Manager

Ramón plans to be a democratic leader, as most of these members have worked well together before (Star is a new employee). All are experts in their areas. Ramón is a project manager for the Design Team, so he will be able to guide the group through the decision-making process.

He sent out an e-mail inviting everyone to the first meeting and attached an agenda. On the agenda he noted the individuals who would speak about certain ideas.

Gómez, Ramón

From: Ramón Gómez
Sent: Tuesday, February 1, 2011
To: Snow, Jenkins, Williams, Howell, and Baker
Subject: RIT meeting 1

Hey all,
Here are the specifics about our first meeting. I can't wait to get started.

Date:	2/8/11
Where:	Room 282
Time:	8:45 am
End:	12:00 pm

Bring your ideas and I will bring the bagels and coffee.
Ramón

2011 Re-Play Team (RIT) Meeting 01

February 8, 2011

Agenda

I. **Housekeeping**
   a. Welcome (Mr. Barnet, president)
   b. Introductions

II. **Report from Design Team (Phoebe)**
   a. Current product line
   b. Products in development

III. **Report from Material Resource (Lars)**
   a. Current significant materials
   b. Any potential new materials

IV. **Discuss potential brainstorming methods**

V. **Set an agenda for the first quarter**

VI. **Additional issues**

Ramón created a brief speech of introduction for Mr. Barnet.

→ See Chapter 16 (Tab 8) for how to write a speech of introduction.

Phoebe and Lars prepared short speeches to report.

→ See Chapter 17 (Tab 9) for how to write a report.

Soon after the end of the meeting, Ramón distributed the minutes to all the members plus Mr. Barnet. He arranged for rooms and necessary equipment for the next quarter's meetings and sent calendar reminders of each date to the members. The team will initially use a creative decision-making process. They plan to visit a local camp for children that just built a complete Re-Play playground. Lars (in Material Resource) even suggested that the group go on a scavenger hunt at the local junkyard and recycling facilities to get ideas.

Tab 9: Review

CHAPTER 17 REVIEW QUESTIONS

1. Explain the difference between a report and a recommendation. Give an example of each.
2. What should you do to prepare for an interview? Discuss preparation prior to the day of the interview, just before the interview, during the interview, and just after the interview.
3. What are the key issues to remember when receiving and giving a review?

CHAPTER 18 REVIEW QUESTIONS

1. What constitutes a small group?
2. What is the difference between social groups and working groups? What are the seven types of working groups discussed in this chapter?
3. What are the five phases of group development? Explain each.
4. List and explain the three different types of leadership styles.
5. List and explain three group task roles, three group interaction roles, and three self-centered roles.
6. What are the six steps of the DECIDE model? Briefly explain each.
7. What should your group consider when planning to present its findings?

TERMS TO REMEMBER

Chapter 17
reports (474)
recommendations (474)
reviews (488)

Chapter 18
small group (494)
small group communication (494)
virtual small groups (494)
social groups (495)
working groups (495)
forming (495)
storming (495)
norming (495)
performing (495)
terminating/reforming (495)
implied leader (496)
designated leader (496)
emergent leader (496)
authoritarian leaders (497)
democratic leaders (497)
laissez-faire leaders (497)
procedural communication (497)
task communication (497)
maintenance communication (497)
group task role (498)
group interaction role (498)
self-centered role (498)
DECIDE model (500)
groupthink (501)

NCA Student Outcomes for Speaking and Listening

The National Communication Association (NCA), in its 1998 report "Speaking and Listening Competencies for College Students," describes the speaking and listening skills students need in order to "communicate more effectively at school, in the workplace, and in society."

The following pages (508–521) provide a quick reference to key places *DK Guide to Public Speaking* addresses the outcomes and abilities from Part One of the NCA's "Expected Students Outcomes for Speaking and Listening: Basic Communication Course and General Education."

NCA defines speaking and listening as follows:

Speaking is the process of transmitting ideas and information orally in a variety of situations. Effective oral communication involves generating messages and delivering them with attention to vocal variety, articulation, and nonverbal signs.

Listening is the process of receiving, constructing meaning from, and responding to spoken and or nonverbal messages. People listen in order to comprehend information, critique and evaluate a message, show empathy for the feelings expressed by others, or appreciate a performance. Effective listening includes both literal and critical comprehension of ideas and information transmitted in oral language.

CONTENTS

Speaking Competencies: Basic Skills   508

Speaking Competencies: Delivery Skills   514

Listening Competencies: Literal Comprehension   516

Listening Competencies: Critical Comprehension   518

NCA information that appears on pages 507–521 comes from the National Communication Association, "Speaking and Listening Competencies for College Students" (Washington, D.C.: NCA, 1998), 7–12. Reprinted with permission of NCA, www.natcom.org.

Note: NCA's outcomes for interpersonal competencies are not included here.

Speaking Competencies: Basic Skills

In order to be a **competent speaker,** a person must be able to compose a message and provide ideas and information suitable to the topic, purpose, and audience. Specifically, the competent speaker should exhibit the following competencies by demonstrating the abilities included under each statement on pages 508–513.

Determine the purpose of oral discourse.

ABILITIES

- Identify the various purposes of discourse.
- Identify the similarities and differences among various purposes.
- Understand that different contexts require differing purposes.
- Generate a specific purpose relevant to the context when given a general purpose.

REFER TO...

Tab 1 STARTING

Overview
Overview of public speaking, *1–23*

Chapter 2
Identify the general purpose of your speech, *50*
Identify the specific purpose of your speech, *58–59*

Tab 6 SPEAKING TO INFORM

Chapter 13
The informative speech, *333–367*

Tab 7 SPEAKING TO PERSUADE

Chapter 15
The persuasive speech, *403–441*

Tab 8 SPEAKING ON SPECIAL OCCASIONS

Chapter 16
Speeches for special events, *443–469*

Tab 9 SPEAKING IN PROFESSIONAL & GROUP SETTINGS

Chapter 17
On-the-job speaking, *471–491*

Chapter 18
Speaking in small groups, *492–505*

Choose a topic and restrict it according to the purpose and the audience.

ABILITIES

- Identify a subject that is relevant to the speaker's role, knowledge, concerns, and interests.
- Narrow the topic, adapting it to the purpose and time constraints for communicating.
- Adapt the treatment of the topic to the context for communication.

REFER TO...

Tab 1 STARTING

Chapter 1
Getting to know your audience and situation, *25–47*

Chapter 2
How do you select a topic? *50–55*
How do you narrow your topic? *56–57*
How do you create a central idea? *58–63*

Tab 6 SPEAKING TO INFORM

Chapter 13
How do you choose a focused informative topic? *338–345*

Tab 7 SPEAKING TO PERSUADE

Chapter 15
How do you choose a focused persuasive topic? *406–417*

Tab 8 SPEAKING ON SPECIAL OCCASIONS

Chapter 16
How do you write a special occasion speech? *448–453*

Tab 9 SPEAKING IN PROFESSIONAL & GROUP SETTINGS

Chapter 17
How do you create a business presentation? *474–479*

Chapter 18
How do groups present their findings? *502–503*

Fulfill the purpose of oral discourse.

ABILITIES

Formulate a thesis statement.

- Use a thesis as a planning tool.
- Summarize the central message in a manner consistent with the purpose.

REFER TO...

Tab 1 STARTING

Chapter 2
How do you create a central idea (thesis statement)?
58–63

Tab 6 SPEAKING TO INFORM

Chapter 13
Identify your central idea, *344*

Tab 7 SPEAKING TO PERSUADE

Chapter 15
Identify your central idea, *415*

Tab 8 SPEAKING ON SPECIAL OCCASIONS

Chapter 16
Focus on a central idea, *451*

Tab 9 SPEAKING IN PROFESSIONAL & GROUP SETTINGS

Chapter 17
Starting (to create a business presentation), *475*
Chapter 18
Create the (group) presentation, *503*

Fulfill the purpose of oral discourse (continued).

ABILITIES

Provide adequate support material.

- Demonstrate awareness of available types of support.
- Locate appropriate support materials.
- Select appropriate support based on the topic, audience, setting, and purpose.

REFER TO...

Tab 2 RESEARCHING

Chapter 3
Locating support materials, *69–107*
Chapter 4
Selecting and testing support materials, *108–135*

Tab 4 PRESENTING

Chapter 10
Using presentation aids, *261–297*

Tab 6 SPEAKING TO INFORM

Chapter 13
How do you conduct (informative speech) research? *346–347*

Tab 7 SPEAKING TO PERSUADE

Chapter 15
How do you conduct (persuasive speech) research? *418–419*

Tab 8 SPEAKING ON SPECIAL OCCASIONS

Chapter 16
Research your speech, *452*

Tab 9 SPEAKING IN PROFESSIONAL & GROUP SETTINGS

Chapter 17
Researching (a business presentation), *476*
Chapter 18
How do groups make decisions or solve problems? *500–501*

Fulfill the purpose of oral discourse (continued).

ABILITIES	REFER TO...

Select a suitable organizational pattern.
- Demonstrate awareness of alternative organizational patterns.
- Demonstrate understanding of the functions of organizational patterns, including:
  - clarification of information
  - facilitation of listener comprehension
  - attitude change
  - relational interaction

Select organizational patterns that are appropriate to the topic, audience, content, and purpose.

Tab 3 CREATING

Chapter 5
Outlining your speech, *137–171*
Chapter 6
Organizing the speech body, *173–193*

Tab 6 SPEAKING TO INFORM

Chapter 13
How do you organize the body of an informative speech? *350–353*

Tab 7 SPEAKING TO PERSUADE

Chapter 15
How do you organize the body of a persuasive speech? *422–425*

Tab 8 SPEAKING ON SPECIAL OCCASIONS

Chapter 16
Create your outline, *452*

Tab 9 SPEAKING IN PROFESSIONAL & GROUP SETTINGS

Chapter 17
Creating (a business presentation), *477*
Chapter 18
How do groups make decisions or solve problems? *500–501*
How do groups present their findings? *502–503*

Fulfill the purpose of oral discourse (continued).

ABILITIES

Demonstrate careful choice of words.

- Demonstrate understanding of the power of language.
- Select words that are appropriate to the topic, audience, purpose, context, and speaker.
- Use word choice in order to express ideas clearly, to create and maintain interest, and to enhance the speaker's credibility.
- Select words that avoid sexism, racism, and other forms of prejudice.

REFER TO...

Tab 3 CREATING

Chapter 7
Introducing and concluding your speech, *195–213*

Tab 4 PRESENTING

Chapter 8
Using language successfully, *215–235*

Tab 6 SPEAKING TO INFORM

Chapter 13
Language, *362*

Tab 7 SPEAKING TO PERSUADE

Chapter 14
Highlight emotive and stylistic language, *375*
What are faulty arguments? *392–399*
Chapter 15
Language, *436*

Tab 8 SPEAKING ON SPECIAL OCCASIONS

Chapter 16
What are the types of special occasion speeches? *454–467*

Tab 9 SPEAKING IN PROFESSIONAL & GROUP SETTINGS

Chapter 17
Presenting (a business presentation), *478*
Chapter 18
Create the presentation, *503*

Provide effective transitions.

- Demonstrate understanding of the types and functions of transitions.
- Use transitions to:
  - establish connectedness
  - signal movement from one idea to another
  - clarify relationships among ideas

Tab 3 CREATING

Chapter 5
What can you use to link your speech parts together? *160–163*

Speaking Competencies: Delivery Skills

The **competent speaker** must also be able to transmit messages by using delivery skills suitable to the topic, purpose, and audience. Specifically, the competent speaker should exhibit the following competencies by demonstrating the abilities included under each statement on pages 514–515.

Employ vocal variety in rate, pitch, and intensity.

ABILITIES	REFER TO...
• Use vocal variety to heighten and maintain interest.	**Tab 2 RESEARCHING**
• Use a rate that is suitable to the message, occasion, and receiver.	**Chapter 4** Use delivery techniques to enhance your materials, *129*
• Use pitch (within the speaker's optimum range) to clarify and to emphasize.	**Tab 4 PRESENTING**
• Use intensity appropriate for the message and audible to the audience.	**Chapter 9** Pitch, volume, rate, pause, variety, *238–241*

Articulate clearly.

ABILITIES	REFER TO...
• Demonstrate knowledge of the sounds of the American English language.	**Tab 4 PRESENTING**
• Use the sounds of the American English language.	**Chapter 9** Pronunciation, articulation, dialect, *242–243*

Employ language appropriate to the designated audience.

ABILITIES	REFER TO...
• Employ language that enhances the speaker's credibility, promotes the purpose, and [promotes] the receiver's understanding.	**Tab 4 PRESENTING**
	Chapter 8 How can you use language effectively? *220–227*
• Demonstrate that the use of technical vocabularies, slang, idiomatic language, and regionalisms may facilitate understanding when communicating with others who share meanings for those terms but can hinder understanding in those situations where meanings are not shared.	**Chapter 9** Pronunciation, dialect, *242–243*
	Tab 6 SPEAKING TO INFORM
	Chapter 13 Language, *362*
• Use standard pronunciation.	**Tab 7 SPEAKING TO PERSUADE**
• Use standard grammar.	**Chapter 15** Language, *436*

Employ language appropriate to the designated audience (continued).

- Use language at the appropriate level of abstraction or generality.

Tab 8 SPEAKING ON SPECIAL OCCASIONS

Chapter 16   What are the types of special occasion speeches? *454–467*

Tab 9 SPEAKING IN PROFESSIONAL & GROUP SETTINGS

Chapter 17   Presenting (a business presentation), *478*
Chapter 18   Create the presentation, *503*

Demonstrate nonverbal behavior that supports the verbal message.

ABILITIES

- Use appropriate paralanguage (extraverbal elements of voice such as emphasis, pause, tone, etc.) that achieves congruence and enhances the verbal intent.
- Use appropriate kinesic elements (posture, gesture, and facial expression) that achieve congruence and enhance the verbal intent.
- Use appropriate proxemic elements (interpersonal distance and spatial arrangement) that achieve congruence and enhance the verbal intent.
- Use appropriate clothing and ornamentation that achieve congruence and enhance the verbal intent.

REFER TO...

Tab 2 RESEARCHING

Chapter 4   Use delivery techniques to enhance your materials, *129*

Tab 4 PRESENTING

Chapter 9   What are the elements of vocal delivery? *238–243*
What are the elements of physical delivery? *244–247*

Tab 5 LISTENING & EVALUATING

Chapter 11   How can you help your audience listen more effectively? *308–311*

Tab 6 SPEAKING TO INFORM

Chapter 13   Delivery, *363*

Tab 7 SPEAKING TO PERSUADE

Chapter 15   Delivery, *436*

Tab 8 SPEAKING ON SPECIAL OCCASIONS

Chapter 16   Practice the speech, *453*

Tab 9 SPEAKING IN PROFESSIONAL & GROUP SETTINGS

Chapter 17   Presenting (a business presentation), *478*
Chapter 18   Create the presentation, *503*

Listening Competencies: Literal Comprehension

In order to be a **competent listener,** a person must be able to listen with literal comprehension. Specifically, the competent listener should be able to exhibit the following competencies by demonstrating the abilities included under each statement on pages 516–517.

Recognize main ideas.

ABILITIES

- Distinguish ideas fundamental to the thesis from material that supports those ideas.
- Identify transitional, organizational, and nonverbal cues that direct the listener to the main ideas.
- Identify the main ideas in structured and unstructured discourse.

REFER TO...

Tab 3 CREATING

Chapter 5   Use balanced main points, *148*
Employ subordination, *148–149*
Transitions, signposts, internal previews, internal reviews, *160–163*

Chapter 6   How do you make a speech out of a strategy? *186–191*

Tab 4 PRESENTING

Chapter 9   What are the elements of vocal delivery? *238–243*
What are the elements of physical delivery? *244–247*

Tab 5 LISTENING & EVALUATING

Chapter 11   Listening, *299–315*
Chapter 12   The speech message, *324–325*

Identify supporting details.

ABILITIES

- Identify supporting details in spoken messages.
- Distinguish between those ideas that support the main ideas and those that do not.
- Determine whether the number of supporting details adequately develops each main idea.

REFER TO...

Tab 2 RESEARCHING

Chapter 4   Selecting and testing support materials, *108–135*

Tab 3 CREATING

Chapter 5   Employ subordination, *148–149*
Chapter 6   How do you make a speech out of a strategy? *186–191*

Tab 5 LISTENING & EVALUATING

Chapter 11   Listening, *299–315*
Chapter 12   The speech message, *324–325*

Recognize explicit relationships among ideas.

ABILITIES

- Demonstrate an understanding of the types of organizational or logical relationships.
- Identify transitions that suggest relationships.
- Determine whether the asserted relationship exists.

REFER TO...

Tab 3 CREATING

Chapter 5 Transitions, signposts, internal previews, internal reviews, *160–163*
Chapter 6 What organizational strategies can you use in your speech? *174–183*

Tab 5 LISTENING & EVALUATING

Chapter 11 Listening, *299–315*
Chapter 12 The speech message, *324–325*

Tab 6 SPEAKING TO INFORM

Chapter 13 How do you organize the body of an informative speech? *350–353*

Tab 7 SPEAKING TO PERSUADE

Chapter 14 Appeal to logos, *379*
What are the parts of an argument? *384–387*
What are the different types of arguments? *388–391*
Chapter 15 How do you organize the body of a persuasive speech? *422–425*

Recall basic ideas and details.

ABILITIES

- Determine the goal for listening.
- State the basic cognitive and affective contents, after listening.

REFER TO...

Tab 5 LISTENING & EVALUATING

Chapter 11 Listening, *299–315*
Chapter 12 The speech message, *324–325*

Listening Competencies: Critical Comprehension

The **competent listener** must also listen with critical comprehension. Specifically, the competent listener should exhibit the following competencies by demonstrating the abilities included under each statement on pages 518–521.

Attend with an open mind.

ABILITIES

- Demonstrate an awareness of personal, ideological, and emotional biases.
- Demonstrate awareness that each person has a unique perspective.
- Demonstrate awareness that one's knowledge, experience, and emotions affect listening.
- Use verbal and nonverbal behaviors that demonstrate willingness to listen to messages when variables such as setting, speaker, or topic may not be conducive to listening.

REFER TO...

Tab 1 STARTING

Chapter 1
Attitudes, beliefs, values, *28–29*
What specific traits do you need to investigate? *30–35*

Tab 5 LISTENING & EVALUATING

Chapter 11
What can prevent effective listening? *306–307*
As an audience member, how can you listen more effectively? *312–313*
Chapter 12
Evaluating speeches, *317–331*

Perceive the speaker's purpose and organization of ideas and information.

ABILITIES

- Identify the speaker's purpose.
- Identify the organization of the speaker's ideas and information.

REFER TO...

Tab 1 STARTING

Chapter 2
Identify the general purpose of your speech, *50*

Tab 3 CREATING

Chapter 6
What organizational strategies can you use in your speech? *174–183*

Tab 5 LISTENING & EVALUATING

Chapter 11
Listening, *299–315*
Chapter 12
Evaluating speeches, *317–331*

Discriminate between statements of fact and statements of opinion.

ABILITIES

- Distinguish between assertions that are verifiable and those that are not.

REFER TO...

Tab 2 RESEARCHING

Chapter 4
Facts, *110*
What do you evaluate in your support materials?
122–125

Tab 7 SPEAKING TO PERSUADE

Chapter 14
Support a proposition of fact, value, or policy, *373*
What are the traditional appeals used to persuade?
376–379
What are the modern appeals used to persuade? *380–383*

Distinguish between emotional and logical arguments.

ABILITIES

- Demonstrate an understanding that arguments have both emotional and logical dimensions.
- Identify the logical characteristics of an argument.
- Identify the emotional characteristics of an argument.
- Identify whether the argument is predominantly emotional or logical.

REFER TO...

Tab 7 SPEAKING TO PERSUADE

Chapter 14
What are the traditional appeals used to persuade?
376–379
What are the modern appeals used to persuade? *380–383*
What are the parts of an argument? *384–387*
What are the different types of arguments? *388–391*
What are faulty arguments? *392–399*

Detect bias and prejudice.

ABILITIES

- Identify instances of bias and prejudice in a spoken message.
- Specify how bias and prejudice may affect the impact of a spoken message.

REFER TO...

Tab 4 PRESENTING

Chapter 8
Be appropriate (with language), *224–225*

Tab 7 SPEAKING TO PERSUADE

Chapter 14
What are the traditional appeals used to persuade?
376–379
What are the modern appeals used to persuade? *380–383*
What are faulty arguments? *392–399*

Recognize the speaker's attitude.

ABILITIES

- Identify the direction, intensity, and salience of the speaker's attitude as reflected by the verbal messages.
- Identify the direction, intensity, and salience of the speaker's attitude as reflected by the nonverbal messages.

REFER TO...

Tab 4 PRESENTING

Chapter 8
What makes language so important? *216–219*
Chapter 9
What are the elements of physical delivery? *244–247*

Tab 5 LISTENING & EVALUATING

Chapter 11
As an audience member, how can you listen more effectively? *312–313*
Chapter 12
The speaker's presentation, *324–325*

Synthesize and evaluate by drawing logical inferences and conclusions.

ABILITIES

- Draw relationships between prior knowledge and the information provided by the speaker.
- Demonstrate an understanding of the nature of inference.
- Identify the types of verbal and nonverbal information.
- Draw valid inferences from the information.
- Identify the information as evidence to support views.
- Assess the acceptability of evidence.
- Identify patterns of reasoning and judge the validity of arguments.
- Analyze the information and inferences in order to draw conclusions.

REFER TO...

Tab 2 RESEARCHING

Chapter 4
What do you evaluate in your support materials? *122–125*

Tab 5 LISTENING & EVALUATING

Chapter 12
The speech message, *324–325*

Tab 7 SPEAKING TO PERSUADE

Chapter 14
What are the parts of an argument? *384–387*
What are the different types of arguments? *388–391*
What are faulty arguments? *392–399*

Recall the implications and arguments.

ABILITIES

- Identify the arguments used to justify the speaker's position.
- State both the overt and implied arguments.
- Specify the implications of these arguments for the speaker, audience, and society at large.

REFER TO…

Tab 5 LISTENING & EVALUATING

Chapter 11
As an audience member, how can you listen more effectively? *312–313*

Tab 7 SPEAKING TO PERSUADE

Chapter 14
What are the parts of an argument? *384–387*
What are the different types of arguments? *388–391*

Recognize discrepancies between the speaker's verbal and nonverbal messages.

ABILITIES

- Identify when the nonverbal signals contradict the verbal message.
- Identify when the nonverbal signals understate or exaggerate the verbal message.
- Identify when the nonverbal message is irrelevant to the verbal message.

REFER TO…

Tab 4 PRESENTING

Chapter 9
What are the elements of physical delivery? *244–247*

Tab 5 LISTENING & EVALUATING

Chapter 11
Listen critically, *313*
Chapter 12
The speaker's presentation, *324–325*

Employ active listening techniques when appropriate.

ABILITIES

- Identify the cognitive and affective dimensions of a message.
- Demonstrate comprehension by formulating questions that clarify or qualify the speaker's content and affective intent.
- Demonstrate comprehension by paraphrasing the speaker's message.

REFER TO…

Tab 5 LISTENING & EVALUATING

Chapter 11
Listen actively, *312*

Glossary

abbreviation A shortened form of a word or phrase, used to represent the full form. (Chapter 8)

acronym A word formed from the initials or other parts of several words. (Chapter 8)

after-dinner speech A speech usually given with the general purpose to entertain but with a relevant message. (Chapter 16)

analogy A way of explaining the unfamiliar by comparing and contrasting it to what is familiar. (Chapter 4)

appeals The means by which speakers prove or establish the arguments they are making. (Chapter 14)

appearance A person's physical choices of dress and grooming practices. (Chapter 9)

appreciative listening Listening for recreation or enjoyment. (Chapter 11)

arbitrary The relationship between a word and what it stands for is random, subjective, or coincidental. (Chapter 8)

argument A reason or a series of reasons given to support an assertion. (Chapter 14)

argument by analogy The conclusion that something will be accurate for one case if it is true for another similar case. (Chapter 14)

argument by authority An argument dependent on the ethos and authority of others whose testimony you use to support a claim. (Chapter 14)

argument by cause An argument that demonstrates a relationship between two events or factors by focusing on the premise that one caused the other to occur. (Chapter 14)

argument by deduction Constructed by offering a series of general statements that then prove the specific claim/conclusion as correct based. (Chapter 14)

argument by induction Predicting probability, this argument reasons from specific cases to a general statement. (Chapter 14)

articulation How completely and clearly you utter a word. (Chapter 9)

attending The phase of hearing when a person pays attention to a particular sound. (Chapter 11)

attention-getter An opening statement that grabs the audience's interest. (Chapter 7)

attitudes Learned persistent psychological responses, predispositions, or inclinations to act one way or feel a particular way toward something. (Chapters 1, 14)

attitudinal anchors The viewpoints an audience finds most acceptable. (Chapter 15)

audience The person or persons receiving the speaker's message and contributing feedback. (Overview, Chapter 1)

audience analysis A systematic investigation of the characteristics that make the audience unique. (Chapter 1)

audience centered A speech that grabs the audience's attention and recognizes their unique characteristics and viewpoints. (Chapter 1)

audio clips Recordings of only sound. (Chapter 10)

authoritarian leaders Leaders who assume and maintain superiority and authority over small groups by telling the groups what needs to be done without asking advice from the groups. (Chapter 18)

background The speaker's and audience's identities and life experiences. (Overview)

bar graphs Visual aids consisting of vertical or horizontal bars that represent specific sets of data. (Chapter 10)

behaviors The unconcealed actions or reactions people have, often in response to stimuli, related to their attitudes, beliefs, and values. (Chapter 14)

beliefs The ideas a person accepts as plausible, based on interpretation and judgment. (Chapters 1, 14)

blatant plagiarism Occurs either when speakers take an entire speech or document and present it as their own or when speakers take parts of information from other sources and link the parts together, creating an entire speech out of someone else's words. (Overview)

block quotation A quotation of more than four lines of text that is not offset by quotation marks but indented more to signal a quotation. (Chapter 4)

blog A Web site or Web page that contains regular postings by its author(s) and allows visitors to post comments. (Chapter 3)

body The central portion of the speech made up of the main points, the multiple layers of subordinate points, and links. (Chapter 5)

brainstorming The act of free associating from one word or concept to another. (Chapter 2)

brief examples Specific instances illustrating a single general notion. (Chapter 4)

browser A tool, like Internet Explorer or Mozilla Firefox, that allows you to surf the Web. (Chapter 3)

causal strategy Used when the audience needs to understand the cause and effect or consequences of something, by either leading up to a particular result or backtracking from the effect to the cause. (Chapter 6)

central idea The concise, single sentence summarizing and/or previewing what a speaker will say during a speech. (Chapter 2)

central processing Occurs when an audience is motivated to think critically about a topic. (Chapter 14)

channel The means of getting the message across, such as a voice over the airwaves or visual messages in the form of nonverbal and visual aids. (Overview)

charts Visual summaries of complex or large quantities of information. (Chapter 10)

chronological strategy Used when moving through steps in a process or developing a timeline. (Chapter 6)

citations The credits for the original sources of the support materials used for a speech. (Chapter 4)

claim An assertion made in an argument. (Chapter 14)

clichés Overused words or phrases that have lost their affect. (Chapter 8)

closed-ended questions Questions that seek short, precise answers (such as "yes" or "no"). (Chapter 3)

coercion The act of forcing a person, via threats or intimidation, to do something against his or her will. (Chapter 14)

cognitive dissonance theory A theory emphasizing the human need to be in a harmonious state and that conflicting attitudes, values, beliefs, ideas, or behaviors can cause an inharmonious or dissonant feeling. (Chapter 14)

common ground The overlap within the speaker's and audience's identities and life experiences. (Overview)

communication apprehension Fears a speaker has about giving a speech. (Overview)

comparative advantage A strategy to convince an audience that one thing is better than another by comparing the two. (Chapter 6)

comparative strategy An organizational strategy using the practices of compare and contrast. (Chapter 6)

comparison The act of pointing out similarities between two or more ideas, things, factors, or issues. (Chapter 4)

conclusion The ending of the speech, which allows the speaker one last moment to reinforce the main ideas as well as "wow" the audience. (Chapters 5, 7)

connotative meaning The emotional and personal reaction a person may have to a word. (Chapter 8)

contrast The act of pointing out differences between two or more ideas, things, factors, or issues. (Chapter 4)

critical listening Listening carefully to a message to judge it as acceptable or not. (Chapter 11)

critical thinking The careful, deliberate determination of whether one should accept, reject, or suspend judgment about a claim or information and the degree of confidence with which one accepts or rejects it. (Chapter 11)

culture The learned patterns of beliefs, values, attitudes, norms, practices, customs, and behaviors shared by a large group of people that are taught from one generation to the next. (Chapters 1, 8)

databases Extensive collections of published works, such as magazine, newspaper, and journal articles, all in electronic form. They contain descriptions, citation information about the articles, and often the full text of the articles. (Chapter 3)

DECIDE model An approach for decision making and problem solving that has six steps: defining the goal, examining issues preventing success, considering alternatives, initiating a decision, developing a plan, and evaluating the results. (Chapter 18)

decoding The process of interpreting messages. (Overview)

definitions Brief explanations designed to inform the audience about something unfamiliar. (Chapter 4)

delivery outline An outline maintaining the structure of the speech while eliminating much of the detail. Used during the speech and contains delivery hints. (Chapter 5)

demagogue A speaker who stirs up the audience's feelings by strong provocation. (Chapter 14)

democratic leaders Leaders who involve group members in the decision-making and/or creative processes. (Chapter 18)

denotative meaning The accepted meaning of a word, which can be found in the dictionary. (Chapter 8)

description The stage of evaluation when the evaluators offer what they saw and heard. (Chapter 12)

descriptive statistics Numerical facts or data that describe or summarize characteristics of a population or a large quantity of data. (Chapter 4)

designated leader A leader elected or appointed by the group when it is formed. (Chapter 18)

design principles Principles relating to the arrangement and placement of various elements of visual aids for optimum effect. (Chapter 10)

dialect The way a culture or subculture pronounces and uses language. (Chapter 9)

direct eye contact The act of a speaker briefly looking into audience members' eyes. (Chapter 9)

doublespeak The use of euphemisms, jargon, inflated language, or nonsensical sentences to disguise or distort the meaning of the message. (Chapter 8)

drawings Maps, sketches, diagrams, plans, or other nonphotographic representations. (Chapter 10)

egocentrism The tendency for an audience to be interested in the topics that relate and matter to them, as well as their need for the speaker to recognize that they are a group of unique individuals. (Chapter 1)

Elaboration Likelihood Model Suggests that people process persuasive messages based on their commitment or involvement by either central processing or peripheral processing. (Chapter 14)

emblems Speech-independent or culturally learned gestures that have a direct verbal translation. (Chapter 9)

emergent leader A group member who evolves as the leader during the early stages of the group's formation. (Chapter 18)

empathic listening Listening for the purpose of giving the speaker emotional support. (Chapter 11)

encoding The process of conveying messages. (Overview)

enthymeme A truncated syllogism that omits an obvious minor premise. (Chapter 14)

enunciation The ability to use distinctiveness and clarity while saying linked whole words. (Chapter 9)

environmental barriers Conditions within the speech location that interrupt the listener's ability to concentrate, such as movement, heat, cold, or hard seats. (Chapters 1, 11)

ethnicity Traits that stem from national and religious affiliations. (Chapter 1)

ethnocentrism The notion that one's culture is superior to other cultures. (Overview, Chapter 14)

ethos Appeal of reliability or credibility. (Overview, Chapter 14)

eulogy A speech presented after a person's death. (Chapter 16)

euphemisms Less direct words or phrases that replace harsh, distasteful, or offensive language. (Chapter 8)

evaluation A detailed description of a speech's successes and/or the improvements needed, which is grounded in justified judgment. (Chapter 12)

evidence The material that proves a claim to be accurate. (Chapter 14)

examples Specific instances or cases that embody or illustrate points in a speech. (Chapter 4)

Expectancy-Outcome Values Theory A theory suggesting that people will evaluate the cost, benefit, or value related to making change in a particular attitude, value, belief, or behavior to decide if it is worth it or not. (Chapter 14)

expert testimony Firsthand knowledge or opinions from a specialist in a field related to the speech's topic. (Chapter 4)

extemporaneous speaking The speaker plans out, rehearses, and delivers the speech from a key-word/phrase outline in a conversational manner. (Chapter 9)

extended examples Detailed stories, narratives, illustrations, or anecdotes allowing the audience to linger on the vivid, concrete images the examples create. (Chapter 4)

external noise Any barrier to effective listening that originates outside of the listener's mind and body, often caused by environmental or linguistic barriers. (Chapters 1, 11)

facial expressions The use of facial features and muscles to convey a speaker's internal thoughts and feelings. (Chapter 9)

facts Verifiable bits of information about people, events, places, dates, and times. (Chapter 4)

fallacy A faulty argument or error in logic. (Chapter 14)

faulty syllogism A flawed argument in which the major premise, minor premise, and/or conclusion is not factual. (Chapter 14)

feedback The verbal or nonverbal message encoded by the audience and decoded by the speaker. (Overview)

figurative analogy Compares and contrasts two essentially different things. (Chapter 4)

fillers Unnecessary sounds, words, or phrases that serve no purpose and do not add to the understanding of the message, such as the word "um." (Chapters 8, 9)

First Amendment U.S. Constitutional amendment establishing freedom of speech by stating, "Congress shall make no law... abridging the freedom of speech, or the press...." (Overview)

flowcharts Charts that diagram step-by-step development through a procedure, relationship, or process. (Chapter 10)

follow-up questions New questions the interviewer produces based on the interviewee's answers to questions during an interview. (Chapter 3)

forming The small group development stage in which the group creates its group identity, seeks guidance and direction from the leader, and determines membership and roles. (Chapter 18)

general purpose The unrestricted aim of a speech. (Chapter 2)

gestures The use of the body or parts of it (hands, arms, eyes, or head) to convey a message or feeling during a speech. (Chapter 9)

graphs Visual representations of numerical information that demonstrate relationships or differences between two or more variables. (Chapter 10)

group interaction role A role in which a small group member helps create and maintain a positive climate and interpersonal relationships within the group.

group task role A role in which a small group member assists the group with completing tasks and the group goal.

groupthink The willingness to conform to what the group thinks at the moment rather than to critically think about the issue and potentially come to a better conclusion.

hearing Occurs when sound waves strike the eardrum and spark a chain reaction that ends with the brain registering the sound. (Chapter 11)

hits A list of Web pages, files, and images related to the term entered into a search engine. (Chapter 3)

hypothetical examples Examples based on the potential outcomes of imagined scenarios. (Chapter 4)

idea bank A list of general words and phrases that could be potential speech topics. (Chapter 2)

identification The human need and willingness to understand as much as possible the feelings, thoughts, motives, interests, attitudes, and lives of others. (Overview)

identity Made up of a person's beliefs, values, and attitudes. (Chapter 1)

identity knowledge The speaker's understanding of what makes the audience distinctive. (Chapter 1)

illustrators Gestures that are speech-dependent or closely linked to what is being said, which help demonstrate the message. (Chapter 9)

implied leader A type of leader that develops when other group members defer to a member because of her/his rank, expertise, or other characteristics. (Chapter 18)

impromptu speaking A delivery method where the speaker has little or no preparation or rehearsal prior to the speech. (Chapter 9)

inferential statistics Draw conclusions about a larger population by making estimates based on a smaller sample of that population. (Chapter 4)

inflection Varying the pitch of one's voice to demonstrate enthusiasm, excitement, concern, and dedication to the topic. (Chapter 9)

informative listening Listening that concentrates on language and detail as well as remembering the knowledge gained by listening for insight or comprehension. (Chapter 11)

informative speaking Gives the audience completely new knowledge, skills, or understanding about a topic or increases their current knowledge, skills, or understanding. (Chapter 13)

internal noise Any physiological or a psychological barrier to effective listening that originates within the body or mind of the listener. (Chapters 1, 11)

internal previews Links to what is next in the speech. (Chapter 5)

internal reviews Links that summarize the information just stated in the previous section of a speech. (Chapter 5)

Internet The massive worldwide network of hardware, connecting millions of computers together so that they can receive and retrieve information. (Chapter 3)

interviews Information-gathering sessions where one person asks the other a series of prepared questions. (Chapter 3)

introduction The opening of a speech used to grab the audience's attention and focus in on the topic. (Chapter 5)

invisible Web Online information that is not accessible through a general search engine but can be accessed through the use of a special gateway such as a database. (Chapter 3)

jargon The technical or specialized vocabulary used among members of a profession. (Chapter 8)

judgment The stage of evaluation where the evaluator offers what was good or not about a speech. (Chapter 12)

justification The stage of evaluation where the evaluator explains why something was good or not about a speech. (Chapter 12)

laissez-faire leaders Leaders who allow their group members complete freedom with the process necessary to reach the group goal. (Chapter 18)

lay testimony Testimony from a peer or an ordinary person, other than the speaker, who bears witness to his or her own experiences and beliefs. (Chapter 4)

line graphs Visuals with numerical points plotted on a horizontal axis with one variable and on the vertical axis with another; the points are then connected to make a line. (Chapter 10)

linguistic barriers Barriers to listening that occur when the verbal and nonverbal messages from the speaker are unfamiliar or misunderstood by the listener. (Chapters 1, 11)

links Words, phrases, or sentences that make a logical connection between the parts of the body of the speech and/or thoughts. (Chapter 5)

listening The conscious learned act of paying attention and assigning meaning to an acoustic message. (Chapter 11)

literal analogy Compares and contrasts two like things. (Chapter 4)

logos Appeals to the audience's ability to reason through statistics, facts, and testimony to reach a conclusion. (Overview, Chapter 14)

main points The essential ideas or claims about a topic that comprise the body of a speech. (Chapters 2, 5)

malapropism The act of selecting an incorrect word that sounds similar to the correct word. (Chapter 8)

manuscript speaking The delivery method used when a speaker reads directly from a word-for-word copy of the speech. (Chapter 9)

Maslow's hierarchy of needs The theory that humans have a hierarchical set of needs that must be met, starting with the lower, more basic needs and progressing to the higher, less basic needs. (Chapters 1, 14)

mean An average of a set of numbers. (Chapter 4)

median The middle value in a set of numbers arranged in increasing order. (Chapter 4)

memorized speaking A delivery method where the speaker delivers a speech from memory exactly as written. (Chapter 9)

message The verbal and nonverbal ideas encoded by the speaker and decoded by the audience. (Overview)

mindfulness The speaker is persistently and conscientiously aware of the distinctions of uniqueness within the audience. (Chapter 1)

mode The number that occurs the most in a set of numbers. (Chapter 4)

models Three-dimensional representations. (Chapter 10)

monotone A vocal quality that is constant in pitch that can be distracting and boring. (Chapter 9)

Monroe's motivated sequence A five-step strategy that motivates an audience to action based on their needs. (Chapters 6, 14)

movement The use of motion and space during a speech. (Chapter 9)

multimedia The combination of multiple presentation aids (still images, graphs, text, sound, and video) into one choreographed production. (Chapter 10)

mythos Appeals to the audience's need for group membership and connection to the group's cultural heritage, traditions, identity, and values and draws upon feelings of patriotism, pride, and valor. (Overview, Chapter 14)

negotiation skill The ability to respond to audience differences through sensitivity, politeness, willing adjustment, and collaboration. (Chapter 1)

no-citation plagiarism Occurs when speakers fail to give source credit to a specific part of their speech that has been taken from another source. (Overview)

noise Any unwanted pleasant or unpleasant barrier that prevents listening and/or interferes with the message and/or feedback. (Overview, Chapter 11)

norming Occurs after the conflict of the storming phase within a small group is expressed and addressed. The members begin to outline necessary tasks and assignments to achieve their goals. (Chapter 18)

objective The part of the specific purpose that describes the outcome or behavior the speaker wants the audience to experience or adopt. (Chapter 2)

open-ended questions Allow for discussion and longer responses. (Chapter 3)

oral evaluations Brief verbal overviews describing what the evaluator saw and felt about a speech. (Chapter 12)

order of intensity strategy An organizational strategy in which main points are arranged in order from least to most, easy to difficult, or neutral to intense. (Chapter 6)

organizational charts Illustrate the structure or chain of command in an organization. (Chapter 10)

parallelism The arrangement of words, phrases, or sentences in similar patterns. (Chapter 6)

paraphrasing Restating material in a simpler format using the speaker's own words. (Chapter 4)

passivity syndrome The act of audience members mistakenly believing that the speaker is entirely responsible for the effectiveness of the message. (Chapter 11)

pathos Appeals to emotions. (Overview, Chapter 14)

pause Slowing down the speaking rate or stopping during a speech for effect. (Chapter 9)

performing The "real work" phase that occurs when the small group conducts the work necessary to make a decision or solve a problem. (Chapter 18)

peripheral processing The act of the audience dismissing a speech because they believe the message to be irrelevant, uninteresting, or too complex to pay close attention. (Chapter 14)

personal testimony The speaker's experience or point of view. (Chapter 4)

personal traits Audience demographics, or traits such as age, gender, sexual orientation, household type, education, occupation, income, and disabilities. (Chapter 1)

persuasion A deliberate attempt, by the speaker, to create, reinforce, or change the attitudes, beliefs, values, and/or behaviors of the listener. (Chapter 14)

photographs Two-dimensional photographic representations. (Chapter 10)

physiological barriers Internal noise such as hunger, sickness, disabilities, and pain that can interrupt the listening process. (Chapters 1, 11)

pictographs Bar graphs that use pictures instead of bars. (Chapter 10)

pie graphs Circular graphs with sections representing a percentage of given quantity. (Chapter 10)

pitch How high or low a person's voice is in frequency, which is determined by how fast or slow the vocal cords vibrate. (Chapter 9)

plagiarism Intentional or accidental use of all or a portion of the words, ideas, or illustrations created by someone else without proper credit. (Overview)

popular sources Publications written for general readers. (Chapter 4)

population The larger group of individuals represented by a small survey group. (Chapter 3)

posture A speaker's body position and stance during a speech. (Chapter 9)

preparation outline The detailed, full-sentence outline of a speech. (Chapter 5)

presentation aids Two- or three-dimensional visual items, video footage, audio recordings, and/or multimedia segments that support and enhance a speech. (Chapter 10)

prestige testimony Firsthand knowledge or opinions from a person known for his or her popularity, fame, attractiveness, high-profile activities, and/or age. (Chapter 4)

primacy model Suggests that the speaker should put the strongest arguments first in the body of the speech to persuade the audience early in the speech. (Chapter 15)

primary sources Original sources of information, such as photographs, autobiographies, and letters. (Chapter 4)

problem–solution strategy An organizational strategy in persuasive speeches demonstrating a problem and advocating a solution. (Chapter 6)

procedural communication The routine communication necessary for a group to function (such as location of meetings and the agenda). (Chapter 18)

pronunciation The standard way or commonly accepted way to make a word sound. (Chapter 9)

proposition of fact An assertion made in a persuasive speech central idea to prove something factual. (Chapter 14)

proposition of policy An assertion made in a persuasive speech central idea that seeks to prove a need for a new or different policy. (Chapter 14)

proposition of value An assertion made in a persuasive speech central idea that seeks to make a value judgment. (Chapter 14)

psychological barriers Internal noise in the form of emotional conditions that may prevent the listener from focusing on and absorbing a message. (Chapters 1 ,11)

psychological traits The needs and motivations of the audience. (Chapter 1)

quotations A form of support material where the speaker directly uses words or passages written by someone else. (Chapter 7)

race The biological differences of humankind based on physical markers, such as color or texture of hair, color of skin and eyes, shape of facial features, and bodily build and proportions. (Chapter 1)

rate The speed at which a person speaks. (Chapter 9)

rationale The stage of evaluation where the evaluator offers a rationale or norm for his or her judgment. (Chapter 12)

reasoning The rational thinking that humans do to reach a conclusion or to justify beliefs or acts. (Chapter 14)

receiving The physiological process of hearing. (Chapter 11)

recency model The speaker begins with the weakest argument and finishes with the strongest to persuade the audience. (Chapter 15)

recommendations On-the-job proposals arguing for a belief or course of action. (Chapter 17)

reflexivity Occurs when a speaker takes a moment to consider him- or herself in relation to the speech and vice versa. (Chapter 12)

refutation strategy An organizational strategy used in persuasive speeches based on countering someone else's argument. (Chapter 6)

remembering The final stage of hearing, in which the listener retains information. (Chapter 11)

reports Forms of informative speaking designed to present business-related information to others, usually

concerning the speaker's profession or expertise. (Chapter 17)

responding The phase of hearing when a response is given to the sounds that have been processed. (Chapter 11)

reviews Performance appraisals or job-related evaluations. (Chapter 17)

rhetorical questions Questions that the speaker does not expect the audience to answer, which are used for effect rather than to gain knowledge. (Chapter 7)

roast A humorous tribute to a person. (Chapter 16)

sample The surveyed portion of a larger population. (Chapter 3)

schemes Speech devices or language techniques that manipulate word order or repeat sounds, words, phrases, sentences, or grammatical patterns. (Chapter 8)

scholarly sources Sources written for readers who are specialists in their academic or professional fields. (Chapter 4)

search engines Specific tools used to locate information on the Web. (Chapter 3)

secondary sources Sources that build upon other (often primary) sources, by citing, reviewing, quoting, and/or paraphrasing the other materials or sources. (Chapter 4)

self-centered role A role in which a small group member focuses on his or her own needs. (Chapter 18)

signposts Words or phrases that signal to the audience where they are with regards to related thoughts or what is important to remember. (Chapter 5)

situation The location and time in which the process of communication takes place. (Overview)

small group A group of at least three and up to about 20 people who unite over time for a common purpose. (Chapter 18)

small group communication Interaction in a small group of people who unite over time for a common purpose, feel a sense of belongingness, and have the ability to influence each other and the outcome. (Chapter 18)

social groups Informal groups that form when individuals unite for the purpose of socializing and participating in group social activities. (Chapter 18)

social judgment theory States that the speaker's persuasion will be easier, tolerated more, and potentially longer lasting if the audience can tie the persuasion to what they find most acceptable. (Chapter 15)

social traits Relate to how the audience is affected by or identifies with other groups of people. (Chapter 1)

sources Any books, magazines, journals, blogs, Web sites, e-mail, interviews, or other such resources that contribute information to the creation of a speech. (Chapter 3)

spatial strategy An organizational strategy recognizing space as a method of arrangement. (Chapter 6)

speaker The person who initiates and is responsible for most of the message. (Overview)

speaking competence How well the speaker communicates with the audience. (Chapter 1)

special occasion speech A speech given to celebrate, commemorate, inspire, or entertain. (Chapter 16)

specific purpose A single statement combining the general purpose, a specific audience, and the speaker's objective. (Chapter 2)

speeches to celebrate Honor or highlight a person, group, institution, place, or an event by praising the subject of the occasion. (Chapter 16)

speeches to commemorate Pay tribute to or remember a person, group, institution, place, or an event. (Chapter 16)

speeches to entertain Have the general goal to amuse, delight, and engage the audience for the purpose of enjoyment with a bit of wisdom or tribute thrown in. (Chapter 16)

speeches to inspire Speeches that motivate, stir, encourage, or arouse the audience. (Chapter 16)

speech of award acceptance The response a speaker gives after receiving an award, prize, or honor. (Chapter 16)

speech of award presentation A speech given to announce the recipient(s) of an award, prize, or honor. (Chapter 16)

speech of inspiration A speech that strives to motivate, encourage, move, or arouse an audience in a positive manner. (Chapter 16)

speech of introduction A speech that introduces the next or main speaker. (Chapter 16)

speech to describe A speech that describes an object, a person, an animal, a place, or an event. (Chapter 13)

speech to explain A speech that explains a concept or issue. (Chapter 13)

speech to instruct A speech that teaches or demonstrates a process. (Chapter 13)

speech to report An oral report or briefing. (Chapter 13)

standard of balance The subpoints under the main point in a speech should be nearly equal to each other in length and weight. (Chapter 6)

statistics Numerical facts or data that are summarized, organized, and tabulated to present significant information about a given population. (Chapter 4)

stereotyping The false or oversimplified generalizing applied to individuals based on group characteristics. (Chapter 1)

storming The phase of group development when the small group begins focusing on its goal and may become complex as power and relationship issues erupt. (Chapter 18)

strategy A plan designed to achieve a goal, particularly concerning the relationship and arrangement of a speech's main points. (Chapter 6)

subpoints Subordinate points that offer information to support and relate back to the main points of a speech. (Chapter 5)

support materials Any information that helps explain, elaborate, or validate a speech topic. (Chapter 3)

surveys Series of questions used to collect quantifiable information from a population. (Chapters 1, 3)

syllogism The classical form of deductive reasoning, featuring major and minor premises and a conclusion. (Chapter 14)

symbolic A word that represents what it is referring to either by association, resemblance, or convention. (Chapter 8)

tables Visuals consisting of numbers or words arranged in rows, columns, or lists. (Chapter 10)

target audience The primary group of people the speaker is appealing to. (Chapter 15)

task communication The necessary interactions a leader must make during small group meetings to keep the group on task to reach its goal. (Chapter 18)

terminating/reforming The fifth phase of group development, when the small group either disbands or reforms with a new goal. (Chapter 18)

testimony Firsthand knowledge or opinions held by someone. (Chapter 4)

toast A speech expressing honor or goodwill to a person, institution, group, or an event that is punctuated by taking a drink. (Chapter 16)

topical strategy Used when there is a strong inherent or traditional division of subtopics within the main topic. (Chapter 6)

transactional process The fluid process of communication where the speaker and the listener participate equally by giving and receiving information to and from one another. (Overview)

transitions Words or phrases signaling movement from one point to another and how the points relate to each other. (Chapter 5)

tribute A speech that commemorates the lives or accomplishments of people, groups, institutions, or events, either with the recipient present or posthumously. (Chapter 16)

tropes Language techniques that transform ordinary words. (Chapter 8)

understanding The phase of the listening process in which meaning is applied to a sound. (Chapter 11)

values The enduring principles related to worth or what a person sees as right or wrong, important or unimportant. (Chapters 1, 14)

variety The fluctuation, change, or adjustment of a speaker's volume, pitch, rate, and pauses. (Chapter 9)

video clips Footage from television, movies, or any other type of video. (Chapter 10)

virtual small groups Assisted by electronic media, these groups function much like other small groups, only they may never or rarely meet face-to-face. (Chapter 18)

visible Web Includes anything accessible online through a general search engine. (Chapter 3)

volume How loud or soft the speaker's voice is. (Chapter 9)

warrants Assumptions that act as links between the evidence and the claim in an argument. (Chapter 14)

Web An information-sharing model built on top of the Internet that allows access to the information. (Chapter 3)

Web sites Consist of multiple, unified pages beginning with a home page, created and maintained by an individual, group, business, or organization. (Chapter 3)

working groups Individuals who meet in a formal atmosphere to work on a specific task. (Chapter 18)

working main points The early drafts of a speaker's main points that are subject to change during the course of research. (Chapter 2)

working outline A brief, usually handwritten, outline of the body of the speech, used to guide the research during the early stages of creating a speech. (Chapters 2, 5)

written evaluations Assessments given in written form. (Chapter 12)

Bibliography

Adams, Katherine and Gloria J. Galanes. *Communicating in Groups: Applications and Skills*. 7th ed. Boston: McGraw, 2009. 12–13. Print.

Aristotle. "De Anima." Trans. J. A. Smith. *The Basic Works of Aristotle*. Ed. Richard McKeon. New York: Random, 1941. 554–581. Print.

—. "De Caelo." Trans. J. L. Stocks. *The Basic Works of Aristotle*. Ed. Richard McKeon. New York: Random, 1941. 404. Print.

—. "Rhetorica." Trans. W. Rhys Roberts. *The Basic Works of Aristotle*. Ed. Richard McKeon. New York: Random, 1941. Print.

Burke, Kenneth. *A Rhetoric of Motives*. Berkeley: U of California P, 1969. viii. Print.

Carson, Rachel L. *Under the Sea-Wind: A Naturalist's Picture of Ocean Life*. 1st ed. New York: Simon, 1941. xiii. Print.

Conan Doyle, Arthur. *The Hound of Baskervilles*. New York: Grossett, 1902. 36. Print.

Corbett, Edward J. and Robert J. Connors. *Classical Rhetoric for the Modern Student*. 4th ed. New York: Oxford UP, 1999. 62–71. Print.

Duarte, Nancy. *Slide:ology: The Art and Science of Creating Great Presentations*. Sebastopol: O'Reilly, 2008. 13, 83. Print.

Ferrell, O. C. and Michael Hartline. *Marketing Strategy*. 3rd ed. Mason: Thomson South-Western, 2005. 236. Print.

Festinger, Leon. *A Theory of Cognitive Dissonance*. Stanford: Stanford UP, 1957. Print.

Fishbein, Martin and Icek Ajzen. *Belief, Attitude, Intention, and Behavior: An Introduction to Theory and Research*. Reading: Addison-Wesley, 1975. 6. Print.

Frymier, Ann Bainbridge and Marjorie Keeshan Nadler. *Persuasion: Integrating Theory, Research, and Practice*. 2nd ed. Dubuque: Kendall, 2010. 34. Print.

Harris, Thomas E. and John C. Sherblom. *Small Group and Team Communication*. 5th ed. Boston: Allyn, 2011. 46-47. Print.

Hofstede, Geert. *Culture's Consequences: International Differences in Work-Related Values*. 2nd ed. Beverly Hills: Sage, 2001. Print.

Lancaster, Lynne C. and David Stillman. *When Generations Collide*. New York: Harper, 2002. 18–32. Print.

Legal Information Institute. "First Amendment." *United States Constitution*. Cornell U School of Law, n.d. Web. 17 Aug. 2010.

Littlejohn, Stephen W. and Karen A. Foss. *Theories of Human Communication*. 9th ed. Belmont: Thomson Wadsworth, 2008. 27. Print.

Lippmann, Walter. "The Indispensable Opposition." *Atlantic Monthly* 164.2 (1939): 188. Print.

Mandela, Nelson. *Long Walk to Freedom: The Autobiography of Nelson Mandela*. New York: Back Bay, 1995. Print.

Maslow, Abraham. *Motivation and Personality*. New York: Harper, 1954. 80–106. Print.

Monroe, Alan H. *Principles and Types of Speeches*. Chicago: Scott, 1935. Print.

Moore, Brooke Noel and Richard Parker. *Critical Thinking*. 4th ed. Mountain View: Mayfield, 1995. 4. Print.

Ogden, Charles K. and Ivor A. Richards. *The Meaning of Meaning*. 8th ed. New York: Harcourt, 1949. Print.

Pelias, Ronald J. and Tracy Stephenson Shaffer. *Performance Studies: The Interpretation of Aesthetic Texts*. Dubuque: Kendall, 2007. 181–195. Print.

Petty, Richard. E. and John T. Cacioppo. *Communication and Persuasion: Central and Peripheral Routes to Attitude Change*. New York: Springer-Verlag, 1986. Print.

Population Reference Bureau. "Traditional Families Account for Only 7 Percent of U.S. Households." *PRB*, Population Reference Bureau, n.d. Web. 22 Oct. 2010.

Sagan, Carl. *The Demon-Haunted World: Science as a Candle in the Dark*. New York: Random, 1996. 209–217. Print.

Samovar, Larry A., Richard E. Porter, and Edwin R. McDaniel. *Communication Between Cultures*. 7th ed. Boston: Wadsworth, 2010. 36–39, 198–207. Print.

Sherif, Muzafer and Carl I. Hovland. *Social Judgment: Assimilation and Contrast Effects in Communication and Attitude Change*. New Haven: Yale UP, 1961. Print.

Sleep Disorders Center. "Relaxation Techniques." *University of Maryland Medical Center*. University of Maryland Medical Center, 3 Aug. 2010. Web. 10 Aug. 2010.

Syrus, Publius. *The Moral Sayings of Publius Syrus, A Roman Slave*. Trans. Darius Lyman, Jr. Cleveland: L. E. Barnard. 1856. 43. Print.

Toulmin, Stephen Edelston. *The Uses of Argument*. New York: Cambridge UP, 1958. 94–145. Print.

Toulmin, Stephen, Richard Rieke, and Allan Janik. *An Introduction to Reasoning*. 2nd ed. New York: Macmillan, 1984. 129–175. Print.

Tuckman, Bruce W. "Stages in Small Group Development Revisited." *Group and Organizational Studies* 2 (1977): 419–427. Print.

United States Census Bureau. "An Older More Diverse Nation by Midcentury." *U.S. Census Bureau Newsroom*. U.S. Department of Commerce, 17 April 2009. Web. 7 June 2009.

Notes

OVERVIEW

1. "First Amendment Attorney Floyd Abrams Talks About Three Decades of Free Speech" *(Center for Individual Freedom*, 15 June 2005), Web, 1 April 2010.

2. Gerald Ford, *A Time to Heal* (New York: Harper, 1979), 50, Print.

3. David G. Myers and Malcolm A. Jeeves, *Psychology through the Eyes of Faith* (San Francisco: Christian College Coalition, 1987), 139, Print.

CHAPTER 1

1. Norman Katlov, *The Fabulous Fanny: The Story of Fanny Brice* (New York: Knopf, 1953), 71, Print.

CHAPTER 4

1. Ed. Robert I. Fitzhenry, *The Harper Book of Quotations*, 3rd ed. (New York: Harper, 1993), 398, Print.

CHAPTER 8

1. Martin Luther King, Jr. "I Have a Dream," Lincoln Memorial (Washington: 28 Aug. 1963), Speech.

2. Sojourner Truth, "Ain't I a Woman?" Women's Convention (Akron: May 1851), Speech.

3. Patrick Henry, "Give Me Liberty or Give Me Death," St. John's Henrico Parish Church (Richmond: 25 Mar. 1775), Address.

4. Hillary Clinton, "Women's Rights Are Human Rights" (Beijing: 5 Sept. 1995), Speech.

5. Ludwig Wittgenstein, Ed. C.K. Ogden, *Tractatus Logico-Philosophicus* (New York: Harcourt, 1922), 149, Print.

CHAPTER 9

1. Although commonly attributed to Aristotle, this quotation originates from Will Durant's summation of Aristotle's ideas in Ethics, book II, chapter 4 and book I, chapter 7. See Will Durant, *The Story of Philosophy: The Lives and Opinions of the World's Greatest Philosophers* (New York: Pocket, 1991), 76, Print.

CHAPTER 11

1. Rachel Naomi Remen, *Kitchen Table Wisdom: Stories that Heal* (New York: Berkley, 2006), 143, Print.

CHAPTER 16

1. Titus Maccius Plautus, Ed. Ferruccio Bertini, *Asinaria* (Padova: R.A.D.A.R., 1968), 104, Print.

CHAPTER 17

1. Marty Blalock, "Why Good Communication Is Good Business," *Wisconsin Business Alumni Update* (Board of Regents of the U of Wisconsin, Dec. 2005), Web, 27 Aug. 2010.

2. Laura Harris, *Surrender to Win* (Austin: Greenleaf Book Group P, 2009), 147, Print.

Credits

PHOTOGRAPHS

OVERVIEW: Tab 1 (front) © Getty Images; **Tab 1 (back):** © imagebroker/Alamy; **2** Columbia College/Megan Pettegrew-Donley; **6** © Image Source/Alamy; **8** © Bryan Mullennix/Alamy; **12** © Realistic Reflections/Alamy; **14** Columbia College/Kaci Smart; **16** © Oliver Knight/Alamy

Chapter 1: 24 Ryan McVay; **26** © Tetra Images/Alamy; **28** (left) © Radius Images/Corbis, (right) © Bryan Allen/Corbis; **29** (left) © Jim Young/Reuters/Corbis, (right) © Jerry Arcieri/Corbis; **30** © INSADCO Photography/Alamy; **36** Roy Hsu; **37** Columbia College/Kaci Smart **38** LINKS/A.collection; **40** hana/Datacraft; **43** U.S. Department of Commerce http://www.ntis.gov/newpage.aspx?np=y&url=http://www.commerce.gov. National Technical Information Service, Alexandria, VA 22312; **44** © Peter Cavanagh/Alamy; **46** © RubberBall/Alamy

Chapter 2: 48 Campus Life; **50** © Mark Sykes/Alamy; **53** © 2010 National Geographic Society; **56** © David Crausby/Alamy; **58** © Rick Barrentine/Corbis; **64** © Beaconstox/Alamy; **66** © ALEXANDRE SILVA/Alamy

Chapter 3: Tab 2 (front) © Ladi Kirn/Alamy; **Tab 2 (back)** Dorling Kindersley; **70** Influx Productions; **72** © Ladi Kirn/Alamy; **80** Universal Images Group; **85** © David Adamson/Alamy; **86** © Jason/Alamy; **90** © Andy Mills/Star Ledger/Corbis; **94** © Kristian Peetz/Alamy; **98** © Serge Kozak; **102** © image100/Alamy; **106** © UpperCut Images/Alamy

Chapter 4: 108 © Wilfried Krecichwost/Corbis; **110** © ImageDJ/Alamy, **116** © Paul Bradforth/Alamy; **120** © James Leynse/Corbis; **122** © Geoffrey Kidd/Alamy; **126** Lester Lefkowitz; **130** © [apply pictures]/Alamy; **134** © UpperCut Images/Alamy

Chapter 5: Tab 3 (front) GK Hart/Vikki Hart; **Tab 3 (back)** © amana images inc./Alamy; **138** © face to face Bildagentur GmbH/Alamy; **140** © Joe Fairs/Alamy; **142** © Micah Hanson/Alamy; **152** © tbkmedia.de/Alamy; **160** © Image Source/Corbis; **164** © Platinum GPics/Alamy; **166** © Fancy/Alamy; **170** © GraficallyMinded/Alamy

Chapter 6: 172 © ZHOU CHAO/epa/Corbis; **174** © Corbis Super RF/Alamy; **184** © Michael Haegele/Corbis; **186** © amana images inc./Alamy; **192** © Francisco Villaflor/Alamy

Chapter 7: 194 © Corbis Premium RF/Alamy; **196** © MARKA/Alamy; **198** © Gabe Palmer/Alamy; **204** Henry Horenstein; **206** © Paul Bradforth/Alamy; **208** © Peter Casolino/Alamy; **210** © Mick Sinclair/Alamy; **212** © Angela Hampton Picture Library/Alamy

Chapter 8: Tab 4 (front) © Sprint/Corbis; **Tab 4 (back)** © Bettman/Corbis; **216** Image Source; **217** DK Images; **220** Jupiterimages; **228** bilderlounge/bilderlounge; **234** © Schlegelmilch/Corbis

Chapter 9: 236 © Hill Street Studios/Blend Images/Corbis; **238** © Odilon Dimier/PhotoAlto/Corbis; **244** © Hill Street Studios/Blend Images/Corbis; **245** (left) © Laura Doss/Corbis, (right) © Tetra Images/Alamy; **246** (top and bottom) © RubberBall/Alamy; **247** (top left) © digitallife/Alamy, (top right) © Inspirestock Inc./Alamy, (bottom left) ColorBlind Images, (bottom right) ERproductions Ltd; **248** iStock Photo; **252** © Number 7/Alamy; **256** © SoFood/Alamy; **258** (top) © S.E.A. Photo/Alamy, (bottom) © Robert Harding World Imagery/Corbis

Chapter 10: 260 Thomas Barwick; **262** Hugh Sitton; **264** (left) RedChopsticks, (right) © Hugh Threlfall/Alamy; **265** © Lew Robertson/Corbis; **266** DK Images; **267** DK Images; **272** Noel Hendrickson; **273** © cambpix/Alamy; **274** Ryan McVay; **276** © Image Source/Alamy; **277** Jon Feingersh; **278** George Doyle; **279** © Blend Images/Alamy; **280** George Doyle; **281** Daly and Newton; **282** Gary John Norman; **283** DK Images; **284** DK Images; **285** DK Images; **286** © WoodyStock/Alamy; **288** © Corbis Premuim RF/Alamy; **292** (top) © WoodyStock/Alamy, (bottom) DK Images; **294** iStock Photo; **296** (top) © Image Source/Corbis, (bottom left) © Peter Arnold, Inc./Alamy, (bottom right) DK Images; **297** DK Images

Chapter 11: Tab 5 (front) © The National Trust Photolibrary/Alamy; **Tab 5 (back)** © Mikhail Kovalev/Alamy; **300** © Simon Jarratt/Corbis; **302** © Jose Luis Pelaez, Inc./Blend Images/Corbis; **304** Stockbyte; **306** Marilli Forastieri; **308** © fStop/Alamy; **312** Floridapfe from S.Korea Kim in cherl; **314** © Blend Images/Alamy

Chapter 12: 316 © vario images GmbH & Co.KG/Alamy; **318** © David L. Moore – Studio/Alamy; **322** Clarissa Leahy; **324** © Simon Jarratt/Corbis; **326** © Eric Audras/PhotoAlto/Corbis; **330** Clarissa Leahy

Chapter 13: Tab 6 (front) © Staffan Widstrand/Corbis; **Tab 6 (back)** © Westend61 GmbH/Alamy; **334** Reza Estakhrian; **336** © Zute Lightfoot/Alamy; **338** © Ocean/Corbis; **346** Andy Ryan; **348** © David Papazian/Corbis; **350** Chris Teso www.christeso.com/photography; **354** Jason Todd; **362** © Inspirestock Inc./Alamy; **364** iStock Photo; **366** Mike Booth/Alamy

Chapter 14: Tab 7 (front) Jamie Grill; **Tab 7 (back)** Colin Hawkins; **370** © Images-USA/Alamy; **372** © chris stock photography/Alamy; **380** © Peter Glass/Alamy; **384** ©

Coaster/Alamy; **388** © Mike Hill/Alamy; **392** © Ken Welsh/Alamy; **400** © mm-images/Alamy

Chapter 15: **402** Blend Images/Jon Feingersh; **404** Jonny Basker; **406** Absodels; **418** Jose Luis Pelaez; **420** Superstudio; **422** © Mettafoto/Alamy; **426** Bernard van Berg; **436** Reza Estakhrian; **438** Chris Ryan; **440** © mm-images/Alamy

Chapter 16: Tab 8 (front) Cynthia Edorh; **Tab 8 (back)** © Image Source/Corbis; **445** © Blend Images/Alamy; **446** © Vstock LLC/Tetra Images/Corbis; **448** © Stefan Zaklin/epa/Corbis; **468** © UpperCut Images/Alamy

Chapter 17: Tab 9 (front) © UK Stock Images Ltd/Alamy; **Tab 9 (back)** © Moment/cultura/Corbis; **472** © image100/Alamy; **474** © LAMB/Alamy; **480** Photo Alto/Alamy; **482** © Corbis Super RF/Alamy; **488** © Blend Images/Alamy; **490** © Yuri Arcurs/Alamy

Chapter 18: 492 Anthony Marsland/Getty Images; **494** © Radius Images/Corbis; **496** © Paul Burns/Blend Images/Corbis; **500** © Sean Justice/Corbis; **502** © Mark Edward Atkinson/Blend Images/Corbis; **504** © Andres Rodriguez/Alamy

TEXT

OVERVIEW: 3 Michelangelo quotation, Michelangelo di Lodovico Buonarroti Simoni (6 March 1475–18 February 1564), commonly known as Michelangelo, was an Italian Renaissance painter, sculptor, architect, poet, and engineer. **5** Martin Luther King, Jr. quotation, Reprinted by arrangement with The Heirs to the Estate of Martin Luther King, Jr., c/o Writers House as agent for the proprietor New York, NY. Copyright 1963 Dr. Martin Luther King, Jr., copyright renewed 1991 Coretta Scott King. Publilius Syrus quotation, Roman author Publilius Syrus, The first century BCE; **7** Relaxation techniques, University of Maryland Medical Center (http://www.umm.edu/sleep/relax_tech.htm#c). Used by permission.; **9** Aristotle quotation, Aristotle (384 BC–322 BC), Greek philosopher; **11** First Amendment text, The United States Constitution; Floyd Abrams quotation, Floyd Abrams, Attorney and Constitutional law expert; **13** Gerald R. Ford quotation, "A Time to Heal," by Gerald R. Ford, 38th President of the United States 1974–1977; **23** Jesse Jackson quotation, Reverend Jesse Jackson. Speech at Anderson College, 4 March 1979. Anderson. Indiana.

Chapter 1: 26 Fanny Brice quotation, Fanny Brice, famous stage, radio, and film star of the 1940s and 1950s. © Norman Katlov, *The Fabulous Fanny: The Story of Fanny Brice* (New York: Alfred A. Knopf, 1953), 71, Print.; **31** Generation trends table, © Lancaster, Lynne C. and David Stillman. *When Generations Collide.* New York: Harper Business, 2002. 18–32. Print.; **32** Maslow's hierarchy of needs illustration, Maslow, Abraham

(1954). *Motivation and Personality.* New York: Harper Collins.; **34** Changes in U.S. population diversity illustration, U.S. Census Bureau; **35** Hofstede's five dimensions of culture table, Samovar, Larry A., Richard E. Porter, and Edwin R. McDaniel. *Communication Between Cultures,* 7th ed. Boston: Wadsworth, 2010. 36–39, 198–207. Print.; **43** Gallup screenshot, Gallup.com; Pew Research Center screenshot, © Pew Research; USA.gov screenshot, www.firstgov.gov; U.S. Census screenshot, U.S. Census; Infoplease screenshot, Pearson Education

Chapter 2: 53 Yahoo! Screenshot, © Yahoo! Used by permission.; Librarians' Internet Index screenshot, Librarians' Internet Index; *Newsweek* cover, From *Newsweek,* 8/13/07 © Harman Newsweek LLC, Inc. All rights reserved. Used by permission and protected by the Copyright Laws of the United States. The printing, copying, redistribution, or retransmission of the Material without express written permission is prohibited. Cover photo courtesy of SOHO/EIT (ESA & NASA).

Chapter 3: 72 Google screenshot, reused by permission of Google, Inc.; Excite screenshot, Copyright IAC Search and Media, www.excite.com, www.life123.com. 2010.; **73** DMOZ screenshot, used by permission of Netscape, Inc., www.dmoz.org; Complete Planet screenshot, Copyright, www.brightplanet.com. 2010.; **74** Monsanto quotation, Copyright "Monsanto Donates Corn and Vegetable Seeds to Haiti." 14 May 2010. www.monsanto.com. Used by permission.; Monsanto screenshot, Copyright, www.monsanto.com, 2010.; **75** UNISEF quotation and screenshot, Copyright "Achieving Zero," from The Believe in Zero Campaign, 2010, www.unicef.org. Used by permission of UNICEF.; **76** Air Force One quotation, White House Blog, July 14, 2010, www.whitehouse.gov; White House screenshot, www.whitehouse.gov, Official White House website; **77** Annette Kennedy screenshot, Copyright Annette Kennedy. David Walker Web Designs. Used by permission.; **78, 79** Columbia College screenshot, Copyright Columbia College, Columbia, MO, www.ccis.edu, 2010. Used by permission.; **81** University of Colorado screenshot, © U of Colorado at Boulder Libraries; **83** J Stor screenshot, Reprinted courtesy of ITHAKA. ITHAKA, Copyright 2010. All rights reserved.; **84** *The Beginner's Guide to Preserving Food at Home* cover, Courtesy of Storey Publication, No. Adams, MA.; **85** *Wall Street Journal* quotation, Copyright *Wall Street Journal,* July 23, 2010; **86** Tom O'Neill quotation, Copyright *National Geographic Magazine,* September 2009. Tom O'Neill, from "Every Bird a King." Used by permission.; **87** Signs of Stroke list and screenshot, Federal Government Website, "NIH, News in Health," www.nih.gov, 2010.; **88** *Journal of Film of Video* text and cover, Copyright 2010 by the Board of Trustees of the University of Illinois. Used with permission of the University of Illinois Press.; **89** *Huckleberry Finn* cover, http://commons.wikimedia.org/wiki/File:E._W._Kemble_-_Adventures_of_Huckleberry_Finn_Cover.jpg; **91** City of Columbia quotation, Official Website, City of

Columbia, MO, www.gocolumbiamo.com, 2010; USA.gov screenshot, U.S. Government Website, www.us.gov, 2010; **92** *The Penguin Dictionary* cover, Copyright *The Penguin Dictionary of American English Usage and Style: A Readable Reference Book, Illuminating Thousands of Traps That Snare Writers and Speakers,* by Paul W. Lovinger. Used by permission.; **93** Quoin definition, By permission from *Merriam-Webster's Collegiate® Dictionary,* 11th ed. © 2010 by Merriam-Webster, Inc. (www.merriam-webster. com); Refdesk screenshot, Used by permission of www.refdesk. com, 2010.; Infoplease screenshot, © Pearson Education. Used by permission.; **103** *Silent Spring* quotation, From *Silent Spring* by Rachel Carson. Copyright © 1962 by Rachel L. Carson. Used by permission of Frances Collin, Trustee. Any electronic copying or distribution of this text is expressly forbidden.; March of Dimes text, Copyright 2010, March of Dimes Foundation. Used by permission.; **106** Even Fairbanks quotation, Copyright "Father Disfigure" by Eve Fairbanks, *Newsweek* online; **107** Apartheid definition, Copyright *The American Heritage Dictionary of the English Language,* 4th ed. 2000, Houghton Mifflin Company. Found at http://education.yahoo.com/reference/dictionary/entry/apartheid.

Chapter 4: 109 Will Henry quotation, Fitzhenry, Robert I., ed. *The Harper Book of Quotations,* 3rd ed. New York: HarperCollins Reference, 1993. 398. Print.; Digital Piracy quotation, Copyright *Webster's New World Finance and Investment Dictionary,* 2003. Reproduced with permission of John Wiley & Sons, Inc.; **111** Kathleen Sebelius text, Kathleen Sebelius, U.S. Director of Health and Human Services. Statements she made in 2009 in various outlets, largely transcripts/statements on CDC.gov and flu.gov.; **113** *New England Journal of Medicine* text, Ojikutu, Bisola O. and Stone, Valerie E., "Women, Inequality, and the Burden of HIV." *New England Journal of Medicine,* Feb. 17, 2005. Copyright © 2005 Massachusetts Medical Society. All rights reserved.; **114** Katie Smith text, Copyright Turner Sports and Entertainment, www.wnba.com, August 3, 2009; President Obama's job approval rating text, Copyright Gallup, Inc. Used by permission.; **128** National Geographic quotation, Copyright *National Geographic,* "Africa's Last Frontier" by Neil Shea, March 2010. Used by permission of the *National Geographic* Society.; Aristotle text, Aristotle (384 BC–322 BC), Greek philosopher; **129** *National Geographic* quotation, Copyright *National Geographic,* "Africa's Last Frontier" by Neil Shea, March 2010. Used by permission of the National Geographic Society.; **130, 132** Douglas Brinkley quotation, Copyright Brinkley, Douglas, "The World According to Tom," *Time.* 15 March 2010.; **135** Nelson Mandela screenshot, Copyright The Nelson Mandela Foundation, http://www.nelsonmandela.org. Used by permission.; Nelson Mandela quotation (Nobel Lecture), Copyright Mandela's Nobel lecture, December 10, 1993. Copyright Nobel Prize, www.nobelprize.org.; Nelson Mandela

quotation ("Our message was"), © *Long Walk to Freedom: The Autobiography of Nelson Mandela.* Back Bay Books, 1995.

Chapter 6: 182 Monroe's Motivational Sequence example text, Monroe, Alan H. *Principles and Types of Speeches.* Chicago: Scott, 1935. Print.; **183** AIDA example text, Ferrell, O. C. and Hartline, Michael. *Marketing Strategy,* 3rd ed. Mason: Thomson South-Western, 2005. 236. Print.

Chapter 7: 199 CDC example text, Centers for Disease Control and Prevention, 2006; *Under the Sea-Wind* quotation, Carson, Rachel L., *Under the Sea-Wind: A Naturalist's Picture of Ocean Life,* 1st ed. New York: Simon Schuster, 1941. xiii. Print.; **200** Darfur example text, *Washington Post,* "In Sudan, Death and Denial" by Emily Wax. *Washington Post* Foreign Service Sunday, June 27, 2004. Page A01 http://www.washingtonpost. com/wp-dyn/articles/A8610-2004Jun26.html Joke example text, http://www.teach-nology.com/jokes/change.html. Used by permission.; **201** President Barack Obama speech, President Barack Obama's speech to Congress, September 9, 2009; **202** Sven-Göran Eriksson quotation, Swedish soccer manager, Sven-Göran Eriksson; **205** Coombs excerpt, Coombs, Robert H. *Handbook of Addictive Disorders: A Practical Guide to Diagnosis and Treatment.* Hoboken: Wiley, 2004. 411. Print. Reprinted with permission of John Wiley & Sons, Inc.; Stanford University survey, The Stanford University School of Medicine Survey, 2006; **208** Neil Armstrong quotation, Neil Armstrong, American astronaut and the first person to set foot on the moon, July 20, 1969.; **213** "Meet Me in St. Louis" lyrics, Lyrics by Andres Sterling, written in 1904 in honor of The Louisiana Purchase.

Chapter 8: Tab 4: Martin Luther King, Jr. quotation, Lincoln Memorial (Washington DC: 28 Aug. 1963) Speech. Reprinted by arrangement with The Heirs to the Estate of Martin Luther King, Jr., c/o Writers House as agent for the proprietor New York, NY. Copyright 1963 Dr. Martin Luther King, Jr; copyright renewed 1991 Coretta Scott King. **215** Sojourner Truth quotation, Sojourner Truth, "Ain't I a Woman?" Women's Convention (Akron, OH: May 1851) Speech; Patrick Henry quotation, Patrick Henry, "Give Me Liberty or Give Me Death," St. John's Henrico Parish Church (Richmond, VA: 25 Mar. 1775) Address; Hillary Rodham Clinton quotation, Speech. "Women's Rights Are Human Rights," First Lady, Hillary Rodham Clinton, at the UN World Conference on Women, Beijing, China, 5 Sept. 1995 by invitation of the UN Secretary General.; **216, 217** Triangle of Meaning text, © Ogden, Charles K. and Ivor A. Richards. *The Meaning of Meaning,* 8th ed. New York: Harcourt Brace Jovanovich, 1949. Print.; **217** Bat (animal) definition, www.merriam-webster. com; Bat (baseball) definition, www.merriam-webster.com; **218** Ludwig Wittgenstein quotation, Ludwig Josef Johann

Wittgenstein (26 April 1889–29 April 1951), 20th century philosopher. Ludwig Wittgenstein, ed. C. K. Ogden, *Tractatus Logico-Philosophicus,* (New York: Harcourt, Brace & Company, 1922) 149. Print.; *Communication Between Cultures* text, © Larry A. Samovar, Richard E. Porter, and Edwin R. McDaniel, *Communication Between Cultures,* Wadsworth Publishing, 5th ed. (August 1, 2003).; **219** Flash mob definition, By permission. From *Merriam-Webster's Collegiate® Dictionary,* 11th Edition. © 2010 by Merriam-Webster, Incorporated (www.merriam-webster.com).; 220 *Friends* quotation, "The One Where Chandler Doesn't Like Dogs," *Friends.* NBC Dir. Kevin S. Bright. 23 Nov. 2000. Television.; **223** Declaration of Independence quotation, United States Declaration of Independence; **227** Barack Obama example text, At the time Illinois Senator Barack Obama, Speech, Democratic National Convention, 2004; **230** Martin Luther King, Jr. example text, Martin Luther King, Jr. "I Have a Dream," Lincoln Memorial (Washington D.C.: 28 Aug. 1963) Speech. Reprinted by arrangement with The Heirs to the Estate of Martin Luther King, Jr., c/o Writers House as agent for the proprietor New York, NY. Copyright 1963 Dr. Martin Luther King, Jr; copyright renewed 1991 Coretta Scott King.; **231** Shakespeare quotation, William Shakespeare, *The Merchant of Venice,* 3:1; **232** Martin Luther King, Jr. example text, Martin Luther King, Jr. "I Have a Dream," Lincoln Memorial (Washington DC: 28 Aug. 1963) Speech. Reprinted by arrangement with The Heirs to the Estate of Martin Luther King, Jr., c/o Writers House as agent for the proprietor New York, NY. Copyright 1963 Dr. Martin Luther King, Jr; copyright renewed 1991 Coretta Scott King,; **233** Hillary Clinton quotation, Excerpt from speech at the Democratic National Convention, 2008, Hillary Rodham Clinton; Winston Churchill quotation, Winston Churchill in a speech to the House of Commons, June 4, 1940; John F. Kennedy ("American vessels") quotation, John F. Kennedy, *Profiles in Courage.* New York: Harper & Row, 1964. 214. Print.; George W. Bush quotation, U.S. President George W. Bush in address to Joint Session of Congress, 20 September 2001; Benjamin Franklin quotation, Benjamin Franklin, one of the founding fathers, leading author, politician, inventor, and diplomat.; Neil Armstrong quotation, Neil Armstrong, American astronaut and the first person to set foot on the moon, July 20, 1969; Richard Nixon quotation, President Richard Nixon, Inaugural Speech, January 20, 1969; John F. Kennedy ("Ask not" and "Pay any price") quotation, President John F. Kennedy, Inaugural Speech, January 20, 1961; Julius Caesar quotation, Reportedly written by Julius Caesar, ancient general and ruler of the Roman Empire.

Chapter 9: 237 Will Durant quotation, Although commonly attributed to Aristotle, this quotation originates from Will Durant's summation of Aristotle's ideas in *Ethics,* Book II,

Chapter 4 and Book I, Chapter 7. See Will Durant, *The Story of Philosophy: The Lives and Opinions of the World's Greatest Philosophers* (New York: Pocket Books, 1991), 76, Print. **240** John F. Kennedy quotation, President John F. Kennedy, Inaugural Speech, January 20, 1961; **241** Jean Paul Richter quotation, Jean (Johann) Paul Richter, German writer, 1763–1825; Ronald Reagan quotation, U.S. President Ronald Reagan, remarks delivered in front of Brandenburg Gate, commonly known as the Berlin Wall, on June 12, 1987; **259** Domesticated dog speech text, "Pet File Facts: Dogs." *BBC Science & Nature.* BBC, Mar. 2004. Web. 9 Nov. 2010.

Chapter 10: 269, 270, 271 Carbon emissions text, Land area loss graph, U.S. diversity graph, and Greenhouse gas emissions graph, Originally published in *Dire Predictions: Understanding Global Warming,* by Michael E. Mann and Lee R. Kump, © 2008 Dorling Kindersley Limited. These graphs based on original data documented in the Fourth Assessment Report of the IPCC.; **282** Nancy Duarte quotation, Duarte, Nancy. *Slide:ology: The Art and Science of Creating Great Presentations.* Sebastopol: O'Reilly, 2008. 13, 18. Print.; **283** Greece country facts, U.S. Department of State, www.travel.state.gov; **284** Greece's people, *Encyclopaedia Britannica;* The Parthenon, www.sacredsites.com; **286** Greece's currency, worldtravelguide.net; **289** Practicing ethics text, www.utsystem.edu/ogc/intellectualproperty/copypol2.htm; **290, 291** PowerPoint screenshots, © Microsoft, Inc. Used by permission.; **292** Greece's currency, worldtravelguide.net.

Chapter 11: 299 "Can you hear me now?" quotation, Verizon Commercial, 2002. © Verizon, Inc.; Rachel Naomi Remen quotation, Rachel Naomi Remen, *Kitchen Table Wisdom: Stories that Heal* (New York: The Berkley Publishing Group, 2006), 143. Print.; **305** Critical thinking quotation, © Brooke Moore and Richard Parker, *Critical Thinking,* 4th ed. Mountain View: Mayfield, 1995. 4. Print.; Carl Sagan quotation, Carl Sagan, (1934–1996) American astronomer, astrophysicist, author, and cosmologist who popularized the natural sciences.; **315** Successful entrepreneur text, www.business.gov/start/start-a-business.html.

Chapter 12: 319 Pelias and Shaffer text, © Pelias, Ronald J. and Tracey Stephenson Shaffer, *Performance Studies: The Interpretation of Aesthetic Texts.* Dubuque: Kendall Hunt, 2007. 181–195. Print.; **320** Sherlock Holmes quotation, *The Hounds of the Baskervilles;* **331** MasterCard quotation, © MasterCard, Inc.

Chapter 13: 355, 357 John Muir quotation, © Muir, J. (1901). *Our National Parks.* New York: Houghton Mifflin.

Chapter 14: 371 Attitudes text, © Fishbein, Martin and Ajzen, Icek. *Belief, Attitude, Intention, and Behavior: An Introduction to Theory and Research.* Reading: Addison-Wesley, 1975. 6. Print.; Beliefs and Values text, Frymier, Ann Bainbridge and Nadler,

Marjorie Keeshan. *Persuasion: Integrating Theory, Research, and Practice,* 2nd ed. Dubuque: Kendall Hunt, 2010. 34. Print.; **376** *Rhetoric* text, "Rhetorica." Trans. W. Rhys Roberts. *The Basic Works of Aristotle.* Ed. Richard McKeon. New York: Random House, 1941. Print.; *Time* magazine cover, © Time Magazine, Inc. January 2010. Used by permission.; **377** Riccardo Conti quotation, International Committee of the Red Cross, www.icrc.org; **380, 381** Alan Monroe text, Monroe, Alan H. *Principles and Types of Speeches.* Chicago: Scott, 1935. Print.; Maslow's hierarchy of needs illustration, Maslow, Abraham. *Motivation and Personality.* New York: Harper & Row, 1954. 80–106. Print.; **382** Cognitive Dissonance Theory text, Festinger, Leon. *A Theory of Cognitive Dissonance.* Stanford: Stanford UP, 1957. Print.; **383** Expectancy-Outcome Values Theory text, Fishbein, Martin and Ajzen, Icek. *Belief, Attitude, Intention, and Behavior: An Introduction to Theory and Research.* Reading: Addison-Wesley, 1975. 6. Print.; Elaboration Likelihood Model text, Petty, Richard E. and Cacioppo, John T. *Communication and Persuasion: Central and Peripheral Routes to Attitude Change.* New York: Springer-Verlag, 1986. Print.; **385** Chickens text, Kilarski, Barbara. *Tending Small Flocks in Cities, Suburbs, and Other Small Spaces* and Luttmann, Rick and Gail. *Chickens in Your Backyard: A Beginner's Guide;* **386** Warrants text, Toulmin, Stephen Edelston. *The Uses of Argument.* New York: Cambridge UP, 1958. 94–145. Print.; **396** Either-or fallacy text, Eldridge Cleaver, Cleaver, E., civil rights leader, *San Francisco Barrister's Club.* San Francisco, CA. Sept. 1968. Speech.

Chapter 15: 408 CQ Researcher screenshot, © CQ Press; **413** Social judgment theory text, Sherif, Muzafer and Hovland, Carl I. *Social Judgment: Assimilation and Contrast Effects in Communication and Attitude Change.* New Haven: Yale UP, 1961. Print.

Chapter 16: 446 Plautus quotation, Titus Maccius Plautus (c. 254–184 BC), ancient playwright, *Titus Maccius Plautus.* Ed. Ferruccio Bertini, Asinaria (Padova, Italy: R.A.D.A.R., 1968), 104. Print.; **455** Senator Chris Dodd's eulogy for Senator Ted Kennedy, © Senator Christopher Dodd, September 2009; **456** Rosalind Russell quotation, Rosalind Russell, great screen and stage star of the 20th Century, Russell, Rosalind and Chris Chase. *Life Is a Banquet.* New York: Random House, 1977. 211. Print.; **461, 462, 463** "Pennies in the American Monetary System," by Brendan Chan, University of Texas at Austin. Reprinted with permission; **464** Speech of inspiration text, John J. Yonker, Senior Minister, First Christian Church, Columbia, MO.; **465** Agnes George de Mille quotation, Agnes George de Mille, actor, dancer, and niece to the great Hollywood producer of the 20th Century, Cecil B. de Mille. Quoted in Evelyn L. Beilenson and Ann Tenenbaum, eds. *Wit and Wisdom of Famous American Women.* White Plains: Peter Pauper Press, 1986. 13. Print.; **466** Kenneth Haigh quotation, Kenneth Haigh, well-known British actor of the early–mid 20th century. *Theatre Arts,* July 1958; **467** Alan Alda quotation, © Alan Alda, great American actor of the 20th and 21st centuries.

Chapter 17: 471 Robert Kent quotation, Robert Kent, former dean of Harvard Business School. Blalock, Marty. "Why Good Communication Is Good Business,"Wisconsin Business Alumni Update, (The Board of Regents of the University of Wisconsin System, Dec. 2005), August 27, 2010, Web.; **482** Ray Kroc quotation, Ray Kroc, founder of McDonald's Restaurants. Laura Harris, *Surrender to Win* (Austin: Greenleaf Book Group P, 2009), 147, Print.

Chapter 18: 495 Small group development text, Tuckman, Bruce W. "Stages in Small Group Development Revisited." *Group and Organizational Studies,* 2 (1977): 419–427. Print.; **499** Group roles table, From Harris & Sherblom, *Small Group and Team Communication,* Table 3.1 "Roles in Group," 46-47. © 2011 by Pearson Education, Inc. Reproduced by permission of Pearson Education, Inc.; **501** The DECIDE Model table, From Harris & Sherblom, *Small Group and Team Communication,* Table 9.2 "Six-Step DECIDE Model of Decision Making and Problem Solving," 154. © 2011 by Pearson Education, Inc. Reproduced by permission of Pearson Education, Inc.

Index

A

Abbreviations, 222
Abrams, Floyd, 10
Abstract words, 223
Acceptance speeches, 459
Accuracy, of support material, 122
Acronyms, 222
Action
    call to, 218, 275, 372, 412, 438, 474
    in Monroe's motivated sequence,
        182, 183, 381
Ad hominem, 395
Ad ignoratiam, 397
Ad populum, 399
After-dinner speeches
    ethical issues for, 460
    example of, 461–463
    guidelines for, 460
Age, 30, 101, 111, 224, 308, 339, 398,
    407, 460, 483, 487
AIDA strategy, 183
Ajzen, Icek, 371, 383
Alexa, 73
Alliteration, 233
AltaVista, 72
American Psychological Association
    (APA), 104, 141. *See also* APA style
Analogy
    argument by, 390
    explanation of, 127
    false, 394
    figurative, 127, 391
    literal, 127, 391, 394
Anastrophe, 233
Anecdotes, 200, 208
Antithesis, 233
Anxiety, 5
APA style
    citing sources using, 105
    examples of, 165
    explanation of, 104, 141
    for source page, 166–168

Appeals
    to commitment, 383
    to ethos, 378
    explanation of, 374
    to gain, 383
    to harmony, 382
    to logos, 379
    to mythos, 377
    to need, 380–381
    to pathos, 376–377
    use of appropriate, 4, 401
Appeal to tradition fallacy, 398
Appearance, personal, 244, 486
Appreciative listening, 304
Arbitrary words, 216
Arguments. *See also* Persuasion;
        Persuasive speeches
    by analogy, 391
    by authority, 391
    by cause, 391
    checklist for creating, 387
    claim of, 385
    by deduction, 388–389
    evidence of, 385
    explanation of, 384
    faulty, 392–399 (*See also* Fallacies)
    format for, 379
    by induction, 390
    organization of, 374, 425
    warrants of, 386–387
Aristotle, 4, 9, 197, 228, 376, 378
Articulation, 243
A9 (search engine), 72
Assonance, 233
Asyndeton, 233
Attending, hearing and, 303
Attention-getters
    in conclusions, 208
    displays of talent as, 203
    example of, 205
    explanation of, 198
    facts and statistics as, 199

    historical references as, 201
    humor as, 200
    for persuasive speeches, 427
    questions as, 201
    quotations as, 199
    references to prior speeches as, 202
    references to self, occasion or
        audience as, 201
    stories, narratives, illustrations or
        anecdotes as, 200
    use of Internet to research, 203
Attention, in Monroe's motivated
    sequence, 182, 183, 381
Attitudes, 28, 371
Attitudinal anchors, 413
Audience
    acknowledging freedom to decide
        by, 375
    adapting to, 46–47
    appropriateness of central idea
        for, 63
    attitudes of, 28, 371
    behaviors of, 371
    beliefs of, 29, 371
    captive, 39
    capturing attention of, 196
    cultural differences in, 9, 222
    effects of noise on, 44–45
    effects of speaking situation on,
        36–39
    eliciting response from, 207, 211
    empathy, 3, 200, 263
    evaluation by, 327
    explanation of, 15
    feedback, 15, 309, 321, 323, 327,
        364, 460, 503
    generational trends and, 31
    harmony with, 382
    identity, 29, 339, 371, 407
    knowledge of, 27, 308–309, 338,
        339, 406–407, 451, 475
    listening to, 311

Audience (*continued*)
for on-the-job speaking, 475
personality traits of, 30–31
for persuasive speeches, 406, 407
presentation aids to suit, 275
presenting challenges to, 209
psychological traits of, 32
references to, 202
responses of, 372
size of, 38
social traits of, 33–35
for special occasion speeches, 451
stereotypes of, 31
strategy selection based on, 185
target, 412
for toasts, 457
values of, 29, 371
view of speaker's credibility, 378
Audience analysis
benefits of, 18, 25, 26–27
checklist for, 412
explanation of, 27
obtaining information for,
40–43, 451
Audience-centered public speaking,
3, 27
Audio clips, 272
Authoritarian leaders, 496
Authoritative warrants, 387
Authority
argument by, 391
faulty use of, 393
Award acceptance speeches, 459
Award presentation speeches, 458

B
Baby Boomers, 31
Background, 15
Balance, in presentation aids, 285
Bar graphs, 270
Begging the question, 396
Behaviors, of audience, 371
Beliefs, 29, 371
Bing, 72
Blatant plagiarism, 10, 104

Block quotations, 128
Blogs, 76
Body language, 254, 375
eye contact, 245
facial expression, 246
gestures, 246
movement, 247
posture, 247
Body of speech. *See* Speech body
Books
citing sources for, 105
as research sources, 84, 89
Brainstorming, 39, 51
Breathing techniques, abdominal, 7
Brief examples, 112
Burke, Kenneth, 3, 313
Business meetings, 480–481
Business presentations
evaluation of, 479
getting started with, 475
methods for, 478
recommendations as, 474
reports as, 472
research for, 476
strategies for, 477

C
Cacioppo, John, 383
Causal strategy
explanation of, 175, 178
for on-the-job speaking, 477
Cause, argument by, 391
Celebration speeches, 447
Central ideas
categories of, 65
creation of, 60–61
evaluation of, 62–63
explanation of, 57
identification of, 58–59, 415
of informative speeches, 344
for on-the-job speaking, 475
in outline, 143
in persuasion, 373
for special occasion speeches, 451
Central processing, 383

Chalkboards, 276
Channel, 15
Character, perception of
speaker's, 378
Charisma, of speaker, 378
Charts, as presentation aids, 268
Chronological strategy
explanation of, 175, 176
for on-the-job speaking, 477
Circle graphs, 271
Citations. *See also* APA style; MLA
style; Sources
APA vs. MLA style for, 105
explanation of, 130
guidelines for, 164
in-text, 151
oral, 130–133
in outlines, 164–165
parenthetical, 151
research notes and, 104–105
Claims, 385
Clarity, 222, 262
Clichés, 223
Clinton, Hillary Rodham, 215
Closed-ended questions, 41, 95
Coercion, 375
Cognitive dissonance
theory, 382
Colloquiums, 502
Color harmony, 283
Color unity, 283
Commemoration speeches, 447
Commercial Web sites, 74
Commitment, appeal to, 383
Common ground, 15
Communication
evaluation to improve, 321
during interviews, 482–487
maintenance, 496
during meetings, 480–481
procedural, 496
process of, 14, 15, 44, 370
during reviews, 488–489
in small groups, 493, 494
task, 496

Communication apprehension, 6–7.
   See also Speech anxiety
Comparative advantage, 179
Comparative strategy
   explanation of, 175, 179
   for on-the-job speaking, 477
Comparisons, 127, 179
Competency, speaker, 378
Completeness, of source material,
   124
Complete Planet, 73
Concluding transitions, 161
Conclusions
   explanation of, 141
   format for, 20
   functions of, 206–207
   for informative speeches, 354, 355
   organization of, 210–211
   in outlines, 145
   for persuasive speeches, 426, 427
   "wow" statements in, 208–209
Concrete words, 223
Confidence, 310
Confidence boosters
   audience knowledge as, 27
   breathing techniques as, 7
   for delivery, 254
   evaluation as, 321, 323
   function of, 5
   good organization as, 174
   grooming and nonverbal messages
      as, 310
   knowledge as, 90
   memory devices as, 189
   on-the-job, 489
   outlines as, 139
   presentation aids as, 263
   in small groups, 498, 503
   solid introductions as, 205
   for special occasion speeches, 456
   step-by-step preparation as, 335
   support materials as, 119, 374
   topic selection as, 51
   vocabulary building as, 229
Connective transitions, 161

Connors, Robert, 231, 392
Connotative meaning, 217, 224
Contrast, 127
Coordination, of main points,
   188–189
Copyright laws, 289
Corbett, Edward, 231, 392
Core beliefs. *See* Values
Creativity
   importance of, 5
   in informative speaking, 334–335
   in presentation aids, 287
Credibility
   elements of, 378
   introductions to build, 197, 205
   presentation aids to promote, 263
   of sources, 118
Critical listening, 305, 313
Critical thinking, 305, 320
Cultural differences
   in audience, 9, 222
   awareness of, 33
   dialect and, 243
   eye contact and, 245
   listening and, 309
   presentation aids to assist with, 263
   in vocal tone, 239
Culture
   delivery and, 245–246
   explanation of, 33, 218
   Hofstede's five dimensions of, 35
   humor and, 200
   language and, 9, 218, 243
Currency, of support material, 123
Cyber-cultures, 218

D
Databases, 82–83
DECIDE model, 500–501
Decision making, group, 500–501
Declarative sentences, 188
Decoding, 15
Deduction, argument by, 388–389
Deep breathing, 7
Definitions, 110

Delivery. *See also* Presentation
   aims for, 21
   appearance and, 244
   articulation in, 243
   dialect in, 243
   dramatic, 129
   to enhance support materials, 129
   eye contact during, 245
   facial expression during, 246
   gestures during, 246
   importance of, 237
   for informative speeches, 362
   for introductions, 197
   movement during, 247
   for on-the-job speaking, 478
   pause in, 240
   for persuasive speeches, 375, 436
   pitch in, 238
   posture during, 247
   pronunciation in, 242
   rate in, 239
   selecting appropriate style for, 5
   variety in, 241
   volume in, 239
Delivery methods
   extemporaneous, 249, 252–255
   impromptu, 251
   manuscript, 250
   memorized, 250
   types of, 248
Delivery outlines
   examples of, 158–159, 171
   explanation of, 158–159
   for extemporaneous speeches,
      253, 254
Demagogue, 399
Democratic leaders, 496
Demographics, 30, 42, 99, 101, 451
Demonstration speeches, 176
Denotative meaning, 217, 224
Denotative meaning of words, 217, 224
Descriptive statistics, 114
Designated leaders, 496
Design principles for presentation
   aids, 282–287

Dialect, 243
Dimensions of culture (Hofstede), 35
Direct eye contact, 245
Directory of Open Access Journals, 73
Dissonance, 382
Diversity, 27, 31, 33, 263
  cultural, 33, 218, 309
  in language, 9, 222
  population, 34
Documentation. *See* Citations
Dogpile (search engine), 72
Doublespeak, 224
Drawings, as presentation aids, 267
Durant, Will, 237

E

Egocentrism, 27
Either-or fallacy, 396
Elaboration Likelihood Model, 383
Emblems, 246
Emergent leaders, 496
Emotion
  appeals to, 4, 182, 376–377
  faulty appeals to, 399
  presentation aids to convey, 263
Empathic listening, 304
Emphasis, design, 286
Encoding, 15
Entertainment speeches, 447
Enthymeme, 389
Enunciation, 243
Environment, 38, 311
Environmental barriers, 22, 45, 307
Equipment, checking, 294–295
ERIC, 82
Ethical issues
  for citations, 151
  for critical listening and critical
    thinking, 305
  for emotional appeals, 182
  for humor, 209
  for impromptu speeches, 251
  for informative speeches, 336
  for on-the-job public speaking,
    473, 476

for persuasion, 92, 181, 371, 372,
  375, 376, 392
for presentation aids, 265
for relating to audience, 31
for small groups, 498, 501
source citations as, 273
for source materials, 122, 125
for special occasion speeches,
  447, 460
of topic selection, 55
use of critical thinking as, 320
for word choice, 218
Ethics, 122, 124, 164, 197, 399.
    See also Ethical issues
  in humor, 200
  when interviewing, 95, 97
  overview of, 8
  in presentation aid use, 289
  in public speaking, 9–11, 22, 25
  in support materials, 122, 418
  Practicing Ethics, 10, 31, 55, 95,
    97, 125, 151, 181, 182, 199, 209,
    218, 251, 265, 273, 289, 305, 320,
    336, 371, 375, 376, 392, 438, 447,
    460, 473, 476, 498, 501
  when using the Internet, 70
Ethnicity, 33, 460, 487
  in language, 9, 243
Ethnocentrism, 9, 377
Ethos, 4, 378
  derived level, 378
  initial level, 378
  terminal level, 378
Ethos-reducing language, 224
Eulogies, 454, 455
Euphemisms, 224
Evaluation. *See also* Speech evaluation
  by audience, 327
  benefits of, 318–321
  explanation of, 319
  of informative speeches, 364–365
  by instructors, 328
  job, 322
  of on-the-job speaking, 479
  oral, 323

of persuasive speeches, 438, 439
  self-, 326
  of special occasion speeches, 453
  written, 323
Evidence, 9, 385
Examples, 112
Excite (search engine), 72
Expectancy-outcome values
    theory, 382
Expert testimony, 111
Extemporaneous speaking
  audience questions following, 255
  explanation of, 249
  presentation aids in, 263
  rehearsal methods for, 252–255
  techniques for, 249
Extended examples, 112, 113
External noise, 45, 307
Eye contact, 245, 486

F

Facial expressions, 246
Facts
  as attention-getting device, 199
  explanation of, 110
  proposition of, 373
Fallacies
  ad hominem, 395
  ad ignoratiam, 397
  ad populum, 399
  appeal to tradition, 398
  begging the question, 396
  either-or fallacy, 396
  explanation of, 392
  false analogy, 394
  faulty emotional appeal, 399
  faulty use of authority, 393
  hasty generalization, 393
  non sequitur, 398
  post hoc ergo propter hoc, 394
  slippery slope, 396
  straw man, 397
Fallacy of exhaustive hypotheses, 396
False analogy, 394
False choice, 396

Faulty emotional appeals, 399
Faulty syllogism, 389
Faulty use of authority, 393
Fear. *See* Speech anxiety
Feedback, 15, 321, 323
    audience, 15, 309, 321, 323, 327,
        364, 460, 503
    giving, 312–313, 328, 329, 364, 479
    nonverbal, 309
    verbal, 303, 309
Ferrell, O. C., 183
Festinger, Leon, 382
Figurative analogies, 127
Fillers, 223
First Amendment, 11
Fishbein, Martin, 371, 383
Flip charts, 279
Flowcharts, 268
Follow-up interview questions, 96
Fonts, 284, 285
Ford, Gerald R., 13
Forming stage of group
    development, 495
Forums, 502
Foss, Karen, 27
Freedom of expression, 11, 473
Freedom of speech, 11
Frymier, Ann Bainbridge, 371

G

Gain, appeal to, 383
Gender, 30, 31, 101, 224, 225, 339,
    407, 460
    interviews and, 483, 487
    language and, 9
Gender-neutral language, 224–225
General purpose
    explanation of, 50, 52
    strategy selection based on, 185
Generation X, 31
Generation Y, 31
Generational trends, 31
Gestures, 246
Google, 72
Google Scholar, 73

Government resources, 90, 91
Grammatical errors, 221
Graphs
    explanation of, 268
    types of, 269–271
Grooming, 244, 486
Group interaction roles, 498, 499
Group membership, 4
Group oral reports, 502
Group task roles, 498, 499
Groupthink, 501
Guided imagery, 7

H

Handouts, 278, 478
Harmony, appeal to, 382
Hartline, Michael, 183
Hasty generalization, 393
Hearing, 302
Helping verbs, 221
Henry, Patrick, 215
Historical events, 201, 203
Hitler, Adolf, 399
Hits, 72
Hofstede, Geert, 35
Hoveland, Carl, 413
Hugh Wire, 73
Humor
    as attention-getting device, 200
    in conclusions, 209
    Internet as source for, 203
Hyperbole, 231
Hyperlinks, 160
Hypothetical examples, 112, 113

I

Idea bank
    explanation of, 51, 53, 54
    informative, 340
    for persuasive speeches, 408, 409
Identity
    audience's, 29, 339, 371, 407
    cultural, 218, 219, 243, 377, 380
Identity knowledge, 27
Idioms, 170

Illustrations, 200, 208
Illustrators, 246
Image unity, 283
Implied leaders, 496
Impromptu speaking, 251
Inclusive language. *See* Language,
    appropriate
Income, 30, 31, 339, 407
Induction, argument by, 390
Inferential statistics, 114
Inflection, 238
Infomine, 73
Information, as purpose of speech,
    50, 52
Informative listening, 305
Informative speeches
    central idea for, 344
    creative process for, 334–336
    delivery of, 363
    evaluation of, 364–365
    explanation of, 336–337
    identifying purpose for, 344
    introductions and conclusions for,
        354–355
    language for, 362
    organizational strategy for, 180,
        350–353, 356–361
    overview of, 334
    preparation outlines for, 348–349,
        356–361
    presentation aids for, 363
    research for, 346–347
    sample construction of, 366–367
    topic choice for, 338–341
    types of, 342
    working outlines for, 345
Inspirational speeches
    example of, 465–467
    function of, 447
    guidelines for, 464
Instructors, evaluation by, 328
Intercultural competence, 27
Internal noise, 45, 307
Internal previews, 162
Internal reviews, 163

Internal summaries, 163
Internet
  citing sources from, 105
  evaluating information from, 71
  language associated with, 218
  library access through, 78–79
  locating icons and graphics
    on, 270
  media-assisted interviews
    and, 97
  overview of, 70
  searching for topics on, 53
  as source for attention-getters, 203
  as source for support
    materials, 419
Internet searches
  blogs and, 76
  commercial Web sites and, 74
  nonprofit organization Web sites
    and, 75
  personal Web sites and, 77
  search engines for, 72–73
Interviews
  dressing for, 96, 483, 486
  explanation of, 94
  to gather support materials, 94–97
  illegal questions during, 487
  locating people for, 94
  media-assisted, 97
  to obtain audience information, 41
  participants in, 484, 490
  preparation to conduct,
    482–483, 491
  as source for support
    materials, 419
  strategies following, 487
  strategies for day of, 486–487
  strategies prior to, 485
Introductions
  attention-getters in, 198–203
  explanation of, 141, 195
  format for, 20
  function of, 196–197
  for informative speeches, 354, 355
  organization of, 204–205

for persuasive speeches, 426, 427
in preparation outlines, 145
references to, 209
Introduction speeches, 456
Invisible Web, 70, 73
Irony, 231

J
Janik, Allan, 392
Jargon, 222
Job applications, 484
Job evaluation, 322
Job interviews
  illegal questions during, 487
  participants in, 484, 490
  preparation to conduct,
    482–483, 491
  strategies following, 487
  strategies for day of, 486–487
  strategies prior to, 485
Jobs, public speaking in, 13
Journals, as research sources, 88
JSTOR, 82, 83

K
Kaczynski, Theodore, 219
Keller, Helen, 216
King, Martin Luther, Jr., 214, 215,
    230, 232
Knowledge
  of audience, 27, 308–309, 338,
    339, 406–407, 451, 475
  identity, 27
  personal, 119
  of situation, 36–39, 339, 407
Kroc, Ray, 482

L
Laissez-faire leaders, 496
Lancaster, Lynne, 30
Language, 215–235. See also Words
  appropriate, 224–225
  clear, 222
  concise, 59, 223
  conversational, 362, 363, 436, 486

correct, 220–221
culturally appropriate, 224–225
culture and, 9, 218, 243, 478
distinctive, 227–233
embellished, 230–231
emotive and stylistic, 375
ethos-reducing, 224
for informative speeches, 362
gender-neutral, 225
meaning of, 216–217
oral style of, 226
for persuasive speeches, 436
offensive, 9, 224
power of, 9, 215, 219
specific, 223
speech devices and, 232–233
unbiased, 224–225
vivid, 228–231
Lay testimony, 111
LCD projector, 280, 281
Leaders, small group, 496–497
Leadership styles, 496
Lecterns, 247
Libraries
  books in, 84
  catalog system in, 81
  database use in, 82–83
  government resources in, 90, 91
  Internet use to access, 78–79
  journals in, 88
  magazines in, 86
  newsletters in, 87
  newspapers in, 85
  overview of, 80
  reference works in, 90, 92–93
  as source for support materials, 419
  special collections and rare books
    in, 89
Library of Congress, 81
Line graphs, 269
Linguistic barriers, 22, 45, 307, 308
Links. See also Transitions
  explanation of, 141
  in outlines, 150, 160
  types of, 161–163

Lippmann, Walter, 301
Listening
    active, 312
    appreciative, 304
    barriers to, 22, 306–307
    to build relationships, 301
    as communicative responsibility, 301
    critical, 305, 313
    effective, 308–311, 328
    emphatic, 304
    explanation of, 302
    to gain knowledge, 300
    informative, 305
    to informative speeches, 364
    to persuasive speeches, 438
    process of, 302–303
    in workplace, 479
Literal analogies, 127, 391, 394
Littlejohn, Stephen, 27
Location, 38
Logos, 4, 379
Lycos (search engine), 72

M
Magazines, 86
Main points
    creation of, 188–189
    discovering your, 186–187
    explanation of, 141, 186
    for informative speeches, 352
    in outlines, 146, 148
    for persuasive speeches,
        416–417, 424
    working, 64
Maintenance communication, 496
Malapropism, 220
Mamma (search engine), 72
Manuscript speaking, 250
Maslow, Abraham, 380
Maslow's hierarchy of needs, 32,
    380, 381
McVeigh, Timothy, 219
Mean, 115
Media
    contemporary, 280

    to create presentation aids, 272–273
    traditional, 281
Median, 115
Meetings, 480–481
Memorized speaking, 250
Memory devices, 189
Message
    creating effective, 310
    evaluation of, 324, 325, 438
    explanation of, 15
Metacrawler (search engine), 72
Metaphor, 231
Metasearch engines, 72
Michaelanglo, 3
Microphones, 239
Millennials, 31
Mindfulness, 27
Misplaced modifiers, 221
MLA style
    citing sources using, 105, 151
    examples of, 165
    explanation of, 104, 141
    for source page, 167, 168
Mode, 115
Models, as presentation aids, 265
Moderator, 502, 503
Modern Language Association (MLA),
    104, 141. *See also* MLA style
Monotone, 238
Monroe, Alan, 380
Monroe's motivated sequence strategy,
    175, 182–183, 380, 381
Mood, 39
Moore, Brooke, 305
Motivational warrants, 387
Movement, 247
Multimedia, 273
Mumbling, 243
Mythos, 4, 377

N
Nadler, Marjorie Keeshan, 371
Narratives, 200, 208
Need, in Monroe's motivated
    sequence, 182, 183, 380, 381

Needs
    appeal to, 380
    Maslow's hierarchy of, 32, 380, 381
    physiological, 32, 381
    safety, 32, 381
    self-actualization, 32, 381
    self-esteem, 32, 381
    social, 32, 381
Negotiation skill, 27
Nervousness, 5
Newsletters, 87
Newspapers, 85, 105
No-citation plagiarism, 10, 104
Noise
    explanation of, 15, 36, 306
    external, 45, 307
    internal, 45, 307
    role of, 44
Nonprofit organizations, 75
Non sequitur, 398
Nonverbal behavior
    eye contact and, 245, 486
    facial expressions and, 246
    gestures and, 246
    movement and, 247
    posture and, 247
    use of appropriate, 3
Nonverbal responses, 303
Norming stage of group
    development, 495
Note taking
    methods for, 103
    source citations and, 104–105
    strategies for, 313, 419

O
Obama, Barack, 201, 227
Occasions, 39, 202
Occupation, 30, 31, 339
Ogden, Charles K., 216
Onomatopoeia, 231
On-the-job speaking
    benefits of skills in, 472–473
    in business presentations, 474–479
    ethical issues related to, 473, 476

On-the-job speaking (*continued*)
  in interviews, 482–487
  in meetings, 480–481
  preparation for, 471
  in reviews, 488–489
Open-ended questions, 41, 95
Oral citations. *See also* Citations
  delivery method for, 132–133
  examples of, 133
  explanation of, 130–131
  types of, 131
Oral evaluation, 323
Oral reports, 474, 475
Oral style, 226
Order of intensity strategy, 175, 178
Organization
  common problems with, 191
  of conclusions, 210–211
  importance of, 5
  of introductions, 204–205
Organizational charts, 268
Organizational strategies
  causal, 178
  chronological, 176
  comparative, 179
  for informative speeches, 350–353
  Monroe's motivated sequence,
    182–183
  for on-the-job speaking, 477
  order of intensity, 178
  overview of, 174
  for persuasive speeches, 374,
    422–425
  problem-solution, 180
  refutation, 181
  selection of, 184–185, 423
  spatial, 177
  topical, 177
  types of, 175
Outlines
  balancing main points in, 148
  benefits of, 137–139
  citations in, 151, 164–165
  covering one issue at time in, 144
  delivery, 158–159, 253, 254

elements of effective, 142
employing subordination in,
  148–149
examples of, 155–159, 170–171
formal links in, 150
format for, 146–147
full sentences in, 143
information at top of, 143
introductions and conclusions
  for, 145
links in, 150, 160–163
parts of, 140, 141
preparation, 20, 154–157, 253,
  348–349
source pages to follow, 141,
  166–169
for special occasion speeches, 451
working, 57, 64–65, 67, 152–153,
  345, 416–417
Oxymoron, 231

P
Panel discussions, 502
Parallelism, 189, 233
Paraphrasing, 128
Parker, Richard, 305
Passivity syndrome, 301
Pathos, 4, 376–377
Pattern principle, 284
Pause, vocal, 240
Peer evaluation, 328, 329
Pelias, Ron, 319
Performance reviews, 488–489
Performing stage of group
  development, 495
Periodical citations, 105
Personal attire, 244, 486
Personal knowledge, 119
Personal testimony, 111
Personal traits, 30–31
Personification, 231
Persuasion. *See also* Arguments
  ethical issues related to, 181, 371,
    372, 376, 392
  explanation of, 369, 370

faulty arguments used for, 392–399
function of, 371–375
identifying purpose for, 50, 52,
  412–414
modern appeals used for, 380–383
parts of argument used for, 384–387
traditional appeals used for, 376–379
types of argument used for, 388–391
Persuasive speeches
  audience for, 406, 407
  body of, 422–425
  central idea for, 415
  creative process for, 404–405
  delivery of, 436
  evaluation of, 438–439
  idea bank for, 408–409
  identifying your purpose for, 50,
    52, 412–414
  introductions and conclusions for,
    426–427
  language use for, 436
  outline for, 420–421
  preparation outline for,
    428–435, 441
  presentation aids for, 437
  research for, 418–419
  selecting and narrowing topic
    for, 410–412
  situation for, 406, 407
  types of, 412–413
  working outline for, 416–417
Petty, Richard, 383
Photographs, 266
Physiological barriers, 22, 45, 307
Pictographs, 270
Pie graphs, 271
Pitch, 238
Plagiarism, 10, 79, 104, 164, 357
Plautus, 446
Policy, proposition of, 373
Popular sources, 118
Population, 98
Population diversity, 34
Positive visualization, 7
Posters, 277

Post hoc ergo propter hoc, 394
Posture, 247
Power, of language, 9, 215, 219
PowerPoint (Microsoft)
  basic information for, 290–293
  benefits of, 280
  posters created with, 277
  printing handouts using, 278
  use of, 288, 478
Practice, 7, 254, 453
Premises, 388
Preparation outlines. *See also* Outlines
  construction of, 420
  examples of, 155–157, 170, 349, 421, 428–435
  explanation of, 20, 154
  for extemporaneous speeches, 253
  for informative speeches, 348–349, 356–361
  introductions and conclusions in, 145
  links in, 150
  for persuasive speeches, 420, 421, 428–435
Presentation. *See also* Delivery
  elements of, 21
  evaluation of, 324–325, 365, 439
  for on-the-job speaking, 478
Presentation aids
  actual items as, 264
  to build redundancy, 363
  charts and tables as, 268
  checklist for, 295
  design of, 282–287
  display of, 275–281
  drawings as, 267
  explanation of, 262
  for extemporaneous speeches, 253
  function of, 21, 262–263
  graphs as, 269–271
  for informative speeches, 363
  media as, 272–273
  models as, 265
  for on-the-job speaking, 478
  for persuasive speeches, 437
  photographs as, 266

previewing, checking and practicing with, 294–295
selection of, 274–275
for small group presentations, 503
Presentation software
  explanation of, 288
  PowerPoint, 290–293
  storyboarding and, 289
Prestige testimony, 111
Previews, 197, 205
Primacy model, 425
Primary sources, 117
Problem-solution strategy
  explanation of, 175, 180
  for on-the-job speaking, 477
Problem solving, group, 500–501
Procedural communication, 496
Procrastination, 257
Pronouns, errors in use of, 221
Pronunciation, 242
Proofs. *See* Appeals
Proposition, in persuasion, 373, 415
Psychological needs, 32
Psychological traits, 32
Public speaking. *See also* On-the-job speaking; Speeches
  audience-centered, 3, 27
  benefits of skills in, 1, 472
  building competence in, 27
  creative phase of, 20
  ethics in, 8–11
  initial considerations for, 18
  listening and evaluating phase of, 22
  method to overcome fear of, 6–8
  occasions for, 12–13
  presentation phase of, 21
  qualities for success in, 2–6, 473
  research phase of, 19
  steps in, 16–22
Publilius Syrus, 5
Purpose
  awareness of, 18
  explanation of, 50
  general, 50, 52, 185
  of informative speeches, 343

for on-the-job speaking, 475
of persuasive speeches, 50, 52, 412–414
of presentation aids, 274
of special occasion speeches, 50, 52, 446–447, 449
specific, 57–59, 414
topic categories to fit, 52

Q
Question-and-answer sessions, 255
Questions
  as attention-getting device, 201
  closed-ended, 41, 95
  follow-up, 96
  interview, 96, 487
  open-ended, 41, 95
  rhetorical, 201, 209, 231
Quotations
  as attention-getting device, 199
  block, 128
  in conclusions, 208
  effective use of, 128, 129
  Internet as source for, 203

R
Race, 33, 101, 224, 339, 407, 460, 487
  language and, 9
Rare books, 89
Rate, of speech, 239
Reagan, Ronald, 241
Reason, appeal to, 4
Reasoning, 379. *See also* Arguments
  faulty, 393–399
Receiving, hearing and, 303
Recency model, 425
Recent events, 201, 203
Recommendations, 474–476. *See also* Business presentations
Reference works, 90, 92–93
Reflexivity, 326
Reforming stage of group development, 495
Refutation strategy, 175, 181
Relationship building, 301

Relevance, 197, 205
Reliability, 4, 118
Religion, 29, 33, 101, 460
    interviews and, 483, 487
    language and, 9
Remembering, 303
Remen, Rachel Naomi, 299
Repetition, 232, 233
Reports. *See also* Business presentations
    business, 474, 475
    group oral, 502
Research. *See also* Sources; Support
    materials
    considerations for, 19
    for informative speeches, 346–347
    to obtain audience information, 43
    for on-the-job speaking, 476
    for persuasive speeches, 418–419
    preparation for, 102, 109
    for special occasion speeches, 451
Research notes
    source citations and, 104–105
    system for, 103
Responding, 303
Responsibility, 10
Reviews, performance, 488–489
Rhetoric (Aristotle), 4, 128, 376
Rhetorical questions
    in conclusions, 209
    explanation of, 231
    in introductions, 201
Rhythm, 232, 287
Richards, Ivor A., 216
Richter, Jean Paul, 241
Rieke, Richard, 392
Roasts, 457

S
Safety needs, 32
Sample, explanation of, 101
Satisfaction, in Monroe's motivated
    sequence, 182, 183, 380, 381
Schemes, 232, 233
Scholarly sources, 118
Search engines, 72–73

Secondary sources, 117
Self, references to, 202
Self-actualization needs, 32
Self-centered roles, 498, 499
Self-development, public speaking
    and, 13
Self-doubt, 51
Self-esteem, 13, 32
Self-evaluation, 326
Senses, language that appeals to,
    228, 229
Sentences, 143, 188
Sexual orientation, 30, 31, 224,
    460, 487
Sherif, Muzafer, 413
Signposts, 162
Silence, 303
Simile, 231
Situation
    adapting to, 44–45
    explanation of, 15
    knowledge of, 36–39, 339, 407
    locating information about, 40–43
    presentation aids to suit, 275
Slides
    creation of, 289–292
    design elements for, 292–293
    tips for presenting, 293
Slippery slope fallacy, 396
Small groups
    decision making and problem
        solving in, 500–501
    developmental stages in, 495
    ethical issues in, 498, 501
    explanation of, 495
    leaders in, 496–497
    members in, 498
    presentation formats for, 502
    roles in, 499
    types of, 495
    virtual, 494
Small-group speaking
    format for, 502
    overview of, 493
    presentation strategies for, 503

Social groups, 495
Social judgment theory, 413
Social needs, 32
Social traits
    cultural dimensions and, 35
    explanation of, 32
    population diversity and, 34
Software. *See* PowerPoint (Microsoft);
    Presentation software
Source page, 141, 166
Sources. *See also* Citations; Research;
    Support materials
    explanation of, 69
    importance of citing, 10
    popular, 118
    primary, 117
    scholarly, 118
    secondary, 117
    selection of, 116
Spatial strategy
    explanation of, 175, 177
    for on-the-job speaking, 477
Speaking. *See also* Delivery
    extemporaneous, 249, 252–255
    impromptu, 251
    informative, 336–337
    manuscript, 250
    memorized, 250
Special collections, library, 89
Special occasion speeches
    after-dinner speeches as, 460–463
    award acceptances as, 459
    award presentations as, 458
    creative process for, 444–445
    eulogies or tributes as, 454–455
    inspiration speeches as, 464–467
    introduction speeches as, 456
    process to write, 448–453
    purpose of, 50, 52, 446–447, 449
    toasts or roasts as, 457
Specific language, 223
Specific purpose. *See also* Purpose
    examples of, 59
    explanation of, 57, 58
    identification of, 414

for on-the-job speaking, 475
  in outline, 143
Speech anxiety, 5, 6, 7, 139, 145,
    307, 317
Speech body
  elements of, 141
  for informative speeches, 350–353
  organization of, 20
  in outline, 141
Speeches. *See also* Public speaking;
    specific types of speeches
  to actuate, 372, 412, 423
  to commemorate special
    occasions, 50, 52
  to convince, 372, 412, 413, 423
  general purpose of, 50
  information as purpose of,
    50, 52
  informative, 333–366
  Internet as source for, 203
  persuasion as purpose of, 50, 52,
    412–414
  preparation for, 256–257
  preparation outlines for, 20
  references to prior, 202
  to stimulate, 372, 412, 423
  tips for practicing, 254, 255
Speech evaluation
  by audience, 327
  benefits of, 318–321
  of central ideas, 62–63
  considerations for, 22
  example of, 330–331
  by instructors, 328
  of message, 324, 325
  methods for, 322
  oral, 323
  overview of, 317
  by peers, 328, 329
  of presentation, 324–325
  self-, 326
  written, 323
Statistics
  applications of, 114–115
  explanation of, 114

Internet as source for, 203
  types of, 114
Stephenson, Tracy, 319
Stereotyping, 31
Stillman, David, 30
Stories
  as attention-getting device, 200
  in conclusions, 208
  Internet as source for, 203
Storming stage of group
    development, 495
Storyboarding, 289
Strategy, 173. *See also* Organizational
    strategies
Straw man fallacy, 397
Subjects. *See* Topics
Subject-verb agreement, 221
Subordination, in outlines,
    148–149
Subpoints
  creation of, 190
  explanation of, 141, 190
  in outlines, 147
Substantive warrants, 387
Suitability, of support material, 125
Sullivan, Annie, 216
Summaries, 207, 211
Support materials. *See also* Research;
    Sources
  accuracy of, 122
  applications of, 106–107, 134–135
  approaches to, 127
  completeness of, 124
  considerations for, 19
  currency or, 123
  definitions as, 110
  delivery techniques for, 12
  examples as, 112–113
  explanation of, 69
  facts as, 110
  government resources to locate,
    90, 91
  for informative speeches,
    346–347, 353
  Internet to locate, 70–79

interviews to gather, 94–98
  libraries to access, 80–89
  oral citations for, 130–133
  paraphrasing or quoting, 128
  personal knowledge as, 119
  for persuasive speeches, 374,
    418, 419
  from primary and secondary
    sources, 116–117
  purposeful use of, 126
  reference works to locate, 90,
    92–93
  from scholarly and popular
    sources, 118
  selection of, 116
  statistics as, 114–115
  suitability of, 125
  surveys to gather, 98–101
  taking notes from, 102–105
  testimony as, 111
  for topics with special demands,
    120–121
  trustworthiness of, 124
  used for arguments, 425
Surveys
  creation of, 99–100
  explanation of, 98
  to gather support materials, 98–101
  method to conduct, 101
  to obtain audience information, 42
  as source for support materials, 419
Syllogism, 388, 389
Symbolic words, 216
Symbols, 284
Symposiums, 502

T
Tables, 268
Talent displays, 203
Target audience, 412
Task communication, 496
Terminating stage of group
    development, 495
Testimony, 111
Thatcher, Margaret, 2, 238

Thesis statement, 57. *See also* Central
    ideas
Time considerations, 39
Time transitions, 161
Titles, in presentation aids, 286
Toasts, 457
Topical strategy
    explanation of, 175, 177
    for on-the-job speaking, 477
Topics
    brainstorming for, 51
    ethical guidelines related to, 55
    idea bank of potential, 51, 53, 54,
        408, 409
    for informative speeches, 338–341
    introduction of, 197
    method to narrow, 56–57, 341,
        410–411
    in outline, 143
    presentation aids to suit, 275
    selection of, 3, 18, 49, 54–55,
        66–67, 341, 410
    sources to support special, 120–121
    strategy selection based on, 185
Toulmin, Stephen, 386, 392
Traditionalists, 31
Traits
    personal, 30–31
    psychological, 32
    social, 33–35
Transactional process, 15
Transitions, 161. *See also* Links
Tributes, 454
Tropes, 231
Trustworthiness, 124

Truth, Sojourner, 215
Tuckman, Bruce, 495

U
Understanding, 303
Unity, in presentation aids, 283

V
Value Dimension model (Hofstede), 35
Values
    of audience, 371
    explanation of, 28
    proposition of, 373
Variety, vocal, 241
Verbal language, 3
Verbal responses, 303
Verbs, helping, 221
Video clips, 272
Viewpoint transitions, 161
Virtual small groups, 494
Visible Web, 70
Visualization, in Monroe's motivated
        sequence, 182, 183, 380, 381
Visualization, positive, 7
Visuals. *See* Presentation aids
Vivid language, 228–231
Vocabulary building, 229
Vocal chords, 238
Vocal fillers, 140
Volume, vocal, 239

W
Warrants, 386, 387
Wasik, Bill, 219
Web, 70, 73. *See also* Internet

Web browsers, 70
Web directories, 73
Web sites. *See also* Internet
    blog, 76
    commercial, 74
    evaluation of, 71
    explanation of, 71
    government, 91
    for nonprofit organizations, 75
    personal, 77
    as presentation aid, 478
Whiteboards, 276
Wittgenstein, Ludwig, 218
Word order, manipulation of, 232–233
Words. *See also* Language
    abstract, 223
    arbitrary, 216
    concrete, 223
    connotative meaning of, 217, 224
    denotative meaning of, 217, 224
    meaning of, 216–217
    symbolic, 216
Working groups, 495
Working main points, 64
Working outlines. *See also* Outlines
    construction of, 65, 67
    example of, 170
    explanation of, 57, 64, 152–153
    for informative speeches, 345
    for persuasive speeches, 416–417
"WOW" statements, 208–209, 211
Written evaluation, 323

Y
Yahoo!, 72

Contents

TAB 1: STARTING

OVERVIEW OF PUBLIC SPEAKING 1
How public speaking helps you 1
Be a successful public speaker 2
  Be audience centered 3
  Select appropriate topics 3
  Be knowledgeable 3
  Use appropriate verbal and nonverbal behavior 3
  Use appropriate appeals 4
  Be creative but organized 5
  Select appropriate delivery styles 5
  Practice again and again 5
  Boost your confidence 5
Overcome a fear of speaking 6
  Face your fear head on 6
  Learn techniques that work for you 6
  Practice, practice, practice 7
Be an ethical public speaker 8
  Be a successful speaker 9
  Be open to differences 9
  Use evidence, logic, reasoning 9
  Be sensitive to language 9
  Cite sources (avoid plagiarism) 10
  Accept responsibility 11
  Support freedom of expression 11
Use the skills 12
  In your public life 12
  In your professional life 13
  In your personal life 13
The process of communicating 14
The creative process for public speaking 16
Using the steps in this book 23

CHAPTER 1: GETTING TO KNOW YOUR AUDIENCE AND SITUATION 25
Why you need to know your audience 26
  Get your audience's attention and good will 27
  Build your speaking competence 27

What you need to know about your audience 28
  Attitudes 28
  Beliefs 29
  Values 29
Traits to investigate 30
  Personal traits 30
  Psychological traits 32
  Social traits 33
Why you need to know the speaking situation 36
What you need to know about the situation 38
  Place and audience size 38
  Time 39
  Occasion 39
Locate information 40
  Stop, think, brainstorm 40
  Interview 41
  Survey 42
  Research 43
Adapt to your audience 44
  Adapt to external noise 45
  Adapt to internal noise 45

CHAPTER 2: SELECTING YOUR TOPIC AND PURPOSE 49
Select a topic 50
  Identify the general purpose 50
  Create an idea bank 51
  Select your topic 54
Narrow your topic 56
Create a central idea 58
  Identify the specific purpose 58
  Identify the central idea 60
  Evaluate your central idea 62
Construct a working outline 64

TAB 2: RESEARCHING

CHAPTER 3: LOCATING SUPPORT MATERIALS 69
The Internet 70
  Search engines 72
  Commercial Web sites 74
  Nonprofit organization Web sites 75

  Blogs 76
  Personal Web sites 77
Using the Internet to access libraries 78
The library 80
  The catalog 81
  Databases 82
  Books 84
  Newspapers 85
  Magazines 86
  Newsletters 87
  Journals 88
  Special collections, rare books 89
On the Internet and in libraries 90
  Government resources 91
  Reference works 92
Interviews 94
  Prepare for the interview 95
  Conduct the interview 96
  Use media-assisted interviews 97
Surveys 98
  Create the survey 99
  Conduct the survey 101
Take research notes 102
  Prepare to research 102
  Use a note-taking system 103
  Know your style manual 104

CHAPTER 4: SELECTING AND TESTING SUPPORT MATERIALS 109
Types of support materials 110
  Facts 110
  Definitions 110
  Testimony 111
  Examples 112
  Statistics 114
Choose types of sources 116
  Primary vs. secondary sources 117
  Scholarly vs. popular sources 118
  Personal knowledge 119
  Topic needs 120
Evaluate support materials 122
  Accuracy 122
  Currency 123
  Completeness 124
  Trustworthiness 124
  Suitability 125
Use materials effectively 126
  Use materials purposefully 126
  Use materials in different ways 127
  Quote and paraphrase 128
  Use delivery techniques 129
Cite sources orally 130
  Collect necessary content 130
  Create and deliver citations 132